Reader's Digest

GREAT
BIOGRAPHIES

*Reader's
Digest*

GREAT
BIOGRAPHIES

*selected
and
condensed by
the editors
of
Reader's
Digest*

The Reader's Digest Association, Inc.
Pleasantville, New York
Cape Town, Hong Kong, London, Montreal, Sydney

READER'S DIGEST CONDENSED BOOKS

Editor-in-Chief: John S. Zinsser, Jr.

Executive Editor: Barbara J. Morgan

Managing Editors: Anne H. Atwater, Ann Berryman, Tanis H. Erdmann,
Thomas Froncek, Marjorie Palmer

Senior Staff Editors: Jean E. Aptakin, Virginia Rice (Rights), Ray Sipherd, Angela Weldon

Senior Editors: M. Tracy Brigden, Linn Carl, Joseph P. McGrath,
James J. Menick, Margery D. Thorndike

Associate Editors: Thomas S. Clemmons, Alice Jones-Miller, Maureen A. Mackey

Senior Copy Editors: Claire A. Bedolis, Jeane Garment, Jane F. Neighbors

Associate Copy Editors: Maxine Bartow, Rosalind H. Campbell, Jean S. Friedman

Assistant Copy Editors: Ainslie Gilligan, Jeanette Gingold

Art Director: William Gregory

Executive Art Editors: Soren Noring, Angelo Perrone

Associate Art Editors, Research: George Calas, Jr., Katherine Kelleher

CB PROJECTS

Executive Editor: Herbert H. Lieberman

Senior Editors: Dana Adkins, Catherine T. Brown, John R. Roberson

CB INTERNATIONAL EDITIONS

Executive Editor: Francis Schell

Senior Editor: Istar H. Dole

Associate Editor: Gary Q. Arpin

Library of Congress Cataloging-in-Publication Data
Reader's digest great biographies.
Contents: v. 1. The Spirit of St. Louis/by Charles A. Lindbergh.
Florence Nightingale/by Cecil Woodham-Smith.
Edison/by Matthew Josephson.
Hans Christian Andersen/by Rumer Godden—[etc.]
1. Biography—Collected works. I. Reader's Digest Association.
II. Reader's digest. III. Title: Great biographies.
CT101.R42 1987 920'.02 86-29816 ISBN 0-89577-259-0 (v.1)

Printed in the United States of America

Contents

Ticker-tape reception – New York

SPOILED NEW YORK

Bryant Park Bank

New York, June 17th, 1927

Pay to the Order of Charles A. Lindbergh

Twenty-five Thousand no/100 Dollars

Payable in funds current at New York Clearing House

$25,000. no/100

Raymond Orteig

Being decorated by
Mayor Jimmy Walker

A CONDENSATION OF

THE
SPIRIT
OF
ST. LOUIS

by
CHARLES A.
LINDBERGH

SOON AFTER landing the *Spirit of St. Louis* at Paris, I agreed to take part in publishing a book about my flight. I was under the impression that the account would be written in the third person, over someone else's name, and that I would confirm its authenticity and contribute a foreword. Instead, a ghostwritten manuscript, in the first person, was submitted to me for approval, and rejected.

Since the project had already been announced publicly, I felt obliged to carry it through, so I wrote a short book which was brought out, in 1927, under the title of *We*. The manuscript was completed in about three weeks. I had little experience in writing, limited facilities for research, and no extra hours to attempt a second draft or to work on shading or balance. Being young, and easily embarrassed, I was hesitant to dwell on my personal errors and sensations. Also, believing in aviation's future, I did not want to lay bare, through my own experience, its existing weaknesses. For reasons such as these, I left out of that story much of interest— which I am now, twenty-five years later, attempting to portray in *The Spirit of St. Louis*.

Throughout the following chapters I have made use of records and documents culled from attics, files, and libraries. In telegrams I have used the originals where they were available, and approximated from memory where they were not. Since it is impossible to describe exactly the wanderings of the mind, I have placed flashbacks out of sequence to attain impressionistic truth. But all incidents in this book are factual, and I have tried to describe them with accuracy.

—Charles A. Lindbergh, 1953

I. THE CRAFT
September, 1926

NIGHT already shadows the eastern sky. To my left, low on the horizon, a thin line of cloud is drawing on its evening sheath of black. A moment ago, it was burning red and gold. I look down over the side of my cockpit at the farmlands of central Illinois. Wheat shocks are gone from the fields. Close, parallel lines of the seeder, across a harrowed strip, show where winter planting has begun. Several men quitting work for the day look up and wave as my mail plane roars overhead. In a few minutes it will be dark, and I'm still south of Peoria.

How quickly the long days of summer passed, when it was daylight all the way to Chicago. April, when we inaugurated the airmail service from St. Louis to Chicago, seems only a few weeks ago. As chief pilot of the line, I had the honor of making the first flight. There were photographs, city officials, and hand-shaking all along the route. But after the first day's heavy load, swollen with letters of enthusiasts and collectors, interest declined. Airmail saves a few hours at most; it's seldom worth the extra cost per letter. Yet week after week, we carry the nearly empty sacks back and forth. We have faith in the future. Some day we know the sacks will fill.

Our contract calls for five round trips a week, landing the St. Louis mail in Chicago in time to connect with planes coming in from California, Minnesota, Michigan, and Texas, so that letters will reach New York City by the opening of the business day. Three of us carry on this service: Philip Love, Thomas Nelson, and I. We've established the best record of all the routes converging at Chicago, completing over ninety-nine percent of our scheduled flights. Paying almost no attention to weather forecasts, we've landed our rebuilt army warplanes on Chicago's Maywood field when older and perhaps wiser pilots ordered their cargo put on a train.

During the long days of summer we seldom missed a flight. But now nights are lengthening; skies are thickening with haze and storm. We're already landing by floodlight at Chicago. Soon it will be dark when we glide down onto that narrow strip of cow pasture called the Peoria airmail field. Before the winter is past, even the meadow at Springfield will need lights. Today I'm over an hour late—engine trouble at St. Louis.

Night flying isn't difficult if you have money to pay for an airport's revolving beacons, boundary markers, and floodlights. But our organization can't buy such luxuries. There's barely enough money to keep going from month to month.

The Robertson Aircraft Corporation, for which we fly, is paid by the pounds of mail we carry, and often the sacks weigh more than the letters inside. Our operating expenses are incredibly low; but our revenue is lower still. Our planes and engines were purchased from army surplus, and rebuilt in our shops at Lambert Field. We call them DHs, because the design originated with De Havilland, in England. Used during the war for bombing and observation purposes, they are biplanes, with two cockpits and with a single, 12-cylinder, 400-horsepower Liberty engine in the nose. The mail compartment is now where the front cockpit used to be, and we pilot from the position where the wartime observer sat.

We've been unable to buy full night-flying equipment for these planes. Red and green navigation lights were installed on our DHs only last week. Before that we carried nothing but one emergency flare and a pocket flashlight. But then this economy proved false and cost us a plane: I lost a DH just over a week ago because I didn't have an extra flare, or wing lights.

I had encountered a solid bank of fog that night, on the northbound flight to Chicago. Turning back, I tried to drop my single flare so I could land on one of the farm fields below; but when I pulled the release lever nothing happened. Since the top of the fog was less than 1000 feet high, I decided to climb over it and continue on my route, hoping to find a clear spot around the airmail field. There I could pick up the Chicago beacon, which had been installed at government expense.

Glowing patches of mist showed me where cities lay; with these patches as guides, I had little trouble locating the outskirts of Chicago, but a thick blanket of fog covered the field. Mechanics told me afterward that they played a searchlight upward and burned two barrels of gasoline on the ground in an effort to attract my attention. I saw nothing.

After circling for a half hour I headed west, hoping to pick up one of the beacons on the transcontinental route. They were fogged in, too. By then I had discovered that the failure of my flare to drop was caused by slack in the release cable, and that the flare might still function if I pulled on the cable instead of on the release lever. I turned southwest, toward the edge of the fog, intending to follow my original plan of landing on some farmer's field by flare light. But my engine spat a few times and cut out almost completely; the main fuel tank had run dry. That left me with reserve fuel for only twenty minutes of flight—not enough to reach the edge of the fog.

I decided to jump when the reserve tank ran dry, and I had started to climb for altitude when a light appeared on the ground —just a blink, but that meant a break in the fog. I circled down to 1200 feet and pulled the flare-release cable. This time the flare functioned, but it showed only a solid layer of mist. I began climbing again.

I was 5000 feet high when my engine cut the second time. I shoved my flashlight into my pocket, unbuckled my safety belt, dived over the right side of the fuselage, and pulled the rip cord. The parachute opened right away. I was playing my flashlight down toward the top of the fogbank when I suddenly heard the sound of an airplane coming toward me. In a few seconds I saw my DH less than a quarter mile away and about on a level with me, circling in my direction. Thinking it was completely out of gasoline, I hadn't cut the switches before jumping. When the nose dropped, from the loss of my weight in the tail, some additional fuel apparently had drained forward, sending the plane off on a flight of its own.

In spite of the sky's tremendous space, it now seemed crowded with traffic. I pushed my flashlight into a pocket and caught hold of the parachute risers so I could slip the canopy one way or the other in case the plane kept pointing toward me. But it passed fully 100 yards away, leaving me on the outside of its circle. The engine noise receded, and then increased as the DH appeared again, still at my elevation. The rates of descent of plane and parachute were approximately equal. I counted five spirals, each a little farther away than the last. Then I sank into the fogbank.

Knowing the ground to be less than 1000 feet below, I reached for the flashlight. It was gone. In my excitement I hadn't pushed it far enough into my pocket. I held my feet together, guarded my face with my hands, and waited. I heard the DH pass once again. Then I saw the outline of the ground, braced myself for impact, and hit—in a cornfield. I got on my feet, rolled up the chute, tucked it under my arm, and started walking through stalks of corn that were higher than my head. I climbed over a fence into a stubble field. There I found wagon tracks and followed them. Ground visibility was about 100 yards.

The wagon tracks took me to a farmyard. As I neared the house, I saw an automobile move slowly along the road and stop, playing a spotlight from one side to the other. I walked over to the car. Several people were in it.

"Did you hear that airplane?" one of them called out as I approached. "Just dove into the ground. God, it made a racket!" He searched with his spotlight, but the beam didn't show much in the haze.

"I'm the pilot," I said. The spotlight stopped moving.

"*You're the pilot?* Good God, how—"

"I jumped with a parachute," I said.

"You aren't hurt?"

"No. But I've got to find the wreck and get the mail sacks."

"It must be right nearby. Get in and we'll drive along the road a piece."

We spent a quarter hour searching, unsuccessfully. Then I accompanied the farmer to his house. My plane, he said, had flown over his roof only a few seconds before it struck the ground. I asked to use his telephone. The party line was jammed with voices, all talking about the airplane that had crashed. I broke in and asked the operator if anyone had reported the exact location of the wreck. A number of people had heard the plane pass overhead just before it hit, she replied, but nothing more definite had come in.

I'd hardly hung up and turned away when the phone rang. My plane had been located, the operator told me, about two miles from the house I was in. We drove to the site of the crash. The DH was a ball-shaped mass. Narrowly missing a farmhouse, it had skidded along the ground for 80 yards, ripped through a fence, and come to rest on the edge of a cornfield. Splinters of wood and bits of torn fabric were strewn all around. The mail compartment was broken open and one sack had fallen out; but the mail was undamaged—I took it to the nearest post office to be entrained.

LIGHTS ARE BLINKING ON in the city of Peoria. I glance at the watch on my instrument board: 6:35. I've made up ten minutes since leaving St. Louis. I nose down toward the flying field, letting the airspeed needle climb to 120 miles an hour. The green mail truck is at its usual place in the fence corner. The driver, standing by its side, lifts his arm in greeting as my plane approaches. And for this admiring audience of one, I dive down below the treetops and chandelle up around the field, climbing steeply until trembling wings warn me to level off. Then, engine throttled, I sideslip down to a landing.

I taxi up to the mail truck, blast the tail around with the engine, and pull back my throttle until the propeller is just ticking over. The driver comes up smiling with the mail sack draped over one arm. It's a registered sack, fastened at the top with a big brass padlock. Good! The weight of that lock is worth nearly two dollars to us.

I toss the sack down into the plane and pass out two equally empty sacks from St. Louis and Springfield. A few dozen letters in, a few dozen letters out, that's the Peoria airmail.

"No fuel today?"

"No, plenty of fuel," I answer. "I've had a good tail wind."

It's a relief to both of us, for twenty minutes of hard labor are required to roll a barrel of gasoline over from our cache in the fence corner, pump 30 or 40 gallons into the DH's tank, and start the engine again.

Leaving the engine idling, we walk over to inspect the field lighting equipment which has been improvised for the night landings of winter. Since the Robertson Aircraft Corporation keeps no mechanics at intermediate stops between St. Louis and Chicago, all the assistance we have comes from the mail-truck drivers. They help us with refueling and starting, keep the wind sock untangled, and hold on to a wing when taxiing is difficult. It's not part of their work, but they're always ready to give us a hand. Now we'll depend on them to arrange the lights for our night landings.

Electric floodlights cost too much, so our corporation bought flares instead. The first shipment has just arrived. The driver unlocks a plank box and takes out a long cylindrical flare. On one end there's a spike that can be stuck into the ground to hold it upright. It will burn for nearly two minutes—long enough if lighted at the right moment.

I show the driver where it should be placed with different directions of wind—always on the leeward end of the landing strip, with a curved sheet of tin behind it for a reflector and to keep the light from blinding the pilot as he glides down. A flare is not to be set off, I tell him, unless he sees the plane's navigation lights blink several times. On moonlit nights we can economize by not using a flare at all.

I'M AN HOUR AND TEN MINUTES behind schedule taking off. The trees at the far end of the field have merged into a solid clump in thickening dusk. The moon is rising in the east.

I welcome the approach of night. The day has been almost cloudless; perfect for flying—almost too perfect, for it requires no ability to hold your course over familiar country with a sharp horizon in every quarter. You simply sit, touching stick and rudder lightly, dreaming of the earth below, of experiences past, of adventures to come. There's nothing to match yourself against—no tricks of wind, no false horizons. The hours are shaped for beauty, not for contest.

The last tint of pink disappears from the western sky, leaving to the moon complete mastery of night. It makes the earth seem more like a planet; and me a part of the heavens above it. I look down toward the ground, at the faintly lighted farmhouses and the distant glow of cities. Those myriad lights, all the turmoil and works of men, seem to hang precariously on the great sphere hurtling through the heavens. I feel aloof and unattached, in the solitude of space. Why return to that sphere, why submerge myself in brick-walled human problems when all the crystal universe is mine? Like the moon, I can fly on forever through space.

Suppose I really could stay up here and keep flying; suppose gasoline didn't weigh so much and I could put enough in the tanks to last for days. How much fuel *could* a plane carry if its fuselage were filled with tanks? René Fonck tried that in his big Sikorsky biplane and crashed in flames on a New York field. If gasoline weighed only a pound per gallon instead of six, there'd be no limit to the places one could fly—if the engine kept on running.

If the engine kept on running! I return abruptly to problems of engine temperature, oil pressure, and rpm. I have fuel enough for another two hours. But long before that I'll be down at Chicago, and the mail will be in the cockpit of another plane, headed for New York City.

I'm annoyed at the thought of landing. It's a roundabout method, this flying the mail to Chicago to get it east. Why shouldn't we carry it direct to New York from St. Louis? There aren't enough letters in that wilted sack to pay for a direct service, but the mail will grow in volume as aircraft improve and more time is saved. There's that Wright-Bellanca, for instance.

15

It has taken off with an incredible weight on some of its test flights. With three Bellancas we could easily carry the mail nonstop between St. Louis and New York, and possibly two or three passengers besides. But one Wright-Bellanca would cost ten or fifteen thousand dollars. Who could afford it? Our DHs cost only a few hundred dollars apiece.

I grow conscious of the limits of my biplane. A Bellanca would cruise at least 15 miles an hour faster, burn only half the amount of gasoline, and carry double the payload.

If only I had one Bellanca, I'd show St. Louis businessmen what modern aircraft could do; I'd take them to New York safely in eight or nine hours. Businessmen think of aviation in terms of barnstorming, flying circuses, crashes, and high costs per flying hour. If they could be made to understand the possibilities of flight, it wouldn't be difficult to finance an airline between St. Louis and New York.

In a Bellanca I could fly all night. Carrying nothing but gasoline, and with the engine throttled down, I could stay aloft for days. Possibly—my mind is startled at its thought—I could fly nonstop between New York and Paris.

NEW YORK TO PARIS—a dream. And yet, if one could carry fuel enough (and the Bellanca might), if the engine didn't stop (and those new Wright Whirlwinds seldom do stop), and if one held to the right course long enough—one should arrive in Europe. The flying couldn't be more dangerous or the weather worse than the night mail in winter.

Why shouldn't I fly from New York to Paris? I'm almost twenty-five. I have more than four years of aviation behind me, and close to two thousand hours in the air. I've barnstormed over half of the forty-eight states, flown my mail through the worst of nights. During my year as a flying cadet, I learned the basic elements of navigation. I'm a captain in Missouri's National Guard. Am I not qualified for such a flight?

When I was a student in college, just flying an airplane seemed a dream. But that dream turned into reality. Then, as a pilot barnstorming through the country for a living, the wings of the Army Air Mail Service seemed beyond reach. But I won them.

Finally, to be a mail pilot appeared the summit of ambition; yet here I am in the cockpit of a mail plane. Why wouldn't a flight across the ocean prove as possible as all these things have been?

This vision born of a night and altitude and moonlight, how will I translate it into an actual airplane flying over the Atlantic Ocean? The important thing is to start; to lay a plan, then follow it step by step. I haven't enough money to buy a Wright-Bellanca. But maybe I could raise the money in St. Louis; I can put up some myself. Then there's the Raymond Orteig prize of twenty-five thousand dollars for the first man to fly from New York to Paris nonstop—that's more than enough to pay for a plane and all the expenses of the flight. A successful trip to Paris might even end up a profitable venture.

There must be men of means with enough vision to take the risk involved. Maybe the Wright Aeronautical Corporation itself would back the project. What could be a better advertisement for their engine than a nonstop flight across the ocean?

The Chicago beacon flashes in the distance. In ten minutes I must land.

IT'S TOO LATE to think more about ocean flights tonight. I crawl into bed, angle cornerwise for room—and lie there unable to turn off thought. What made Fonck's Sikorsky crash? Was the frail structure simply overloaded, or did he make an error in piloting technique? After his takeoff was started, about halfway down the runway, one of the auxiliary landing gears came loose and dragged up a cloud of dust. The plane swerved, straightened—engines still wide open. It reached the end of the runway without gaining speed enough to fly, and crashed—in flames. Fonck and his copilot escaped from the wreckage almost uninjured, but the navigator-mechanic and the radio operator lost their lives. Newspaper accounts are so conflicting it's hard to judge. The big plane had taken off beautifully on its lighter load tests, and there was good reason to believe it could carry enough fuel for the Paris flight. The dragging of the auxiliary landing gear probably held it on the ground. I should think Fonck would have cut his switches when the gear broke loose. But who am I to judge his crisis-action while I lie snugly here in bed? He had to decide in seconds what his critics have had days to talk about. And what pilot is immune to error?

What I don't understand is why the plane was not stripped of every excess ounce of weight. Its cabin, luxuriously finished in leather, contained a bed, two radio sets, and special flotation bags in case of a landing at sea. And it certainly doesn't take four men to fly a plane across the ocean.

Well, if I can get a Bellanca, I'll fly alone. If there's upholstery in the cabin, I'll tear it out. I'll take only a few concentrated rations, a little extra water, and a rubber boat for emergency.

Now I must get a few hours' sleep.

THE ALARM CLOCK'S shattering ring seems to reach down through a dozen layers of blankets. It's a drugged awakening. For a moment I almost believe that flying isn't worth such a terrific effort to overcome bodily desire. I start to reset the clock, so I can sleep for ten minutes more. But this morning is not like other mornings. This is the dawn of a new life, a life in which I'm going to fly across the ocean to Europe!

All during my flight to St. Louis I turn over plans in my mind. How can I get the airplane I need? I probably won't succeed if I simply go to the Wright corporation and say that I want a Bellanca for a New York-to-Paris flight. Without either cash in hand or well-established references, they'd have little interest in my ideas. Even if I could persuade them that the value of the flight would justify taking the chance involved, they'd probably want to have their Bellanca flown by a better-known pilot. There are lots of men more experienced than I.

I'll have to get men with both influence and money to go into the project with me. Then I can say I represent a St. Louis organization which intends to purchase an airplane for the New York-to-Paris flight, and that we are considering, among others, the Bellanca. That would put the Wright corporation in the position of trying to sell their product to me instead of my trying to sell an idea to them. They might go into partnership with us. And if they won't, I can try other manufacturers.

I have a few thousand dollars, invested for me by my mother in Detroit. This includes childhood savings, small amounts sent home from my pay as a flying cadet, and profits from my years of barnstorming. It's a reserve I've built up slowly and carefully to safeguard my flying career—to cover a crashed plane, or a bad season. Well, a financial reserve isn't quite as important as it used to be. Now that I'm an experienced pilot, I can always get some kind of a job flying.

For the St. Louisans who might be interested in taking part, I have two major arguments. First, that a nonstop flight between America and Europe will place St. Louis in the foreground of aviation. Second, that a successful flight will cover its own costs because of the Orteig prize. But to whom shall I go with my project? I have friends in the city, but most of them are aviators, too, and men in aviation seldom have much money.

LAMBERT FIELD lies in farming country about 10 miles north-west of the St. Louis business district. There are no runways, but the clay sod is good surface for any aircraft. The field's major commercial activity is carried on by the Robertson Aircraft Corporation, built and managed by the three Robertson brothers. A little stove-heated office, two frame warehouses for airplane and engine parts, and half of a civilian hangar house its operations. The corporation's major income results from the sale of reconditioned army training planes, engines, and spares.

Except on weekends, when the National Guard squadron comes out, there are seldom more than a half-dozen pilots on Lambert Field, and their chief activity is training students. One can always make a few extra dollars and build up flying time by instructing.

Those of us who instruct know Lambert Field as a child knows his own yard. And in every azimuth there's a reminder of some past incident of flight. At this spot, George Harmon was killed when his pilot stalled on a left chandelle. Against an east wind, one takes off over the cornfield where Captain Bill spun in after his Jenny's engine failed. (By some miracle he wasn't hurt.) There's where Smith and Swengrosh died when they lost a wing in a loop. On the side of that ditch is where Bud Gurney broke his arm in a parachute spot-landing contest. The pigpen by the white farmhouse is where O. E. Scott once nosed over.

Scotty is manager of the field, and pilot of the new Travel Air which was bought last year by Harold Bixby. Since Bixby, a St. Louis banker, bought the plane, several of the city's businessmen have started flying. Harry Knight, the broker, is taking lessons. And Earl Thompson, the insurance executive, has a golden-winged Laird. I've given him a little instruction now and then. Thompson is the kind of man who'll listen to my ideas. I'll telephone tomorrow for an appointment.

I PUSH THE DOORBELL and step back on the porch to wait. Earl Thompson said he could see me at once at his office or spend an evening with me at his house the next week. I chose the latter. It seemed less likely that one could sell a flight across the ocean at an office desk.

A maid shows me to the living room. Mr. Thompson comes in, shakes hands, motions me to a chair. I feel uncomfortable in the soft upholstery.

"Mr. Thompson," I begin, "I've come to ask your advice about a project I'm considering."

He smiles and nods encouragement.

"You've heard about the Orteig prize of twenty-five thousand dollars for a nonstop flight between New York and Paris. I'd like to try it. It would advance aviation, and it would advertise St. Louis."

I explain that I want to get a group behind me to finance the project and give me the prestige I'll need in dealing with aircraft manufacturers.

"I can furnish two thousand dollars myself," I say. "But the right kind of plane will probably cost at least ten thousand."

Mr. Thompson's face becomes serious. "What kind of plane would you get for that flight, Captain?" he asks.

"I think the Wright-Bellanca could make it," I tell him.

"But that's a land plane—and it has only one engine, hasn't it?" His voice is as disturbed as his question. "I'd want you to have a flying boat, or a plane with enough engines so you wouldn't have to land in the water if one of them stopped. Have you considered using a three-engined Fokker, like Commander Byrd's?"

I was afraid of that. Businessmen are always conservative. But at least he's taking my idea seriously.

"Well," I argue, "a flying boat can't take off with enough fuel. And I'm afraid a trimotored Fokker would cost at least thirty thousand. Besides, I'm not sure three engines would really add much safety on a flight like that. The plane would be overloaded with fuel anyway, and if one engine stopped over the ocean, you probably couldn't get back to land with the other two. You know Fonck had three engines, but that didn't help him any when his landing gear gave way. A single-engined plane might be safer, everything considered."

"Well, you know a lot more about airplanes than I do," Mr. Thompson says. "But I don't like the idea of a single engine out over the ocean."

We spend the rest of the evening talking about the flight. Mr. Thompson is interested and encouraging, but cautious and greatly concerned about the risks involved. After all, his business is insurance.

"THERE's a Fokker man here. He's up with Major Robertson, talking about a St. Louis agency."

I'm eating late breakfast at Louie De Hatre's lunch stand, after bringing in the Chicago mail. At the counter one learns immediately about everything new on the field. The possibility of a Fokker agency is real news. For me, it's a chance to get some accurate information about the big trimotored monoplane's performance and cost. I watch the door to Major Bill Robertson's little office until he emerges with the stranger—a stocky man in city clothes. They stroll over to the lunch stand, and we are introduced. Pilots, mechanics, and students gather, sit on benches, lean against walls, listening to stories of Tony Fokker's genius, of the safety and efficiency of multiengines. The Fokker salesman's "line" is good.

A phone call comes for Major Robertson. The Fokker man and I walk over toward the hangar. "I'd like to talk to you about a project we're considering here," I tell him. "But I'm going to ask you to hold what I say in confidence for the present."

He nods assent.

"A group of St. Louis men are thinking of buying a plane for the New York-to-Paris flight," I say. "We've been considering a Fokker."

He's looking at me intently now.

"We'd like to know whether you can build a plane that could carry enough fuel to make that flight, how much it would cost, and how soon it could be delivered."

"The Fokker company has made a study of that flight," the salesman tells me courteously but without enthusiasm. "Mr. Fokker can design a plane with enough range to reach Paris with a good reserve of fuel. The company can deliver it by next spring, if the order is placed now. It would cost about ninety thousand dollars."

Ninety thousand dollars! I try to keep my face as expressionless as his, but my mind whirls.

"Of course," he adds, "the company would have to be satisfied with the competence of operating personnel before they would be willing to sell a plane for such a flight."

I pass over this as though it didn't apply to me. "That's much more than we had planned on. The figure I heard quoted—"

The salesman doesn't wait for me to finish. "Oh, our standard trimotors are much less. A plane for long range would have to be specially built, you see. It would need a large wing, and extra tanks in the fuselage. The landing gear would have to be beefed up. It would be a different airplane entirely. The Fokker company's reputation would be at stake."

"We've also considered using a single-engined plane," I tell him. "How much would it cost to build a single-engined Fokker with enough range for—"

The salesman breaks in again. "We would not be interested in selling a single-engined plane for a flight across the ocean."

I feel embarrassed, as though I were an adolescent boy broaching an ill-considered venture to a tolerant but disapproving parent. I slip away as soon as I can, and walk out along a narrow dirt road to farmlands beyond. I need time, alone, to think.

The two men I've talked to about a New York-to-Paris flight are both prejudiced. One of them looks on the risk from the standpoint of an insurance executive. The other wants to promote multiengined airplanes. But Earl Thompson is interested in the flight—that's the important thing.

I decide to try to purchase the Wright-Bellanca. The Wright corporation will certainly have confidence in its own engine; and since they don't make a multiengined plane, they should be in sympathy with my arguments against one.

Next week I have an appointment to talk to Major Albert Bond Lambert, for whom the St. Louis field is named. During the World War, he commanded a school for balloon pilots. He is among the most active leaders in midwestern aviation.

MAJOR LAMBERT sits at his desk, alert, serious, looking at me through thick eyeglasses. His gray hair is thinning where he parts it in the center. He's immaculately dressed. "That's quite a flight, Slim. Do you really think it can be done?" he asks.

"Yes, sir, but I need help. If the manufacturers know that responsible people are behind me, they'll give me all the information I want about performances, and I'll be in a good position to trade on prices, too."

Major Lambert doesn't raise any question about flying boats or multiengines. He has lived through too many years of aviation; he knows there's danger involved in all flying.

"If you can get the right fellows together, Slim," he says, "you can count on me for a thousand dollars."

A thousand dollars! With my own money, that's three thousand dollars already. And Mr. Thompson is with me, even though he hasn't promised any definite amount. I have an organization under way, so it's time to talk to Bill Robertson.

"*Wheeuuu . . .*" Major Robertson whistles. "It doesn't seem possible to put enough gasoline for thirty-five hundred miles in an airplane. What does a Bellanca cost?"

"My guess is about ten thousand dollars. Major Lambert says he'll put in a thousand if I can get the right kind of men together, and I can put in two thousand myself. Earl Thompson is interested. I haven't asked anybody else."

Bill hesitates, then he says, "We'll help as much as we can, Slim, but you know we're losing dollars every day."

"I know, Bill. I didn't come to you for money. You can help in two other ways. I want to be able to say that the Robertson Aircraft Corporation is behind me; and I need your permission to arrange the mail schedule so I can get away for two or three days at a time when it's necessary."

"You can say we're behind you," he says. "But I don't know about the schedule. You know the post office won't take excuses if the mail doesn't go through. Can Phil and Nellie handle it?"

"I think we can keep it running all right, Bill. You can tele-graph me if a plane goes down and I'll take the first train back. If I have to be away too much, we'll train another pilot."

"Well, fix it up with Phil and Nellie, Slim. Say, that flight ought to be worth a lot for advertising. The *Post-Dispatch* might be willing to put up enough money to cover the whole thing. You could paint the paper's name on the fuselage. I know one of the editors. Why don't we go down and talk to him?"

I'm not too happy about the *Post-Dispatch* suggestion. There's something wrong about flying a billboard to Paris; it's like blocking out a mountain vista with a beer advertisement. Still, I've got to look into all possibilities.

"You make the appointment," I tell him.

I STAND in the doorway of the post office, reading an Associated Press dispatch.

BYRD TO FLY ATLANTIC

POLE CONQUEROR PREDICTS OCEAN CROSSING NEXT YEAR

BRIDGEPORT, CONN., Oct. 28 (AP).—Con-quering the Atlantic Ocean by air from New York to London or Paris in a heavier-than-air machine would be accomplished next summer, Lieut. Commander Richard E. Byrd declared here tonight, intimating that he himself would attempt the journey.

That's formidable competition. Commander Byrd is experienced at organizing, and he knows how to get financed. And what about those French pilots who say they are going to win the Orteig prize by flying from east to west? For weeks there have been rumors to the effect that they are ready to take off. And the other American projects I've read about. A lot of people want to be first to make the nonstop flight.

"THE Post-Dispatch wouldn't think of taking part in such a hazardous flight. Across the Atlantic with one pilot in a single-engine plane? We have our reputation to consider!"

Major Robertson and I sit uncomfortably in front of the editor's desk. The Post-Dispatch is not impressed either with the advertising value of a flight to Paris or with my plan for making it. We get up, shake hands, and leave.

"I'm going to talk to the Wright people before we proposition anybody else," I tell Bill. "I want to know just what the Bellanca can do, and how often Whirlwind engines fail. If I'd had accurate data, I could have put up a better argument to that editor."

But how am I going to contact the Wright corporation? No friend of mine knows anyone in the organization, even indirectly. It won't make a very good impression if I just arrive at the reception desk and say I want to talk to one of the officers.

I've got to remember that New York isn't St. Louis. Here in St. Louis I'm well known in aviation circles. I can get a good reference from anyone connected with Lambert Field. But I'm unheard of in New York and at Paterson, New Jersey, where the Wright Aeronautical Corporation has its plant.

I can write a letter to them mentioning our group, our interest in the Paris flight, and our wish to discuss purchasing the Bellanca. I can say that I plan to be in New York in the near future, and that I will phone for an appointment. But the corporation might write back for the names of my partners in the enterprise, and I could only say that three men in St. Louis have more or less committed themselves provided I can get together a large enough group to finance the project adequately. Such an answer probably wouldn't get any further reply.

I might telegraph the Wright corporation. But I'd like to do something even more out of the ordinary. Why not *telephone* them all the way from St. Louis? It would probably cost at least five dollars, but a long-distance call would carry a prestige which no letter or telegram, signed by an unknown pilot, could possibly have. I'll tell them that I'm coming to Paterson to discuss buying the Bellanca for the New York-to-Paris flight. A long-distance phone call and a 2000-mile train trip ought to impress them.

IT'S MY TURN to fly the mail tonight. Ten minutes away from Peoria trees ahead disappear in fog and twilight. There's not a chance to get there. I take up a compass course back toward Springfield. It looks as though I'll have to entrain the mail.

In the distance, the cloud layer glows dimly. That's Springfield. It's too dark to tell exactly where I am. I shift course five compass degrees and watch for the straight row of lanterns that the mail-truck driver hangs on fence posts along the southern border of our mail field.

Four of six lanterns are still burning when I find the pasture. Night's black brush has swept over posts and poles, trees and earth, leaving no contrast between them—only four dim points of light, a yard above the ground, and several farmhouse windows for horizon.

A burst of engine—10 feet above a lantern—blackness— keep the tail up—ready with the throttle. Bump, let her bounce once, stick forward, back, a little power; let her roll—how near is the fence? Taxi back toward the lanterns.

There's nobody on the field. I pull up close to the fence corner, swing into wind, cut switches, turn off the fuel valve, unsnap the belt, and climb out of my cockpit. A sharp ridge dents the sole of my sheepskin moccasin: the ground is starting to freeze. We've had a telephone installed on one of the poles, a party line, and I put in a call for the Springfield post office.

"This is the flying field—Pilot Lindbergh. I've got to entrain the mail. Peoria's closed in."

"We'll send a truck out. Is there anything else you need?"

"That's all, thanks, but could you notify St. Louis?"

"We'll get a wire right off."

I walk out along the fence line, gather up the lanterns, and station them around my plane. From the looks of the weather, it's not likely that I can take off before sunrise. If I drain the engine and tie my DH to the fence, I can ride to town on the mail truck and get a night's sleep. But then it would take two men, at least, to start up tomorrow morning, even if I pour boiling water into the radiator. Once a Liberty cools off, it's a devil's job to get it running again. And you can't ask help from just anybody who comes along—it takes training to handle either throttle or propeller. I'd probably have to phone for a mechanic to be flown up from Lambert Field. No, I'll stay with the plane and start the engine every twenty minutes. That will keep it warm.

It feels good to move around; the air is sharp, my flying suit comfortably warm. I walk out into the pasture's darkness. Why shouldn't I telephone Wright tomorrow for an appointment? But before taking the train east, I'd have to go back to St. Louis for my clothes. It wouldn't be good technique to present myself at the Wright corporation's offices in boots, breeches, and a three-day-old shirt. But a captain's uniform is the only good suit I own, and one just doesn't wear an officer's uniform on personal business. My business suit goes back to college days; it's shiny and worn, and never did fit very well. I want something better than that, and I'll need a felt hat and an overcoat. All the success-ful businessmen I know wear felt hats and overcoats—they give an impression of dignity and influence.

Car lights are coming along the road from the south. It's probably the mail truck. I go back to the plane and unstrap the hatch to the mail compartment. The truck pulls in through the gate. Mr. Conkling, the postmaster, is driving.

I jump down off the fuselage, and we shake hands. "Tie your plane down and come in for supper with us," he says.

"I'd like to," I tell him as I hand over the mail sacks, "but I can't leave it that long. The engine would freeze up."

"Well, can't we send you something to eat?"

"No, thanks. I'm not hungry."

I'm used to going without meals, and I don't want him to

bother making another trip out from town. Postmaster Conkling climbs back into the truck.

"Good-by and good luck," he calls. "We notified both St. Louis and Chicago that you got down all right."

The truck grinds off, and I'm alone on the field. The time is 7:15. I'd better start the engine before it gets too cold. It's really a stunt for one man, and a very dangerous stunt. The trick of handling a propeller is to make your muscles always pull away from it. If you lean against a blade, on contact, you're asking for broken bones. I put a lantern on the ground next to my cockpit, and line up the other three in front and a little to the left of the propeller. I chock the wheels, tie the stick back with my safety belt, check switches, give the engine three primer shots, retard spark, close throttle, run back to the propeller, catch one blade with my left hand, scrape over frozen ground with my moccasins as I pull a cylinder through compression. It takes all the strength I've got—the oil's beginning to thicken. How fast an engine cools in winter!

One, two, three, four blades through. Leave the fifth sixty degrees below horizontal. Back to the cockpit. Throttle one-half inch open. Switches on. Back to the propeller—10 feet to the right side. Got to watch this; I should have two men pulling on my arm, and a mechanic in the cockpit. Run—grip the blade—throw my weight against it—angle forward to clear its bone-shattering strength—let go—catch balance—back for another try. There's a *ping* this time—the blade moves forward, stops as I trip away. No action on the third blade. On the fourth she hits—one, two cylinders—the engine catches. I stumble as the blade jumps from my hand, break the fall with my arm and shoulder. I scramble up and around the wing to the cockpit. Ease on throttle, a roar from the engine—she's safe now. I unsnap the belt from the stick and climb into the pilot's seat. I'll idle for five minutes, then switch her off for twenty. It's 7:35. I have nine hours to pass before dawn.

I'll have to be in the air for nearly forty hours between New York and Paris. How long can an engine run without attention? How long can a pilot stay awake? It seems ages since I got out of bed yesterday morning; actually it's less than twenty hours.

World War I DH before conversion for mail service

T. Nelson   Lindbergh   P. Love

Lindbergh, 1926

Lambert Field 1925

"IF YOU WANT A REALLY GOOD SUIT, have it tailor-made," says Captain Littlefield. I've selected the most neatly dressed officer in my National Guard squadron for advice on clothing. "A tailored suit looks better and lasts longer," he goes on. "It's worth the extra cost. I know a good tailor in the city. I'll give you his address."

In St. Louis I read the items on the sales slip: 1 overcoat, blue; 1 hat, gray felt; 1 pair gloves, fur-lined; 1 scarf, silk; 2 pair sox, wool; 1 necktie, silk; 1 suitcase, leather. He hasn't filled in the prices yet. Good Lord, that's going to run close to a hundred dollars, and there's still my suit to pay for. I can economize on shoes and shirts; the ones I wear with my uniform will do.

It bothers me to think that I'm buying these clothes just to make an impression on the Wright corporation—they won't add a penny's worth to my ability as a flyer. But right now the impression I make may be as essential to my Paris flight as my plane will become later.

"I WANT to put in a call to the Wright Aeronautical Corporation at Paterson, New Jersey. Yes, anybody who answers." I've never talked that far over the phone. I hope the connection's good.

I hear clickings, buzzings, snatches of words and numbers.

"Here's your party."

Another girl's voice comes on: "Wright Aeronautical."

"I'd like to speak to one of your officers, please," I tell her, trying to hide all trace of excitement in my voice.

"What officer do you want?" she asks.

"One of your executive officers."

"Which executive officer?" Her voice is insistent, and a little annoyed now. Somehow I've got to break through this.

"I am calling long-distance from St. Louis, Missouri. I want to talk to one of your executive officers—on business." I say it slowly and firmly.

"Hold on a minute, please."

The next voice is a man's.

"I'm calling from St. Louis," I repeat. "My name is Charles Lindbergh. I represent a group of men here who are interested in buying a plane for the New York-to-Paris flight. I'd like to talk to you about the Bellanca. When would it be convenient for you to see me in Paterson?"

"Did you say you're calling from St. Louis?" the man asks.

"That's right."

He's impressed. My phone-call money is well spent.

"We'll be glad to see you any day," he says. "Just let me know when you can come, and we'll set the hour."

II. NEW YORK
November, 1926

THE WRIGHT FACTORY has all the appearances of a successful business organization. As I step through the door I feel that my new clothes are paying off. The girl at the desk smiles. Yes, she's been told to expect me. She calls a number on her phone. "Captain Lindbergh is here," I hear her say.

"This way, please."

The girl leads me down a corridor to a room near the end. A man rises from his desk in greeting.

"So you're interested in the Wright-Bellanca," he says. "Sit down, won't you?"

"Yes, sir. I'd like to have all the information you can give me about the Bellanca. We're also interested in Whirlwind engines."

"I can get all the data you want on Whirlwind engines, but at the moment we can't quote a price on the Bellanca. We're negotiating to sell both the plane and the manufacturing rights to the Huff-Daland Company. You see, the Wright corporation never intended to manufacture aircraft. We built the Bellanca to show how a Whirlwind could perform in a modern plane—it was really a demonstration of our engine. Of course if the deal doesn't go through, we may still be interested in selling the plane."

"How soon will you know whether the Bellanca is for sale?"

"You'd better talk to Giuseppe Bellanca about that. I've arranged for you to meet him. You may want to talk to the Huff-Daland people, too."

"MY PLANE IS FULLY CAPABLE of flying nonstop from New York to Paris," says Giuseppe Bellanca, leaning forward intently from a lounge in the Waldorf-Astoria. He is a serious, slender man—straight black hair, sharp-cut features, medium height. One feels, in his presence, capability, confidence, genius. "It will only be necessary to put a big gasoline tank in the cabin," he adds.

"Is the landing gear strong enough to take off with such a load of fuel?" I ask.

"Yes; I have built the landing gear especially strong."

"How many hours do you think your plane could stay in the air without refueling, if the pilot kept it throttled down to minimum flying speed?" I ask.

"It could stay up for more than fifty hours, Captain Lindbergh. That would break the world's endurance record."

"It might be a good idea to try to break the endurance record, as an engine test, before starting a flight over the ocean."

"I think that would be wise. The plane is capable of it."

In Giuseppe Bellanca I have a friend. He's as much interested in the New York-to-Paris flight as I am. We talk about cruising speeds, fuel requirements, takeoff distances. He has at his fingertips the answers to practically everything I want to know.

"Well," I say finally, "thank you for all your help."

We get up, shake hands.

"I hope that you are able to buy my plane, Captain Lindbergh," he tells me.

I take the train west that night. When I get to St. Louis, I'll be able to tell about an airplane that's able to make the flight, and a designer who's anxious to have his plane bought for that purpose. Then, if I can raise enough money, I'll make a cash offer to whoever owns the Wright-Bellanca.

As soon as I reach Lambert Field, I wire Bellanca: IMPORTANT TO KNOW AS SOON AS POSSIBLE WHETHER PLANE CAN BE PURCHASED FOR ST. LOUIS TO PARIS FLIGHT STOP WOULD GREATLY APPRECIATE YOUR KEEPING ME POSTED ON DEVELOPMENTS. LINDBERGH.

It's essential to keep my project alive. This leaves the next move up to Bellanca.

After lunch I drive into the city to tell Mr. Thompson and Major Lambert about my eastern trip.

DAYS PASS, AND NO ANSWER from Bellanca. Then, on the morning of December 4, I get a telegram: SORRY LONG UNAVOIDABLE DELAY WILL BE GLAD TO HELP YOU IN ANY WAY TO OBTAIN PURCHASE OF WRIGHT BELLANCA AND PREPARE SAME FOR PARIS FLIGHT BUT IF UNABLE TO BUY WRIGHT BELLANCA I OFFER THREE MOTOR PLANE FOR TWENTY NINE THOUSAND DOLLARS WHICH IS EXCEPTIONALLY ADAPTED FOR PARIS FLIGHT. BELLANCA.

Good Lord! I thought Bellanca was one man who wouldn't advocate multiengines. Even if I had twenty-nine thousand dollars, how long would it take to build a trimotored plane?

I'm still turning this problem over in my mind when a telegram arrives from the Huff-Daland Company, indicating that negotiations for purchase of the Wright-Bellanca have been broken off. So I wire the Wright corporation: ESSENTIAL TO KNOW AS SOON AS POSSIBLE WHETHER BELLANCA CAN BE PURCHASED FOR ST. LOUIS TO PARIS FLIGHT. LINDBERGH.

Four days pass. I send another message.

This reply arrives: REGRET THAT WE DO NOT DESIRE AT THIS TIME TO HAVE WRIGHT BELLANCA USED FOR TRANSATLANTIC FLIGHT SUGGEST FOKKER OR HUFF DALAND THREE ENGINE PLANES. WRIGHT AERO.

Well, that's definite enough. But perhaps Bellanca can build another single-motored plane. I'll wire him to let him know my interest is still keen: WRIGHT CORPORATION REFUSES SELL BELLANCA STOP WHEN COULD YOU DELIVER SIMILAR SINGLE ENGINE PLANE FOR PARIS FLIGHT AND WHAT WOULD PRICE BE. LINDBERGH.

FOR DAYS, nothing has flown on Lambert Field except our mail planes. Turbulent winds, and mud alternating with frozen ground, have brought student training to a standstill. I've had plenty of time to work on my Paris project, and I've gotten nowhere. Bellanca hasn't replied to my latest telegram. Aside from Mr. Thompson and Majors Robertson and Lambert, I've found no one willing to take part in financing a flight across the ocean. Prospective backers consider the risk too great—if not for their bank accounts, then for their reputations. I've not been able to convince them that flying the ocean is no more dangerous than a winter on the mail. They want no share in the criticism

33

they think would come from sending a young pilot to his death.

The winter is almost half over. Each day makes my failure more complete. In France and in America, aircraft for the transoceanic flight are being built and tested, while I do nothing but think over plans. I must make a final effort or give up my dream. I'll ask Love and Nelson to take over the mail schedules completely for a few days. Then I'll lay my Paris project before every businessman in St. Louis I can get an appointment with.

"SLIM, you ought not to be running around worrying about raising money. You've got to put all your attention on that flight if you're going to make it."

I'm talking to Harry Knight in his brokerage office. I met Knight, who is president of the St. Louis Flying Club, on the airfield last summer when he was taking flying lessons. He's a stocky, abrupt young man, not much older than myself.

"Let me talk to a friend of mine in the bank," he says. "Maybe we can take care of the financial end for you. How much money is it going to take?"

His words strike like the flash of an airfield's beacon on a stormy night.

"If we can get the plane and engine manufacturers to stand part of the expense, I think ten thousand would be enough. Otherwise it might cost as much as fifteen thousand."

"You're talking about a single-engined plane. Wouldn't a tri-motor be better for that kind of flight?" he asks.

I start in with my old arguments again. "It would cost twenty-nine thousand to get a trimotored plane from Bellanca. The Fokker company wants ninety thousand for one of theirs. Multiengined planes are more complicated; there are more things likely to go wrong with them. The greatest danger lies in weather, and in takeoff with a full load, not in engine failure—"

Knight suddenly swings around in his chair and picks up the telephone. "Get me Harold Bixby at the State National Bank," he says, and then: "Bix, how about coming over here for a few minutes?"

Within ten minutes Bixby knocks on the door. He's a man

you like right away—smiling and full of humor. But his brown eyes are penetrating.

Harry Knight outlines my project.

"You think a plane with a Whirlwind engine can make a flight like that?" Bixby asks.

"Yes, sir," I answer. I tell him about my trip to New York and my talks with the Wright corporation and Bellanca. "It might work to put an oversize wing on an existing fuselage," I say. "But there's not time to do a lot of building. I want to be ready to start as soon as the weather breaks next spring."

"Slim, don't you think you ought to have a plane with more than one engine for that kind of flight?" Bixby asks.

Harry Knight laughs. "That's what I asked him, Bix, but he doesn't think it would be much safer."

"I don't believe a Paris flight would be any more dangerous than a winter on the mail line," I say. "A pilot can't fly without taking *some* risk. I've weighed my chances carefully—"

Bixby breaks in. "Yes, you've only got a life to lose, Slim. But don't forget, I've got a reputation to lose." Then he surprises me by adding, "You let us think about this for a day or two, and talk to some of our friends. If you're going to make the flight, we've got to get started right away. Come down and see me next Wednesday, ten a.m., at my office."

IT'S SNOWING on the Springfield pasture. I've just flown through sleeting rain. I taxi slowly, wings rocking with gusts of wind.

"Here's Chicago weather. It don't look so good," the Springfield mail-truck driver says, handing up a folded sheet of paper. It doesn't look so good here either. I've just measured the ceiling at 300 feet, and darkness isn't far away. I wait until the driver starts unbuckling the mail hatch, then throw his message over the far side of my cockpit, unread. Chicago reports are so unreliable that I don't want to condition my mind with them. I'd rather judge weather ahead as I fly.

"Those Chicago fellows just look out the window before they call Springfield," Nelson told me once. "If they can see a few blocks down the street, they say the weather's good. If a little haze fuzzes up the lamps, they say it's all closed in. But let's not discourage them. Maybe someday they'll get better." One thing is certain: they can't get any worse. And at least we've got the principle of weather reports established.

I know there's bad weather ahead tonight. Love had to entrain the southbound mail. If he couldn't take off in daylight, there's not much chance of my getting through in darkness. But somehow I've got to get back to St. Louis to make a 10:00 a.m. appointment with Harold Bixby. If I can get through to Chicago, I'll start at daybreak on a southbound ferry flight.

Flakes of snow melt against my cheeks as I take off.

Is something wrong with the engine? It's like that first, vague, uncomfortable feeling which precedes the outward manifestation of an illness. I cut the left switch, then the right. The engine vibrates, spits, and sputters. I turn back toward Springfield's pasture. It's not over five minutes since I left.

The mail driver is waiting for me.

"Too thick?" he asks, stomping his feet to keep warm.

"No, it was lifting a little. My engine started cutting out." I crawl forward. "Put a stone behind the wheels, will you, so she doesn't blow backward while I look at the distributors."

I find the trouble—a loose spring.

"Hang up the lanterns and wait here twenty minutes," I tell the driver. "I want to try again."

He nods, gives me a hand pulling through the propeller, waves me off the field.

Twenty miles north of Springfield it stops snowing. Thirty miles north, the stars are out and there's not a cloud in the sky. I find Chicago cloud-covered, but the ceiling has lifted to at least 500 feet.

"Think you're a mail pilot, don't you?" Love, feet apart, hands in pockets, stands beside my fuselage as I climb down. His DH rests silently behind its chocks, half hidden in the darkness.

"Oh, it was a little thick; but nothing to worry about," I answer, making the most of his embarrassment. He'll find out soon enough that I've come in with clearing skies.

Everett, our Chicago mechanic, is grinning. He has that crewman's intuition which tells him whether a flight has been tough or not. He feels pretty sure I've come through without much trouble. "We'll have to leave one of these planes out tonight," he remarks.

This is the moment to lay down my joker. "Oh, I'm going to ferry back just as soon as we can refuel. We don't want *two* planes up here at Chicago."

"Slim, are you crazy?" Love asks. "You're not going back into that stuff tonight!"

"Just stand by and watch," I say.

"DO YOU MIND WAITING? Mr. Bixby is still in conference. He'll be through in just a few minutes."

The secretary smiles and leaves. It's ten o'clock. I sit down in a corner chair at the State National Bank of St. Louis. I glance sidewise at the people waiting with me. They must be facing problems similar to mine. I shift in my chair. My clothes bind; my collar sticks around my neck.

"Hello, Slim! I'm sorry I had to keep you waiting."

Bixby slips in through one of those waist-high mahogany, semiprivate gates. I stand to shake hands.

"You're taking on a tough job," he says, "but we've talked it over and we're with you. From now on you'd better leave the financial end to us." His cheeks wrinkle back in confidence as he speaks. "You put in your two thousand dollars. We'll arrange whatever organization we need. You concentrate on the plane and getting ready for the flight. We want to be sure it's a practical proposition. Don't get obligated before we meet again. But let us know as soon as you have something definite lined up."

I'm really going to fly to Paris! It's no longer just an idea. My most difficult problems are solved—organization and finance.

Now I must find a plane. I'll sound out all the aircraft builders in the United States. The Travel Air Company at Wichita is producing a monoplane along the general lines of the Wright-Bellanca—it might do. I've also read of a high-wing monoplane built by a company named Ryan, out in San Diego. The Travel Air Company is nearer. I'll telegraph them first and ask whether they'd consider building a plane for the St. Louis–Paris flight.

I WAKE SOON AFTER DAWN. As I fry potatoes and eggs for breakfast, I list items to be covered on this new day of the new life I've entered. For it is a new life; I'll now bend every thought and effort toward one objective—landing at Paris.

We'll have to select and train another pilot for the mail route. It will be difficult in winter; but most of the beacons are now installed, and days are getting longer. Then I must notify the National Guard that I'll be absent for weeks or months.

A reply comes back quickly from Travel Air. They won't accept the order. What about the Ryan company? I'll try them. I'll sign the message "Robertson Aircraft Corporation," as Major Bill gave me permission to do.

FEB. 3, 1927. RYAN AIRLINES INC., SAN DIEGO, CALIFORNIA: CAN YOU CONSTRUCT WHIRLWIND ENGINE PLANE CAPABLE FLYING NONSTOP BETWEEN NEW YORK AND PARIS STOP IF SO PLEASE STATE COST AND DELIVERY DATE. ROBERTSON AIRCRAFT CORP.

FEB. 4, 1927. CAN BUILD PLANE CAPABLE OF MAKING FLIGHT COST ABOUT SIX THOUSAND WITHOUT MOTOR AND INSTRUMENTS DELIVERY ABOUT THREE MONTHS. RYAN AIRLINES.

Six thousand dollars! With the engine, that would make about ten thousand. It's well within my budget. But does the Ryan company understand what it's offering to undertake?

FEB. 5, 1927. RYAN AIRLINES INC., SAN DIEGO, CALIFORNIA: COMPETITION MAKES TIME ESSENTIAL CAN YOU CONSTRUCT PLANE IN LESS THAN THREE MONTHS STOP PLEASE WIRE GENERAL SPECIFICATIONS. ROBERTSON AIRCRAFT CORP.

FEB. 5, 1927. GAS CAPACITY THREE HUNDRED EIGHTY GALLONS CRUISING SPEED ONE HUNDRED MILES PER HOUR LOADING ONLY TWELVE AND HALF POUNDS PER FOOT AND TWENTY POUNDS PER HORSEPOWER STOP CAN COMPLETE IN TWO MONTHS FROM DATE OF ORDER STOP WILL REQUIRE FIFTY PERCENT DEPOSIT. RYAN AIRLINES.

Bill Robertson

Harold Bixby

Harry Knight

Major Lambert

The Bellanca

René Fonck and Igor Sikorsky with
biplane designed for N.Y.-Paris competition

Three hundred and eighty gallons! That's a tremendous load of gasoline for a 200-horsepower engine. But 100 miles per hour is excellent cruising speed.

Two months—that would let me start tests sometime in April. I could be ready to take off when the weather breaks in spring.

Bixby and Knight look at the telegrams I lay before them.

"I've never heard of the Ryan company."

"Can they build a plane with enough performance, Slim?"

"Ryan mail planes have a pretty good reputation," I answer.

"Well, I certainly wouldn't turn them down because we haven't heard of them," Knight tells me. "They probably haven't heard of us, either. What kind of plane do they make?"

"It's a high-wing monoplane, like Bellanca's, only it's got an open cockpit, and the span is shorter."

"At least they're anxious to build us a plane," Bixby says. "Do you want to go out to California and talk to them?"

"I can't very well size up the Ryan people until I see them."

"How soon can you start?"

"Within a week. I don't know how long I'll be away, of course. If we decide to buy a plane, I'll stay in California while it's being built. I'll take care of my own expenses on this trip."

"No, you won't," Bixby says. "We're in this with you. We'll split up on all those things."

A ROBERTSON MECHANIC hands me a telegram as I jump down from the front cockpit of my training plane on Lambert Field. I tear open the envelope and read: FEB. 6, 1927. WILLING TO MAKE ATTRACTIVE PROPOSITION ON THE BELLANCA AIRPLANE FOR PARIS FLIGHT STOP SUGGEST YOU COME NEW YORK SOON POSSIBLE SO WE CAN GET TOGETHER IN QUICKEST MANNER STOP WIRE ME CARE COLUMBIA AIRCRAFT CORPORATION 5104 WOOLWORTH BUILDING NEW YORK. BELLANCA.

Bellanca must have organized a new company and bought his plane from the Wright corporation. His message came just in time; in two more days I would have left for California.

The Wright-Bellanca is at last available; and now I have the financial backing to buy it. I'll be ahead of everyone else. I'll have the best plane for the flight, and plenty of time to test it before weather clears in the spring. I'll get big fuselage tanks put in, fly nonstop to St. Louis, fill them up, and break the world's endurance record. After that, we'll have the Whirlwind torn down and inspected to see if any parts show excessive strain or wear; and we'll give the plane a final going-over. Then I'll be ready to take off for Paris whenever conditions are best. Meanwhile I'll study methods of long-range navigation.

I wire Bellanca that our St. Louis organization is complete, and that I'm coming to New York.

"CAPTAIN LINDBERGH, I want you to meet Mr. Levine, chairman of the board of directors of the Columbia Aircraft Corporation. And this is Mr. Chamberlin, our pilot." Bellanca, smiling and pleasant, introduces me.

"So you want to buy our Bellanca?" Mr. Levine's eyes size me up as he speaks. "Who is in your organization at St. Louis?"

As I list my partners, I can see that Levine is impressed.

"You have your money all raised?" he asks.

"No, only part of it," I answer. "We're not going to raise much money until we know what plane we're going to buy. We can raise the money all right, but we think the manufacturer ought to contribute something, too. A flight to Paris would be worth a lot in advertising."

"We would contribute to such a flight," Levine tells me. "The Bellanca is worth twenty-five thousand dollars. For that flight, we will sell the plane for fifteen thousand."

Fifteen thousand dollars! I thought I could cover the entire project for that amount—fuel and tests included. "That's considerably more than we expected to pay," I say. "Is it the lowest price you'd consider?"

"Fifteen thousand dollars is cheap for our Bellanca," he replies. "We could not take less. Remember it is the only existing plane capable of flying from New York to Paris!"

"It can easily break the world's record for nonstop range," Chamberlin adds.

"I'll have to talk to my partners in St. Louis before I can give you a definite answer," I say.

"WHAT WOULD YOU THINK of naming your plane the *Spirit of St. Louis?*"

Bixby's question strikes vaguely through my ears. I'm staring at the words on a slip of paper in my hand—FIFTEEN THOUSAND DOLLARS. This check can be traded for the Wright-Bellanca.

The *Spirit of St. Louis*—it's a good name. "All right, let's call it that."

"When do you plan on starting back to New York?" Knight asks.

"I'll take the train this afternoon," I tell him.

"We'll start setting up a *Spirit of St. Louis* organization while you're away," Bixby says. "Let us know as soon as you can when you'll be here with the plane."

"The gas tanks have to be made, but they can be installed later. I'll try to land the Bellanca on Lambert Field within a week."

"We'll be out to meet you—good luck!"

"OF COURSE we reserve the right to select the crew that flies our plane."

I stand, dumbfounded, in the Columbia Aircraft Corporation office. The fifteen-thousand-dollar cashier's check lies conspicuously on Mr. Levine's polished desk top.

"You understand we can't let just anybody pilot our airplane across the ocean," he adds.

I feel more chagrined than angry. Here's a point there can be no trading over. "I'm afraid there's been a misunderstanding," I say. "This is a St. Louis project. We'd naturally want to work with you closely in planning for the flight; but if we buy a plane, we'll pick our own crew."

"Columbia Aircraft can't afford to take a chance with our airplane," Levine replies. "We would select a good crew. Your organization would have all the credit for the flight."

"As far as I can see, we'd be paying fifteen thousand dollars for the privilege of painting the name of St. Louis on the fuselage," I tell him. "If you'd stated these terms when I was here before, it would have saved me a two-thousand-mile train trip. Is the Bellanca for sale or isn't it? If it is, we can close the deal. If it's not, I want to look for another plane."

"Yes, yes, it's for sale," he insists, "but we know better than anybody else how to fly the Bellanca. It would be wise for you to let us manage the flight to Paris. Think it over."

"There's no use thinking it over," I say definitely. "We either buy the plane outright or we don't buy it. Will you accept this payment, or must I find another plane?"

I pick the check up from the desk top.

"You are making a mistake," Levine argues. "The Bellanca is the only airplane that can fly between New York and Paris."

I start out the door.

"Wait—call me tomorrow."

"There's no use waiting," I tell him, "unless you'll reconsider your terms."

Levine hesitates. "Call me tomorrow at eleven," he says.

AT ELEVEN O'CLOCK I call Levine.

"Good morning," he says. "Have you changed your mind?"

Too angry to reply, I hang up, step outside, and stride up Madison Avenue. It's overcast, cold, and windy. Crevices in the sidewalk hold filthy chunks of ice; taxis surge at the traffic lights. Crowds of people, with problems of their own, flow by, filter through traffic, seep in and out of stores. Brisk walking, and the cold February air, gradually clear my mind.

One company after another has turned me down. If I go out to San Diego, will the Ryan offer collapse, too? This is the third week of February. Even if Ryan can build a plane in two months, it would be late April before I could be back in New York, ready to take off for Paris. Levine already may have decided to let Chamberlin make the New York-to-Paris flight. I'm behind all my competitors—so far behind, in fact, that most of them don't know I exist.

It is reported that Lieutenant Commander Davis is well along with his plans for a New York-to-Paris flight, and that Major General Patrick, Chief of the Army Air Corps, has authorized the Huff-Daland Company to sell him a stripped-down, three-engined bomber. It has been announced that Commander Byrd is going to try for the Orteig prize in a new trimotored Fokker, and there are rumors that Sikorsky is building another multiengined biplane for Fonck. Several transatlantic planes may be undergoing final tests in Europe—the French have been pretty secretive about their projects.

Of course there's always the Pacific Ocean. I don't think anybody is preparing for a transpacific flight.

"LET'S STICK to the Paris flight, Slim," Harry Knight is saying. "That's the idea we started out with."

I'm back after the dreary train trip from New York.

I have just suggested that it might be wise to give up plans for flying the Atlantic and concentrate on a transpacific flight. But Knight and Bixby have no thought of quitting. Until this moment I didn't realize how firmly they stand behind me.

"You may decide that Ryan can do a pretty good job," Bixby says. "We're not whipped yet."

III. SAN DIEGO
February, 1927

THE RYAN AIRLINES factory is an old, dilapidated building near the waterfront. I feel conspicuous driving up to it in a taxicab. There's no flying field, no hangar, no sound of engines warming up; and the unmistakable smell of dead fish from a nearby cannery mixes with the banana odor of drying dope.

I open the door to a small, dusty, paper-strewn office. A slender young man advances to meet me—clear eyes, intent face. He is Donald Hall, chief engineer for Ryan Airlines. Another young man moves up beside him: Walter Locke, in charge of the purchasing department. Within a few minutes, A. J. Edwards, sales manager, arrives—genial and stocky.

B. F. Mahoney, president of the company, is broad shouldered, smiling, young—in his late twenties, I judge. "Before we get down to business," he says after shaking hands, "we'd like you to see what we're doing in the factory."

He opens a door at the back of the office and we step down onto the factory floor. A half-dozen workmen are scattered about, splicing cables, drilling holes, installing instruments and levers, attending to the infinite details of aircraft construction. They glance up from their jobs—sizing me up, no doubt, as a prospective customer. Another plane sold? A few more weeks of pay secure? A small aviation company like this must live from hand to mouth.

We climb upstairs to a big loft of a room. Two men are fitting ribs to spars of straight-grained spruce. Another is brushing a second coat of dope into a cotton-clothed aileron. Mahoney thumps his fingers on a rudder's fabric. "Look at that construction," he says, pointing to the framework, "strong and simple."

We start back downstairs. I count the fuselages under construction—two in framework stage, one about ready for its wing—not much business to keep a factory going.

"Where do you test your planes?" I ask.

"Our flying field is at Dutch Flats," Edwards answers. "It's out on the edge of the city."

"The field isn't very big," Mahoney adds, "but it's convenient. We'll take you out there later on. You'll want to meet our pilots."

We sit down on desks and tables. "Well, we'd like to build your plane," Mahoney says. "What do you think of our proposition?"

"Your telegram quoted a price of six thousand dollars, without engine," I reply. "How much would it cost, complete?"

"If we put in a J-Four Whirlwind, the completed price would run between nine and ten thousand dollars," Mahoney says. "If you want one of the Wright corporation's new J-Five engines, it would run ten thousand or better."

"I'd much rather fly a J-Five," I say. "I want a metal propeller, and I'll need good instruments—the best we can get."

"We can't give you an exact figure until we know just what you want us to put in," Mahoney answers, "but I'll tell you what we'll do. We'll give you the engine and the extra equipment at cost."

"Fair enough. How about performance? Are you sure you can build a plane that will take off with enough fuel for the flight?"

"It'll be tough, but we believe we can do it. And we can start building the plane as soon as you place the order."

"Could we depend on delivery in two months?"

"I think so, but I wouldn't want to promise."

"I guess the next step is for me to talk to your engineer about construction details."

"All right," Mahoney agrees. "You probably won't want us around. Why don't you and Hall go off somewhere together?"

Donald Hall and I go to his bare but spacious drafting room next to the wing loft.

"We can't use the standard Ryan fuselage," Hall says. "Also, the wingspan will have to be considerably increased, which means we'll have to move the tail surfaces aft to maintain stability and control. And that means the engine will have to be moved forward. When it comes right down to it, I've got to design a completely new fuselage and a different type of landing gear."

He begins to sketch. A slightly lopsided monoplane takes form on the sheet of paper before us. "The main gas tank will have to be under the wing, in the fuselage, with its center of gravity close to that of the airplane. Now, where are we going to put the cockpits for you and the navigator?"

"I only want one cockpit," I tell him. "I'll do the navigating myself. I'd rather have extra gasoline than an extra man."

Hall picks up the idea instantly: "Well, of course that would be a big help from the standpoint of weight and performance—particularly range. It would keep the length of the fuselage down and probably save about three hundred and fifty pounds. That's at least fifty gallons more fuel, which would give you a good reserve. But are you sure one pilot alone can make a flight like that? It's going to be something like forty hours in the air, you know. Exactly how far is it between New York and Paris by the route you're going to follow?"

"It's about thirty-five hundred miles. We could get a pretty close check by scaling it off a globe. Do you know where there is one?"

"At the public library. I've got to know what the distance is before I can make any calculations. My car's right outside."

"IT'S THIRTY-SIX HUNDRED statute miles." The bit of white grocery string under my fingers stretches taut along the coast of North America, bends down over a faded blue ocean, and strikes—about at right angles—the land mass of Europe. It isn't a very scientific way of finding the exact distance, but the answer is accurate enough for our first calculations.

"The plane ought to carry fuel for four thousand miles in still air," Hall says. "Maybe that isn't enough. You may want to follow the ship lanes. Suppose you run into a head wind—"

"I'm going to fly straight," I tell him. "I don't plan on detouring at all. What's the use flying extra hours over water just to follow the ship lanes? If I run into a head wind, I'll turn back and try again. If the plane can make four thousand miles in still air, that's plenty. That's four hundred miles reserve plus whatever tail wind I pick up. I won't start without a tail wind."

Hall makes some calculations on the back of an envelope. "Maybe we'd better put in four hundred gallons of gasoline instead of three hundred and eighty."

MAHONEY leans forward in his office chair. Hall has just described the changes he wants to make in the Ryan design.

"We can't afford to waste money," Mahoney says, "but the company's reputation goes along with this plane. Can you make those changes and still get it built in sixty days?"

"We can if the men will work overtime," Hall replies.

Mahoney turns to me. "You give us the order, and we'll start. It'll be ten thousand five hundred and eighty dollars, with a J-Five engine—special equipment extra; at cost."

FEB. 24, 1927. HARRY H. KNIGHT, ST. LOUIS, MO.: BELIEVE RYAN CAPABLE OF BUILDING PLANE WITH SUFFICIENT PERFORMANCE STOP COST COMPLETE WITH WHIRLWIND ENGINE AND STANDARD INSTRUMENTS IS TEN THOUSAND FIVE HUNDRED EIGHTY DOLLARS STOP DELIVERY WITHIN SIXTY DAYS STOP RECOMMEND CLOSING DEAL. LINDBERGH.

FEB. 25, 1927: SUGGEST YOU CLOSE WITH RYAN FOLLOWING TERMS . . .

It's from Harry Knight. The chafing, frustrating weeks of hunting, first for finance and then for a plane, are over. I can turn my attention to the flight itself.

Except for the loss of time, there are great advantages in building a new plane instead of buying a standard model. Every part of it can be designed for a single purpose, every line fashioned to the Paris flight. Knowing intimately both the strengths and weaknesses of my plane, I'll be able to tax the one and relieve the other according to conditions which arise. By working closely with the engineer, I can build my own experience into the plane's structure, and make the utmost use of his theories.

DONALD HALL and I sit down on the long, curving beach at Coronado Strand. It's pleasantly warm in the morning sun.

"Where are we going to put the cockpit?"

"I'd like to have it behind the gas tank," I say.

"But then you couldn't see straight ahead," he argues. "The tanks would be directly in front of you."

"We always look out at an angle when we take off," I tell him. "The nose of the fuselage blocks out the field straight ahead, anyway."

"I'm not referring to takeoff," Hall says. "I'm thinking of forward vision in normal flight."

"There's not much need to see ahead in normal flight. When I'm near a flying field, I can watch the sky ahead by making shallow banks. Why don't we leave the cockpit in the rear? All I need is a window on each side. The top of the fuselage could be the top of the cockpit. A cockpit like that, without any projections, wouldn't add any resistance and ought to increase the range by a hundred miles. I think we ought to give first consideration to efficiency in flight; second, to protection in a crackup; third, to pilot comfort. A rear cockpit covers all three."

"Cockpit in the rear, then," Hall says. "Now, what night-flying equipment do you want?"

"None. We can't afford the weight."

"Do you want gages on your gasoline tanks?"

"No, that would mean extra pounds. I'll measure fuel consumption with my watch."

"How about a parachute?"

"Same answer. That would add almost twenty pounds."

Hall makes some notes on his pad. "Well, if you don't have to carry those things, it will make it a lot easier for me," he says. "But I'm not satisfied with the size of the M-Two tail surfaces. They ought to be bigger for good stability in cruising flight."

"Wouldn't bigger surfaces cut down the range?"

"A little, but not very much."

"Let's put everything into range," I say. "I don't need a very stable plane. I'll have to be watching the compass all the time anyway. I don't plan on going to sleep while I fly, and we can't afford to spend time on anything that isn't essential."

"All right, then. Now let's talk about range."

We conclude that the minimum requirement for fuel will be enough to fly between New York and Paris over the great-circle route in still air. Of course that requires a theoretical reserve. An engine in flight doesn't operate with perfect settings, and a pilot doesn't navigate with perfect accuracy. We decide that the plane should be designed around a theoretical range of 4000 miles, as Hall originally suggested.

But how does one navigate along a great circle, crossing 3600 miles of earth and ocean? My navigation has always been carried out on maps which I checked with landmarks on the ground—lakes, towns, bends in rivers, and railroad tracks. At night there were familiar lights below. Flying the Atlantic will be different. I'll have to change my heading by time and theory alone. Ship captains sail by sextant sights on the sun and stars. Why can't I do that, too? How does one lay out a great-circle route? Does it require much knowledge of mathematics?

I could undoubtedly get the information I need from some of the naval officers stationed at San Diego, but I hesitate to ask them for advice. There's enough skepticism about my flight now, without adding to it by showing how inexperienced I am in long-distance navigation. No, I can't afford to inquire openly about such an elementary procedure as the construction of a great-circle course. But there'll be ship chandlers in San Diego who carry charts. I'll see what I can buy there.

49

"I WANT A SET OF CHARTS covering the North Atlantic Ocean," I tell the clerk. He looks up in obvious surprise.

"The *Atlantic*? Sorry, we supply only Pacific shipping. You might get Atlantic charts at San Pedro."

The salesman at the San Pedro store pulls out two oblong sheets. "I think these are what you want," he says.

They're Mercator projections and they extend inland far enough to include New York and Paris. Then, like stumbling over a nugget of gold, I see a gnomonic projection covering them both. I remember learning in the army's navigation class that a great circle on the earth's surface translates into a curve on a Mercator chart, but becomes a straight line on a gnomonic projection because all maps are distorted in one way or another.

Rummaging around still further, I locate a time-zone chart of the world, a chart of magnetic variation, and others showing prevailing winds over the Atlantic for April, May, and June. I buy them all.

HALL HAS CLEARED a table for my use in his drafting room. It's an uninspiring place, with damp-spotted walls and an unshaded light bulb hanging down on a wire cord from the ceiling. But there's enough room to spread out my charts and drawings; and, locked in, we work in relative seclusion.

I find, printed on the charts I bought, ample instructions for laying out my great-circle route. With instruments Hall lends me, I draw a straight line between New York and Paris on the gnomonic projection. Then I transfer points from that line, at 100-mile intervals, to the Mercator projection, and connect these points with straight lines. At each point, I mark down the distance from New York and the magnetic course to the next change in angle. I choose 100-mile intervals because, wind and cruising speed considered, it seems likely that the *Spirit of St. Louis* will cover about that distance each hour. I ink my route in and measure off its time zones. The distance scales at exactly 3610 miles.

I stand looking down at the completed chart. It curves gracefully northward through New England, Nova Scotia, and Newfoundland, eastward over the Atlantic, down past the southern tip of Ireland, across a narrow strip of England, until it ends sharply at the little dot inside of France marked "Paris." Life itself will depend on the correctness of that curving black line and the numerals I've marked along its edges. I'd feel better if I could get some confirmation of my figures and my angles.

The public library downtown has texts on navigation. But it's not as easy to find great-circle latitudes and longitudes through logarithmic formulas as it is to pick them off charts. It takes a long time to work out each position. After spending several days at this task, I reach a point in the Atlantic 1200 miles beyond the coast of Newfoundland. My mathematical route and my charted route coincide so closely that it seems time wasted to continue checking.

Should I buy a sextant and study celestial navigation? Could I handle a sextant while flying a plane? That at least is something I can ask the naval officers on North Island—no one expects an airplane pilot to know much about celestial navigation.

"YOU MIGHT GET a sun line," a blue-uniformed officer tells me, "but I don't think you could hold a sextant steady enough to take a bubble sight at the same time you fly the plane. You ought to carry a navigator on a flight like that."

"How much do your aircraft radios weigh, and how far can you get direction with a loop?" I ask.

"I can't answer those questions," he says. "Radio isn't my specialty. But come out to North Island and I'll introduce you to the experts there."

I find that naval radios are much too heavy for my single-engined plane. So Hall and I decide to increase the tank capacity to 425 gallons—we'll trade radio and sextant weight for extra gasoline. What I lose in navigational accuracy I hope to gain twice over in total range.

I HAVE DIVIDED my reserves for the flight into two categories: reserves for success, and reserves for failure. I am dependent on my reserves for success to land on the airfield at Le Bourget. I am dependent on my reserves for failure to let me live if I can't get through to Paris, and, if possible, to save my plane.

Extra fuel is my greatest reserve for success. With it, I can ride through night and detour storms. Prevailing westerly winds form a reserve which costs me nothing. And the long coastline of Europe—I can be hundreds of miles off course when I strike it, and still reach Paris.

The ability to turn back is my greatest reserve for failure. For more than 1000 miles after I leave New York I'll be within easy reach of land. If weather becomes too thick, if I encounter head winds, or if some engine roughness indicates danger, I can turn back and start the flight again.

But suppose my engine fails over the Atlantic, what emergency equipment shall I take with me? Safety at the start of my flight means holding down weight for the takeoff. Safety during my flight requires plenty of emergency equipment. Safety at the end of my flight demands an ample reserve of fuel. It's impossible to increase safety at one point without detracting from it at another. I decide to buy a small, black rubber raft that's displayed in the window of a sporting-goods store downtown; it weighs only ten pounds. I'll also need a knife, flares, water, and some food.

WANAMAKER BEHIND NEW YORK-PARIS FLIGHT

WILL FINANCE BYRD VENTURE WITH $100,000

May Race with Fonck

NEW YORK, March 2.—Rodman Wanamaker will back Commander Byrd's attempt to fly non-stop from New York to Paris next spring. A huge three-engined Fokker monoplane, now under construction, is to be used for the trip. It is expected that the machine will be ready by May, the earliest month weather conditions will be suitable for a transatlantic flight.

... The Sikorsky Company announced recently that a big plane was being built for the Atlantic flight. It is reported that the pilot will be Capt. René Fonck, the French ace who crashed on Roosevelt Field on an attempted take-off for Paris last September.

LEGION BACKS DAVIS NEW YORK-PARIS FLIGHT

PLANE TO HAVE 4,600 MILE RANGE

MARCH 14.—Lieut. Commander Noel Davis plans to take off from Mitchel Field, Long Island, in June for a non-stop flight to Paris. He will fly a Keystone Pathfinder biplane with additional fuel tanks in the fuselage which will give a flying radius of fifty-four hours. The big ship, christened "The American Legion," will be powered with three Wright Whirlwind engines.

NUNGESSER TO FLY ATLANTIC

FRENCH ACE ANNOUNCES PARIS TO NEW YORK FLIGHT THIS SUMMER

PARIS, March 26.—Captain Charles Nungesser, one of the top aces of the World War, said today that he would pilot a French-built plane across the Atlantic this summer. He will be accompanied by Lieut. Coli, the famous one-eyed airman, as navigator. The machine they expect to use will have a single 450-horsepower engine, and carry 800 gallons of gasoline.

Every few days a new article about the progress of trans-atlantic projects appears in the paper—Byrd, Fonck, Davis, Nungesser. And Chamberlin is almost certainly getting the Bellanca ready. I'm clearly in a race against time, with the odds against me.

The construction of the *Spirit of St. Louis* moves along as fast as Hall can produce drawings from his board. The factory manager starts work on less important items without waiting for drawings. Everyone is taking a personal interest in my flight; hours of voluntary overtime become normal. Hall often goes to the factory at five o'clock in the morning to inspect the previous day's progress before the men arrive. Work on other planes has almost stopped. It's less than three weeks since I arrived in San Diego, yet skeletons of the fuselage and wing have taken form.

I've completed my general plans. I'll take off from New York at daybreak. That will give me sunlight for my fuel-overloaded hours, and put me over Newfoundland before dusk. I should strike Ireland before nightfall of the second day. I'll have to find Paris and land after dark. I'll be a little tired by that time, but I'll have a lightly loaded plane.

Hall now estimates the range of the *Spirit of St. Louis* to be 4100 miles, at the most economical cruising speeds. Even with no help from wind, that would put me over Paris with 500 miles of fuel in my tanks—a reserve to ease the mind of any pilot.

To get maximum range, throttle and mixture controls must be correctly set. It would help if I had an instrument which would show exact consumption of gasoline with each different adjustment of the engine. I've tried to get such an instrument, but apparently there is no satisfactory fuel-flow meter for aircraft. So I'm designing one myself.

MAR. 28, 1927. CHARLES A. LINDBERGH: COMMITTEE ADVISES CHANGES IN WING AREA AND LOADING APPROVED. HARRY H. KNIGHT.

That means our formal entry has just been accepted by the contest committee of the National Aeronautics Association, which administers the rules for the Orteig prize. Sixty days must elapse between a pilot's entry and his flight, according to the regulations, so I won't be eligible until the end of May. If I start before that, and get to Paris, we'll lose twenty-five thousand dollars!

I send a return wire, saying that the *Spirit of St. Louis* will be ready for its test flights sometime in April.

THE WHIRLWIND ENGINE arrives from Paterson. We gather around the wooden crate as though some statue were to be unveiled. It's like a huge jewel, lying there set in its wrappings. Here is the ultimate in lightness of weight and power—223 horses compressed into nine delicate, fin-covered cylinders of aluminum and steel. On this intricate perfection I'm to trust my life across the Atlantic.

The inner organs of this engine—its connecting rods, cams, gears, and bearings—will be turning over many hundred times each minute—sparks jumping, teeth meshing, pistons stopping and reversing at incomprehensible speeds. And I'm demanding that this procedure continue for forty hours if need be!

On the Ryan factory floors the workmen are out to set a record in construction time. And I make a point of spending part of each day at the factory. In good weather I often go out to Dutch Flats and fly one of the company's machines. None of them has a Whirlwind engine; but they perform well with their wartime Hispanos, and they teach me the characteristics of high-wing monoplanes.

ENDURANCE PLANE SMASHES WORLD'S RECORD

CHAMBERLIN AND ACOSTA
MORE THAN TWO DAYS IN AIR

NEW YORK, April 14.—Clarence D. Chamberlin and Bert Acosta yesterday landed their Bellanca monoplane on Roosevelt Field, Long

55

Island, after 51 hours, 11 minutes, and 25 seconds aloft, exceeding by nearly six hours the previous endurance record which was established in August, 1925, by two French Army officers, Drouhin and Landry, at Etampes.

WANT TO FLY ATLANTIC

Both flyers are anxious to be the first to make the New York to Paris flight, across the Atlantic Ocean. Charles A. Levine, chairman of the Columbia Aircraft Corporation, which plans to build Bellanca Aircraft, said that preparations would be rushed to permit the Bellanca to be the first plane to complete the New York to Paris flight.

Well, that's the record I'd hoped to break. Maybe I still can break it. In the *Spirit of St. Louis* I'll have the extra pilot's weight in fuel. Other things being equal, that should give me a 50-gallon advantage over the Bellanca. But as far as the New York-to-Paris flight is concerned, there's no use blinding myself to reality. Almost everyone else would have to fail before my project can succeed—and everyone else seems to be getting along fine. I started too far behind. I probably won't even fly to New York, to say nothing of taking off for Paris.

AMERICA CRASHES ON TEST FLIGHT

BYRD, BENNETT, AND NOVILLE INJURED, FOKKER PILOTING CRAFT AT TIME

NEW YORK, April 16.—The big trimotored Fokker monoplane which Commander Richard Byrd and his crew were preparing for the trans-atlantic flight between New York and Paris crashed at Teterboro airport at 6:00 o'clock this afternoon. The machine was coming in for a landing after its first trial flight when it overturned, injuring three of the four members of its crew. The accident may force Commander Byrd to abandon his plans for a transoceanic flight this spring.

The Fokker has cracked up! The nose structure, holding the center engine, collapsed and crushed Floyd Bennett's leg.

That's one of the things I don't like about big planes and forward cockpits. If a small plane, like the *Spirit of St. Louis*, with the cockpit in the rear, noses over, the pilot isn't likely to be hurt at all.

THE THIRD WEEK of April is crammed with the endless details which precede the completion of a new airplane. An atmosphere of tension and expectancy pervades the entire factory. Each workman has some finishing touch to add before he's ready to call his job completed. They all sign their names on the front wing spar, before the fabric covering is added, "to ride along on the flight for good luck."

My equipment is all bought—flying suit, canteens, army rations, rubber raft, knife, pump, repair kit, flares—everything within the weight allowance I've set. At first I couldn't find any red flares. Then I bought four of the kind railroads use for danger signals. I've got each one sealed up watertight in a piece of bicycle inner tube.

NUNGESSER PLANE COMPLETES TEST

DROUHIN ENTERS CONTEST

APRIL 22.—Competition in the New York to Paris flight contest has intensified with the entry of M. Drouhin, the French aviator whose duration flight record was broken recently by Bert Acosta and Clarence Chamberlin.

Two other French contestants are known to be preparing planes for the transatlantic flight. M. Tarascon will fly a Bernard-Marie-Hubert plane, with a Gnome-Rhone-Jupiter engine. M. Coste plans to pilot a Breguet, with a Hispano-Suiza engine.

Meanwhile, the work of repairing Commander Byrd's Fokker monoplane, *America*, is under way. It should be completed in from two to three weeks.

I'm not going to let these press reports worry me. In another week the *Spirit of St. Louis* will be ready for flight. I'll make the light-load tests from the Ryan company's field at Dutch Flats. It's a smooth, grassless area, like a dry lake bed, boxed in by roads and telephone wires. It will do while the tanks are only partly filled with fuel, but we'll have to make our heavy-load tests elsewhere; for them, I'll need clear approaches and 3000 or 4000 feet of run.

Hall suggested that we use the parade grounds on the abandoned army post at Camp Kearney. The conditions are almost ideal: there's a long, level strip available for a runway, lying almost exactly parallel to prevailing winds. The mountains are far enough back to be out of the way for landing, and there's nothing at all to clear on takeoff, not even a fence.

If we run our tests at Camp Kearney, we may be able to get them over with before the newspapers find out what we're doing. Reporters and photographers have become a problem in recent weeks. What started as a pleasant relationship with local journalists now involves elements of tension. On the one hand, publicity is an important asset to this project. On the other hand, we have to concentrate our attention on the tests and the accuracy of data. A slight error can cause a crash.

The only serious disadvantage of the old parade grounds is that its surface is scattered over with stones, many larger than a man's fist, and capable of bursting a tire on takeoff or landing. We'll just have to pick up and get rid of the biggest ones.

Telegrams are coming in fast these days.

WASHINGTON, D. C. CHARLES A. LINDBERGH: YOUR LICENSE NUMBER TRANSATLANTIC SHIP IS N DASH X TWO HUNDRED ELEVEN STOP TRANSPORT LICENSE WILL BE MAILED TOMORROW CARE ROBERTSON AIRCRAFT. E. KINTZ, DEPARTMENT OF COMMERCE.

PATERSON, N.J. WHEN USING FIRST CLASS AVIATION GASOLINE THERE IS NO CARBURETOR INTAKE ATTACHMENT NECESSARY STOP AFTER ARRIVING EAST WE WILL FIT ENGINE WITH CARBURETOR AIR HEATER IF FOUND DESIRABLE. WRIGHT AERONAUTICAL CORP.

That's good. I was concerned about the cold of altitude and night. But if I don't have to use a carburetor air heater, it will save several pounds of weight.

HOLMSTEAD, PA. 15.5 DEGREES SETTING PROBABLY NECESSARY ON YOUR MONOPLANE TO GET TAKEOFF WITH HEAVY LOAD FUEL ECONOMY WILL BE IMPROVED ON HIGHER PITCH SETTING STOP IF TAKEOFF IS SATISFACTORY WITH 15.5 SETTING SUGGEST TRY 16.5 AS THIS WILL IMPROVE FUEL ECONOMY. STANDARD STEEL PROP. CO.

It's a good suggestion. We'll try it out. The higher the pitch, the more the range.

NEW YORK, N.Y. CHARLES A. LINDBERGH: LEARN YOU HAVE CHOSEN MOBILOIL B FOR YOUR FLIGHT STOP HAVE ADVISED ST. LOUIS REGARDING MOBILOIL SUPPLIES ON YOUR ARRIVAL THERE STOP GLAD TO OFFER ALL POSSIBLE ASSISTANCE BOTH HERE AND ABROAD STOP BEST WISHES FOR SUCCESS. VACUUM OIL CO.

That's another problem off my mind. My plans are meshing smoothly. In three or four more days we'll haul the *Spirit of St. Louis* to the flying field and assemble fuselage to wing.

BELLANCA IN
CRACK-UP

NEW YORK, April 24.—The Bellanca transatlantic monoplane narrowly escaped disaster today when part of the landing gear tore loose on take-off. Only Chamberlin's great skill as a pilot saved what might have been a serious accident. He landed so gently on the one sound wheel that only minor damage was sustained by the Bellanca.

Both Bellanca and Sikorsky are top designers. Why did their landing gears fail? Is some strain caused by these heavily loaded takeoffs being overlooked in engineering calculations? May there also be a hidden weakness in the *Spirit of St. Louis?* I must talk to Donald Hall about it.

This morning we hauled the finished plane to Dutch Flats.

By taking off the landing gear on one side, it was easy enough to move the fuselage through the big doorway of the factory's ground floor; but the wing in the loft created an unexpected problem. When Hall concluded that 10 feet should be added to the standard M-2 span, no one thought about getting a 46-foot wing out of the room where it was built. For a time it looked as though we'd have to tear out a section of the wall; but careful measurement showed that we could get by if we tipped the wing over at an angle and removed the loft's double doors.

Such a delicate structure required careful handling. Fortunately an empty boxcar was standing on the railroad siding next to the factory, and all hands turned out to push the boxcar into a position which would form the first step downward from the loft. Then, with a contractor's derrick, we maneuvered the wing onto the car top, and from the car top down to a waiting truck. The workmen who weren't tugging at guy ropes watched from open doors and windows as though some child of theirs were going away. Their part is done. For two months theirs has been the active part, while I stood by watching their craftsmanship. Now, the roles are reversed, and I'll have the field of action. The success of their efforts depends upon my skill, and my life upon their thoroughness.

DAVIS AND WOOSTER KILLED

AMERICAN LEGION CRASHES ON TAKE-OFF

HAMPTON VA., April 26.—Lieut. Commander Noel Davis and Lieutenant Stanton H. Wooster lost their lives today on the last of the trial flights of the huge trans-Atlantic plane in which they were to attempt a flight to Paris next week.

The tragedy occurred when the machine was carrying almost the equivalent of its full load for the trans-Atlantic trip. The big machine came down in an area of marsh land, not far from Langley Field.

My God! Every one of the big multiengine planes built for the New York-to-Paris flight has crashed—Fonck's Sikorsky, Byrd's Fokker, and now Davis's Keystone! Four men have lost their lives, three have been injured. Even the Bellanca has cracked up.

TODAY I'm going to test the *Spirit of St. Louis*. What a beautiful machine it is, resting there on the field in front of the hangar, trim and slender, gleaming in its silver coat! For me, it seems to embody the whole future of aviation.

The cockpit is still unfamiliar and strange in spite of the hours I've spent sitting in it on factory and hangar floors. The chief mechanic turns the propeller over several times.

"Contact!"

"Contact!"

He swings his body away from the blade as he pulls it through. The engine catches, picks up quickly as I crack the throttle—800 revolutions per minute, every cylinder hitting, oil and fuel pressures normal, the temperature already up. I check controls, moving them from one position to another in a last attempt to get their feel. This is considerably different from any cockpit I've been in before. The big fuel tank in front of me seems doubly large, now that I'm actually to fly behind it.

I open the throttle slowly—1000 ... 1200 ... 1400—wide. The fuselage trembles with power, and I feel the wheels crowd up against their chocks. I cut first one magneto and then the other—not a miss or a jerk in the engine.

I signal the chocks away. A young mechanic ducks under the wing to pull them out. The *Spirit of St. Louis* rolls lightly over the baked-mud surface of the field. How strange it is to taxi with such a wide wheel tread! I glance again at the wind sock on the hangar, at instruments, valves, and levers, at the field ahead, the sky above.

My cockpit is a little blind, but I can see ahead well enough by leaning to one side. I've never felt a plane accelerate so fast before. The tires are off the ground before they roll 100 yards. The plane climbs quickly, even though I hold its nose well down. There's a huge reserve of power. I spiral cautiously upward—500 ... 1000 ... 2000 feet. I straighten out and study my instruments. They're all working properly. I circle over the factory. Little figures run outdoors to see the machine they built actually flying overhead. I rock my wings, and head across the bay.

I have no time for gazing; there are tests to run, and men waiting anxiously for my reports. Ailerons ride a bit too high. The fin needs slight adjustment. I note these items on my data board, and push the stick over to one side. The wing drops rather slowly, but we expected that. The response is good enough for a long-range airplane.

I straighten out, pull into a stall, and let go of the stick. The nose drops and has no tendency to come back up. The dive steepens until I force the plane back to level flight again. I take my feet off the rudder, and steer with stick alone. The fuselage veers the opposite way to the ailerons. It's clear that stability isn't a strong point with the *Spirit of St. Louis*. But we didn't design the plane for stability.

What top speed can I make? That's one of the crucial tests. I drop down to 1000 feet, level off, and open throttle. The indicator starts to climb: 100, 115, 120, 128 miles an hour. That's encouraging. I throttle down and head toward San Diego. I do two or three stalls on the way back to get the feel of the plane and practice for its landing.

"How's the control, Charlie?"

"Good enough, but she needs some adjustment." I let the engine idle while I describe the results of the flight.

"Say, you ran only a hundred and sixty-five feet before your wheels left the ground—only six and one-eighth seconds." Hall is enthusiastic over the performance.

IT'S 5:40 A.M., May 4, the day of my final speed and load tests. A morning fog is lifting when I take off and head toward the army's speed course along Coronado Strand. As I climb over San Diego Bay, I find it still half covered with low, rolling clouds which obscure the buoy markers I must use. I decide to drop in at Rockwell Field and try out the roughness of its surface. I'd like to use it as my departure point from San Diego.

I slip down on the final glide and straighten out just before my wheels touch. Bumps and hummocks are worse than I expected.

Several officers are waiting on the line as I taxi in. They saw my plane coming down, and want to inspect it at close range. Most of them are still skeptical about my flight; but they extend a hearty welcome, and invite me to spend the morning and stay for lunch.

"Thanks, but we've got to run tests today. I'll have to take off as soon as the fog clears."

"Well, how about coming over to the club while you're waiting?" they insist.

"I'd like to, but I'd better size up the field first. I want to take off with a fairly heavy load when I leave for St. Louis, and some areas are probably a little smoother than others."

"We'll drive you over it."

"Thanks, but I'd rather walk. I can get a better idea of what it's like."

I want to dig my heels into the surface, see the height of grass on my legs, and study contours of earth by zigzagging back and forth across them. If Rockwell Field turns out to be too rough, then I'll take off for St. Louis from Camp Kearney.

When I return to the hangars, the day is beginning to feel warm and the clouds are fading away. A mechanic swings my propeller, and another holds a wing strut as I taxi out from the line. I do a chandelle off the field, to show how well the *Spirit of St. Louis* performs, and head toward the speed course. I fly over it once to locate its markers. Then, at a distance of about two miles from the nearest one, I turn back, nose down to 50 feet above the water, and push the throttle wide open. At times the indicator jumps to over 130 miles an hour. I press my stopwatch as the first buoy streaks by under the wing. I can't see the next, but I know it's dead ahead. Now the third buoy is in sight, a black dot in the distance. I press my watch again as I pass above it, throttle back, and climb several hundred feet while I fill in the time on my data board. One flight back over the buoys in the opposite direction, two more round trips to average with the first, and the high-speed runs are finished.

Now I fly to Camp Kearney for the load tests. On my way I jot down the relation of airspeed to engine revolutions for Hall. By the time I'm over the parade grounds there's only one more test to make. I pull the throttle back, take a pencil from my pocket, and pick up the data board. The nose rises, a wing drops. I reach for the stick—and a gust of air snatches the data board from my hand and carries it through the open window! All the figures I've collected this morning go fluttering down toward a brush-covered hill below! I bank sharply and watch the board, flashing as it catches sun, land in the branches of a thick bush about 200 yards from the edge of a clearing. Now it's only a white spot among brownish-green leaves.

The clearing looks big enough to land on with one of the company's Hisso-Standards. I circle around for several minutes, locating in my mind the exact position of the data board. When I'm sure I can spot its bush again, I fly back to Camp Kearney.

Hall, Edwards, and several mechanics are waiting beside a gasoline truck parked on a corner of the parade grounds. And there's Mahoney, a little to one side, leaning against his car. Apparently the secrecy of our plans has been well kept, for there isn't a newspaperman in sight. Hall's face lengthens when I tell him about the data board. It will have to be retrieved or all the morning's tests must be run again. Mahoney sends a mechanic to the nearest telephone, with orders to have one of the Hisso-Standards sent over from Dutch Flats. Meanwhile we fill the center wing tank with gasoline for our first load test. After that, we'll add 50 gallons for each flight, until Hall gets enough measured points to check his theoretical curves.

When the Standard arrives, I climb in to go hunt for the data board. Over the brush patch again, I find the board still clearly visible. I stall down into the clearing and stop rolling with several yards to spare. Leaving the engine idling, I crawl through thick bushes to where I think the board should be. After hunting for several minutes without result, I remove my coat, spread it on top of some branches, return to the clearing, and take off again in the Standard.

In the air, I see my coat is at least 50 yards from the data board. I land again, but am still unsuccessful in my search; so

The Raymond Orteig $25,000 Prize

Feb. 26, 1927

PARIS · NEW YORK — NEW YORK · PARIS
Trans-Atlantic Flight

(Under the rules of the Fédération Aéronautique Internationale of Paris, France, and National Aeronautic Association of the United States of America of Washington, D. C.)

ENTRY FORM

Name of Aviator Entrant (in full) Charles A. Lindbergh.
Address % Mr. H. H. Knight, 401 Olive St., St. Louis, Missouri.
Aviator's F. A. I. Certificate No. 6286 Issued by National Aeronautic Ass'n.
Aviator's Annual License No. 295 (1927) Issued by National Aeronautic Ass'n.
PARTICULARS RELATING TO THE AIRCRAFT INTENDED TO BE USED.

Type, (Monoplane, Biplane, Hydroaeroplane, Fl
NYP Ryan Monopl
Wing area in sq. ft. 290
Make and type of engine Wright
Approximate capacity of Fuel Tanks

I, the undersigned, Charles L.
of % Mr. H. H. Knight, 401 Oli
for the Raymond Orteig "New York-P

1. I agree to observe and abide b
governing the contest, and to comply
regarding the contest, which may be giv
Association of the United States of Am

2. In addition to, and not by the wa
under the said Rules and Regulations, I
of the United States of America and the
mond Orteig, the donor of the New Yor
or any fellow competitor, against all clai
flight or descent made by me whether or
own actions or out of the acts, actions or
present at such ascent or descent.

3. I enclose my certified check for $25
$25,000 Prize, being Entrance Fee, and req
tional Aeronautic Association of the Unit

Signature Charles A. Lindbergh
Address % Mr. Harry H. Knight,
401 Olive St.
St. Louis, Mo.

(Notary Seal.)

Subscribed and sworn to before me
this 15th day of Feb. 1927.
Date Feb. 15, 1927. E. Oberhelmann
My commission expires May 9 1927
This blank is to be executed and forwarded with certified check to The Contest Committee of the National Aeronautic Association at No. 1623 H Street, Washington, D. C., and notice thereof immediately communicated to

The Secretary of the Trustees of the
Raymond Orteig Twenty-Five Thousand Dollar Prize
c/o Army and Navy Club of America
30 West 44th Street, New York City

3

Commander Byrd's Fokker "America"

Nungesser and Coli's French-built plane

Fatal crash of the American Legion

I leave the coat in a new location and take off once more. This time, coat and data board are only 20 feet apart. I land, pick them both up, and head back to Camp Kearney.

The *Spirit of St. Louis* is ready for its first load flight when I arrive. Hall takes the data sheets as though they contained directions to a lost gold mine. We're several hours behind schedule, and anxious to finish tests before any major change in weather. A quartering wind close to seven miles an hour has already sprung up. We'll have to work fast to finish before dark.

The first two or three takeoffs are easy. But as we keep putting in 50-gallon increments of gasoline, the run lengthens and the wheels jerk up and down over loose stones until I wonder how tires can be built to stand the strain. At the 300-gallon test, the plane is off the ground in twenty seconds; but the tires take a terrific beating, and the landing is even rougher than the takeoff.

"Do you want us to put in fifty gallons more?" the chief mechanic asks.

"It's too late for another flight today," I say, looking toward the west.

"I don't think you ought to take a heavier load across those stones anyway," Mahoney says, examining tires and landing gear.

I had intended to take off with loads up to 400 gallons; but if I keep on, and a tire blows, it may wreck our whole project. After all, one can carry tests so far that instead of adding to safety they increase the overall danger. I'll probably never land with as much as 300 gallons again, so I've already exceeded any future requirements. I'll have to take off with 125 gallons more at New York, but the field there will certainly be smoother. I think Mahoney is right; we'll call it enough.

When I get back to the city, I telegraph my partners that the tests are satisfactorily completed, and that I'll be ready to start east within forty-eight hours. I had planned to run a series of gasoline-consumption checks before leaving California, but I'll save at least a day by doing that on my flight between San Diego and St. Louis. My fuel-flow meter doesn't work; it looks as though I might as well discard it.

NUNGESSER OVER ATLANTIC

DUE IN NEW YORK TOMORROW

PARIS, May 8.—As the sun rose above the horizon this morning, Captains Charles Nungesser and Francois Coli started their transatlantic flight westward to New York.

There was a breath-taking moment during the long take-off, when Captain Nungesser tried to lift his machine, but failed. He was successful, however, on the next attempt. . . .

That's the first time a plane loaded for the New York-Paris flight has actually gotten off the ground. Nungesser and Coli are experienced men. I spend most of the day studying charts and data I've assembled for a Pacific flight.

NUNGESSER SIGHTED OFF CAPE RACE

FRENCH AIRMEN REACH NOVA SCOTIA

TRANSATLANTIC FLYERS OVER BOSTON

CROWD AT BATTERY WAITS ANXIOUSLY

NUNGESSER, COLI LOST

PARIS FEARS WORST

NAVY READY FOR SEARCH

Step by step newspaper headlines follow Nungesser and Coli from their takeoff at Paris, only to have them vanish like midnight ghosts. Now no one seems to be sure that they were *ever* sighted after their plane left the coast of France. Accidents, delays, and tragedies have combined to leave only the Bellanca poised for the New York–Paris flight.

THE *Spirit of St. Louis* is ready in its hangar. For two days I've been waiting on weather. A storm hovers over the Rocky Mountains and the Southwest, making even a daylight flight questionable. And I want to fly to St. Louis through the night.

I've gone down to the weather bureau each afternoon to look over maps and forecasts. Each time it has been the same story: mountaintops in clouds, low visibility in passes, heavy rain, local reports of ice and hail. I wait here helplessly because of an area of opaque air.

Possibly I can get through if I fly by daylight. Most of my friends advise against an overnight flight to St. Louis. Even in perfect weather, they say, flying over the mountains at night is taking too much chance. But for me, the experience of 800 miles of darkness will be the best training I can get for the far more difficult flight across the ocean.

I've never flown through an entire night. I want to find out how accurately I can hold my course between sunset and sunrise, without any checkpoints on the ground. A nonstop overnight flight across deserts, mountains, and prairies to St. Louis also will do much to answer the people who talk about my lack of experience in long-distance flying.

TODAY, I VISIT the weather bureau with more hope than usual, for the low-pressure area has shown signs of moving eastward. The weather bureau chief spreads his meteorological charts. I can tell by his expression that good news awaits me. I can probably take off tomorrow and expect fair weather all along my route. I should even have a tail wind most of the way!

The Bellanca hasn't started yet, and Byrd's Fokker isn't ready. If I follow close on the tail of this storm, I may get to New York before the weather permits anybody else to leave for Paris. But that will mean cutting out the St. Louis ceremonies my partners have planned. We intended to christen the plane, and Bixby wrote that the chamber of commerce wants to hold a big luncheon while I'm there. How will my partners feel about my using Lambert Field as little more than a refueling point en route to New York? It really isn't fair to them. After all, it's a St. Louis project. I planned the flight to be from St. Louis to Paris, with a stopover at New York. Yet, if I'm to be successful, I can't waste time on ceremonies.

IV. ACROSS THE CONTINENT
May 10–12, 1927

THIS IS THE DAY of takeoff. I pack a small suitcase, which I'll lash to the left side of the fuselage, beside my seat. Since the fuel tanks will be only slightly over half full for a 1500-mile flight, I can afford the luxury of carrying a suitcase. I'll need business clothes in St. Louis and New York. After that I'll leave everything behind except what I wear.

I stop for a few minutes to say good-by to the men in the factory. I don't want to start east too early, for I plan on meeting daybreak over Kansas. That's far enough from St. Louis to hold down my angular correction if I've drifted off course. Also, it will give the sun a chance to burn morning mists away. I've set 4:00 p.m. as departure time. That will leave nearly three hours of daylight during which I can turn back or land if anything goes wrong.

At 3:15 reporters and photographers are already on the field.

I wish my earth-inductor compass was working; but a bearing froze on one of the test flights and we can't get parts out here to repair the damage. The Pioneer Instrument Company telegraphed that they'll have a new compass ready in New York when I arrive. They're also going to put in a newer type of liquid compass for me. The one in my cockpit now has excessive deviation; but it's good enough for my trip across the country. In a compass, I prefer steadiness to accuracy of reading. As long as the deviation chart is correctly made out, it's easy to subtract or add a few degrees to one's magnetic course.

At 3:40 I crawl into my flying suit. It's uncomfortably hot in this California sun, but I can't very well put the suit on while I'm in the air—and I'll certainly need it over the mountain ranges tonight. We warm up the engine. Then I wave good-by, taxi into position, and ease the throttle open. As I pick up speed, I hold the tail low to put as much load as possible on the wings and reduce strain on the landing gear.

The *Spirit of St. Louis* is in the air soon after its wheels start clattering over the hummocky portion of the field. It's 3:55, Pacific time. I check instruments, pull the throttle back slightly, begin a wide, climbing turn to the left, and set my compass heading for St. Louis.

The coastal range of mountains is only a few miles east, lying about at right angles to my route. I cross over valley orchards, and climb with bush-green foothills, using just enough power to keep a safe altitude above their crests.

I look down on boulder-strewn mountainsides. What a hopeless place for a forced landing! There's not a level area in sight to which I could glide in emergency. A pilot has to trust his engine above terrain like this. To my right are the Superstition Mountains; to my left, the San Jacinto peaks. Ahead, the coastal range breaks down into sharp-shadowed desert ridges.

A GREAT VALLEY stretches out before me, sun-scorched, sage-flecked, veined with dry, stony creek beds. Soft desert colors merge into one another until I'm not sure whether the sands are more yellow or pink. In the middle of this valley is the Salton Sea—a pale blue wash which seems to have neither depth nor wetness. My course lies directly across it, toward the crinkled Chocolate range beyond. Men have died of thirst trying to cross such burning wastes on foot or muleback. I glance automatically at the two canteens of water beside me in the cockpit.

Sunset finds me over purple valleys, dusk-filled canyons, and silhouetted cliffs of Arizona, climbing toward night. Threads of steel on the ground below are barely visible in gathering twilight—tracks of the Santa Fe, my last checkpoint of day.

It's getting cold. I draw on boots, then mittens. Three and a quarter hours out now. The altimeter is up to 8000 feet, and

I'm still climbing to stay well above the ridges. Ground details are obscured by a haze which has been forming since sunset. The moon is almost overhead, several days from full. I can't see far ahead, but below me, the general contours of earth are perceptible in outline. I run my flashlight over the instrument board. Every needle is in place. I fill out the log and settle back in my cockpit.

THE ENGINE JERKS!—again!—again!—the danger sign I know so well. It splutters, jumps, begins to vibrate. I grip the stick, and glance toward earth. I'm over mountains—bare ones—no trees. That's all I can tell. Haze is thicker; but I still see outlines with the moon. I ease back on the throttle; the engine shakes the entire plane. I pull the mixture control back, slowly, to its stop. The coughing goes on.

A forced landing over mountains at night? There's just the barest possibility that I can stall down into some moonlit area without crashing my plane beyond repair. But I'm over one of the wildest regions of Arizona, with close to 200 gallons of gasoline in my tanks. I stare at the earth. There's not a single light on its surface. Thousands of feet below I see a huge treeless desert slope, curving up the side of a mountain. I've seen such mountain slopes before—cut by arroyos, spattered with stones, without a level spot where wheels can roll.

The Whirlwind is still putting out some power. But I'm slowly losing altitude. Should I turn back now and try to find a better place to crash? No, there are only more mountains behind.

I glance at the altimeter. I'm still several thousand feet high. I may be able to postpone the forced landing for a long time.

What can the trouble be? It sounds like fuel mixture, but I've tried the mixture control in different positions without success. Three pounds pressure—that's normal. It can't be ignition when the engine runs as well, or as badly, on one magneto as on the other. Is there water in the carburetor? We strained every drop of fuel carefully. Is something broken in the engine?

I open the throttle wide and pull it back again. The coughing decreases slightly. I open the mixture control cautiously. That helps, too. Yes, the engine is definitely running better. I keep circling. I'm no longer losing altitude. *Perhaps I won't have to land.*

I keep working with mixture control and throttle, to reduce the shaking. By just the right jockeying of these levers I find that I climb slowly, gaining back part of the altitude I've lost. I was down to 7000 feet above sea level at the lowest point—within 2000 or 3000 of the ground, as near as I could judge. Now, I'm up to 7500. I glance at the clock—8:07. It seems hours, yet it's been only fifteen minutes since the missing started. Should I try to spiral until daybreak? Should I take up my heading east across the Rockies, toward sunrise and level Kansas plains? Should I turn back toward California?

I have plenty of fuel in the tanks. But turning back would destroy the check on navigation which is my main object in this flight. It's extremely important to see how far off route I am when the sun rises. If serious errors have crept into my navigational techniques, I must learn about them before I start across the ocean. The fuel-consumption data I had hoped to get is already thrown off—spiraling, climbing, and using an extra 100 rpm to keep the engine warm make it almost valueless. But I can run another test on that during the flight from St. Louis to New York. What I need now is a check on navigation. So I'll try to hold to the route I laid out in San Diego.

Twenty minutes pass; the Whirlwind runs better. I feel confidence returning. Maybe my trouble is caused only by altitude and the cold air of night. I'll use more power and watch the mixture control carefully. I stop spiraling and take up my St. Louis course, setting the throttle at 1750 rpm, climbing steadily to get above the mountain peaks.

THE USE of more power is working: the engine sometimes runs for several minutes between coughing spells. I'm over 13,000 feet now. I wonder if that long, snowcapped ridge, reaching to outer limits of the moonlight, is the Continental Divide. I clear summits by about 500 feet.

Mountains melt quickly into foothills, and foothills roll out into level plains. I see the lights of four villages, stringing north and south. They're probably tied together by a railroad. I ease my stick forward to lose altitude and reach warmer air. Soon, if I've not drifted north of route, I'll be over the panhandle of Oklahoma.

TWELVE O'CLOCK, San Diego time—halfway to Lambert Field. I've been in the air for better than eight hours—much longer than any flight I've made before. The Whirlwind runs smoothly now, with the throttle well advanced. I'll have a carburetor heater put on at New York. The warning I got tonight may save my life over the North Atlantic, flying in still colder air.

Stars are fading in the sky ahead—the first sign of morning. East's horizon sharpens. A tinge of pink precedes the birth of day. I see outlines of fields below—straight-edged shades, one darker than another; and here and there is a raveled line which marks a creek bed. I'm somewhere over Kansas. That's almost certain. In a few more minutes I'll know.

A red disk bumps up the sky's edge, and a barn roof glints sharply. Spinning windmills point northwestward. Oil derricks are scattered around ahead. Now to find where I am on the map. Train tracks come angling in from the northwest, and run on toward a small city several miles away, under my right wing. Another roadbed enters my field of vision from east of north, converging with the first on the same little city. I unfold the map of Kansas.

Soon I find the pattern I'm looking for—the same lines, the same angles, villages and towns where villages and towns should be. My location is definite. There must have been a strong tail wind during the night; and I've held a higher rpm than I intended. I'm nearly 50 miles south of my route!

WELL, THE FLIGHT has been successful. I mark down instrument readings for the last time. In a few minutes more I'll be landing. I see the outline of Lambert Field. How green it has become! It was a muddy brown in February.

Several men are standing in front of the National Guard hangars as I approach. It's only eight o'clock, local time. Figures run out of buildings as I flash overhead. Fifty feet off the ground now. I ease the stick back slightly—20 feet, 10, 5. Over the center of the field, I pull up steeply in a climbing turn—300, 700, 1000, 1500 feet. Lambert Field never saw a plane with such a combination of range, speed, and climb.

I circle once, and point my nose toward St. Louis—I promised to fly over the business district before landing.

THE *Spirit of St. Louis* touches ground fourteen hours and twenty-five minutes from takeoff. No man ever traveled so fast from the Pacific Coast before. I taxi up in front of the National Guard hangars. Every person in sight is walking or running toward my plane. Bill and Frank Robertson come up to welcome me. I climb out of my cockpit and answer reporters' routine questions.

Soon we're walking over to Louie's for breakfast.

"Any news from Nungesser and Coli?" I ask.

"There's a report that a British ship picked them up at sea," one of the reporters replies. "But we can't get confirmation."

"Has the Bellanca taken off yet?"

"No. The last report is that they're going to take off Saturday, if the weather's good enough. Have you heard about the warning from the State Department?"

"No. What is it?"

"Our embassy in Paris says it might be misunderstood if an American plane lands in France before there's definite word about Nungesser and Coli."

"The Bellanca is going to make the flight anyway," somebody else says. "What do you think you'll do, Slim?"

"I don't know," I answer. "I'll at least go through to New York. If Nungesser and Coli are lost, it seems to me it's up to the rest of us to carry on what they attempted."

While we're eating Louie's ham and eggs, Harold Bixby and Harry Knight arrive. Soon my other partners begin phoning and assembling. I show them the *Spirit of St. Louis,* tell them about the flight, and of the results of our tests in San Diego.

"How long can you stay in the city, Slim?" Bixby asks. "We've got a half-dozen dinner invitations for you."

"I'll stay as long as you want me to," I answer. "But I think I ought to go right on to New York. If I don't, somebody else will beat us to the takeoff. Unless weather holds them down, the Bellanca crew will probably start before I can anyway. But they may not get through the first time they try."

"That's what we thought you'd say, Slim. It's going to disappoint a lot of people, but you're right. We had some things lined up for you tomorrow, but we'll cancel them all. You'd better stay here and get some sleep tonight. Take off in the morning if you want to."

How could one have better partners?

V. ROOSEVELT FIELD
May 12–20, 1927

I TAKE OFF from Lambert Field at 8:13 a.m. Over the Missouri-Mississippi junction, grain fields ripple in a northwest wind. The *Spirit of St. Louis* has grown with those crops: I conceived the flight last fall when the wheat was planted, and I'm getting under way with the green blades of spring.

I've caught up with the tail of the storm that delayed my San Diego takeoff. Will the Allegheny Mountains be clear? If only the bad weather hovers over the Atlantic and holds my competitors on the ground for two or three more days.

At the end of the seventh hour, Manhattan appears below me: building-weighted, wharf-spined, teeming with life. What contrast to the western spaces I have crossed! I feel cooped up just looking at it.

Beyond those suburbs on Long Island lies what looks like a field, and a second, and, not far away, a third. I bank to circle all three, while I study size and surface.

Mitchel is well kept, but the sod looks rough; Curtiss, where I'm about to land, is much too small for the heavy-load takeoff of the Paris flight. Roosevelt is large enough, and it's the only one that has a runway laid out approximately east and west. If the wind blows in the direction of that runway when I want to start, Roosevelt will be the best.

I circle over Curtiss. A number of men with cameras have

scattered out onto the field, some of them right where I want to touch my wheels. I gun the engine, bank out of the way, and slip down to land at an angle with the wind. Almost as soon as my plane comes to a stop it's surrounded by photographers. I shout at them to keep clear of the propeller, but no one pays attention. Why can't they wait until I taxi to the line and stop my engine?

Several mechanics come out to guard my propeller and lead me to a place in front of one of the hangars. I cut switches, and someone chocks the wheels. A crowd packs around the cockpit, pushing and shouting. A man who obviously has some authority works his way through with difficulty.

"I'm Casey Jones, airport manager," he says, extending his hand in welcome. "We've got one of the hangars ready for you." His glance sweeps around the cockpit, over instruments and controls.

Casey Jones, the famous Curtiss test pilot! What aviator hasn't heard of him? Another man comes up beside him, slender, mustached. "I'm Dick Blythe," he says. "I represent the Wright corporation. They've instructed me to offer you all the help we can give."

"I won't need a whole hangar," I say, "just room for my plane. I'd like to have an expert mechanic check over the engine."

"The best Whirlwind men in the country are right here waiting," Blythe says. "I think you know Ken Boedecker, one of our field service representatives. And this is Ed Mulligan. He's assigned exclusively to your plane. I handle public relations. Now, how about letting the camera boys get a picture of you? Some of them have a deadline to make."

There's a milling about of reporters as I climb down from the cockpit. I stand, as requested, with one hand on the propeller of the *Spirit of St. Louis*.

Each moment I feel more uncomfortable. It's not like San Diego or St. Louis. These cameramen curse and jostle one another for position, while they take pictures from every conceivable angle. Some kneel or crouch; a few even lie on the ground to point their lenses at me. They take photographs head on, from the quarter, from the side; distant shots, close-ups, motion pictures, and stills.

They must have enough pictures to last forever. I start to leave. They crowd nearer. Cameras come within three or four feet of my face. I turn away and begin walking toward the nearest hangar. Photographers run in front. Reporters close in around me; there must be a dozen of them.

"When're you going to start for Paris?"

"Tell us about your flight from California."

"What do you think about Nungesser?"

I don't get a chance to answer any of the questions. Somebody slaps me on the back, somebody else pulls sideways on my arm.

"Now, fellows," Dick Blythe breaks in, "let's get this organized so it's fair to everybody."

I slip into the side door of a hangar while Blythe makes arrangements for a mass interview. Mechanics push the *Spirit of St. Louis* into the hangar. We stretch a rope across the entrance so people can see the plane but not touch it. It's past six, eastern daylight time—too late to accomplish much today.

"I'll want to phone about my compass in the morning."

"You won't have to bother about that," Boedecker tells me. He introduces a man from the Pioneer Instrument Company.

"I've got your earth-inductor compass here," the man says, "all ready to put in."

To my amazement, I find that all the organizations I planned to contact have their representatives right here on Curtiss Field, ready to do whatever they can to help me.

"Captain, I've got the press representatives all together now," says Blythe. "They're waiting for you in the hangar office. But a few photographers didn't get a picture when you landed, and if they don't, some of them may lose their jobs. New York editors are pretty tough."

I stand in front of the *Spirit of St. Louis* again, feeling awkward and foolish. Instead of "a few" photographers, there are more than before.

Then I'm led to the reporters, waiting in a large office at the side of one of the hangars. There must be twenty or thirty of them, standing, leaning, draped on desks and chairs—all looking at me intently. In among them are scattered more photographers, with flashbulbs attached to their cameras. The questioning starts at once.

"When are you going to take off for Paris?"

"My engine needs servicing, and I'm having new compasses installed," I answer. "After that's done, I'll take off as soon as the weather clears up enough."

Questions about the plane are covered quickly. Then subjects are raised which I feel are too personal or too silly to discuss.

"Do you carry a rabbit's foot?"

"How do you feel about girls?"

"What's your favorite pie?"

It's dark by the time I reach my room at the Garden City Hotel.

DURING SUPPER my newly made friends bring me up-to-date on New York-to-Paris flight developments. Byrd has a lease on Roosevelt Field, but I can probably get permission to use the runway. Close to a mile long, it's really the only place for a heavily loaded takeoff. The *America*, Byrd's trimotored Fokker, has just been rebuilt after the crack-up at Teterboro. Chamberlin's Bellanca, the *Columbia*, is on Curtiss Field, only a few hundred feet away from the *Spirit of St. Louis*.

"Why hasn't the Bellanca taken off yet?" I ask.

"Weather and personnel trouble," Blythe tells me. "The route forecasts have been bad, and there's been a lot of squabbling about who is going to fly with Chamberlin."

The Wright corporation is in the enviable but difficult position of having its Whirlwind engines in all the New York-to-Paris planes. Its engineers and mechanics have been instructed to help put each engine and plane in the best possible condition, as a matter of policy. The corporation's interest doesn't end with the engine, Boedecker explains, for the engine is no better than its installation; and if something goes wrong with a plane that forces it to land in the ocean, the engine will probably get the blame regardless of the real cause.

Blythe tells me that public interest has become intense—what with a long record of crashes, with four men killed, two missing, and three injured, and with three planes waiting only on weather or minor adjustments before taking off for France.

Before I arrived at St. Louis yesterday, New Yorkers had paid relatively little attention to my project. But when I landed on Lambert Field, nonstop and overnight from California, their attitude underwent a rapid change. Then came my swift flight through to New York. The trim lines of the plane, the solo crossing of the continent, and my actual presence here, have created extraordinary elements of competition and suspense. Most in question is the ability of a man to fly 3600 miles alone. People say that mine is a fool's venture.

"What do you think of that?"

I read the clipping placed beside my fork:

THINKS NUNGESSER
TRIED TOO MUCH

HALIFAX, N.S., May 10 (AP).—Captain Charles Nugnesser made "the mistake of endeavoring to fly his machine the entire distance himself," in the opinion of Major A. S. Shearer of the Royal Canadian Air Force. The Major said he considered it a physical impossibility for one man to pilot an airplane across the Atlantic for forty hours. . . .

"Well, I've stayed awake over forty hours more than once, working pretty hard most of the time, too," I say. "I don't see why I shouldn't be able to fly that long, sitting down."

After supper we drive back to Curtiss Field. "What's the latest news of Nungesser and Coli?" I ask.

"Same story. One headline says they've been picked up; the next says they haven't. Some of the French papers printed an account of the plane's landing at New York. They even quoted Nungesser's first words to the American press."

Mulligan has the cowlings off when we arrive, and is working efficiently and quietly on my engine. Boedecker pulls off his coat and starts working, too. Blythe goes out to talk to reporters. I decide to take out the six dry batteries to save weight; I can carry an extra flashlight in my pocket.

"You've certainly got the rival camps stirred up," Blythe tells me when he comes back. "The press boys say it looks as though mechanics are going to work all night on both the Fokker and the Bellanca."

IT'S THE MORNING of May 13. Blythe has brought the New York papers to my room. I stare at them, slightly dazed.

BELLANCA PLANE, SPURRED BY LIND-BERGH'S ARRIVAL, IS READY TO GO

SPIRIT OF ST. LOUIS AND AMERICA JOIN THEIR RIVAL HERE FOR THE HOP-OFF

LINDBERGH HERE, READY FOR SEA HOP

CHAMBERLIN AND LINDBERGH SET TO GO

What promises to be the most spectacular race ever held—3,600 miles over the open sea to Paris—may start tomorrow morning. Observers look to Lindbergh as a dark horse in the race. He arrived yesterday afternoon, ahead of schedule, after a fast seven and a quarter hour flight from St. Louis. The trim, slender lines of his silver-coated monoplane impressed pilots and mechanics alike.

"You've taken the show," Blythe says. "The boys don't know how to size you up. They can't laugh off your flight from California. At any other time that would be a big story in itself."

"How's the weather over the Atlantic?" I ask.

"Still bad."

"Let's get some breakfast."

AT THE HANGAR on Curtiss, a crowd has already assembled to see the *Spirit of St. Louis*. Mulligan comes up to me with a piece of cowling in his hands.

"Where's the propeller?" I ask.

"Over at the Curtiss company," he says. "We found a crack in the spinner. They're fixing up a new one for you."

"They said they wouldn't send a bill for the work," Boedecker adds, "so we didn't wait to ask you if it was all right. Outside of that, your engine's checked and set to go."

It's extraordinary. Here's the Curtiss company, one of the Wright corporation's chief competitors, repairing my spinner for nothing. Everywhere I turn it's the same. Bellanca and Chamberlin stop by to wish me well. Commander Byrd comes to the hangar to extend a welcome, and to offer me the use of Roosevelt Field for my takeoff. He's spent much more effort and money than I have in preparing for the Paris flight, and he must be just as anxious as I am to be first to land on Le Bourget; yet he gives me the use of his runway, free of charge.

I work on the *Spirit of St. Louis* most of the morning, with mechanics and instrument experts. Mulligan installs a carburetor air heater to prevent a recurrence of the trouble I had on the flight between San Diego and St. Louis. After lunch I walk to Roosevelt Field to go over the runway, foot by foot. The surface tends to softness, and I wish it were a little wider; but on the whole, it will give me a longer and better takeoff run than I expected to find.

I must take the Pioneer Instrument man on a flight to check my compasses. It will surprise everyone to see how quickly the *Spirit of St. Louis* can take off and climb. A car bumps out over the field to pick me up, and a motorcycle policeman escorts us back to the hangar, where two more uniformed officers are stationed at the doors. Inside, someone hands me another group of papers. "You won't like these very much," he says.

A big front-page picture of myself is below the tabloid headline: FLYIN' FOOL HOPS TODAY. I'm supposed to be ready to take off for Paris at any moment!

Depending on which paper I pick up, I find that I was born in Minnesota, in Michigan, or in Nebraska; that I learned to fly at Omaha, at Lincoln, or at San Antonio. I'm told that my nickname is "Lucky," that I land and take off by looking through periscopes, that I carry "devices" on my plane which will enable me to "snatch a snooze" while steering a "beeline" for Paris.

MY PROBLEMS are shifting from aviation to reporters, photographers, business propositions, and requests for autographs.

The moment I step outside the hangar I'm surrounded by people and protected by police. Even at the hotel, newspapermen fill the lobby and watch the entrance so carefully that I can't walk around the block without being followed. There's never a free moment except when I'm in my hotel room. That's why Ken Lane, chief airplane engineer for Wright, Ed Mulligan, Dick Blythe, and I are sitting here waiting for room service to send up our supper on trays.

There are knocks on the door and conversation stops. "Telegram, sir!" I give the bellboy a dime and tear open the envelope.

CAPT. CHARLES A. LINDBERGH   DETROIT MICH.
CURTISS FIELD, LONG ISLAND, N.Y.   MAY 13, 27
ARRIVE NEW YORK TOMORROW MORNING. MOTHER.

Good Lord! She's been reading the newspaper stories that say I'm likely to crash on takeoff, like Fonck and Davis, or be lost at sea, like Nungesser and Coli. She's coming to Long Island to be near me in this period of danger. Probably the Detroit reporters have been phoning her every hour. My father died three years ago, and it is hard for her to be alone through all this; but Curtiss Field is the last place where she should be. I don't want to leave her to the tabloid press when I take off for Paris; and before that, I should concentrate every minute on my preparations. I'll telephone—no, her train's already left.

I put the telegram in my pocket, and conversation begins again.

"There are more damn crazy ideas floating around this place than I've ever heard before," says Blythe. "Some man's got a young dancer who's worked out an act to symbolize the flight between New York and Paris. He wants to get her out here in costume and have her photographed doing a split on the propeller of the *Spirit of St. Louis*."

"On the *propeller?*"

"Yeah—horizontal."

"I should think it would be pretty difficult."

"Well, we're not going to make the test."

The phone rings. It's another weather report. The Atlantic is still partly covered with areas of fog and storm, and there's not much sign of improvement.

"You ought to visit the New York weather bureau, Captain," Blythe says. "Doc Kimball could give you a lot of dope. He's working out charts for Byrd, you know. The boys say he's good."

"I'd like to do that tomorrow," I answer. "I wonder if—"

The door bursts open and two men stride into the room carrying press cameras. We all jump from our chairs.

"Say, who do you think you are?" Lane demands.

"We're here to get a picture of Lucky Lindy shaving and sitting on the bed in his pajamas."

The men look at me, grin, start adjusting their cameras.

"No! Get out!" We push them from the room.

It may be bad public relations, but I'm not going to have my private life invaded to *that* extent.

MY MOTHER spent one day with me, and left. She felt she had to have that day, she told me. The stories in the papers and the phone calls from reporters in Detroit disturbed her so that she had to see me before I took off—to talk to me—to make sure I really wanted to go and felt it was the right thing to do. Then, she said, she would return home. She had never meant to stay, because she knew that would take my attention from the flight.

MONDAY EVENING, May 16. The *Spirit of St. Louis* is ready to take off, but my route to Paris is still covered with fog and storm. These have been the most extraordinary days I've ever spent, and I can't call them very pleasant. Newspaper, radio, and motion-picture publicity has brought people crowding out to Curtiss and Roosevelt fields until the police are faced with a major traffic problem. Last Sunday, *The New York Times* said, there were thirty thousand people!

And hundreds of letters have come to the field, addressed to me. I've opened only a few. The writers want me to send autographs, want to give me advice, want to show me inventions, to offer me business propositions, to share with me their viewpoints on religion.

Our project has been successful beyond my wildest dreams. We've brought attention to St. Louis, helped focus everybody's eyes on aviation and its future, shown what kind of flights a modern plane can make; and my reputation as a pilot has been established. *The New York Times* is going to buy the story of my flight and syndicate it throughout the country.

All this is very satisfactory. But the way the tabloid people have acted has left me with no respect for them whatever. They must think I'm a cowpuncher, just transferred to aviation. Now they're calling me "a lanky demon of the air from the wide open spaces."

DR. KIMBALL had his latest weather map spread out when I visited his bureau in New York City. A grand person, he went to no end of trouble explaining its details to me. He was disturbed about my intention to follow the great-circle route rather than the ship lanes. He said he couldn't get enough information that far north to forecast the weather properly. I explained that I'm willing to take a chance on weather in order to save distance; and that if the weather proves too bad I can change my course to the south after I'm under way.

On the strength of Dr. Kimball's forecasts of continuing poor conditions, I've accepted a number of invitations to visit private homes. Today I had lunch with Colonel Theodore Roosevelt, Jr., at Oyster Bay.

I found a local doctor waiting to talk to me when I returned to the field. He was concerned about the effects of fatigue and eyestrain on my flight. He had brought me a small first-aid kit, and a pair of colored spectacles for protection from the sun. I didn't think I'd need either, but I slipped them into my map pocket because his arguments were good, and you feel grateful to men like that who want only to help.

Bill MacCracken, Assistant Secretary of Commerce for Aeronautics, has flown up from Washington. The new federal regulations require navigation lights on night-flying aircraft, but I've left them off to save weight and complication.

"Could I have permission to fly without lights on this particular trip?" I inquired.

MacCracken smiled. "Well, you probably won't encounter much night traffic up where you're going," he said. "I think we can give you a special dispensation, just this once."

I REALIZE MORE every day how great an asset lies in the character of my partners in St. Louis. Byrd has been delayed by elaborate organization, and by Wanamaker's cautious insistence on a "scientific" test program for the *America*. In the Bellanca camp there are arguments about who is to go, the route to be followed, and whether or not to carry a radio. My partners, on the other hand, haven't interfered in any way. They've stuck to Bixby's original proposition that they would take care of the finances, and leave the technical end of the flight to me.

Earlier this week I phoned Harry Knight and told him that if I'm going to be first to Paris I'll probably have to start before I'm eligible for the Orteig prize. The sixty days specified in the contest rules haven't passed since my entry was accepted. "To hell with the money," Knight said. "When you're ready to take off, go ahead."*

IT'S THURSDAY AFTERNOON, May 19, one week since I landed in New York. A light rain is falling. Fog shrouds the coasts of Nova Scotia and Newfoundland, and a storm area is developing west of France. It may be another week or two before I can take off. I wouldn't be so concerned about weather if the moon weren't already past full. Soon it won't be any use to me.

I've been ready to take off since daybreak Monday, watching

---

*In the end, the advance notification requirement was waived and the Orteig prize was awarded to Lindbergh in June, 1927.

every report and sign of weather, listening to every rumor about my competitors' plans. Weather reports are so discouraging that I leave the *Spirit of St. Louis* under guard and drive off with friends to a Broadway show. Dick Blythe has arranged for us to go backstage—it ought to be fun.

"Shall we call Doc Kimball for another report?" Lane asks, as we drive across Forty-second Street to the theater.

"Yes," I say, "I think we'd better."

We park at the curb, while Blythe phones the bureau. When he comes out I know by his face and gait that he has news.

"Weather over the ocean is clearing," he announces. "The low-pressure area over Newfoundland is receding, and a big high is pushing in behind it. Of course conditions aren't good all along your route—it may take another day or two for that."

But there's a chance I'll be able to take off at daybreak. Thoughts of the theater vanish. We start immediately for Curtiss. Will the *America* and *Columbia* crews be there, getting ready, too? They probably had this weather report some time ago. I can't fly over to Roosevelt Field tonight—the haze is too thick, the ceiling too low. We'll put about 100 gallons of gasoline in the tanks before taking the *Spirit of St. Louis* out of its hangar. But most of the fueling will have to be done after daybreak, when the plane is in takeoff position.

We stop for a quick dinner and to lay plans for the night. Lane offers to take charge of fueling and putting my plane through a final inspection; Boedecker and Mulligan will help. And there's the recording barograph to be fastened inside the fuselage by the representative of the National Aeronautics Association. Somehow we'll have to locate him before morning. The barograph marks time and altitude on a slowly revolving cylinder of paper. Without it, the record of my flight won't be officially accepted.

"You'd better prepare yourself for some unpleasantness in France," one of my friends tells me at dinner. "A fellow just back from Europe says the feeling over there isn't very friendly toward Americans. He thinks that no American ought to make the flight so soon after Nungesser and Coli have been lost."

At the airfield, I'm surprised to find no sign of preparation in the Byrd or Chamberlin camps. It seems that everyone else is waiting for confirmation of the indications of improving weather. This is the opportunity I've been wishing for. Dr. Kimball will be extremely cautious about saying the time is opportune, knowing that life and death are involved in his decision. My competitors can wait for him to give the word, if they want to. I'll take that responsibility on my own shoulders, where it belongs. I'll be ready at daybreak, and decide then whether or not to start.

WITH PLANS MADE and work quietly under way, I leave for my hotel to get whatever sleep the night still holds for me. But rumors of activity in my hangar have already spread; reporters and others are waiting in the lobby. One man asks me to sign a motion-picture contract; another wants me to make a series of appearances on the stage. I tell them that I can't think about the future until after I reach Paris.

It's close to midnight when I get to my room and lie down. I let my head sink into the pillow and my mind relax. All my work is done, all arrangements made. Competent men have charge of the final servicing of the *Spirit of St. Louis*. I ought to have been in bed three hours ago—there are only two and a half hours left in which to sleep. But how could I have foreseen the sudden change in weather? I've been caught off guard. Well, this is one of the emergencies that fill a flying life, and you keep reserves to meet them. But how much better it is to start a day fully rested.

If only the weather is good in the morning. If only there's a little wind along the runway, not across it. I can't take off, heavily loaded, with a strong crosswind. How much crosswind should I attempt to take off with—what angle—what velocity? If only I could get a good sleep—could put off starting for one more day. But if I let a day of good weather pass, Chamberlin will probably start ahead of me. Now I've drawn even with them at last—no, I'm ahead of them. I won't lose that advantage for the sake of a little sleep. There's still two hours for some rest.

But I'm wide awake. Usually when I lie down tired I fall asleep in an instant. After a day's work in open air I need only to shut my eyes and all problems leave my mind. The days in New York have been tiring—there's no question about that—but in an unhealthy sort of way.

Well, I'll be away from it all in the morning. I must stop my mind from rambling. It's already 1:15. There's only an hour left. But did I make a mistake in telling Lane to fill all the gasoline tanks? I'll have to get 450 gallons into the air—the tanks came out 25 gallons oversize. I'll gain 160 miles' more range; but at a cost of 150 pounds of extra load. How much weight can an airplane lift? When does it just refuse to climb?

My watch says 1:40—almost time to dress. I'll lie and rest a few minutes more. The night is past; the new day has begun, and with it, revived hope, interest, life.

I GET TO THE FIELD a little before 3:00. It's hazy, and light rain is falling. There's a small crowd outside the hangar, and several police officers are at the door.

"Didn't my message get through, Slim?" Lane asks.

"No. What was it?"

"We've found a way to haul your plane up over the rise to Roosevelt Field," he tells me. "You won't have to fly it. We've got a truck standing by. I said to let you sleep until just before daybreak, and we'd have everything set for you to take off."

"Is anybody else getting ready to start?" I ask.

"It doesn't look like it."

"What are the last reports on weather?"

"Still not too good, but it's improving."

I slip out through the big, half-open door, and stare at the glowing mist above Garden City. That means a low ceiling and poor visibility—streetlights thrown back and forth between wet earth and cloud. The ground is muddy and soft. Conditions certainly aren't what one would choose. But the message from Dr. Kimball says that fog is lifting at most reporting stations between New York and Newfoundland. A high-pressure area is moving in over the entire North Atlantic. The only storms listed are local ones, along the coast of Europe.

Clearing along the American coast, clearing over the Atlantic, only local storms in Europe. What does a low ceiling matter at

New York? If clouds here leave room to slip beneath, I'll start at daybreak. If I can't get through, I can turn back. I order the *Spirit of St. Louis* taken to Roosevelt Field.

Mechanics tie the plane's tail skid to the back of a motor truck and wrap a tarpaulin around the engine. Reporters button up their raincoats. Men look out into the night and shake their heads. The truck starter grinds. My plane lurches backward. Shrouded, lashed, and dripping, it looks awkward and clumsy— completely incapable of flight. We are escorted by motorcycle police, pressmen, aviators, and a handful of onlookers. It's more like a funeral procession than the beginning of a flight to Paris.

VI. NEW YORK TO PARIS
May 20–21, 1927

THIRTY REVOLUTIONS low, tires bulging, a soft runway, a tail wind, an overload. I glance down at the wheels. They press deeply into the wet, sandy clay. The engine's roar throbs back through the fuselage and drums heavily on taut fabric skin. I close the throttle and look out at tense faces beside my plane.

The wind changed at daybreak, changed after the *Spirit of St. Louis* was in takeoff position on the west side of the field, changed after all those barrels of gasoline were filtered into the tanks, changed from *head* to *tail*—five miles an hour *tail!*

But it's only a breath, barely enough to lift a handkerchief held in the hand. If we move the plane, it may shift again as quickly as it did before. Taking off from *west* to *east* with a tail wind is dangerous enough—there are only telephone wires and a road at the far end of the field—but to go from *east* to *west* would mean flying right over the hangars and blocks of houses beyond—not a chance to live if anything went wrong.

And there's no time. I'm already late—it's long past dawn. The plane would have to be towed 5000 feet over the muddy runway; I couldn't taxi—the engine's too light and would overheat.

My cockpit quivers with the engine's tenseness. Sharp explosions from the exhaust stacks speak with confidence and precision. But the *Spirit of St. Louis* isn't vibrant with power as it's always been before. I'm conscious of the great weight, and of the fragility of wings that now have to lift 5000 pounds—more than they ever carried before.

The long, narrow runway stretches out ahead. Over the telephone wires at its end lies the Atlantic Ocean. The mechanics, the engineers, stand behind the wing, their eyes intently on mine. If I shake my head, I'll be welcomed back into their midst, back to earth and life. A shake of the head, and we'll be laughing and joking together, laying new plans, plodding over the wet grass toward hot coffee and a warm breakfast—all men of the earth. A nod, and we'll be separated—perhaps forever. The decision is mine.

Thirty revolutions low! "It's the weather," the mechanic said when I climbed into the cockpit. "They never rev up on a day like this." But his encouraging words failed to hide the apprehension in his voice and eyes. He stands there helplessly, with tightened jaw, waiting for my signal.

I lean against the side of the cockpit and look ahead, through the idling blades of the propeller, over the runway's wet and glistening surface. A curtain of mist shuts off the horizon.

Those carefully laid performance curves of ours have no place for mist, or a tail wind, or a soft runway. And what of the 30 revolutions lost? No, I can turn to no formula, the limits of logic are passed. Now, the final judgment must be made by experience, instinct, intuition. When all the known factors have been considered, after equations have produced their final lifeless numbers, one measures a field with an eye, and checks the answer beyond the conscious mind.

I lean back in the wicker seat, running my eyes once more over the instruments. Nothing wrong there. They all tell the proper story. Wind, weather, power, load—gradually these elements stop churning in my mind. It's a decision of feeling, as when you gauge the distance to be jumped between two stones across a brook. Something within you disengages itself from your body and travels ahead with your vision to make the test. You can feel it try the jump as you stand looking. Then uncertainty gives way to the conviction that it can or can't be done. Sitting in the cockpit, the conviction surges through me that the wheels *will* leave the ground, that the wings *will* rise above the wires, that it *is* time to start the flight.

I buckle my safety belt, pull goggles down over my eyes, turn to the men at the blocks, and nod. Frozen figures leap to action. A yank on the ropes—the wheels are free. I brace myself against the left side of the cockpit, sight along the edge of the runway, and ease the throttle wide open. Action brings confidence and relief.

But, except for noise and vibration, what little effect the throttle has! The plane creeps heavily forward. Several men are pushing on wing struts to help it start—pushing so hard I'm afraid the struts will buckle. How can I possibly gain flying speed? The *Spirit of St. Louis* feels more like an overloaded truck than an airplane.

Gradually, the speed increases. The engine's snarl sounds inadequate and weak, carrying its own note of mechanical frustration. There's none of the usual spring forward; the stick wobbles loosely from side to side. But we're going faster—men begin stumbling off from the wing struts.

A hundred yards of runway passes. The last man drops off the struts. The stick's wobbling changes to lurching motion as ailerons protest unevenness of surface. How long can the landing gear stand such strain? I keep my eyes fixed on the runway's edge. I *must* hold the plane straight. Controls begin to tighten against the pressure of my hand and feet. There's a living quiver in the stick. I have to push hard to hold it forward. Slight movement of the rudder keeps the nose on course. Good signs, but more than a thousand feet have passed. Is there still space?

Pace quickens—turf becomes a blur, the tail skid lifts off ground, I feel the load shifting from wheels to wings. The runway's slipping by quickly. The halfway mark is just ahead, and I have nothing like flying speed. But the engine's turning faster and the propeller's taking better hold—I can tell by the sound. I can't look at instruments—I must hold the runway, not take my eyes from its edge for an instant. An inch off on stick or rudder, and my flight will end.

The halfway mark streaks past. Seconds now to decide—close the throttle, or get off? I pull the stick back firmly, and *the wheels leave the ground*. Then I'll get off! The wheels touch again. I ease the stick forward—almost flying speed, and nearly 2000 feet of field ahead. A wing drops, lifts as I shove aileron against it—the entire plane trembles from the shock. Off again, then back onto the runway. I could probably stay in the air; but I let the wheels touch once more—lightly, a last bow to earth, a gesture of humility before it.

The *Spirit of St. Louis* takes herself off the next time, full flying speed, the controls taut, alive, straining—and still 1000 feet to the web of telephone wires. Now, I *have* to make it! I keep climbing slowly, each second gaining speed. If the engine can hold out for one more minute—5, 20, 40 feet—wires flash by underneath—*20 feet to spare!*

Green grass and bunkers below—a golf links—people looking up. A low, tree-covered hill ahead—I shallow-bank right to avoid it, still grasping the stick tightly as though to steady the plane with my own strength. The *Spirit of St. Louis* seems balanced on a pinpoint, as though the slightest movement of controls would cause it to topple over and fall.

The plane's climbing faster—200 feet aboveground. Now I'm high enough to steal glances at the instrument board. The tachometer needle shows 1825 rpm—no sign of engine overheating. I move the throttle back slowly—a glance at the terrain ahead—a glance at the tachometer—1800, 1775 rpm. Pull the stabilizer back a notch. The airspeed's still over 100 miles an hour. I throttle down to 1750—the tail stays up—the controls are taut!

On the instrument board in front of me, the earth-inductor compass needle leans steeply to the right. I bank cautiously north and begin the first 100-mile segment of my great-circle route to Paris. It's 7:45 a.m., eastern daylight saving time.

THE CURTAIN OF MIST moves along with me. I can see three miles ahead, no more. Even at that distance details merge with haze. I pull the map of New York State from its cloth pocket at my side. I must get a check on the compasses, watch for landmarks, make sure that the places I fly over on the earth's surface correspond to the symbols crossed by the inked line on my map.

The great landscaped estates of Long Island pass rapidly below: mansion, hedgerow, and horse-jump giving way to farms and woodlands farther east. I hold my plane just high enough to clear treetops and buildings on the hills. By flying close to the ground, I can see farther through the haze.

The engine has withstood its test of power. It's throttled down, turning smoothly and easily. The *Spirit of St. Louis* seems to form an extension of my own body, ready to follow my wish as the hand follows the mind's desire—instinctively, without commanding.

I settle back in the cockpit, running my eyes carefully over the instruments, between glances at the ground. Fifteen minutes out and all readings normal. I shift from center wing tank to nose tank. Fifteen minutes flying on each of the five fuel tanks should leave enough airspace to stop overflow, and every drop of gasoline must be saved.

As I look out, a newspaper plane banks steeply and heads back—probably trying to get a scoop on the others. I hadn't noticed them during the first few minutes after takeoff. They drew in closer, cameras sticking out of cockpits and cabin windows, and I was startled to find that newspaper companies would hire planes to follow the *Spirit of St. Louis*. The plane rocks slightly—turbulent air! I glance up at the heavily loaded wings. Bumps are light, but the tips flex up and down too far for comfort. I'm passing over Port Jefferson and its harbor full of boats. Air's usually rough where land and water meet. I fly through uneasy seconds until Long Island's coast is behind. Then, within 1000 yards of the shoreline, air smooths out like glass. And at almost the same moment, the pilot of the last escorting plane dips his wing in farewell, and turns back toward land.

I'm alone at last, over the first short stretch of sea on the route to France. The surface is calm. There's hardly a sign of movement beneath the oil-smooth sheen of its skin. It's only 35 miles to the Connecticut shore, but I've never flown across that much water before. Long Island Sound comes as an advance messenger, welcoming and yet warning me of the empire that lies ahead—of the trackless wastes, the great solitude of the ocean.

Haze thickens behind me until the coastline becomes lost. There's not a boat in sight. Only a few spiraling gulls and dark bits of refuse on the water show that land is near. I'm the center point in a circle of haze moving along with me over the glassy water—gray haze over gray water, the one mirrored in the other until I can't tell where sea ends and sky begins.

I relax in the cockpit—this little box with fabric walls in which I'm to ride across the ocean. It's a compact place, designed to fit me so snugly that no ounce of weight or resistance is wasted. I can press both sides of the fuselage with partly out-stretched elbows. The instrument board is an easy reach for-ward for my hand, and a thin rib on the roof is hollowed slightly to leave clearance for my helmet. There's room enough, no more, no less.

A pilot doesn't feel at home in a plane until he's flown it for thousands of miles. At first it's like moving into a new house. The key doesn't slip in the door smoothly; the knobs and light switches aren't where you put your hand. Later, after you've used the key a hundred times, it turns easily in the lock; knobs and switches leap to meet your fingers on the darkest night. My test flights in California, the long hours of night above deserts and mountains of the Southwest, the swift trip over the Alle-ghenies to New York, have removed the feel of newness from the *Spirit of St. Louis*. Each dial and lever is in proper place; and the slightest pressure on controls brings response.

I'm glad this flight to Paris hasn't become a race. There are hazards enough without adding human competition. Now I can set my throttle for range instead of speed, hoarding gasoline for that worried hour when extra fuel means saving the flight.

What advantages there are in flying alone! I know now what my father meant when he warned me, years ago, of depending too heavily on others. He used to quote a saying of old settlers in Minnesota: "One boy's a boy. Two boys are half a boy. Three boys are no boy at all." By flying alone I've gained in range, time, flexibility, freedom. My movements haven't been re-stricted by someone else's temperament, health, or knowledge.

NEW ENGLAND'S TREE-COVERED HILLS harden from the northern haze. Scattered ships and launches ply back and forth offshore. I fold up the map of New York, and pull out one of Connecticut. The first state is passed; the first salt water crossed. It gives me a feeling of accomplishment.

Inland, there's not much room between green hills and clouds. I climb slowly, and push out the periscope built by one of the workmen in the factory at San Diego. Its field of vision isn't large, but it shows the country directly ahead well enough to warn of a high summit in my line of flight. I don't have to lean over to one side for a better view. I can take off my goggles and sit quietly in the center of the cockpit.

I cross the Thames River between Norwich and New London. Over the valley, the ceiling is higher. Ahead, the haze is clearing, and the cloud base is lifting rapidly. I angle five degrees northward to pick up my great-circle route.

It's 8:52 a.m. The second hour begins. I mark down the instrument readings on my log, and reset the earth-inductor compass.

Rhode Island is already beneath me. How these northeastern states are crowded together! I'm accustomed to the great distances of the West, where an inch on the map represents many miles on the ground, and where railroads are often an hour's flight apart.

I look down on small fields spread out in stream-fed valleys and sloping toward heavily wooded hills. They're filled with cattle, gray boulders, and moist green crops of spring—so unlike the big farms of my Mississippi Valley, with their miles of straight fence lines. Here, the tumbledown stone walls run every which way. Highways and villages are everywhere. I can't keep count of them on the map. And the railroads are too close together to make good checkpoints.

Providence is under my left wing. The Massachusetts line runs through the city's eastern suburbs. The *Spirit of St. Louis* has flown over the whole of Rhode Island in the time it takes to walk a single mile. *And the sky is clearing*. In the distance, dazzling white strips between gray bunched clouds show where the sun is breaking through.

97

The skyline under the wing seems to be dividing. Below the straight but still vague line of the natural horizon, a darker irregular line has formed—the Atlantic Coast! There, above it, is the great ocean itself—real, wet, and endless—no longer simply an idea or a blue tint on paper. I pull out my Mercator projection map of the North Atlantic. I worked endless hours on this chart in California, measuring, drawing, rechecking each 100-mile segment of its great-circle route, each theoretical hour of my flight. But only now, as I lay it on my knees, do I realize its full significance. A few lines and figures on a strip of paper, a few ounces of weight, this strip is my key to Europe. With it, I can fly the ocean.

As the third hour begins, I enter instrument readings in my log. Cape Cod, a low, bluish hook of land, dents the horizon to my right. Rapidly fading out of sight behind me is the coastline of the United States. Looking ahead at the unbroken horizon and limitless expanse of water, I'm struck by my arrogance in attempting such a flight. I'm giving up a continent, and heading out to sea in the most fragile vehicle ever devised by man.

My first real test of navigation is at hand. For more than two hours, I'll be out of sight of land. When I left the coast of Massachusetts, I was on the great-circle route to Paris. When I strike the coast of Nova Scotia, I'll know exactly how many degrees I've deviated from it. Between the two there's nothing but water beneath my plane.

I nose down closer to the low, rolling waves—100, 50, 20 feet above their shifting surfaces. I come down to meet the ocean, asking its favor—the right to pass for thousands of miles across its realm. The earth released me on Long Island; now I need approval from the sea.

I drop down till my wheels are less than a man's height above the rollers. The ocean doesn't seem hostile; it has rather a cold hospitality. There will be a polite relationship between us. I'll have only the air to contend with.

Miles slip by quickly. The *Spirit of St. Louis* is like a butterfly blown out to sea, dancing up and down above the water. As a child, on the banks of the Mississippi, I used to watch butterflies dance up and down with their own fancy and the currents of air. A touch of wing to water, and they were down forever—just as my plane would be.

After a while, flying next to the water grows tiresome. When I'm low, I have to keep a firmer grip on controls, and rivet my attention to the space between wheels and water. When I'm high, I can settle back comfortably, touching stick and rudder just enough to keep the compass needle centered. I climb up 100 feet and search the horizon for signs of life.

It's 10:52 a.m. The fourth hour. I mark down a third set of instrument readings on the log sheet. About 300 pounds of fuel have been consumed; the plane's almost a barrel's weight lighter. I ease the throttle back to 1725 rpm, and lean out the fuel mixture, reduce the amount of gasoline mixing with the air passing through the carburetor. The airspeed drops to 104 miles an hour. I have to pull the nose up a trifle—enough to warn me against reducing power further.

There are ripples on the water—a northwest breeze. That's too much from the side to be of value. What I need is a west wind; or better, one from the southwest. A side wind's not a good omen. With a large high-pressure area over the ocean, I had hoped for a tail wind on this portion of my route. What does it mean, this unexpected direction?

I'M A LITTLE TIRED. The sun beating in through the window overhead makes the cockpit uncomfortably hot. My legs are stiff and cramped. But that won't last more than three or four hours. The dull ache will get worse for a time, and then go away. I've experienced the feeling before. It begins after about three hours of flying, and ends at about seven. I wish the desire for sleep could adapt itself to a long-distance flight as easily.

It would be pleasant to doze off for a few seconds. But I mustn't feel sleepy at this stage of the trip! I'm less than a tenth of the way to Paris. I sip some water from the quart canteen at my side. Below it are five sandwiches in a brown paper bag; but I'm not hungry. And anyway, it's easier to stay awake on an empty stomach. The lack of sleep I feel now, at eleven o'clock in the morning, is a grain of sand compared to the mountain that will tower over me when dawn breaks tomorrow.

I think of dawns on the mail route, after a late flight the night before. They brought moments when only pride kept me from landing in some pasture, cutting my engine, and slumping back in my cockpit to sleep. Those moments were always at dawn. I awoke with the sunrise. But this is different: I want to sleep in broad daylight, before noon of the first day.

I'll climb up 200 or 300 feet and stop looking ahead for boats. There's not much danger of hitting one, and watching my periscope mirror is an added strain. In glancing from compass to water and out to the horizon where land should soon appear, my eyes fasten on a band of mud sticking to the right wing's lower surface. I want to reach out, scrape it off, and polish the fabric; but it's an arm's length too far away. Now, I'll have to look at it helplessly during all the rest of the flight. Thirty-three hours to get that mud off the wings—

I'm half asleep! I cup my hand into the slipstream and deflect fresh air against my face. Check the instruments—that will help. I slide the periscope back into the cockpit. There's been no ship for many miles, and I'm too high to strike a mast anyway. I can at least save its resistance; on such a long flight that should save a gallon or two of fuel. Possibly it will compensate for the mud. A pound of resistance saved is worth several pounds of weight. From the start, I've planned this flight on the basis that no detail is too small to be considered. To save extra ounces, I've made my own flying boots out of light material, bought small flashlights, and cut unneeded areas from my charts.

THE FIFTH HOUR. Land ahead! A huge green mass extends back to a hilly horizon: Nova Scotia! The low, grassy coast, curving in under my right wing, is backed by growths of spruce and pine. I forget about being tired. Here's a vital point in the flight. How accurately have I held my course? I climb higher. When you fly low, you gain intimacy but lose perspective. There are probably a dozen river mouths, capes, and villages on your map, and when you don't know your position, you need to be high enough to see the entire geographical community.

From 1000 feet, I find a peninsula on my left, a cape on my right, a tongue of sea stretching inland far ahead. I've made my landfall at the mouth of Saint Mary Bay. I've covered 440 miles in four hours and nineteen minutes, an average of 102 miles an hour.

At San Diego I'd decided that an error of five degrees would mark reasonably good navigation. Now, I've held within only two degrees of the great circle on my chart. I'll be well satisfied if I can hold that close to route.

The country under my plane is spotted with forests, lakes, and marshes. Gray boulders wart up everywhere—one sees them even underwater where it's shallow. The lakes are smooth as glass, not a breath of air blowing across them. It won't make any difference which way I land if the engine fails.

A forced landing: years of barnstorming with rebuilt army planes and engines have trained me to keep that possibility always in mind. You never know, with such equipment, when an engine will stop running. I study the ground, my eyes searching for the place I'd choose to land in case of engine failure. Not a farmer's field in sight. My mind now takes fiendish pleasure in planning a landing—on hills, in marshes, in tree clumps; it visualizes the best technique to use, carrying me along in its excursions until my ears can almost hear the motor cough, and my body feel the impact of the wheels and wings.

Its 12:52 p.m., the sixth hour; it's lunchtime in New York. What a contrast between my cockpit, high over Nova Scotian wilds, and the silvered settings of a city table! What magic is carried in an airplane's wings—breakfast-to-lunch in time equals New York-to-Nova Scotia in distance. Flying has torn apart the relationship of space and time. I drop my hand to the bag of sandwiches, but I'm not hungry. A drink of water will do.

In hanging up the canteen, I let my map slide toward the window. One corner flutters in a puff of air. I jerk it away with a start. Suppose my chart blows out, as my data board did on that test flight in California? My key to Paris would be gone; I'd have to turn back. "Plenty of fuel, all readings normal, but the chart blew out the window." What an explanation that would make!

But why not put the windows in? They're in their rack, an arm's reach behind me. I carried them because they were worth more than their weight in fuel. They'll smooth out the flow of air along the fuselage; smoother flow means less resistance; less resistance means more speed; and more speed will result in additional miles of range.

I open the cockpit ventilator and start to slip the left window into place when I realize that a new factor has to be considered, one of those factors engineers can't measure, yet one on which all performances must rest—the condition of the pilot. Windows would cut down the flow of air through the cockpit. They'd interfere with my communion with water, land, and sky. They'd insulate me from a strength I'll need before my flight is done.

No, I'll leave the windows in their rack and sacrifice their efficiency to mine. It's a new experience. Always before, I've had a reserve of energy and skill on which my plane could draw; now, for the first time, I'm taking a favor from my plane. It makes the *Spirit of St. Louis* seem more a living partner in adventure than a machine of cloth and steel.

THE SKY HAS been filling slowly. A solid mass of clouds now blocks out the north—tremendous, dark, and foreboding. Angular streaks of gray break the horizon ahead into segments— rainsqualls. Lakes and ponds below are wave-roughed; white beaches of foam have formed against leeward shores. It takes a gale to whip up water like that—40 or 50 miles an hour.

The wind mounts in velocity and blows directly across my route. I should crab toward it at an angle of twenty-five degrees to compensate for drift. But that would leave my plane pointing into the great black body of the storm. I won't change my heading for the time being. I'll let wind drift me where it will. Winds which arise suddenly on the edge of storms often change just as suddenly and blow in another direction.

But now, as I approach these storm clouds, the air really gets rough. Wing tips flex with rapid, jerking movements, and the cockpit bumps up, down, and sideways. I buckle my safety belt. The plane is 500 pounds lighter than on takeoff; but with a ton of fuel left on board, it's still dangerously overloaded. A violent gust might easily snap a spar or fitting. The wings were never designed for such a wrenching! I feel as though the storm were gathering my plane in its teeth as a dog picks up a rabbit.

A parachute would be useless over the ocean. Over Long Island and New England, I flew too low to use one, and when I get to Europe, the wings will be so lightly loaded that I won't have to worry about turbulence. This is the only portion of the route where I might need a parachute. Everything considered, I was right when I decided not to bring one. But logic's not enough to calm my senses. They know what it's like to feel fittings snap in air—the physical jolt, the mental shock.

During a combat maneuver once, in Texas, our pursuit squadron of SE-5s had located the "enemy" below us, some 5000 feet aboveground, and nosed down to attack. I was flying left wing, with a Lieutenant McAllister on my right. We reached a pretty high speed in our dive, closing in to confirm the "kill." Then we pulled up. I'd kicked left rudder, as I hauled back on the stick, into what I thought was empty sky.

Then it happened. I heard the snap of parting metal and the crunch of wood as my forehead bumped the cockpit's cowling and my plane cartwheeled through the air. I yanked the throttle shut as muscles tensed body back in place. There, canted sidewise, less than a dozen feet away, was the fuselage of another SE-5. Our wings were ripped and locked together. Both planes seemed to hang motionless in space. I saw McAllister reach for his safety belt and half rise in his seat. Then we began to rotate in the air. A trailing edge of the broken top wing folded back over my cockpit and vibrated against my helmet, shaking sight from my eyes and thought from my brain—except for the imperative idea of clearing the wreckage with my parachute.

By that time I had the rubber safety band removed and my belt unbuckled. Wires were howling; wooden members snapping; my cockpit had tipped toward the vertical. Our planes were revolving like a windmill. I pushed past the damaged wing, hooked my heels on the cowling, and kicked backward into space. My parachute had no more than flowered out when the wrecked planes plummeted past me, and McAllister's chute came swinging down out of the mist above. We angled with the wind toward a plowed field that was ideal for parachute landings. And in slightly over an hour, we were back in the air again—members in the Caterpillar Club: that exclusive and unorganized group of flyers whose lives have been saved by the silkworm's product.

THE FIRST SQUALL isn't large. But with each succeeding one clouds grow darker, rain is heavier, and lightning flashes down on trees and rocks. Finally I give up my course and turn eastward to skirt the edges of the more violent storms. I weave in and out, flying now through a cloudburst, now under a patch of open sky; returning to my heading, then leaving it again rather than drill through the heart of a storm. Water lashes over the wings, turns the propeller into a whitish disk of vapor, trickles along silver surfaces, eddies behind screwheads and fittings; seeps into my cockpit, splashing over flying suit and charts, moistening my lips, freshening the air I breathe.

Can the ignition system stand such a drenching? I haven't tested the *Spirit of St. Louis* in a cloudburst. I don't dare check the magnetos now; but not a single cylinder has missed.

Gradually the wind swings southward, until at last it blows southeast, and then begins to die. From northwest to southeast— it's a good omen; that's the way the wind should veer if the storm area is small.

THE SEVENTH HOUR, still over Nova Scotia. Six hundred miles out, three thousand miles to go. Squalls are lighter, and patches of blue sky are larger. But I've got to be cautious about too much optimism. I'm at a point in my flight where I have the feeling of great accomplishment without having experienced the major strain of effort. Fatigue to a body is like air resistance to a plane. If you fly twice as fast (if you continue twice as long), you encounter four times the resistance (you become several times as tired). But elements of mind and body don't follow such clear, sharp curves of physics; they jump erratically to peaks, and back to depths, and then may strike an average for a time. The cool freshness of the rain, the concentration required in flying through the squalls, and the satisfaction of entering the seventh hour of my flight have brought me to a peak of confidence and hope.

A wilderness now lies beneath my wings. Valleys are filled with the deep green of virgin timber. Flocks of duck rise out of lakes and marshes. I think of childhood nights on our farm, when I lay awake listening to my father's stories of hunting and trapping around such lakes as these.

My grandfather must have found a country like this when he immigrated to America from Skane in the southern part of Sweden. My father was only a few months old then. Traveling westward, the family settled, and built a log cabin on the Sauk River's bank, in the new state of Minnesota.

As soon as my father was old enough to carry a gun, it was his job to keep the family supplied with meat. Since ammunition was scarce, his rounds were counted, and a bird was demanded in return for each round fired. When he missed a shot, he tried to hit two birds with the next. My father had spoken of it casually. Now, as I look down on this game-filled land, I understand his casualness better. It wouldn't be so difficult to kill two birds with one shot when they're as thick as that.

Several small farms line the river ahead—fields walled in by timber. Cattle wade across the water, their shadows falling sharply on its surface. One of my father's stories was about fishing from a riverbank on the homestead. Sioux massacres in the Minnesota Valley and raids northward had left settlers nervous. It had been several years since the uprising, but fear remained in children's minds. One day, my father suddenly saw shadows move along the edge of a pool upstream: Sioux warriors! He lunged backward into hazel brush as he looked up to see—not warriors, just farm cattle, like those below me now.

Are there Indians in these forests, too, here in Nova Scotia? I can only guess as I fly over hills and valleys, now 50 feet, now 500 above the ground. In flying, you get to know the external character of a country; but you have little contact with its inner life. You *see* the land below you, but you don't *feel* it; until you set foot on ground it remains foreign soil. A Nova Scotian hilltop is 50 feet away. I can see pine needles but I can't smell their fragrance; the pines are swaying, but I hear no sound of wind. At times I feel as separated from the country below me as though I were looking through a giant telescope at the surface of another planet.

THE EIGHTH HOUR of flight. On the ground, patches of old snow appear in hollows and on the north side of boulders. I left summer back on Long Island this morning. Only a few minutes ago, I flew through the showers of spring. Now I'm over a land just emerging from winter. And my route continues to angle northward for more than 1000 miles.

I'm flying along dreamily when I see a narrow white band on the horizon to my right. *There's fog on the Nova Scotian coast.* It brings me to attention like ice water dashed in the face.

Fog—the most dreaded of all enemies of flight. Will Cape Breton Island and Newfoundland be hidden by a sheet of blinding white? Will I be able to check my course over Newfoundland?

I begin climbing, while my eyes search the ground for some landmark that shows on my map. It's important to know my exact position before venturing out over that sea of white.

I can find no checkpoint on the ground. The best map of this country I could buy contains nothing but lightly tinted space and a few wriggling lines for rivers. But as I near the coast, what seemed a great fogbank from the distance turns out to be only a long, narrow strip hovering above shore. The ocean beyond is sparkling blue in sunlight.

Along the coast of Cape Breton Island the air is crystal clear. But inland, a new cloud bank is forming, so it seems wiser to remain near the sea. My eyes wander up to the taut, silvered wing outside my window. It's difficult to realize that air is rushing past that motionless surface at nearly 100 miles an hour. One of the miracles of flying is that when you look out at your wings you see neither movement nor support. It's not until you put your arm outside, and press hard against the slipstream, that you sense the power and speed of flight.

Barely a tremor of turbulence is left. The engine's even vibration, shaking back through the fuselage's steel skeleton, gives life to cockpit and controls. Flowing up along the stick to my hand, it's the pulsebeat of the plane. Let a cylinder miss once, and I'll feel it as clearly as though a human heart had skipped against my thumb.

My cockpit is small, and its walls are thin; but inside this cocoon I feel secure. It makes an efficient, tidy home, one so easy to keep in order that its very simplicity creates a sense of satisfaction and relief.

Thirty hours to Paris! What a simple statement, when there's a chasm of eternity to cross. Who could look at the sky, at the mountains, at the chart on my knees, at the motionless wings of my plane, and still think of time in *hours*? In the *Spirit of St. Louis*, I live in a different frame of time and space.

I became minutely conscious of the weld marks on the steel tubing, a dot of radiolite paint on the altimeter's face, the battery of fuel valves. How detached the intimate things around me seem from the world below. How strange is this combination of proximity and separation. That ground—seconds away— thousands of miles away. This air, stirring mildly around me. That air, an inch beyond, rushing by with the speed of a tornado. These minute details in my cockpit. The grandeur of the world outside. The nearness of death. The longness of life.

It is the ninth hour. The coastline stops wandering back and forth, and turns abruptly northwest—the end of Cape Breton Island. Now, 200 miles to Newfoundland; after that, the great body of the Atlantic.

The sea is as welcome a change as the coast of Nova Scotia was. I nose the *Spirit of St. Louis* down toward the wild and lonely shore, down so low that I can see the wetness of the pebbles on the beach. I level out at 20 feet above the water— above a rougher, greener, colder-looking ocean, with whitecaps breaking off to streaks of foam. There are no marks of human life along the coast, not even a plank of wreckage rotting on the beach.

The cloud layer which was forming in the north remains behind with the peaks of Cape Breton Island. Now it's time to angle back onto my great-circle route. If I leave Newfoundland on my plotted course, accurate navigation will be simpler.

I look down at my Mercator projection. Fifteen degrees

subtracted from my heading would put me back on the great circle by the time I reach Newfoundland's southern coast. Still, there may be clouds on the mountains, as there were on Cape Breton Island. Then I'd be better off to the eastward, where I could follow up Placentia Bay and cross over the neck of land at its head into Trinity Bay, which opens to the ocean.

My flight plan argues against detours unless forced by weather that I can't fly above or through—but striking Placentia Bay would scarcely add the mileage and there'd be plenty of time to get back onto the great circle during long hours over the ocean. Besides, if I set my course for Placentia Bay, and the mountains are clear, I can fly over the little city of St. John's. Someone there will surely send a message back to say I have passed.

Those men back on the field at Long Island, who worked all night long that I might start, are probably waiting for some sign that I haven't crashed. My partners in St. Louis also have a right to know that when I start over the ocean all is well. The men at the factory in San Diego who built the *Spirit of St. Louis* —by this time they'll have heard that I got off the field with full tanks. They, too, will want to know where I am at nightfall. And my mother, teaching in Detroit—she's probably been wondering and worrying all day. How well I remember the expression on her face that winter evening when I told her I wanted to leave college and learn to fly. "All right," she said. "If you really want to fly, that's what you should do. Only I can't see the time when we'll be together much again." Her prophecy came true. I haven't been home for more than a few days at a stretch since then. But we went barnstorming together in southern Minnesota in the summer; and she's flown back and forth between Chicago and St. Louis with me on the mail route, riding on the sacks. I know what a message of my welfare would mean to her tonight.

But I've already drawn enough on my reserves by detouring squalls and leaving windows out. Misdirected sentiment could result in death. A message back from Newfoundland tonight is less important than to land in France tomorrow.

Yet suppose I have a forced landing on the ocean. There'd

be an advantage in people's knowing that I went down some-where east of St. John's. If I can't charge a gallon of fuel to sentiment, I *can* charge it to safety. I reset my compass and turn the *Spirit of St. Louis* slightly toward the south.

NOW, UNTIL Newfoundland's coast appears, I'll have nothing to do but follow the compass and add one set of readings to my log. I twist around in the cockpit to a new and momentarily more comfortable position, and sleep comes filtering in. It comes like that early turbulence of storm squalls, barely per-ceptible at first, satisfying to the body, alarming only in the warning it carries to conscious portions of the mind.

Why is the desire to sleep so much stronger over water than over land? Is it because there's nothing to look at, no point different from all others to rivet one's attention to—nothing but waves, ever changing and yet changeless; no two alike, yet monotonous in their uniformity? Hold the compass needle on its mark, glance at the instruments occasionally; there's nothing else to do.

If I could throw myself down on a bed, I'd be asleep in an instant. In fact, if I didn't know the result, I'd fall asleep just as I am, sitting up in the cockpit—I'm beyond the stage where I need a bed, or even to lie down. My eyes feel dry and hard as stones. The lids pull down with pounds of weight against their muscles. Keeping them open is like holding arms outstretched without support. After a minute or two of effort, I have to let them close. Then I press them tightly together, forcing my mind to think about what I'm doing so I won't forget to open them again; trying not to move stick or rudder, so the plane will still be flying level and on course when I lift them heavily.

It works at first, but soon I notice that the minute hand of the clock moves several divisions forward while I think only seconds pass. My mind clicks on and off, as though attached to an elec-tric switch with which some outside force is tampering. I try letting one eyelid close at a time while I prop the other open with my will. But the effort's too much. Sleep is winning. My whole body argues dully that nothing is quite so desirable as sleep. My mind is losing resolution and control.

I pull the *Spirit of St. Louis* up 200 or 300 feet above the water, shake my head and body roughly, flex muscles of my arms and legs, stamp my feet, breathe deeply, and squirm about as much as I can while still holding the controls.

My body is shaped by the seat's design. My hand is tied to the stick and my feet to the rudder by cords of instability. Even the angles of my joints are fixed. But shaking clarifies my mind a little—enough to make new resolutions. I will *force* my body to remain alert. I will *force* my mind to concentrate—never let it get dull again. I simply can't think of sleep. I have an ocean yet to cross. Sleep is insignificant compared to the importance of this flight. It will interfere with my judgment, my navigation, my accuracy of flying. It can come later, after I land at Paris and have the *Spirit of St. Louis* put safely away in some hangar. All this I tell myself savagely—and futilely. The worst part about fighting sleep is that the harder you fight the more you weaken your resistance to it. The very exertion of staying awake makes you sleepier.

The cramped feeling I had in my legs has left, as I knew it would. Only dull aches in my back and shoulders remain. I would almost welcome sharper pain. It might help to stay awake. I'm like a man lost in a blizzard, feeling the weight of sleep on his shoulders as though his coat were made of lead, wanting nothing so much as to fall down in the softness of a snowbank and give way to irresponsible sleep, yet realizing that beyond such relaxation lies the eternity of death.

I WAS CAUGHT in a blizzard once, in Minnesota. Deep midwinter snow had made roads impassable except to man and horse. I was seventeen years old then, and I'd just taken on a dealership for milking machines and farm engines. Early that morning, I'd saddled one of my ponies and started out for the little town of Pierz. I'd ridden from one barn to another until evening found me almost 30 miles from home.

Snow was falling lightly when I started back. I'd pulled my fur hat down, buttoned my sheepskin collar around my face, and almost gone to sleep in the saddle, leaving navigation to my pony. I don't know how many miles had passed when a change in rhythm jolted me alert. The pony had stopped walking. He stood quivering—legs spread apart as though he were afraid of losing his balance and toppling into snow. I dismounted, spoke to him, and led him on. He could walk alone, but my weight on his back had been too much. He was getting old, and the day had been long.

I made the rest of the way home on foot, some 15 miles, my pony following behind. The first hour was easy enough, even pleasant as a change. Then the heavy winter clothing began to bear down on my shoulders, and my felt-lined boots grew heavier with every step. The snow lashed against my eyes, drifted over the road, held back my plodding feet.

Sometime after midnight the blizzard stopped, and it turned cold—that bitter cold in which a quickly drawn breath strikes into lungs with pain. Hoarfrost formed on the fur of my cap. My pony's hoofs crunched into the silence of the night. As hours passed I lost consciousness of muscles moving. My legs swung back and forth like clock pendulums, as though they were part of a machine on which my upper body rode.

Oh, how I wanted to lie down in a snowbank and sleep! Finally, I hooked the bridle reins over my arm, fell into the snow, and for two or three minutes let every muscle forget its responsibility—while the pony stood above me, head down, also resting. I could lie, and rise, and make my body walk, and stop, and walk again. I wasn't bound to a cramped position in a cockpit.

I *must* keep my mind from wandering. It must be kept on its proper heading as accurately as the compass. I'll review my plans for navigation. Then I'll concentrate on some problems. If the wind keeps on increasing and swinging tailward, I ought to average over 100 miles an hour through the night. A strong tail wind would put me over Europe well ahead of schedule. But suppose the wind shifts north or south during the night, and blows me hundreds of miles off route. (This ought to be a line of thought to stay awake on!) The night has always formed a gap in my plans for navigation.

Since I'll have to get to Europe by dead reckoning, I'll correct my heading for the wind at nightfall. If it's blowing in a different direction at daybreak, I'll estimate that it blew half the night in one direction and half in the other.

My watch will help indicate my position as I approach Europe. If I sight land on or ahead of schedule, it will probably be Ireland, for Ireland lies farther west than any other country. If my landfall comes a little late, that may be caused either by a head wind holding me back from Ireland or by a crosswind drifting me north to Scotland. If I fly for two or three hours beyond my estimated time of crossing, and still there's only sea ahead, I'll probably be south of route. If I make a landfall in daylight, or even in moonlight, I'll know what country I'm over. But suppose there's fog? Well, I'll simply hold my course until ... until ... There's trouble in the cockpit—I've been half asleep again. The compass needle's a full ten degrees right of its mark! I bank the *Spirit of St. Louis* back on course, gripping the stick as though hundreds of pounds of strength, rather than ounces, were required on the controls.

I stare out at the horizon, dragging my eyes back to check the compass, making them look blearily at instruments, performing routine duties of flight. Suddenly I become aware of a difference—one of my senses is banging on a distant door, shouting for attention—there's an essential message I must have. It's like the moment of confusion that precedes alertness, when you've been startled from a deep sleep—who? what? where? And then life clarifies.

The ocean ahead has assumed a different texture, brighter, whiter—an ice field! It turns dazzling white in sunlight as it slides in beneath my wing. Great white cakes are jammed together, with ridges of crushed ice pushed up around the edges, all caught and held motionless in a network of black water which shows through in cracks and patches. A quarter mile in from the field's edge the sea smooths out, the waves disappear, and there's not a sign of movement among the blocks of ice. As far as I can see ahead, the ocean is glaring white. Despite the noise and vibration of the engine, I feel surrounded by frozen silence.

The brilliant light and the strangeness of the sea awaken me, make my mind the master of my body once again. Any change,

I realize, stimulates the senses. Even the changing contours of the ice cakes help me to stay awake. I must look for differences, and emphasize them. I can fly high for a while and then fly low. I can fly first with my right hand and then with my left. I can shift my position a little in the seat, sitting stiff and straight, slouching down, twisting sidewise. I can create imaginary emergencies in my mind—a forced landing, the best wave or trough to hit. A swallow of water now and then will help. And there's the hourly routine of the log readings.

It's 4:52 p.m.; the tenth hour. I nose down, catching up to the shadow of my plane, which has been gliding fleetly on ahead. The largest cakes are 50 or 60 feet across. I could bounce my wheels on them with a half-inch movement of the stick. I feel I could reach down and plunge my hand into freezing water, or close my fingers on a chunk of ground-up ice. I'm conscious of desolate solitude.

What would I do now if my engine failed? If an essential part of my engine broke, I'd be down in thirty seconds. I'd only have time to bank left into wind, cut the switch, pull my stick back, and pancake onto ice. What then? There'd certainly be no rescue ships steaming through an ice field. Staying with the wreckage would mean only a few more days of life. I'd have to start traveling as soon as my clothes were dry. My eyes pick out the best routes to follow as I imagine walking over the ice field.

I decide that this flight is no more dangerous than flying mail for a single winter. Still, the idea that he would as likely have crashed in an Illinois forest wouldn't give much comfort to a man crawling across those ice cakes.

I remind myself that I wasn't bound to carry the night mail. I'm not bound to be in aviation at all. I'm here only because I love flying. Of course there's danger; but a certain amount of danger is essential to the quality of life. I don't believe in taking foolish chances; but nothing can be accomplished without taking any chance at all.

One day when I was a child in Minnesota I was playing upstairs in our house on the riverbank. The sound of a distant engine drifted in through an open window. Automobiles had been going past on the road quite often that summer. But no automobile engine made that noise. It was approaching too fast, and it was on the wrong side of the house! I ran to the window and climbed out onto the tarry roof. It was an airplane—a frail, complicated biplane, with the pilot sitting out in front between struts and wires. I rushed downstairs to tell my mother.

There had been a notice in the *Transcript*, she said, about an aviator who had come to our town. He was carrying passengers from a field over on the east side of the river. But rides were unbelievably expensive, a dollar for every minute in the air! And anyone who went up took his life in his hands.

I was so greatly impressed by the cost and danger that I pushed aside my desire to go up in a plane. But as I grew older, I learned that danger was a part of life not always to be shunned. It often surrounded the things you liked most to do. It was dangerous to climb a tree, to swim down rapids in the river, to go hunting with a gun, to ride a horse. You could be killed as quickly on a farm as in an airplane.

I never felt safer, and never came closer to being killed, than when a gangplow turned over behind my tractor. I had just tripped the plow lift and started to turn at the field's end when bright steel flashed by my head and thudded heavily on the ground. The lift mechanism had jammed, upsetting the entire gangplow. If I hadn't turned my tractor at the moment I pulled the trip lever, I would have been crushed on the seat.

I center the earth-inductor compass needle, and drop down closer to the ice field.

WHEN I WAS ELEVEN, I learned to drive my father's Ford, and at twelve I chauffeured him around the country. That car had seemed terribly dangerous at first. You could get your arm broken cranking the engine. You could skid off an embankment or collide with someone at any intersection. But as my driving experience increased, so did my confidence. There were foils against danger—judgment and skill. If you clasped your thumb and fingers on the same side of the crank handle, a backfiring engine wouldn't break your bones. If you adjusted speed to road conditions, skids and collisions could be avoided. Twenty miles an hour had seemed an excessive speed when I started driving. A decade later, 60 was safe enough on a clear stretch of pavement. I learned that danger is relative, and that inexperience can be a magnifying glass.

WHEN I WAS a sophomore at the University of Wisconsin, I decided to give up my course in mechanical engineering and learn to fly. One of my friends tried to persuade me not to leave my studies. He said a pilot's life averaged only a few hours in the air, and cited wartime figures to prove his point. But I'd grown tired of the endless indoor hours of university life. I longed for open earth and sky. I chose a school in Lincoln, Nebraska, and enrolled for a course in the spring.

I'd never been near enough to a plane to touch it before entering the doors of the Nebraska Aircraft Corporation's factory. I can still smell the odor of dope, still see the brightly painted fuselages on the floor, still marvel at the compactness of the Hispano-Suiza engine which turned the force of 150 horses through its little shaft of steel.

On April 9, 1922, at the age of twenty, I made my first flight. The plane had been hauled out from the factory the day before, wings stacked and padded carefully in a big truck, fuselage trailing behind. I stood on the airfield, watching riggers attach wings; watching mechanics strain in fuel, tune up the engine; watching the engineer test cable tautness with his fingers and measure wing droop with a knowing eye.

Behind every movement was the realization that man took life in hand to fly, that death lay in each bolt and wire and wooden strut—waiting for an angled grain or loosened nut to let it out. The rigger wound his copper wire with a surgeon's care. The mechanic sat listening to his engine and watching his gages as a doctor would search for a weakness in the human heart. An error meant a ship might crash; a man might die.

How clearly I remember that first flight. The mechanic throws his leg and body backward as his arms jerk the propeller down. There's a deep cough, vicious spitting. The mechanic regains his balance, takes his place by the wing tip. Miraculously his fingers haven't been chopped off by that now invisible blade. The cylinders bark out their power and merge into a deep roar. I am belted down in the front cockpit, goggles and leather helmet strapped tight on my head. Beside me is a younger boy, one of the workmen from the factory. He, too, has never flown before.

The roar grows louder. Wings begin to tremble. The engine's power shakes up my legs from the floorboards, beats down on my head from the slipstream, starts a flying wire vibrating. I twist about to look back at the pilot. His eyes study the instruments—no trace of a smile on his face.

The engine quiets. The pilot nods. A mechanic from each side ducks in and unchocks a wheel. We taxi downwind, bumping over sod clumps, to the end of the field. A burst of engine—the tail swings around into wind.

Now! The roar becomes deafening, the plane lurches forward through a hollow in the ground; the tail rises, the axle clatters over bumps, trees rush toward us, the ground recedes. We are up, past riggers and mechanics, over treetops, across a ravine. Trees become bushes; barns, toys; cows turn into rabbits as we climb. I lose all conscious connection with the past. I live only in the moment in this strange, unmortal space, crowded with beauty, pierced with danger.

Why can't I keep the compass needle centered? I skid the Spirit of St. Louis *back onto course again.*

I WAS A NOVICE when we made that flight at Lincoln five years ago. But the novice has the poet's eye. He sees and feels where the expert's senses have been calloused by experience. Contact tends to dull appreciation. Now, to me, houses and barns are no longer toys. I look down a mile on some farmer's dwelling much as I would view that same dwelling a horizontal mile away. I can translate the textures and shadings of the ground. I can easily see through the tricks of wind and storm and mountains, but I have never seen the earth below so clearly as in those early days of flight.

I was the Nebraska Aircraft Corporation's only student that

spring. Ira Biffle was my instructor. Biff was impatient, quick, and picturesque of tongue. We got along together well enough. But he'd lost the love of his art, and I found it hard to get time in the air. When rain was falling or wind blew hard, of course, flying was out of the question for a new student. On such days, I rode my motorcycle to the factory and spent hours watching the craftsmen work. A would-be aviator had to learn how to care for his plane in the field. Tail skids and shock absorbers broke, ribs snapped, and wing covering ripped all too easily. You had to know how to bind the ends of rubber rope, how to lap a propeller hub to its shaft, hundreds of details.

But on mornings of calm, clear weather, I felt it was my right to receive the instruction I had paid for. And Biffle was often nowhere to be found. Sometimes he would come out to the field in time to make a half-dozen takeoffs and landings before dusk. But often he didn't come at all.

Then the corporation's only training plane was sold to Erold Bahl, the best flyer around Lincoln. I'd had about eight hours of flying instruction, even though I hadn't yet soloed. Maybe I could get Bahl to let me go barnstorming with him.

EROLD BAHL WAS serious, mild mannered, slender. There was no showmanship about him—he flew in ordinary business clothes. He never wore an aviator's helmet and breeches like the rest of us. I waited until I found a chance to talk to him alone.

"You don't need somebody to help when you're out barnstorming, do you?" I asked. "I'd pay my own expenses."

"I don't need any help—" he said. Then, hesitating a moment as he looked at me, he continued, "But if you want to go along badly enough to pay your own expenses, I'll take you."

We left on our first barnstorming trip in May. I kept the plane wiped clean, pulled through the propeller, and canvassed the crowds for passengers. "You're working hard," Bahl told me, after a few days, "and you're making me extra money. From now on, I'll pay your expenses."

I felt secure flying with Bahl. He'd take off in weather that would keep most pilots on the ground; but he handled his plane perfectly, and he never did any silly stunts. I once suggested that we might draw a bigger crowd if I stood out on one of the wings while we flew over town. "You can climb out of the cockpit if you want to," he said, "but watch how you step on the spars, and don't go farther than the inner-bay strut the first time." Those simple instructions gave me my start as a wing walker.

That summer, a parachute maker named Charlie Harden came to Lincoln to demonstrate his product. I watched him strap on his harness and helmet, climb into the cockpit and, minutes later, a black dot, fall off the wing 2000 feet above our field. At almost the same instant, a white streak behind him flowered out into the delicate, wavering, gossamer muslin of a parachute.

I stood fascinated while he drifted down, swinging with the wind, the chute's skirt weaving with its eddies, lightly, gracefully, until he struck the ground and all that fragile beauty wilted around him into a pile of wrinkled, earth-stained cloth.

Later, I found Harden in a corner of the factory where wing coverings were made. He and his young wife were busy sewing, cutting, and stitching the long, triangular strips of a new parachute. Piles of white muslin lay all about them.

"You want to jump?" They both eyed me keenly.

"I'd like to make a double jump," I said.

"You want to do a double jump the *first* time?" Harden's tone was disapproving—I had to think fast.

"I want to see what it's like. I—I might want to buy a parachute. It isn't more dangerous with two chutes than with one, is it?"

Harden's handbills said that he had used as many as ten parachutes in one descent, and claimed the utmost reliability for the products he made and sold. My questioning of his parachutes' safety, and the prospect of a sale, had the effect I was after.

"All right, if the school will give you a plane, I'll let you use my chutes."

"How much does one cost?" I asked.

"If you really want to buy one, you can have it for a hundred dollars cash—harness, bag, and all."

Is that a small boat on ahead? No, of course not—just a shadow on a chunk of ice.

THE STIFF, double-canvas straps of the harness dig into my legs and press down on my hipbones. The big parachute bag lies awkwardly out on the right wing, its top lashed to the strut. It's a long way out along that panel, but you have to be sure the parachute will clear the plane's tail as you jump. I'm to jump when we reach 2000 feet. But it's hard to see safety inside that dirt-smeared canvas sack bulging on the wing. My heart races, and my throat is dry.

The plane banks toward the field. I sink down on the wing, buttocks on spar, legs dangling on top of patchwork fields. I snap the parachute hooks onto my harness. The parachute bag shifts forward on the wing. I look back—the pilot nods. I let myself down on drift and flying wires—they bite into my fingers as I swing free beneath the wing.

The flying field is more than a mile ahead; it's too soon to jump. I dangle under the wing panel. Two ropes from my harness run up above my head and disappear into the parachute bag. A bowknot holds the bag's canvas lips together. It's all that holds me to the plane. Eyes dry in wind. Clothes flutter against skin. The roar of the engine dies—that's the signal! I reach up and pull the bow's end. Tightness of harness disappears, the wing recedes, white cloth streaks out above me.

Harness tightens on legs, on waist. My head goes down—muscles strain against it and tilt it back. The canopy opens round and wide. I swing lazily, safely.

But there's a second step to take. I must leave plenty of altitude. The ground has already risen—fields are larger. I yank the knife rope which cuts the line lashing the second chute to the first, and the white canopy ascends. This time I know what to expect: the harness will tighten and—but why *doesn't* it tighten? It didn't take so long before! Air rushes past. My body tenses, turns, falls—good God—

The harness jerks me upright—my parachute blooms white. Earth and sky come back to place; I'm controlled by gravity once more. Now, danger is behind.

120

Life changed after that jump. I noticed it in the attitude of those who came to help gather up my chute. I'd stepped suddenly to a new level of daring.

Science, freedom, beauty, adventure: what more could you ask of life? Aviation combined all the elements I loved. There was science in each curve of an airfoil, in each angle between strut and wire, in the gap of a spark plug or the color of the exhaust flame. There was freedom in the unlimited horizon, on the open fields where one landed. A pilot was surrounded by beauty of earth and sky. Adventure lay in each puff of wind.

I began to feel that I lived on a higher plane than the skeptics of the ground; one that was richer because of its very association with the element of danger they dreaded, because it was freer of the earth to which they were bound. Who valued life more, the aviators who spent it on the art they loved, or these misers who doled it out like pennies through their antlike days? I decided that if I could fly for ten years before I was killed in a crash, it would be a worthwhile trade for an ordinary lifetime.

But I needed more experience before I could fly a plane of my own. The corporation had just sold a plane to "Banty" Rogers, a wheat rancher from Bird City, Kansas. He hadn't yet learned to fly himself, but he'd teamed up with a pilot he introduced as "Cupid" Lynch—a man who handled aircraft with extraordinary skill. The school paid Lynch for giving me a few more instruction flights before the plane was taken away.

Out of the blue, Lynch said one day, "How'd you like to go barnstorming with me this summer?"

"I can start anytime," I told him.

Lynch grinned. "Well, I'll see what it's like when I get out to Bird City. My guess is that Banty'll be tied up with the harvest in a few more weeks. You and I could put on a real show with a little wing walking and a parachute jump. Don't count on it, but I think I'll be sending you a telegram before long."

The school owed me about two more hours of instruction. In a three-cornered deal with the school and Harden, I traded these, the wages due me, my claim to the right to solo, and twenty-five dollars in cash, for a new muslin parachute.

After Charlie Harden left, I was the only parachute jumper

on the field at Lincoln. Just as people used to say, "*There's a pilot,*" when Biff walked by, they'd speak of me as "the parachute jumper" in low tones.

If flying was considered dangerous, wing walking and parachute jumping were regarded as suicidal. But the hazards of aviation only loomed high to the ignorant. If you were careless, you could be killed. But if you kept alert, studied the rules, and flew within your skill—well, Orville Wright and Glenn Curtiss and a dozen others showed what could be done.

The same principles applied to parachute jumping. Parachutes never failed to open if they were properly made and packed. You could usually glide a parachute out of the way of trees; and even if you did land in branches, you weren't likely to get hurt badly if you kept your legs together.

As for wing walking, it was almost as easy to hang on to the struts and wires of an airplane as to climb up through branches of a high tree with the wind blowing hard. You had to get used to the slipstream's whipping blast; but it didn't reach out as far as the inner-bay struts. After you got there, you could hold on with one hand and look around quite comfortably.

There were lots of tricks in exhibition work—closely guarded secrets of professional circus flyers. Ownership of a parachute made me an apprentice in the craft, and gave me the right to be taught its skills. From a young mechanic I learned that a wing walker didn't really hang by his teeth from a leather strap attached to the landing gear's spreader bar. He simply held the strap in his mouth while his weight was safely supported by a thin steel cable hooked to a strong harness underneath his coat.

I'm tired of holding my plane up off the ice. I shift the stabilizer adjustment back again.

IN MID-JULY, 1922, Lynch's telegram arrived, asking me to join him for the season, and to bring my parachute. I didn't expect to make much money, but I knew that all my expenses would be paid. I settled my boardinghouse bill, stored my motorcycle in the factory basement, packed up parachute and suitcase, and climbed on a grimy old day coach that clanked slowly along the rails westward through Nebraska and Kansas. Bird City was almost at the end of the line—a few score houses and a few hundred people, surrounded by a sea of wheat.

Rogers and Lynch met my train at the station. "You and I are going to barnstorm the towns nearby, Slim," Lynch said as we drove to the plane.

"How about starting out with a jump at Bird City?" Rogers asked. "I'd like the people here to see you." He was grinning and enthusiastic.

"All right." I was anxious to get up into the air again.

I met another aviation enthusiast on the Rogers Ranch—his black-and-white fox terrier, Booster.

"That dog just naturally takes to flying," Lynch said as Booster leaped into the car, his clipped tail vibrating like a fly's wing.

"He's liked to ride in my car ever since he was a pup," Rogers added. "But he'll leave the car any day to ride on my tractor. He chases rabbits that jump out of the wheat—they're his greatest interest in life. But he'll leave the tractor for the airplane every time."

Booster became the mascot for our Standard. At first, he rode with me in the front cockpit on cross-country flights. Then, we fastened a rubber mat to the turtleback and bought him a harness so we could snap him loosely into place. As soon as we started the engine, he'd jump onto the stabilizer, run up to his mat, and hook his forepaws around the cockpit cowling. The pilot's head formed his windshield. He had no sense of altitude or fear. Once, when we were coming in to land, he tried to jump off 50 feet above the ground to chase some big jack rabbits. There was an unmistakable expression on Booster's face when he saw rabbits, and a tenseness to his body. At altitudes of 1000 feet or so, cows brought the same reaction. As far as animals were concerned, he never seemed able to relate altitude to size.

During the rest of that summer and early fall, I was a wing walker, parachute jumper, and mechanic. Lynch and I flew over the fields of Kansas, across the badlands of Nebraska, along the Big Horns of Wyoming, to the rimrocks of Montana.

123

DAREDEVIL LINDBERGH I was billed in huge black letters on the posters we threw out above towns and villages. People came for miles to watch me climb back and forth over wings, and finally leap off into space. Ranchers, cowboys, and storekeepers in town, followed with their eyes as I walked by.

FIVE YEARS have passed now since I learned to fly. I've spent almost two thousand hours in the air—twice the average flyer's lifetime back in 1922. But there've been close calls—many of them. Vivid images flash through my mind—treetops rushing toward my underpowered plane during a takeoff in Minnesota; a rudder bar kicked off its post in a bank near the ground at St. Louis; the blur and bump of air from a fighter missed by inches in a Texas sky; jumping from my mail plane, out of fuel, 13,000 feet above the earth, and twisting back and forth, down through the black, flashing belly of a storm.

I've flown for the love of flying, done the things I wanted most to do. I've simply studied carefully whatever I've undertaken, and tried to hold a reserve that would carry me through. I believe the risks I take are justified by the sheer love of the life I lead. Just being in the air on a flight across the ocean to Paris warrants the hazard of an ice field below.

I look down. The ice field angles off into the distance under my right wing. The sea ahead is covered with waves again, fit companions to the biting air and arctic sky. The wind, strong and almost west, blows me along swiftly. The horizon is still clear; no trace of fog.

For 30 miles along Burin Peninsula, my course parallels a coast of bare granite mountains, dented with bays and jutted with capes. The sun is nearing the horizon; already, shadows cut sharp lines from cliff to cliff, and higher summits almost reach the sun. I've never been as conscious of the minuteness of my plane or of the magnitude of the world. On my right, the ocean extends limitlessly.

Nungesser and Coli may have crashed somewhere among those mountains. Any one of those cliff-lined valleys could hold a shattered plane. Searching expeditions haven't found a trace. But from the start it was almost a hopeless hunt. A plane is hard enough to find in the wilderness when you have some indication of where it crashed. Searching for Nungesser and Coli, with no accurate clue to follow, was only a gesture, the payment of a debt felt by living men to their lost brothers.

I think of the day I saw Nungesser in St. Louis. He was clear-eyed and quick. He'd come to give an exhibition with his pursuit plane. I stood nearby, watching the great French war ace, thinking of the combat clashes from which he had so narrowly escaped. I wonder if *he* concluded that flying the ocean was less dangerous than, say, a single combat in the air.

THE ELEVENTH HOUR of flight: over Placentia Bay, Newfoundland. It's only six o'clock in New York. I've flown more than an hour eastward by the sun. Think of man competing with the speed of the earth's rotation: think of covering an hour's sun travel since this morning. Why, if I flew a little farther north, the *Spirit of St. Louis* could move around the world as fast as the sun itself!

How far away St. Louis is, yet how closely tied to my presence here at this moment. If it weren't for St. Louis, I'd probably still be barnstorming, or piloting an army plane as lieutenant in the air corps. It was chance that took me to St. Louis in the first place. In 1923, the year of my solo flight, I spent the summer barnstorming in Minnesota. But when fall came passenger business fell off; the days got so chilly that people didn't like to ride in an open cockpit. So I pointed my OX–5-powered Jenny toward St. Louis. In my hotel the night before, I'd read in the local paper about the International Air Races being held that very week at Lambert Field.

In barnstorming one seldom met other flyers, and never saw modern airplanes. A visit to an organized airport was a special event, and there I was, only a few hours' flight from the races. There'd be dozens of pilots, and the newest planes, and racers that could attain the incredible speed of over 200 miles an hour. What fun it would be to land on Lambert Field with my Jenny and view the show as an insider.

But at Lambert, instead of gliding down onto a welcoming airport, I found one of the races under way. Large military planes were banking steeply around a brightly painted pylon in front of the crowd. Obviously the airport was closed to common traffic. I circled, high in the air, until I saw several other barnstorming planes sitting on a hillside a mile or so away. I landed in the weeds beside them, and learned from their pilots that special hours were set aside for visiting aircraft to arrive at the races.

In late afternoon, I flew over to Lambert and staked my Jenny down at the end of a row of civilian planes. Wherever I'd been before, a pilot was accorded great prestige. Cars speeded out from town with offers of help and transportation; people assembled from nearby farms; often schools were let out so children could watch the flying. But at Lambert Field, I soon realized, the ordinary pilot was not far ahead, in standing, of the layman in the crowd.

I ate a hamburger lunch, and wandered about the field alone, studying different types of aircraft, and growing more conscious of my unshined boots and unpressed clothes in contrast to the neatly tailored uniforms of military pilots. The small amount of baggage he could carry made it difficult for a barnstormer to keep neat, living as he did in daily contact with oil and dust. When darkness came, I looked for a place to spend the night, but every available room in the nearby towns had been rented. So with my bundle under one arm (I couldn't afford the weight or stiff-cornered bulk of a suitcase in my Jenny) I walked half a mile to the tracks and boarded a streetcar for St. Louis.

The next day, I spent hours looking up into the sky, watching maneuvers I had never seen, and walking from one plane to the next. I was so fascinated by it all that I felt I must take my Jenny into the air when the field was thrown open to visiting pilots at the end of the day's program; not for any good reason, but just to be in the same sky with the others.

I unlashed the wings, blocked the wheels, set the throttle, swung through my propeller, climbed into my cockpit, and started the warm-up. I pushed the throttle wide open. Everything was perfect. But as I throttled down I heard shouts of rage behind me. I looked back to discover a great cloud of dust thrown up by my slipstream. In it I could see gesticulating pilots and a half-dozen other planes. I'd been used to flying from sod-covered pastures, not from a crowded and newly graded airport, baked dry by Missouri's sun. It never occurred to me that I was blowing dust on other people's aircraft.

An air-race official emerged from the cloud, hanging onto his hat with both hands, face and clothes yellow with dust. He outlined his opinion of my judgment as a pilot in no uncertain terms: "God Almighty! Don't you know enough to taxi out on the field before you warm up your engine? What's your name? How in hell did you get here?" He spluttered out questions so fast I didn't have time to answer any of them. "Get out and lift your tail around. Hold that throttle down while you taxi! All right, damn it, go ahead!"

The incident left me feeling like a forty-acre farmer stumbling through his first visit to the state fair. I taxied carefully out and took off; but the joy was gone from wingovers, banks, and spirals. A crowded airport wasn't my environment. The sooner I could get back to the freedom of farm fields and open prairies, I decided, the better. Maybe I'd leave St. Louis in the morning.

Then, shortly after I landed, I ran into Bud Gurney, who had come down to the races from Lincoln. Together we wandered around, meeting other pilots, mechanics, and stunt men. Talk always wound around shop, of course. Was I going to sell my Jenny at St. Louis? There were a lot of buyers at the races, also people who wanted to learn to fly. I could sell my plane with a course of instruction thrown in. Barnstorming wasn't very good in the South, and fields were scarce in the other states. "Why don't you stay at Lambert and do some instructing?" Bud asked.

That question stuck in my mind. A year and a half ago I'd been a student. How I'd admired the pilots who sat in the front cockpit—so experienced, so capable, so confident. Now, with two hundred and fifty hours in the air and a plane of my own, *I* had a chance to be an instructor.

I was told that I didn't need any license. I was just expected to know how to fly, and to use good judgment.

"Slim, I met a fellow who might buy your plane," Bud informed me later. "You'd have to teach him how to fly. Let's go talk about it."

127

He introduced me to a young Iowan. I set a price on my Jenny, with a solo flight guaranteed, and closed the deal. Instruction flights would begin as soon as the meet was over.

My throat's a bit dry. I can afford a swallow of water, and still stay well within my ration.

I FOUND AN open welcome among the handful of pilots, as more planes in the air brought bigger crowds to the airport; bigger crowds meant more people who would watch for a time and then gather courage to make a flight themselves—at five dollars a head.

St. Louis is a city of winds, and the air above Lambert Field is usually rough, which made it difficult to teach a student how to land properly. Since turbulence is often least in early morning, my pupil and I began our day by practicing takeoffs and landings. After that, we worked on the Jenny, and lunched at Louie's stand. When the wind died down, we would start again: takeoff and landing, takeoff and landing, skid, slip, and stall. I soon discovered that I was learning as much about flying as my student. A pilot can never duplicate intentionally the plights that a student gets him into by accident. When you're flying yourself, you know in advance whether you're going to pull the stick back, push it forward, or cut the throttle. You think of a maneuver before you attempt it. But you're never sure what a student is going to do. He's likely to haul the nose up and cut the gun at the very moment when more speed is needed. If you check his errors too quickly, he loses confidence in his ability to fly. If you let them go too long, he'll crash you. You must learn the exact limits of your plane: not how high the tail *should* go in takeoff, but how high it *can* go without disaster; not how to avoid a wind drift when you're landing, but how much drift there *can* be when the wheels touch, without a ground loop or blown tire resulting. And as you learn how to keep a student out of trouble, you become a better pilot yourself. As you instruct him in the primary art of flying, he instructs you in its advanced phases.

Late in the fall of 1923 I soloed my Jenny student. And not

With Erold Bahl's yellow Tourabout

C.A.L.
and his Harden
parachute

Booster goes flying

C.A.L. ready to take Booster up.

SOUTHERN ILLINOIS HARD ROAD BASEBALL
ASSOCIATION CARTERVILLE TEAM PRESENTS

Vera May Dunlap's

Flying Circus

In conjunction with their opening game

Sat. & Sun., May 9 & 10

At Carterville Base Ball and Aviation Field

1 MILE SO. OF CARTERVILLE AT CROSS ROADS

Carries Mills vs. Carterville

By special arrangements Vera May Dunlap will appear
IN PERSON and will positively stand erect on top of the
upper wing of the airplane without any visible means of
support whatsoever while her pilot loops the loop, defying
all laws of gravitation. Miss Dunlap carries with her a
fleet of airplanes under the personal direction of Capt.
Frank T. Dunn, the Canadian Ace. The only flier who
has successfully looped the bridge on a navigable stream.
Also Herbert Budd in the swing of death. T. Gurney the
fastest wing walker and aerial performer in the world.
Enslow, Hissel, Mann, Armstrong and Brown, pilots. Last
but not least is Lt. Chas. A. Lindberg who saved his life by
jumping from an aerial collision on March 6, 1925 in Kelly
Field, Texas. He is now in the U. S. Air Service and will
positively be in Carterville May 9-10. Herbert Budd will
change from the top of one plane to another without any
rope ladder. Admission to the ball game, including the
airplane circus will be

50 cents

The gates will b
cars free. Miss
planes with lice
to ride $3.00. L
some will contai

Carterville B

long afterward I took the examinations for appointment as a flying cadet in the Air Service of the Army. The appointment came through, and in March, 1924, I entered flying school in Texas. A year later, I'd become a full-fledged second lieutenant in the Organized Reserve Corps. I had applied for authority to take examinations for a commission in the Regular Army Air Service; but the War Department hadn't answered. So I returned to St. Louis. There was a hospitality about the city, a fellowship at Lambert Field, that I'd found nowhere else in my travels. Now that I was in civilian life again, what better place to start looking for a job?

There'd been plenty to do at Lambert Field—instructing, passenger carrying, taxi flights. The Robertson Aircraft Corporation offered me the position of chief pilot if their bid for the St. Louis–Chicago airmail route was accepted. I barnstormed through Missouri, Illinois, and Iowa. August of 1925 found me carrying passengers at the National Guard encampment near Nevada, Missouri. There, I received a letter from the president of The Mil-Hi Airways and Flying Circus, at Denver, Colorado, offering me a flying job at four hundred dollars a month.

Denver was within gliding distance of the Rockies. That would give me a chance to explore the air currents around canyons, slopes, and ridges. I could study the effect of turbulence, about which aviators knew so little and speculated so much. The mail contract had not yet been awarded. I flew back to St. Louis, and boarded a train for the West.

At Humphrey's Field, outside of Denver, I found that The Mil-Hi Airways and Flying Circus consisted of one old Hisso-Standard, with a huge green dragon painted on each side of the fuselage. This time the rear cockpit was mine. The inner-bay strut was for someone else's parachute, and the wings for some-one else's feet.

Our contracts with fair officials usually called for daytime acrobatics and fireworks at night.

"Whatever you do, don't get caught in the air after dark," a pilot had warned me when I was a student. "You're up there, you've got to land—and you can't see to do it."

The first time I tried the nighttime fireworks exhibition, I persuaded a dozen drivers to line their cars up along the edge of the field so I could take off and land across the beams from their headlights. It was more difficult with only one car for a marker on a dark night, but on several occasions that was all I could get.

Once I got caught without any lights at all, circling a Colorado town I'd never seen before. We had a contract for night fireworks there. But four passengers had come late to ride, at our previous location, and we'd stayed on after our planned departure time. We'd still have gotten through before darkness if the engine hadn't run short of oil en route. I had to throttle down and land outside the nearest village. By the time we found a car to take us to town, bought our oil, and got the cans back out, the sun had set. The president of Mil-Hi Airways, Wray Vaughn, was with me on that trip.

"Maybe we'd better tie down here," I'd suggested. "It's pretty hard to pick out a landing strip in dusk."

"We'll lose two hundred and fifty dollars," Vaughn argued. "It's the last night of the fair. I know where the field is. It'll only take us fifteen minutes to get there. Let's try it."

I was as anxious as he to make that money. I pushed the engine, and we flew low. The western sky was still bright when we reached the town and started circling, but you couldn't see much on the ground. It was essential to land right away, but Vaughn couldn't pick out the field. After several circles, ditches and fences had merged with darkness, and I couldn't see what was below. I headed toward more open country.

"Get your belt tight," I shout to Vaughn. "Brace your arms against the cowling."

Vaughn nods, follows my instructions calmly.

There's a big, dark area—probably a stubble field. There's a roundish patch near the center, not quite as dark—probably a strawstack. There are several blotches just beyond one end— probably trees. I bank and take my gliding distance, grateful for those meager clues. Are there prairie-dog holes, ditches, cows, or posts in that black area? We won't know until we hear a shattering of wood—or feel wheels clatter over the ground.

"Well, we had luck that time," I say as we climb down from our cockpits.

"There's a car coming," Vaughn says. "I'll flag him down."

"Okay. I'll be there in a few minutes." I walk over the field. It's smooth, and plenty big enough—I couldn't have picked a better one by day. I turn back. The car lights stop. I hurry toward them.

"These men say they'll take us into town," Vaughn calls to me. "Maybe we can still put on the show. Our contract doesn't expire till midnight."

"There's not much wind. The plane'll be all right where it is," I say. I climb into the back seat of the car.

"I'll find the fireworks," Vaughn says. "You get the boards and hardware."

It's half past nine when we get back to the field. We unload fireworks, boards, bail wire, hammer, saw, and nails. Stars are bright. The air is calm. I taxi the plane up close to the fence. Two automobiles turn on their lights to help us work. The owner of another takes me back and forth over the field to make doubly sure there aren't any posts or holes in the area I'll have to use.

It's half past eleven before we get the racks wired into place and the Roman candles fastened on. There are only thirty minutes to go, and I have 2000 feet to climb. All cars have left but one. We make a final check of our efforts.

"You know these fireworks are going to be wasted," I say. "Everybody in town will be in bed."

"Our contract says 'midnight'," Vaughn replies firmly. "We've done our best, and we can't afford to lose that money."

The plane starts smoothly. I warm it up and swing around for takeoff. But what's the matter? Downfield there are only two faintly glowing spots, like the eyes of a big animal. The car's battery must be going dead!

"Get him to drive you out so you can throw your flashlight on the strawstack," I call to Vaughn. "I've got to see *something* when I take off. Try to get another car before I land. If you can't, then flash your light up at me when I fly overhead after the show. Keep flashing it at the plane until I'm on the ground."

It's 11:40 when I get in the air. The city's pretty well asleep; more than half its lights are out. I've got to mark the stubble field's position in my mind. I'll be in a real jam now if I get lost. Let's see: that line of streetlamps points about ten degrees northward. Four times its length projected southwest should about bring me overhead.

By 11:50 I'm over the fairgrounds, at 1800 feet—high enough—and there's no more time. The bombs are in a box at my side. I pick one up, pull off the cap, rub the igniter, toss it over the cockpit's rim. One, two, three, four, five, six—green, red, and purple streamers arch out, fall, and fade. That ought to attract attention down below. I toss a second bomb out; pick up a third. There are seven seconds between ignition and explosion. But don't count on more than five after the fuse starts burning. There, that's the last one—it bursts a brilliant red.

Now for the Roman candles. I turn east for position, nose down, and close the switch. Trails of flame stream backward, four below each upper wing. Colored sparklers blossom out between them. I pull up into a loop. My plane's brilliance blinds me to the stars, but the city's sprinkling of lights gives me a reference for gravity's direction. There's my fiery trail below. I dive through it, loop again, bank over in a spiral. The candles sputter, fade into night. Now the flares ignite. They're so bright that people half a mile away can read a newspaper's printed page. For me, it's like driving a chariot of the sun. I can't even see the instruments in the cockpit. I shade my eyes with one hand and look straight down until the flares burn out.

My eyes adjust slowly to the blackness of the night. I pull the watch from my pocket: 11:57. We've completed our contract with three minutes to spare. I ease back on power, find my row of streetlamps, angle off at ten degrees. Down in the great dark sea ahead are only a half-dozen pricks of light. Well, there'll be no flashes until my engine's heard.

I should be about over the stubble field now. Can that be the signal? There are regular blinks to the south, probably half a mile away. I glide lower, circle at 500 feet. There's no longer a difference in shade between prairie and stubble. Even the strawstack is lost to sight. The blinks seem as weak as the flame of a match. But we agreed that they would mark the straw-stack. I ease back on the throttle and sink down toward the hard, black bottom of the night. Thank God for the length of Colorado fields.

WINTER FOUND ME back in St. Louis, instructing, test-flying, and laying plans for the airmail route to Chicago. The Robertson Aircraft Corporation had been awarded the contract, and had appointed me chief pilot, in charge of operations. Mail flying was to start with good weather in the spring. Meanwhile, I had to hire two other pilots, select equipment, survey the routes.

I enlisted in the 110th Observation Squadron of the 35th Division, Missouri National Guard, and was soon promoted to first lieutenant. I instructed pilots in new flying techniques and lectured on navigation, parachuting, and aerodynamics.

It was during that winter I met the men who later formed *The Spirit of St. Louis* organization. Only eight months ago—it seems as many years—I was sitting in the reality of my mail cockpit, dreaming of a plane that would fly across the sea. The dream has become the reality; and the reality, the dream. Placentia Bay, the strange, is my world, there below me; and the Midwest, the familiar, my object now of imagination. Whatever a man conceives of he can attain, if he doesn't become too arrogant and encroach on the gods.

Is aviation too arrogant? I don't know. Sometimes, flying feels too godlike to be attained by man. Sometimes, the world from above seems too beautiful, too wonderful, too distant for human eyes to see, like a vision at the end of life forming a bridge to death. Is man encroaching on a forbidden realm? Is aviation dangerous because the sky was never meant for him? When one obtains too great a vision is there some power that draws him from mortal life forever? Will this power smite pilot after pilot until man loses his will to fly? Or, still worse, will it deaden his senses and let him fly on without the vision? In developing aviation, in making it a form of commerce, in replacing the wild freedom of danger with the civilized bonds of safety, must we give up this miracle of air? Will men fly through the sky in the future without seeing what I have seen, without feeling what I have felt? Is that true of all that we call human progress—do the gods retire as commerce and science advance?

I CLIMB HIGHER as I approach Avalon Peninsula. Bleak mountain summits glow coldly against a deepening sky. The wind lifts me up and carries me with it over the mountains, blowing hard, rocking my wings as it swirls past ridges and stirs in valleys. Each crevice fills with shades of gray. The empire of night is expanding over earth and sea.

This is my last hour of America and of day. I fly low across these last mountains, close to their granite summits, exploring ledges and crevasses no man has seen before, the ground now 50 feet, now 1000 feet beneath. I've never felt so carefree of terrain. Why should I concern myself with engine failure? From now on, the explosion of the engine will be inseparable from the beat of my heart. As I trust one, I'll trust the other.

THE TWELFTH HOUR begins. Hazy in the light of sunset, a great finger of water points down between the ridges on my left. The gray mass behind it, scarcely perceptible in the distance, is Conception Bay. Skirting the Newfoundland coastline timidly, a scratch of man across this tremendous wilderness, lies the winding track of a railroad. Looking at bay and mountains, I become aware of the roadbed as one notices a thread lying on a parlor floor.

I've covered 1100 miles in eleven hours, an average of exactly 100 miles an hour in spite of the detours I had to make around storms in Nova Scotia. I must be making a mile every thirty seconds now, with this wind on my tail. That would put St. John's just over a quarter hour's flight ahead. How surprised people there will be when they see the *Spirit of St. Louis* swoop down from the sky and head straight out into the Atlantic and the night!

No plane en route to Europe ever flew over Newfoundland before without landing. Commander Albert C. Read used it as a refueling point for his transatlantic flight in 1919. Three of the Navy's big multiengined flying boats left Newfoundland; but only Commander Read's NC-4 arrived at Fayal, in the Azores, the next morning. Their four engines hadn't helped much when the NC flying boats ran into low visibility and fog; but their boat hulls helped a lot. The weather forecast had been wrong. They encountered an area of storm, and after daybreak all three flying boats lost their bearings. Two of them landed in open ocean and were damaged too badly to take off again, but they stayed afloat. One managed to sail through heavy seas to Ponta Delgada. The other, after drifting for several hours, was found and taken in tow by a ship. It sank later, but everyone on board was rescued.

How secure those naval aviators must have felt, when they started out, inside their big hulls. But they paid heavily in range for what they gained in seaworthiness. I've got a better chance of reaching Europe than they had of reaching the Azores. I have a more reliable engine, improved instruments, and a continent instead of an island for my target.

I'm certainly better off than John Alcock and Arthur Brown—and they got across the ocean in their twin-engined Vickers bomber after burrowing through hundreds of miles of fog and storm. They took off from Newfoundland a month later than Commander Read, and crash-landed in an Irish bog. And Harry Hawker and MacKensie Grieve—they went down in mid-Atlantic with their landplane when its engine overheated. But a Danish ship rescued them.

All those flights took place only eight years ago. What leaps forward aviation has made since then! I still have fuel in my tanks for more range than they were able to take off with.

I come suddenly upon the little city of St. John's—flat-roofed houses and stores, nestled at the edge of a deep harbor. It's almost surrounded by mountains. Farther ahead, the entrance to the harbor is a narrow gap with sides running up steeply to the crest of a low coastal range which holds back the ocean. Fishing boats are riding at buoys and moored at wharves.

Twilight deepens as I plunge down into the valley. Mountains behind screen off the colors of the western sky. There's no time to circle, no fuel to waste. It takes only a moment to dive down over the wharves, over ships in the harbor, and out through the gap, that doorway to the Atlantic. Mountainsides slip by on either wing. Great rollers break in spray against their base. The hulk of a wrecked ship lies high upon the boulders.

Here, all around me, is the Atlantic—its expanse, its depth, its power, its wild and open water. Flying swiftly through that gap in the mountains was like diving into a cold pool. A minute ago I was a creature of the land, stripping for that final plunge. Now I'm a creature of the ocean, sensing the coolness of the water, thinking of the continent behind.

I've reached the point where real navigation must begin. I'm a little ashamed of having detoured to St. John's: I'm 90 miles south of the great circle. All the way to Ireland, I'll have this extra factor to consider in setting my compass heading. In addition to wind drift and magnetic variation, I'll have to compensate for starting so far south. A change in navigation would be easy enough on a chart board, with a protractor and a straight-edged rule; but in this narrow cockpit I must estimate new angles roughly with my eye. And I'm tired. I look down at the ocean. Wind streaks are hard to see in the dusk—gray threads raveling across black water. This will be my final estimate. The figures I use now will have to last all through the night. The surface velocity looks close to 30 miles an hour. I wish I had some experience in estimating wind from waves.

Suddenly I become aware of a white pyramid below me—an iceberg, lustrous white against the water. Ahead are several more. So that's why surface ships stay south in warmer waters! Well, I'm flying high enough to miss these drifting crags. Here and there a wisp of fog hangs low above the waves.

Soon there are icebergs everywhere—white patches on a blackened sea; sentries of the Arctic. The wisps of fog lengthen and increase until they merge to form a solid layer ahead; but, separating as I pass above them, they leave long channels of open water in between—stripes of gray fog and black water across my course. With every minute I fly, these channels narrow; until finally all the ocean is covered with a thin, undulating veil of mist. At first it doesn't hide the denser whiteness of the icebergs, but makes their forms more ghostlike down below. Then, the top of the veil slopes upward toward the east—

real fog, thick, hiding the ocean, hiding the icebergs. I ease the stick back slightly, take five miles from my speed, and climb over the fog.

THE THIRTEENTH HOUR, 7:52 p.m. Twelve hundred miles behind. One-third of the flight completed: a satisfying fraction. I've left the coast of Newfoundland under the best conditions I ever hoped for—on schedule, plenty of fuel, and a tail wind.

I've flown an hour and a quarter from each of the outer wing tanks, and a quarter hour from the center wing tank. I'll run through the night on fuselage and nose tanks, leaving the gasoline in the wing tanks for reserve. If anything goes wrong with the fuel pump, I can feed from the wings by gravity alone; and in case the big fuselage tank should spring a leak, every hour I use from it will be that much ahead.

Instrument readings are all normal. The engine sounds smoother than at the beginning of the flight. Possibly it's the night air; possibly it's simply the smoothness a well-cared-for engine gains during the early hours of its life.

I've been climbing slowly to stay above the top of the fog-bank, watching a light haze form in the air around me, wondering how thick it will grow. Day has almost vanished; just a trace of it left, a wash on the western sky, only enough to illumine the gray mist rollers beneath my plane. The fog, the icebergs, and the gathering haze caused me to neglect the sky. Now the few faint stars, twinkling down through the window above me, seem more important than all the world below.

You fly by the sky on a black night, and on such a night only the sky matters. Sometime near the end of twilight, you find that the heavens have drawn your attention subtly from earth; instead of glancing from the compass down toward ground or sea, your eyes turn upward to the stars.

I wonder if man ever escapes from worldly bonds so completely as when he flies alone above clouds at night. When there's no cloud layer beneath him, then, no matter how high he may ascend, he is still conscious of the surface of the earth by day and of its mass by night. While flying over clouds in daytime, there's something about the motherly warmth and light of the sun that imparts a feeling of the earth below. You sense it down there underneath, covered only by a layer of mist which may draw apart at any moment to leave the graceful contours of land or the sparkling sea, clear and naked in sunlight. But at night, over a stratus layer, all sense of the planet disappears. You know that down below, beneath that heavenly blanket, *is* the earth, but it's an intellectual knowledge—knowledge tucked away in the mind, not a feeling that penetrates the body.

The airspeed has dropped to 85 miles an hour, and the altimeter shows 2000 feet; but the fog is climbing as fast as my plane. Well, let the haze thicken, let the fog climb! I can't expect good weather for all the 3600 miles between New York and Paris. If there's to be an area of fog and storm, this is probably the best place for it to begin. Much of my overload is gone; there's nothing ahead but ocean for almost 2000 miles, and the chance that a storm will be that large is slight. If I make the whole flight without meeting anything worse than those scattered squalls in Nova Scotia, I'll feel as though I'd been cheating, as though I hadn't earned success. A victory given stands pale beside a victory won.

It's very dark. Only a half dozen of the brightest stars, directly overhead, pierce the haze. The luminous dials of the instruments stare at me with ghostlike eyes. The hands of the clock, which I haven't changed from their New York setting, show 8:35. I glance at my altimeter: 5000 feet, and still climbing. The cloud layer—you can hardly call it fog at this altitude—is dimly perceptible in the haze. Its gray shoals rise faster than my plane; it's less than a hundred feet from my wheels.

I can't see what lies ahead. I'll either have to climb faster or give up the stars and follow instruments blindly through the night. But those glowing lines and dots seem so much less tangible, so much less secure, than the stars overhead. The stars have always been there. I watched them through the screen of a sleeping porch when I was a child; drove under them on Minnesota roads with my father and mother; flew under them night after night with the mail. I can trust the familiar constellations following each other slowly through the heavens. As long as I can hold on to them I'll be safe.

With a strong tail wind, I'm gaining on my estimate of fuel; I can afford to spend a gallon or two for altitude. I open the throttle and pull the nose a little higher. In the morning I'll regain some of that fuel as I glide down.

I think again of the cautious phrases in Dr. Kimball's forecast: "Most Atlantic coast stations report the fog clearing, and indications are that weather along the route will continue to improve." That has all come true. "A large high-pressure area is forming over the North Atlantic," the forecast continued, "and there are local storms off the coast of Europe."

A high-pressure area over the North Atlantic. It's probably only a small storm ahead, nothing very high or dangerous.

I fly with my head thrown back, looking up through the skylight at the handful of stars above me, glancing down at intervals to make sure my compass heading is correct. When you can see stars close to the horizon it's easy to hold on course. But looking straight up for guidance is like dangling at the end of a rope; it's almost impossible to keep from turning slightly.

The stars blink on and off as haze thickens, then thins out again. I hold on to them tightly, dreading the blind flying that lies ahead the moment I let them go, hoping I can climb above the haze into the crystal blackness of the higher night—hoping, climbing, and yet sinking deeper every minute.

Soon the haze becomes so thick that, except for those dim points of light, it might as well be cloud. At any moment those stars may blink their last, leaving me stranded, like a diver whose lifeline has been cut. I'd thought I could climb above the fog and leave it beneath me. Now I know what a formidable enemy it is. Its forces have been in ambush all around me, waiting only for the cool of night to show their form.

If I start flying blind, God only knows how many hours of it lie ahead. It might go on through the entire night—the monotony of flying with my eyes always on the instrument board; the strain of flying by intellect alone, forcing the unruly senses of the body to follow the doubted orders of the mind—the endless bringing of one needle after another back to its proper position, and then finding that all except the one my eyes hold tight have strayed off again. The *Spirit of St. Louis* is too unstable to fly well on instruments. If I relax pressure on stick or rudder for an instant, the nose veers off course.

And there's the question of staying awake. Could I keep sufficiently alert during the long hours of flying with my eyes glued to the instruments, with nothing more to stimulate my mind than the leaning of a needle? It was difficult enough to stay awake over the ice fields southwest of Newfoundland, when my eyes could travel the whole horizon, and with the piercing light of day to stir my senses. How would it be with fog and darkness shutting off even the view of my wing tips? It would be like a dream, motionless yet rocketing through space, led on and on by those glowing dials two feet in front of me. A dream that could turn into a nightmare as alarming as engine failure.

It might end—how might it end? What do you feel in the rending, crashing instant that must exist between life and violent death? Excruciating pain? Have you time to realize that life is ending? Is consciousness forever blotted out, or is there an awakening as from a dream, as from a nightmare? What waits after life, as life waits at the end of a dream? Do you really meet your God, or does nothingness replace your being?

I WAS ONCE BRACED for the impact of death. It was during an emergency parachute jump. I had been running tests on a new biplane, designed and built at Lambert Field. I'd been doing acrobatics at an altitude of about 2500 feet. Tailspins were the last items on my test list. I tried two full turns to the left, and found my controls useless—blanketed out by wings and fuselage. Full rudder and stick had no effect. Bursts from the engine did no good. The plane kept right on spinning, nose high, flat, lunging slightly. I rode it down for close to 2000 feet, fighting the controls. Then a glance at the ground showed no more time. I rolled out of the cockpit, pulling my rip cord the instant I passed under the stabilizer. Dizzy spinning pressures stopped. But the ground was right there, leaping at me. Trees and houses looked tremendous.

My chute opened quickly; but I'd dropped faster than the plane. The canopy had no more than billowed open to check my fall, when I looked up to see the plane less than 100 feet away, pointed directly at me.

I saw the stroke of death coming. I was helpless. I braced my body for the impact—propeller, wing, or whatever death's instrument might be. Every muscle, every nerve, was tensed for the tearing blow on flesh. Danger had swept all detail from my mind—it was as clear as a pane of glass. It had no thoughts of past or future, or of the swinging parachute, or of the closeness of the ground beneath my feet.

If death ever cracks the door that lets life's senses peek beyond life's walls, it should have cracked it then. In mind and body I'd arrived at the very second of impact. But that door stayed shut. The parachute's shroud lines had gotten twisted in the jump, and they swung me around awkwardly. In the fraction of time it took to turn my head from right to left, the plane passed, and somehow missed me. The pilots who had watched told me later that I hadn't been more than 350 feet high when I jumped. You couldn't come much closer to death than that. And yet I've known times when the nearness of death has seemed to crack the door—times when I've felt the presence of another realm, a realm my mind has tried to penetrate since childhood. . . .

IT'S SUNDAY in Little Falls. I press my stomach against a windowsill of the yellow brick Buckman Hotel and look out onto the dirt street, one story below. Several carriages are lined up in front, horses tied carelessly to the hitching rail. A farmer's heels click on the new cement sidewalk. The Minnesota sky is whitish blue. The morning is starting to get hot.

I'm five years old and it's to be my first day in church. Mother has dressed me in a gray flannel suit, long black stockings, felt hat, and brown kid gloves—terribly uncomfortable. Church! How I dislike that word, although I'm not quite sure what it means. It's keeping me away from the farm, where we usually drive on Sunday mornings. Before our house burned down last summer we lived on the farm all the time.

I have to go to church because my father is going to be a congressman in Washington, and the family of a man who holds such an important position is expected to go to church.

It's even hotter in church than behind our team of horses on the crunching road. There's no movement of leaves outside the window. No breath of air comes through. A smell of too many people weights the sticky dampness. My legs itch under tight stockings, and the stiff edges of my new suit press sharply against my skin. The words of the preacher echo from high wood walls, merging with each other until all are meaningless to my ears: he mentions God, and death, and another life.

Through the years of my childhood, God remained vague and disturbing. You heard of Him in storybooks, in the cursing of lumberjacks, in the blessing of an old aunt. He seemed to have a lot to do with people who died—and there was nothing more disturbing than death.

On our sleeping porch, I lay awake in evenings, staring out at the sky, thinking about God and life and death. If God existed, why didn't He show Himself to people, so there'd be no argument about it? No, God was as remote as the stars, and less real—you could at least see the stars on a clear night. . . .

They are dim, blinking, gone—no, I can still see them. I rip through years of time, from a sleeping porch in Minnesota to a cockpit above the Atlantic. I feel a sudden desire to tear the pane out of the skylight, to remove all obstruction between my eyes and those points of light above. Glass forms too great a barrier between us. Seeing the stars through that window is like touching water through a rubber glove.

They blink off again. I open the throttle to 1700 rpm to get above the haze. There must still be close to 300 gallons in the tanks, and in clear air I can make up in my own efficiency what I lose in fuel range by climbing. I may even gain a stronger tail wind at higher altitudes.

I discover that my ability rises and falls with the essential problems that confront me. What I *can* do depends largely on what I *have* to do to keep alive and stay on course. If there were no alternative, I could fly blind through fog night and day. The love of life is sufficient guarantee for that. But there *is* an alternative, the alternative of climbing faster; and that I choose.

My head is thrown back to look upward. My neck is stiff. Hold on to those stars.

Ready for a game of catch

With Dingo

At age eight with father

I WAS NEVER CONVINCED that going to church in Little Falls that Sunday had any effect on my father's job in Washington. I simply accepted the fact that his election to Congress brought certain changes in life for me. Among the most disagreeable were the winters my mother and I spent in the nation's capital.

For me, the city formed a prison. Red brick houses replaced the woodlands on our farm. Concrete pavement jarred my heels. It was the clank of streetcars, not the hoot of an owl, that woke me at night. Through long winters, I counted the weeks and days until spring, when we would return to Minnesota.

My father's office was in a great marble building that covered an entire block. I used to roller-skate around it. My father was often at his desk before dawn and late at night. Congressmen spent most of their days indoors, seldom feeling wind or rain on their faces. They even had a tunnel built so they could walk back and forth to the Capitol without being exposed to weather. My father didn't like that tunnel. He used to take me for long walks outdoors whenever he had time. Sometimes we'd stop in the House lobby on the way home, and I'd get a ten-cent glass of apple cider.

I spent many hours on the House floor with my father. There were usually plenty of empty seats. But it reminded me of church. It was always too hot and rather stuffy, and the speeches went on like sermons; sometimes you got a headache as you listened. . . .

A headache—why does my head press against the skylight's rib? Something isn't right in the plane. But of course—the air cushion I'm sitting on—it's been expanding as I climb and the atmospheric pressure becomes lower! I open the valve for a few seconds, to lower my position and make sure the fabric won't burst.

WASHINGTON DID HAVE its interesting hours, though. On vacation days my mother and I visited the parks and buildings of the city. It was near Washington that I attended my first air meet. We rode out of the city to Fort Myer, Virginia, where a half-dozen airplanes were lined up in front of the plank-built grandstand. One of the planes took off and raced a motorcar around the oval track in front of us. Another bombed the chalked outline of a battleship, with oranges thrown down by hand. A third had a forced landing in the woods half a mile or so away. As it dropped below treetops, a lot of men began running toward the place where it went down.

THE ALTIMETER shows 9300 feet. Stars are brighter and there are more of them. That means I'm gaining on the storm. And the throttle isn't yet wide open; I still have a reserve of power. I finish the log entries of the fourteenth hour and switch off the flashlight. The clouds are still within a few hundred feet of my wheels. There's no doubt now that a storm area lies ahead. I keep climbing slowly, rising to meet it, thankful it didn't come before a third of my fuel was gone.

How high do storm clouds usually rise? We mail pilots often discussed that question, and ideas varied. But after the discussion was over, you went away with little more knowledge than you had when you arrived—and more respect for storms. I'll climb to 15,000 feet, I decide, and no higher. Above that altitude, air's too light to support efficiency of either plane or pilot. The engine would lose power, the wings would grasp for substance, and lack of oxygen would dull my own perception when difficult flying required still more alertness. If clouds rise above 15,000 feet, I'll throttle down again, reset the stabilizer, and sink into the body of the storm.

MY EYES on the stars, I travel with their light-years back through time. I'm in the railroad station at Detroit. There he is at the gate, a little to one side of the crowd, face beaming, familiar white mustache and gold-rimmed spectacles, an old black felt hat raised high in his hand to attract our attention—Grandfather! He's always there to meet us when we arrive. He takes a suitcase in each hand as he greets my mother, and we start toward the streetcar.

It's half a block from the car line to his gray frame house on West Elizabeth Street. Lilac bushes by the steps are in full bloom, fresh against the city's carboned earth and sooty walls. We turn in off the flagstones and stop in front of the low porch, while my grandfather searches for his key ring. A metal plaque on the door says: C. H. LAND, DENTIST.

Inside, I rush back toward the kitchen to find my grandmother. On the way I pass the stuffed head of the big Rocky Mountain sheep that I use as a target for my unloaded rifle, the safe that holds platinum foil and bright sheets of dental gold, the cabinet full of polished stones and fossils. Each wall and corner has its treasures, to be recounted through the days ahead.

Upstairs next, to wriggle out of my traveling suit and into clothes which can be rubbed against the black grime of central Detroit. My grandparents have struggled futilely against that grime. Years ago Grandfather invented an air-conditioning system for the house—big wooden frames of cheesecloth through which an electric fan sucked air, straining it clean of soot. But dirt soon clogged the layers of cloth and seeped in through cracks, until washing and dusting seemed to spread it rather than keep shelves and windows clean.

Grandfather is a scientist who invents all sorts of things: from baby rockers to high-temperature gas furnaces. His specialty is the development of porcelain dentistry. The basement and half the rooms on the ground floor of his house are filled with tools, machinery, chemicals. The walls of these laboratories enclose a unique world. Here, I live amid turning wheels, the intense heat of muffle furnaces, the precise fashioning of gold and platinum. My grandfather gives me the freedom of his laboratories, excepting only the most delicate instruments and dangerous chemicals. He shows me how to mix clay and make molds, how to cast metal, handle electrically charged wires, polish my Minnesota carnelians on his dental wheels. The benches we work on are littered with forceps and plaster casts, patterns for gas furnaces, old teeth, blowpipes, and bottles with dust-covered labels.

At dinner table, I listen to talk about the latest discoveries of science. I can appreciate, even though I can't always understand, the clear-cut language of science. It doesn't hum in my ears like a church sermon or a political speech. Science confronts opinion with facts; men are measured by what they really do. It doesn't matter whether you believe in God, or whether you are a Republican. Your experiment works, or it doesn't. A machine will run, or it won't. I think that when I grow up, maybe I'll become a scientist.

THERE WERE TIMES when I considered taking up biology and medicine so I could explore the mysteries of life and death. But those sciences belonged to well-grounded, brilliant minds; their study was intricate, and my school marks were poor in the subjects they demanded as a background.

Our family travels made it difficult to be a good student. My mother and I always arrived in Washington after classes started in the fall, and left before they ended in the spring. Until I entered college I had never completed a full academic year. Nor did I study very hard; in class my mind often wandered.

I did come from a family of physicians. My mother's uncle Edwin was the doctor in attendance at my birth. My grand-uncle Gus was a doctor in Milford, Michigan. And my grand-uncle Albert, also a doctor, lived only about three blocks away from my grandparents on Elizabeth Street. I bicycled up to his office-home whenever I had the chance. He showed me medical specimens, and gave me sugar pills.

We were all proud of Great-grandfather Edwin. He'd been one of the best doctors in Detroit, and a very active man. In addition to attending to a big practice, he ran a pharmacy, published the *Homeopathic Observer*, and fathered eleven children in two marriages. He was extremely religious. In his Bible he underlined all the words of Christ in red, and all those of the Disciples in blue. He used to write the Lord's Prayer on a piece of paper the size of a dime to entertain his grandchildren. On Sundays he often preached in a little wooden church on the shore of Orchard Lake, not far from a farm he had bought. My mother told of seeing him wade out into the cold water to baptize new members of the congregation. No sprinkling on the head for him. He believed in ducking them right under.

As a doctor, Great-grandfather Edwin lived in close contact with both life and death. There didn't seem to be any conflict in his mind between science and God. He had faith in some quality that was independent of the body.

IT'S HARD TO BE AN AGNOSTIC up here in the *Spirit of St. Louis*, aware of the frailty of man's devices, a part of the universe between its earth and stars. If one dies, all this goes on existing in a plan so perfectly balanced, so wonderfully simple, so incredibly complex, that it's far beyond our comprehension— worlds and moons revolving; planets orbiting suns; suns flung with apparent recklessness through space. There's the infinite magnitude of the universe; there's the infinite detail of its matter—the outer star, the inner atom. And man conscious of it all—a worldly audience to what if not to God?

It's nine o'clock. I've reached an altitude of 10,000 feet, and clouds are still rising up to meet me. It's cold at this altitude. I zip the flying suit across my chest. It's cold enough for mittens and my wool-lined helmet, too, but not for flying boots—I'll let them go until later. Too much warmth would make me want, still more, to sleep.

I must straighten out my neck before it cramps permanently in this thrown-back position. I turn from the stars to the instrument dials. I fix my eyes now on the glowing dots an arm's length before me, now on the points of fire millions of miles away. I travel with their vision back and forth.

As I fly through the body of night, haze lessens, and I discover that I'm among cloud mountains—great shadowy forms, awesome in their magnitude, in their weird, fantastic shapes. Huge pillars push upward thousands of feet above the common mass. Black valleys and chasms open below me to unfathomed depth.

There's no possibility of flying above those mountains, higher than any clouds I ever saw before, and the valleys are narrowing. So I can't follow the valleys; I'll have to challenge the mountains themselves. Flying through an occasional thunderhead will be less tiring than spending hours on end down in the writhing body of the storm. A few minutes of blind flying isn't that much to dread. It may even be a welcome change, sharpen my dulled senses, break up the monotony of routine flight.

Then I'll hold my course, stay above the stratus layer of the storm, and tunnel through the thunderheads that rise directly on my route. I tighten my belt, push the nose down a bit, and adjust the stabilizer. I prepare mentally and physically for blind flying.

The body must be informed sternly that the mind will take complete control. The senses must be lined up in strictest discipline, while logic replaces instinct as commander. If the body feels a wing dropping, and the mind says it is not (because the turn-indicator's ball and needle are still centered), the muscles must obey the mind's decision no matter how wrong it seems to them. If the eyes imagine the flicker of a star below where they think the horizon ought to be, if the ears report the engine's tempo too slow for level flight, if the nerves say the seat back's pressure is increasing (as it does in a climb), the hands and the feet must still be loyal to the orders of the mind.

It's a terrific strain on the mind to turn from bodily instinct to the cold impartiality of needles moving over dials. For the mind is accustomed to relying on the senses. They're trained to keep the body upright on the darkest night; to hold a blind man's balance; to catch a stumble in an instant. Blind flying requires absolute discipline. The mind must operate as mechanically as the gyroscope which guides it. The muscles must move as unfeelingly as gears. If the senses get excited and out of control, the plane will follow them, and that can be fatal. If the senses break ranks while everything is going right, it may be impossible, with the plane falling dizzily and needles running wild, to bring them back into line.

Wings quiver as I enter the cloud. Rough air jerks the *Spirit of St. Louis* about as though demons were pulling at fuselage and wings. Everything is uniform blackness, except for the exhaust's flash on passing mist and the glowing dials in my cockpit. What lies outside doesn't matter. My world is compressed within these fabric walls.

Flying blind is difficult enough in smooth air. In this swirling cloud, it calls for all the concentration I can muster. The turn and bank indicators, the airspeed, the altimeter, and the compass, all those phosphorescent lines and dots in front of me, must be kept in proper place. When a single one strays off, the rest go chasing after it like so many sheep, and have to be caught quickly and carefully herded back into position again.

It's cold up here at—I glance at the altimeter—10,500 feet. *Cold*—good Lord, there *are* things to be considered outside the cockpit! How could I forget! I jerk off a leather mitten and thrust my arm outside the cockpit. My palm is covered with stinging pinpricks. I pull the flashlight from my pocket and throw its beam onto a strut. The entering edge is irregular and shiny—*ice!* And as far out into darkness as the beam penetrates, the night is filled with countless, threadlike, horizontal streaks.

I've got to turn around, get back into clear air—quickly! But in doing so those instrument needles mustn't move too far or too fast. Mind, not body, must control the turn. My senses want to whip the *Spirit of St. Louis* into a bank and dive it out of the thunderhead, back into open sky. But the mind retorts, "Steady, steady. If you turn too fast, the plane may get out of control."

I keep pressing the rudder cautiously until the turn-indicator's needle creeps a quarter inch to the left. I push the stick over just enough to hold the proper bank. The airspeed drops 10 miles an hour. The altimeter shows a 100-foot descent.

I open the throttle another 50 revolutions. I don't dare push the stick forward very much to gain speed. The *Spirit of St. Louis* is too close to the top of the main cloud layer. There were less than 1000 feet to spare when I entered the thunderhead. That endless stratus layer is probably full of ice, too. If I drop down into it, I may never see the stars again.

The altimeter needle falls 200 feet, 300 feet. I push the throttle wide open—I *must* stay above that vast layer of cloud at the thunderhead's base. The airspeed rises to 100 miles an hour. I bank again and glance at the altimeter: 10,300 feet. Good, it's gone up a little. I throw my flashlight onto the wing strut. Ice is thicker!

The earth-inductor needle begins moving backward, jumping erratically. Level out wings—about the right heading. Now, if the turn indicator doesn't ice up for a few minutes more—I put my hand out the window again—the pinpricks are still there.

Steady the plane—but the air's too rough. Is the turn indicator icing? It seems to move back and forth more slowly. Everything depends on its working till I get outside this cloud. Just two or three more minutes . . .

My eyes sense a change in the blackness of my cockpit. I look out through the window. Can those be the same stars? Is this the same sky? How bright! How clear! What safety I have reached! Bright, clear, safe? But this is the same hazy air I left a fraction of an hour ago. I've simply found security where I left danger, flying over a major storm, above a frigid northern ocean. I was in the thunderhead for ten minutes at most; but it's one of those incidents that can't be measured by minutes. Such periods stand out like islands in a sea of time. It's not the limitless vista of experience, not hours or years that are most important. It's the islands, no matter how small. They impress the senses as they draw the eye at sea. Against them, years roll in and break, as waves upon a coast.

How much ice has accumulated on the plane? I move my flashlight from one spot to another. There's none on the bottom surface of the wing; but a thin layer forward on the strut tells me that it's also clinging to the airfoil's entering edge. There's not enough weight to make much difference, but what about resistance? Will the change in contours have a great effect on speed? The airspeed needle shows a five-mile drop. Have those few minutes in the cloud cost me five miles an hour cruising?

I turn southward, skirting the edge of the cloud pillar. I'll have to fly around these thunderheads. But can I? There are more masses ahead, and fewer stars. Will they merge into one great citadel of storm? Will I follow up a canyon in the heavens, as I often have on earth, to see it disappear against a mountain ridge? Or can I find real passes in these clouds, as I've found them in the mountains, where a plane can slip between the icy walls?

In the blackness of night, and in the haze that still contaminates the sky, one cloud merges into another so I can't distinguish edge from center point. I have to bank as I approach, and follow around the vague wall of mist until I can again take up my compass heading.

Would it be wiser to change my course entirely, and fly around the whole storm area? That's what my fuel reserve is for. Is this the emergency in which to use it?

Great cliffs tower over me, ward me off with icy walls. There'd be no rending crash if my wing struck one of them. They carry a subtler death. A crash against an earthly mountain is like a sword stroke: one flash and it's over. But these mountains of the heavens enmesh intruders. They toss you in their inner turbulence, lash you with their hailstones, poison you with freezing mist. It would be a slow death, a death one would have long minutes to struggle against, trying blindly to regain control of an ice-crippled airplane, climbing, stalling, diving, whipping, always downward toward the sea.

For the first time the thought of turning back seriously enters my mind. I can climb another 5000 or 6000 feet. The canyons up there may be wider. If they're not, and I can find no passes east or southward, I'll have to turn back—back 1400 miles to New York, back for another start from that narrow, muddy runway on Long Island. And when I got back, I'd have been about thirty hours in the air. Think of flying long enough to have reached Ireland, and ending up at Roosevelt Field!

I could try diving quickly to a lower level, where the air may be too warm for ice to form. No, it would be a fool's chance. As far north as Newfoundland and in the cold of night, icing conditions probably extend down to the waves themselves.

The pillars of cloud multiply and thicken. I follow narrow passageways between them, weaving in and out around thunderheads. Dark forms blot out the sky on every side, but stars drop down to guide me through the passes.

THE FIFTEENTH HOUR, 9:52 p.m. Fourteen hundred miles behind. Twenty-two hundred miles to go. All readings normal. I make the log entries and shine my flashlight onto the wing strut again. The coating of ice is thinner. It's evaporating slowly. When will it all be gone—in an hour, two, or five? I don't know.

The haze is clearing. I can see cloud silhouettes against a star-brightening sky. I bank toward the southern edge, and settle back in my cockpit.

In keeping his heading by the stars, a pilot must remember that they move. In all the heavens, there is only one he can trust not to lead him off course—Polaris, faint star of the northern pole. Those other more brilliant points of light, which at first seem motionless, too, sweep through their arcs so rapidly that he can use them only as temporary guides.

As a child, I'd lie on my bed in Minnesota and watch the stars curve upward in their courses, rising over treetops, climbing slowly toward our roof. I would curl up under my blankets and web the constellations into imaginary scenes of celestial magnitude—a flock of geese in westward flight, God's arrow shooting through the sky. I'd make my wishes on the stars, and drift from wakefulness to sleep. There was no roar of an engine in my ears, no sound above the wind in leaves except the occasional whistle of a train, far away across the river.

That whistle was the only note to break the peace of night, to connect me to the modern world in which fate and my father's business made me spend my winters. That train would carry me back to Washington in September, as it carried me westward to our farm in June. It followed the steel cords which tied marble buildings and deliberative halls to my fields and rolling hills a thousand miles away in Minnesota.

Wheels clatter on tracks. The tempo changes as our train curves and brakes across the bridge. Downriver I see the great tops of Norway pine that mark our farm. Our train slows, jerks, stops—"L-l-little-e-e Fa-a-a-l-l-l-s." I jump down onto the boardwalk, and turn to wait for my mother. Winter's school is over. Summer has come.

It's a two-mile walk to our farm, past Engstrom's hardware store, past Wilsczek's butcher shop, past the swinging-doored saloons. We stop at Ferguson's grocery to order food for the week. Along with it, the one-horse delivery cart will bring our suitcases and trunk.

Our road bends south around the yellow brick church, then west to the Coultas home, where my dog has spent the winter. From a flower-filled yard with picket gate he bounces out to meet me—red-haired, white-chested, barking, wriggling Dingo.

We start down the sandy street together. Soon I'll be out of city clothes—in overalls, barefooted. Here's the path through hazel brush. Here's the shortcut through the gravel pit where I sometimes find carnelians. Here we strike real country, for the telephone poles stop. "La-a-l-l-y bo-o-o-o-s-s-y. La-a-l-l-y bo-o-o-s-s-y"—the Sandstrom girls are calling their cattle. Here's the Johnson farm, with its pasture rolling over to the river—the brindle cow staked out in thick green grass.

Now the road jogs away from the river to take in a strip of woodland. It widens and straightens for its half-mile stretch southward between the white-cedar fence posts of our farm. There's our gray barn, and the tenant's horses. Trees and flowering honeysuckle bushes screen our house. I throw open the iron gate, run under oaks and poplars along a deeply shaded footpath, feet kicking through last October's leaves.

I turn the key in the padlock, jerk open the rusting hasp, push through our kitchen door. Dingo wedges past my legs, and Mother is close behind. A cool, musty smell surrounds us. There's been no one in the house all winter. We throw doors and windows wide open, light the cookstove, start unpacking boxes. Between tasks I run out to see that the swing ropes are still there, that the tree seat hasn't blown away, that I can still keep my balance on my stilts. There's the maidenhair patch to visit, the bluffs on the creek to slide down. I have my guns to clean and hawks to hunt. Dingo has gophers to catch. There are neighbors' boys to swim and play with under noonday suns ahead. . . .

THE EARTH-INDUCTOR compass needle is halfway to the peg! I bank the *Spirit of St. Louis* toward its proper heading. The needle moves up slowly, fluctuating; then overshoots the line and drops down on the other side. I've never seen it act like that before. Is the earth-inductor failing, or am I half asleep and flying badly?

I shine my flashlight on the liquid compass overhead. It, too, is swinging. I center the turn indicator, and hold the plane's nose straight toward a star. But the needle is still top-heavy, and the liquid compass's swinging doesn't stop. Something's seriously wrong. I haven't depended too much on the earth-inductor compass. It's a new and complicated instrument, just past the experimental stage. But the liquid compass! It's almost as essential for it to work as for the engine to keep running. I never heard of *two* compasses failing at the same time.

I look at the liquid compass again, as though trying to steady it by concentration alone. The card is rocking through an arc of more than sixty degrees—more than ninety degrees at times. Is it possible that I'm entering a magnetic storm? Most pilots scoff at their existence. They say magnetic storms are figments of imagination, like air pockets—just an excuse for getting lost— to explain away mistakes in navigation. Do magnetic storms really occur, then?

The earth-inductor needle's wobbling back and forth from peg to peg. There's no use in paying any attention to it. But the liquid compass hesitates between oscillations, and remains fairly steady for several seconds at a time. I set my heading by these periods of hesitation, and hold it by the stars—except when a thunderhead gets in the way. As long as the stars are there, I can hold a general easterly direction; but there'll be little accuracy to navigation. God only knows where I'll strike the European coast. But if the liquid compass gets any worse, and high clouds shut off the sky, I won't know whether I'm flying north, south, east, or west.

It would be easier to set a course if I could read the liquid compass without a flashlight. While the flashlight's on, I can't see the stars; and it's hard to watch the compass overhead and the instruments on the board at the same time.

On what delicate devices flight depends: a magnetized bar of steel, slender as a pencil lead, reaching for the North Pole thousands of miles away, swinging with each bump of air, subject to the slightest disturbance, barely strong enough to point; yet without its directive force the engine, the plane, the skills of the pilot become meaningless.

Stars drop lower. Valleys between thunderheads widen. I no longer have to look up through the window on top of the fuselage to find a stable point in space. Cloud outlines are sharp and the sky seems lighter. Can it be the first faint warning of the moon's approach? I turn to the south window—the night has a deeper shade. Yes, it must be the morning rising of the moon—a luminous wash, barely perceptible, on the northeastern wall of night.

I'd almost forgotten the moon. Now it's coming to my aid.

Every minute will bring improving sight. As the moon climbs higher in the sky, its light will brighten, until finally it ushers in the sun. The stars are already fading. This far north, there have been only two hours of solid darkness.

Gradually, as light improves, silhouettes give way to shadings. In the reflected light of the moon, clouds seem more akin to it than to the earth over which they hover. They form a perfect setting for that strange foreign surface one sees through a telescope trained on the satellite of the world. Formations of the moon, they are reality combined with the fantasy of a dream—volcanoes and flat plateaus; great towers and bottomless pits. There are shapes like growths of coral on the bed of a tropical sea, or the grotesque canyons of sandstone and lava at the edge of Arizona deserts—first black, then gray, now greenish in the cold, mystical light.

Far ahead, a higher cloud layer is forming, thousands of feet above my level—glowing, horizontal strips, supported by thick pillars from the mass below. Will these clouds finally merge to form one great mass of opaque air? Must I still turn back? *Can* I still turn back? North, south, and west, clouds rise and tower.

Starting the sixteenth hour, with 1500 miles behind me, I'm not halfway to Paris, but halfway between New York and Ireland. After I flew out through that gap in the mountains at St. John's, Ireland became, subconsciously, more of an objective for me than Paris. A long flight always divides up into such mileposts—the first state, the first shoreline, the first 100 miles—there's always some objective reached to give the feeling of accomplishment. My log of them is filling. In it I've placed the continent of North America, Newfoundland, the first day, the blackness of the first night. Next, still quite far away, will be the dawn.

THE MOON is a little higher, and too far north. I've let the plane veer off course again. If only those compasses would steady down, I could stop cramping my neck to see the stars, and rest. That's what I want most now—to rest. Why try to hold a steady course? Why worry about a trivial five- or ten-degree error? I can't possibly miss the whole continent of Europe.

I shake myself violently, alarmed by my weakness. No matter how inaccurate my navigation, it must be the best I can do. The more my compasses swing, the more alert I must stay to compensate for their errors. I cup my hand into the slipstream, diverting a strong current of air against my face, and breathe deeply. I let my eyelids fall shut for five seconds; then raise them against tons of weight. Protesting, they won't open wide until I force them with my thumb and lift the muscles of my forehead to keep them in place.

My fingers are cold from the slipstream. I draw my mittens on again. Shall I put on flying boots? I'd have to take my feet off the rudder pedals, and do most of the work with one hand. The *Spirit of St. Louis* would veer off and I'd have to straighten it out a dozen times before I got the boots on. It's too much effort. I'd rather be a little cold.

I draw the flying suit's wool collar across my throat. Should I put the windows in now and gain that mile or two of speed from streamlining? Those windows, resting idly in their rack, pushing down on the plane with their three or four pounds of unused weight, still rankle in my mind—50 miles of range thrown away. There's still time to make them pay a profit on their passage. But the same argument that kept them out before prevails again. If I shut myself off even partially from outside air, the lure of sleep may prove beyond resistance.

How wonderful it would be if this really were a dream, and I could lie down on a cloud's soft quilt and sleep. I've never wanted anything so much. I'd pay any price—except life itself. But life itself *is* the price.

I've *got* to do something to clear my head. I've *got* to do a better job of navigation. How shall I compensate for the night's errors? When morning breaks, what estimate will I make of my position? I force my hands to unfold the chart on my knees and slant the flashlight's beam across its surface. The white paper glares back into my night-accustomed eyes as though it were reflecting a midday sun. I pull the eastern half of the chart from the map pocket and join it to the western.

This cockpit was never made for spreading out charts. The paper wrinkles; the ends hang down and flutter in swirls of air.

I need four hands—one for the stick, one for the flashlight, and one for each strip of paper. I try holding the stick between my knees and the flashlight under my chin. It works for a moment; then comes that out-of-balance feeling which tells me the plane's veering off again. I shut off the light, pull the stick back, and look up through the skylight to find stars. There are none. The glaring whiteness of the chart has blinded me to such vague pinpricks.

Gradually sight returns. I find the stars, and straighten out on what I estimate the course to be. I piece the charts together again, flying entirely by instruments, so that my wind-dried eyes work always in an even light. But the *Spirit of St. Louis* refuses to be left unattended for five seconds. As soon as I look down at the charts the plane starts cutting up like a spoiled child piqued by a moment's neglect.

Finally I give up trying to hold the charts, and visualize them in my mind while I watch the moon and stars. I've worked over them until their features are as plain as a familiar face on memory's screen. I can see the outline of the European coast almost as clearly as though I were looking at the charts themselves. It's best to angle northward, in the direction of nearest land; yet fate's been pushing me farther and farther south—I may be pointed at the Bay of Biscay instead of Ireland.

The Bay of Biscay! Its name strikes back in memory to my childhood in Minnesota, to a ditty my father used to sing as we drove along winding dirt roads on crystal summer nights, looking up at the moon and stars just as I'm looking up at them now. The words run through my mind:

> *All through the Bay of Biscay,*
> *That gallant vessel sailed,*
> *Until one night among the sailors,*
> *They raised a merry row . . .*

For me, that song has always been connected with night, stars—and sleep, for I was young and usually very sleepy when he sang. And here I am, at night, dependent on the same stars; flying, possibly, toward the Bay of Biscay itself. I shout out the words of the song as loudly as I can. Singing may help to keep me awake and pass the hours until dawn. Maybe that's why my father used to sing, along those lonely Minnesota roads—to help keep awake, as I must keep awake tonight.

THE SEVENTEENTH HOUR. It's midnight in New York, and I've covered about thirty degrees of longitude since takeoff. Here, it's two o'clock in the morning, if I think in daylight-saving terms. Dawn isn't many hours away. The moonlight is brilliant. Objects in my cockpit are taking form again; I can almost read the figures on the charts. Clouds are clear and sharp, lightly veiling the moon as they pass. From a distance they block the sky completely, except for corridors lit by the rising moon; but as I approach they separate into layers and isolated masses, with fields of stars between.

I look up at the compass. Good; it's steadier than usual—it's almost stopped oscillating! The earth-inductor needle, too, has regained some of its precision—it no longer wobbles with every bump of air. Am I getting out of the magnetic storm?

The haze is almost gone. I throw the beam of my flashlight out onto the wing struts. There's no trace of ice remaining. It's warmer in the cockpit, pleasantly warm. My hands are warm, too, and moist. I pull off my mittens and press an arm out against the slipstream. The air has more the feel of a tropical sea. It's changed completely within the hour. I lay my mittens on the floor and zip down my flying suit.

I'm about 500 miles from Newfoundland. Maybe I've crossed the border of the Gulf Stream. Down below, the water, too, will be warm. It's like crossing a stormbound mountain range to find a sunbathed valley just beyond.

All through the storm, my instincts were anchored to North America; in an emergency, I would have turned back. Now, my anchor is in Europe. It's been shifted by the storm behind me, by the moon's rising in the east, by the breaking sky and warmer air, and the possibility that the Gulf Stream may lie below.

Unless the clouds below me break, too, there's nothing to do until sunrise except hold my heading, shift fuel tanks, and fill in the log each hour. There's no need to watch dials carefully.

Earlier, if they had forecast trouble, the sooner I noticed it and turned back the better chance I had of reaching land. Now, no matter what the dials show, I'll continue on my course as long as engine can hold plane in air. Before, I'd been flying away from safety. Now, every mile I cover brings me closer to it.

IT'S MY EIGHTEENTH HOUR in the air. For unmeasurable periods, I seem divorced from my body, as though I were an awareness spreading out through space, unhampered by time or substance, free from heavy human problems. My body requires no attention. It's not hungry. It's neither warm nor cold. It's resigned to being left undisturbed while the weightless element that has lived within it flashes through the skies.

This essential consciousness expands through the universe; I am a part of all existence, powerless but without need for power; immersed in solitude, yet in contact with all creation.

Awakening from my celestial excursion, I find the clouds around me covered with a whiter light. Night is giving way to day. Dawn! It's tremendously important, but how dull appreciation is. My senses perceive it only vaguely, separately, indifferently, like pain through too weak an anesthetic. It is intellectual knowledge, and physically I'm like an automaton.

With the faint trace of day, the desire to sleep falls over me in quilted layers. I've been staving it off with difficulty during the hours of moonlight. Now it looms all but insurmountable. This is the beginning of my greatest test. This will be the worst time of all, this early hour of the second morning—the third morning since I've slept.

I've lost command of my eyelids. When they start to close, I can't restrain them. They shut, and I shake myself, and lift them with my fingers. I stare at the instruments, wrinkle forehead muscles tense. Lids close again, regardless. My body has revolted from the rule of the mind. Every cell of my being is on strike, sulking in protest, claiming that nothing in the world could be worth such effort; that man's tissue was never made for such abuse. My back is stiff; my shoulders ache; my face burns; my eyes smart. It seems impossible to go on longer.

I've struggled with the dawn often enough before, but never

with such a background of fatigue. If I can hold out for one more hour, the sun will be over the horizon and the battle won. Each ray of light is an ally. With each moment after sunrise, vitality will increase.

Something's wrong on the instrument board—the compass needle has strayed ten degrees off course while I have been making resolutions to keep it on its mark. I tense my muscles, shake my body, and bounce up and down in the cockpit. I simply *must* keep that compass needle in the center—good God, it's off again. This is like a feverish dream.

I've got to find some way to keep alert. *There's no alternative but death and failure*, I keep repeating, using the thought as a whip on my lagging mind. I try running fast on the floorboards with my feet for as many seconds as the *Spirit of St. Louis* will hold to course. Then I clamp the stick between my knees while I simulate running with my hands. I push first one wing low and then the other, to blow fresh air through the cockpit and change pressure on my body. I shake my head until it hurts; rub the muscles of my face to regain feeling. I pull the cotton from my ears, fluff it out, wad it in again.

I'll put my mind on the sunrise, watch the clouds brighten. As that dazzling ball of fire climbs into the sky, night's unpaid claims will pass. The desire for sleep will give way to waking habits of the day. And yet I'm not sure—it's never been like this before—I never wanted so badly to sleep—

I TAKE OFF my helmet, rub my head, pull the helmet on again. I drink some water from the canteen—that helps. Possibly if I eat a sandwich—but my mouth wants no food, and eating might make me sleepier. Should I have taken along a thermos of coffee? No, it wouldn't have any effect when I'm feeling like this. If I could get down through the clouds and fly close to the waves, maybe that would help me stay awake, as it did yesterday. But there isn't enough light yet. I'll have to wait another hour.

Shaking my body and stamping my feet no longer works. It's more fatiguing than arousing. I'll have to try something else. I push the stick forward and dive down into a high ridge of cloud, pulling up sharply after I clip through its summit. That wakes me a little, but tricks don't help for long. They're only tiring.

My mind strays from the cockpit and returns. My eyes close, and open, and close again. But I'm beginning to understand vaguely a new factor which has come to my assistance. It seems I'm made up of three personalities, three elements. There's my body, which knows definitely that what it wants most in the world is sleep. There's my mind, constantly making decisions that my body refuses to comply with, and which itself is weakening in resolution. And there's an element of spirit which seems to become stronger instead of weaker with fatigue, a directive force that has taken control over both mind and body.

When my body cries out that it *must* sleep, this third element replies that it may relax but not sleep. When my mind demands that my body stay alert, it is informed that alertness is too much to expect under these circumstances. And when my mind argues back that to sleep would be to fail, and crash, it is reassured that while it must not expect alertness it can be confident there'll be no sleep. This force knows and holds a limit I can't define, letting my mind and body stay relaxed as long as the plane flies reasonably straight and level, giving the alarm to both when needles move too fast or far. So far, no farther, the plane can dive or climb. Then I react from my stupor, level out, shake myself to half awakeness—and let the needle creep again. I'm asleep and awake at the same moment. My eyes, under their weighted lids, are a part of this third element. They seem completely disconnected from my body, to have within themselves no substance, to be conscious rather than to see.

I'm thankful we didn't make the *Spirit of St. Louis* a stable plane. The very instability which makes it difficult to fly blind or hold an accurate course now guards me against excessive errors. It's again a case of the plane and me compensating for each other. When I was fresh and it was overloaded, my quick reactions held its nose from veering off. Now that I'm ridden by sleep, its veering prods my lagging senses.

The clock's minute hand shows a quarter of two. It's almost time for my hourly routine of log and tanks and heading. Previously, I've looked forward to this as welcome diversion, as something to sharpen my senses, to bring movement to cramped muscles. Now, the effort seems too much to bear. It's all I can do to rouse my senses sufficiently to pull out the pencil and lay the log sheet on my chart.

The nineteenth hour. Eighteen hundred miles behind, eighteen hundred to go. Halfway to Paris. Once this was a point I planned on celebrating. But now it seems unimportant. I have as far to go as I've come. I must fly for eighteen endless hours more.

Shall I shift fuel tanks again? I've been running a long time on the fuselage tank. Let's see—it's best not to let the center of gravity move too far forward, so the plane won't dive under the surface in case of a forced landing. I turn on the nose tank and shut off the flow from the fuselage tank. I put another pencil mark on the instrument board to register the eighteenth hour of fuel consumed.

I let the compass heading go for another hour. What difference do two or three degrees make when I'm letting the nose swing several times that much to one side or the other of my heading? Sometime I'll have to make an estimate of my position; right now, it's beyond my ability. I can work it all out after sunrise.

The clouds turn from green to gray, and from gray to red and gold. I realize that it's day. The last shade of night has left the sky. Clouds, dazzling in their whiteness, cover the ocean below, rise in mountains at my side, and—that's why I've waked from my dazed complacency: towering ahead is a sheer white wall!

I'm in it—engulfed by the thick mist, covered with the diffused, uniform light which carries no direction and indicates no source. Mechanically, I hold my hand out into the slipstream. The temperature of air is well above freezing—no danger from ice.

Flying blind again. The turn indicator must be kept in center. That's the most important thing. Then the airspeed needle must not be allowed to drop or climb too far. At the same time, I have to keep the earth-inductor needle somewhere near its lubber line.

167

The knowledge of what would happen if I let those needles get out of control does for me what no amount of resolution can. Danger, when it's imminent and real, cuts like a rapier through the draperies of sleep. Let the turn indicator move an eighth of an inch or the airspeed change five miles an hour, and I react in an instant.

It's not a large cloud. Within fifteen minutes the mist ahead brightens and the *Spirit of St. Louis* bursts out into a great, blue-vaulted pocket of air. But there are clouds all around—stratus layers, one above another, with huge cumulus masses piercing through and rising far above. I cut now across a sky valley surrounded by towering peaks of white.

Another wall ahead. More blind flying. Out in the open again. But only for minutes. When I leave a cloud, drowsiness advances; when I enter the next, it recedes. All my attention is concentrated on the task of simply passing through.

The twentieth hour, 2:52 a.m. I tunnel by instruments through a tremendous cumulus mass. As I break out, a glaring valley lies across my path, miles in width, extending north and south as far as I can see. The sky is blue-white above, and the blinding fire of the sun itself has burst over the ridge ahead.

I nose the *Spirit of St. Louis* down, losing altitude slowly, 200 feet or so a minute. At 8000 feet, I level out, plumbing with my eyes the depth of each chasm I pass over. In the bottom of one of them I see, like a rare stone perceived among countless pebbles at your feet, a darker, deeper shade, a different texture—the ocean! Its surface is splotched with white and covered with ripples. Ripples from 8000 feet! That means a heavy sea.

It's one of those moments when all the senses rise together, and realization snaps so acute and clear that seconds impress themselves with the strength of years on memory. It forms a picture with colors that will hold and lines that will stay sharp throughout the rest of life—the broad, sun-dazzled valley in the sky; the funnel's billowing walls; and deep down below the hard, blue-gray scales of the ocean.

I've got to get down where I can see waves and wind streaks, find out how much the wind has changed, begin to grapple with problems of navigation.

I nose down steeply. The sun's rays flood through the fuselage window, cut across the cockpit, touch first this instrument, then that. Whitecaps sparkle on distant water. Layer after layer of thin gray clouds slip by. My ears clear, and stop, and clear again from change in pressure. My air cushion wilts until I feel the hard wicker weaving of the seat.

Two thousand feet now—under the lowest clouds. The sea is fairly writhing beneath its skin—great waves—breakers—streaks of foam—a gale wind. From the northwest? I straighten out and take up compass course. I'm pointed obliquely with the waves—yes, the wind's northwest. It's a quartering tail wind! It's probably been blowing that way all night, pushing me along on my route, drifting me southward at the same time.

A tail wind across the ocean! How strong is it? I can judge better close to the surface. I ease the stick forward and begin a slow descent. Curtains of fog hang down ahead and on each side, darkening the air and sea, shutting off the horizon. I nose down to 1000 feet, to 500, to 50 feet above huge waves. The wind's probably blowing 50 or 60 miles an hour, scraping whitecaps off and carrying the spray ahead like rain over the surface. The whole ocean is covered with ragged streaks of foam. It's a fierce, unfriendly sea—I feel naked above it, as though stripped of all protection, conscious of the terrific strength of the waves, of the thinness of the cloth on my wings, of the dark turbulence of the storm clouds.

Now it's essential to lay out a definite plan of navigation. The wind aloft is probably stronger than it is down here. If it is also from the northwest, and if it didn't shift during the night, I must be well ahead of schedule and south of my course.

Whatever estimate I make of my position is just a guess; but right or wrong, I've got to make some estimate. When I left Newfoundland, I set my heading ten degrees northward to compensate for drift. Should I now allow five degrees more? I look at the waves again. The wind streaks are more tail than side—my route curved southward during the night. Fifteen degrees might be too much. Then for over an hour I haven't reset the compass at all; that leaves me headed an extra two degrees toward the north.

169

Still, I have a strong feeling that I'm too far south to strike Ireland unless I change my heading. But there aren't enough facts to back it up. I must consider only the known elements in navigation. Suppose I crank in five degrees to the earth-inductor compass, then if I don't make a landfall by—

The waves ahead disappear. Fog covers the sea. I have only time to reset the altimeter and start climbing. A hundred feet above water, in rough air, is no place for blind flying. Turbulence is severe. The safety belt jerks against me. Needles jump back and forth over dials until I can follow only their average indications. I push the throttle forward and hold 95 miles an hour until the altimeter shows 1000 feet. Problems of navigation fade against the immediate need of holding the *Spirit of St. Louis* level and on course. I'll figure it all out accurately after the fog has passed.

The fog doesn't pass. I go on and on through its white blankness, flying automatically again through eyes which register but do not see. . . .

"CHARLES!"

I hardly hear my nurse's voice above my heartbeat. I've slipped away from her guard to stare fearfully around the gray barn's corner. A huge column of smoke is rising from our house, spreading out, and blackening the sky. Then that's why I was jerked away from my play so roughly and rushed down the kitchen steps. Our house is burning down! A hand grasps my arm and pulls me behind the barn. "Charles, you *mustn't* watch!"

It was a dreary winter that came after the burning of our house, in 1906. We rented a small flat in Minneapolis. I missed the roomy freedom of the farm. Tired of books and toys, and of pressing my face against a frosted window, I move aimlessly about, experiment with any new thought. Why can't I hold ten marbles between ten toes? How long can a cream-filled chocolate last if I eat it with a pin?

THE NOSE is down, the wing low, the plane diving and turning. I've been asleep with open eyes. I'm certain they've been open, yet I have all the sensations of waking up—lack of memory of

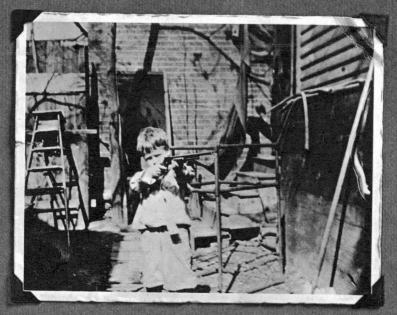

Target practice

Hunting and boating in Minnesota

intervening time, inability to comprehend the situation for a moment, the return of understanding like blood surging through the body. I kick left rudder and pull the stick back cornerwise. My eyes jump to the altimeter. No danger; I'm at 1600 feet. In a moment, I'll have the plane leveled out. But the turn indicator leans over the left—the airspeed drops—the ball rolls quickly to the side. A climbing turn in the opposite direction! My plane is getting out of control!

The realization is like an electric shock. In a matter of seconds I have the *Spirit of St. Louis* back in hand. But even after the needles are in place, the plane seems to be flying on its side. I know what's happening. It's the illusion you sometimes get while flying blind that your plane is no longer in level flight, that it's spiraling, stalling, turning, that the instruments are wrong.

There's only one thing to do—shut off feeling from the mind and keep the needles where they belong. Gradually, when the senses find that air isn't screaming through the cowlings as it would in a dive, that wings aren't trembling as they would in a stall, that there's really no pressure on the seat as there would be in a bank, they recover from their confusion.

As minutes pass and no new incident occurs, I fall into the state of eye-open sleep again. I fly with less anguish when my conscious mind is not awake. I'm not sure whether I'm dreaming through life or living through a dream.

"HOW MANY do you want, Boss?"

My father dumps another turtle into the boat with his oar. It's the summer of 1911. The lake is full of turtles—red, green, and yellow, sunning themselves on top of a thick growth of weeds. They try to dive as we approach, but some become entangled in the matted stems, and these we catch.

"Get that little one, Father!"

It flips in beside me. I want the babies for my pen—a series of sandboxes, dishpans, and stone-islanded tubs that I've connected with special turtle walkways.

Father always calls me "Boss," but he's not fooling me. I know who's going to decide when we'll start home, and when we'll go on the next expedition. If I were really boss, we'd stay here tomorrow, too, and go to Squaw Lake next week. Squaw Lake has the best fishing I've ever seen.

Father taught me how to fish, just as he taught me how to handle turtles, and how to swim and hunt. But it was Grandfather Land who started me off with a gun. He made me a present of a 22-caliber rifle when I was six, and my uncle Charles showed me how to shoot it at a target in the basement. Father thought six was young for a rifle, but he'd let me walk behind him with a loaded gun at seven, use an axe as soon as I had strength enough to swing it, drive his Ford anywhere at twelve. My freedom was complete. All Father asked for in return was a sense of responsibility on my part—

THE AIRSPEED'S DOWN to 80 miles an hour, and the nose is sixteen degrees off course! I warn myself of relaxation's dangers. It's all very well to go half asleep in high clear air, but flying blind at low altitude is a matter of life and death! It's no use. Simply telling myself that I must hold those needles on their marks has no effect. There's a power beyond my will's control which knows exactly where the danger limit lies, and which realizes that as I become more skilled in using instruments, the need for concentration accordingly decreases. This power has taken over the direction of my flight, knowing better than I how far down the wing or nose can drop before an emergency has to be declared and the alarm given to my senses.

With each minute, my confidence increases. At first, my conscious mind didn't trust its ghostlike, newly made acquaintance. But now, when crises come, when sleep presses close and hard, it gives over command entirely, as an ailing man gives over a business he once thought no one else could run.

I wish I could blow up the air cushion. But I can't fly blind with only my knees against the stick. The seat is hard and painful. Pain doesn't help one to stay awake, as I thought it would.

THE TWENTY-FIRST HOUR. I'm half an hour late for instrument readings. But I can't control those needles and make entries in my log. It's not worth the effort anyway. I'll let it go until the air's clear again—let resetting the course go, too. I'll just mark the hour of fuel consumed. I reach forward and add one more line to the group under "nose tank."

Shall I go on blind, or climb above the clouds? I'm flying at 1500 feet; the monotony of this changeless, opaque mist creates a longing for either sea or sky. Since I'm completely shut off from the sea, my mind grasps at the idea of climbing back into sunlight and the crystalline upper world. But I decide to continue blind for one hour more.

My throat is a little dry. I reach for the canteen. No, just reaching throws the plane off balance. I don't need water. It's more important to keep the needles centered; every time I use an extra muscle they go jumping off.

IT'S APRIL, 1918, and our high school superintendent has offered full scholastic credit to students who leave classes to work on farms. I'd like to join the army and fly a Scout, like Eddie Rickenbacker and the pilots of the Lafayette Escadrille; but I'm only sixteen, too young to enlist, so I'm going to help raise the food we need to win the war. Father has bought a carload of western heifers, and another of western sheep. We'll make our hundred-and-twenty-acre farm produce all the food it can.

I'm taking my school books with me, but it's a gesture; there won't be much studying after a full day's labor on the farm. Father's going to buy a tractor, so I can plow and seed our fields. He'll be away most of the time. He has a law office in Minneapolis now, and business interests often take him East. I'll have charge of the farm. I must start right in, for there are fences to mend, and the barn needs fixing for cows—

Eight degrees right rudder.

LIGHT FROM my kerosene lantern throws soft shadows on the floor. The sun went down more than an hour ago. The year 1919 is two weeks old. My fingers strip out last drops of milk. It's stuffy here in the barn. Air reeks of cows' breath, bodies, and manure. Tongues rasp up last scraps of bran. Teeth go on munching hay. I don't dare let in more air tonight. It's thirty-seven degrees below zero outside. Steam puffs out from nostrils, and windows are a half-inch thick with frost.

I separate cream, feed calves, then check sheep in the lower barn. Snow squeaks against my boots as I cross the road and follow the path to our chicken coop. A tree cracks through the night's silence like a rifle shot. A million stars light up the sky.

Swing the nose back south.

IT'S JUNE OF 1920; I'm taking a train to Minneapolis. This afternoon I must interview prospective tenants for our farm. I've got to find someone who'll take charge, for I'm to enter the University of Wisconsin in the fall. I'm going to be a mechanical engineer.

I didn't plan on running the farm permanently. I started because of the war, and kept on because I loved the life and our Minnesota home. But two years out of school are enough. Even now I may be too rusty for engineering college. I have my high school diploma; but I haven't studied, and I've forgotten a lot.

Whether I graduate from the university or not, there are two things I want to do. I want to pilot an airplane, and I want to go to Alaska. Vilhjalmur Stefansson says Alaska is our modern frontier. It holds adventure and opportunity.

I SHAKE MY HEAD and thumb my eyelids open. Four fifty a.m., New York time! The twenty-second hour. I grope for the pencil in my pocket, and take my eyes from the turn indicator long enough to add another fuel mark to the group under "nose tank." There are twenty of those marks now on the instrument board. I switch over to the right wing tank; log entries can go until the air's clear.

Will the fog never end? Does this storm cover the entire ocean? Except for that small, early morning plot of open sea, I've been in fog or above it for nine hours. But I shouldn't complain—the weather's no worse than I expected. The only thing that's seriously upset my plans is the sleepless night before I started. If this were the first morning without sleep instead of the second, blind flying would be a different matter.

Sometimes the impression of movement ceases, and I seem to be just hanging in space—unrelated to any outside point of reference, hypnotized by the instruments. Over and over again, I fall asleep with my eyes open, knowing I'm falling asleep, unable to prevent it; having the sensations of falling asleep, as one does in bed at night; and then, seconds or minutes later, having all the sensations of waking up.

The fog dissolves, and the sea appears. Flying 200 feet higher, I wouldn't have seen it, for the overcast is just above me. There's no sun; only a pocket of clear air. Ahead, another curtain of mist. I push the stick forward. Waves are mountainous, even higher than before. If I fly close to their crests, maybe I can stay below the next area of fog.

I drop down until I'm flying in salt spray whipped off white-caps by the wind. But the fog is too thick. It crowds down between the waves themselves. A gull couldn't find enough ceiling to fly above this ocean. I climb. The air's rougher than before, swirling like the sea beneath it.

Before I reach 1000 feet, waves show again, vaguely, but in a moment they're smothered by mist. I climb. Strips of blue open and close like shutters, while layers of clouds shuffle past one another. It looks as though the storm is breaking. I pull out my air cushion, blow it up, stuff it back under me quickly, and straighten out the plane. I pour a little water down over the dryness of my throat.

A light rain streaks by, trickles over struts and wings, splashes through cracks and around corners into the cockpit. Flecks of cool water strike my face. Rain may be an indication of better weather close ahead.

I stare at the instruments, both conscious and asleep, and the fuselage behind me becomes filled with ghostly presences—vague, transparent forms riding weightless with me in the plane. Without turning my head, I see them as clearly as though they were in my normal field of vision. There's no limit to my sight—my skull is one great eye, seeing everywhere at once.

These phantoms speak with human voices—friendly, vapor-like shapes, passing in and out through the walls of the fuselage. First one and then another presses forward to my shoulder to speak above the engine's noise, and then draws back among the group behind. At times, voices come out of the air itself, clear yet far away; familiar voices, advising on my flight, discussing problems of navigation, reassuring me, giving me messages of importance unattainable in ordinary life.

All sense of substance leaves me. There's no longer weight to my body, hardness to the stick. The feeling of flesh is gone. I'm almost one with these vaporlike forms behind me. I'm still attached to life; they, not at all; but at any moment some thin band may snap and there'll be no difference between us.

At another time I'd be startled by these visions; but on this fantastic flight I'm so far separated from the earthly life I know that I accept whatever circumstance may come. I live in the past, the present, and the future, here and in different places, all at once.

IT'S JUNE, 1915. Father's coming down the icehouse road. I hop down the steps to meet him. It's late afternoon. A cool breeze has followed midday's blistering sun. My father leans his bicycle against an oak tree, and we walk along the garden path. We talk of our plans, for next week we start on a most important expedition. From the headwaters of the Mississippi, we will make a rowboat voyage through forest, swamp, and rapids, until we arrive again at the banks of our farm.

Six degrees right rudder.

THE TRAIN TAKES US north to Bemidji, and a car tows our white, clinker-built rowboat to Lake Itasca. My father rows along the lakeshore, searching for the river outlet. Water is clear and satin-smooth. Fish splash rings upon the surface. Turtles slither off their logs.

We find the river—up here it's only a brook—and wind slowly down through grass banks, tamarack, and pine. Sun alternates with shower. There are noises in the brush.

Turn east, turn north, turn south, and west. You'd think a river had no purpose. But we can trust the Mississippi. We know that regardless of where it wanders, it will finally take us

to our farm. We portage around rapids. Clouds pinken in the west. Spaces between tree trunks darken. We ground our boat, pitch our tepee tent, and light the cooking fire.

Flames play with forest shadows. Two bass fry in the pan. An owl hoots in the distance. Water gurgles over stones. We stand in smoky air to keep mosquitoes away, and eat, and talk—

THE *Spirit of St. Louis* bursts into brilliant sunlight, dazzling to fog-accustomed eyes. The ocean is not so wild and spray-lashed. The wind's strength has decreased and shifted toward my tail. I nose down closer to the waves.

Brilliant light, opening sky, and clarity of waves fill me with hope. I've probably passed through the body of the storm. Clouds still lie ahead and on each side, but there are channels of clear air between, so future periods of blind flying should be shorter. I'm free of the instruments. I can look around again. The gravitation of life is strong.

The twenty-third hour. For over three hours I've entered nothing in the log. What difference does it make? The clerk-like details of a log are of trivial importance. I'm over ten hours out from Newfoundland. In less than eight hours more, if the wind holds and I'm not too far off course, I should strike the Irish coast. Eight hours is only a little longer than the trip between St. Louis and New York.

Sea, clouds, and sky are all stirred up together—dull gray mist, blinding white mist, patches of blue, mottling of black, a band of sunlight sprinkling diamond facets on the water. I fly above, below, between cloud layers, sometimes with my wings almost in the breakers' foam. It's like playing leapfrog with the weather. These cloud formations help me to stay awake. They give me something on which to fix my eyes in passing, but don't hold my stare too long.

The wind continues to decrease. I climb to 500 feet. Now and then I have to fly blind for a few minutes, but never for long. A cloud arches above me, like a great bridge. If I pulled back on the stick, I could almost loop around it. That would help to keep me awake. But looping bridges isn't part of a transatlantic flight—

SUNLIGHT FLASHES AS I EMERGE from a cloud. My eyes are drawn to the north. There, only five or six miles distant, a coastline parallels my course—purple, haze-covered hills; clumps of trees; rocky cliffs.

But I'm in mid-Atlantic, nearly a thousand miles from land! Have I been flying north instead of east? Is it the coast of Labrador or Greenland that I see?

I shake my head and look again—the shoreline is still there. But I couldn't have been flying north: the sun and the moon both rose on my left, and stars confirmed that my general direction was toward Europe. I know there's no land between Greenland and Iceland to the north and the Azores to the south. But I look down at the chart for reassurance, for my mind is no longer certain of its knowledge.

No, they must be mirages, fog islands sprung up along my route. But so apparently real! I bank north; then, before the *Spirit of St. Louis* turns ten degrees, I straighten out again. It's nonsense to be lured off course by fog islands. But if those islands aren't real, how will I recognize Europe when I reach it?

Another island lies across my route ahead, wooded and hilly. As I fly toward it, my eyes almost convince my mind that it *is* land. Then, like the desert mirage that turns to burning sand, shades of gray and white and purple disappear. Boulders are only shadows next to sunlight. Trees and rolling hills become crevasses in the fog. Beaches are but wisps of mist; and the surf, a line of whitecaps on the sea.

CLOUDS BREAK and lift as the angle of the sun increases. The horizon is now sharp and bright. Navigation can't be neglected any longer. Each apathetic hour adds hazard to my flight. I feel shame, like dull internal pain. I've believed that fatigue and hardship are the real tests of character; now, confronted by them, I'm failing. I'm capable only of holding my plane aloft, laxly pointed toward a heading I set some hours ago. No extra energy remains. I'm as strengthless as the vapor spirits to whom I listen.

The sun is out half the time now. Its rays beat down through the top window. My flying suit is uncomfortably hot. Behind me in the fuselage, the drift indicator is lying in its rack. The movement of an arm would slip it into the brackets on my window. I'd only have to line up its parallel hairs with the foam's apparent path. Then I could read off my exact angle of drift, and offset it on the compass. So simple. So impossible. Why did I think I could fly the *Spirit of St. Louis* straight while I lean out over the eyepiece of a drift indicator?

The twenty-fourth hour. But I won't bother starting to keep the log again. Its sequence has been broken, and the effort of filling in its columns is out of all proportion to any future value. The fuel valves can stay where they are, too—no need of shifting them each hour. I pencil one more fuel score on the instrument board, and go on struggling vaguely with my navigating problems.

Twenty-three hundred miles from New York. Thirteen hundred miles to Paris. Then it's only 700 miles to Ireland—probably not over 600 with the tail wind that's been blowing. I left Newfoundland—when did I leave Newfoundland? I seem no longer able to deal with figures. St. John's was 11¼ hours from New York, and I'm now 23 hours from New York . . . 11 from 23 is . . . twice 11 is 22 . . . then 11 and 12 make 23. Twenty-three . . . what do I want with 23? . . . I'll have to start again . . . in a minute or two, after my mind is clearer. . . . I'll let my mind rest, and start again.

I HAVE NOT been a good student at the University of Wisconsin. For just so long, I can sit and concentrate on work, and then I'm off to the shores of Lake Mendota; to the gymnasium swimming pool; to my motorcycle and distant country roads.

Eleven different schools I went to, from the District of Columbia to Redondo Beach in California, and there wasn't one that I enjoyed. Their memory chafes like a slipping rope against the flesh of childhood.

Ten years of school were like that—mining for knowledge, burying life—studying in grade school so I could pass examinations to get into high school—studying in high school so I could pass examinations to get into college—studying in college so—but there I broke the chain. Why continue studying to pass examinations to get into a life I didn't want to lead—a life of factories and drawing boards and desks? In the first half of my sophomore year I left college to learn to fly.

From the army flying school in Texas, I was graduated top man in my class. There, I'd really gotten down to business, worked on my studies. An Air Service pilot's wings were like a silver passport to the realm of light. With them went a second lieutenant's bars, and the right to fly all military airplanes.

Right rudder, fifteen degrees.

I SHIFT SIDEWAYS in the seat, move joints, tense muscles, hunt for a pad of flesh my bones haven't half pushed through. Any change, any stimulation helps. It's less a question of pain or pleasure than of attaining any feeling at all. I drink deeply from the canteen.

Now I'll get back to navigation. I'm twelve hours out from Newfoundland. At 100 miles an hour, that would put me less than 700 miles from the Irish coast. But with the tail wind, I may be within 400 miles of the Irish coast at this moment. No, it's better not to count on the wind. I'll calculate my course at an even 100 miles an hour and stay with my original estimate of navigation. But what correction shall I make for drift, for the detours around thunderheads?

Right rudder, ten degrees.

IT WAS IN THE ARMY flying schools that I learned the elements of navigation—how to swing a compass; how to lay a course.

I was barnstorming in southern Minnesota when I first heard about the Texas training fields of Brooks and Kelly. It was a summer evening in 1923. I was wiping off my Jenny's cowlings when a touring car drove up. The people in it were not passengers, as I had hoped. They came to watch, and talk of flying.

"How's business?" one of the men asked me.

"Not too good," I answered, going on with my work.

"This town's barnstormed out," the man continued. "Where are you going next?"

"First town with a good field near it."

"It must be a hard way to make a living. Why don't you enlist in the army as a flying cadet?"

"I've got a plane of my own. Why should I want to be a cadet?" I was annoyed by the implication that I lacked experience as a pilot.

"Oh, you can barnstorm around with OX–Five Jennies all right; but the only way you'll get to fly the big ones is to join the army. They train you on DHs with Liberty engines. You don't know what flying's like until you hold four hundred horses on your throttle."

He'd used the right bait. Who wouldn't want to fly a Liberty engine? I hung my gasoline-soaked rag over the drift wire. "If a commercial pilot enlists, can't he fly army planes without going to cadet school?"

"No, you have to go through the whole course. Takes a year, but you get a lieutenant's commission if you graduate—"

Right rudder, four degrees.

THE LURE of De Havillands and Liberties won out. I'd written a letter, obtained recommendations through my father, reported at Fort Snelling for an interview, and taken entrance examinations at Chanute Field, Illinois. Then Leon Klink and I flew south with his Canuck. Klink was an automobile dealer in St. Louis who'd been taking flying lessons at Lambert Field. He wanted to try cross-country flying, and I wanted to keep my hand in at the controls until I heard from the War Department about my examinations. We made many stops, for the fuel tank held only 23 gallons—enough to fly for two and a half hours. If we left a half hour in reserve for locating a field, which was often difficult, our plane had a range of 150 miles.

In Pensacola, Florida, I received notification from the War Department that I had passed my examinations satisfactorily. I was to report for enlistment in time to enter the March 15, 1924, class of flying cadets at Brooks Field, San Antonio.

It was a full month to the middle of March. "Why don't we work our way across to the Pacific?" I suggested to Klink.

"Whenever we find a place where a lot of people want to ride, we'll hold over and make some money."

Klink was always ready for adventure; the idea of a transcontinental flight appealed to him. We figured that if we averaged only one passenger flight a day, there was time to make California. I could enlist on the coast, and take a train back to Texas.

We added 10 gallons to the Canuck's gasoline capacity by lashing a cylindrical can, bought at a local hardware store, next to the fuselage on each lower wing. That gave us an hour more in the air. It was quite a job leaning out of the cockpit, into the slipstream, and unlashing one of those cans; and then lashing it back again, empty. But with the aid of a steam hose slipped over the nozzle, I hardly spilled a drop. This extended our range so greatly that we were able to follow the Gulf of Mexico's coast all the way to Pascagoula, Mississippi, before we landed. On the next flight we made New Orleans; then Lake Charles; then Houston, Texas. At Rice Field, outside of Houston, we found a hangar full of surplus army equipment. We bought three 9-gallon wing tanks, and attached them to the Canuck. With the regular fuselage tank and the two 5-gallon cans, this gave us a cruising range of about 400 miles.

At Brooks Field, San Antonio, our load-carrying troubles began. We'd filled both our cans and all our tanks with gasoline. We got into the air but the Canuck couldn't climb 50 feet aboveground. I landed, and we left one of the 5-gallon cans behind. Klink carried the other on his lap, to save air resistance.

There were no good fields around Camp Wood, Texas, our next stop, so we landed in the town square: the largest open area we could find that was smooth enough to land on. People came running from all directions as we taxied to a corner. Horses were hitched to posts; stores were locked; school was let out. A crowd surrounded the Canuck in no time at all. What was wrong? Where had we come from? Where were we going?

All would have been well if the wind hadn't veered southeast during the night; but the next morning, buildings blocked our takeoff direction from the square. There was a possibility that

I could use one of the adjoining streets as a runway. I looked over the street carefully, walking up and down its center. There was a depression a few hundred feet from the point where I'd have to start. To get off before the depression, I'd have to pass between two telegraph poles, about 50 feet from my starting point, and only two or three feet farther apart than the span of the upper wings.

One regularly drove a car between objects with only a few inches clearance. Why shouldn't it be done with an airplane? I marked the exact center of the street between the poles, and we pushed the Canuck into position.

I thought I was rolling precisely along the center of the street, but I failed by three inches to clear the right-hand telephone pole. The pole held my wing, while the plane's momentum carried the fuselage around and poked its nose right through the board wall of a hardware store. The propeller was shattered, of course, and the engine stopped at once. But pots and pans kept crashing down inside the store for several seconds.

The hardware dealer, instead of being angry, appeared quite pleased. When we tried to pay for the damage we'd done, he refused to accept a cent. The advertising value, he said, was worth much more than the cost of the few boards needed for repairs.

Aside from the propeller and wing tip, there was nothing broken on the Canuck. We wired Houston for a new prop and a can of dope to be expressed to Camp Wood. With the help of the crowd, we pushed our plane back into the square. Three days later, we were ready to start again. The wind blew in the right direction that morning, and we took off. The Canuck flew as well as ever.

A half hour before sunset we began looking for a place to come down for the night. There wasn't a town within sight, but beside the railroad ahead of us we saw a section house and three old boxcars which, we learned later, was Maxon, Texas. A quarter mile to the west lay a long, sloping, irregularly shaped area of relatively smooth ground. Clumps of cactus were scattered over it, but there was room for our wheels and wings to pass between them. We landed with an east wind. The section boss and a number of Mexican hired hands rushed over from the boxcars to meet us and help tie down the plane.

When we woke at Maxon, a westerly breeze was blowing down the slope of the prairie strip. A hill to the east prevented our taking off downwind; and rolling uphill would take so long to get flying speed that we'd be in sagebrush and cactus before our wheels left the ground.

Hiring some Mexicans to help us, we spent the entire morning cutting out a longer runway for the Canuck. We made an up-slope takeoff with only the main fuel tank full, but the plane had no power for climbing. The wheels, rising only about four feet, scraped through sagebrush.

We stalled over a gravelly wash and slapped through a clump of cactus leaves on the far side. Then a Spanish bayonet—a yucca plant with spine-tipped leaves—loomed up above the foliage ahead. It was too late to land. I was too low to bank. I tried to zoom, but pulling the stick back did no good. As wing and trunk collided, I jerked the throttle closed, to crash. The six-inch trunk of the plant smashed fabric, nose, and spar. I'd expected it to shear right through our wing; but the bayonet imbedded itself in the middle of the panel, and rode on with us through the brush—green blades rising from the parchment-colored fabric like an orchid on a limb.

The landing gear bumped along without collapsing as sage and cactus brought us to a stop. We climbed out to find our damage extraordinarily light. Some turnbuckles needed tightening, and we had a few long tears in the fabric on the under surfaces of the wings, but except for the area the bayonet went through, not a single rib was shattered.

Our attention had been so concentrated on the plane that we didn't notice a freight train stop on some tracks 100 yards away.

The fireman was running toward us. "Need any help there?" he shouted as he jumped over cactus. "We were afraid somebody got hurt," he added breathlessly as he came closer.

"Thanks, but I guess there's not much help you can give us," I said. "We'll just have to patch the plane up again."

"You'll need to go to the city for repairs. Can't get anything out here, you know. We'll take you along in the cab if you like. But we gotta start right off—have to get the track clear."

"You climb on board and get what material you can," I told Klink. "I'll stay and work on the plane."

Klink went all the way to El Paso to get dope, two lengths of crating board, some nails and screws, a can of glue, several balls of chalk line, and enough cotton cloth to repair the wings. We borrowed an axe, a butcher knife, a needle, and a spool of thread from the section boss. We hewed the crating boards down roughly to size with the axe, cut them into proper lengths with an old hacksaw blade from our engine's tool kit, and whittled off edges, thick spots, and splinters with the butcher knife. We used up most of our dope shrinking the cord wrapping. The body of the wing patch, and the long rents in wing fabric which I'd sewed together while Klink was away, had to be left flabby and untreated.

I scraped up over the cactus on my next takeoff attempt at Maxon. It was close, but a steady east wind helped, and the front cockpit was empty. We'd been on the ground for eight days. Our time had run out. Klink had decided to go on to California by train, while I flew back to Brooks Field.

Right rudder, seven degrees.

THE CANUCK was in sorry shape when I landed on Brooks Field. The airstream's whipping had worn away undoped cloth until several square feet of skeletal ribs and spars were exposed. The rips I'd sewn up were frayed and sagging, and one wheel had no tire—I'd pulled it off after the inner tube had ripped beyond repair.

I'd hoped to recondition the plane in spare hours, but the commanding officer held a different view. I was sitting on my barracks bunk when his messenger arrived. There were a dozen other cadets in the bay.

"Which one of you fellers flies that plane that's out in the hangar?" demanded the corporal who'd been sent to inquire.

"I do." I stood up as I spoke. All eyes turned on me—here was a cadet who was actually a pilot. I felt wise and proud.

"Major says get that damn thing off Brooks Field." The stern-faced corporal wheeled and left, heels clicking on the oiled wood floor.

I took off again on a tireless wheel, aileron dropped to make up for missing fabric. Fortunately, Stinson, a commercial airfield, was only a mile or two away, and they were glad to have me leave the plane for repair. It meant business, and any aircraft that could land was welcome.

Our flying training started in April of 1924. I was assigned to a lanky sergeant named Bill Winston—good-natured, skillful, cautious—one of the finest pilots on Brooks Field. The Hisso-Jennies the army used for training were like the civil aircraft I'd been piloting, except that they were heavier and carried their throttles on the left side of the fuselage.

A new plane, and changing hands on the stick, threw me off a little; my first landing was not three-point. But Master Sergeant Winston turned me loose for solo after three rounds of the field. "You know how to fly all right," he said. "You've just got to get used to this Jenny. Later on I'll try you out in acrobatics."

In Texas, I was in the unique position of being an army student at Brooks and a civilian instructor at Stinson. As soon as Klink returned from California, I began showing him the techniques he would have to use in getting the Canuck back to St. Louis. I spent mornings practicing acrobatics, sat through hours of ground school in the afternoon, instructed in the evening, and studied at night.

There was so little contact between army and civilian personnel in the area that I don't think the officers at Brooks knew I flew at Stinson. A mile of mesquite and cactus divided the two fields as though it were an ocean. And in many ways they seemed continents apart. At Brooks, you walked erect, saluted, made sure your uniform was properly buttoned. The grounds were neat, the barracks swept, the hangars in perfect order. Then you took a winding, cactus-studded path—it was so hidden that you had to know exactly where it started—and ended up where there wasn't any discipline at all. Stinson's flyers wore what they liked; paper scraps and pop bottles littered hangar corners; wrecks of airplanes lay around like unburied skeletons on the prairie grass.

At Brooks, by the end of June, nearly half of our class had been washed out. Those of us who remained felt like veterans, though by no means secure. We had close to eight months more.

Photography, motors, map making, radio theory, military law—twenty-five courses we took in our first half year of training. Somehow the schedule dropped behind, so they worked us Saturdays, too. Lectures on navigation, meteorology, and rigging alternated with formations, transition, and cross-country flights.

Eight degrees right rudder.

IN SEPTEMBER, thirty-three "veteran" cadets moved ten miles westward, from Major Royce's Brooks to Major Hickam's Kelly Field, for advanced training. We left Jennies behind. Kelly's students flew De Havillands. "Now just remember, DHs aren't built like Jennies," we were told. "They've got power to pull you through more; but if you once stall them, it takes a lot of altitude to recover. And you can't stunt them—no rolls or loops. Their wings aren't tied on that strong; if you pull the stick back too hard, they're liable to leave you."

We were trained in gunnery and bombing; taught how to intercept enemy aircraft, hold tight formations, follow signals quickly in the air. At graduation, as commissioned officers, we were all assigned to one of the air service's four branches—pursuit, bombardment, observation, or attack. I'd aimed for pursuit, and I got it.

THE SUN blinks on again in my cockpit. The cloud's shadow has passed. The ocean stretches ahead to the horizon, its brilliance smarts my eyes. This dawn-created stupor should have vanished with the morning twilight. Why can't I break these elastic bonds of sleep? The day will grow no brighter, and I'm still carrying on the vaguest kind of navigation. I'm losing time. I'm losing fuel—mixture control and throttle are only roughly set. My eyes stay shut for too many seconds at a time.

Crash landing in Leon Klink's Canuck

Kelly Field bomb range

Operations office,
Brooks Field

C.A.L.'s barracks, Brooks Field

JOIN THE
ARMY AIR SERVICE
BE AN AMERICAN EAGLE!

CONSULT YOUR LOCAL DRAFT BOARD. READ THE ILLUSTRATED BOOKLET AT ANY RECRUITING OFFICE, OR WRITE TO THE CHIEF SIGNAL OFFICER OF THE ARMY, WASHINGTON, D. C.

I strike my face sharply with my hand. It hardly feels the blow. I strike again with all the strength I have. My cheek is numb, but there's none of the sharp stinging that I counted on to wake my body. No jump of flesh, no lash on mind.

Paris is over a thousand miles away! I must be prepared to strike a fog-covered European coast hundreds of miles off course; and, if necessary, to fly above clouds all the hours of another night. How can I pass through such ordeals if I can't wake my mind and stir my body? Can I even reach the Irish coast? The alternative is failure and death! *Death! For the first time in my life, I doubt my ability to endure.*

The stark concept of death has more effect than physical blow or reasoned warning. It imbues me with enough power to communicate the emergency to my body's senses, to whip them from their lethargy. *Life itself is at stake.* This time I'm not just saying so. *I know it.*

I shake my head and body. I flex arms and legs, compress muscles of chest and stomach, stamp feet on floorboards, bounce up and down. *I'll break this spider web of sleep!* But what I need most of all is *breath*—the instrument board is vague—my brain swims—

Instinct tells me the key to life is air. I lean to the side of the cockpit, grip the sill, push my head dizzily out. Am I gliding or climbing? Is one wing down? Waves are gone from the ocean—there's no horizon to the sky. I'm passing out—maybe it's carbon monoxide from the exhaust—

The fresh blast of the slipstream washes over my face, rushes into my mouth and nostrils, forces my eyelids open, fills my lungs with breath. Can I hold on to consciousness? I must—I'm too close to the water—less than 100 feet—to let go for an instant. Breathe deeply, force the eyes to see. Each gulp of air is medicine—but has it time to work? There's not enough area to my lungs—sea, sky, and instruments merge in night— God give me strength—

No, I'm not going over the precipice. The ocean is green again, the sky's turning blue, clouds are whitening. Instrument faces stare at me, numbers come in focus. I've been hanging over the chasm of eternity, holding on to the ledge with my fingertips; but now I'm gaining strength, consciousness is coming back.

The *Spirit of St. Louis* is climbing slowly. My mind and my senses join. The seriousness of the crisis has startled me to awareness. I've finally broken the spell of sleep. The sight of death has drawn out the last reserves of strength.

I feel as though I were recuperating from a severe illness. It's like knowing the crisis has passed. The fever leaves; a sense of health returns, and you feel increasingly normal. You become aware of life's quality again. I sit quietly, looking out, letting confidence build up. How beautiful the ocean is; how clear the sky is; how fiery the sun! Whatever coming hours hold, it's enough to be alive this minute.

I'm wide awake. In three minutes it will be 7:52, New York time, the beginning of the twenty-fifth hour. I watch the hand creep forward—7:50 . . . 7:51 . . . 7:52—exactly one day since takeoff. At this moment yesterday, I'd just cleared the telephone wires at the end of the runway on Long Island.

I mark another fuel line on the instrument board, and turn to navigation. I have a strong impression that I've drifted south. I unfold the charts on my knees, and begin to estimate the southward factors.

First, the detours around thunderheads during the night. It seemed a great distance at the time, but as I look back from the objectivity of day and sunlight, I remember that most of my detours were only fifteen or twenty degrees to the southward. After the moon rose, I made several to the north in partial compensation. Probably the distance deviated from my route was somewhere between 25 and 50 miles. But the stars lure a pilot southward with their movement through the heavens, when he follows them, no matter how stubbornly he tries to compensate by change in heading. I'll add an estimated 10 to 20 miles to southward for this.

The next factor is one I don't know how to estimate. The compass swinging seemed as much one way as the other in the magnetic storm. I took for granted that the card was in its right position during the steadier periods. What else could I do? This factor I'll class as an unknown, an X quantity in my equation.

The last factor, which disturbs me most of all, is the direction and velocity of the wind aloft. I flew over clouds for seven hours, at high altitude, without any indication of the wind. I have reasons to hope that a strong tail or quartering tail wind blew me far along. Possibly it also drifted me many miles southward. This, too, must be treated as an X quantity.

Now, the northward compensations. For the last seven hours I've been lax about changing compass headings. That would leave me somewhat north of the course on my chart, but probably not over 5 or 10 miles. Much more important is the northward error caused by hours of lethargic and inaccurate flying, when the compass needle leaned so far and so frequently to the left of its lubber line. How far this carried me off course is as uncertain as the wind drift. But it was definitely to the north. And since an estimate must be made, I'll put it at between 25 and 50 miles.

My equation contains southward errors of 35 to 70 miles, northward errors of 30 to 60 miles, and two X quantities. The most practical approach to a solution seems to lie in assigning probable maximum values to the X quantities—first in one direction and then in the other.

Suppose the wind blew constantly from the north at 50 miles an hour. In seven hours I would have drifted 350 miles southward. Adding 70 miles for thunderhead detours and star-steering errors would make 420 miles. If I allow 50 miles for compass swinging, it brings the total to 470 miles. From this must be subtracted the 25 miles estimated minimum error caused by faulty flying. That leaves 445 miles. And finally, there's the estimated minimum of 5 miles I angled northward because the compass heading wasn't changed. The result gives me a probable maximum southward error of about 440 miles.

I look down at the chart. Four hundred and forty miles would take me off the edge of the strip. If I'm that far south and hold my present heading, I'll strike the coast of Europe where the Bay of Biscay scallops farthest into France—and after darkness. I'll have to fly over half a thousand more miles of ocean than if I make my landfall on the Irish coast. It will be hard to locate my position even if the moon shines through a clear sky.

Maybe it would be better to turn twenty degrees northward, even though I strike Ireland well above my route. Then I'll have a good chance of locating my position before darkness. If I can do that, I'll find my way to Paris through the blackest night.

But suppose a south wind blew at 50 miles an hour above the clouds last night. It's possible that the *Spirit of St. Louis* is north of course: 350 miles for wind, plus 50 miles for letting the compass needle wander, plus 50 miles for swinging, plus 10 miles for not changing my heading on time, makes a total of 460 miles. Subtracting 25 miles for detouring the thunderheads and 10 miles for following the stars leaves 425 miles. If I'm that far north of route, I'll hit the Scottish coast. If I subtract another twenty degrees from my heading, on a mistaken theory that I'm too far south, I may miss the British Isles entirely! That would mean striking the foggy, fjorded coast of Norway in the night.

Suppose, which thank God is probable, that the wind aloft was both strong and tail. If it blew 50 miles an hour from the west, I'm within 300 miles of Ireland at this moment. Then there's no need to turn northward; even if I'm south of course, I'll strike the French coast before nightfall.

Certainly any major change in heading involves a dangerous risk. It seems wisest to fall back on the basic plan of navigation I laid out in San Diego: compensate only for known and highly probable factors until I estimate my position to be 100 miles east of the meridian cutting the western Irish coast. At that time, if land is still unsighted, subtract thirty degrees from my heading. Then, regardless of how the winds blew or how faulty my navigation had been, I could hardly miss striking somewhere on the western coast of Ireland, or the southern end of England, or the northern coast of France.

I'll estimate that I've averaged 120 miles an hour since I left Newfoundland. That would put me 1560 miles east of St. John's. Suppose I lost an hour in climbing, detouring, compass swinging, and poor flying. I'd be 420 miles from Ireland. I'll let my known northward and southward errors cancel out. They're all estimates, and there's not enough difference between them to justify a change in course.

So all those lethargic hours may not have been squandered. Maybe I haven't lost much efficiency by giving way to dreams and sleep. And by resting, I've built up strength to fit me for the morning, afternoon, and night. I'm probably better off than if I could have forced myself to stay alert. I settle back and let my eyes sweep leisurely over the sea and horizon on both sides. If I've drifted far south of my route, I may at any time see ships.

The sun is overhead, burning between clouds. I wish I could land and lie under the shade of my wing. Some of the pleasantest hours of my life have been spent in such shade—waiting for the Nebraska wind to calm when I was learning to fly; waiting for a fuel truck to drive out from some Missouri town; waiting for passengers on Kansas fields. It's a sociable place, under a wing, and good for business, too. People like to come and sit beside you. They start asking questions about flying, and telling about their farms. Pretty soon they begin kidding each other into taking a flight over town.

I SEE a sun-baked plateau near the city of Red Lodge in Montana. It's midafternoon. Cupid Lynch and I are sitting in the shade of our Standard's lower panel. We have been idle all day.

"It's too hot for anybody to fly now," I say. "Maybe we'll get some passengers this evening."

"Maybe we're going to get a passenger right now," Lynch says, pointing.

A car has left the main road, and is curving upslope toward our strip of prairie. It is large, new, and brightly painted. The car skids to a showy stop, and a tanned man, wearing a Stetson, springs out. He looks like a rancher. Lynch and I get to our feet to meet him. The stranger's eyes sparkle and his teeth show white as he strides toward us.

"Howdy! Turner's my name. What'll ya charge to fly me over the town?" he asks.

"Ten dollars" Lynch tells him.

"That's a deal."

We strap our passenger down tightly in the front cockpit, and Lynch takes off between patches of prickly pear.

Close to a quarter hour passes before the Standard returns.

The rancher, beaming, jumps down from his cockpit, hands Lynch a ten-dollar bill, walks jauntily to his car, and spins his wheels over the gravel to a skidding, jack-rabbit start.

"Slim, in all the years I been flying, I never had a ride like that." Lynch's face is half amused, half serious, as we search for cactus-free ground under the wing. "I've heard about fellows like him, but I never met one before. After we got in the air, he twisted around and shouted: 'TAKE ME LOW DOWN THE MAIN STREET.' We were charging him a pretty fair price for the flight, so I just couldn't say no. I took a chance on the engine cutting, and flew him along the storefronts, about a hundred feet high. Everybody in town was running out and looking up. First thing I know, the son-of-a-bitch pulls out two pistols and begins shooting past the wings. He had the guns empty before I could do a damn thing. While we're taxiing in, he turns around with that grin all over his face and yells: 'I SHOT THIS TOWN UP A'FOOT, AN' I SHOT THIS TOWN UP A'HOSSBACK, AN' NOW I SHOT THIS TOWN UP FROM A AIRPLANE.'"

THE TWENTY-SIXTH HOUR. I'm cruising at 1575 rpm, at an airspeed of 93 miles an hour. By now the engine has burned about 300 gallons of fuel. The *Spirit of St. Louis* is light enough to throttle down still farther, possibly to 1525 rpm. To get maximum range, it's necessary to take a little less power from the engine with every hour that passes. I reach for the throttle, but specters of fog and darkness rise in my mind. I hope to reach the coast of Europe before dark. If I throttle down, I may not.

Fifty rpm could make the difference between day and night. Shall I build up a fuel reserve against the possibility of spending the entire night over a fog-covered continent? Or shall I draw on my reserves now to increase the probability of a daylight landfall? Security and caution demand the conservation of fuel. Success and adventure argue for a higher speed. With plenty of fuel, I can get down without a crack-up, regardless of the weather. Flying faster will give me a better chance of finding Paris.

But if security were my prime motive, I'd never have begun

this flight at all—I'd never have learned to fly in the first place. I open the throttle to 1650 rpm, reset the mixture control, and watch the indicator needle rise 7 miles an hour. It seems very little extra speed for such a sacrifice, but it will add up to 50 miles by sunset.

I see a dark object moving through the water. I search the surface—yes, there it is again, a porpoise, the first living thing I've seen since Newfoundland. Fin and sleek, black body curve gracefully above the surface and slip down out of sight.

The ocean is as desolate as ever. Yet a complete change has taken place. I feel that I've safely recrossed the bridge to life—broken the strands which have been tugging me toward the universe beyond. Why do I find such joy, such encouragement in the sight of a porpoise? What was there in that flashing glimpse of hide that means so much to me, that even makes it seem a different ocean? Is there some common tie between living things that surmounts even the barrier of species?

This ocean, which for me marks the borderland of death, is filled with life; life that's foreign, yet in some strange way akin; life that welcomes me back from the universe and makes me part of the earth again.

Nine fifty-two on the clock—the twenty-seventh hour since takeoff. The compass needle leans toward one side. I nose back onto course. Somehow I still can't keep the plane from swinging left, from following my instinctive feeling that Ireland lies north. I decide to do nothing but watch the compass needle.

It's like the first cross-country flight I made as pilot of my own airplane. I was so busy studying the map and trying to make it correspond to the ground below, that I let my plane veer off course just as the *Spirit of St. Louis* is veering now.

That was in May, 1923. I was on my way home to Minnesota with a Jenny I'd bought at Souther Field in Georgia. I'd gone there with a few hundred dollars in my pocket, in checks and cash. "That's a good place to buy Jennies cheap," I'd been told.

I'd paid five hundred dollars for my Jenny. It was more than I planned on, but only half the price first asked; and I got a brand-new Curtiss OX-5 engine in the deal, a fresh coat of olive drab dope on all surfaces, and an extra 20-gallon tank installed in the fuselage. My father had helped me buy the Jenny, so I still had money left for the trip home, and I hoped to make at least out-of-pocket expenses by taking up passengers in the towns where I landed.

When my Jenny was assembled and the paint all dry, I faced my greatest problem: I hadn't flown in six months, and I'd *never* soloed. Everybody at Souther Field assumed I was an experienced pilot when I arrived alone to buy a plane. They didn't ask to see my license, because you didn't have to have a license to fly an airplane in 1923. There were no instructors on the field, and anyway I didn't want to spend more money on instruction.

"Well, she's ready. When are you going to test her out?" The chief mechanic handed me my plane graciously with word and gesture. It was obvious that he expected me to say, "Let's push her out on the line." So that's what I said. After all, I'd had eight hours of instruction from Ira Biffle just one year before. I'd had a little "stick time" flying with Bahl, and a little more with Lynch. Souther Field was big and smooth. I thought I'd be able to get my Jenny into the air and down again without cracking up. I climbed into the cockpit, warmed up the engine, and taxied downwind to the farthest corner of the field.

How I wished I'd had my training in Jennies instead of Standards! I'd flown in a Jenny for only thirty-five minutes at the flying school, just enough to realize that it had quite a different feel.

There wasn't any halfway about flying. It wasn't like starting to drive an automobile. You couldn't stop if anything went wrong. Once you decided to take the air, you needed all the speed and power you could get. But I could taxi across the field a few times to get a little practice and a better feel of controls. I could lift the wheels two or three feet off the ground, cut the throttle, taxi back, and try again. After I gained confidence in my landing ability, I'd climb straight ahead and make a full circle of the field.

I headed directly into the wind and opened the throttle—cautiously. The Jenny swerved a little. I straightened out, opened the throttle more. The tail lifted up a bit too high. I pulled back on the stick—the tail skid touched; I pushed forward, pulled back—before I knew it, I was in the air! I cut the throttle—dropped too fast—opened it wide—ballooned up, right wing low—closed the throttle—yanked back on the stick—bounced down on wheel and wing skid.

Nothing broke, but it was a hard landing. I didn't want to repeat that experience. What an exhibition I'd made! And they'd probably been watching me from the line, too. They'd know now that I'd never soloed. I was sweating all over. I needed time to think. I decided to wait for a time when the air was completely calm. I wished I could have switched off the engine and stayed right there in the middle of the field, but of course the mechanics would have driven out in their cars to ask what the trouble was. I turned and taxied slowly back toward the hangars.

A stranger sauntered out to meet me—young, heavyset, and smiling—dressed in pilot's costume of breeches and boots. He said his name was Henderson. It was the first time I'd seen him on the field.

"Why don't you let me jump in the front cockpit before you try that again?" he said.

I could feel my cheeks turning red. "The air's a little rough, and I haven't flown since October," I replied. "I'm going to wait until it's smoother."

"Lots of pilots are in the same spot," he said, laughing. "It's pretty hard to make expenses through the winter. I'll give you some time while I'm waiting for the ship I bought. Don't worry," he added, "it won't cost you anything. I haven't much to do for the next day or two." He stepped into the front cockpit. I taxied out onto the field again and plunged up into air. It was a lot easier when I knew someone was there to check any serious errors I might make. I circled widely and came down to a two-point, bouncy landing. After a half-dozen takeoffs and landings, my new friend pulled back the throttle and said, "You won't have any trouble. You're just a little rusty from not flying for so long. Why don't you wait until the wind dies down this evening and then make a few hops yourself?"

It was nearly five o'clock when I started the engine again. The air was almost calm and there was no one on the field. I taxied out, took a last look at the instruments, and opened the throttle.

No matter how much training you've had, your first solo is far different from all other flights. You are hopelessly beyond help, entirely responsible, and terribly alone in space. There's no hand to motion the nose down before a stall, no other head to check your fuel or watch your rpm. You can choose your point of the compass, and fly on as long as you like. But if you get lost from your field, the penalty is more severe than words of reprimand and laughter.

I kept climbing that day, higher and higher, over red plowing, green forests, and shanty homes of Georgia. Souther Field, with its lines of buildings, shrank in size below me. I climbed until my altimeter needle covered the dot at 4500 feet. I might not have stopped climbing then, but the sun was almost touching earth, and dusk makes landing difficult for the amateur's eyes. I was happy to finish my first solo flight without cracking up.

I spent a week at Souther Field, practicing takeoffs and landings. Then I felt it was time to start barnstorming. I'd built up nearly five hours of solo, and my funds were getting low. I decided to detour west, through the southern states, to Texas, and then north to Minnesota. Every barnstorming pilot I knew had flown in Texas; it seemed to be a badge of the profession.

"You're heading over some of the worst territory in the South," a pilot told me when he heard of my plans. "If you're bound to go to Texas, I'd advise you to follow the Gulf Coast."

But my engine was new; and my inexperience great. I'd not be bluffed by a few swamps and hills. Surely, with more than four hours of fuel in my tanks, I'd be able to find fields large enough to land on. It would be interesting to see what the South's worst flying territory was like.

I sent my suitcase home by Railway Express. Then I rolled up an extra shirt, a pair of breeches, a toothbrush, some sox, spark plugs, tools, and other spare equipment in a blanket, and strapped the bundle down in the front cockpit with the seat belt. On a May morning I took off and set course for Montgomery, Alabama.

I made Meridian, Mississippi, before sunset, and headed west again the following morning. The sky was full of great white clouds, the horizon broken by local storms. For half an hour, I saw no checkpoint on the ground that conformed with the small-scale map I had bought in a drugstore. Then I put too much significance in the angling tracks of a railroad, and changed my course to the right. I kept on flying in a direction I thought was westward. I had no compass. I'd bought one the day before I left Souther Field. But in my hurry to get started I'd wrapped it in my blanket roll, planning to install it sometime when weather held me on the ground. Now it was out of reach.

The territory below grew wilder—mostly swamp and timber. Storms became thicker and heavier. After an hour had passed, I decided to land, ask where I was, and fill up my tanks. The fields below were small, hilly, and most of them plowed. To land in furrows meant an almost sure nose-over for a Jenny. At last I found a pasture that had two well-sodded slopes, with a small meadow between. I circled, landed, coasted down the near slope, across the meadow, and stopped rolling halfway up the slope on the far side. I felt highly professional.

A small but dark storm area was drifting in my direction, and only a mile or two away. I wanted to get my plane into a grove of pine trees at one side of the slope behind me, and tie the wings down before strong wind gusts arrived. So I opened my throttle, and taxied across the little meadow at the highest speed I dared. It was too late to stop when I saw a ditch ahead, almost completely hidden by grass. I had barely time to pull the throttle shut. There was the crash of wood as my wheels dropped in and the propeller struck the ground. The tail rose like a seesaw until it was almost vertical.

I climbed out and surveyed the damage. The plane was splattered with mud, but nothing was broken except the propeller. Raindrops began to patter on fabric. Treetops were boiling in the wind. Several men and boys came running up.

"What's the name of the nearest town?" I asked.

"Well, if you go northeast, you come to Maben. If you go southwest, you come to Mathiston."

"What's the closest big city?"

Refueling Jenny while barnstorming

Mrs. Lindbergh, Sr. in southern Missouri

Countryfolk gathered to see an airplane

"Well, if you go about a hundred miles south, you come to Meridian. That's about the biggest one we got around here."

Meridian, Mississippi! That's where I'd started from—I'd flown *north* instead of west! I had thought I was in Louisiana.

By that time a crowd was assembling in spite of the rain—old people, young people, babies, and dogs. We hauled down the fuselage and pushed my Jenny out of the ditch into the grove of pines. I tied the wings to trees, and rode into Maben with a storekeeper who had locked up his place of business when he heard of my landing and driven out to see for himself what had happened.

Before leaving Souther Field, I'd invested twenty dollars in two extra propellers as a safeguard for my summer's barnstorming. I telegraphed for one of them to be expressed to Maben. Then I checked into Maben's hotel. The next afternoon, I installed the compass in my cockpit.

Four degrees right rudder.

THREE DAYS LATER, the new propeller arrived. I lapped it onto the engine shaft, while a large part of the population of Maben, Mathiston, and the surrounding country watched me work.

On the test flight, my takeoff was easy, and my landing fairly good, but constant rains had kept the field soft. I taxied back carefully around the ditch end, and announced that I was ready for passengers. While I was waiting for the propeller, I had talked half a dozen townsmen into promising to fly with me. Most of them were right there, gathered around my plane.

It took several minutes of persuasion to get the first Mississippian in my cockpit. After that, they came fast. I stopped my engine only when it was necessary to pour gasoline in the tanks. That day, I took in enough money to pay for new propeller, gasoline, and hotel bills, and leave me a profit besides.

I stayed in Maben for two weeks, and carried close to sixty passengers. People flocked in from the surrounding country. Some traveled for 15 miles in oxcarts, just to see my Jenny fly. I could have carried many more passengers, but the rains continued, and each flight rutted the meadow until the Jenny didn't have enough power to pull through the mud. I had looked over the surrounding country for a better field, but there was none. I said good-by to my southern friends and headed west again, for Texas.

How simple it all was! If you got lost, you landed and inquired; if you were short of fuel, you phoned the nearest oil company to send out a truck. If you were tired, you stretched out on the grass; and if you wanted to sleep, you slept.

I'm five degrees off course. Got to be more careful.

AT MARSHALL, MINNESOTA, I joined my father. He was running as a candidate for the United States Senate that year. I had suggested that he make some of his campaign trips in my Jenny, and he had agreed to the idea. Now I was to take him for his first ride in an airplane.

If Father had any fear of flying, he didn't show it, although I thought his lips were tighter set than usual when I strapped him down. He began his aerial campaign that day by throwing out printed circulars above the town. Our handbills hit the town; he enjoyed the ride, and started plans immediately for going up again.

That also was the year I landed at our Minnesota farm. I'd looked forward to bringing my own airplane home ever since I began flying. It was a luxury to which I'd promised to treat myself as soon as I'd made a little extra money and developed enough skill. By early fall I felt I'd amassed enough of both. I barnstormed my way north, past Minneapolis, past St. Cloud, and pointed my nose one morning in the direction of Little Falls.

There it is, lying nakedly below me, river and creek, fields and woodlands—our farm. It has never fully exposed itself to my eyes before. How well I know each detail! How little I've understood the whole! In the past, I've seen our farm as a surgeon views his patient—all parts hidden but the one on which he works. Now, I embrace its entire body in sight and consciousness at once. I see the bare curves of our western hill, the dells of our eastern twenty. Cow trails tie barn to pasture, gate to gate, wind in and out through trees.

I gauge the wind's direction from silvered poplar leaves, stall over the fence, land tail skid first, stop rolling with plenty of room to spare.

Daniel Thompson, our old Norwegian hired hand, comes to meet me. He stands looking first at the plane, and then at me, and then chuckles in a sort of bewilderment. Of course he knows I learned to fly last year, and he's used to seeing me drive all sorts of farm machinery; but the airplane resting here where we used to unhitch our hay wagon is almost too much for him.

"How's the farm, Thompson?" My eyes sweep over the neglected field.

"All in weeds."

It's true. There are no crops in the fields, no wheel marks on the road that crosses the creek, no fresh cow dung on the path we follow. The house is padlocked. Our tenants had failed to make a living on the farm, and had left.

"They're starting to cut timber in the valley," Thompson says as we walk toward the house.

Yes, I know. The survey for the new Pike Rapids dam showed that our valley would be flooded, so all the trees will have to go—the great white oak where my father and mother camped while the first house was being built, the crabapple orchard by the riverbank, the tall linden whose branches filtered stars.

I knew that day that childhood was gone. My farm on the Mississippi would become a memory, of which, sometime, I'd tell my children, just as my father told me of his fields and forests on Sauk River. As the modern railroad divided his family homestead, a modern dam would submerge the acres of our farm.

I SHIFT ARMS on the stick. My left hand, now free and aimlessly exploring the pockets of the chart bag, fingers the shiny little first-aid kit and the dark glasses given me by that doctor on Long Island. I hook the wires over my ears and look out on a shaded ocean. It's as though the sky were overcast again. I don't dare use the glasses. They're too comfortable, too pleasant. They make me want to sleep.

I slip the glasses back into their pocket, pull out the first-aid kit, and idly snap it open. It contains adhesive tape, bandages, and a pair of scissors. Not enough to do much patching after a crash. Tucked into one corner are several capsules of aromatic ammonia—smelling salts. If they revive people who are about to faint, why won't they revive people who are about to fall asleep? A whiff of one of these capsules should sharpen the dullest mind and sting the sleep from eyes.

I crush a capsule and hold it cautiously several inches from my nose. There's no odor. I move it closer, slowly, until finally it touches my nostrils. I smell nothing! My eyes don't feel the slightest sting, and no tears come to moisten their dry edges. I inhale again with no effect, and throw the capsule out the window. I realize how deadened my senses have become, how close I must be to the end of my reserves.

I lean out into the slipstream again, to breathe the fresher air. I nose down to the water, gliding along swiftly with lightened fuel load and faster turning engine. I force the wheels as close as I dare to the waves, playing with their crests to stimulate my senses. I sharpen the blade of skill on the stone of danger.

I fly in tight formation with my shadow, less than 10 feet above the waves. I'm tempted to touch tires on the water to break monotony and see spray fly up. Is that a piece of driftwood? No, it's moving; it's a gull, wheeling low over the waves. A second sign of life! I twist around to watch the flapping wings pass behind my tail. There's another gull in the distance, a speck rising and lowering against the southern sky. This is becoming a populated ocean. What are gulls doing here so far from land? I've heard that they follow ships all the way from America to Europe, dropping down to pick up scraps of refuse. Then have I drifted south to the ship lanes? But there's not a ship in sight; not a sign of refuse on the surface.

The shadows in my cockpit assume a different angle. The wind decreases. Foam no longer streaks the sea. Cumulus clouds mirror white on the deep blue water. A light haze replaces midday's crystal clarity. Gray areas in the distance mark scattered squalls; they're ominous, and not many miles away.

I've already spent fuel to increase my chance of a daylight landfall, so it's essential to stay underneath the clouds. I'll climb above them only as a last resort. Even if the sky becomes completely overcast the cloud base may stay high. If I can see only a few miles when I strike the coastline, I should be able to locate my position in daylight.

If vision is cut down by haze, I'll fly low over the first town I come to, and let the signboards tell me which country I'm in. Maybe I can read the name of the town on the railroad station, as I've done so often on cross-country flights at home.

The greatest test of my navigation will come if I make a landfall in darkness, when hills merge into valleys and railroad intersections are impossible to see. Then I'll have to establish my position from the general contour of the coast—the bays, the peninsulas—and set a compass course from the lights of one major city to those of another, checking the distance between them against the airspeed and the clock. If I find my position to be on the coast of northern Ireland, for instance, I'll set course first for Dublin, then for Birmingham, next London, and finally for Paris. All four cities are so large that I should be able to find them if there's any ceiling at all.

I'M FLYING along dreamily when it catches my eye, that black speck on the water two or three miles southeast. I realize it's there with the same jerk to awareness that comes when the altimeter needle drops too low in flying blind. I squeeze my lids together and look again. A boat! A small boat! Several small boats, scattered over the surface of the ocean.

All drowsiness departs. I bank the *Spirit of St. Louis* toward the nearest boat and nose down. Fishing boats! *The European coast can't be far away!* Those little vessels are Europe. Are they Irish, English, Scotch, or French? What fishing bank are they anchored on? How far from the coast do fishing banks extend? Thoughts press forward in confused succession. After the hours of solitude, here's human life and help and safety.

I feel as secure as though I were circling Lambert Field. I could land alongside any one of those boats, and someone would throw me a rope and take me on board where there'd be a bunk I could sleep on, and warm food when I woke up.

The first boat is less than a mile ahead. I dive down 50 feet above its bow, dropping my wing to get a better view. There's no sign of life on deck. Can all the men be out in dories? I climb higher as I circle. No, there aren't any dories. I can see for miles, and the ocean's not rough enough to hide one. Are the fishermen frightened by my plane? Possibly they never saw a plane before. *Of course* they never saw one out so far over the ocean. Maybe they all hid below decks when they heard the roar of my engine. But if the crews are so out of contact with the modern world that they hide from the sound of an airplane, they must come from some isolated coastal village above which airplanes never pass. And the boats look too small to have ventured far from home.

I fly over to the next boat bobbing up and down on the swells. Its deck is empty, too. But as I drop my wing to circle, a man's head appears, thrust out through a cabin porthole, motionless, staring up at me. In the excitement and joy of the moment, I decide to make that fisherman come out of the cabin and point toward the Irish coast. No sooner have I made the decision than I realize its futility. He probably can't speak English. Even if he can, he'll be too startled to understand my message, and reply. But I'm already in position to dive down past the boat. It won't do any harm to try. I've talked to people before from a plane, flying low with throttled engine, and received as answer a nod or an outstretched arm.

I glide down within 50 feet of the cabin and shout:

"WHICH WAY IS IRELAND?"

How extraordinary the silence is with the engine idling! I look back under the tail, watching the fisherman's face for some sign of understanding. But an instant later, all my attention is concentrated on the plane. For I realize that I've lost the "feel" of flying. I open throttle, and watch the airspeed indicator while I climb and circle. As long as I keep the needle above 60 there's no danger of stalling. Always before, I've known instinctively just what condition my plane was in—whether it had flying speed or whether it was stalling, and how close to the edge it was riding. I didn't have to look at the instruments. Now, the pressure of the stick no longer imparts its message clearly to my hand.

When I pass over the boat a third time, the head is still at the porthole. It hasn't moved or changed expression since it first appeared. I feel baffled. Why don't the fishermen gather on the decks to watch my plane? Why don't they pay attention to my circling and shouting? These aren't vessels of cloud and mist. They're tangible—sails furled, ropes coiled neatly on the decks, masts swaying back and forth with each new swell. Yet the only sign of crew is that single head, hanging motionless through the cabin porthole.

I want to stay, to circle until the crew comes out on deck. I want to see them standing and waving. Since my last contact with other men, I've been planets and heavens away, until only a thread was left to lead me back to earth and life. I've followed that thread with swinging compasses, through lonely cloud canyons, over pitfalls of sleep, past the lure of enchanted islands, fearing that at any moment it would break. Now I've returned to earth, and I want an earthly greeting, a warmer welcome.

Shall I fly over to another boat and try again to raise the crew? No, I'm wasting minutes of daylight and miles of fuel. I straighten out the *Spirit of St. Louis* and fly on eastward.

Land *must* be somewhere near. When I first saw those boats their bows seemed to point my direction like signposts, saying: "This way to Paris." But as I leave them behind, a few black dots on an endless waste of ocean, reason argues that I know nothing more about my latitude than I did before. They might be north of Scotland; they might be south of Ireland. They might be anywhere along the coast. There's no way to tell. And it's dangerous to take for granted that land is very near; even small boats sometimes venture far to sea. What can I do but continue on the course I set before?

Patches of blue sky above me are shrinking in size. To the north, heavier storm clouds gather.

TEN FIFTY-TWO A.M., New York time—about three o'clock in the afternoon here. The twenty-eighth hour is beginning. I keep scanning the horizon through breaks between squalls. Any one of those rain curtains may hide a ship or another fishing fleet. The air is cool, fresh, and pleasantly turbulent. I fly 100 feet or so above the ocean—now under open sky, now with rain streaming over wings and struts.

Is that a cloud on the northeastern horizon, or a strip of low fog? *Can it possibly be land?* Framed between gray curtains of rain, not more than 15 miles away, a purplish blue band has hardened from the haze: flat below, like a waterline, curving on top, as hills do.

If that's Ireland, I'm two and a half hours ahead of schedule. I don't intend to be tricked by another mirage; but I'm no longer half asleep. I bank the *Spirit of St. Louis* toward the nearest point of what might be land. I stare at it intently, not quite daring to believe my eyes, keeping hope in check to avoid another disappointment, watching the shades and contours unfold into a coastline—a fjorded coastline coming down from the north and bending toward the east. Barren islands guard it. Inland, green fields slope up the sides of warted mountains. This *must* be Ireland. It can be no other place than Ireland. The fields are too green for Scotland; the mountains too high for Brittany or Cornwall.

I climb to 2000 feet so I can see the contours of the country better and look for prominent features to fit the chart on my knees. The mountains are old and rounded, the farms small and stony. Rain-glistened dirt roads wind narrowly through hills and fields. Below me lies a great tapering bay, a long, bouldered island, a village. Yes, there's a place on the chart where it all fits—line of ink on line of shore—Valentia and Dingle Bay, *on the southwestern coast of Ireland!*

I can hardly believe it's true. I'm almost exactly on course, closer than I ever really hoped to come. The wind above the storm clouds must have blown fiercely on my tail. In edging northward, intuition must have been more accurate than reasoned navigation.

The southern tip of Ireland! Over two hours ahead of schedule; the sun still well up in the sky. I circle again. There's no question about it; every detail on the chart has its counterpart below. I spiral lower, looking down on the little village. There are boats in the harbor, wagons on the stone-fenced roads. People are running out into the streets, looking up and waving.

Here's a human welcome. I've never seen such beauty before—fields so green, people so alive, a village so attractive.

One appreciates only after absence. For twenty-five years I've lived on the earth, and yet not seen it till this moment. For nearly two thousand hours, I've flown over it without realizing what wonders lay below—snow-white foam on black rock shores, the hospitality of little houses, the welcome of waving arms. During my entire life I've accepted these gifts of God to man, and not known what was mine until this moment. It's like rain after drought; spring after a northern winter. I've been to eternity and back. I know how the dead would feel to live again.

I circle a third time, then straighten out. Only 600 miles to Paris. There are golden hours of the afternoon still left, and the long evening twilight. There'll be less of night to Paris than on a single flight over my airmail route in December. Now I'm dealing with distances and methods of navigation I can measure in terms of past experience, and if the weather holds, night flying will be easy.

I look ahead at the weather. There's only water ahead where land has been, and storms instead of breaking sky! What's happened? What's wrong now? The compass needle almost centers on its mark, and I've not changed the setting on the dial. It's too wrong; so terribly wrong there must be a simple answer. Collect thoughts, blink eyes, shake head—start again.

There *is* a simple answer. I look back; and there behind me, less than a mile away, lies Valentia and the Irish coast. I was watching first the earth and then the chart with such intentness that in straightening out, I took up the reverse heading to my course. I'm pointed back over the ocean, a hundred and eighty degrees from Paris!

I bank steeply around and set my course southeastward, cutting across the bouldered fjords, flying low over the hilltop farms, the rock fences, and the small, green fields of Kerry. I check the engine: all cylinders hitting. And all instrument readings are normal.

There's only one more island to cross—only the narrow tip of an island. I look at England's outline on my map. As Nova Scotia and Newfoundland were stepping-stones from America,

Ireland and England are stepping-stones to Europe. Yesterday, each strip of sea I crossed was an advance messenger of the ocean. Today, these islands below are heralds to a continent.

It's as though a curtain has fallen behind me, shutting off the stagelike unreality of this transatlantic flight. It's been like a theater where the play carries you along until you forget you're only a spectator. You grow unaware of the walls around you, of the program clasped in your hand, even of your body, its breath, pulse, and being. You live with the actors and the setting, in a different age and place. It's not until the curtain drops that consciousness and body reunite. Then, you turn your back on the stage, step out into the night, under the lights of streets, between the displays of store windows. You feel life surging in the crowd around you, life as it was when you entered the theater, hours before. Life is real; it always was. The stage, of course, was the dream. All that transpired there is now a memory, shut off by the curtain, by the doors of the theater, by passing time.

Striking Ireland was like leaving a theater—phantoms for actors; cloud islands and temples for settings. The ocean behind me is now an empty stage; the flight across is already like a dream. I'm over villages and fields, back to land and wakefulness and a type of flying that I know. I'm myself again; that third, controlling element has retired. My mind is again in command, and my body follows out its orders with precision.

THE TWENTY-NINTH HOUR. I run my eyes over the instruments and shift to the nose tank. I'll leave the nose tank on until it runs dry, so the center of gravity will be well to the rear if I'm forced down on some field along the coast. The heavier the tail, the less chance of nosing over. Also, I want to get a check on fuel consumption. None of the tanks has run dry yet, and I'm still figuring gallons per hour by theory.

The wind is strengthening; cumulus clouds mottle the sea with their shadows. Scattered squalls, one after another, emerge from the haze—light squalls, light haze, a clearing sky. I can see almost to the horizon. The mellowness of late afternoon blends with the approaching end of my flight. The heavy chores of the day—the great difficulties of the flight—are over. The remaining hours are routine. I have plenty of fuel, plenty of power.

It's incredible that so much weight can be moved through the air so far. The gasoline left in my tanks when I reach France will weigh more than all the mail one of our DHs can carry between St. Louis and Chicago. Why, if I had refueled at an airport in Newfoundland, and then refueled again in Ireland, I could have brought thousands of letters to Paris—a huge pay load!

The year will surely come when mail is flown every day from America to Europe. Airmail will cost much more than ship mail; but letters can be written on lightweight paper, and there'll be people with such pressing business that they can afford the higher price of postage. And improved aircraft should make flying safer. Weather will be the greatest problem. We'll have to find some way to fly through sleet, and land in fog.

Possibly everyone will travel by air in another fifty years. I'm not sure I like the idea of millions of planes in flight. Of course I want to see aviation develop into important branches of industry and commerce. But I love the sky's unbroken solitude. I don't like to think of it cluttered up by aircraft, as roads are cluttered up by cars. I feel like the western pioneer when he saw barbed-wire fence lines encroaching on his open plains. The success of his venture brought the end of the life he loved.

The engine jerks against its mounting! I stiffen as though I'd had an electric shock. Irregular spluttering replaces the exhaust's sharp rhythm. Instinctively I push forward on the stick and sit rigidly. Am I to be brought down on this trivial arm of ocean? Have I grown too confident, too arrogant?

But nothing serious is wrong. The nose tank simply ran dry, as I intended it to. I turn on the center wing tank, shut off the nose-tank valve, close the throttle and mixture control, and being working the wobble pump. The jerking and coughing stop. I ease the throttle forward. Power surges through the plane. The engine smooths out. The airspeed rises. I take up course.

IT'S THE THIRTIETH HOUR: 12:52 p.m., New York time; about 5:30 here. I'm just over four hours from Paris. By turning the engine faster, I can reach France before darkness. If there should be a thick haze beneath low clouds over the English Channel it would be difficult to cross at night, for there'll be few lights, and no differences in shading between air and water. But if I can reach the French coast in daylight, then only fog or violent storms can hold me back from Le Bourget.

I open the throttle to 1725 rpm and watch the airspeed mount to 110 miles an hour. That will take me to England well before sunset, and leave just enough time to get back to Ireland by dark if Cornwall is covered with fog.

Of course a return to Ireland would probably mean giving up a nonstop flight to Paris. There'd hardly be enough fuel left to circle through the night and then fly 600 miles after the fog cleared. A half hour ago, in the joy of my landfall, I felt that nothing would induce me to lose contact with the surface of the earth again. The security I'd regained seemed more important than any success I could achieve. But with each passing minute the idea of turning back becomes more repulsive. I begin reconsidering my decision not to climb above a fog. There may be fog over England and the Channel while the continent beyond is clear. After flying over storms and ocean, I'm not going to be defeated by a narrow strip of weather. No, I won't let a little fog frighten me now. I'll fly over Paris by dead reckoning if need be, and then decide whether to go on or turn back.

Judging from the nose tank, I have enough fuel to reach Rome. I can certainly get that far if this tail wind keeps blowing. How surprised people back home would be if I cabled them from Rome instead of Paris! I unfold the map of Europe. Rome is about 700 miles beyond Paris, and not far south of my great-circle route extended eastward. It's a shame to land with nearly a thousand miles of fuel in the tanks. Why waste all that gasoline after carrying it across the ocean? I could circle Paris, if it's clear, dip my wings, and fly on to Rome. Think of it: a flight of almost 4300 miles nonstop.

No, this flight is from New York to Paris; I planned and organized it with the intention of landing at Paris. I didn't start out to see how far I could fly. If Paris is covered with fog, that's different; then I can go on with a clear conscience. But first I must exert every effort to land at the destination I set.

ALL READINGS ARE NORMAL. The sky is broken, the sea light, the horizon veiled in haze. From my altitude of 1500 feet, I count half a dozen ships. At any moment now England's shoreline will be in sight.

For aviators approaching from the sea, a coastline appears in one of two guises. When air is crystal clear it announces itself delicately, subtly, as a fine, dark line, barely breaking the evenness of the horizon; rising, growing, flowering gradually, giving one plenty of time to adjust to its presence, its shades of color, its intricacies of character and shape. But in heavy haze or fog it can loom up with terrifying suddenness, not even leaving time to turn from its crushing impact. On one day, it uses the curvature of the earth as a cloak. On another, it veils itself with shades of mist and weather. Welcoming hills in sunlight are deadly bluffs in storm; and a summit higher than the rest may be either a flyer's beacon or his grave.

The coast of England is well above the horizon when I see its outline, pale and whitish in the haze. There's no fog over Cornwall. I can let go of Ireland completely, and move forward another notch in the ratchet of my calculations. If by any dwindling chance I still have to turn back from Paris, I now have England for a haven.

Above the sheer Cornish cliffs, rising straight up out of the sea, farm fields break off abruptly where their soil has tumbled down into encroaching waves. As a schoolboy I read of the slowly changing surface of the earth, of clam fossils found on hilltops, of glaciers building and melting, of land masses that disappeared, of drifting continents and dried-up seas. But all these things were measured on a time scale that made little impression on my mind—hundreds of centuries. Here, I see the earth actually in the modeling. The signs below are fresh and unmistakable. The road, the houses and barns on top of the cliff, are all set back from the precipice, leaving a strip of green fields along the edge, a few generations' worth of land to delay the inevitable collapse into sea.

One fifty-two p.m., New York time. The thirty-first hour begins. Cornwall is more populated and prosperous than Ireland, and less rugged. How different from America it is, with its miniature farms neatly divided by hedge and stone fences, and its narrow, sod-walled roads running crookedly between slate-roofed villages. How can a farmer make his living from fields so small? He'd barely get started with a plow before the hedge at the far end would turn him back. No wonder there are so many one-horse carts. It wouldn't pay to buy modern machinery for such acreage. A hundred of these fields would fit into a single Kansas wheat ranch.

It was from such farms and villages as these that Englishmen set out to build a new life in America. The men and women down below are children of those who stayed at home, still carrying on the traditions of our forefathers. I'm a child of those who left—flying back generations later. Most of my mother's forebears came from England. My great-great-grandfather, William Gibbon Lodge, sailed to America soon after the War of 1812. Our family's written records begin with his wife, Harriet Clubb, of Tunbridge, Kent. She had reservations in regard to Americans, to judge from her diary: "We walked about in the Battery Gardens," she wrote, soon after arriving in this country, "and had a good look of the American ladies, who are anything but pretty. They are small, scraggy, and rather prudish looking. Nature does not appear to have done so much for them as for the vegetation which is luxuriant in the extreme. The men are likewise far from being so good-looking or gentlemanly as the English."

Now it's *my* turn to get a first impression of the *English*. I drop down to 500 feet. People raise their heads as I fly over them. What do they think when they see my plane? Do any of them realize I've flown across the Atlantic, or do they regard me as simply a British pilot on a local flight? Even if they heard of my takeoff from their local radio or press, they wouldn't expect me to fly through their particular sky so soon.

There's the English Channel—shoreline darkening against pale gray of distant water. I've crossed England so quickly! It seems so small, in keeping with the miniature farms below. Why, I'll be over the sea again within twenty minutes of the time I struck the Atlantic Cornish coast! It's only three hours since I sighted Ireland. One more hour to the coast of France! I can't accustom myself to the short distances of the Old World. I look down at my map. All England is no larger than one of our midwestern states.

There, on my left, is Plymouth, and the same harbor from which the *Mayflower* once sailed, against weeks of adverse winds and hardships. Yesterday, I flew almost over Plymouth Rock, on the coast of Massachusetts. Beyond, the green, indented, rolling coast parallels my course for another thirty miles. The horizon is sharpening, and the sky ahead is clear.

From Start Point of England to Cape de la Hague of France is 85 miles. In the past, I would have approached an 85-mile flight over water with trepidation. This evening, it's just part of the downhill glide to Paris.

Haze slowly covers up the Channel coast behind. Only a few ships are left in sight. I start climbing—1000, 2000 feet. The sun behind me is low. This is the last water, this little bit of ocean.

The thirty-second hour. A strip of land, 10 miles or so in width, dents the horizon. Cape de la Hague—the coast of France! It comes like an outstretched hand to meet me, glowing in the light of sunset. From this very coast, thirteen days ago, Nungesser and Coli set out for the westward flight across the ocean. They took off from Le Bourget, where I am soon to land. Why were they lost? Were they caught at night in a mountainous cloud of ice? Could they have flown off through starlit passageways, and lost the thread of earth entirely? Aviation has great power, but how fragile are its wings. How slight a mishap can bring one down—a microscopic flaw in a fitting, a few crystals of ice in a venturi tube, the lack of an hour's sleep.

The sun almost touches the horizon as I look down on the city of Cherbourg, embracing its little harbor. France itself is 2000 feet underneath my wing. It's only 200 miles to Paris, and half of that will be in twilight.

I slip the Mercator projection into its pocket for the last time, and draw out the map of France. Ahead, the sky is clear. On my left, several ships punctuate the sea. On my right, chimney smoke points toward Paris. My route passes over 15 miles of land and then parallels the coast of Normandy to Deauville.

Before now, I haven't dared plan beyond landing on Le Bourget. What *will* I do after I land? First, of course, I'll get the *Spirit of St. Louis* put away in some hangar. Then, I'll send a cable home, giving my time of landing. The speed I've made will surprise everyone back there—nearly three hours ahead of schedule—an average of more than 100 miles an hour. After that, I'll find some place to spend the night. Everything else can go until morning.

These arrangements would be simple enough back home. They'll be more difficult in a foreign country—I don't speak a word of French. I didn't get a visa before I took off—I wonder how much trouble that will cause. I'm so far ahead of schedule that I may not find anybody waiting for me on the field. But one of the pilots or mechanics will probably speak a little English.

During the first two or three days there'll be newspaper interviews and photographs to endure. I'll have to buy a new suit of clothes, and a half-dozen odds and ends. I haven't brought even a toothbrush or an extra shirt with me. Later on, I'll take a day or two off to walk through the streets and buildings of Paris.

Possibly I can make a flying tour through Europe. It wouldn't be very expensive—mostly hotel bills and gasoline and oil. People over here will surely want to see the plane that's flown nonstop all the way from the United States to France. I can probably get permission to land wherever I want to go. I could fly to England, spend a day or two in London, and then hop over to Ireland—something draws me back to those green fields and boulders. I could go up to Scotland, visit Sweden, Denmark, and Norway, and stop off in Germany on the way. After that, there's still Russia—and Italy and Spain, and all those Balkan countries. When I'm ready to leave Europe, I can fly on around the world, through Egypt, and India, and China, until I reach the West by flying east.

As a matter of fact, how *will* I return home? *Why not* fly on around the world? The scarcity of airports in Asia is no problem for a plane that can fly 4000 miles nonstop. If I crossed the Pacific in the north, between Siberia and Alaska, I probably wouldn't ever need to take off with more than a half load of fuel. And haven't I barnstormed for weeks at a time without seeing an airport?

Flying on around the world would show again what modern airplanes can accomplish. Besides, it's beneath the dignity of the *Spirit of St. Louis* to return to the United States on board a boat. I'll make the westward flight back over the route I've just followed. There'd be head winds, of course, flying westward, and the danger of striking fog over Newfoundland and Canada. If I take off from Ireland instead of France, I might fly all the way to St. Louis nonstop. I can see the pilots and mechanics on Lambert Field running up to my plane.

"Where did you come from?"

"I came from Ireland."

"From Ireland—when did you leave?"

"I left yesterday."

I would say it all casually, just as though I'd landed on a routine mail flight from Chicago.

THE THIRTY-THIRD HOUR. Almost 3500 miles from New York. I've broken the world's distance record for a non-stop airplane flight. Southward lies the dusk-touched coast of Normandy. Little boats sail in toward shore, leaving only their wakes as signs of movement to an airman's eye. I cross the coast exactly on course, over Deauville. The western sky is still red with sunset. What more I see of France, before I land, will be in this long twilight of late spring. I nose the *Spirit of St. Louis* lower and study the farms and villages—the signs I can't read, the narrow, shop-lined streets, the walled-in barnyards, the well-groomed, fertile fields.

People come running out as I skim low over their houses—blue-jeaned peasants, white-aproned wives, children scrambling between them, all looking up to search for the noise above their roofs. Four twenty on the clock. That's nine twenty here. Why, it's past suppertime! I hold the stick with my knees, reach in the paper bag and pull out a sandwich—my first food since takeoff. I uncork the canteen. I can drink all the water I want now—plenty more below if I should be forced down between here and Paris. But how flat the sandwich tastes! It's an effort even to swallow. I'm hungry and I go on eating, but I have to wash each mouthful down with water.

Night is now masking out details on the ground. Color is gone. Only shades remain—woods darker than fields; hedgerows, lines of black. Lights twinkle in villages and blink in farmhouse windows. The rest of the flight will be in darkness. I climb to 2000 feet. A light flashes from the darkness, miles ahead. I stare at the area and wait. On our mail route at home, you count eleven between flashes. Another flash—yes, it's an air beacon! And there are two more, blinking dimly in the distance. It must be the airway between London and Paris. From now on everything will be as simple as flying into Chicago on a clear night.

Down under my left wing, angling in from the north, winding through fields submerged in night, comes the Seine, shimmering in the faint remaining light of evening. With the air clear and a river and an airway to lead me in, nothing but engine failure can now keep me from reaching Paris.

I throw my flashlight on the engine instruments. Every needle is in place. For almost thirty-three hours, not one of them has varied from its normal reading—except when the nose tank ran dry. For every minute I've flown there have been more than seven thousand explosions in the cylinders, yet not a single one has missed.

The *Spirit of St. Louis* is a wonderful plane. It's like a living creature, gliding along smoothly, happily, as though a successful flight means as much to it as to me, each of us feeling life and death as keenly, each dependent on the other's loyalty. *We* have made this flight across the ocean, not *I* or *it*.

Within the hour I'll land, and strangely enough I'm in no hurry to have it pass. I haven't the slightest desire to sleep. My eyes are no longer salted stones. There's not an ache in my body. I want to sit quietly in this cockpit and let the realization of my completed flight sink in. Europe is below; Paris, just over the earth's curve in the night ahead—a few minutes more of flight. It's like struggling up a mountain after a rare flower, and then, when you have it within arm's reach, realizing that satisfaction lies more in the finding than the plucking. Plucking and withering are inseparable. I want to prolong this culminating experience of my flight. I almost wish Paris were a few more hours away.

I'm at 4000 feet when I see it, that scarcely perceptible glow below, as though the moon had rushed ahead of schedule. Paris is rising over the edge of the earth. The thirty-fourth hour since my takeoff on Long Island will soon start. Myriad pinpoints of light emerge, a patch of starlit earth under a starlit sky—the lamps of Paris: straight lines of lights, curving lines of lights, squares of lights. Gradually avenues, parks, and buildings take form; and there, far below, a little offset from the center, is a column of lights pointing upward, changing angles as I fly—the Eiffel Tower. I circle once above it, and turn northeast toward Le Bourget.

Now it's 4:52 on the clock—9:52, Paris time. Le Bourget isn't shown on my map. But I was told that it is northeast of the city. So I penciled a circle on my map, about where Le Bourget ought to be; and now the *Spirit of St. Louis* is over the outskirts of Paris, pointed toward the center of that circle.

A beacon should be flashing on such a large and important airport. But the nearest beacon is fully 20 miles away, and west instead of east of Paris. I bank slightly, so I can search the earth directly ahead. There's no flash. But I'm probably far above the beacon's beam. From my altitude, I should be hunting for a darkened patch of ground, bordered by straight-lined, regularly spaced points of light, with a few green and red points among the yellow.

Yes, there's a black patch to my left, large enough to be an airport. And there are lights all around it. But they're neither straight nor regularly spaced. I bank left to pass overhead. Are those floodlights in one corner of the dark area? They're awfully weak, hardly bright enough for landing aircraft.

It looks like an airport. But why would an airport be in such a congested section? There are thousands of lights along one side, probably from a large factory. I'm almost overhead now. Those *are* floodlights, and they show the edge of a field. I point my pocket flashlight toward the ground, and key out a message. There's no response.

I circle. Yes, it's definitely an airport. I see part of a concrete apron in front of a large, half-open door. But is it Le Bourget? Well, at least it's a Paris airport. I spiral lower, keeping close to the edge of the field. I'll give those lights along the southern border a wide berth when I come in to land. There may be high factory chimneys rising among them.

As I bank, new details emerge from night and shadow. I see a line of big hangars, outlined vaguely, near the floodlights. And now, from the far side of the field, I see that all those smaller lights are automobiles, not factory windows. They seem to be congested on a road behind the hangars. It's a huge airport. The floodlights show only a small corner. It *must* be Le Bourget.

I'll drag the field from low altitude to make sure its surface is clear. After that, everyone down there will know I want to land. If they have any more lights, they'll switch them on.

I sweep my flashlight over the instrument board in a final check, fasten my safety belt, and nose the *Spirit of St. Louis* down into a gradually descending spiral.

I circle several times while I lose altitude, trying to penetrate the shadows from different vantage points. At 1000 feet I discover the wind sock, dimly lighted, on top of some building. It's bulged, but far from stiff. That means a gentle, constant wind, not over 15 miles an hour. My landing direction will be over the floodlights, angling away from the hangar line.

I straighten out my wings and let the throttled engine drag me on beyond the leeward border. Now the steep bank into wind, and the dive toward ground. It is a strange descent. I'm wide awake, but the feel of my plane has gone. My movements are mechanical, uncoordinated, as though I were coming down at the end of my first solo.

I see the whole outline of the hangars now. Two or three planes are resting in the shadows. There's no time to look for more details. The lighted area is just ahead. It's barely large enough to land on. I nose down below the hangar roofs, so low that I can see the texture of the sod, and blades of grass on high spots. The ground is smooth and solid as far as the floodlights show its surface. I can tell nothing about the black mass beyond. But those several pinpoints in the distance look as though they

DIMANCHE
22
MAI 1927

EXCELSIOR

Lorsqu'en part d'une erreur on n'arrive jamais à la vérité.

LINDBERGH A TRIOMPHÉ

L'AVIATEUR AMÉRICAIN

Franchissant l'Atlantique, il est venu New-York à Paris en 33 h. 27 minutes.

COMMENT IL A PU SE DIRIGER SON AVION

*In the hangar
at Le Bourget*

*With Ambassador
Herrick (right)—Par...*

mark the far border. Since Le Bourget is a major airport, the area between is probably also clear—I'll have to take a chance on that.

I start a climbing turn. No one turns on more lights. I level off for the downwind stretch. The motorcars are still jammed in traffic. There's no sign of movement on the ground.

I'm a quarter-mile downwind now. I bank around for final glide. The airspeed's at 90 miles an hour. I'll overshoot if I keep on at this rate. Stick back, close the throttle. I can hardly hear the engine idling—is it too slow? It mustn't stop now. The silence is like a vacuum in my ears. I open the throttle for a quick burst—but I'm going much too fast.

In spite of my speed, the *Spirit of St. Louis* seems about to stall. My lack of feel alarms me. I've never tried to land a plane without feel before. I want to open the throttle wider, to glide faster. But the needle points to 80 miles an hour. The *Spirit of St. Louis*, with most of its fuel gone, is lightly loaded. Even at this speed I'll overshoot the lighted area before my tail skid strikes the ground. No, I'll have to pull the nose higher instead of pushing it down. I'll have to depend on the needle, on judgment more than instinct; the edge of perception is very dull. It's better to come in fast, even if I roll into that black area after I land. And it's better to come in high—there may be poles or chimneys at the field's edge.

It's only 100 yards to the hangars now—I'm too high, too fast. Careful—mustn't get anywhere near the stall. I've never landed the *Spirit of St. Louis* at night before. Below the hangar roofs now—straighten out. A short burst of the engine. Over the lighted area, sod coming up to meet me. Deceptive highlights and shadows—careful—easy to bounce when you're tired. The wheels touch gently—off again—back on the ground— off—back—the tail skid, too. Not a bad landing, but I'm beyond the light—can't see anything ahead. The field *must* be clear—uncomfortable though, jolting into blackness. Slower, now—the *Spirit of St. Louis* swings around and stops rolling, resting on the solidness of earth, in the center of Le Bourget.

I start to taxi back toward the floodlights and hangars—but the entire field ahead is covered with running figures!

Afterword

BECAUSE of the warnings I had been given in America, I was completely unprepared for the welcome that awaited me on Le Bourget. I had no idea that my plane had been so accurately reported along its route between Ireland and Paris—over Dingle Bay, over Plymouth, over Cherbourg. When I circled the airport it did not occur to me that any connection existed between my arrival and the cars stalled in traffic on the roads. When my wheels touched earth, I had no way of knowing that tens of thousands of men and women were breaking down fences and flooding past guards.

I had barely cut the engine switch when the first people reached my cockpit. Within seconds my open windows were blocked with faces. My name was called out over and over again. I could feel the plane tremble with the pressure of the crowd. I heard the crack of wood behind me when someone leaned too heavily against a fairing strip. Then a second strip snapped, and a third, and there was the sound of tearing fabric; souvenir hunters were going wild. I decided to get out of the cockpit and try to find some English-speaking person who would help me organize a guard to hold back the crowd.

I opened the door, and started to put my foot down onto ground. But dozens of hands took hold of my legs, my arms, my body. I found myself prostrate, up on top of the crowd, in the center of an ocean of heads that extended as far out into the darkness as I could see. My head and shoulders went down, and up, and down again, and up once more. It was like drowning in a human sea. I heard several screams. I was afraid that I would be dropped under the feet of those milling, cheering people.

I tried to sit up, to slip down into the crowd. It was useless. It seemed wiser to relax as much as I could, and let time pass. Countless minutes later, I felt my helmet jerked from my head. Firmer hands gripped my body. And suddenly I was standing on my feet—on European ground at last. With strong arms linked solidly in mine, I began moving slowly, but unnoticed, through the crowd.

In the week I spent in Paris, I pieced together the story of what happened that Saturday night at Le Bourget. Despite skepticism about my flight, the French authorities had prepared for my reception. Police, reinforced by two companies of soldiers, were detailed to the airport when reports of my plane's being sighted over Ireland, England, and Normandy brought automobiles pouring out from Paris by the thousands. After I landed, my plane was supposed to be guided toward the administration building, where I was to be met by a reception committee of French and American officials. Press photographers and reporters were assigned to appropriate positions.

When the crowd broke down steel fences and rushed out onto the field, police and soldiers were swept away in the rush. Two French aviators, Detroyat and Delage, found themselves close to me in the jam of people. Delage grabbed Detroyat's arm and cried, "Come—they will smother him!" Detroyat, who was in his military uniform, was able to exercise some authority over the men who had me on their shoulders. Once my feet were on the ground, it was too dark for my flying suit to be very noticeable. Meanwhile, my helmet had somehow gotten onto the head of an American reporter. Someone had pointed to him and called out, *"There is Lindbergh!"* The crowd had taken over the reporter and left me free.

Delage rushed to get his little Renault, while Detroyat maneuvered me to the outskirts of the crowd. When the car arrived, I said that before leaving I wanted to be sure a guard had been placed around the *Spirit of St. Louis.* Communication was difficult: my ears were still deafened from the flight; I spoke no French; my new friends, only a little English; and in the background were the noises of the crowd. My plane was being taken care of, they told me. I should not try to go back to it—there was no mistaking their tones and gestures.

We drove into a big hangar, and I was taken to a small room on one side. My friends motioned me to a chair and put out most of the lights—so I would not be discovered by the crowd. Did I need food, drink, the attention of a doctor? Would I like to lie down? they asked. I had only to tell them what I wanted.

I didn't feel like lying down, and I had no need whatever for a doctor; but I was greatly worried about my plane. I received assurances that everything possible was being done to take care of it. I asked what customs and immigration formalities I had to go through, and received mostly smiles and laughter in reply. I decided that the best thing for me to do was just to wait and let events develop. Was there any word of Nungesser and Coli? I asked. Faces lengthened. No, no news had come.

I stayed with Delage while Detroyat went to search for an officer of higher rank. He found Major Weiss of the Bombardment Group of the 34th Air Force Regiment. The major could not believe that I was sitting in a hangar's darkened room. "It is impossible," he told Detroyat. "Lindbergh has just been carried triumphantly to the official reception committee." The reporter with my helmet had been taken, struggling, to the American ambassador before the mistake in identity was finally established. But Major Weiss followed Detroyat, and on seeing me insisted that I be taken to his office on the military side of Le Bourget—about a mile away. So we climbed into the Renault again and drove across the field.

About an hour later the Honorable Myron T. Herrick arrived at the hangar and I was introduced to him. After extending a welcome and inquiring about my welfare, he said he was going to take me back with him to the embassy. I accepted gladly; but I asked to see the *Spirit of St. Louis* before we left the field.

Ambassador Herrick nodded. A discussion in French followed, and I was assured again that the *Spirit of St. Louis* had not been badly damaged; it had been placed in a locked hangar, under a military guard. I needed to sleep, it was suggested. There would be time enough to see the plane after that.

I couldn't put the cracking wood and ripping fabric from my mind that easily. I was anxious to find out what repairs would have to be made. I didn't know, then, that the French authorities wished to have all repairs completed before I saw the plane. I argued that I wanted to get some items from the cockpit.

So we climbed into Delage's car and drove to the hangar in which the *Spirit of St. Louis* had been placed. The plane's fuselage was full of gaping holes, and some souvenir hunter had torn a grease reservoir off the engine. But no serious damage had been done. A few hours of work would make the plane airworthy again.

It was then time for me to rejoin Ambassador Herrick and drive with him to Paris. But since my friends couldn't find him, they decided to take me to the embassy themselves. So the four of us started out—Weiss, Delage, Detroyat, and I—in the Renault. Nobody looked twice at the car as we wound about through the crowd.

When we reached the end of a long avenue in the city, Delage parked at the curb near a great stone arch. My friends took me through the arch and I found myself standing silently with them at the tomb of France's Unknown Soldier, with its ever burning flame. They wanted my first stop in Paris to be at the Arc de Triomphe, they said. We arrived at the American Embassy, far ahead of Ambassador Herrick. He had searched for me all over Le Bourget. And then his car had become involved in the traffic jam between airport and city. It was three o'clock when the ambassador reached home. By that time a small crowd—mostly newspapermen—had assembled in the street outside. At Herrick's suggestion they were invited in, and I spent a few minutes answering questions and telling them about my flight. Paris clocks marked 4:15 in the morning before I went to bed. It had been sixty-three hours since I had slept.

I woke that afternoon, a little stiff but well rested, into a life which could hardly have been more amazing if I had landed on another planet instead of at Paris. The welcome I received at Le Bourget was only a forerunner to the welcome extended by all of Europe. It was a welcome which words of appreciation are incompetent to cover. But the account of my experiences abroad, of my homecoming to the United States, and of my gratitude to the peoples of Europe and America, belongs to a different story.

FLORENCE
NIGHTINGALE

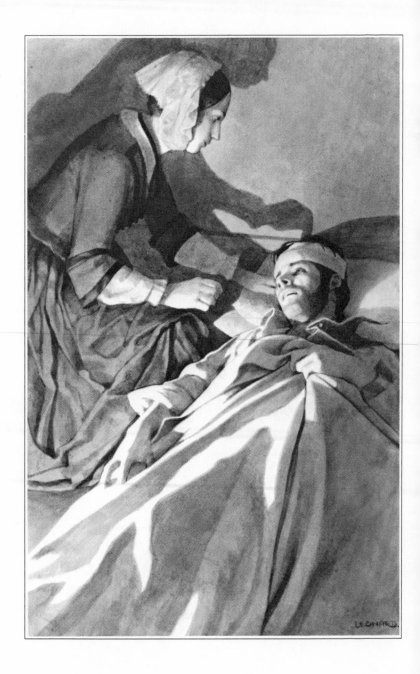

FLORENCE NIGHTINGALE

by
CECIL
WOODHAM-SMITH

ILLUSTRATED BY
MICHAEL LEONARD

God bless Miss Nightingale,
May she be free from strife;
These are the prayers
Of the poor soldier's wife.

Thus ran a popular English song of 1855. And indeed, to thousands of sick and wounded British soldiers in the Crimean War, Florence Nightingale was their symbol of hope, their ministering "Lady with the Lamp." Yet the lives she saved and the revolution in health care she began during that war were only part of the contribution she made to medicine.

A woman who could be both charming and ruthlessly demanding, she reformed nursing and made it a respectable profession, radically changed hospital administration, and struggled to improve the wretched condition of the British soldier. All her life, in fact, she had to struggle; first, against her Victorian family, who did not share her dedication to her cause, and later, against the politicians and medical authorities who lacked the vision to support her pioneering work.

Florence Nightingale comes to life in these pages, a woman of character ruled by compassion, unafraid to challenge the accepted cruelties of a man's world.

Chapter 1

IT WAS SOMETHING NEW to call a girl Florence. Within fifty years thousands of girls all over the world would be christened Florence in honor of this baby, but in the summer of 1820, when Fanny Nightingale fixed on the name for her daughter, it was new.

Novelty was the fashion in 1820. Europe was still rejoicing in the liberty which followed the Napoleonic wars. Freedom to travel had returned, and Europe was thronged with travelers. Fanny and William Edward Nightingale had been traveling in Europe since their marriage in 1818. They already had one daughter, born in Naples in 1819 and christened by the Greek name for her birthplace, Parthenope. For her second confinement Fanny chose the city of Florence. When a second girl was born there on May 12, 1820, Fanny decided she too should be named after her birthplace.

Fanny and W.E.N., as he was always called, though both handsome and intelligent, were not a well-matched couple. Fanny was six years older than W.E.N. In 1820 she was thirty-two, extremely beautiful, generous and extravagant, indefatigable in the pursuit of pleasure. In the art of making people

237

comfortable, in the arrangement of a house, the production of good dinners, she possessed genius.

She came from a remarkable family. Her grandfather, Samuel Smith, had been celebrated for the riches he had amassed as a merchant and for his humanitarian principles. His son William, Fanny's father, devoted his wealth to collecting pictures and fighting for the weak, the unpopular and the oppressed. In the House of Commons, where he sat for forty-six years, he was a leading Abolitionist, championed the sweated factory workers, and battled for the rights of Dissenters and Jews. His children did not inherit his altruism. There were five sons and five daughters, all good-looking, with immense zest for living and amazing health. "We Smiths never thought of anything all day long but our own ease and pleasure," Fanny wrote fifty years later.

Fanny was the beauty of the family; yet Fanny did not marry. In 1816 she fell in love with the Honorable James Sinclair, a younger son of the Earl of Caithness. His character was allowed to be good and his intentions disinterested, but he possessed no income beyond the pay of a captain in the Ross-shire militia. In letters, full of kindness and unanswerable common sense, William Smith pointed out the absurdity of a woman of Fanny's habits contemplating life on an income of scarcely four hundred a year and declined, in justice to his other children, to assume the support of her future family. Fanny pleaded in vain that her affections were entirely given away, but by 1817 the affair was at an end.

Fanny was now nearly thirty and William Edward Nightingale was nearly twenty-four. She had known him since he had been an awkward lanky schoolboy, immensely tall, immensely thin, with a habit of always standing upright propped against mantelpieces and doors because he disliked folding himself into a chair. At twenty-one he had come into a fortune left him by his uncle, and had gone up to Cambridge. There he proved, though lazy, to be clever. He gained a reputation for wit. His height and remote gentle manners gave him distinction.

In 1817 W.E.N. became engaged to Fanny. He was very much in love. Fanny's rich beauty warmed his reserved temperament, and for a short time he thawed. The period was brief. Normally, as Fanny wrote later, "Mr. Nightingale is seldom in the melting mood."

Fanny's family did not approve of the engagement. They were fond of W.E.N., but they had no faith in his character. He was clever but he was indolent, hated making up his mind, hated taking action—he was not the husband for Fanny. Within six months, however, they were married and had gone abroad. Fanny believed she would be able to mold W.E.N. She intended him to become one of the prosperous, cultivated and liberal-minded country gentlemen who played an important part in English public life. They would have a beautiful house, a fine library, maintain an interest in the arts and entertain.

After nearly three years abroad Fanny began to feel it was time they came home, and in 1821, when Florence was a year old, the Nightingales left Italy, accompanied by maids, footmen, valet, coachman and cook. W.E.N. had made a quick trip to England to have work started on a new house of his own design. He gave it a vaguely Gothic air, and called it Lea Hurst. But no sooner was it finished than Fanny realized that Lea Hurst was inadequate. The only attraction was its wonderful view. The situation was inaccessible, the house cold. Above all, it was too small a house in which to entertain. (Fanny's standards of accommodation descended to her daughter. Twenty years later at a dinner party Florence denied that Lea Hurst was anything but a small house. "Why," she said, "it has only fifteen bedrooms.")

In 1825, therefore, W.E.N. bought Embley Park, near Romsey, in Hampshire. It was a good-sized square house of the late Georgian period. London was reasonably near, and Fanny would be within easy reach of her two married sisters, Mrs. Nicholson at Waverley Abbey, and Mrs. Bonham Carter at Fair Oaks near Winchester. By the time Florence was five, the pattern of the Nightingales' life was fixed; summer at Lea Hurst, the rest of the year at Embley Park, visits to London in spring and autumn.

W.E.N. proceeded to turn himself into an English country gentleman. He shot, fished, hunted, did a great deal for his tenants, and took part in local politics. Fanny looked forward to the day when he would stand for Parliament.

Fanny's life ran smoothly. The only shadow was cast by Florence. Called Flo (as Parthenope was Parthe or Pop), she promised to grow up more than ordinarily good-looking. She was lightly built, singularly graceful, with thick bright chestnut hair and a delicate complexion. But she was not an easy child.

Both Fanny and W.E.N. loved children. A stream of cousins spent their holidays at Embley and Lea Hurst, and almost invariably Fanny had a couple of family babies in the house. "Kiss all babies for me" is a frequent ending to the first letters Flo wrote home when she was sent to stay with relatives. Flo's childhood was filled with gardens to play in, ponies to ride, and a succession of dogs, cats and birds to be looked after.

Yet she was not happy. If she had been an ordinary naughty child, Fanny would have understood her, but she was not naughty. She was strange, passionate, obstinate and miserable. She had an obsession that she was not like other people, that she was some sort of monster. She was afraid of meeting strangers, especially children, lest they discover her secret. She doubted her capacity to behave like other people, and refused to dine downstairs, convinced she would betray herself by doing something extraordinary with her knife and fork. At first she was overwhelmed with terror and guilt at the gulf which separated her from everyone round her. Surely she ought to be like everyone else? But almost before she had grown out of babyhood, guilt and terror were succeeded by discontent. Miss Nightingale recorded that as early as the age of six she was aware that the rich smooth life of Embley and Lea Hurst was distasteful to her. She began, like many imaginative children, to escape into a dream world, to tell herself stories in which she played the heroine.

Though she shrank from meeting people, she was not self-sufficient. She was a child who craved sympathy and attached herself with vehemence to anyone whom she felt to be sympathetic. Her childhood was a series of passions—for her governess Miss Christie, for W.E.N.'s younger sister "Aunt Mai," for a beautiful older cousin. When the governess left, and when Aunt

Mai married, the violence of Florence's feelings made her physically ill.

She did not attach herself to her mother. As a child she was a copious letter writer, and her letters show her consciousness of a want of sympathy in Fanny. When she writes to others, her pen flies on, with a total disregard of spelling, telling them of the adventures of Nelson the dog, of a local suicide, a good crop of apples, and Aunt Mai's new baby. "Aunt Mai calls her new baby the Thing, don't you think that is very disrespectful?" Writing to Fanny, the flow is checked; her letters are formal and short. She assures her mother that she is wearing the boots to strengthen her ankles, she is endeavoring to improve her spelling, she is trying to be more good-natured.

The companion of her childhood was her father. W.E.N. was a man to enchant a child. He loved the curious and the odd, and he loved jokes; he had a mind stored with information and the leisure to impart it. He was a lonely man, and it was with intense pleasure he discovered companionship in his daughters. Both were quick; both learned easily, but the more intelligent, just as she was the prettier, was Flo.

It was a difficult situation for Parthe, the elder. Flo—strange, passionate, uncomfortable little thing—had something about her which struck people as exceptional. Flo led and Parthe followed, resentfully. Parthe was possessive towards Flo, she adored Flo, but she was bitterly envious. In 1830 Flo wrote to Parthe from Fair Oaks: "Pray dear Pop, let us love each other better than we have done. It is the will of God and Mama particularly desires it."

W.E.N.'s plan for their education brought about the final division between the girls. In 1832 he determined to teach them himself. A governess was engaged for music and drawing, but the girls learned Greek, Latin, German, French, Italian, history and philosophy from their father. W.E.N. was exacting, and Parthe rebelled. Florence and her father both had the same regard for accuracy, the same cast of mind, at once humorous and gloomy, the same passion for abstract speculation. Parthe resented their companionship, but she did not want to struggle with Greek verbs. While Florence was with W.E.N. in the library, Parthe would be busy with Fanny, arranging flowers, entertaining friends, writing innumerable letters to the vast Nightingale family's connections.

On Florence's fourteenth birthday W.E.N. calculated she had already twenty-seven first cousins and nearly two dozen aunts and uncles by blood and marriage. Fanny's brothers and sisters, the energetic handsome Smiths, had the strongest possible family feelings. Not only major events, weddings, births, deaths, but the choice of a place for a holiday, the dismissal of a cook, provoked correspondence with aunts, uncles, cousins and grandmothers.

To Florence all this was an intolerable waste of time. "I craved," she wrote, "for some regular occupation, for something worth doing instead of frittering time away on useless trifles." To her only three families were of importance—the Nicholsons, the Bonham Carters, and the family of Aunt Mai, now Mrs. Sam Smith of Combe Hurst, Surrey.

Aunt Mai was a person of importance to the Nightingales. She was W.E.N.'s sister; and, should he have no son, the property he had inherited from an uncle would pass to her. In 1827 she had married Fanny's younger brother, Sam Smith. It was then seven years since the birth of Florence, Fanny was nearly forty and there was no sign of another child. It was almost certain that, if Aunt Mai had a son, he would eventually inherit Embley and Lea Hurst, and the marriage which linked the two families more closely together was welcomed. In 1831 a son was born, and Fanny behaved admirably. The situation was not easy for her. Not only was Aunt Mai mother of the heir, she was also the object of Florence's extravagant devotion. Nevertheless, Fanny's affectionate relations with Aunt Mai were unclouded. Aunt Mai's son was given a privileged position in the Nightingale family. When he was a few days old he was laid in Florence's arms: "My boy Shore," the eleven-year-old Flo proudly called him. Devotion to Shore, pride in him, and Shore's devotion to her grew into one of the most important relationships in her life.

At Embley and Lea Hurst there were comfort, security and affection; there were intelligence and companionship. And yet beneath the surface there was no peace; Florence was brought up in a hothouse of emotion, the result of a literary fashion. Romanticism had penetrated English life, and ordinary wives and mothers were reproducing the behavior of the heroines of Byron and Chateaubriand. Women prided themselves on their excessive sensibility, and "delicacy" was universal. Fanny, Parthe and Florence were all considered "delicate," though Fanny lived to be ninety-two, Florence ninety and Parthe seventy-five.

Miss Nightingale was indelibly impressed by this atmosphere. Though her extraordinary mind owed its quality to uncompromising clarity and realism, her character throughout her life contained the contradiction that she was emotional, prone to exaggeration and abnormally sensitive.

The summer of 1834 brought a turning point for the family— W.E.N. was invited to stand for Parliament as candidate from Andover. He went into the contest full of enthusiasm and hope, and Fanny saw her plans for W.E.N.'s entry into public life maturing. But she was defeated. W.E.N.'s seat was lost because he refused to purchase votes. His first contact with practical politics left him profoundly disillusioned, and he resolved never to enter political life again. He ceased now to adapt himself to the character of a country gentleman Fanny had planned. He gave up hunting, spent more time teaching Florence and took to passing the greater part of each day in his library. His natural home, he was fond of saying, was in "the quiet and the shadows." But such a life was unbearable to Fanny. She transferred her ambitions to her daughters.

They were sixteen and seventeen in 1835. Next year, or the year after, they must be launched in society. But now Embley was discovered to be inadequate for this. Six more bedrooms must be added, new kitchens built. Fanny proposed that, while the alterations were carried out, they should make an extended tour abroad with the girls. W.E.N. agreed. He loved Europe. The alterations to Embley were started at once, and the Nightingales fixed a date to leave.

At this moment, in the midst of bustle, plans, discussions, Florence received what she believed to be a call from God.

IT IS POSSIBLE to know a great deal about Miss Nightingale's inner life because she had the habit of writing what she called "private notes." She was unhappy in her environment, she had no one to confide in, and she poured herself out on paper. A very large number of her private notes exists. She wrote them on anything that came to hand—odd pieces of blotting paper, backs of calendars, margins of letters; sometimes she dated them, sometimes not. Sometimes they cover several foolscap pages, sometimes consist of one sentence. From time to time she also kept diaries; but it was in her private notes, written from girlhood to old age, that she recorded her true feelings.

It was in one of these that she wrote: "On February 7th, 1837, God spoke to me and called me to His service." She heard, as Joan of Arc had, a voice outside herself, speaking to her in human words.

She was not quite seventeen and her dream world was often more actual to her than the real world. But the voices which spoke to her were not a phenomenon of adolescence. Nearly forty years later she wrote in a private note that her "voices" had spoken to her four times. Once on February 7, 1837, the date of her call; once in 1853 before going to her first post at the Hospital for Poor Gentlewomen in Harley Street; once before the Crimea in 1854; and once after the death in 1861 of Sidney Herbert, her most influential friend and protector.

Her path was not made clear. God had called her, but what form that service was to take she did not know. The idea of nursing did not enter her mind. She doctored sick pets; she was especially fond of babies. Her protective instincts were strong, but they had not yet led her to the knowledge that God had called her to the service of the sick. Meanwhile she was at peace, full of confidence and faith. God had spoken to her once; presently He would speak to her again.

ON SEPTEMBER 8, 1837, the Nightingales crossed from Southampton to Le Havre. The next day they left Le Havre in brilliant weather in a traveling carriage which W.E.N. had designed. It was enormous, drawn by six horses, ridden by postilions. On the roof were seats for servants and for the family to admire the scenery. The girls sat on the roof, the postilions sang and cracked their whips, and the carriage lumbered down the straight roads of France.

Florence was in transports of delight. She recorded in her diary that at Chartres she sat all night at her window enchanted by the beauty of moonlight on the cathedral. Yet for all her rhapsodies she remained precise. Each day she noted in her diary the exact hours of departure and arrival and the exact distance covered.

On December 15 they drove into the gay town of Nice, where there was a large English colony. With startling suddenness, cathedrals and scenery vanished from Florence's diary and letters. She developed a passion for dancing and wrote to her favorite cousin and most intimate friend, Hilary Bonham Carter, that at the biggest ball of the season she danced every quadrille. When the time came to leave Nice for Italy, she was heartbroken.

Her tears dried themselves with remarkable speed. From the city of Florence Fanny wrote her sister that the Grand Duke of Tuscany was "exceedingly distinguished and polite," the balls at the ducal palace "exceedingly fine," and that Flo had been "much noticed." The opera in Florence was one of the best in Europe, and Flo, "music mad," persuaded Fanny to take her three times a week. She did more than go into transports. She kept a book in which she made a detailed comparison of the score, libretto and performance of every opera she heard. Her mind demanded something hard to bite on, and the romantic extravagance of her emotion crystallized surprisingly into facts and figures.

By the following autumn the Nightingales were back in France. W.E.N. proposed to spend some months in Paris and took an "extremely splendid" apartment in the Place Vendôme, with gilt mirrors and velvet draperies in the dining room, crimson satin and ebony cabinets in the salon. Fanny intended if possible to enter intellectual society and had an introduction, of which she had great hopes, to one of the most celebrated women in Paris—Miss Mary Clarke.

Without money or beauty, though with excellent family connections, Mary Clarke had made herself a major figure in the political and literary world of Paris. Every Friday night Cabinet ministers, dukes, bishops, scholars and writers crowded the drawing room of her apartment at 120 rue du Bac.

Mary Clarke's personal appearance was odd. She was very small, with the figure of a child; her eyes were startlingly large and bright, and at a period when women brushed their hair smoothly she wore hers over her forehead in a tangle of curls. Guizot, the French statesman, said that she and his Yorkshire terrier patronized the same *coiffeur*. Yet though she had no ordinary feminine attractions, men were devoted to her, and many men wished to marry her. The celebrated author Chateaubriand delighted in her. "Boredom is impossible where she is," he declared.

She entered distinguished circles partly through her close friendship with Claude Fauriel, the renowned medieval scholar. In 1837 Mary and Fauriel had been on terms of intimacy for more than fifteen years. He dined with her almost every night, was invariably present at her parties and behaved as master of the house; yet Mary's reputation was unblemished. There was in fact no cause for scandal. They were friends, not lovers. Mary loved Fauriel, but he had never asked her to marry him, had offered her only devoted friendship.

The Nightingales were not the kind of connection which appealed to Mary Clarke. She did not care for young ladies. She was, however, "absurdly fond" of children. She acknowledged Fanny's letter of introduction by inviting the Nightingales to a "children's soiree."

One afternoon near Christmas they drove up to 120 rue du Bac, and walked into a drawing room crowded with dancing, singing children. In the midst of them, clapping her hands, was a strange little figure who Florence realized must be Mary Clarke. The children began to play blindman's buff, and without ado Florence picked up her skirts and joined in. It was the happiest possible introduction. She was never so unselfconsciously gay as with children.

Immediately Mary Clarke fell in love with the whole family, most of all with Florence, but also with W.E.N.'s remote charm,

Fanny's rich beauty and kindness, and Parthe's elegance. They christened her "Clarkey," and she turned their stay in Paris into a carnival. She took the girls to parties, to studios, to concerts, to the famous salon of Madame Recamier. They met Chateaubriand, and were paid the great compliment of being invited to hear him read his memoirs.

Florence was wildly happy. She had a "passion" for Clarkey; she was beginning an important friendship with Julius Mohl, an Oriental scholar of great distinction who was hopelessly in love with Mary Clarke. For the first time in her life young Florence was breathing the air of freedom. One of the deepest impressions she received was made by Clarkey's friendship with Claude Fauriel. She observed that Clarkey and Fauriel met daily, that Fauriel had great respect for Clarkey's mental powers and treated her as an equal; above all, that this close intimacy was accepted by everyone without disapproval.

She acquired a belief in the possibility of a close friendship between a man and a woman on terms which did not include passion, and which did not provoke scandal. It was a belief she never lost and one which was to regulate her conduct throughout her life.

In April the family left Paris, as Fanny wished to spend the season in London and have the girls presented at Court. Fanny was well satisfied. The tour had shown her that in Florence she possessed a daughter who promised to be exceptional. Florence's success in the intellectual world of Pàris pleased her as much as her success at balls. She was graceful, witty, vividly good-looking. Her hair was of unusual beauty, thick, glossy and wavy. Fanny's pride in Florence was immense, her hopes for her brilliant.

They were doomed. Florence's conscience was awake, and the brief halcyon period was over. It was two years since God had spoken to her. Why had He not spoken again? The answer was evident—she was not worthy. She had forgotten God in the pleasure of balls and operas, in the vanity of being admired. In March 1839, before she left Paris, she wrote in a private note that, to make herself worthy to be God's servant, the first temptation to be overcome was "the desire to shine in society."

Chapter 2

With the return of the Nightingales to London the first great struggle of Miss Nightingale's life began. It was divided into two stages and lasted fourteen years. First she groped within herself for five years before she reached the certainty that her "call" was to nurse the sick; next a bitter conflict with her family followed, and nine more years passed before she was able to nurse.

In April 1839 Fanny and William Nightingale had no inkling of Florence's secret life of aspiration and despair.

Since the alterations to Embley would not be finished by June, Fanny decided to spend the whole season in London. Her sister, Mrs. Nicholson, was also bringing out two girls, and the families united to take a floor of the Carlton Hotel. On May 24 Florence and Parthe were presented at the Queen's Birthday drawing room. Florence, in a white Paris dress, looked, wrote Fanny, "very nice," and "was not nearly as nervous as she expected."

The girls were caught up in a whirl of gaiety. Once more her "call" vanished from Florence's mind; she became absorbed in dresses and balls. She was deliriously happy, perpetually excited, and had been seized by a "passion" for her cousin Marianne Nicholson.

Marianne was dazzlingly beautiful and had exceptional musical gifts, but her moods were unpredictable, and her capacity to love was reserved for her own family. Of all her brothers and sisters, the one she adored the most was Henry. By an unhappy chance, Henry fell desperately in love with Florence. She did not love him, but for a long time she encouraged him because he brought her closer to Marianne.

In September the family moved back to Embley, though the builders were still at work. Settling the house filled the next months, and it was not until the New Year that Florence could draw breath.

She was furiously discontented with herself; towards justifying her "call" she had done nothing. Her life was hateful; impossible that God should have bestowed the gift of time on His female creatures to be used as Fanny wished her to use it. "Faddling twaddling and the endless tweedling of nosegays in jugs," Clarkey called it.

Miserable, bored, Florence became unwell. She was rescued by Aunt Mai. They were now devoted friends, no longer fond aunt and adoring little niece but equals. Aunt Mai possessed many of W.E.N.'s qualities—intellectual curiosity, humor—and she placed Florence above ordinary humanity, above the claims even of her husband and her children, and became her protector, interpreter and consoler. Aunt Mai's tact, her energy, her flow of words were inexhaustible, and in innumerable letters she endeavored in a flood of apologies and explanations to make life easier for Florence. In January 1840 she persuaded Fanny that "Flo would be all the better for a little change," and Florence was allowed to pay a visit to Aunt Mai and her family at Combe Hurst.

At once her spirits soared. London was buzzing with gossip of Queen Victoria's wedding, and Florence wrote a lively account of the ceremony. She went to several dinners and to the opera, received a flattering number of valentines and spent a great deal of time with Aunt Mai's children.

But beneath the gay surface were agony and despair. It was three years since she had been "called" and she still did not know to what. How was she to make herself worthy so God could give her instructions?

Perhaps she would find life more satisfactory if she studied mathematics. Mathematics, she had told Clarkey, gave her a sense of certainty. She and Aunt Mai began to work together, getting up before it was light to avoid disturbing the routine of the house. She became ecstatic. If only her parents could be persuaded to let her do this instead of doing worsted work and practicing quadrilles!

In March Aunt Mai wrote Fanny a letter. "I am much impressed with the idea that hard work is necessary to give zest to life in a character like hers, where there is great power of mind and a more than common inclination to apply. *So* I write to ask you if you in any way object to a mathematical master. . . ."

Fanny did object. Her daughter's destiny was to marry, and what use was mathematics to a married woman? "I don't think you have any idea of half that's in her," Aunt Mai wrote back. But Fanny would not give way.

In the middle of May Florence went back to Embley. That summer Fanny had a series of house parties. Clarkey came for a long visit, and Fanny's new friends, Lord Palmerston and his wife, were constantly at Embley. They brought with them their son-in-law Lord Ashley, better known by his subsequent title of Lord Shaftesbury, the reformer and philanthropist.

And still Florence was not satisfied. The previous autumn she had complained that she had no one to talk to; now she complained she had too many. She had said she must have intelligent conversation; now she said she must have time for study. She worked at mathematics in her bedroom, and rose in the small hours to read philosophy and study Greek. She was discontented with life, even more discontented with herself. She blamed herself for her bad temper at home, for her unworthiness before God, as still she did not know what God had called her to do.

Among her cousins her most intimate friend was Hilary Bonham Carter, a year younger than herself. She was unusually pretty and had a talent for painting; a self-portrait shows a charming little pointed face framed in heavy bands of soft hair. When in 1838 her father had died she had become the support of her mother, a nervous, impractical woman overwhelmed by the responsibility of bringing up a large family unaided. Florence was passionately attached to Hilary, and made her the confidante of her difficulties.

By 1841, after nearly two years at home, she had achieved nothing but desperate unhappiness. She loathed life at Embley, where she never had a moment to herself; every day was filled with the performance of endless needless tasks which provoked the asking of endless needless questions. She had a feeling of oppression; she felt herself pursued by servants, guests, relations in a clutching, demanding horde. She had no leisure. Christmas 1841 was spent at Waverley. Fanny described the festivities as "awesome." Eighty people slept in the house. There was a huge masked ball which went on until five o'clock in the morning, succeeded the following night by an amateur performance of *The Merchant of Venice*.

By 1842 Florence was becoming a figure in intellectual society, though she was only twenty-two. She danced beautifully yet possessed a surprising degree of learning, had great vitality and was an excellent mimic. During the London season that year she was "very much noticed" by the new Prussian ambassador, the Chevalier Bunsen, a Biblical scholar and Egyptologist of world reputation and a close friend of Queen Victoria and Prince Albert. Florence went constantly to the Bunsens' house and was addressed by the Chevalier as "my favourite and admired Miss Nightingale."

She had achieved a success, and could not help feeling satisfaction, yet she reproached herself bitterly. "All I do is done to win admiration," she wrote in a private note. She cared too much, she went on, for "the pride of life."

The temptation to shine was greatly increased when, at a dinner party at the Palmerstons', she was introduced to Richard Monckton Milnes. Richard was thirty-three. Heir to a great estate in Yorkshire, he was a brilliant figure in society and in literary and political circles. "He always put you in a good humour with yourself," said Thackeray. "He treated all his fellow mortals as if they were his brothers and sisters," Florence later wrote. He loved children, and it was largely owing to his efforts that young criminals ceased to be jailed with adults and were sent to reformatories instead.

During the summer Richard Monckton Milnes came several times to Embley. He was falling in love with Florence, and by the end of July he was treated as one of the family.

Sometime in that summer, however, Florence had taken the first step towards the fulfillment of her destiny. England in 1842 was in the grip of what has passed into history as "the hungry forties." Everywhere were starvation, sweated labor and dirt. Diseased scarecrows swarmed not only in the airless undrained courts of London but in the "black filth" of rural cottages; workhouses, hospitals and prisons were overflowing. Florence wrote in a private note: "My mind is absorbed with the idea of the sufferings of man. . . . All the people I see are eaten up with care or poverty or disease."

She knew now that her destiny lay among the miserable, outside her little world of ease and comfort. But what form it was to take, she still had no idea.

That autumn in London she asked the Chevalier Bunsen: "What can an individual do towards lifting the load of suffering from the helpless and miserable?" In reply, the Chevalier mentioned the work of Pastor Fliedner at Kaiserswerth, on the Rhine, where Protestant deaconesses were trained in the institution hospital to nurse the sick poor. Florence's attention was not arrested; she had not yet begun to think of nursing. But when, in July 1843, the Nightingales went to Lea Hurst, she began to spend the greater part of her day in the cottages of the poor and sick, and to badger her mother for medicines, food, bedding, clothes. When the time came to go back to Embley, Florence wanted to stay at Lea Hurst, but Fanny thought her daughter's interest in nursing was unreasonable, and would not hear of it.

Florence's misery was increased by a terrifying discovery. She records in a private note that she suddenly realized the extent to which the habit she called "dreaming" had enslaved her. She fell into "trance-like" states in the midst of ordinary life, while, for instance, she was making conversation at a dinner party. She could not control herself. Was there nothing for her but dreaming? Had she better close her eyes and find what satisfaction she could in a false paradise of consoling visions?

Yet she was approaching a secret decision of the utmost importance and some time in the following spring the knowledge came to her that her vocation lay in hospitals among the sick. At last, seven years after her "call," her destiny was clear. "Since I was twenty-four," she wrote later, ". . . there never was any vagueness in my plans or ideas as to what God's work was for me."

In June Dr. Samuel Gridley Howe, the American philanthropist, came to Embley. On the night of his arrival Florence spoke to him privately: "Dr. Howe, do you think it would be unsuitable and unbecoming for a young Englishwoman to devote herself to works of charity in hospitals and elsewhere as

Catholic sisters do?" He gave a sincere answer: "My dear Miss Florence, it would be unusual, and in England whatever is unusual is thought to be unsuitable; but I say to you 'go forward,' if you have a vocation for that way of life, act up to your inspiration and you will find there is never anything unbecoming or unladylike in doing your duty for the good of others. Choose, go on with it, wherever it may lead you, and God be with you."

She had reached the turning point of her life, but she confided in no one. The word "hospital" had not yet been uttered to her family; she was well-advised to hesitate before introducing it; it was a dread word.

In 1844 hospitals were places of wretchedness, degradation and squalor. "Hospital smell," the result of dirt and lack of sanitation, was so overpowering that persons entering the wards for the first time were seized with nausea. Wards were crammed with beds. Even decency was impossible.

The patients came from slum tenements called "rookeries," from hovels, from cellars where cholera lurked. Gin and brandy were smuggled into the wards and fearful scenes took place, ending by half-dying creatures attacking each other in frenzy or writhing in fits of "screaming horrors." The sick came into hospitals filthy and remained filthy. The nurses did not wash them; "it was common practice to put a new patient into the same sheets used by the last occupant of the bed, and mattresses were sodden and seldom if ever cleaned."

Yet the real obstacle would not be physically disgusting conditions, but the notorious immorality of hospital nurses. "It was *preferred*," wrote Miss Nightingale, "that the nurses should be women who had lost their characters, i.e., should have had one child." Nurses slept in the wards they nursed, and it was not unknown for nurses of male wards to sleep in the wards with the men. Drink was the curse of the hospital nurse, as of the patients.

Life in this setting was what Florence Nightingale was now considering. But a year passed and she became more wretchedly unhappy; in vain had she dug after a plan which could conceivably result in her going to work in hospitals. Eight years had

253

passed since her "call," and not merely had she accomplished nothing, she had slipped backwards—she had lost the sense of walking with God. She reproached herself bitterly.

The strain was too great, and when she went with her family to London in February 1845, she was ill as soon as she arrived. On March 1 she was in bed in the Burlington Hotel, suffering from bronchitis. Outside was thick yellow fog, candles were lighted though it was only two in the afternoon, but in spite of them and a large fire the fog hung in the room. In deep depression she wrote to Clarkey: "You ask me why I do not write something. . . . I had so much rather live than write. . . . I think one's feelings waste themselves in words, they ought all to be distilled into actions and into actions which bring results. . . ." She had become indifferent to pleasure, she was not disappointed to be ill. Her only regret was for a new dress, "a beautiful new violet," which she was to have worn when she went to "a lecture given by Faraday to expound his new discoveries about electricity."

Before she left London in the spring of this year she received a shattering blow: Henry Nicholson proposed for the last time and insisted on a definite answer. She refused him. Henry was heartbroken and the Nicholsons were furious. Florence had, they said with justice, encouraged Henry. Marianne ended her friendship with Florence, and the loss to Florence was a catastrophe.

She was approaching a mental collapse when two serious illnesses in the family saved her. In August of 1845 she went with her father to visit her grandmother, found her seriously ill, and was allowed to stay and nurse her. Hardly was her grandmother convalescent when Mrs. Gale, the girls' old nurse, was taken ill at Lea Hurst. Florence was again allowed to take care of the sick, and when Mrs. Gale died Florence was holding her hand.

For a short time Florence and her mother drew closer; her heart was melted by Fanny's kindness at this time, and one of the few intimate letters she ever wrote to her mother described Gale's death: "Did I tell you one night she was very suffering and I was doubting whether I should speak to her, something

good about the weary and heavy laden, when she said quite distinctly 'Oh I was so well, quite well till now, but I've been sadly off my teas and breakfasts of late.' Oh my dear Mum, life is nothing so much as profoundly ridiculous after all. Is that what the eternal spirit is talking about, when it is communing in its dream with the unspeakable presence, and perhaps with the other invisible spirits on the eve of becoming like them?"

These two nursing episodes brought a certain amount of emancipation. Since Florence had proved herself capable, it was difficult to forbid her to nurse. In the autumn there was an unusual amount of sickness in Wellow, the village near Embley, and she took an active part.

And now she moved forward another step—she realized the necessity of training in nursing. The discovery came as a shock. It was universally assumed that the only qualification needed for taking care of the sick was to be a woman. Ignorance was complete and its consequences disastrous. "I saw a poor woman die before my eyes this summer because there was nothing but fools to sit up with her, who poisoned her as much as if they had given her arsenic," she wrote to Hilary Bonham Carter.

In 1844, when she first knew with certainty that her vocation lay among the sick in hospitals, she had not had the actual practice of nursing in her mind. She too had thought that the qualities needed to relieve the misery of the sick were tenderness, sympathy and patience. Now her short experience had already shown her the necessity for training, for expert skill. She must learn how to nurse if she were to fulfill her destiny. How could she? There was perhaps one avenue by which she might succeed.

The idea was bold. Her plan was to persuade her parents to allow her to go for three months to Salisbury Infirmary, only a few miles from Embley. The infirmary was a well-known hospital, and the head physician, Dr. Fowler, was an old friend. He held advanced views, and she thought he might support her.

In December 1845 the Fowlers came to stay at Embley, and Florence proposed her plan. The Nightingales were horror-struck. A storm burst. "Mama was terrified," she wrote to

Hilary. Parthe had hysterics. Florence persisted, and her mother's terror passed into furious anger—Florence wanted to "disgrace herself."

The Fowlers, embarrassed, "threw cold water." W.E.N., coldly disgusted, went away to London. Was it for this he had educated a charming daughter? Florence was left defeated, helpless, hopelessly depressed. "No advantage that I can see comes of my living on," she wrote Hilary. "I shall never do anything and am worse than dust and nothing. . . ." But the story of her "call" Florence confided not even to Hilary.

Chapter 3

ONE OF THE EXTRAORDINARY FEATURES of Miss Nightingale's life is the passage of time. She starts with a "call" in 1837. Seven years pass before she finds out what she has been called to do. Nine more years pass before she gains freedom in 1853 to pursue her vocation. Sixteen years in all, during which the eager susceptible girl was slowly hammered into the steely powerful woman of genius. The last eight years, after her failure in 1845, were years in which suffering piled on suffering, frustration followed frustration, until she was brought to the verge of madness.

The bonds which bound her were only of straw, but she did not break them. She could act only when she felt moral justification, and she felt no moral justification. She spent sleepless nights, wrestling with her soul, seeking with tears and prayers to make herself worthy to receive the kindness of God. And dreaming enslaved her more and more as she carried out the duties of a daughter. Many of her dreams centered upon Richard Monckton Milnes. She imagined herself married to him, performing heroic deeds with him.

Throughout the winter she was unwell, and to be unwell at Embley was to have life made unendurable by Fanny's fussing. "Oh if one has but a toothache," she wrote in a private note of 1846, "what remedies are invented! But if it is something the matter with the *mind* . . . it is neither believed nor understood." Yet, in spite of her wretchedness, she was making progress. She started, in secret, to study hospital reports and Blue Books—the first Blue Books dealing with public health had just been published.

She got up before dawn and wrote by candlelight. Notebook after notebook was filled with facts, indexed and tabulated. She wrote privately to M. Mohl and the Bunsens for reports on hospitals in Paris and Berlin. In the cold dark mornings she laid the foundation of the vast knowledge of sanitary conditions which was to make her the first expert in Europe. Then the breakfast bell rang, and she came down to be a Daughter at Home.

So month followed month—it seemed uneventfully, but in her character a profound change was taking place. "I feel," she wrote in 1846, "as if all my being were gradually drawing together to one point." She decided that her longing for affection was too powerful for safety, and she began deliberately to detach herself from human relationships. Love, marriage, even friendship, must be renounced. But she could not bring herself yet to face losing Richard Monckton Milnes. The desire to be loved died hard.

And there were happy days, as when in June the Nightingales went to Oxford and Milnes went with them. They lunched at Christ Church with Professor Buckland, the famous naturalist, who kept animals at liberty in his rooms. Florence "invited a Bear of 3 months old to lunch, who climbed like a squirrel for the butter on the table . . . which went to his head and he became obstreperous. Mr. Buckland rebuked it, at which it became violent and was carried out in disgrace. . . . When we came out it was still storming and howling on its hind legs. I said, 'I'm going to mesmerise it.' Mr. Milnes followed the suggestion and in $\frac{1}{2}$ minute the little bear began to yawn, in less than 3 min. was stretched fast asleep on the gravel."

In October the Chevalier Bunsen sent her the yearbook of the Institution of Deaconesses of Kaiserswerth. Now with overwhelming joy she realized that this was what she had been seeking. At Kaiserswerth she could have training where the religious atmosphere, the ascetic discipline, placed the nurses above suspicion. But she did not dare mention Kaiserswerth to her mother. Fanny was busier, more successful than ever, and Embley was filled for autumn parties.

At this point Florence found consolation in a new friend. Through Clarkey, who after Fauriel's death in 1844 had married Julius Mohl, she met Selina Bracebridge and her husband, Charles. Selina understood Florence. In retrospect Miss Nightingale wrote: "She never told me life was fair and my share of its blessings great and that I *ought* to be happy. She did not know that I was miserable but she felt it. . . ."

Selina Bracebridge was a remarkable woman, beautiful in a regal style, intellectual, artistic and possessing an extraordinary warmth of character. She and her husband were well-known travelers. Charles Bracebridge had an enthusiasm for the cause of Greek freedom, and had taken part in a revolt against the Turks. Generous, impetuous, irascible, he combined intense family pride with a passion for liberty. He dressed picturesquely in wide hats and flowing cloaks, and was "the kindest of friends and one of the best and noblest of men," Miss Nightingale wrote. "All his life he was fighting battles against cruelty and oppression."

Like Fanny, Selina Bracebridge prided herself on collecting interesting people, and in particular young writers. The Bracebridges were rich, had no children, and entertained a great deal. Fanny warmly encouraged the friendship. Selina was twenty years older than Florence, a very happily married woman. She might induce Florence to accept Richard Monckton Milnes. Selina and her husband became family friends, and she was given a pet name by the Nightingales, the Greek character sigma—Σ.

The importance of Selina to Florence was overwhelming. Selina never doubted that the struggles in Florence's soul were the long agonies through which something of immense importance would eventually be born. She made Florence the main object of her life, pouring out on her an extraordinary affection, partly worship, partly maternal love.

In the autumn of 1847 Florence broke down completely. For the past eighteen months she had been ailing. The morning hours of secret toil were a physical strain, her life in public a continual irritation; she grew thin, slept badly. The autumn months at Embley always brought commotion—Clarkey wrote that the Nightingales "lived in a state of endless faddle which wore poor Flo out." In September she wrote to Clarkey that she could not face "the prospect of three winter months of perpetual row." She was rescued by the Bracebridges, who persuaded Fanny to let them take Florence to Rome with them. The fuss was enormous, Parthe was overcome at the idea of separation, but on October 27 the party left England.

"OH, HOW HAPPY I WAS! I never enjoyed any time in my life as much as my time in Rome," Miss Nightingale wrote. Once more as soon as she left home she was transformed. With Σ she was free. They wandered about Rome on foot, eating meals of vegetables and bread in small restaurants and practicing their Italian; they bought chestnuts from a street vendor, filled their handkerchiefs with them and walked all the way to the Villa Mellina, talking and eating; they stayed to watch the sunset, running all the way home and being late for dinner. And no one scolded.

Miss Nightingale was intoxicated with Rome. Fifty years later she could still describe every street, every turning, every building in minute detail. One of the great moments of her life was her first sight of the Michelangelo ceiling in the Sistine Chapel. "I did not think I was looking at pictures but straight into Heaven itself," she wrote to Parthe. For the rest of her life she had prints of the Sistine frescoes hanging in her room.

She danced out the old year of 1847. "This is the most unbroken freedom from dreaming I have ever had." She was well all the six months she was in Rome.

And there she met Sidney Herbert. Their strange and fatal intimacy began in picture galleries and churches; each was destined to exercise an extraordinary influence on the other, each in meeting the other had met his fate; but no portent indicated that this was the most important moment of their lives. The acquaintance opened with Florence's introduction by Σ to Liz Herbert, a remarkably beautiful girl who had been "almost like a daughter" to Σ. Formerly Elizabeth à Court, she had married Sidney Herbert, heir presumptive of the Earl of Pembroke, and they were in Rome on a postponed wedding tour. She was immediately attracted by Florence and they became intimate friends.

Fate had heaped blessing upon blessing on Sidney Herbert's head. He was astonishingly good-looking, tall, broad-shouldered, graceful. He had great wealth; he lived at Wilton, one of the most beautiful houses in England; his wit and social talents were famous. He secretly belonged to an association the members of which were pledged to give away a large part of their incomes in private charity. And yet, with so much goodness, brilliance, beauty and success, he was without zest for life. He longed only for the quiet—the peace of Wilton.

It was impossible. Riches, high office, power, responsibility descended on him. He found the burden almost intolerable and turned for consolation to religion. He built a new church at Wilton, he worked to improve the condition of the poor, he was in the process of building and endowing a convalescent home, and into these and other plans Liz also threw herself heart and soul, desiring to share her husband's every activity and thought.

When Florence returned to England her friendship with the Herberts, a profound satisfaction to Fanny, grew ever closer. Through them she met a circle of extremely influential people also interested in hospital reform. Public opinion was awakening, the Herberts and their friends were eager for information, and Miss Nightingale by now had an enormous mass of it at her fingertips. She gradually became known as an expert on hospitals and public health.

The Herberts knew of her plan to go to Kaiserswerth and approved. Surely her mother must allow herself to be convinced. In September 1848 a heaven-sent opportunity offered. Because of her uncertain health, Parthe was ordered to take a cure at Carlsbad, and the Nightingales planned to go on to Frankfurt, where Clarkey and M. Mohl were staying. Kaiserswerth being nearby, Florence's plan, still unknown to her family, was to "visit the deaconesses and perhaps fit in a little training."

But 1848 was the year of revolution in Europe. When disorders broke out in Frankfurt, W.E.N. thought it wiser to stay in England and take Parthe to Malvern. Florence's reaction was violent. It was God Himself who had cut her off from Kaiserswerth because she was sinful. She went down into the depths of depression; the short period of comparative happiness was over.

She succumbed to dreaming, helplessly, shamefully. She dreamed of fame, of Richard Monckton Milnes. To escape from dreaming she sought relief in nursing the poor of the village of Wellow. Fanny and Parthe became irritated: it was unnecessary for Florence to go into the "black filth" of the cottages, actually touching sick people and even making their beds; she would bring an infectious disease into the house and kill her sister. She visited her sick in secret, running back breathless through the muddy lanes to be in time for dinner. W.E.N., who hated dirt, disease and ugliness, was disgusted. He told Florence she was being theatrical; if she wanted something to do, let her work in the village school. She did for a time, but she failed. "I was disgusted with my utter impotence," she wrote. "I made no improvement. . . . Why should I? . . . Education I know is not my genius."

In March, when the Nightingales went to London for the season, Florence was in a mounting delirium of self-reproach and frustration. Dreaming became uncontrollable. She was convinced that she was going insane. In this wretched state another blow fell. Richard Monckton Milnes, after seven years, would be put off no longer. He insisted on a definite answer—would she marry him or not? She refused.

It was an act which required extraordinary courage. She was deeply stirred by him, she called him "the man I adored"; and she renounced him for the sake of a destiny which it seemed impossible she would ever fulfill. In a private note she analyzed her reasons. She wrote several versions; she began it, broke off, returned to it again. "I have an intellectual nature which requires satisfaction and that would find it in him. I have a passionate nature which requires satisfaction and that would find it in him. I have a moral, an active, nature that requires satisfaction and that would not find it in his life. . . . I could be satisfied to spend a life with him in combining our different powers in some great object. I could not satisfy this nature by spending a life with him in making society and arranging domestic things." But she could not always be rational. With a pencil that trembled, and dug itself into the paper, she wrote again, "Life is desolate without his sympathy." And yet she would not give way.

Fanny was disappointed and furiously resentful. She determined that Florence should not have her own ungrateful way, and what had begun as genuine maternal solicitude for her daughter's welfare turned into a contest of wills in which love and kindness were forgotten. By the autumn Florence's mental and physical state was pitiable. Fanny and Parthe nagged her unceasingly, and she adopted a policy of silence, which they found intensely provoking. She was far from well and fainted on several occasions; sometimes her mind became a blank and she looked at people wildly and vaguely, not hearing what was said to her.

Σ once more intervened, and persuaded Fanny to let the Bracebridges take Florence to Egypt and to Greece. A journey to Egypt was an adventure in 1849. But in Florence's state the brilliant landscapes of the Nile meant little.

Now Σ acted on her own responsibility. They were to travel home from Greece by land; she chose a route through Berlin and suggested that while they were there Florence should visit Kaiserswerth. Florence was too wretched to be grateful. Her only relief was in the companionship of animals. On the Nile she had found two chameleons which slept on her bed. She had been sorry to part with them, "they were such company." She was traveling now with two tortoises, called Mr. and Mrs. Hill, a cicada named Plato, and Athena, a baby owl, which she had rescued from some boys at the Parthenon. Athena became devoted to her and traveled everywhere in her pocket. At Prague Athena ate Plato.

But in Berlin, as soon as Miss Nightingale began visiting hospitals and charitable institutions, her spirits revived. "All at once I felt how rich life was." On July 31 she reached Kaiserswerth for her first visit. When she left two weeks later, she felt "so brave as if nothing could ever vex me again." She was well, brimming with vitality. In less than a week she had dashed off a pamphlet of thirty-two pages, telling the women of England, women "going mad for the want of something to do," of work, happiness and comradeship waiting for them at Kaiserswerth.

On August 21 she reached Lea Hurst and "surprised my dear people, sitting in the drawing room, with the owl in my pocket. Sat with Mama and Parthe. Rode with Papa." Happiness lasted only a few hours. Fanny was furiously angry; the visit to Kaiserswerth was shameful, a disgrace. Florence must be forced to do her duty, made to stay at home and engage in the pursuits proper to her upbringing and station.

Five years had passed since her attempt to enter Salisbury Infirmary; she was no longer a girl but a woman of thirty, and she had accomplished nothing. Only her determination persisted. "Resignation!" she had written in 1847. "I never understood that word!" A new struggle began, more bitter, more unhappy than ever before.

THE CONFLICT had changed its character for the worse. Fanny had begun by sincerely wishing for Florence's happiness, sincerely believing what she wished to do would ruin her life. That point was passed. There was justification for Miss Nightingale's sense of guilt: she evoked the worst from each one of her family; normally kind, normally generous, they behaved to her as to no one else. Fanny's obstinacy, Parthe's possessiveness, W.E.N.'s hatred of unpleasantness, became mania. The most furious opposition to Florence came from Parthe. She was thirty-one, and she had achieved only moderate success; the successes, the lovers, the popularity were Florence's, not hers.

She cast herself as the adoring indispensable sister who could not be left out of Florence's growing celebrity and success. But what if, instead of creating a brilliant, interesting life for Parthe, she went off to lead a sordid existence of her own? The possibility drove Parthe frantic.

Fanny and W.E.N. accused Florence of heartlessness: for nearly a year she had been away; Parthe had been left behind to mope, and her health had suffered. They demanded that Florence should devote herself entirely to Parthe for six months. Parthe triumphed; she made little scenes and was coaxed out of them; she sketched with Florence, sang with Florence, wandered with her in the garden, chattered of poetry and art. The effect on Florence was devastating. Stupid with frustration she was carried on Fanny's merry-go-round from Lea Hurst to Embley, Embley to London and back to Embley again.

In despair, she reproached herself. "What is to become of me," she wrote. "I can hardly open my mouth without giving dear Parthe vexation—everything I say or do is a subject of annoyance to her." "Oh dear good woman," she wrote of Fanny, "when I feel her disappointment in me it is as if I were going insane . . . what a murderer am I to disturb their happiness. . . . What am I that their life is not good enough for me?"

When the six months ended, Florence went immediately to Wilton to stay with Liz Herbert. That summer her attitude to life began to change. The absurdity of her slavery to Parthe, the encouragement of the Herberts had forced her eyes open. Her sense of guilt lessened, and at long last she saw herself as the victim, not the criminal. On June 8, 1851, she wrote a private note on her family in a new vein. "I must expect no sympathy or help from them. I must *take* some things, as few as I can, to enable me to live. I must *take* them, they will not be given to me. . . ."

A fortnight later, she had arranged to go to Kaiserswerth. There was a final scene with her mother and Parthe "which was so violent that I fainted." The following day she left.

IN 1833 PASTOR THEODOR FLIEDNER and his wife had converted a summerhouse in their garden into a refuge for a destitute discharged prisoner. From this beginning had grown the Kaiserswerth Institution. By 1851 it included a hospital, an infant school, a penitentiary, an orphan asylum and a school for training schoolmistresses. Life was Spartan, work rigorously hard, the food such as was eaten by peasants. "Until yesterday," wrote Miss Nightingale to Fanny in July 1851, "I never had time even to send my things to the wash. We have ten minutes for each of our meals, of which we have four. We get up at 5; breakfast $\frac{1}{4}$ before 6. . . . Several evenings in the week we collect in the Great Hall for a bible lesson. . . . I find the deepest interest in everything here and am so well in body and mind. . . . Now I know what it is to live and to love life. . . . I wish for no other earth, no other world than this."

Florence slept in the orphan asylum and worked there and in the hospital. She was even present at operations, which was considered almost indecent. Miss Nightingale always denied she had been "trained" at Kaiserswerth. "The nursing there was nil," she wrote later, "the hygiene horrible. The hospital was certainly the worst part of Kaiserswerth. But never have I met with a higher tone, a purer devotion than there."

Towards the end of her stay the Herberts visited her, and Herr Fliedner told them that "no person had ever passed so distinguished an examination, or shown herself so thoroughly mistress of all she had to learn as Miss Nightingale." She was completely happy; her heart overflowed and she made one last effort to be reconciled with her mother and Parthe. She repeated what she had tried to explain a hundred times before but never so gently, so affectionately. "Give me time, give me faith. Trust me, help me. . . . My beloved people I cannot bear to grieve you. Give me your blessing." Neither Fanny nor Parthe responded. She never appealed to them again.

In October Florence joined her mother and sister at Cologne. "They would hardly speak to me. I was treated as if I had come from committing a crime." A miserable party traveled towards England. Florence was seething with plans. She was wild to train in earnest, this time in one of the great London hospitals.

Once more her plans were doomed. At Embley, Parthe was better because her sister was at home, and W.E.N. would not go away for treatment of an inflamed eye unless Florence went with him. If the claims of family affection were strong the claims of suffering were stronger. She entered the cage once more. "O weary days—oh evenings that never seem to end," she wrote at this period. "Women don't consider themselves as human beings at all. . . . I know nothing like the petty grinding tyranny of a good English family."

In March the Nightingales went to London for the season, and the restrictions imposed on Miss Nightingale reached absurdity. She was treated as a schoolgirl, her movements controlled, her letters read, her invitations supervised; yet she was a woman of over thirty with a distinguished circle of her own. Among her friends in 1852 were Elizabeth Barrett Browning, George Eliot, Lord Shaftesbury, Lord Palmerston, Arthur Stanley, later Dean of Westminster Cathedral, and his sister Mary Stanley, who was her slavish admirer.

W.E.N. became uneasy. It was borne in on him at last that his wife and daughter were treating Florence badly. He became her secret ally. Parthe and Fanny prolonged the struggle, but victory had in fact been won when she went to Kaiserswerth. Her suffering was no longer despair, it was rebellion. Dreaming tortured her no longer. She possessed herself now, and she was at peace.

But as Florence proceeded openly to plan, Parthe's health grew steadily worse. In August 1852 she had a mental breakdown. She was taken to see the Queen's physician, Sir James Clark. Sir James, who was an admirer of Miss Nightingale, told Florence that Parthe's only chance of regaining normal balance was to learn to live without her. Florence described this as "a terrible lesson which tore open my eyes as nothing less could have done. My life has been decided thereby." The burden of her responsibility for Parthe had been removed, and she began quietly to separate herself from home. She was making plans to go to Paris, and by the end of October she had obtained an authorization from the Council of the Sisters of Charity in Paris allowing her to work in their hospitals and institutions.

She did not wish to go to Paris without Fanny's consent. There was a financial difficulty, W.E.N. was nervous, and she shrank from a quarrel; Fanny must be brought round. Clarkey was called in to try her hand at persuasion. She did not sympathize with Miss Nightingale's "craving after sisters of charity and hospitals," but it was her philosophy that "everyone should do as they please and be agreeable about it. . . . Flo should be perfectly free to do her own foolishness, or her own wickedness, if she likes. It is only by knocking their heads that brats learn not to knock them . . . you know my passion for freedom."

Though Fanny fought obstinately she could not continue to fight. Once more she was persuaded, implored by the Herberts, the Bunsens, by the Bracebridges, by Aunt Mai. She retreated, contesting every inch of the way. How, for instance, was Florence to travel to Paris? She refused to allow Florence to be accompanied only by her maid. It turned out that Lady Augusta Bruce was going to Paris in the second week of November and would be delighted to have Miss Florence Nightingale as a traveling companion. Florence, who was in London staying with the Herberts, began to pack her trunks.

At this stage a great-aunt was taken ill. The journey to Paris was canceled and Florence went to nurse her through her last illness. On New Year's Eve Miss Nightingale was back at Embley.

Fanny now saw how Florence's presence exasperated Parthe. She gave way—partially. Florence might go to Paris for a short time on a visit to Clarkey, but the horrid name of the Sisters of Charity was not to be mentioned. Parthe was furious, possessiveness and jealousy consuming her with a twin flame. She wrote angrily to Clarkey: "I believe [Florence] has little or none of what is called charity or philanthropy, she is ambitious— very and would like well enough to regenerate the world. . . . Here she has a circle of admirers who cry up everything she does or says as gospel and I think it will do her much good to be with you, who, though you love and admire her, do not believe in the wisdom of all she says *because* SHE says it. I wish she could be brought to see it is the intellectual part which interests her, not the manual. When she nursed me everything which intellect and kind intention could do was done but she was a shocking nurse."

Yes, there was, in spite of the gentleness, the sympathy, the charming intelligence, something about Florence which chilled. She did not know what personal feelings were, in a private note she wrote that never in her life did she recollect being swayed by a personal consideration. She lived on a different plane, frighteningly and infuriatingly remote.

On February 4 Miss Nightingale arrived at 120 rue du Bac

to stay with Clarkey. Her plan was to make a survey of all the hospitals in Paris. She spent a month visiting hospitals, infirmaries, almshouses and institutions, watching doctors examine patients and witnessing operations. She drew up a detailed questionnaire which she circulated to hospitals in France, Germany and England; she accumulated an enormous collection of reports, illustrating hospital organization and nursing arrangements in hospitals throughout Europe. To assemble and digest this mass of information in a single month was a remarkable feat. Her long hours of toil in the chilly dawn bore fruit— already she was not a student but an expert. Eight years had been spent in keeping her away from hospitals but she was as much at home in them as if she had lived in hospitals all her life.

Arrangements had been made for her to enter the hospital of the Sisters of Charity in the rue Oudinot, to undergo a training in nursing. The day of her entry had been fixed—when Fate struck again. Her grandmother was taken ill, and she was recalled to England to nurse her through her last days.

At this point Liz Herbert told her of an opening in London which caused her to give up her idea of training in a hospital. The Institution for the Care of Sick Gentlewomen in Distressed Circumstances was to be reorganized, and the committee, of which Lady Canning was chairman, were looking for a superintendent to undertake the reorganization. Liz Herbert suggested Florence, and on April 18 there was an interview. "I was delighted with Miss N's quiet sensible manner," Lady Canning wrote to Liz. "I am sure she must be a most remarkable person. It is true that [she] looks very young but . . . I hope the old matron or housekeeper will . . . supply the young Miss N's deficiencies in years." Miss Nightingale had suggested she should bring, as her personal attendant, a "superior elderly respectable person" at her own expense.

When the news was broken to the family Parthe had to be put to bed, Fanny had to be given sal volatile, and meals were sent away untouched. W.E.N. took refuge in the Athenaeum Club. He did, however, take one vital step—he decided to allow Miss Nightingale five hundred pounds a year.

Negotiations with the committee were trying. Their hesitations centered upon Miss Nightingale's social position. She was a young lady in society—was it not peculiar for a young lady to wish for such a post; should a lady nurse one who was not a lady; was it nice for a lady to be present at medical examinations and, worse still, at operations? Despite everything, by the end of April Miss Nightingale had successfully completed her negotiations. She was to live at the institution; she was to receive no remuneration; but she was to be in complete control not only of the management of the institution but of its finances.

On July 13 she went to London with Aunt Mai to supervise the alterations to the institution's new premises. On August 12, 1853, she went into residence at Number 1 Harley Street.

IN THAT SUMMER OF 1853 Miss Nightingale was moving in her natural element. Keeping a firm hand on her committee, she issued precise instructions. Her requirements were revolutionary. She had a scheme for saving work by having hot water "piped up to every floor." She wanted a "windlass installation," a lift to bring up the patients' food. She wrote to Lady Canning: "The nurse should never be obliged to quit her floor, except for her own dinner and supper, and her patients' dinner and supper (and even the latter might be avoided by the windlass we have talked about). Without a system of this kind, the nurse is converted into a pair of legs. *Secondly*, that the bells of the patients should all ring in the passage outside the nurse's door *on that story* and should have a valve which flies open when its bell rings, and *remains* open in order that the nurse may see who has rung."

Her committee became dazed. Sent out on expeditions to unknown parts of London to view windlass installations and systems of bells with valves, they had the sensation of having released a genie from a bottle. They were, she said, "children in administration." The accounts of the institution were in confusion; the two committees that managed the institution, a Ladies' Committee and a Gentlemen's Committee, quarreled with each other, and the doctors did the same.

During her first week Miss Nightingale and her committee had a serious difference. She was determined the institution should be nonsectarian; the committee was determined it should be Church of England. She wrote to Clarkey: "My Committee refused me to take in *Catholic* patients, whereupon I wished them good morning, unless I might take in Jews and their Rabbis to attend them. So now it is settled, and *in print* that we are to take in all denominations whatever, and allow them to be visited by their respective priests and Muftis, provided *I* will receive the obnoxious animal at the door, take him upstairs myself [to] his patient, make myself *responsible* that he does not speak to, or look at, *anyone else*, and bring him downstairs again in a noose, and out into the street. And to this I have agreed! And this is in print! Amen."

Miss Nightingale was not what her committee had expected. She gave devotion generously, and she did an immense amount of practical nursing in the institution herself, but her genius was of an unromantic character. She perceived that unorganized devotion and self-sacrifice were useless. To bring about a balanced expenditure, to put in the best possible kitchen stove, to provide patients with clean beds and good food—these were more effectual than to sit through the night cheering the dying moments of the patient expiring from scurvy and bedsores. But they were not so picturesque.

By December she had learned how to get her own way with the committee. "When I entered 'into service' here," she wrote to W.E.N., "I determined that, happen what would, I NEVER would intrigue among the Committee. Now I perceive that I do all my business by intrigue. I propose, in private, to A, B, or C, the resolution I think A, B, or C, most capable of carrying in Committee, and then leave it to them, and I always win." On December 3 she wrote to W.E.N.: "I am now in the heyday of my power. . . . Lady —— who was my greatest enemy is now, I understand, trumpeting my fame through London." And her patients worshipped her, writing her innumerable adoring letters.

As soon as the institution was running smoothly, however, she became restless. In the spring of 1854 she began to visit hospitals and collect facts to establish a case for reforming conditions for hospital nurses. She began to think about a training school capable of producing a supply of respectable, qualified nurses. Rumors reached Embley, and Fanny and Parthe broke into new lamentations, but Florence was not at home to be reproached in person. The eager, oversusceptible girl became the elegant, composed, independent woman of genius. It was now beyond anyone to stop Miss Nightingale in her course. Fanny's reproaches trailed into silence and were heard no more.

In the summer of 1854 cholera broke out in the miserable, undrained slums of London. Hospitals were overcrowded; many nurses died; many, afraid of infection, ran away. In August Miss Nightingale went as a volunteer to the Middlesex Hospital to "superintend the nursing of cholera patients." The patients, brought in every half hour, were chiefly wretched, drunken prostitutes. From one Friday afternoon until Sunday afternoon Miss Nightingale was never off her feet in her care of them. From the Middlesex Hospital she went to Lea Hurst, where Mrs. Gaskell, the famous author, was staying. Mrs. Gaskell's letters give a vivid firsthand view of Florence at this time.

"I wish you could see her," she wrote. "She is tall; very slight and willowy in figure; thick shortish rich brown hair; very delicate colouring; grey eyes which are generally pensive and drooping, but which when they choose can be the merriest eyes I ever saw; and perfect teeth, making her smile the sweetest I ever saw. . . . She has a great deal of fun and is carried along by that, I think. She mimics most capitally. . . ."

And yet a week later Mrs. Gaskell was chilled. Beneath the fascination, the sense of fun, the gentle hesitating manner, there was the hard coldness of steel. "She has no friend—and she wants none. She stands perfectly alone, halfway between God and His creatures. She is so excessively gentle in voice, manner, and movement, that one never feels the unbendableness of her character when one is near her," and again: "This want of love for individuals becomes a gift and a very rare one, if one takes it in conjunction with her intense love for the RACE—but she is really so extraordinary a creature that anything like a judgment of her must be presumptuous."

What Fanny felt about the astonishing daughter whom she had never understood, she told Mrs. Gaskell one day, with tears in her eyes. "We are ducks who have hatched a wild swan." But it was not a swan they had hatched: in the famous phrase of Lytton Strachey's essay, it was an eagle.

The summer of 1854 marked the end of a chapter. The long, agonizing apprenticeship was over and the instrument uniquely fitted for its purpose was forged. In March 1854 England and France had declared war on Russia. In September the allied armies landed in the Crimea. Harley Street and Middlesex Hospital had been a dress rehearsal. Now the curtain was about to go up on the play.

Chapter 4

To the British people the invincibility of the British army was an article of faith. It was taken for granted that the nation which had beaten Napoleon at Waterloo could not be defeated. But since Waterloo forty years of economy had run their course. Before the army sailed the processes by which the troops were to receive food and clothing, to be maintained in health and cared for when wounded or sick, had already fallen into confusion.

In the spring of 1854, however, confidence was complete. The guards were a magnificent body of fighting men as they marched through London to embark. The crowds which cheered them did not know that behind these splendid troops were no reserves. They were doomed to perish, and when they perished their ranks were to be filled with raw recruits made "pretty perfect in drill in sixty days."

The first operation was not to be in the Crimea, but in Romania, then a Turkish province, where the Russians were besieging the Turks. A British base was established at Scutari on the Asian shore of the Bosporus, and in June 1854 the British army disembarked at the Black Sea port of Varna. A cholera epidemic broke out; the army became an army of invalids, accomplished nothing, and the Turks raised the siege in Romania on their own. The allies then proceeded to the true objective of the war, the destruction of the great naval base recently constructed by the Russians at Sebastopol, on the Crimean peninsula.

The plan of a descent on Sebastopol had been discussed in the press, but it had never been officially intimated to the supply departments. Consequently, when the British army embarked at Varna to go to the Crimea, there were not enough transports there to take both the army and its equipment across the Black Sea. Thirty thousand men were crammed in, but pack animals, tents, cooking equipment, medicines and stores were left behind. Twenty-one wagons only were brought for thirty thousand men going into action. On September 14 the army disembarked at a cove with the sinister name of Calamita Bay. "My God," exclaimed Dr. Alexander, first-class staff surgeon to the Light Division, "they have landed this army without any hospital transport, litters or carts or anything." Cholera still raged, and more than a thousand cholera cases were shipped back to Scutari.

A week later, the British and the French won the hard-fought battle of the Alma, and the wounded paid the price of the abandonment of the army's hospital equipment. There were no bandages, no chloroform, no morphia. The wounded lay on the ground or on straw mixed with manure in a farmyard. Amputations were performed without anesthetics; the victims sat on tubs or lay on old doors; the surgeons worked by moonlight because there were no candles or lamps.

At Scutari were enormous barracks, the headquarters of the Turkish artillery. These barracks and the hospital attached had been handed over to the British, who assumed that the hospital, known as the General Hospital, would be adequate. The unexpected cholera epidemic produced total disorganization. The first thousand cases had filled the hospital to overflowing; drugs, sanitary conveniences, bedding, doctors were insufficient. While Dr. Menzies, senior medical officer, was struggling with this crisis, he was notified that the battle casualties from the Alma and a thousand more cholera cases were on their way. He was ordered to convert the artillery barracks into a hospital. It was an impossible task. The vast building was bare, filthy and dilapidated; and there was no hospital equipment to put in it.

Meanwhile the sick and wounded were enduring a ghastly journey across the Black Sea. Men with amputations were flung about the decks screaming with pain. When they arrived at the Barrack Hospital there were no beds. They lay on the floor wrapped in the blankets saturated with blood and ordure in which they had been lying since they left the battlefield. No one could attend them because there were not sufficient doctors. Some of them lay without even a drink of water all that night and through the next day.

Such scenes of horror were nothing new in Britain's military annals. But the earlier horrors had remained unknown. England rang with the story of Scutari because with the British army was the first war correspondent, William Howard Russell, of *The Times* of London. Russell was an Irishman with an Irishman's capacity for indignation, and in dispatches published in early October he furiously described the soldiers' sufferings. His revelations burst on the nation like a thunderclap, and on October 13 Sir Robert Peel opened "*The Times* Fund" for supplying the sick and wounded with comforts. The same day *The Times* published another dispatch from Russell. "The manner in which the sick and wounded are treated is worthy only of savages. . . . The French are greatly our superiors. Their medical arrangements are extremely good, their surgeons more numerous and they have also the help of the Sisters of Charity . . . these devoted women are excellent nurses." The next day a letter in *The Times* demanded angrily, "Why have we no Sisters of Charity?"

All this was read by Sidney Herbert, who in December 1852 had been appointed Secretary at War, and was now responsible for the treatment of the sick and wounded. The administration of the British army was then divided between two ministers, the Secretary for War and the Secretary at War. The Secretary at War was responsible for the financial administration of the army, and since the criminally inadequate arrangements had been executed in his name, the blame must lie at the door of Sidney Herbert. His situation was painful. It was not only that one of the main objects of his life was to improve conditions for the British private soldier, but his political position was now extremely delicate. His mother had been Russian, and the famous Vorontsov road, to be of such overwhelming importance to the British army in the Crimea, led to the Vorontsov palace at Yalta which belonged to his uncle. A storm of national fury burst on his head. The military authorities, enraged by the interference of *The Times*, refused to admit that anything was wrong, but Herbert was not convinced and acted on his own responsibility. On October 15 he wrote inviting Miss Nightingale to go to Scutari in command of a party of nurses.

She was already arranging on her own to sail for Constantinople with such a party. On Saturday, October 14, she had written asking Liz Herbert to negotiate her release from Harley Street. Would Sidney approve? "And are there any stores for the Hospital he would advise us to take out."

This letter crossed Sidney Herbert's to her. The terms of his letter were considered by Miss Nightingale to be her charter. She was to go as an administrator, not as an angel of mercy. The overwhelming consideration was that she should advance the cause of nursing. "There is but one person in England that I know of who would be capable of organising and superintending such a scheme," he wrote. "You would of course have plenary authority over all the nurses, and I think I could secure you the fullest assistance and cooperation from the medical staff, and you would also have an unlimited power of drawing on the Government for whatever you thought requisite for the success of your mission. . . ."

On Monday Sidney Herbert called on her at Harley Street. The number of nurses in the party was fixed at forty. She was doubtful of her ability to control more than twenty, but he insisted that twenty would not be a sufficiently large number to make the experiment impressive.

On Wednesday, October 18, Sidney Herbert placed Miss Nightingale's appointment before the Cabinet. It was unanimously approved, and next day she received a formal confirmation. She was appointed "Superintendent of the Female Nursing Establishment of the English General Hospitals in Turkey," and her authority was defined: "Everything relating to the distribution of the nurses, the hours of their attendance, their allotment to particular duties is placed in your hands, subject of course to the sanction and approval of the chief medical officer; but the selection of the nurses in the first instance is placed solely under your control." Precise as these instructions appeared, they contained a flaw. The words "in *Turkey*" were subsequently contended to limit her authority to Turkey, and to exclude her from the Crimea.

Her appointment caused a sensation. No woman had been so distinguished before. Fanny and Parthe were ecstatic. Forgetting they had brought her to the verge of insanity by their opposition, congratulating themselves on the scope of experience which qualified her for her mission, they hastened to London to share in the excitement. In the confusion of packing, the owl Athena was left shut in an attic, where she was found later dead. When the lifeless body was put into Miss Nightingale's hands, she burst into tears. "Poor little Beastie," she said, "it was odd how much I loved you." It was the only sign of emotion she showed on the eve of departure.

She had made up her mind to start on Saturday, October 21. In four days nurses had to be engaged, their uniforms made, their tickets and berths reserved. The Herberts had asked the Bracebridges to accompany her; Σ and her husband had agreed and Mr. Bracebridge took over the financial and traveling arrangements.

The headquarters of the expedition were at the Herberts' London house. Florence's friend Mary Stanley was a member of the Herberts' circle who was interested in nursing. She, Mrs. Bracebridge and two other ladies sat all day in the dining room prepared to receive a rush of applicants—but few came.

Only thirty-eight women who could conceivably be considered suitable presented themselves. Most of the candidates came from the humblest class—"Maid of all work," "Very poor," "Has been for a few days in St. George's Hospital." Mary Stanley wrote, "One alone expressed a wish to go from a good motive. Money was the only inducement." The nurses were to receive twelve to fourteen shillings a week with board, lodging and uniform; after three months' good conduct they received sixteen to eighteen shillings.

Each nurse signed an agreement submitting herself absolutely to Miss Nightingale's orders. Misconduct with the troops was to be punished by instant dismissal. No young women were accepted, the majority being stout elderly old bodies. Miss Nightingale wrote later from Scutari that in future "fat drunken old dames of fourteen stone and over must be barred, the provision of bedsteads is not strong enough." A uniform was provided, but each nurse was to take underclothing, four cotton nightcaps, one cotton umbrella and a carpetbag. No colored ribbons or flowers were allowed.

Fourteen nurses who had experience of serving in hospitals were engaged; the remaining twenty-four were all members of religious institutions. The party was nonsectarian; nurses, insisted Miss Nightingale, were to be selected "with a view to fitness and without any reference to religious creed."

With the assistance of an old friend she had met in Rome, Manning, the priest who later became Cardinal, it was arranged that ten Roman Catholic nuns, five from Bermondsey and five from Norwood, should join the party, and that they should be completely under Miss Nightingale's control. A nun nursing for Miss Nightingale must take her nursing orders from Miss Nightingale and not from her mother superior; and the mother superior must take her nursing orders from Miss Nightingale and not from the bishop. It was an extraordinary concession for Manning to have obtained, and, as far as the original nuns were concerned, it worked with perfect smoothness. The Bermondsey nuns were among the most valuable members of the party. Their superior, known as Reverend Mother Bermondsey, became one of Miss Nightingale's dearest friends.

Three other religious bodies were approached: St. John's House, a High Church sisterhood; the Sellonite Anglican sisterhood; and an evangelical body, the Protestant Institution for Nurses. The Sellonites sent eight sisters who had had experience of nursing cholera, and St. John's House sent six. The Protestant Institution flatly refused—their nurses were to be controlled only by their own committee. The refusal was unfortunate. As a result, twenty-four of the thirty-eight were either Catholic nuns or High Church sisters. This was later to become a problem.

278

Miss Nightingale refused to admit benevolent "ladies," as such, into her party. All must be nurses; all must eat the same food and wear the same uniform, except the nuns and sisters, who were allowed to wear their habits. The uniform consisted of a gray tweed dress, a gray worsted jacket, a plain white cap and a short woolen cloak. This was not designed to make the wearer look attractive, but Scutari was a disorderly camp, and a distinguishing dress was necessary to protect both the person and the reputation of the nurses.

On Saturday morning, October 21, 1854, the party left London for Marseille. Among the Nightingale papers is preserved a small black notebook containing three letters, the only personal papers Miss Nightingale took with her to Scutari. One from Fanny bestowed the maternal blessing Florence had so long sought in vain; one from Manning commended her to the Protection, Worship and Imitation of the Sacred Heart; the third was from Richard Monckton Milnes—"So you are going to the East . . . you can undertake that, when you could not undertake me."

On October 27 the party sailed from Marseille on a fast mail boat, the *Vectis*, and headed straight into a gale. Miss Nightingale, a wretchedly bad sailor, was prostrated by seasickness. On November 3, still in atrocious weather, the ship, "blustering, storming, shrieking," rushed up the Bosporus. Constantinople, in the pouring rain, looked like a washed-out daguerreotype. On the opposite shore stood the enormous Barrack Hospital of Scutari. Everyone was on deck eager to see the goal. "Oh, Miss Nightingale," said one of the party, "when we land don't let there be any red tape delays, let us get straight to nursing the poor fellows!" Miss Nightingale, gazing at the gigantic building, replied: "The strongest will be wanted at the washtub."

They were to go to the hospital at once, because wounded were expected from the battle of Balaclava. The nurses with their carpetbags and umbrellas were lowered from the *Vectis* into painted caïques, the gondolalike boats of the Bosporus, and rowed across to Scutari. As the caïques approached a rickety landing stage, the nurses shrank at the sight of a bloated carcass of a horse, washing back and forth on the tide and pursued by a pack of starving dogs. A few men, limping and ragged, were helping each other up the muddy slope to the hospital. The nurses disembarked, climbed up after them, and passed through the enormous gateway of the hospital, that gateway over which Miss Nightingale said should have been written "Abandon hope all ye who enter here."

FROM THE EUROPEAN SHORE of the Bosporus, the great quadrangle of the Turkish barracks glimmered golden, magnificent as a palace, but at close quarters romance vanished. Vast corridors with floors of broken tiles and walls streaming damp stretched for miles. Later Miss Nightingale calculated there were four miles of beds. The building was a hollow square with towers at each corner. One side had been gutted in a fire and could not be used. Within the vast ramifications of the barracks were a depot for troops, a canteen where spirits were sold, and a stable for cavalry horses. Deep in the cellars were dark and noisome dens where more than two hundred women who had been allowed to accompany the army drank, starved, gave birth, carried on their trade as prostitutes and died of cholera.

The only communication with Constantinople was by boat. At Scutari were the principal cemeteries of Constantinople, but no markets or shops. There were only tents and sheds used as drinking shops and brothels which had sprung up round the barracks.

These were obvious drawbacks, but the vast building hid a more fatal secret. Sanitary defects made it a pesthouse. The majority of the men who died there died not of the wounds or sickness with which they arrived, but of disease they contracted in the hospital. When Miss Nightingale arrived on November 5, 1854, food, drugs and medical necessities had already run short, and winter was swiftly advancing. There were men, both there and in England, who saw the approach of disaster. But the system under which the health of the British army was administered defeated them.

Three departments were responsible for the health of the army and the organization of its hospitals: the commissariat, the purveyor's department, and the medical department. Forty years of economy had cut them to the bone. The purveyor's department had been reduced to four persons, and at the outbreak of war it was extremely difficult to find anyone with experience to send out as a purveyor in chief. Mr. Ward, "poor old Ward," the purveyor at Scutari, was over seventy years of age. His staff consisted of two inexperienced clerks and three boys who also acted as messengers. Mr. Filder, the commissary general, had three clerks to conduct the whole business of supplying the army in the Crimea.

The method by which the hospitals were supplied was confused. Mr. Filder said later to one of the investigating commissions that he had never understood where his duties ended and the purveyor's began. Relations between the doctors and the purveyor, who supplied invalid foods, were even more obscure. A doctor might order a special diet, but it depended on the purveyor whether the patient received it or not. Beyond making a requisition, the doctor was powerless.

The commissary general and the purveyor themselves had only a limited power. Certain goods only might be supplied—those listed in a series of "warrants" naming definite articles. Extraordinary shortages resulted. The regulations of the British army laid down that each soldier should bring his pack into the hospital with him, and his pack contained a change of clothing and utensils for eating. These articles were consequently not on the purveyor's warrant. But most of the men who came down to Scutari had abandoned their packs at the orders of their officers and were therefore without shirts, knives or spoons. Nevertheless, the purveyor refused to consider any requisitions for these articles.

The Barrack Hospital was the fatal fruit of this system. When Dr. Menzies, senior medical officer at the Barrack Hospital, was abruptly instructed to turn the Turkish barracks into a hospital for the Alma casualties, all he could do was send for "poor old Ward." How the purveyor was to conjure hospital equipment out of the drink shops and tombs of Scutari at a moment's notice was not the doctor's concern. Mr. Ward had no authority to expend sums of money in the open market, and many of the articles required were not on his warrant. He had to requisition the commissariat on the proper forms. The commissariat wrote on the forms "None in store," and the matter was closed. The wounded arrived and were placed in the filthy, dilapidated building. Having no shirts, they lay naked.

The destruction of the British army in the Crimean campaign was materially assisted by the attitude of officer to private soldier. Savage physical suffering was endured by officers and men alike, and the officers were courageous, stoical, physically tough. But they regarded the men they commanded as "the scum of the earth." Miss Nightingale was repeatedly told: "You will spoil the brutes." The medical authorities were enraged by what they considered unreasonable demands—clean bedding, soup, hospital clothing were "preposterous luxuries" for what the officers called "blackguards" or "animals."

The doctors at Scutari had received the news of Miss Nightingale's appointment with disgust. They were understaffed, overworked; it was the last straw that a youngish society lady should be foisted on them with a pack of nurses. They had no choice but to submit, for Miss Nightingale was known to have powerful backing. Opinion was divided as to whether she would turn out a well-meaning, well-bred nuisance or a government spy.

However, on November 5 the nurses were escorted into the Barrack Hospital with every appearance of flattering attention. When they saw their quarters, the picture abruptly changed. Six rooms, one of which was a kitchen and another a closet ten feet square, had been allotted to forty persons. The same space had previously been allotted to three doctors and, in another part of the hospital, similar space was occupied solely by a major. The rooms were damp, filthy and unfurnished, but Miss Nightingale made no comment and the officials withdrew.

Fourteen nurses, they decided, would sleep in one room, ten nuns in another; Miss Nightingale and Mrs. Bracebridge would share the closet; Mr. Bracebridge and the courier-interpreter would sleep in the office; Mrs. Clark, who was to be cook, and her assistant must go to bed in the kitchen. There was one room upstairs for the eight Sellonites. They went upstairs, and hurried back. The room was still occupied—by the dead body of a Russian general. Mr. Bracebridge fetched two men to remove the corpse while the sisters waited. The room was not cleaned, and there was nothing to clean it with. There were no beds, no bedding, no food, no means of cooking food. While the nurses and sisters unpacked, Miss Nightingale went down into the hospital and managed to procure tin basins of tea. As the party drank it she told them what she had discovered.

The hospital was totally lacking in equipment. It was hopeless to ask for furniture. There were not even the ordinary necessities of life. The nurses must use their tin basins for everything, and must limit themselves each to a pint of water a day for washing and drinking, including tea.

There was nothing to sleep on but wooden benches built in round the rooms, and lying on them that night the nurses tried to console themselves by thinking how much greater were the sufferings of the wounded. The rooms were alive with fleas, and rats scurried beneath the benches all night long.

The doctors ignored Miss Nightingale. She was to be frozen out. Only one of them would use her nurses or the supplies she had brought with her. Though in London she had been assured that there was now a positive profusion of medical comforts at Scutari, she had bought a large quantity of miscellaneous provisions and stores in Marseille. Now, when she could supply what was wanted, her stores were refused. She realized that she must wait until the doctors asked her for help. She must demonstrate that she and her party were prepared to submit completely to the doctors' authority.

To do nothing demanded self-control. Miss Nightingale could accept the hard fact that they could never succeed against official opposition, but she came into conflict with her nurses. She made them sort and mend old linen, count her stores, while the cries of the men were unanswered. For nearly a week they were kept shut up in their quarters making shirts, pillows and slings. This was not what they had left England to accomplish. They blamed Miss Nightingale.

She was first able to get a footing in the hospital through the kitchen. To cook anything at the Barrack Hospital was practically impossible. The sole provision for cooking was thirteen Turkish copper caldrons, each holding about four hundred and fifty pints. Tea was made in the unwashed coppers in which meat had just been boiled. It was undrinkable. The meat for each ward was issued to the orderly for the ward. The orderly would tie it up, put some distinguishing mark on it, like a rag or an old nail, and drop it into the pot. The water did not generally boil; the fires, made of green wood, smoked abominably. When the contents of the coppers were distributed, the joints were sometimes almost raw. The orderly then carried the meat into the ward and divided it up, usually on his bed.

The food was almost uneatable by men in good health; as a diet for cholera and dysentery cases it produced agonies. The torture endured by the men when the pangs of hunger were superimposed on diarrhea was frightful.

The day after Miss Nightingale arrived she began to cook "extras" in her own kitchen. She had bought arrowroot, wine and beef essences and portable stoves in Marseille. Ships bringing wounded from Balaclava began to unload. With the doctors' permission, she provided pails of hot arrowroot and port wine for the survivors, and within a week her quarters had become an extra diet kitchen. For five months this kitchen was the only source of invalid food. She strictly observed official routine, nothing being supplied without a requisition signed by a doctor.

Cooking was all she had managed to accomplish when, on November 9, the situation changed. A flood of sick poured in on such a scale that a terrible crisis arose, and prejudices and resentments were for the moment forgotten.

Chapter 5

IT WAS THE OPENING of the catastrophe. The destruction of the British army had begun. These were the first of the flood of men suffering from dysentery, scurvy, starvation and exposure who were to pour down on Scutari all through the terrible winter. Over in the Crimea on the heights above Sebastopol the army was marooned. Seven miles below the heights lay

Balaclava, the British base, which had been a tiny fishing village. No steps had been taken to make it sanitary, and the army which marched in was stricken with cholera. The single narrow street was a disgusting quagmire. Piles of arms and legs amputated after the battle of Balaclava, with sleeves and trousers still on them, had been thrown into the harbor and could be seen dimly through the water. The whole village smelled of putrefying bodies.

On November 5 the Russians had attacked at Inkerman, on the heights above Sebastopol. In a grim battle fought in swirling fog the British were victorious. But the victory was not reassuring. The British troops were exhausted. Their commanders were shaken by the revelation of Russian strength. It was evident that Sebastopol would not fall until the spring. The British army was going to winter on the heights before Sebastopol, and it not only had no supplies but no means of transporting supplies. Churned by the wheels of heavy guns, the one wagon track which linked Balaclava with the camp on the heights had become impassable.

Icy winds blew, and the troops, without shelter, drenched by incessant rain, had no fuel. Every bush, every stunted tree was burned, and the men clawed roots out of the earth to gain a little warmth. They slept in mud, ate hard dried peas and raw salt meat. The percentage of sickness rose and rose.

The first transports loaded with sick landed at Scutari that November 9 without notice. The doctors, overwhelmed, turned to Miss Nightingale. Her nurses began with desperate haste to stuff bags with straw. These were then laid down in wards and corridors. There were no pillows, no blankets. Even the supply of bags gave out as day after day the sick poured in, until the miles of corridors were lined with men lying on bare boards. The unwashed rotten floors crawled with vermin. As the Reverend Sidney Godolphin Osborne, a volunteer chaplain, knelt to take down dying messages, his paper became thickly covered with lice.

The doctors worked "like lions," but some men were there for two weeks without seeing a surgeon. There were no screens or operating tables. Amputations had to be performed in the wards in full sight of the patients. One of Miss Nightingale's first acts was to procure a screen from Constantinople so that men might be spared the sight of the suffering they themselves were doomed to undergo.

She estimated that in the hospital at this time there were more than one thousand men suffering from acute diarrhea and only twenty chamber pots. Huge wooden tubs stood in the wards and corridors for the men to use. The orderlies disliked the task of emptying these, and they were left unemptied for twenty-four hours on end. "The mortality . . . is frightful. . . . This is only the beginning of things," Miss Nightingale wrote. The classification between wounded and sick broke down, for the wounded began to catch fevers.

Fate had worse in store. The Crimea was devastated by a storm of hurricane force. Tents were reduced to shreds, horses blown for miles. Every vessel in Balaclava harbor was destroyed, among them a large ship loaded with warm winter clothing and stores for the troops.

Winter then began in earnest with further storms of sleet and winds that cut like a knife as they howled across the bleak plateau. Dysentery, diarrhea, rheumatic fever increased by leaps and bounds. More shiploads of sick inundated Scutari, the men so ragged and so swarming with vermin they told the nurses to keep away. "My own mother would not touch me," one of them said. By the end of November the administration of the hospital had collapsed. Through all the departments there was a paralyzing fear of incurring any responsibility, of exceeding instructions.

And then in the confusion a light began to break. It dawned on harassed officials that there was one person in Scutari who had money and the authority to spend it—Miss Nightingale.

She had at her disposal from various sources a sum amounting to more than thirty thousand pounds of which seven thousand pounds had been collected by her personally; and Constantinople was one of the great markets of the world. During the gathering catastrophe, it became known that whatever was wanted, from a milk pudding to an operating table, the thing to do was to "go to Miss Nightingale." Each day she ascertained what articles were lacking in the purveyor's store. The goods were then bought in Constantinople, and were issued by her but only upon official requisition, duly signed by a medical officer. Gradually the doctors ceased to be suspicious.

One of her first purchases was two hundred hard scrubbing brushes and sacking for washing the floors. She insisted on the huge wooden tubs in the wards being emptied promptly. Her next step was to arrange to have the men's clothes washed by the women who lived in the cellar beneath the hospital.

By the end of December Miss Nightingale was in fact purveying the hospital. During the period of two months she supplied, on requisition of medical officers, about six thousand shirts, two thousand socks and five hundred pairs of drawers. "I am a kind of General Dealer," she wrote Sidney Herbert in January, "in knives and forks, wooden spoons, tin baths, cabbages and carrots, operating tables, towels and soap, small tooth combs, precipitate for destroying lice, scissors, bed pans and stump pillows." She even fitted an entire regiment with warm clothing when Supply had declared such clothing unprocurable—Supply was compelled to get all its goods from England.

Outside Sebastopol conditions grew steadily worse. Early in December Lord Raglan, the commander in chief, announced that a further five hundred sick and wounded had been shipped to Scutari. It was impossible to cram any more cases into the hospital, and Miss Nightingale pressed to have the burned-out wing put in order. But the cost would be considerable, and no one had the authority to do it. Miss Nightingale took matters into her own hands. She engaged two hundred workmen, and paid them partly out of her own pocket and partly out of *The Times* fund. By the time the transports arrived, with eight hundred men instead of five hundred, two new wards and a corridor were ready for them. Received by Miss Nightingale and her nurses with clean bedding and warm food, "we felt we were in heaven," one of them said.

The affair caused a sensation. It was the first important demonstration of what men at Scutari called the "Nightingale power." Respect for the "Nightingale power" was increased when it became known that her action had been officially approved by the War Department and the money she had spent refunded to her.

To Miss Nightingale herself these victories were incidental. Her mission was to prove the value of women as nurses. Unhappily, no difficulties with doctors or purveyors were as discouraging as her difficulties with the nurses themselves.

"I came out, Ma'am, prepared to submit to everything. But there are some things, Ma'am, one can't submit to. There is caps, Ma'am, that suits one face and some that suits another. If I'd known, Ma'am, about the caps, I wouldn't have come, Ma'am." This, Miss Nightingale wrote, was the kind of question which had to be adjusted while "we are steeped up to our necks in blood." To convince nurses and sisters of the necessity for discipline was almost impossible. They could not understand why a man who desperately needed stimulating food should have to go without until the nurse had been authorized by a doctor. It was felt that Miss Nightingale was determined to increase her own power and cared nothing for the sick. Reluctance to obey her instructions was constant, and many of her nurses heartily disliked her.

However, she had managed to establish herself, and her nurses were fully occupied. On December 14 she wrote Sidney Herbert a cheerful letter, listing "what we may consider as having effected." She never wrote quite so cheerfully again. Later that day she suddenly discovered, through a letter from Liz Herbert to Mrs. Bracebridge, that forty-six more nurses were due to arrive at Scutari the next day under the leadership of Mary Stanley.

Miss Nightingale had not been consulted on the dispatch of this new party, and it was in direct contravention of her agreement with Sidney Herbert. More serious, the party was consigned not to her but to Dr. Cumming, a senior medical officer; she had been publicly passed over.

She was furiously angry, and on December 15 wrote Sidney Herbert again. "The quartering them *here* is a physical impossibility, the employing them a moral impossibility. You must feel I ought to resign, where conditions are imposed on me which render the object for which I am employed unattainable." And she pointed out, "The proportion of Roman Catholics which is already making an outcry you have raised to 25 in 84. Dr. Menzies has declared that he will have two only in the General Hospital."

On Sidney Herbert's part there was honest misunderstanding. He was harried, in poor health, almost worked to death, possessed of a wife who was prone to be swept away emotionally. In the confused mind of Mary Stanley there was a mixture of jealousy of Miss Nightingale and religious fervor—she had secretly determined to become a Roman Catholic. And behind Mary Stanley was the formidable figure of Father Manning, who wished to focus on the nuns of his church the fame and glory which surrounded the Scutari nurses.

Mr. Bracebridge spoke angrily of "Popish plots," and that, Miss Nightingale said, was ridiculous. She and Manning remained friends, and she said on several occasions that he had always treated her fairly. But the arrival of Mary Stanley's party dealt her mission a blow from which it never completely recovered. Before it, she was well on the way to complete success. After it, though she achieved personal triumphs, her authority was not established until her mission was almost ended; and the original purpose of the undertaking became obscured by a fog of sectarian bickering.

The high percentage of Catholics and High Church Anglicans in her original party had already provoked an outcry in England. It was Miss Nightingale's fate to be attacked by both sides, to have to endure what she called the "Protestant Howl" and the "Roman Catholic Storm." If Mary Stanley had publicly announced her intention of joining the Roman Catholic Church, Sidney Herbert would not have allowed her to go to Scutari. She not only kept it secret but took with her Mother Frances Bridgeman of Kinsale, an Irish nun of ardent temperament who openly avowed that her mission was spiritual. Her fifteen Irish nuns considered they were under no obligation to obey anyone but Mother Bridgeman, and Mother Bridgeman acknowledged only the authority of her bishop. The entire constitution of the party was contrary to all Miss Nightingale's known rules.

Besides the nuns, there were nine "ladies" and twenty-two "hired nurses." Many of these were ludicrously without experience, one old woman, Jane Evans, having spent her life looking after pigs and cows. Out of the whole forty-six no fewer than twenty had come out with the intention not of nursing but of being "assistant ecclesiastics."

When, on December 15, their ship anchored outside Constantinople, Mr. Bracebridge went on board and advised the party not to disembark. There literally was not a vacant corner in Scutari, and food, water and fuel were seriously short. Dr. Cumming also rebuffed them, declining flatly to employ the nurses and ladies in the hospitals. Temporarily a house belonging to the British Embassy could be lent them, and there they must go until arrangements could be made to send them home. Miss Nightingale, in a cold fury, refused to take any responsibility. It appeared, however, that owing to the lavish style in which the party had traveled, they had spent all of the fifteen hundred pounds with which they had started and were penniless. Florence offered to lend Mary Stanley ninety pounds from her own income, and it was unwillingly accepted. Later she lent another three hundred pounds. Mary Stanley wrote to Liz Herbert that it needed "all her love for Flo" not to feel hurt at being treated so *officially*.

Harassed as Miss Nightingale was, however, she soon saw that it would be disastrous to send the party back. A scandal would do her cause irreparable harm. So on December 24 she suggested a compromise. Some of the Irish nuns should be taken at once into the Barrack Hospital, and to make room for them the Norwood nuns, who had come in the first party and were not experienced in hospital nursing, should be sent home. This arrangement would not increase the number of Roman Catholic nuns in the hospital, which was something Dr. Cumming refused to contemplate.

The compromise did not work. A storm burst immediately. The sisters from Norwood, bathed in tears, bitterly resented being sent home. Mother Bridgeman refused to allow her nuns to enter the Barrack Hospital without her—it would be "uncanonical." She declared they must have their own Jesuit

chaplain and refused the ministrations of the resident Father. Miss Nightingale was on her feet constantly and on her knees dressing wounds for eight hours at a time; but instead of rest she had arguments with Mary Stanley and Mother Bridgeman. Loud-voiced, voluble, Mother Bridgeman was christened by Miss Nightingale "Mother Brickbat."

In the second week of January she at last received Sidney Herbert's answer to her letter. He accepted full blame, confirmed her authority, implored her not to resign, and authorized her to send the second party home. Liz wrote, equally penitent for her part in it all. Miss Nightingale was moved; the letters were "most generous and I deeply feel it." Throughout the misfortunes caused by Mary Stanley's party she never again reminded Sidney Herbert that he was responsible for their ever having arrived at all.

Mary Stanley by now found herself utterly disillusioned. She no longer wished to go to the Barrack Hospital—it was foul and vermin-infested; she had found fleas on her dress. At the end of January it was suggested that the Turkish cavalry barracks at Koulali should be turned into a hospital, and Mary Stanley determined to take it over and run it in her own way. With a group of her ladies and nurses and with Mother Bridgeman and ten of her nuns, she went off to Koulali, refusing to ask Dr. Cumming's permission and declaring she would arrange the purveying of the hospital herself.

At the same time Lord Raglan suggested that nurses be sent to the General Hospital at Balaclava. Miss Nightingale did not wish to send them because the hospital was so filthy and the orderlies so undisciplined, but she was unwilling to refuse Lord Raglan. Reluctantly, therefore, she allowed eleven volunteers to go, some of them from Mary Stanley's party, under the control of the superior of the Sellonite sisters. Thus Mary Stanley's party was dispersed.

Mary Stanley's own reign at Koulali was short. It was to be run on the "lady" plan. There were to be maids to do the menial tasks. The ladies were not to wear uniform. Liz Herbert sent "white furred coats" and was asked for straw bonnets.

Koulali was not ready when Mary arrived. The second day

three hundred sick were carried in. There were no beds, no food. Sacks were hastily stuffed with straw, ladies made lemonade. That night Mary Stanley went round the wards and discovered her health would not stand the strain. More sick poured in, and she became hysterical. Mortality rose, until Koulali's rate was the highest of any hospital in the Crimea. In March Mary Stanley went home, leaving a bill for eighty-two hundred pounds for purveying Koulali which the authorities had to pay.

At this difficult juncture in the history of nursing, Miss Nightingale's position was strengthened by Queen Victoria. On December 14 the Queen had sent gifts to the men and a personal message to Miss Nightingale. Would she suggest something the Queen could do "to testify her sense of the courage and endurance so abundantly shown by her sick soldiers?" Miss Nightingale was already pressing Sidney Herbert to change a regulation affecting the sick soldier's pay; ninepence a day was docked from the pay of the sick soldier in the hospital, even though his sickness was the result of active service, while the wounded man was docked only fourpence ha'penny. Now she wrote to the Queen asking her to have the deduction made the same for sickness as for wounds. The Queen acted immediately. On February 1 it was announced that the men's pay would be rectified as from the battle of the Alma. If the arrival and conduct of Mary Stanley and her party had shaken Miss Nightingale's prestige, Queen Victoria assisted materially to restore it.

In January 1855 the sufferings of the British army before Sebastopol began to reach a fearful climax. Still no stores had reached the army. What had happened to them? the investigating committee demanded later. Huge quantities of supplies had been sent out. Much of this unquestionably vanished in the Turkish customs house, a "bottomless pit," but Miss Nightingale declared that most stores never reached the men because of "Regulations of the Service." Shiploads of cabbages were thrown into the harbor at Balaclava on the ground that they were not consigned to anyone. Twenty thousand pounds of lime juice arrived for the troops on December 10, 1854, but none was issued until February. Why? Because no order existed for the inclusion of lime juice in the daily ration. Meanwhile, on January 2, of twelve hundred sick men arriving at Scutari, eighty-five percent were cases of acute scurvy. For want of lime juice and vegetables the men's teeth were dropping out; in some cases they were losing toes.

In January 1855 there were twelve thousand men in the hospital and only eleven thousand in the camp before Sebastopol. It was, Miss Nightingale wrote, "calamity unparalleled in the history of calamity." In this emergency she became the rock to which everyone clung. Her calmness, her resource, her power to take action raised her to the position of a goddess. The doctors came to be absolutely dependent on her, and the men adored her. "If she were at our head," they said, "we should be in Sebastopol next week."

Sidney Herbert had asked her to write to him privately in addition to her official reports. She somehow found energy to write him more than thirty letters of enormous length, crammed with practical suggestions for the reform of the present "system —or no system." Her facts and figures were freely used by Herbert and other members of the Cabinet, and important changes made in British army organization during the Crimean War were based on her recommendations.

IN SPITE OF IMPROVEMENTS in the Barrack Hospital, cleaner wards and lavatories, adequate food, the mortality climbed. At the end of December an epidemic, described as "Asiatic cholera" or "famine fever," broke out among the emaciated men of the British army. Four surgeons and three nurses died in three weeks, and "poor old Ward," the purveyor, and his wife. The officers on their rounds began to be afraid to go into the wards. And even when, at last, the number of men in the sick transports decreased, the mortality figures in the Barrack Hospital continued to rise.

In England fury succeeded fury. A great storm of rage, humiliation and despair had been gathering. Through reading the *Times* dispatches of William Howard Russell, the public had realized "with what majesty the British soldier fights." And these heroes were dead. The men who had stormed the heights at Alma, charged with the Light Brigade at Balaclava, fought the grim battle against overwhelming odds in the fog at Inkerman, had perished of hunger and neglect. Even the horses which had taken part in the Charge of the Light Brigade had starved to death.

On January 26 a motion was brought forward in the House of Commons to appoint a committee "to inquire into the condition of the Army before Sebastopol." It was a vote of censure on the government, and it was carried in an uproar. The government fell and Sidney Herbert went out of office. But Miss Nightingale's position was not weakened. The new Prime Minister was her old friend, Lord Palmerston. The two offices of Secretary for War and Secretary at War were combined and held by Lord Panmure, who was instructed to show consideration for her wishes and opinions.

At the end of February, Lord Panmure sent out a sanitary commission to investigate the hospital and the camps. This commission, said Miss Nightingale, "saved the British Army." Their discoveries were hair-raising. They described the sanitary defects of the Barrack Hospital as "murderous." Beneath the magnificent structure were sewers of the worst possible construction. The building stood in a sea of decaying filth; the porous plaster walls were soaked in it. Every puff of air blew poisonous gas through the pipes of numerous open privies into the wards.

Nurses had noticed that certain beds were fatal. Every man put in these beds quickly died. They proved to be the beds nearest the privies, where the gases were worst. The water supply was not only insufficient, it was contaminated. The commissioners had the channel opened through which water for the hospital flowed, and found the water supply passing through the decaying carcass of a horse. They ordered the precincts of the hospital to be cleared, and five hundred and fifty-six handcarts full of rubbish and twenty-six dead animals were removed. They had the sewers flushed, the walls limewashed to free them from vermin, and they tore out benches and shelves which were harboring rats. The effect was instant: the mortality rate began to fall. In the Crimea spring came with a rush; the bleak plateau before Sebastopol was bathed in sunlight and carpeted with crocuses and hyacinths. The men's rations improved. The survivors of the fearful winter lost their unnatural silence and began once more to curse and swear.

The emergency was passing, and as it passed opposition to Miss Nightingale awoke again.

Chapter 6

BY THE SPRING OF 1855 Miss Nightingale was physically exhausted. She was a slight woman who had never been robust, and was now living in almost unendurable hardship. When a flood of sick men came in she was on her feet for twenty-four hours at a stretch.

"She had an utter disregard of contagion," wrote the Reverend Sidney Godolphin Osborne. "The more awful any particular case, especially if it was a dying man, the more certainly might her slight form be seen bending over him, administering to his ease and seldom quitting his side until death released him." She estimated that during that winter she witnessed two thousand deathbeds. The worst cases she nursed herself.

One of the nurses described accompanying her on her night rounds. "It seemed an endless walk. . . . As we slowly passed along the silence was profound; very seldom did a moan or cry from those deeply suffering fall on our ears. A dim light burned here and there, Miss Nightingale carried her lantern which she would set down before she bent over any of her patients. I much admired her manner . . . it was so tender and kind."

The troops worshipped her. "What a comfort it was to see her pass even," wrote a soldier. "She would speak to one, and nod and smile to as many more; but she could not do it all you know. We lay there by hundreds; but we could kiss her shadow as it fell and lay our heads on the pillow again content."

This was work hard enough to have crushed any ordinary woman; yet, she wrote, it was the least of her functions. The crushing burden was the administrative work. Her quarters were called the Tower of Babel. She slept in the storeroom in a bed behind a screen; in the daytime she worked at a little unpainted deal table in front of it. All day long a stream of callers thronged in, officers, nurses, doctors, asking for everything from writing paper to bandages. Every time there was a pause she snatched her pen and went on writing, for there was no one capable of acting as her secretary. Requisitions, orders, records, immense correspondence must all be written by herself.

It was terribly cold, and she hated cold. Her breath congealed on the air; the ink froze in the well. Hour after hour she wrote on; the staff of the hospital declared that the light in her room was never out. She wrote for the men and sent home their dying messages. She wrote for the nurses, many of whom had left children behind. She wrote official reports, official letters. Papers were piled round her in heaps; they lay on the floor, on her bed. Often in the morning Mrs. Bracebridge found her still in her clothes on her bed, where she had flung herself down in a stupor of fatigue.

She spared herself nothing—but the joy had gone out of the work. The high spirit, the faith which had sustained her through the first months of her mission faded as she learned the power of official intrigue. As she wrote to Sidney Herbert, "The real hardship of this place is that we have to do with men who are neither gentlemen nor men of education nor even men of business, nor men of feeling, whose only object is to keep themselves out of blame."

She crossed the path of such a man, Dr. John Hall.

Dr. John Hall, Chief of Medical Staff of the British Expeditionary Army, had been kept occupied in the Crimea since the autumn of 1854, but the hospitals of Scutari were also under his control and he had no intention of allowing them to get out of hand. His name had been associated with an unsavory case in which a private had died after a brutal flogging, and he was known throughout the army as a strict disciplinarian. He did not believe in chloroform, and warned his officers against its use. "The smart use of a knife is a powerful stimulant and it is much better to hear a man bawl lustily than to see him sink silently into the grave."

Just before Miss Nightingale's arrival, Dr. Hall had been sent by Lord Raglan to inspect the hospitals at Scutari. He had reported that "the whole hospital establishment has now been put on a very creditable footing and nothing is lacking." It was a fatal statement. He had committed himself. Henceforward he had to stand by what he had said, and his subordinates had to back him up. After Sidney Herbert had heard the truth from Miss Nightingale, he wrote Lord Raglan: "I cannot help feeling that Dr. Hall resents offers of assistance as being slurs on his preparations."

By the spring of 1855 Dr. Hall was boiling with rage. One of the government investigating commissions had reported unfavorably on his hospitals, and, worse, he himself had been censured by Lord Raglan. He judged the time had come to assert himself. He knew his powers and he had his friends. One of his friends was a Dr. Lawson, whom he now appointed as senior medical officer at the Barrack Hospital to replace Dr. Menzies. Dr. Lawson had recently been censured by Lord Raglan for callous treatment of the sick aboard a transport ship. For this he had been relieved of his duties—only now to assume them in another place.

Miss Nightingale received the news of his appointment with horror. Dr. Lawson was a walking reminder of what the medical department could do. Dr. Hall knew how to protect his own, and how to punish the disloyal. He was absolute master of his department, and no Nightingale power, no Sidney Herbert could save those who offended him. Terror swept over the Scutari medical staff. The doctors began to succumb to Lawson's influence and avoid Miss Nightingale. They slipped back into a state of mind in which hospital equipment was thought an unnecessary extravagance.

But despite Dr. Lawson the work of the Sanitary Commission was having rapid effect. The hospital's mortality rate had fallen by April to 14.5 percent and by May 19 was down to 5.2 percent. Thanks to Miss Nightingale, there were plenty of drugs, surgical instruments, baths and medical comforts. Food had been miraculously improved by a famous London chef, Alexis Soyer, who had come out in March. In manner he was a comic-opera Frenchman, but Miss Nightingale recognized his genius and became his friend. Armed with authority from Lord Panmure, Soyer attacked the kitchens. As he walked the wards with his tureens of excellent soup, the men cheered him.

With the Barrack Hospital reasonably satisfactory, Miss Nightingale determined to go to the Crimea. There were two large hospitals at Balaclava. One was the General Hospital under Dr. Hall's personal direction; the other a collection of huts called the Castle Hospital on the heights above Balaclava harbor. Disquieting news had reached Miss Nightingale of the conduct of the female nurses, particularly at the General. And now the fatal flaw in her instructions appeared. Dr. Hall maliciously asserted that, as "Superintendent of the Female Nursing Establishment in the English Military Hospital in *Turkey*," she had no jurisdiction over the Crimea. It was with his support that the nurses there, most of whom had come out with Mary Stanley, were defying her authority.

Nevertheless, on May 5, six months after she had landed at Scutari, Miss Nightingale stepped ashore in Balaclava, and went at once to report to Lord Raglan. She rode, says Soyer, who was one of her party, "a very pretty mare which by its gambols and caracoling seemed proud to carry its noble charge." Afterwards, she visited a mortar battery outside Sebastopol, where the astonishing sight of a lady accompanied by gentlemen in glittering uniforms produced "an extraordinary effect." The news spread like wildfire that the lady was Miss Nightingale, and the soldiers rushed from their tents and "cheered her to the echo with three times three." The party then cantered home, Miss Nightingale looking exhausted. It was, she said, the unaccustomed fresh air.

The next morning she began her inspection. It was a depressing task. The hospitals were dirty and extravagantly run, the nurses inefficient and undisciplined. She was received with hostility and insolence. She ignored it, and gathered herself together to do battle. But before she could do anything, she collapsed. The senior medical officer was hastily summoned, and a statement was issued that Miss Nightingale was suffering from Crimean fever.

All Balaclava, says Soyer, was in an uproar. A solemn cortege transported her to the Castle Hospital on the heights, four

LEONARD

soldiers carrying her on a stretcher. By this time she was delirious and very ill. At Scutari the men, when they heard, "turned their faces to the wall and cried," a sergeant wrote home, and throughout England the tidings were received with consternation.

For more than two weeks she hovered between life and death. In her delirium she was constantly writing. She thought her room was full of people demanding supplies, and that an engine was inside her head. In the height of the fever all her hair was cut off.

When at last she was out of danger it was Lord Raglan himself who, after a long visit at her bedside, telegraphed home the good news. Strangers passed it on to each other in the streets. As she recovered she was frantic to settle the Balaclava problems but her weakness was extreme. The doctors advised her to go to England. She refused. It was arranged that she should be taken to Scutari on a transport and occupy a house belonging to one of the chaplains who had gone home on sick leave.

The house had windows opening onto the Bosporus—the most famous view in the world, which, she said, she had never had time to look at—and a green tree in a garden behind. For the next few weeks she lived in a world of the convalescent, a world filled with small things. Sidney Herbert had sent her a terrier from England, and she had an owl, given her by the troops to take the place of Athena, and a baby. The baby belonged to a Sergeant Brownlow, and spent the day, while its mother washed for the hospital, in a pen which she could see from her bed.

By July she was better. Her cropped hair was growing in little curls which gave her a curiously touching and childish appearance. Dr. Sutherland, her doctor, told her the fever had saved her life by forcing her to rest, and implored her to spare herself. She dared not. Storm clouds were gathered in the Crimea. Lord Raglan had died, and his successor, General Simpson, was against "pampering the troops." Moreover, the War Office had not passed on to the new commander in chief the official instructions as to her position. Every day her authority was being more flagrantly disregarded.

She was gathering her strength to return to the Crimea when a fresh blow fell. The Bracebridges wished to go home. For nine months they had shared the fearful sights, the horrible smells, the petty slights. It was given out that they would come back in the autumn, but she knew they would never return. As soon as they sailed on July 28 she went back to her quarters at the Barrack Hospital, retaining the chaplain's house and sending her nurses there by turns to rest.

The medical authorities did not welcome her; they felt that the state of the hospital was now satisfactory. There was an unwillingness to consult her. Some of the admirable work of the Sanitary Commission was being undone. Trouble with the nurses was continuous. A few suffered from drink; others got married. One morning six of her best nurses came into her room followed by six corporals or sergeants to announce their impending weddings. On one occasion an emissary from a Turkish official called on her with an offer to purchase a particularly plump nurse for his master's harem.

Much more serious trouble followed. After Mrs. Bracebridge went home Miss Nightingale appointed a Miss Salisbury to take charge of the "Free Gift" store at a salary. The "Free Gifts" were voluntary contributions sent from England for the men. Among the gifts were articles of value as well as groceries, wines, clothing; it was necessary to keep careful track of them to ensure that they were fairly distributed. From the moment Miss Salisbury took up her post, she began thieving on a considerable scale. A search was ordered and the results were staggering. In her room every box, every package, every cranny was crammed with stolen goods.

Miss Nightingale summoned the new military commandant, General Storks. The wretched Miss Salisbury was now groveling on the floor and sobbing, imploring Miss Nightingale not to prosecute, but to send her home at once. Miss Nightingale wished to avoid a scandal, so she and General Storks agreed. It was a grave mistake.

Miss Salisbury, back in England, declared she had been ill-treated. Miss Nightingale refused to let the gifts be used, and Miss Salisbury had abstracted them in order to give them to the poor fellows for whom they were intended. Why had not the police been called in if what Miss Nightingale asserted was true? Miss Salisbury was soon in conference with Mary Stanley, and a formal complaint against Miss Nightingale was submitted to the War Office. Mr. Hawes, the Permanent Under-Secretary, chose to take the complaint seriously. An official letter was written to Miss Nightingale and General Storks requesting them to justify their conduct.

When the action of the War Office became known in London the Nightingale family felt that someone must go out to be with Florence. On September 16, therefore, Aunt Mai arrived at Scutari. She burst into tears at sight of Florence, thin and worn. And the web of partisan intrigue, irritations and discourtesies in which Flo was forced to live horrified her.

At the end of that month a new tempest blew up in the Crimea. Dr. Hall and the Reverend Mother Bridgeman— "Mother Brickbat"—without informing Miss Nightingale, had effected a large-scale transfer of nurses to the General Hospital, Balaclava, where Mother Bridgeman was to be superintendent. When Miss Nightingale considered the situation she came to the conclusion that her personal resentment must be swallowed. Sebastopol had fallen, evacuated by the enemy, and the end of the war was only a question of time. She was desperately anxious not to come to shipwreck at the eleventh hour. She went to the Crimea determined, in her favorite phrase, "to arrange things," ready even to conciliate Dr. Hall and Mother Bridgeman.

At first it seemed that she might succeed. And then a copy of *The Times* for October 16, 1855, arrived from London, and all her work was undone. It contained a report of a lecture given at Coventry by Mr. Bracebridge, a furious and inaccurate attack on British army authorities and doctors. Other papers reprinted the allegations and it was believed that Miss Nightingale herself had instigated this assault on the army medical department.

Miss Nightingale objected in the strongest possible manner to the lecture, but the damage had been done. She contemplated the wreckage of her endeavors with despair. "I have been appointed a twelvemonth today," she wrote, "and what a twelvemonth . . . of experience which would sadden not a life but eternity. . . ."

As if she had not enough to endure she was taken ill again in Balaclava. But in a week she was working once more, ignoring humiliations as long as female nursing in military hospitals might emerge as a unified undertaking at the end of the war. No official statement had yet come to establish her authority, and Dr. Hall gave out that she was an adventuress and to be treated as such. Minor officials treated her with vulgar impertinence. The purveyor refused to honor her drafts.

In November she was hastily summoned back to Scutari, where a new cholera epidemic had broken out. Her prestige in the Crimea had never been so low, or her difficulties so great, when an astonishing demonstration of public feeling in England placed her in the position of a national heroine whom no one could afford to ignore.

A LEGEND had been growing as survivors of the British army came home and told the story of Miss Nightingale and the Barrack Hospital. The legend was born, and gained strength in cottages and tenements, in beerhouses and gin shops. In topical doggerel, innumerable songs were written about her. A verse of one of them, still popular at regimental reunions fifty years later, runs:

> Her heart it means good for no bounty she'll take,
> She'd lay down her life for the poor soldier's sake;
> She prays for the dying, she gives peace to the brave,
> She feels that the soldier has a soul to be saved.
> The wounded they love her as it has been seen,
> She's the soldier's preserver, they call her their Queen.
> May God give her strength, and her heart never fail,
> One of Heaven's best gifts is Miss Nightingale.

Quantities of a biography were sold, price one penny. "Miss Nightingale" appeared everywhere in prints and in Staffordshire figures, the likenesses all imaginary because she objected to having her portrait circulated. Ships, racehorses, lifeboats were named after her. Strangers called at Embley and asked to be allowed to see her desk.

The successive tidings of her illness, her recovery and her determination to stay at her post until the end of the war had raised public feeling to the boiling point. A committee was formed to honor her, with the dukes of Cambridge and Argyll, Sidney Herbert and Richard Monckton Milnes as members, and public meetings were held throughout the country. So much money came in that it was decided to set up a Nightingale Fund, to enable her to "establish . . . an institute for the training of nurses." After the formation of the fund Queen Victoria, to "mark her warm feelings of admiration," presented a brooch, a Saint George's Cross in red enamel surmounted by a diamond crown, inscribed: "To Miss Florence Nightingale, as a mark of esteem and gratitude for her devotion towards the Queen's brave soldiers from Victoria R. 1855."

Miss Nightingale was not gratified; praise, popularity, jewels left her unmoved. In regard to the fund, she wrote the committee that she could accept it only if it was understood that there was great uncertainty as to when she would be able to employ it. The fact was that reform of nursing no longer filled her horizon. She had set herself a new and gigantic task—to reform the treatment of the British private soldier.

A mystical devotion to the British army had grown up within her. In the troops she found the qualities which moved her most. They were victims; her deepest instinct was to be the defender of victims. They were courageous; she instantly responded to courage. And their world was not ruled by money. The supreme loyalty which made a man give his life for his comrade, the courage which enabled him to advance steadily under fire, were displayed by men who were paid a shilling a day.

She did not sentimentalize the British private soldier. Queen Victoria offered to send eau de cologne for the troops, but Miss Nightingale said someone had better tell her a little gin would be more popular. She accepted and loved the troops as she accepted and loved children and animals. She called herself the mother of fifty thousand children. "Give them opportunity

. . . and they will use it. Give them books and games and amusements and they will leave off drinking," she wrote Parthe.

It became clear to her that she must look after the troops not only when they were ill but when they were well. In May 1855, after strenuous opposition, she had opened a small reading room in the hospital. The authorities feared that the men would get above themselves if they read instead of drank, and she was accused of "destroying discipline." However, their conduct was excellent. She found that many of them could neither read nor write, and asked if she might engage a schoolmaster. This was absolutely refused by the military commandant.

She discovered the men drank their pay away because they were dissatisfied with the official method of sending money home. They believed they were defrauded. She made it a practice to sit in her room one afternoon a week and receive the money of any soldier in the hospital who desired to send it to his family. About one thousand pounds a month was brought in, involving her in a very large amount of extra work. When the men rejoined their regiments they wished to continue sending money home. She submitted a scheme to the authorities, but it was refused.

In her letter of thanks for Queen Victoria's brooch, she laid before the Queen the men's difficulties in remitting money home. The Queen sent the letter down to a Cabinet meeting. Palmerston, the Prime Minister, thought it excellent, but Panmure said it only showed that she knew nothing of the British soldier. He wrote to the commander in chief in the Crimea: "The great cry now, and Miss Nightingale inflames it, is that the men are too rich; granted, but it is added that they have no means to remit their money home. . . . The soldier is not a remitting animal . . . there are many so selfish and brutish, whose appetite is their God, and everything is offered up to gratify its sensual longings. You must change the class of the British soldier if you would have it otherwise." Lord Panmure proved wrong. Offices where money orders could be obtained were opened and seventy-one thousand pounds was sent home in less than six months. It was, said Miss Nightingale, all money saved from the drink shops.

In the summer of 1855, when General Storks became commandant, she found at last an enthusiastic collaborator; working hand in hand they brought discipline and order to the Barrack Hospital and its neighborhood. By September one large recreation room, called the Inkerman Coffee House, was opened for the army; then a second one, in the courtyard of the Barrack Hospital, for patients. By the spring of 1856 four schools had also been opened. "The lectures," she wrote, "were crowded to excess so that the men would take the door off the hut to hear. Singing classes were formed, and the men got up a little theatre for themselves. Football and other games for the healthy, dominoes and chess for the sick, were in great request. A more orderly population than that of the whole Command of Scutari in 1855–1856 it is impossible to conceive."

It was an astonishing achievement. During the winter of 1855–1856 the picture of the British soldier as a drunken intractable brute faded away never to return.

In every other direction, however, the good that Miss Nightingale had done was being undone, and she was tormented by official spite. Most heartbreaking of all was the case of Miss Salisbury and the "Free Gifts." Night after night she sat up wrestling with her statement for the War Office. "They are killing me," she told Aunt Mai. When 1856 dawned she had lost much weight, was troubled with continual laryngitis and found it difficult to sleep. In the dark icy cold she paced her room obsessed by failure. Aunt Mai wrote Mrs. Herbert that Florence often seemed about to faint with exhaustion, and lay on the sofa unable to speak or eat. Yet if anyone came to see her she pulled herself together.

In the early months of 1856, her difficulties reached a climax.

In London there had been an extensive whitewash of officials accused of negligence in the disastrous winter of 1854–1855. Dr. Hall had become Sir John Hall, KCB ("Knight of the Crimean Burial grounds I suppose," wrote Miss Nightingale). He had been circulating round London a "Confidential Report" on Miss Nightingale and her nurses which had been written by the chief purveyor in the Crimea and which was a tissue of unfounded accusations and malicious libels. Miss Salisbury's stories were also being believed; and Mary Stanley, while writing Florence letters of devoted affection, was busily spreading rumors. Meanwhile Mother Bridgeman and the Hall faction were openly declaiming their intention of routing her out of the Crimea.

On February 20 she had written to Sidney Herbert asking him to urge the War Department to telegraph a statement of her powers to the authorities in the Crimea. It had not come. When in March the Land Transport Corps asked her to send ten nurses to Balaclava, the situation was such that she doubted if she dared to do it. There were, however, indications that Sir John Hall was a trifle uneasy. He had recently disclaimed association with the "Confidential Report," and now he wrote her a suave letter inviting her to bring the nurses. She accepted, but with so little faith in his goodwill that she took with her everything she and her nurses could need, not only food but stoves.

On the day she left for Balaclava a dispatch, establishing her position in terms far beyond anything of which she had ever dreamed, reached the Crimea. The dispatch had a curious history. In October 1855 a certain Colonel Lefroy had appeared, first in Scutari, then in the Crimea. He was, in fact, engaged on a secret mission. He was to observe and report to Lord Panmure the truth about the state of the hospitals. Reaching home in February, Colonel Lefroy pressed Miss Nightingale's case with warmth. She had asked for an official telegram defining her position, but Colonel Lefroy went further; he wished her to have the unique distinction of her name in General Orders, the bulletin issued daily by the commander in chief and posted in every barrack and mess. Lord Panmure took his advice. As Secretary of State for War he addressed a dispatch to the commander of the forces with a desire that it be promulgated in General Orders. It read in part: "Miss Nightingale is recognised by Her Majesty's Government as the General Superintendent of the Female Nursing Establishment of the military hospitals of the Army. No lady, or sister, or nurse, is to be transferred . . . without consultation with her."

The dispatch was published in General Orders on March 16, 1856, and left no room for question about her authority. It was triumph. It was complete defeat for the Hall party, the Stanley party, the Salisbury party. Her struggle was all but over, and the war was all but over, too.

On April 29 peace was at last proclaimed. English and Russian soldiers got drunk together; Lord Panmure wrote to the commander in chief in the Crimea on the importance of bringing the army home without beards. But Miss Nightingale felt no exultation. "Believe me when I say that everything in the Army (in point of routine versus system) is just where it was eighteen months ago. . . . In six months all these sufferings will be forgotten."

The nurses began to go home by detachments. Every nurse was to be provided for. No one was to be "thrown off like an old shoe." Those Miss Nightingale did not feel she could ask the government to assist she helped out of her private pocket. One thing only she implored—that they should keep out of print.

On July 16, 1856, the last patient left the Barrack Hospital and Miss Nightingale's task was ended.

The nation passionately desired to honor her. She had emerged from the war with the only great reputation on the British side. The government offered a man-of-war to take her home. Committees met, triumphal arches were planned; there were to be bands, processions, addresses. She rejected everything. She did not enjoy her fame; she was afraid of it. Her reputation stood so high that whatever she did must disappoint expectations. And she was bereaved, a haunted woman. She began to write private notes again: "Oh my poor men, I am a bad mother to come home and leave you in your Crimean graves. . . ."

On July 28 she embarked at Constantinople for Marseille, traveling incognito with Aunt Mai as "Mrs. and Miss Smith." She left Aunt Mai in Paris and went on alone to England. At eight in the morning she rang the bell at the convent of the Bermondsey nuns. She spent the morning in prayer and meditation with the reverend mother. In the afternoon she took the train north, still alone, and in the evening walked up from the station to Lea Hurst.

Parthe, Fanny and W.E.N. were in the drawing room, but

Mrs. Watson, the housekeeper, was sitting in her room in front of the house. She looked up, saw a lady in black walking up the drive, looked again, shrieked, burst into tears and ran out to meet her.

TWO FIGURES emerged from the Crimea as heroic, the soldier and the nurse. In each case a transformation in public estimation took place, and in each case the transformation was due to Miss Nightingale. Never again was the British soldier to be ranked as the scum of the earth, nor the nurse pictured as a tipsy, promiscuous harridan. Miss Nightingale had stamped the profession of nurse with her own image. She ended the Crimean War obsessed by a sense of failure. Yet, in the midst of the muddle and the filth, the agony and the defeats, she had brought about a revolution.

Chapter 7

SHE SAID she had seen Hell, and because she had seen Hell she was set apart. Between her and every normal human pleasure, every normal human enjoyment, stood the memory of the wards at Scutari. Again and again she wrote, "I can never forget."

She was pursued not by ghosts but by facts, the facts of preventable disease. The mortality of the Crimean disaster had been the ghastly fruit of the system which controlled the health administration of the British army. The system was in operation still, murdering men as surely as it had in Scutari. She, and she alone, it seemed, had discerned this self-evident truth. The summons to save the British private soldier had come to her.

She obeyed the summons but she resented her fate. She wept for herself. She grew angry; the benevolence so marked in her youth faded. Her astonishing mind developed; her penetration, iron will, scrupulous sense of fair play became still more extraordinary. But the woman of her early years ceased to exist.

She was so exhausted it seemed madness to contemplate work. But the urgency of the situation drove her. Action must be taken while the Crimean disaster was fresh in the nation's mind. What could she do? Lord Panmure was in Scotland shooting grouse. Sidney Herbert was in Ireland fishing for salmon. She besieged him with letters, and he wrote her candidly that he thought her overwrought.

She became frantic; delay was fatal. And yet—a false step was fatal too. Special difficulties, she felt, confronted her. She was a woman—that was bad; she was a popular heroine, which was worse. The two together formed a pill which officialdom would never swallow. Any scheme known to emanate from her she felt would be instantly rejected simply because it did come from her.

She therefore set out to destroy her fame deliberately as a matter of policy. The authorities expected that on her return she would make revelations. She neither revealed, nor attacked, nor justified herself. She was laying aside a powerful weapon; at the moment adoration of her had reached an extraordinary pitch. But "the buz-fuz about my name has done infinite harm," she wrote. "In no way will I contribute by making a show of myself." Instead, with infinite patience and self-effacement, she set out to win the authorities over to her side.

Suddenly she was given a dazzling and unexpected opportunity. Queen Victoria, staying at Balmoral Castle in Scotland, wished to hear the story of Miss Nightingale's experiences with the army, not only officially but privately.

Her first meeting with the Queen lasted for more than two hours and was a triumphant success. She stayed near Balmoral with her old friend the Queen's physician, Sir James Clark, and was commanded to the castle again and yet again. She went with the royal party to church. On several occasions she dined informally. Most important of all, the Queen paid her private visits. One day she appeared suddenly quite alone, driving a little pony carriage, and took Miss Nightingale off for a long walk. Another day she came over unannounced, spent the afternoon, stayed to tea, and there was "great talk."

It was, however, only a first step. Miss Nightingale had recommended a royal commission to investigate, scientifically, sanitary conditions in the army. But before the warrant for a royal commission could be issued, the Queen must be advised to do so by the Secretary of State for War. Lord Panmure must be convinced of the necessity for army reform. Panmure, whose enormous head, crowned with thick upstanding tufts of hair, had earned him the nickname "the Bison," was a difficult subject.

Though he hated detail, and had a habit of procrastinating, he was a man of character. The Queen arranged for Miss Nightingale to meet him at Balmoral. Her success exceeded all expectations—Lord Panmure succumbed to the spell which drunken orderlies, recalcitrant nurses and suspicious officials had been powerless to resist. It seemed that she had obtained everything: a royal commission was to be drawn up in accordance with her suggestions.

The prospect was rosy when she went to London on November 1 to stay with her family at the Burlington Hotel. She drew up a list of possible commissioners, balancing civilians and military men. Sidney Herbert, though far from well, finally agreed to accept the chairmanship. When Lord Panmure called on November 16, her charm worked again. Her main objective at this meeting—defining the scope of the investigation—was achieved. The commission's scope was to be general and comprehensive, "comprising the whole Army Medical Department and the health of the army at home and abroad."

And then, inexplicably, nothing happened. The official announcement of the royal warrant to set up the commission, which should have been made within the next few weeks, never came. It was Miss Nightingale's first experience of the heartbreaking disappointments in store for the reformer bold enough to challenge British government departments. She paced her room, raged, incited her fellow workers to action. Her shrewd eye had penetrated the Bison's secret. "My Lord is," she wrote, "the most bullyable of mortals." It was true. Miss Nightingale, so very persuasive, pushed him one way; when he returned to the War Office the officials who opposed her plan pushed him the other.

"I will never leave him alone till it is done," she vowed. But her personal relations with him remained pleasant, and their

correspondence was conducted with arch playfulness. "Here is that bothering woman again," she wrote. Panmure jestingly called her "a turbulent fellow" and sent her presents of game. But by March 1 she was in despair. She wrote to Sidney Herbert: "Three months from this day I publish my experience of the Crimea Campaign and my suggestions for improvement, unless there has been a fair and tangible pledge by that time for reform."

It was a threat which could not fail to make the Bison uneasy. Public opinion was at last turning in the direction of army reform; and once the tide had turned, Panmure was not the man to resist. On May 5 the royal warrant was issued, and the following week the commission began to sit.

THE STRAIN on Miss Nightingale was enormous. Three months before, she had been an invalid; now, she was working night and day not only on the commission but on her own confidential report on health administration. The strain was intensified by the emotional conflicts inseparable from Nightingale family life.

Fanny and Parthe were profuse in expressions of affection, but behaved with total want of consideration. The only place at the Burlington where Miss Nightingale could work was a little inner room opening off the outer drawing room. In the outer room Fanny and Parthe entertained friends, and interrupted her whenever the fancy took them. A carriage was provided for them, but not for her. She used cabs or even the public omnibus when she went out to visit hospitals, barracks, infirmaries. She would return almost fainting with exhaustion, to be scolded by Fanny and Parthe because she would not go to parties. It was clear to her that they coveted not her companionship but reflected glory from her celebrity.

When the commission began to examine witnesses, pressure on her increased. The summer became a nightmare, heavy with heat. The rooms at the Burlington were dark and airless, the sky perpetually gray. But Florence would not leave London.

Her position was extraordinary. The men around her christened themselves the "band of brothers," the Burlington Hotel was "the little War Office." They delighted to call her "the commander in chief." She collected the facts, she drew the conclusions, she taught them to the men who were her mouthpieces. She coached Sidney Herbert before each sitting of the commission, prepared a memorandum on each witness who was called. "These men seem to make her opinions their law," wrote Fanny to W.E.N.

Her demands on them were fantastic; yet once within her orbit it was impossible not to be fascinated. She pressed especially hard on Sidney Herbert. She repeated again and again, "Without him I can do nothing." His prestige, his power with the House of Commons, were the means by which the commission was raised to first-class importance. His powers were incomparable—if only she could get him to devote them to the work. But he complained of his health; he suffered from depression and general malaise. They were the first symptoms of mortal disease, but to Miss Nightingale, driving herself by sheer will, his complaints were "fancies."

He did not shrink from her white-hot energy, her implacability—he needed its vitalizing warmth. The fundamental differences between their two characters gave their collaboration its immense value. But because they were so different complications ensued. Miss Nightingale, so prone to hero worship, lavished no admiration on Sidney Herbert while he was alive; her eulogies were written after his death. She was impatient with him, she grumbled at him; and Sidney Herbert, renowned for his urbanity and gentleness, scolded her for her irritability and impatience. Only the words used by him at the end of every note he wrote her, "God bless you," spoke of the affection between them. The tie which united them was so strong that it did not need support. "We were identified," she wrote to Clarkey in 1861. "No other acknowledgment was needed."

Working together they were unequaled. Her industry, energy, and passion for facts, his incomparable talents as a negotiator, were a combination impossible to resist. "He was a man of the quickest and the most accurate perception I have ever known," she wrote. "Also he was the most sympathetic. His very manner engaged the most sulky and the most recalcitrant witnesses. He never made an enemy or a quarrel in the Commission."

As the commission proceeded, as witnesses were examined, it became evident that they were succeeding beyond all hopes. The case for reforming the living conditions of the British army was proving unanswerable. In July came the turn of the most important witness of all, Miss Nightingale herself. Should she testify in person? She was convinced she should not. And how much should she say? Sidney Herbert did not want to "make bad blood by reviving controversies." In the end she did not appear in person, but submitted written answers to questions. Her evidence was read by the commissioners and agreed to be conclusive.

Occupying thirty pages of the report of the commission, it is a verbatim reproduction of part of that great work which she completed in the same month, *Notes on Matters affecting the Health, Efficiency and Hospital Administration of the British Army*. This confidential report, addressed only to Lord Panmure, is a work on the grand scale, and burns with an urgency which still strikes the reader with a physical shock. She used the Crimean campaign as a test case, a gigantic experiment in military hygiene. "It is a complete example of an army after falling to the lowest ebb of disease and disaster from neglects committed, rising again to the highest state of health and efficiency from remedies applied."

In six long and detailed sections she examines the Crimean disaster. Let the past, she pleads, be buried, but alter the system so that the soldier is more humanely treated in the future. She goes on, in the most important part of the book, to prove that living conditions in the barracks of the British army in time of peace were so bad that the rate of mortality in the army was always double, and in some cases more than double, the rate of mortality of the civilian population outside. In a phrase that became the battle cry of the reformers she declared: "Our soldiers enlist to death in the barracks." It was a challenge no government could afford to ignore.

Miss Nightingale decided to defer presenting the *Notes* to Lord Panmure when it became evident that the commission's report would be written in August. Lord Panmure could shelve her confidential report but could not suppress the findings of a royal commission—though he would certainly try to evade the bothers involved in carrying out its recommendations. Once more the Bison had to be bullied.

On August 7, 1857, Sidney Herbert wrote to him and pointed out in suave terms that the disclosures the report would make were sensational. The government would certainly be attacked. He suggested the government should protect itself by taking measures to remedy the worst of the abuses before the report came before the House. He then outlined a plan drawn up by Miss Nightingale. Four subcommissions, with executive powers, were to be appointed at once by Lord Panmure. Sidney Herbert was to be chairman of each. The four commissions would: (1) put the barracks in sanitary order; (2) found a statistical department for the army; (3) institute an army medical school; (4) completely reconstruct the army medical department. The fourth Miss Nightingale called the "wiping commission" because its wide scope enabled the reformers to wipe the slate clean and start afresh.

In mid-August Panmure was shooting grouse, but, forced to come south on War Office business, he was "caught on the wing," and after a long discussion agreed to the plan "in general terms." Sidney Herbert then left for Ireland to fish for a month, "with a lighter heart after seeing Pan," he wrote to Miss Nightingale. "But I am not easy about you."

Before this letter reached her, Miss Nightingale, still toiling in the heat at the Burlington, had a complete collapse.

"I must be alone," she suddenly broke out to Parthe. "I have not been alone for four years." She refused to go to Embley, she refused to be nursed. She did consent to take a cure at Malvern, but she must be quite alone.

She was very ill, so ill that it was generally thought she must die. For once her iron will was defeated and she was forced to stay in Malvern for over a month. Her pulse raced, and she was given two cold-water packs a day to bring it down. It was not until the end of September that she went back to the Burlington, accompanied by Aunt Mai once more.

The collapse of August 1857 was the beginning of Miss Nightingale's retirement as an invalid. Since her return from the

Crimea, though she had felt exhausted and ill, she had had strength, she said, to "rush about." Though she had refused to attend public functions she had seen her friends. From now on she had strength only to work.

She not only became an invalid; she used her illness as a weapon. When Parthe proposed coming to London, Florence's reply was to have an "attack"—"excessive hurried breathing with pain in the head and heart." When W.E.N. insisted on coming, she had another and he retreated. While her life, as Aunt Mai wrote, "hung by a thread," it was too much for her to see her family. After several further efforts Parthe and Fanny gave way. They came to London for the season but they went to another hotel.

Fortunately a new interest was absorbing the family. In the previous summer Fanny, writing to W.E.N. from the Burlington, had described a visit from Sir Harry Verney. Sir Harry was owner of the historic mansion of Claydon House, in Buckinghamshire; he was fifty-six years old, a widower, and one of the handsomest men in England, immensely tall with aristocratic features. During the summer of 1857 he had asked Florence to marry him, and she had refused him. During the winter he stayed at Embley, and it began to be evident that he was becoming attached to Parthe. The engagement was announced in April and the marriage took place at Embley in June 1858.

The prospect of becoming Lady Verney occupied Parthe's mind; the business of marrying a daughter delighted and distracted Fanny. At last Florence was left alone.

A HUSH FELL over her life. In her new rooms at the Burlington she lay prostrate, convinced, as everyone round her was, that she had at most a few months to live. Aunt Mai came to stay and make her last days easy. Aunt Mai's son-in-law, Arthur Hugh Clough, the poet, became Florence's slave, wrote notes for her, delivered reports, was content, as she put it, "to do the work of a cab horse." The Nightingales, cowed, remained at a distance. Aunt Mai and Clough became the twin guardians of a shrine.

It was a strange, hothouse existence, led under the shadow of impending death. And in this atmosphere, lying on the sofa in the drawing room, seldom sitting up and almost never going out, Miss Nightingale proceeded to toil as she had never toiled before.

Lord Panmure was again being rent apart by conflicting pressures. He lost his nerve and revoked the "wiping" subcommission. Appalled, Sidney Herbert forced Panmure to see him, and after a long and stormy interview this subcommission was reinstated. It became clear to Miss Nightingale that whichever side could frighten Panmure more would be victorious.

She devised a new idea. Public opinion was the reformers' strongest weapon. She would instruct public opinion in the truth about the army through a press campaign. The outlines, the facts, even the headings for articles were supplied to contributors by her. She signed nothing herself, not even her own pamphlet, *Mortality in the British Army*, which was one of the earliest, if not the earliest, presentations of statistical facts by means of pictorial charts—Miss Nightingale believed she invented this method.

By the end of 1857 Panmure had given way. All four subcommissions were set up in December. In May a series of resolutions on the health of the army was moved in the House of Commons, to deafening cheers. One of her collaborators wrote Miss Nightingale: "To you more than to any other man or woman alive will henceforth be due the welfare and efficiency of the British Army. I thank God that I have lived to see your success."

Throughout the summer of 1858 she was at the Burlington, going out of London only twice for a week's cure of "fresh air and water packs" at Malvern. She traveled by railway in an invalid carriage attended by Aunt Mai. She was carried in a chair, and usually her bearers were old soldiers, who carried her as if she were a divinity. A space was cleared on the platform, curious onlookers were pushed back, voices were hushed and the stationmaster and his staff stood bareheaded as she was carried into the carriage. She was already becoming a legend.

Though she cut herself off from the world her rooms at the Burlington were a hive of industry. She had made her rooms cheerful with new carpets and curtains at her own expense, a friend sent flowers and plants from the country every week, and Fanny supplemented the Burlington catering with game, hothouse fruit, eggs and cream. Miss Nightingale was very ready to provide her fellow workers with breakfast, luncheons and dinners. She visited no one, but very eminent visitors came to her. The Queen of Holland, the Crown Princess of Prussia, the Duke of Cambridge called on her regularly.

In the spring of 1858 she had begun an important friendship. Captain Douglas Galton was the army's leading expert on barrack construction, and his support was to be vital to the success of the barrack subcommission. Miss Nightingale met and corresponded with him almost daily. He was also a family connection, for he was married to the beautiful Marianne Nicholson. Marianne had not spoken to the Nightingales since Florence had refused to marry her brother Henry, but she now became reconciled to them. Though Florence was too busy to see Marianne she wrote her kind letters and was godmother to one of the Galton children.

At the same time developments of great importance for the future were taking place. India had passed from the government of the East India Company to the government of the Crown, and appalling reports were received of sanitary conditions there. Miss Nightingale had been pressing for a royal commission to deal with the health of the army in India. Now she seemed likely to succeed. The first Secretary of State for India to be appointed was Lord Stanley, who was her admirer and friend.

All too soon the sky darkened. Sidney Herbert's health was breaking down. He had never been robust, and in 1857 he had had, as chairman, to grapple with the enormous tasks of obtaining and setting up the four subcommissions and then of administering them. The work was crushing, physically. Inspection of barracks meant constant traveling, there was opposition, commanding officers were insolent; the commissioners were kept waiting on barrack squares in cold and wind. Physical exertions were succeeded by the grueling labor of drafting and revising regulations. From the beginning of 1858 a marked deterioration in his health began.

Never did a man receive less sympathy. Miss Nightingale, who believed she was on her deathbed, had small consideration for lesser ailments. She drove him. And he was urged on no less relentlessly by his wife. Far from resenting his work with Miss Nightingale, Liz encouraged it; this was the part of her husband's life which she most thoroughly shared. She clung to Florence because through her she drew nearer to Sidney.

Thus goaded, Sidney Herbert struggled through 1858; the next year he was appointed Secretary of State for War. It was, on the face of it, a triumph. What could not Sidney Herbert do for army reform in the place of Panmure? But only now did it become clear that the basic difficulty was the administrative system of the War Office itself. Before reforms could be carried through, the War Office itself must be reorganized. Sidney Herbert must nerve himself to yet another gigantic task. He felt he had no choice but to accept it. His duty lay clear before him, though he knew he was not equal to the task. In consultation with Miss Nightingale he set to work "to simplify procedure, to abolish divided responsibility."

She approached this new task with a determination so grim that it was almost despair. The exhilaration of the early days was gone. She was being crushed by the weight of her labors. She had no secretary. The compilation of statistics, the noting down of columns of figures, the laborious comparisons were done by herself. The physical effort of writing down the enormous number of words she produced each day was staggering. At the end of the summer of 1859 she had another collapse. But now the attitude of her circle towards her physical condition was changing. Aunt Mai's family became impatient. Two years had passed since she had gone to the Burlington. A serious sacrifice had been made. Uncle Sam wrote that she "formed the absolute ingredient in the inner life of her domestic circle." His grievance did not stop at Aunt Mai—his daughter Blanche's life had been broken up by Florence's absorption of Clough, her husband.

At the end of September 1859 Uncle Sam did his best to persuade Aunt Mai to leave Florence. Miss Nightingale was very angry. Aunt Mai's presence in London was essential to the work.

Since Florence was the instrument chosen to do the work, if she suffered the work must suffer. She insisted that Aunt Mai must return. In October she still had Aunt Mai and Clough to slave for her in the Burlington and outwardly everything was the same. Difficulties were piling up, however; the task of War Office reform became daily more complicated and laborious; above all, there was the constant menace of Sidney Herbert's failing health.

TO CONTEMPLATE THE WORK which Miss Nightingale performed for the army produces a sensation of weariness. It is too much. No one person should have driven herself to accomplish all this. What must not these mountains of paper, of reports and letters, have cost in fatigue, in strain? And yet by 1859 this was only a part of her labors.

She had experience of civilian as well as military hospitals that no other person in Europe possessed. Her knowledge and her genius were such that inevitably she was drawn into the field of public health.

In 1859 she published a book on hospital construction, *Notes on Hospitals*, which went into three editions, and made a point still revolutionary even to educated people: that the answer to mortality in hospitals was better ventilation, better drainage and a higher standard of cleanliness. "It may seem a strange principle to enunciate as the very first requirement in a Hospital that it should do the sick no harm," she wrote. From then on she was repeatedly asked for advice on hospital construction, not only in England but also in India, Prussia, Holland and Portugal. This meant dealing with masses of details, from how to pipe water to what color to paint the walls—"the palest possible pink," she recommended. She wrote hundreds of letters to ironmongers, engineers and architects.

She also advocated a uniform system of registering patients and classifying diseases. With this in view she drafted model statistical forms to "enable us to ascertain the relative mortality of different hospitals, as well as of different diseases." The forms were adopted in most London hospitals. She found statistics "more enlivening than a novel" and loved to "bite on a hard fact." Hilary Bonham Carter wrote that however exhausted Florence might be the sight of long columns of figures was "perfectly reviving" to her.

At the same time her interest in nursing reform had never diminished, though it had been pushed for a while into second place. With the Nightingale Fund of forty-five thousand pounds at her disposal she began in 1859 taking steps to establish her training school at St. Thomas's Hospital.

While she worked on this plan she wrote a little book on nursing for the use of the ordinary woman, which became the most popular of her works. *Notes on Nursing* is a book of great charm, sympathetic, sensible, full of pungent sayings. Neither its good sense nor its wit have dated it and it can be read with as much enjoyment today as when it was published. Fifteen thousand copies were sold within the first month, and it was translated into French, German and Italian.

It is impossible to doubt, after reading it, that Miss Nightingale was a gentle and sympathetic nurse. She understood that the sick suffer almost as much mental as bodily pain. "Apprehension, uncertainty, waiting, fear of surprise, do a patient more harm than any exertion. Remember he is face to face with his enemy all the time, having long imaginary conversations with him." She spoke of the "acute suffering" caused a sick person by being so placed that it is impossible to see out of the window; of the "rapture" brought to an invalid by a bunch of brightly colored flowers. She loved babies and recommended visits from the very young. "No better society than babies and sick people for each other." She attacked "invalid food," as a result of which, she declared, thousands of patients are annually starved.

In a series of pungent paragraphs she cut to pieces the current idea of a nurse. "No *man*, not even a doctor, ever gives any other definition of what a nurse should be than this—'devoted and obedient.' This definition would do just as well for a porter. It might even do for a horse." "It seems a commonly received idea among men, and even among women themselves, that it requires nothing but a disappointment in love, or incapacity in other things, to turn a woman into a good nurse."

Early in the summer of 1860 the scheme for the nurses' school at St. Thomas's went through. The idea was not universally welcomed. A strong party in the medical world thought training nurses would merely result in their trespassing on the province of the doctors. Within St. Thomas's itself, the senior consulting surgeon argued that nurses were "in the position of housemaids" and needed only the simplest instruction, such as how to make a poultice. In this atmosphere of criticism both the resident medical officer and the matron, Mrs. Wardroper, showed courage in committing their hospital to the scheme.

Mrs. Wardroper, a gentlewoman by birth, had been left a widow with young children at the age of forty-two, and had then taken up nursing, learning in the hospital wards. She was to be superintendent of the Nightingale Training School for twenty-seven years, and a great part of the success of the school was due to her. "Her force of character was extraordinary," Miss Nightingale said of her, "and she seemed to learn from intuition."

The object of the school was to produce nurses capable of training others for posts in hospitals and public institutions. They were not to undertake private nursing. Surrounded as they were by opposition eagerly waiting to fasten on a single false step, they must be above suspicion. The future of nursing depended on how these young women behaved themselves. As a result, candidates to become Nightingale probationers were subjected to minute examination and there was great difficulty in finding young women of suitable character.

In July 1860 the Nightingale school opened therefore with only fifteen candidates. The training was to last for one year. The probationers lived in a nurses' "home" on an upper floor of St. Thomas's. Each had a bedroom to herself. Each wore a brown uniform with a white apron and cap. Her board, lodging and uniform were provided by the Nightingale Fund, and she was given ten pounds for her personal expenses during training —a standard of life which nurses had never been offered before. The girls worked hard, attending daily lectures by the staff of St. Thomas's Hospital. They were required to take notes and to pass examinations both written and oral; they acted as assistant nurses in the wards and received practical instruction from surgeons and sisters. Every month a report entitled "Personal Character and Acquirements" was filled in by Mrs. Wardroper, who exercised the closest possible individual supervision.

Strictness was necessary. The Nightingale nurse must establish her character in a profession proverbial for immorality. Flirtation was punished by instant dismissal. No girl was permitted to leave the home alone; two must always go out together. "Of course we always parted as soon as we got to the corner," one of them wrote.

It soon became evident that the school was succeeding. Within a few months a flood of applications was being received to bespeak the services of Nightingale probationers as soon as their training was completed.

It was at this time that, through Clough, Miss Nightingale met Benjamin Jowett, the great Regius Professor of Greek at Balliol College, Oxford. In appearance he was short, cherubic and strikingly handsome on a miniature scale. He spoke in a small piercing voice, and undergraduates nicknamed him the "downy owl." Between Miss Nightingale and Jowett acquaintance quickly became intimacy. Jowett pressed her to marry him. She refused, but their friendship was unaltered. They corresponded constantly, and she leaned on the devotion and advice of "my darling Jowett," as she called him.

She needed friendship, for in 1860 the work which meant most to her, the work which she had been doing for the army, received a critical setback. Sidney Herbert's health finally collapsed.

His breakdown came at the worst possible moment. War Office reorganization could be pushed through by Sidney Herbert alone. "One fight more. The last and the best," Miss Nightingale wrote him; let him nerve himself to this final task and he should be released, be allowed to resign his office.

In 1860 another blow fell. Aunt Mai returned to her family. She had been away from them for two and a half years, and it was undeniable that Florence, who had taken her from them in 1857 because she was dying, was still alive. Aunt Mai's decision provoked intense bitterness. Florence refused to see her. Miss Nightingale's bitterness was for the work—not herself. Aunt Mai had dealt the work a fatal blow by depriving her of the sympathy of the one nearest and dearest to her.

She could not be left alone. In June 1860 Hilary Bonham Carter came to take Aunt Mai's place and stayed until the following year. Clough remained faithful, but his health, like Sidney Herbert's, was causing anxiety.

Sidney Herbert was now nearly at the end of his powers. He was pronounced to be suffering from kidney disease, incurable and at an advanced stage. The doctors enjoined complete rest as his only choice; but that choice neither Miss Nightingale nor his wife would allow him to contemplate. Nor did he contemplate it himself. In the pitched battle between the forces of reform and the forces of bureaucracy, Sidney Herbert was the pivot. He struggled on.

But by the end of May 1861 what she demanded he no longer had the power to attempt. He spent the mornings on a sofa drinking gulps of brandy until he had the strength to crawl to the War Office. He was dying on his feet; an examination, made after his death two months later, showed disease so far advanced that it was a miracle he had been able to work at all for the past year.

When on June 7 he wrote to Miss Nightingale telling her he must resign, she replied bitterly. Her anger he had always been able to bear, but he could not endure her unhappiness. "Poor Florence"—he used the phrase often. "She gave up so much." Ill and harried as he was, he went to face her. A terrible interview took place. She was consumed with grief and rage, she would not see that she had before her a dying man. By failing to endure—and who could be asked to endure more than she had endured?—he was dooming the British army.

He bore it all. He did not justify himself. On July 9 he came once more to the Burlington to say good-by to her. He could no longer walk easily, and he was brought in a carriage and assisted up the stairs.

She never saw him again. He managed to reach Wilton, the place where he loved every spot as though it were a living person, and early in the morning of August 2, 1861, he died. His last words were for her: "Poor Florence—our joint work unfinished."

Miss Nightingale was overwhelmed by the news. Anguish, despair rushed in on her like the bursting of a dam. She collapsed, and was seriously ill for nearly four weeks. The structure of her existence had been destroyed at a single blow. And now that he was dead an extraordinary change took place in her. While Sidney Herbert was alive she had been the hand, he the instrument. Now he was dead she called him her "Master," and she who had criticized him never uttered now a word that was not praise. She developed an intense possessiveness about him. "I understood him as no one else," she wrote. At the Burlington she shut herself up for a fortnight, writing an account of Sidney Herbert's work for the army.

At the end of this memoir Miss Nightingale gave some striking figures. In the three years during which Sidney Herbert was Secretary of State for War only one-half of the men who entered the army died per annum (on home stations) as had previously died. Such was the immediate and startling result of better food, more warmth, more sanitation and more fresh air. Sidney Herbert, she wrote, should be remembered "as the first War Minister who ever seriously set himself to the task of saving life." He died before his work was done and no outstanding reform is associated with his name, but he succeeded in making the health of the British soldier an issue of first-class importance, which no subsequent administration could ignore.

When Miss Nightingale had finished writing her memoir she left the Burlington forever. It was haunted, she could never bring herself to go back there. She retired to Hampstead, where she isolated herself completely. To overwhelming grief was added blank despair as report after report reached her of Sidney Herbert's work being undone.

Within three months she received another mortal wound: Arthur Hugh Clough died in Italy. She was totally unnerved. "Now hardly a man remains," she wrote Douglas Galton, "of all those I have worked with these five years. I survive them all. I am sure I did not mean to."

Chapter 8

SHE WAS CONVINCED that her lifework was ended and on Christmas Eve 1861 she became dangerously ill. After this last illness she became bedridden and did not leave her room for six years. She moved from house to house but could not walk.

Yet she had nearly fifty years still to live, full of extraordinary accomplishments. For the next four years every problem affecting the health and sanitary administration of the British army was referred to her. Ministers, undersecretaries wrote to her daily asking for information and assistance. She drafted minutes, drew up regulations, wrote official memoranda, composed instructions; and with her genius for financial administration she devised a cost-accounting system for the army medical services which was still in use eighty years later.

Douglas Galton, in charge of all army construction, leaned on her judgment as Sidney Herbert had, and through him she exercised close authority over plans for new barracks and hospitals. This toughest and driest of work was only occasionally enlivened by a gleam of humor. In 1863, when Galton sent her plans for a model cavalry barracks, she sent them back with a request that the horses should be provided with windows. "I speak from actual personal acquaintance with horses. And I assure you they tell me it is of the utmost consequence to their health and spirits when in the loose box to have a window to look out of. A small bulls eye will do."

In the meantime, another vast undertaking had come into her life. Sidney Herbert had left her a frightful legacy in the Indian sanitary commission. Back in those hopeful days of 1858, when he and Miss Nightingale had asked for such a commission, she had discovered not only that no satisfactory records of army conditions in India existed but that it was hopeless to obtain in London even ordinary documents relating to India. She decided to collect firsthand information and had accordingly, in 1859, consulted with experts and drafted a *Circular of Enquiry* which was sent to every military station in India.

As the reports came in through 1860-1861 she analyzed them,

with the assistance of Dr. Farr, a statistical expert. These station reports eventually filled one thousand pages of the commission's report. Though Miss Nightingale was not a member of the commission, she was invited to submit "remarks" on the station reports.

By August 1862 she had completed the remarks under the title *Observations by Miss Nightingale*. They are among the most readable of her writings, and fiercely provocative. She showed that for years British troops in India had been dying like flies, at the rate of sixty-nine per thousand, from camp diseases rendered a hundred times deadlier in India by the tropical climate and the proximity of natives living in filth.

As to the barracks, one report stated that "300 men per room were accommodated without inconvenient overcrowding." "What is *convenient* overcrowding?" asked Miss Nightingale. Floors were earth, varnished with cow dung. Most stations contented themselves with describing their water as "smells good" or "smells bad." No drainage existed, and few lavatories. Means of washing were practically nil.

Miss Nightingale had her *Observations* privately printed and sent out in 1862, to whet public appetite for the fuller information contained in the commission's report, which did not appear until the following year.

India was in the public mind, and Miss Nightingale had no difficulty in arranging for the report the most comprehensive press campaign she had yet achieved. She sent advance copies of the report to influential journalists, and by the time it was officially issued, feature writers had had time to acquaint themselves with the essence of the two enormous volumes. She was confident that the report would be read, not only by members of Parliament, but by the public, but disaster followed. It appeared that an attempt was made to suppress the disclosures most unpalatable to the government.

The government was experiencing immense difficulties in India and being subjected to a great deal of criticism. In official circles, many thought the report exaggerated. At the War Office and the India Office Miss Nightingale's share in the report was well-known and strongly resented.

Unknown to her the clerk to the commission prepared a new and shorter edition: shorter because it left out the station reports on which it was based. It was executed with so little competence that reference was repeatedly made to passages which had been eliminated. This edition was to be the only one on sale to the public and was to be the edition presented to both houses of Parliament.

Miss Nightingale could do nothing; it was impossible to set up and reprint the 2028 closely printed pages of the original report. Finally, she was allowed to rewrite the abridged edition. It was manifestly not only unjust but absurd that the only form of the report available should omit the evidence she had worked for years to obtain at the instruction of the government.

Now she began to work on setting up the administrative machinery which should put the report's recommendations into practice. She had to serve not two masters but three. Before any sanitary measures could be taken for the army in India, the War Office, the India Office and the government of India itself must all agree to act. All recommendations emanating from the commission were suspect because it was a War Office commission. Yet the strongest opposition of all came from within the War Office itself.

There was no obligation for the War Office or the India Office to act on the recommendations of the report: they must be persuaded, threatened, cajoled into action. She "baited" Lord Stanley, who had succeeded Sidney Herbert as chairman of the commission, but she could not infect him with a sense of urgency. In time, however, an official dispatch was sent to India recommending the formation of sanitary commissions, and Miss Nightingale was asked to prepare a list of suggestions for improvements which might make the foundation of a sanitary code for India.

An outcry followed, and the report was once more attacked; the picture it gave was totally false. So powerful were the protests that action ceased, and Miss Nightingale was driven from rage to despair. All through the summer she stayed in London, ill, miserable and alone. All her gigantic labors seemed once more to be dissolving into thin air.

Suddenly, however, the scene changed. On November 20, 1863, Lord Elgin, viceroy of India, died, and Sir John Lawrence was appointed successor.

This appointment opened a new period in Miss Nightingale's life. Lawrence was the first of a series of Indian officials of the highest rank who became her intimate friends, and through whose affection and admiration she gained an inside influence in Indian affairs, where her position became even more remarkable than her position at the War Office. She had never been to India, she never did go to India, and yet she was considered an expert on India and consulted on its affairs by men who had lived there all their working lives.

Sir John Lawrence had first called on her when she was in the midst of her work on the station reports in 1861. Both felt an instant attraction. He had striking personal beauty, his height, curling golden hair and flashing blue eyes evoking admiration and awe and in part accounting for his power over native races. He was chivalrous, incorruptible and deeply religious. When the mutiny of 1857 broke out he was governor of the Punjab. His swift action and personal courage, and above all his popularity and influence with the native population, prevented upper India from rising.

When his appointment as viceroy was announced Miss Nightingale's delight knew no bounds. It seemed that a golden age must be about to dawn, and even Lord Stanley allowed himself to be optimistic. "Sir J. Lawrence's appointment is a great step gained," he wrote to Miss Nightingale on December 1, 1863. "I believe now there will be little difficulty in India." He went on to make a remarkable suggestion. The new viceroy must be instructed in the Indian sanitary question; he wished him to learn from Miss Nightingale. With a lifetime spent in India behind him, the viceroy was to come to be taught by an invalid lady who had never been to India in her life. Sir John had only a week before he sailed. But he called on December 4, 1863. The interview, wrote Miss Nightingale, was one never to be forgotten. The viceroy remained with her for several hours, the Indian sanitary report was discussed in detail, and he declared himself "heart and soul for Sanitary Reform." The machinery for putting the recommendations of the report into practice was to be set up at once: at last it seemed that the mountain that was India was being moved.

In January 1864 Miss Nightingale completed her *Suggestions in regard to Sanitary Works required for the Improvement of Indian Stations*. It laid down a schedule of essential works relating to drainage, sanitation, water supply, barrack and hospital construction. It was the first sanitary code for India, the starting point from which, she hoped, great new projects, bringing health and prosperity to millions, would be developed.

Once more hope faded. The *Suggestions* were sent to the War Office, but nothing happened, and Sir John Lawrence wrote repeatedly asking what had become of them. In April Miss Nightingale discovered the truth: the India Office had been offended by a letter sent by the War Office inquiring what action was proposed on the recommendations of the Indian sanitary commission. The India Office, in short, did not intend to have action proposed to it by the War Office, so the *Suggestions* were still in a pigeonhole at the War Office.

When, finally, the *Suggestions* were officially approved Miss Nightingale had copies printed at her own expense and sent out to Sir John Lawrence. Across two continents her burning zeal infused him with new strength. Sir Henry Bartle Frere, the governor of Bombay, told her "men used to say that they always knew when the Viceroy had received a letter from Florence Nightingale; it was like the ringing of a bell to call for Sanitary progress."

Sanitary work in the army in India rapidly advanced through the help of the commander in chief, Sir Hugh Rose. He took immediate action on those recommendations in the Indian sanitary report which affected regiments. Recreation rooms and workshops were opened, regimental gardens laid out to provide troops with vegetables; libraries, savings banks, lectures and courses of instruction in trades started. The regulation two drams of spirits a day was reduced to one. In July 1864 he wrote to the War Office describing what had been done, and the dispatch was forwarded to Miss Nightingale. On August 11 she wrote to Douglas Galton: "It is quite worth while, all that has been suffered, to have this letter from Sir Hugh Rose. And I forgive everybody everything."

Sir Hugh Rose achieved a great deal for the army, but all other plans seemed hopelessly bogged. Delay succeeded delay; 1864 passed into 1865 and still nothing substantial had been done in India. Once more Miss Nightingale was in despair. The constructive campaign had once more faded away. Were the disappointments, the reverses she endured, the common lot of the reformer? She refused to admit it. She was convinced that she was singled out by a malignant fate. She beat herself against the callousness and indifference of the world, and such was the power of her extraordinary nature that in middle age she continued to feel as violently, as blindly, as if she were a girl.

Her life meanwhile was closing in. Every hour must be given up to work. She could not spare time even to see her most intimate friends. "Clarkey darling," she wrote in June 1865, "how I should like to be able to see you, but it is quite quite impossible. I am sure no one ever gave up so much to live who longed so much to die as I do. . . ." She had by now moved into a house which W.E.N. bought for her at 10 South Street, backing onto the gardens of Dorchester House. She could enjoy sunlight, trees and birds, and here at last she lived alone.

Distinguished visitors who had once called on her in a steady stream were no longer received. Her emotions found an outlet in affection for her cats. She worked with a cat "tied in a knot round her neck." As many as six cats wandered about her room and made "unseemly blurs" on her papers. On many of her letters and drafts is still to be seen the print of a cat's paw.

But though she had longed to be alone, the specter of solitude stalked her. In September of 1865 Hilary Bonham Carter died of cancer. Of the friends of her youth Florence had loved none more than Hilary. Through her first winter in her own house she was ill and unhappy. A great consolation was her friend Jowett, who encouraged her to turn once more to Greek, which she read through the long pain-ridden nights. Friendship with him took the only form in which friendship could have been fitted into her life; there was constant and intimate communication, but the communication was by letter.

Even Jowett could bring no interruption to the routine of work. Gigantic though her Indian labors were, the other calls on her were as exacting—public health in England, nursing reform, hospital construction. And, past forty-five, she was slowing down. "I do the work in three hours I used to do in one," she told Clarkey. But she would not spare herself on that account. She had also become deeply involved in district nursing, and this was now to lead her, through another social reform, back to her earliest function.

In 1861 she had received a letter from a Mr. William Rathbone of Liverpool, the eldest son of a dynasty of shipowners. As a young man he had witnessed the miseries endured by the poor who were ill in their own homes. In 1859 he founded district nursing, starting with one trained nurse. Since one nurse proved ludicrously inadequate, he decided to establish, at his own expense, a body of trained nurses to nurse the sick at home. Finding that nurses of the type he required did not exist, he wrote to Miss Nightingale asking her advice.

She gave his scheme "as much consideration," he wrote, "as if she herself were going to be the Superintendent," and the following year, at her suggestion and at his expense, a training school opened in connection with the Royal Liverpool Infirmary, and proved an unqualified success.

Rathbone was a man Miss Nightingale could appreciate, and they became intimate friends. When, in January 1864, he undertook to reform the nursing of sick paupers in workhouse infirmaries, he asked her to send a staff of trained nurses and a matron to the Liverpool Workhouse Infirmary. He would again guarantee the cost; but it would not be easy to obtain permission from the authorities to introduce the nurses.

A long battle ensued. "There has been as much diplomacy and as many treaties and as much of people working against each other, as if we had been going to occupy a Kingdom instead of a Workhouse," Miss Nightingale wrote to the Reverend Mother Bermondsey in September 1864.

At last, in May 1865, twelve Nightingale nurses and a matron, Miss Agnes Jones, entered the Liverpool infirmary. The experiment was at first to be confined to the male wards only, and to one workhouse only. It was a task to daunt the boldest. Fortunately the matron was a young woman of remarkable character and qualifications—"pretty and young and rich and witty"—but beneath the prettiness was the soul of a martyr. Miss Nightingale's work in the Crimea had inspired Agnes Jones to become a nurse. She had trained at the Nightingale school, where she was the best probationer Mrs. Wardroper ever had. She had nursed in great London hospitals, but until she came to Liverpool, she said, she did not know what sin and wickedness were. The wards were an inferno, the hordes of pauper patients more degraded than animals. "It is like Scutari over again," Miss Nightingale told her.

Gradually, under Miss Nightingale's influence, Agnes Jones's genius as a nurse and an administrator made "wonderful changes." By 1867 Miss Jones had convinced both the medical staff and the public authorities of the economy as well as the humanity of having trained nurses care for the pauper sick.

It was triumph, but short-lived. In February 1868 Agnes Jones died of typhus and there was no one to take her place. After so much had been achieved, it seemed that the work would collapse for want of one intelligent nurse-administrator to carry it on.

It was the old problem. The obvious solution for this cata-strophic shortage was for educated women of a good type to become nurses, but the "ladies" and "nurses" controversy which had caused so much heartburning in the Crimea was still raging. Though Miss Nightingale had for so long maintained that nurses were not "scrubbers" and that women of upper, middle and lower classes were equally able to go through the training, few people could yet visualize the professional woman, trained, efficient and highly paid, whom she wished to call into existence.

"We can't find the women—they won't come," she wrote bitterly in one of a number of contemptuous diatribes against her own sex. But even when the right type of woman was found, difficulties remained. The very fervor which inspired the Nightingale nurses created problems. Miss Nightingale did not want fanatics; she did not want warfare. No one knew better than she that the way to improvement did not lie through rebellion. As in the Crimea, authority must not be flouted but converted. "Women are unable to see that it requires wisdom as well as self denial to establish a new work."

It was a difficult lesson to teach. "Do you think," she wrote to a rebellious nurse in 1869, "I should have succeeded in doing anything if I had kicked and resisted and resented? I have been shut out of hospitals, obliged to stand outside the door in the snow, have been refused rations for as much as 10 days at a time for the nurses I had brought by superior command. And I have been as good friends the day after with the officials who did these things—have resolutely ignored these things FOR THE SAKE OF THE WORK."

It had been as an administrator to advance the cause of nursing that she had first gone to the Crimea. The crisis caused by Agnes Jones's death in Liverpool brought her full circle. Though she was called into service with some of the old urgency during the Franco-Prussian War, and though Indian affairs continued pressing, Miss Nightingale's major concern for the rest of her working life was again her first concern: to bring into being a body of efficient, educated, professional nurses.

In 1872 she threw herself into the reorganization of the Nightingale Training School. She had always held that nurses' training, or indeed any education, was made up of two aspects of equal importance: the acquisition of knowledge and the development of character. So, when she had tightened up the technical training, she appointed an assistant superintendent, the "Home Sister," who was to make herself the girls' friend, encourage them to read poetry and go to church, and generally to keep the Nightingale nurses "above the mere scramble for a remunerative place."

It was from now on Miss Nightingale herself who dominated the school. She made herself personally acquainted with every probationer. It was work with human beings again, work for which she had longed. After long dry years of toiling at administration, her life was rich once more.

To her girls she held the place, if not of a mother, then certainly of a favorite aunt. Fruit, game, jellies, creams flowed from her to the Nightingale Home. When a nurse went to a new post, Miss Nightingale sent flowers to welcome her. Nurses who were traveling found her manservant waiting at the train with a luncheon basket. Nurses who were run-down were sent to the seaside at her expense. Her girls were encouraged to feel that she was always behind them. She never ceased in countless letters, in numberless interviews, to hold up before their eyes not only a high standard of efficiency but a sense of the presence of God.

She was repaid. They constantly came to seek her advice. From all over the world they wrote to her, addressing her as "Dear Mistress," "Beloved Chief," "Dearest Friend." She made the Nightingale school as much an expression of her own personality as if she had presided over it in the flesh.

By 1887 at least sixteen British hospitals had superintendents who had been trained at her school. Parties of nurses under Nightingale-trained superintendents had gone to the United States, Australia, Canada, India, Ceylon, Germany and Sweden. Four other training schools modeled on hers had been established. She had indeed, as she put it, "raised nursing from the sink," and she had finally succeeded in founding, after much tribulation, a successful school for midwives.

Since 1880 Miss Nightingale had held the threads of the district-nursing movement in her hands. But finance was a constant difficulty. It was Queen Victoria who solved this. Her Majesty decided to devote the major part of the money which had been presented on her jubilee by the women of England as the "Women's Jubilee Gift" to the cause of "nursing the sick poor in their own homes by means of trained nurses." So the Jubilee Institute for Nurses was founded, a monument both to the Queen and to Florence Nightingale.

Chapter 9

FLORENCE HAD ALWAYS MEANT the break with her family to be permanent, and though she had kept in touch with her parents by letter, her visits to them had been very few. The first for many years had been in the summer of 1866, when

Fanny was seventy-eight, and suffering both from failing eyesight and from the effects of a carriage accident.

Fanny in her old age was much to be pitied. Parthe, for so long her companion, was now immersed in her own life as mistress of the historic mansion of Claydon, "very much the fine lady," a success both as a hostess and as a novelist. Without her, Fanny was very much alone. When in August 1866 W.E.N. had to go to Lea Hurst, Miss Nightingale agreed to stay with her mother at Embley.

Elaborate arrangements were made to receive the illustrious invalid, and the reunion began tenderly enough. "I don't think my dear mother was ever more touching and interesting to me than she is now in her state of dilapidation," Florence wrote to Clarkey. But soon the old irritation and disapproval crept in; the visit was not easy for either of them.

It was another two years before she again went home. Mr. Gladstone, who had become Prime Minister, regarded an army as an undesirable and unchristian institution, and opposed increased expenditure on soldiers' welfare. His accession to power was a severe blow to Miss Nightingale, and Jowett urged her to leave London, to slow down, to change her way of life.

She had indeed begun to change. She was then forty-eight and thought of herself as old. Though she complained to M. Mohl that "one must be as *miserably* behind the scenes as I am to know how *miserably* our affairs go on," she had earlier said, "I am becoming quite a tame beast." And she told Clarkey, "I assure you I don't let things corrode into me now."

The three months she spent at Lea Hurst that summer marked the change. She read the novels of Jane Austen and the plays of Shakespeare. "I don't know whether Hamlet was mad, he would certainly have driven me mad." She had long talks with W.E.N. on metaphysics. She found her mother "more cheerful, more gentle than I ever remember . . . far dearer than ever before."

At the end of September, she went back to South Street. But now she worked in a less frenzied atmosphere. And a new influence for reasonableness had come into her life. Hilary's brother Henry Bonham Carter had been made secretary of the Nightingale Fund, and though devoted to Miss Nightingale he would not be her slave. When it was getting late he used to say, "Now I must go home to dinner." He was an excellent man of business and invaluable to her, but his soul remained his own.

Miss Nightingale still had legendary prestige and enormous popular appeal, and while she had these she could not be without power, no matter who was Prime Minister. Throughout 1870 and 1871 she debated the possibility of "seeking office" again. But by 1872 her influence seemed to be at an end. She was, however, overwhelmed with vitally important nursing matters, and with the reorganization of the Nightingale school.

And now the time came when she was forced to return home for more than a visit. Fanny was eighty-three, W.E.N. seventy-seven, both were ailing, and the management of their properties had become peculiarly difficult. Miss Nightingale found herself elected, most unwillingly, into being the man of business of the family. She was imprisoned again.

Her father and mother clung to her, and her heart forbade her to abandon them. Embley stifled her, and the thought of the work piling up in London was agony. In the spring of 1873 she could bear it no longer. She must be in London; Parthe was ill and could not help. Florence moved her mother to South Street, but by the end of June Fanny became unwell and Florence, chafing, had to move with her back to Embley.

Jowett suggested that she write some essays on the idea of God. The subject attracted her and became her chief solace. She needed a "taste of heaven in her daily life"; her own had become a round of coaxing servants and humoring her parents.

Worse, however, was to follow. In January 1874 her father slipped on the stairs, and died instantly. The affection between them had been very deep. But grief took second place in the innumerable anxieties which arose out of his death.

Embley and Lea Hurst were now the property of Aunt Mai. The settling of the estate was left to Florence. And there was Fanny. Fanny, now helpless, blind, unwanted, had a claim which it was impossible to reject. The only solution was for Miss Nightingale to stay with her at Lea Hurst after which Fanny craved and longed. The next six years she described as "the hardest of my life." Every minute which could be snatched from domestic problems was devoted to trying to preserve some part of her work. Fanny's mind was so dim that Parthe and Clarkey thought she was making an unnecessary sacrifice. But she could not leave her mother to strangers. The tenderness which helplessness and suffering evoked in her were on Fanny's side now. Release came in February 1880, when Fanny died peacefully at the age of ninety-two.

The conflict which had embittered Miss Nightingale's life was over. All her life, resentment against Fanny and Parthe had been a poison working within her. During these last difficult years resentment had melted away, and she had become reconciled with both. She became gentler, calmer, even tolerant.

Failure began to weigh less heavily on her. Had she achieved nothing, need she reproach herself quite so desperately? On New Year's Eve, 1879, Jowett had written to her: "There was a great deal of romantic feeling about you 23 years ago when you came home from the Crimea. . . . And now you work on in silence, and nobody knows how many lives are saved by your nurses in hospitals; how many thousand soldiers who would have fallen victims of bad air, bad drainage and ventilation, are now alive owing to your forethought and diligence; how many natives of India (they might be counted probably by hundreds of thousands) in this generation and in generations to come have been preserved from famine [and] oppression . . . by the energy of a sick lady who can scarcely rise from her bed. The world does not know all this, or think about it. But I know it and often think about it, and I want you to, so that you may see what a blessed life yours is and has been. . . You are a Myth in your own lifetime. Do you know that there are thousands of girls about the ages of 18 to 23 named after you?"

She could look back without regret and now she found she could do more—she could look forward. At the age of sixty she was beginning to hope. On June 30, 1881, she wrote to Clarkey: "I want to do a little work, a little better, before I die."

Opportunity was on its way. At the moment she became free, opportunities to work for India, for nursing, even for the army, presented themselves once more. Throughout the years she had been continually working on the problems of India. Irrigation was a major issue, which led her to the land question, to rights of tenure, to education, to communication. She became involved in each one.

IN 1887 QUEEN VICTORIA celebrated her Jubilee, and Miss Nightingale, too, considered 1887 her Jubilee year: her "voices" had called her first fifty years earlier. Old age had come and she accepted it. The storms had passed and tolerance had replaced the uncompromising desire for perfection. Her health had improved and her mind was at rest.

Few human beings have enjoyed a fuller, happier old age than Florence Nightingale. For the first time personal relationships became of paramount importance to her. Though she had never married, she enjoyed the pleasures of matriarchy. In the lives of a large circle of young people—the children of Aunt Mai's son Shore, the son and daughters of Arthur Hugh Clough, and the stepchildren of Parthe—she came to hold the place of a powerful, generous and respected grandmother.

In old age an extraordinary atmosphere of peace flowed from her. She was formidable still; she would see only one person at a time and she bent her whole attention on her visitor, making you feel, it was said, like a sucked orange, but she was animated now by the purest benevolence. To confide in her was irresistible. Clough's son brought her his love affairs, Shore's daughters their examination papers. And her sympathy extended itself beyond her family to her butcher, to the policemen on duty near her house, to everyone who served her. Their family affairs received her earnest consideration; their health was the object of her solicitude.

To enter her house was to receive an instant impression of whiteness, order and light. Her bedroom had French windows opening onto a balcony; there were no curtains, only blinds, the walls were painted white, and the room was bathed in light. A stand of flowering plants stood in the window, kept filled throughout the year by William Rathbone. The room conveyed an exquisite and fastidious freshness. Flowers were never faded; vases sparkled like crystal.

On her good days she got up after luncheon and received visitors in the drawing room, lying on a couch, wearing a black silk dress and a scarf of white net or lace round her head. The walls of this room were hung with the Sistine Chapel engravings which she had bought when she was a young woman in Rome.

As her character blossomed into benevolence, her physical appearance changed. The slight, tall, willowy girl whose elegance had struck everyone who saw her, the emaciated, mature woman with lines of suffering deeply engraved on her face, underwent a surprising metamorphosis. She became a dignified stout old lady with rather a large good-humored face. Even the shape of her head seemed to change; the face became wider, the neck shorter, the brow much more prominent. A relative, introduced to her as a boy, retained as his recollection that she looked "so jolly."

In 1890 Parthe died. During her illness Miss Nightingale had gone down to Claydon, where she became an essential part of the Verney family life, until Sir Harry's death in 1894.

In 1893 a great grief awaited her: she lost Jowett. During the past few years they had drawn even closer. "The truer, the safer, the better years of life are the later ones," he had written to her in 1887. "We must find new ways of using them, doing not so much but in a better way."

After 1896, she never left the South Street bedroom, but her mind and spirit remained as vigorous as ever. And year by year her legend grew. In the year of Queen Victoria's Diamond Jubilee, 1897, the Victorian Era Exhibition included a section showing the progress of trained nursing, planned around Miss Nightingale.

Then the darkest of shadows fell across the tranquil radiance as she began slowly to go blind. Still she looked forward with an undaunted spirit. Lady Stephen, one of Aunt Mai's granddaughters, was sitting with her one day and spoke of a friend who had recently died. Lady Stephen said that after a busy life he was at rest. Miss Nightingale at once sat bolt upright. "Oh *no*," she said with conviction, "I am sure it is an *immense* activity."

In 1901 darkness closed in on her. Her sight failed completely, and she was not always aware of her surroundings. In 1906 it was necessary to tell the India Office that it was useless to send papers on sanitary matters any longer to Miss Nightingale. She lay inert, unconscious, her hands, still pretty in old age, folded peacefully outside the bedclothes.

And now when she had passed beyond the power of the world to please or pain, a shower of honors fell on her. In November 1907 the Order of Merit was bestowed on her by King Edward VII, the first time it had ever been given to a woman. In the following year she received the Freedom of the City of London. The legend surrounding her silent, inert figure burst into new life.

She knew nothing. But the iron frame which had endured the cold and fevers of the Crimea, which had been taxed and driven and misused in forty years of gigantic labors, still lived on. The end came on August 13, 1910. She fell asleep about noon and did not wake again.

In an immensely long will, which finds a place in collections of legal curiosities, she divided her possessions with meticulous detail. She expressed a wish "that no memorial whatever should mark the place where lies my Mortal Coil"; if this proved impossible she wished her body "to be carried to the nearest burial ground." A simple cross without her name, only with initials, and date of birth and death was to mark the spot. She also directed that her body should be given "for dissection or post-mortem examination for the purposes of Medical Science."

This was not done. But in deference to her wishes the offer of a national funeral and burial in Westminster Abbey was declined. She was buried in the family grave at East Wellow, and her coffin was carried by six sergeants of the British army. Her only memorial is two lines on the family tombstone, "F.N. Born 1820. Died 1910." She had lived for ninety years and three months.

EDISON

A CONDENSATION OF

EDISON

by
MATTHEW
JOSEPHSON

ILLUSTRATED BY
JOHN FALTER

Who can imagine our world if Thomas Edison had not lived in it? Out of his fertile inventive genius sprang the high-speed telegraph, the electrified railroad, the phonograph, the talking motion picture and, of course, the incandescent lamp, which alone would have brought him worldwide fame.

His beginnings, however, were not auspicious. He set out at the age of twelve to make his own way in the world, first as a trainboy selling candy, fruit and newspapers to railroad passengers, then as a young telegrapher transmitting dispatches during the Civil War. From the age of twenty-one, when he patented his first device (an electric vote recorder in which no one was interested), throughout the rest of his eighty-four years, a remarkable array of inventions flowed from his workshop, yielding more than a thousand patents and making Edison a multimillionaire.

Here, then, is the incredible story of the boy who became "The Wizard of Menlo Park," whose extraordinary creative imagination transformed our world and continues to benefit our lives.

I. Childhood and Boyhood

THE VILLAGE OF MILAN, OHIO, where Thomas A. Edison was born, now seems a rural backwater, with its old tree-shaded central square and its quiet lanes of white wooden frame houses. In its heyday Milan was one of the boomtowns of the Middle West, where a man of energy might well grow up with the country. For over twenty years a flood of immigrants from the East Coast, mainly Yankees, but also recent arrivals from Europe, had been moving up the Erie Canal to settle on the virgin soil of the Western Reserve.

Here Edison's father, Samuel Ogden Edison, Jr., a native of Canada, had halted in the summer of 1838, and put down his stakes. Like a good many of his fellow immigrants he had left his troubles behind him and had journeyed to thriving Ohio in the hope of bettering his fortune.

Milan was situated on the Huron River, eight miles inland from Lake Erie; but at the time Samuel Edison, Jr., arrived, construction work on a canal extending northward to the navigable part of the river, and so giving access to Lake Erie's broad waterway, was going on full blast. Sam Edison, experienced in the lumber trade, looked at the busy scene and resolved to take up the business of supplying timber and roofing material for the greater Milan that was to come.

Edison, who in his youth was something of a hothead, had departed from Canada rather suddenly, about six months earlier. The descendant of a hardy and restless clan, part Dutch and part English, he was then still in his early thirties. Unhappily, he had been forced to leave his wife and four young children behind him in Ontario Province until he could establish himself in the States. With the help of his family he was able to raise a little money and for seven or eight months he worked zealously to set up his shingle mill. Some help was given him also by an American friend, Captain Alva Bradley, a future merchant prince whose ships and barges plied Lake Erie.

By the spring of 1839 Edison had hired a few men and was ready for business. Now at last he was able to bring his wife and children across the lake on one of Bradley's barges. After living in temporary quarters for about a year, the Edisons purchased, for the sum of $220, a town lot of an acre on Choate Lane, situated at the edge of the hogback, or bluff, that overlooked the Huron Canal Basin where the shingle mill stood. Here, in 1841, Sam Edison with his own hands built a tidy house of wood-frame and brick construction, using lumber from his own mill. It was to be the Edisons' home for many years.

THE 1830's AND 1840's marked the height of the canal craze in America. Before the coming-of-age of the Iron Horse, states and towns all but ruined themselves to finance the waterways that would give this nation a desperately needed transport system. Thus Milan boomed. Six hundred wagons a day arrived from points within a radius of 150 miles, enough to fill twenty vessels and barges with 35,000 bushels of wheat each day. Soon fourteen grain warehouses lined the basin, most of them roofed with Sam Edison's seasoned pine shingles. For a period everything and everyone here seemed to prosper, including Sam Edison.

The Edison family reunion in the United States was signalized by the arrival of more children. Sam's wife, Nancy, had brought four with her on coming to Ohio in 1839: Marion, the eldest daughter, then ten; William Pitt, eight; Harriet Ann, six; and

Carlile, four. Now, in 1840, Samuel Ogden II followed, and four years later, Eliza. Unfortunately, the Lake Erie region is subject to severe winter storms; the Edison children suffered sorely from colds and from infantile diseases. Soon after being brought to Milan, in 1841, Carlile died at the age of six. Then soon afterward, to Nancy Edison's great sorrow, the lately born Samuel II and Eliza were taken from her in their infancy. Within a few years half of her children were dead.

Nancy Edison, the daughter of a Baptist minister, the Reverend John Elliott, was of Scotch-English and Yankee descent. She had been a schoolteacher before she married and was very different in character from the Edisons; she was small in size, but she showed much patience and inner strength against adversity. She was more than usually intelligent and had absorbed from her own estimable family, the Elliotts, a love of learning as well as devotion to religion.

She was already middle-aged when, in the dead of winter, she awaited the birth of her seventh, and last-born, child. It was to be a son with fair hair, large blue eyes, and a round face, who strikingly resembled the mother but seemed unusually frail and perhaps, as the Edisons said, "defective." His head was so abnormally large that the village doctor thought he might have brain fever. Nancy greatly feared for the life of this new child, who arrived in the world during the early hours of February 11, 1847, following a night of heavy snowfall. Later that morning Sam Edison, Jr., ran along the hogback to get medicine at the pharmacist's in the village square, announcing to all his neighbors that a son had been born to him. The parents christened the boy Thomas, after a brother of the father, and added the middle name "Alva" in honor of their friend Captain Bradley. Thus, Thomas Alva Edison.

ONE MORNING in 1853 a knot of people gathered together in the cobbled square of Milan to look on at a strange rite: Sam Edison, the lumber and feed dealer, was whipping his youngest son, Alva, in the village square. It was like a scene out of the time of the Puritans in New England.

The youngest Edison boy was something of a problem child.

He was of a decidedly mischievous bent and was forever falling into scrapes. The latest and most serious of these had resulted in the burning of his father's barn in the yard below the house. Alva had set a little fire inside the barn "just to see what it would do," as he innocently enough explained it. The flames had spread rapidly; though the boy had managed to escape from the barn, the whole town might have gone up in smoke if there had been a strong wind. Hence his father had devised a punishment to fit the crime.

While in later years Alva spoke with marked affection of his mother, there is no record of his having ever said anything complimentary on the subject of his father. He was always a loyal son. However, the little that he did say in recollection suggested clearly that there was no understanding between them. ". . . My father thought I was stupid, and I almost decided I must be a dunce," was one of Edison's few plain references to his parent.

His father said on a number of occasions that he could make nothing of his son and that the boy seemed wanting in ordinary good sense. He was trying, he was vexing, he was forever curious, and forever asking "foolish questions." The harsh punishment visited so publicly on Alva, meanwhile, did not serve to make him mend his ways, or even to keep him from playing his little tricks on people. He seemed to be one who just grew in his own way.

THE TALES collected about his childhood show him to have been a grave infant who seldom cried. For some years he slept in a crib in the tiny windowless attic room under the eaves which he shared with two other much older Edison children, Harriet Ann and Pitt.

He seems to have had few childhood companions, and he played alone with his toys a good deal of the time. One of his earliest memories was the sight, in 1850, of long trains of prairie schooners drawn up in the narrow roads of Milan; these people, he was told, were going to the gold fields of California. But where was "California"? and what was "gold"?

As soon as he could talk he began to ask his parents and everyone else his interminable questions. There were so many "whys" and "wheres" and "whats" that Sam Edison said that he often felt himself reduced to exhaustion. Alva's mother, however, was more patient.

"Why does the goose squat on the eggs, Mother?"

"To keep them warm," she replied.

"Why does she keep them warm?"

"To hatch them, my dear."

And what was hatching? "That means letting the little geese come out of the shell; they are born that way."

"And does keeping the eggs warm make the little geese come out?" he went on breathlessly.

"Yes."

That afternoon he disappeared for hours. At length his father found him "curled up in a nest he had made in the barn, filled with goose eggs and chicken eggs. He was actually sitting on the eggs and trying to hatch them." Such a little goose he was— yet a *logical* goose!

Toward the age of five or six, there was a whole phase of misadventures and scrapes. Once he fell into the canal and had to be fished out. On another occasion he disappeared into the pit of a grain elevator and was almost smothered before he was rescued. He was nothing if not inquisitive.

Down at the canal basin there was the big steam-driven flour mill of an eccentric Yankee named Sam Winchester. Often the small Edison boy would be found with his nose pressed against the back window of Winchester's shop watching the strange things being done there. His father scolded him severely for hanging about that place and spanked him for going there again after being warned not to do so. The mysterious Winchester ("The Mad Miller of Milan") was not grinding flour, but was constructing a passenger balloon. The hydrogen he had used for this purpose had burned down his first flour mill. The boy Tom Edison knew about these experiments and about Winchester's first, abortive attempt at flight. Some years later, during a second trial, Mr. Winchester managed to ascend into the air, then was wafted slowly in the direction of Lake Erie, never to be seen again.

Finally there was one tragic accident in which the boy was involved that deeply troubled Edison's parents and that he himself never forgot. He recalled the whole affair in notes written long afterward:

> When I was a small boy at Milan, and about five years old, I and the son of the proprietor of the largest store in the town, whose age was about the same as mine, went down in a gully in the outskirts of the town to swim in a small creek. After playing in the water a while, the boy with me disappeared in the creek. I waited around for him to come up but as it was getting dark I concluded to wait no longer and went home. Some time in the night I was awakened and asked about the boy. It seems the whole town was out with lanterns and had heard that I was last seen with him. I told them how I had waited and waited, etc. They went to the creek and pulled out his body.

Why had he not called for help? Why had he said nothing on returning home? A country boy knew what drowning meant. Was he silent because he felt guilty and feared that he would be censured and beaten? His parents could not help showing their distress at his "strange" behavior. Was this boy "without feelings"? Doubtless they applied the switch again, though whipping did no good. The boy could not but sense his father's disappointment and disapproval of him and feel, though dimly, the weight of this.

WHAT DOOM, what blight suddenly fell upon the future metropolis that was Milan, Ohio? What happened, simply, was that the Lake Shore and Michigan Southern Railroad came in 1853, but bypassed Milan and ran instead through Norwalk to Toledo.

As Thomas Edison said in later years, there was "a collapse of the family fortunes," caused by the reduction of canal tariffs at Milan in competition with the railroad and a depression in the town that "undermined the social standing of Samuel Edison, forcing him to leave his picturesque home and begin his life anew. . . . This transpired in the year 1854."

Once more the Edisons were on the move, by train and carriage to Detroit and thence by paddle ship up the St. Clair River to Port Huron, Michigan, where they were to settle. Sam Edison had learned that a railroad being extended northward from Detroit would eventually connect with a Canadian line at this point.

Their new home was a large and solidly built house with columned balconies, set in a grove of pine trees. From its big windows there were fine views over the river and lake. The rooms were spacious, and there were four huge fireplaces; the grounds included an orchard, a large vegetable garden, and several outbuildings. There was only one thing wrong with this fine dwelling: the Edisons no longer owned their home, but rented it. Sam Edison used his remaining capital to engage in the lumber, grain, and feed trade.

As the Edison fortunes declined, for Sam was no steady provider, his wife emerged as the real head of the family. It was she who worked with compulsive energy, cooking and weaving, sewing and crocheting. It was she who struggled to keep the family afloat with the aid of her children, and it was she who educated her youngest son.

On their arrival at Port Huron, Thomas Alva fell seriously ill of scarlet fever. For this or other reasons the boy's entrance into grammar school had been postponed. In the autumn of 1855, when he was more than eight, he was finally enrolled as a pupil in the one-room school of the Reverend G. B. Engle. Mr. Engle, it is related, liked to implant his lessons in his pupils' minds with the help of a leather strap; his wife, who aided in the work of instruction, was said to be even harsher in her methods. It is not surprising, therefore, that the Edison boy, who had been growing up according to his own will, as a sort of child of nature, proved to be somewhat difficult in the classroom.

After he had been at the school about three months, he overheard the schoolmaster one day saying of him that his mind was "addled." In an outburst of temper, Tom Edison stormed out of the schoolroom and ran home, refusing to return.

The next morning his mother came to see the schoolmaster, and an angry discussion followed. Her son backward? She considered him nothing of the sort and believed she ought to know, having taught many children herself in her youth. The upshot was that she removed the boy from school and declared that she would instruct him herself.

The schooling received from the Engles, according to Edison's later recollections, was utterly "repulsive"—everything was forced on him; it was impossible to observe and learn the processes of nature by description, or the English alphabet and arithmetic only by rote. For him it was always necessary to observe with his own eyes, to "do things" or "make things" himself.

Unlike the other boys in the little town, he stayed at home all day, and every morning, after his mother's preliminary house-work was done, she called him to his lessons and taught him his reading, writing, and arithmetic. The affection between mother and son was very strong, especially in these years, when Nancy Edison's relations with her husband grew less happy. She taught her son not only the three R's, but she implanted in his mind the love of learning.

Believing that her son was far from being dull-witted, she read to him from such books as Gibbon's *Decline and Fall of the Roman Empire*, and Hume's *History of England;* also literary classics ranging from Shakespeare to Dickens. Instead of being bored by these works of serious literature, he grew fascinated and at nine was inspired to read such books himself. He soon became a very rapid reader.

Nancy Edison also sensed, or discovered by chance, the real direction of her son's interests; for one day she brought forth an elementary book of physical science, R. G. Parker's *School of Natural Philosophy*, which described and illustrated various scientific experiments that could be performed at home. Now his mother found that the boy had truly caught fire. This was "the first book in science I read when a boy, nine years old, the first I could understand," he later said. Here, learning be-came a "game" that he loved. He read and tested out every experiment in Parker; then his mother obtained for him an old *Dictionary of Science*, and he went to work on that. He was now ten and formed a boyish passion for chemistry, gathering to-gether whole collections of chemicals in bottles or jars, which he ranged on shelves in his room. All his pocket money went for chemicals purchased at the pharmacist's and for scraps of metal and wire.

Thus his mother had accomplished that which all truly great teachers do for their pupils: she brought him to the stage of learning things for himself, learning that which most amused and interested him, and she encouraged him to go on in that path. It was the very best thing she could have done for this singular boy.

A corner of the cellar in the Port Huron house was Thomas A. Edison's first laboratory. There, after the age of ten, he secluded himself, often all day long, absorbed in his study of simple chemicals and gases and in the design of his first homemade telegraph set. Other boys might play in the fields or fish in the river; but Tom Edison buried himself in his cellar laboratory, with his elementary manuals and his chemical and electrical outfits.

"Thomas Alva never had any boyhood days; his early amusements were steam engines and mechanical forces," his father commented. Actually, through his own kind of intellectual *play*, the Edison boy was intensely happy—though his father could not understand this. He was also, despite his steam-engine models, very much a boy.

Up to the age of fourteen, and even afterward, he continued to show such high spirits that it was hard to hold him down. Bouts of horseplay alternated with prolonged sessions in elementary physical science and chemistry belowstairs. Accidents occurred, the muffled sounds of explosions sometimes reaching the parents from the cellar. "He will blow us all up!" the anxious father would exclaim. But his mother remained staunch in his defense. "Let him be," she said. "Al knows what he's about."

ABOVE ALL THINGS, Tom loved to work over models of the telegraph, introduced into practical, everyday usage not long before his time by Samuel F. B. Morse. By 1848 the telegraph flashed intelligence over a network extending from New York and Boston, via Albany, as far as Chicago. As a boy, Edison followed with intense excitement news of the pioneering bands of young telegraphers who extended their long lines of wire

359

across the prairies, over the Indian-infested deserts and the mountains, to California—so that the continent was first spanned, not by the railroad, but by the telegraph—in 1861, during the opening months of the Civil War.

It was in no way remarkable therefore that Edison in 1858, at the age of eleven, like hundreds of other youths of that time, had his own homemade telegraph set and had begun to practice the Morse code. He became absorbed in learning all that he could of the new electrical science.

What was electricity? Tom Edison kept asking people. A Scotsman, who was a station agent on the new railway that came to Port Huron, finally explained that "it was like a long dog with its tail in Scotland and its head in London. When you pulled its tail in Edinburgh it barked in London."

In working with his first crude telegraph made of scrap metal, Edison the boy was approaching, unwittingly, the mainstream of electrical experiment.

More than pocket money, however, was needed for his expanding "laboratory" in the cellar. He was now bent on making a proper Morse sending-and-receiving set of his own, and these were hard times for the Edisons. At the age of eleven Tom, with the help of a friend, Michael Oates, embarked upon his first commercial venture. The two boys laid out a large market garden and tried raising vegetables. A horse and cart were hired, and soon Tom was driving about the town trucking onions, lettuce, cabbages, and peas. Evidently the business was sponsored and supervised by his mother; the first summer's harvest, so he claimed, netted all of "two or three hundred dollars." Was he a merchant prince in embryo? However, he quickly tired of this work, as he says, for "hoeing corn in a hot sun is unattractive. . . ."

Even before the railway was formally opened at Port Huron, young Edison had learned that there would be a job on the daily train for a newsboy, who would have the concession of the "candy butcher" to purvey food and sweets to the passengers. He was only twelve, and small for this work, but the family's situation was such that no schooling for the boy could be considered, and Tom was faced by the early necessity of gaining his own living. It was Sam Edison who selected the job and negotiated with the railroad people for his son's employment. But Nancy Edison strongly objected and Tom had to use "great persistence" in bringing his mother around to his idea. He promised that during the long layover of the daily train at Detroit, he would use his time to read books; he would also have money with which to continue his scientific self-education.

An early photograph shows him in a worn old cap and roughly clad, yet most attractive and intelligent-looking, with his fine brow, his wide jaws, and his big smile. The local railroad officials, at any rate, gave him the job.

THE "MIXED TRAIN" of passengers and freight departed from Port Huron daily at 7:00 a.m. on a journey of more than three hours to Detroit, waited over there most of the day, and returned again to Port Huron at 9:30 p.m. As the train pulled out of the station, a lively urchin, carrying a basket almost bigger than himself, quickly scrambled on board and then made his way through the carriages, calling out: "Newspapers, apples, sandwiches, molasses, peanuts!"

Tom Edison was a cheeky fellow and thoroughly enjoyed this new life of movement and active commerce with all sorts of people. In those days he had, as he himself said, a sort of "monumental nerve." Not only did he dispense a stock of candies along with newspapers and magazines, but he also won permission from the conductor to store a quantity of fresh butter, berries, vegetables, and fruit in the baggage car of the train, which he disposed of at retail along the route. The report of an old news dealer of Detroit shows that he was an honest boy who always did business for cash and paid promptly. He returned home each day long after dark, and gave his mother a dollar from the day's earnings.

There was so much he could learn merely by using his keen eyes. At the railroad yard in Detroit he could watch the men switching cars, or repairing valves and steam boilers. Waiting in the station he observed closely the operations of telegraphers, then beginning to signal train movements between stations.

In Detroit, already a city of over 25,000, he was left to his own devices all day, wandering about with a little money to spend on equipment or books, and talking with men in machine shops. "The happiest time of my life was when I was twelve years old," he said afterward. He was away from home, which was hardly a happy place nowadays; he was away from his father; he was on his own.

After he had been working on the railroad for a year or so, he thought of a way of occupying his leisure time during the layover in Detroit. Since the baggage and mail car had a good deal of empty space, he had the idea of installing his little cellar laboratory at one end of it. The trainman was won to compliance; soon Tom had transported his stock of bottles, test tubes, and batteries, and ranged them neatly on shelves that were fitted to the back wall of the car. This was, no doubt, the world's first mobile chemical laboratory.

There he was, adrift on the train like Huckleberry Finn on his raft, restless, inventive, audacious, an almost legendary picture of the eternal American boy making his way in life. But the real picture is not always so pleasing. The hours away from home were long and wearying; leaving at dawn, the young boy would return at ten or eleven at night. There were the sudden blows of life to be borne, even danger to be faced as bravely as he could, at twelve and thirteen.

Then, as if to make life all the harder, there came to him the cruel affliction of deafness. From the symptoms, as described by himself and others, his deafness seems to have been traceable to the aftereffects of scarlet fever suffered in childhood, and to have developed through periodic infection of the middle ear that was unattended.

He was, thus, permanently disabled when not yet thirteen. There could be no thought of returning to school for he would not hear his teachers. The prospects for a handicapped boy of a poor family were certainly not good. Nevertheless, he was able to go on working as a trainboy.

It was his habit to make light of his misfortunes. The loss of one of his most vital senses was sometimes represented by him as an advantage or an "asset." He could concentrate, could think something through without interruption. But his intimates declared that he had never really been glad that he was deaf. In the privacy of his brief diary he wrote truthfully, years later, these words of infinite sadness: "I haven't heard a bird sing since I was twelve years old."

That the loss of hearing brought him, in effect, to an important turning point in his life was true. He tended to be more solitary and shy; became more serious and reflective; drove himself to more sustained efforts at reading and study. He had been only "playing," hitherto, with his books and his "experiments." Now he put forth tremendous efforts at self-education, for he had absolutely to learn everything for himself. And whereas he had earlier appeared immature or lighthearted, he now seemed serious, or rather old for his years. It was then that he came to enjoy spending so many long hours alone, wholly lost in his elementary experiments with wet cells and stovepipe wire and his first crude telegraph instruments.

In Detroit, during the hours of layover, he found his way to the public library, becoming in 1862 one of its earliest members. He was given a card numbered 33 and paid the substantial fee of two dollars for it. He relates:

> My refuge was the Detroit Public Library. I started with the first book on the bottom shelf and went through the lot, one by one. I didn't read a few books. I read the library. . . .

THE YEARS when he rode back and forth on the Grand Trunk Railway coincided with some of the most dramatic events in American history. There was the insurrection and the hanging of John Brown, the election of Abraham Lincoln, the firing at Sumter, and the opening of the Civil War. He had noticed that when reports of a battle were printed his newspapers sold faster than on other days. He therefore made it his practice to go to the composing room of the Detroit *Free Press* and inquire what the headlines were on the advance galley proofs for that day's edition, so that he might better estimate his needs.

One day in April 1862 the first accounts of an immense battle between the armies of Grant and Johnston at Shiloh reached the newspaper office by telegraph. Learning that the *Free Press* would carry huge display heads announcing a battle in which 60,000 were then believed to have been killed and wounded, the trainboy conceived a splendid little stroke of business for himself.

> Here was a chance for enormous sales, if only the people along the line could know what had happened. I rushed off to the telegraph operator and gravely made a proposition. . . .

At Edison's request, a short bulletin was to be wired by the Detroit train dispatcher to the railroad stations along the road to Port Huron, and the telegraphers there would be asked to chalk it up on bulletin boards in the depots, before the train arrived. For this free telegraph service Tom Edison would pay the friendly Detroit telegrapher with gifts of newspapers and magazine subscriptions.

Thus forearmed, the boy went to the office of the newspaper's managing editor to ask for a thousand copies of the paper, an uncommonly large assignment, since usually he took but two hundred, and he asked for this on credit. The managing editor examined the ragged boy whose expression, however, was resolute enough. "I was a pretty cheeky boy, and felt desperate," he himself recalled later. The authorization was given him and, with the help of another boy, he lugged huge bundles of the newspaper to the train and folded them up.

His device worked even better than he had hoped. In his own vivacious way Edison related:

> When I got to the first station on the run . . . the platform was crowded with men and women. After one look at the crowd I raised the price to ten cents. I sold thirty-five papers. At Mount Clemens, where I usually sold six papers, the crowd was there too. . . . I raised the price from ten cents to fifteen. . . . At Port Huron . . . I was met by a large crowd. I then yelled: "Twenty-five cents, gentlemen—I haven't enough to go around!" It was then it struck me that the telegraph was just about the best thing going, for it was the notices on the bulletin board that had done the trick. I determined at once to become a telegrapher.

It is noteworthy that one of the chief attractions of the telegraph for him was also connected with his bad hearing. *With the telegraph he could hear.* He relates, ". . . From the start I found that deafness was an advantage to a telegrapher. While I could hear unerringly the loud ticking of the instrument I could not hear other and perhaps distracting sounds. . . ."

After learning all he could by studying the apparatus of the dispatching telegraphers, he made an improved sending-and-receiving set of his own device, and rigged up a line from his home to that of a young neighbor a block away. Later, when he was fifteen, he set out a long line of stovepipe wire running about a half mile, strung out on trees, to the home of James Clancy, who sometimes helped him at news vending. On returning home, though it was 10:00 p.m., he would stay up and "play" for hours at sending and receiving messages.

At the beginning of 1862 Tom developed a sudden interest in the craft of printing, and thought of becoming a journalist and starting his own newspaper. With some money he managed to save at the time of Shiloh, he purchased a small secondhand press, together with some old type; in a short time he had taught himself to set type and run a hand press. Now, putting aside his chemicals, he undertook the venture of editing, printing, and selling a small local newspaper, which was produced in that same baggage car.

The *Weekly Herald*, issued from a branch of the Grand Trunk Railway, at eight cents a copy, had a circulation of about four hundred. It covered local news and gossip, reports of the railroad service, changes of schedule, and occasional bits of war news received over the wires almost before the regular newspapers had them. But in almost every other line of his text occurred such errors of orthography as "valice," or "villian," or "oppisition," which probably hampered the progress of his gazette.

An adventure of another kind also belongs to this period. Late in the summer of 1862, he had descended at the Mount Clemens station and was waiting on the platform while the train switched back and forth shunting a heavy boxcar out of a siding. The boxcar finally rolled toward the station, when Edison noticed that the little three-year-old son of the stationmaster was playing right on the main track, in the path of the car. In an instant he had thrown aside his bundle of papers, dashed toward the child, and snatched him up in time to avoid the car. The stationmaster, J. U. Mackenzie, was called out, and young Edison handed him his baby, whose life he had saved by his quick action.

Mackenzie was filled with gratitude and expressed a desire to repay him. He had noticed how Tom Edison hung over his telegraph table constantly. On the instant, the happy idea came to Mackenzie of offering to teach the boy to be an operator. Edison fairly leaped at the proposal. He had at that time, in the care of his mother, a hundred or a hundred and fifty dollars from his business coup after the Battle of Shiloh. Mackenzie invited Edison to come and board with his family for a couple of months, while taking his lessons in telegraphy every night and assisting the train dispatcher. He now gave up half of his newspaper route to another boy so that he could stop off at Mount Clemens and study. He was only fifteen and a bit undersized. But in a few months he would be a real telegrapher.

II. The Wanderyears

THOMAS EDISON's wanderyears began when he was only sixteen. In those days the strange new tribe of telegraphers, known as Lightning Slingers, were generally young men already noted for their nomadic or Bohemian habits, traveling light, pitching their tents for a brief season at one place, then journeying on to another that seemed to offer greener pastures. The young Edison could find work almost anywhere, because the need for telegraphers was so urgent during the Civil War.

As a tramp operator Edison traveled thousands of miles in the Middle West, South and East. His apprenticeship was to be uncommonly long, and he was to be well acquainted with hardship, which he bore with the rollicking spirit usually affected by the brethren of the key, many of them hard-drinking, free-living fellows. His "university" was to be the rough, workaday world during a turbulent era of war and reconstruction; it was nightwork in shabby telegraph or railroad offices; it was solitude and study in squalid rooming houses.

He might have lost his way or gone downhill, like so many others, in that long, often unhappy interlude of his youth. Yet when these arduous years were gone and he had come to manhood, something of iron had entered into him. What he had seen and learned marked him with sharply individual traits of character and mind.

BY THE WINTER of 1863 he had absorbed all that Mackenzie could teach him and he returned to Port Huron. There the operator at the little telegraph office in Thomas Walker's jewelry and bookstore had gone off to war, and the place was offered to Tom Edison. The volume of telegrams handled was small; but even this Edison would neglect, to pore over Walker's file of back numbers of the *Scientific American*, or play with electrical circuits of his own device. What vexed Mr. Walker more was that the impetuous boy would make free with his fine watchmaking instruments, using them to cut wires or work on corrosive primary cells.

The following May Edison went to work as a night-shift railroad dispatcher at Stratford Junction, about forty miles from Port Huron. The job required that he await messages and signal trains or stations according to a stated schedule. Traffic, however, was light; Edison found ways of occupying the hours of this night-owl life by reading or by working over some mechanical device.

On the Grand Trunk Railway it was the rule to have the station operators signal to the office of the train dispatcher at certain hours, to guarantee that they were attentive to their duty. Edison's "sixing" signal, so-called, came over quite punctually at the right hours. But after a while it was noticed at the central control office that, when the train dispatcher there tried to reach Stratford Junction following Edison's signal that he was on the alert, no response came. This was queer; the train dispatcher's office soon investigated the new operator.

What was discovered was that the youth had devised a clockwork attachment, having a wheel with a notched rim, which, at a given hour, automatically transmitted by telegraph the dots and dashes making the "sixing" signal. The device was

conceived with a purpose; for in the small hours of the night, with no train movements to signal, he had formed the habit of taking catnaps. The railroad officials, however, were not amused at Edison's ingenuity.

In one year, when he was seventeen, Tom Edison held four jobs in as many different towns. After losing his job at Stratford, he went to a railroad junction at Adrian, Michigan, at seventy-five dollars a month; then, on being fired for some small act of insubordination, he moved on to Fort Wayne, only to be dismissed soon afterward. Next we find him listed as a second-class operator on the payroll of Western Union's office at Indianapolis. By mid-February 1865 he had shifted to Cincinnati's large Western Union headquarters. He was a rolling stone in those days; his low rating gave him little tenure. In most cases he was fired, either because he was not amenable to office discipline, or was at times inattentive to his duties.

Another cause of trouble was his continual monkeying with some paraphernalia or "invention" that would make the routine work of telegraphy less irksome or allow it to be done more expeditiously. On being sacked again, he would make his way to another town by means of a railroad pass, or on his legs.

Arriving in a strange town to apply for a job, he would usually rent a cheap back room in a boardinghouse, then fill up most of the room with tools, balls of wire, batteries, bottles of chemicals, books. His pockets usually bulged with metal scraps, pliers, and other instruments of the electrician's trade. All the money beyond that needed for his wretched meals he devoted to the purchase of books and equipment, sometimes spending his entire wages an hour after having received half a month's salary.

Edison often lived in vermin-infested bedrooms. The Western Union office in Cincinnati, formerly the site of a large restaurant, was also menaced by armies of rats. One of Edison's first inventions was a "rat-paralyzer," a contrivance made up of two metal plates insulated from each other and connected with a main battery. This machine he laid out in the cellar, and when a rodent chanced to place its forefeet on one plate and its hindfeet on the other, then, as one of his telegrapher friends, Milton

Adams, phrased it, "it would render up its soul and depart this earthly sphere."

In Cincinnati Edison made the acquaintance of another telegrapher, Ezra T. Gilliland, a man of some education and with some skill at mechanical invention; their minds seemed to run in the same path and they became close friends—who were to meet again in later years.

There was a trade union organized at the Cincinnati office when Edison worked there. A delegation of five men from Cleveland simply blew into town, recruited a local branch for the National Telegraph Union, then determined to celebrate the event with a spontaneous walkout and many rounds of beer for all hands. Arriving after the workers had gone—and knowing nothing then of labor unions—Edison found only the office boy on hand. Meanwhile the press report wires clamored for attention. All that night he manipulated the wires single-handed, doing a good deal of "guessing" whenever he fell behind; he was still there in the morning when the office manager arrived. The manager was told, though not by Edison, of what had happened. He studied the files of press copy hanging on the hook, then turned to the lone operator and said, "Young man, I want you to work the Louisville wire nights. Your salary will be a hundred and five dollars."

Edison had been receiving much less than that hitherto. He had long hoped to be advanced to the rank of a first-class operator regularly taking press copy as fast as mind and hand could go. This was promotion indeed.

OUT OF THOSE VAGABOND YEARS there is little of actual accomplishment for Edison to show, save his experience of the world of men, and the knowledge of his trade. On the other hand there are many bits of evidence to be seen, during those careless years, of Edison's growing mechanical resourcefulness.

The telegraph, in the days before the telephone was invented, held a place of enormous importance. It had entered into use about fifteen years before Edison came to it. Technical improvements were being regularly introduced; yet in the sixties installation was still faulty, cables "leaked" current badly under river crossings, and the Morse register which had lately come into use often faltered under pressure, leaving blanks to be filled in by the operator's imagination.

While he was in Indianapolis in the autumn of 1864, Edison, then seventeen and a half, conceived the idea of a repeating device by which the impressions received from a Morse register could be recorded on a strip of paper and played back on a second instrument at the convenience of the receiving operator, and at a speed he could regulate. The beauty of this scheme was that at periods when a great rush of press copy came at high speed, it could be received at leisure and its messages copied in Roman letters with complete accuracy instead of in haste. It was an ingenious repeating system, but it broke down under pressure.

> The crash came [Edison said] when there was a big night's work—a presidential vote, I think—and copy kept pouring in at top speed, until we fell two hours behind. The newspapers sent in frantic complaints, an investigation was made, and our little scheme was discovered.

Use of the duplicating register was forbidden, and Edison was removed from the press copy desk. Yet experiment with innovations in telegraphic apparatus remained an obsession with him.

A year or so later, after the end of the war, he drifted away from Cincinnati, to work at first in Nashville and then in Memphis, Tennessee. These places were then still under military occupation but telegraphers were in high demand and received as much as $125 a month and rations.

At that time connections by wire between New Orleans and New York were completed only by long detours, that is, by retelegraphing in roundabout fashion from one city to another, with much loss of time and attendant error. Edison then adapted his old repeater device, made up of two Morse registers. "I was the first person to connect New Orleans and New York directly . . . just after the war. I perfected my repeater, which was put on at Memphis and worked without a hitch."

Shortly after this he went to Louisville. The streets were icy, but Edison, having spent his money buying apparatus and books, had no overcoat; his shoes were broken and shapeless, and he was penniless. Fortunately, he found work at the Louisville telegraph office, thanks to his demonstrated skill. At the age of nineteen, as an operator, it was said, he had few equals. Now he conquered his wandering habit for more than a year and, save for a brief excursion or two, remained fixed.

During this period of more than a year, when his life assumed some regularity, his self-education went forward more rapidly. He even tried to teach himself foreign languages. He was, then, no ordinary "tramp operator" but a studious fellow with his nose often in books and mechanical treatises.

Using the crude instruments of electrical science that were then to be found in provincial cities, he measured and tested things, often trying new combinations of electrical circuits of varying strength and polarity. During those early fumbling investigations he observed many things unseen by others, and acquired experience that was to serve him well.

As he described this phase of his life afterward, his mind was in a tumult, besieged by all sorts of ideas and schemes. During the fairly stationary year in Louisville the "mysteries of electrical force" as applied to the telegraph, and all the future potentialities of electricity obsessed him night and day. It was then that he dared to hope that he would become an inventor—like the famous Samuel F. B. Morse, one of America's "kings of fortune."

There were so many things to be invented! At Memphis, just prior to his coming to Louisville, Edison had pottered about busily with new electrical circuits, over which he hoped to send two messages at the same time. At Louisville's Western Union office he became, once more, passionately absorbed in schemes for reconnecting wiring and batteries for duplex transmission.

He was desperate, feeling himself near a solution, and appealed to a fellow telegrapher who had some savings. If he could but have the loan of one hundred dollars and a little time he would complete his apparatus. But the other would not entrust his capital to the shabby youth of nineteen. As it happened, a duplex apparatus was not long afterward patented by another inventor, J. B. Stearns, of Boston. Edison always believed that by ill luck and the niggardliness of that man in Louisville he had missed the opportunity to precede Stearns.

In the late autumn of 1867 Edison made his way back to the parental home in Port Huron, as penniless and hungry as ever. It was a sad homecoming. His mother, whom he greatly loved, was transformed by grief. They were about to lose the big "house in the grove" which had been the Edisons' spacious home these thirteen years. To Nancy Edison's bitter disappointment, they were forced to move to temporary quarters until a new dwelling could be found. The whole family now made great moan at the evil days that had befallen the Edisons, and the father betook himself elsewhere as often as possible.

It was not a home to remain in any longer than Tom Edison could manage. On the other hand, there was nothing for the mother to be happy over in the erratic career of her Alva. Though he earned a good living for those days, and aided his parents whenever he could, he usually had nothing to show for his labors. In contrast, his elder brother Pitt, employed for long years in the office of the local horsecar line, seemed a solid citizen.

"After stopping for some time at home, I got restless, and thought I would like to work in the East," Edison recalled. A friend had written him from Boston, and Edison wrote inquiring if there was an operator's job there. The reply advised him to come at once to the Western Union office in that city.

Boston was then not only America's "hub of culture," but also her foremost center of scientific learning. At this stage of his development Edison sensed that he needed contact with better sources of technical knowledge and equipment. In the 1850's Boston had already well-established manufacturers of fine electrical equipment. There he would likely find the answers to many problems in electrical science that now tormented him.

How would he travel almost a thousand miles in winter without money? He had lately rendered some assistance to the Grand Trunk Railway by helping to repair their broken electric cable across the St. Clair; and the railway repaid him with a free pass over its line to Boston.

Well might Mr. Horace Greeley of the *Tribune* urge young

men to "go West" to seek their fortune; Edison, a son of the West, determinedly rode eastward. Unlike his early wanderings, this remove was purposeful.

AFTER A HAZARDOUS JOURNEY delayed by blizzards, Edison finally arrived in Boston, walked to the office of Western Union, and applied for a job. With his wide-brimmed hat, his long hair, and baggy clothes, he looked like a real jay from the woolly West. George Milliken, the manager, however, on being shown a letter in Edison's neat writing and receiving assurance that the youth could take press copy for hours on end at breakneck speed, was impressed. After a five-minute interview he hired Edison, proposing that he begin work at 5:30 p.m. that same day.

His fellow workers thought to initiate the ragged stranger from Michigan by "putting up a job" on him. It was arranged that he should be assigned to the Number One New York wire to receive voluminous press copy for the Boston *Herald*, without making it known to him that he would be expected to keep pace with one of the fastest senders in New York. Edison suspected that something was afoot from the way the Boston operators stood by, looking over his shoulder. The New York operator began slowly, then ran on at top speed, while Edison not only kept pace with him, but sometimes paused to sharpen a pencil, letting the sounder run on. Then the sender began to slur his words, sticking the signals, but Edison was used to this style. Finally, opening the key, he made a telegraphic aside: "Say, young man, change off and send with the other foot." That "broke up" the New York man, and, in disgust, he turned his instrument over to someone else.

Soon Edison was established in a hall bedroom on Exeter Street, together with an old acquaintance, Milton Adams, following his singular routine of working at his telegraph sounder at night and staying wide-awake most of the day. In the old bookshops on Cornhill he could browse over books, which together with the chemical and metallic junk he accumulated soon filled up his room. Back in the telegraph office by evening, he would sit and draw and dream, until reminded by the chief operator that he must attend to his work. His job was to him a distasteful bondage offering no avenue for his real desires and ambitions.

It was at this time that he bought a secondhand copy of Michael Faraday's two-volume work, *Experimental Researches in Electricity*. It was a red-letter day for him. Edison said in after-years that this first encounter with the great English scientist's journals was one of the decisive events of his life. Though he had worked up to an early hour of the morning at the telegraph office, Edison began reading the *Experimental Researches* when he returned to his room at 4:00 a.m. and continued throughout the day that followed.

Here at last, for his guidance, was the lucid exposition of Faraday's long searches in the field which most fascinated the young Edison. Best of all, the account of the experiments was wholly free of complicated mathematical formulas. To Edison Faraday appeared as "the Master Experimenter," whose laboratory notes communicated the highest intellectual excitement— and hope as well. He was filled with determination to learn all he could by repeating the experiments recorded in the master's journals.

To his roommate, Adams, he exclaimed, "I am now twenty-one. I may live to be fifty. Can I get as much done as he did? I have got so much to do and life is so short, I am going to hustle." With that he snatched some pie and coffee, and went off to work on the run, without having slept at all.

FROM REPEATED ALLUSIONS he made in later times, we know that Edison's mind was haunted for ten years by the problems and possibilities of multiplex telegraphy. He now proceeded to carry out a continuous series of experiments with telegraphic apparatuses. If he could but send two messages over one wire telegraphy would be made cheap!

Boston fairly teemed in those days with "addicts" of science and with skilled artisans who were would-be inventors. Visiting their shops, studying their products, Edison was kindly received and greatly stimulated. And the Bostonians noticed the stamp of his mind.

In June 1868 a journal carried an article on the subject of "Mr. Thomas A. Edison, of the Western Union Office, Boston," and his invention of a "mode of transmission both ways on a single wire . . . which is interesting, simple and ingenious." This youthful experiment was hardly of prime importance. But the interest it aroused, the fact that a little capital was now offered him to pursue his experiments, made him determined to throw up his job at Western Union and devote his full time to his own projects.

In January 1869 a brief notice in a small telegraph trade journal reported that Thomas A. Edison, formerly an operator, "would hereafter devote his full time to bringing out his inventions." Other notices or advertisements indicated that he had models of his "double transmitter" for sale at four hundred dollars; that he was associated with George Anders in the manufacture of alphabetical dial instruments for private telegraph lines; and that he was located at Charles Williams's shop on Court Street.

From now on he was, at his own risk, an inventor of the free-lance type. There was, perhaps, no vocation in life he might have chosen that would have been more perilous. It was proverbial that inventors for the most part starved, went mad, or at least were ruined in the end. To make an invention, even to possess the talent to do this, was not enough. Capital and plant and the commercial ability to win acceptance for one's product from the public were needed.

At this period numerous electrical experimenters in Boston were devising all sorts of machines that were merely adaptations of the Morse telegraph, such as fire alarms, call boxes, dial telegraphs, printing telegraphs, and stock quotation tickers. Edison had by now got several irons of his own in the fire. More important, he had been able to persuade several Boston "capitalists" to invest money in his schemes, small sums to be sure, but more than he had ever seen. Shy he might be, but about an idea close to his heart he could become surprisingly eloquent. One Bostonian advanced him five hundred dollars, in return for a half share in future profits from his duplex telegraph. At about the same time he had persuaded another man to invest one hundred dollars as his partner in the development of a telegraphic vote-recording machine.

Having observed the great loss of time attending roll calls for voice votes in Congress and state legislatures, Edison designed an electric vote recorder. This simple telegraphic contraption, a crude forerunner of the present-day voting machine, was capable of taking down votes from a legislative gathering by electromagnetic impulse. This was his first operative invention, for which patent was filed in October 1868 at the United States Patent Office in Washington. It was granted, June 1, 1869, as No. 90,646, his first recorded patent.

Edison and his associates then hastened to approach the Massachusetts legislature. When the apparatus was rejected, they went on to Washington and demonstrated the machine before a committee of Congress authorized to purchase such equipment. To the aspiring inventor the committee chairman said chillingly:

"Young man, that is just what we do *not* want. Your invention would destroy the only hope that the minority would have of influencing legislation. . . . And as the ruling majority knows that at some day they may become a minority, they will be as much averse to change as their opponents."

The idea of hastening the process of vote-taking was abhorrent. "I saw the force of his remarks," Edison recalled, "and was as much crushed as it was possible to be at my age. The electric vote recorder got no further than the Patent Office."

On the sad return journey to Boston, Edison did a heap of thinking and came to the conclusion that hereafter he must confine his efforts to inventing products that were certain to be in "commercial demand." Otherwise his chances of survival as a free-lance inventor were nil.

DURING THE "GILDED AGE" after the Civil War, speculators in gold and securities on all the financial exchanges were greatly dependent on Morse's telegraph. Market quotations were rushed by wire to distant cities and to newspapers. But the mounting pace of speculation required still more complex and swift mechanisms; thus, in 1866 the Gold Exchange in New

York had seen the appearance of a telegraphic gold indicator, invented by Dr. S. S. Laws. Connected by wire to outside brokers' offices, the indicator transmitted numerals—denoting momentary changes in the dollar prices of gold—as electrical impulses which could be received in the subscribing brokerage houses on dial instruments which resembled the fare registers in trolley cars.

A year later, a Boston inventor, E. A. Callahan, developed a superior telegraphic apparatus called the "stock ticker." This machine was able to print full stock market quotations as well as gold prices by wire on a moving paper tape.

After giving much study to the Callahan apparatus, Edison in 1868 conceived of a number of refinements which he incorporated in his own model of the stock ticker. This was his second invention in order of patents applied for; and for its development he acquired another backer who lent him some money.

A Boston company exploiting Edison's stock ticker succeeded in persuading about thirty subscribers to rent it from them. For a while Edison helped to erect a number of private lines leading from the subscribers' offices to the Gold Exchange in Boston, as had already been done on a larger scale in New York. At this time he also engaged in the business of making and selling private telegraph systems, and had several men working with him to make this apparatus in the one-room workshop that he had hired.

In his early twenties Edison was already a "whirlwind of activity," sleeping little and working at all hours of the night and day. His relations with those who backed his first stock ticker, however, became unpleasant; after differences arose between the partners, his patent rights were sold off to a large telegraph company and, thanks to his want of business experience, Edison received almost nothing for his work on this venture. But he had other irons in the fire and soon turned all his attention to them.

They related to the development of an efficient multiplex telegraph, one that would be capable of carrying two messages over a single wire. Such a duplex telegraph instrument had been invented in earlier years by Europeans, but its impulses remained slow. Joseph B. Stearns, of Boston, had greatly improved the operation of this duplex. With Stearns's apparatus two messages could be sent over the same wire at the same time, but only in opposite directions.

At this period, Western Union had already purchased Stearns's patents and was trying out his device on an experimental basis. Duplexing, if successful, would halve the cost of all telegraph traffic. Edison hoped that his own apparatus would have features that would make it more effective than the older inventor's.

When he felt himself ready for a large-scale trial of his duplex system, he asked for permission to dismantle the whole Boston office of Western Union and reconnect its wiring and batteries according to his new system. This privilege being refused him, he applied to the managers of a rival concern, the Atlantic & Pacific Telegraph Company. The head of their Rochester office showed interest and invited him to try his apparatus over the company's wires between that city and New York.

Edison raised eight hundred dollars on a loan from E. B. Welch, of Boston, to whom he gave both his personal note and an agreement allowing the other man a big share of the profits in the event of success. A model of the new duplexing apparatus was completed and, with the highest hopes, he set off for Rochester. Before leaving, he had sent minute written instructions to an expert telegrapher who was to work at the other end of the line, in New York. Edison arrived in Rochester on Saturday, April 10, 1869, and waited at the Atlantic & Pacific Telegraph Company's office until the early hours of Sunday morning, when the wires would be entirely clear, so that his experimental trial could begin.

When at last he began to signal, Edison could get no response whatsoever from New York. As he later described the trial, the telegrapher at the New York end failed to do his part. The trouble may have been due to electrostatic charges, or there may have been other "bugs" he had not yet eliminated. After repeated trials carried out on several successive days, Edison gave up and made his way back to Boston.

The moment was desperate. His more or less profitable undertakings had been disposed of for a bagatelle. He was deep in debt thanks to the fiasco of his duplex transmitter. Of late, he seemed to have gone from failure to failure, and now his credit in Boston was virtually ruined. There was no chance of finding new patrons for his experiments. His only hope was to get out of Boston, reach the bigger center of New York, and try his luck there.

He blandly borrowed a few dollars from one of his telegrapher friends and set off for New York by boat, arriving the next morning with not a coin left in his pocket. All his possessions, tools, and equipment had been left behind; he would have to send for them when he could afford to do so. In effect he had burned his bridges behind him, and not for the first time.

NEW YORK, already a vast metropolis and full of uproar, thanks to its endless traffic of horsecars, drays, and carriages, exhibited indifference to the nomad who, on a spring day, landed at a West Side dock to seek his fortune.

He might look like a country boy still, but there were probably not ten persons in America who knew the tricks he had with currents, relays, and resistances. He was, so to speak, full of his genius. That morning he was also as hungry as he had ever been in his life and had nothing with which to buy his breakfast. He set off on a long walk uptown to find one of his friends of former days who might lend him a small sum of money or even allow him to sleep on the floor of his room, until he found a job. But the only friend he had in New York was not at home, and on his first day there he had to "walk the streets a whole night long."

III. Pluck-and-Luck Edison

BY NOW Edison was not unused to being down on his luck. But the adventures that befell the emaciated young inventor shortly after he arrived in the great city unnoticed and unwelcome led to an extreme change in his fortunes.

After much walking about New York he found a telegrapher

he knew, but was able to borrow only one dollar of him. One of his next calls was on Franklin L. Pope, electrical engineer and telegraph expert, who was then employed at the headquarters of the Gold Indicator Company, on Broad Street. Pope already knew of Edison, as one who had made a stock ticker of his own in Boston.

Talking with the young stranger, Pope could not but appreciate his mettle. He invited Edison to make headquarters in his, Pope's, office and to work at his experiments in the machine shop of the Gold Indicator Company. While waiting for a job to turn up, Edison could study the mechanism of the Laws central transmitter, which was under Pope's superintendence and was still undergoing improvements.

For several nights, at Pope's kind suggestion, Edison even slept on a cot in the Gold Indicator's battery room, living frugally on five-cent meals of apple dumplings and coffee, while above his head millions of dollars were swiftly changing hands. Meanwhile, during the daytime, Edison inspected and familiarized himself with the Laws gold indicator. During the postwar boom when gold speculation reached its peak, this ponderous piece of telegraphic clockworks had assumed immense importance, having almost completely displaced messenger boys or runners as the prime instrument for distributing financial intelligence.

Edison was examining the mechanism of the indicator one day, when suddenly the whole central transmitting instrument came to a stop with a great crash. Pope was on hand and quickly went to work to find out the cause of stoppage. But in the excitement of the moment, he could detect nothing wrong. Dr. Laws himself came rushing forth from his office to learn what the trouble was, and, being even more agitated than Pope, was no more helpful.

Meanwhile, it was as if the heart of Wall Street had suddenly stopped beating. Laws's clients, finding the dial instruments in their offices had halted, grew frantic and sent messenger boys to bring back reports of market quotations. Within a few minutes a mob of three hundred messengers were trying to fight their way into the Gold Indicator Company's office. Franklin Pope, in the melee, seemed to forget everything he knew. Dr. Laws lost his head and began to yell at everyone. A business he had struggled to build up during four years, one which now had attained an annual revenue of $300,000, was threatened with immediate and total ruin.

Edison, in the meantime, had been quietly engaged in looking over the machine himself and soon ascertained the cause of the trouble. He went up to Pope and Laws, who seemed to be holding a shouting match, and managed to convey to them his belief that he had spotted the trouble. One of the many contact springs had broken off and dropped between two gear wheels, stopping the whole mechanism, he said.

"Fix it! Fix it! Be quick, for God's sake!" Laws yelled at him.

The young stranger then carefully removed the broken contact spring, and proceeded to reset the dial back to zero; linemen, in the meantime, set their receiving instruments in unison with the central transmitter. Within two hours Gold Indicator's quotations were being ground out again and communicated all over the Street.

Dr. Laws, having become much more composed, inquired about Edison, learned that he was out of work, and invited the youth to see him at his private office the next morning. The upshot was that Dr. Laws offered to engage him at once, at a larger salary than he had ever received, to work over the mechanical maintenance of his plant, assisting Pope. Though feeling "rather paralyzed," as he put it, Edison maintained his aplomb. Yesterday he was starving; today he was comparatively rich.

A FRUITFUL and prosperous period had opened for Edison. In July, Pope, who had befriended him, resigned from his position to go into business on his own as a consulting electrical engineer, and Edison took his place. His earnings were now advanced to three hundred dollars a month, a princely salary!

Throughout that summer he worked on improvements in the gold indicator, incorporating in its mechanism an alphabetical wheel and printing device. Gold Indicator could now offer a full stock-quotation service, such as its competitor, Gold &

Stock Telegraph, already boasted. That rival company had been bought out by the all-powerful Western Union, the "octopus" of telegraph companies. Rather than contend against Western Union, Laws wisely chose to accept an offer of consolidation and retired from the field with an independent fortune.

Edison had fulfilled his assignment so well that he seemed to have worked himself out of a job. But he had other ideas; indeed he was on the verge of establishing himself on his own as a free-lance inventor.

On October 1, 1869, *The Telegrapher* displayed a half-page advertisement announcing the formation of the new firm of Pope, Edison & Company as "electrical engineers" and "constructors of various types of electrical devices and apparatus." This is believed to have been the first announcement of a professional electrical-engineering service in the United States, the idea of it being credited jointly to Pope and Edison. The two men also had a sleeping partner, J. L. Ashley, publisher of *The Telegrapher*, who donated his journal's advertising space to the enterprise, in lieu of cash.

In the interests of economy, it was arranged that Edison should board with his friend Pope at the latter's home in Elizabeth, New Jersey. Part of an old shop was rented in Jersey City, near the yards of the Pennsylvania Railroad, in which Edison was to carry on experimental work. He would rise at six, have breakfast, catch the seven-o'clock train to Jersey City, and stay at his work until nearly one in the morning, when he would take a train back to Elizabeth. This iron regime was maintained all that winter; there was the half-mile walk from the station at Elizabeth to Pope's house, and Edison later remembered being nearly frozen on his early morning and nightly walks in the winter of 1870. What did it matter if it was cold? He was doing the things he had longed to do.

Edison completed work on a new type of "gold printer" which was to be made by Pope, Edison & Company and rented to subscribers, who were mostly importers and currency dealers. The rental price, set at twenty-five dollars a week, moreover, was low and offered competition to similar services of Western Union. As so often happened in such cases, Western Union took steps to eliminate this competitive threat by buying up the new service within six months. Pope, Edison & Company realized fifteen thousand dollars by this transaction, Edison receiving five thousand as his share.

He was already flourishing in his trade of inventor, but this was the first large sum he had realized from such work. He had recently begun to send money to provide for his parents.

In the year that followed his arrival in New York, he took out seven patents covering a whole series of refinements in the telegraphic art. The telegraph was Thomas A. Edison's first great love, the primary invention out of which many other innovations were to flow. Although these early inventions were of minor importance they showed distinctive skills and insights.

He could see that even his invention of small parts or refinements for so "commercial" a machine as the printing telegraph possessed a considerable value. What galled Edison, however, was that while he did almost all the work, his two partners got the lion's share, the silent partner Ashley receiving as much as Edison, though he had invested no capital. In the summer of 1870, Edison therefore terminated his partnership agreement with the other two men, in friendly fashion. "I got tired," he said dryly, "of doing all the work with compensation narrowed down to the point of extinguishment by the superior business abilities of my partners."

His real "market," after all, was the giant Western Union Telegraph Company, or its subsidiary, Gold & Stock Telegraph, headed by General Marshall Lefferts, a former Army telegrapher who was one of the best informed of the Western Union executives. By 1870 it was noteworthy that Western Union employed a whole team of inventors. Now Lefferts decided to bring Edison, the youngest of the new crop of inventors, into the company's stable.

For Lefferts had been observing that Edison showed a real expertise. This smooth-shaven youth with the big head and broad brows might look like a rustic or a plain mechanic, but one could feel the cunning behind his devices. In order to reserve Edison's entire services for his company, Lefferts now offered to advance him money at regular intervals for the cost of all research and experimentation on their assignments. Edison accepted the proposal.

ONE OF the worst "bugs" that troubled the early wire printing services was their way of suddenly "running wild" and printing crazy figures. After Edison had turned in a whole series of minor inventions to Western Union, he was asked to work on the improvement of their Callahan stock printer, which also occasionally ran wild.

Within about three weeks he was back in Lefferts's office, and before a group of the company's directors he gave a demonstration of a successful unison-stop device that promptly brought stock tickers in outside brokers' offices into alignment with the central station transmitter, whenever they began to print wild figures.

The device made a profound impression on the capitalists; it was obvious it would save much labor and trouble. Even Callahan, whose machine Edison thus completed, said afterward in somewhat grudging praise that a ticker without the unison device would be impracticable and unsalable. At this stage of affairs money had been owing to Edison for some time on account of a whole series of telegraphic inventions.

"Well, young man"—thus Lefferts addressed him—"the committee would like to settle up the account. . . . How much do you think they are worth?"

Edison remembered afterward that he was uncertain about what to demand. He had thought to ask five thousand dollars, but might manage with three thousand. "General, suppose you make me an offer," he said at length.

Lefferts then said, "How would forty thousand dollars strike you?"

Feeling "as near fainting as I ever got," Edison managed to stammer that the offer seemed fair enough. He was asked to come back in three days, when a contract would be ready, and the money also.

The contract, when presented to him, seemed as "obscure as Choctaw," and he signed without reading it. A check with his name on it was handed to him, the first he had ever held. When he went to a Wall Street bank the money was duly paid, in a big pile of ten- and twenty-dollar bills about a foot in thickness.

According to his own account, on receiving his precious bundle of greenbacks he drew his big loose overcoat about him and departed by ferry and train for Newark, where he was living at the time in a dingy boardinghouse. There he sat up all night, unable to sleep for fear of being murdered for the sake of his great hoard.

In the morning he returned to New York to inquire about some way of disposing of his heavy encumbrance of legal tender. Friends advised him to go back to the same bank and open a deposit account; which he did, receiving a little book testifying to the transaction.

Oh, the paradoxes and mysteries of money! Greenbacks now seemed to be raining down from heaven upon the same unwitting head that, only yesterday, did not know where to lay itself.

IN THE WINTER OF 1871 Edison wandered about the industrial section of Newark looking for a good location for the manufacturing shop he was to establish. He had received from Western Union orders for 1,200 stock tickers, to be manufactured over a period of several years—orders totaling nearly half a million dollars. After climbing many stairs in dingy buildings, he found what he wanted, at his price, on the top floor of a three-story structure at 4–6 Ward Street. Soon horse-drawn vans arrived with a quantity of machinery he had purchased.

Many mechanics came to Ward Street in response to advertisements he had inserted in the newspapers. To their surprise they found the proprietor to be a young man of only twenty-four. In this district of small shops, it was rumored that he had struck it rich.

Within thirty days he had spent virtually all the fortune he had just won for equipment of all sorts. His mood, nevertheless, was of the highest optimism, as shown by one letter to his parents in that winter of 1871, in which he wrote:

> . . . I have a large amount of business to attend to. I have one shop which employs 18 men and am fitting up another which will employ over 150 men. I am now what "you" Democrats call a "Bloated Eastern Manufacturer."

But his great anxiety was on the score of his mother, reports of whose ill health reached him. He had not been home in three years and did not know when he would find time for a visit. Indeed, he longed to see his mother once more and show her that her hopes in him had not been misplaced. But that winter he was unable to go to her, and after that it was too late. On April 11, 1871, a telegram arrived from Port Huron telling him that Nancy Edison had died two days before. He hurried home to Michigan to attend her funeral, and kneel beside her grave in the cemetery by Lake St. Clair; then he returned quickly to Newark to lose himself in work.

Later he learned that a few weeks after his mother's death, his father, aged sixty-seven, had formed a connection with one of the local dairymaids, aged seventeen, whom he was eventually to marry.

IN ITS HEYDAY, the great Western Union was an outstanding example of the marriage of capital and applied science; it was indeed the principal initiator of the new electrical industry in this country. Western Union's directors distinguished themselves in the two decades following the Civil War by subsidizing scientific invention more actively than did any other industrialists. The company encouraged inventors by paying them; but while thus sponsoring their work it also took control of their products. The valuable patents of Edison, as of other men, became the property of the giant telegraph company. And when Edison went off to Newark to manufacture stock printers for the company, Marshall Lefferts saw to it that the young man took as his partner one William Unger, said to have been Lefferts's business associate. The firm name was, therefore, Edison & Unger.

Now began an intensively active and happy period of Edison's life, during which he developed, from a sort of master tech-

nician whose task was to perfect—often by simplifying—the crude inventions of others, into an original creator with a flair for truly strategic inventions. At Edison & Unger's he began assembling about fifty men to turn out stock tickers. In hiring workers Edison looked for skilled craftsmen, advertising especially for men who had "light fingers."

There was, for example, John Ott, a youth of twenty-one whom he had first engaged as an assistant at the smaller Pope, Edison & Company shop in Jersey City. A more remarkable mechanic still was Charles Batchelor, a black-bearded young Englishman who had been sent to the United States to install special machinery at the Clark Sewing Thread Mills in Newark. Another hardworking and well-loved member of the original force was John Kruesi, a Swiss clockmaker, who could construct almost any form of instrument or machine he might be called upon to make. Then there was Sigmund Bergmann, a German, who could then scarcely speak English but who showed himself a keen and diligent mechanic.

These skilled men made up the core of the original crew who learned to manufacture electrical equipment under Edison, who was himself still in the learning stage. He was only twenty-four, younger than most of his men, yet he directed his people and assumed complete responsibility for everything going on in his plant. For Edison by now had a sense of the uniqueness of his inventive talent. As master in his own shop, he showed an irrepressible enthusiasm, like that of a child, and his endless curiosity about everything intrigued his co-workers. He was decidedly the egoist, but one who knew how to ally the devotion of other men with his ego drives, for he had an intuitive knowledge of human psychology.

When undertakings of unusual moment absorbed him, he would go about his shop "laying bets with the men" or offering them prizes to continue their work without stopping until some experimental model he had assigned was brought to working order. When the results of some prolonged period of labor were unusually pleasing to him, he might declare a holiday and invite all hands to go fishing with him.

He could be the complete eccentric, too, in his business methods. "I kept only payroll accounts. I kept no books. I preserved a record of my own expenditures on one hook, and the bills on another hook, and generally gave notes in payment. The first intimation that a note was due was the protest; after that I had to hustle around and raise the money. This saved the humbuggery of bookkeeping, which I never understood."

ONLY A FEW MONTHS after he had organized the shop at Ward Street, Edison set aside a room on the top floor as his laboratory, with far more elaborate equipment than he had ever possessed before. During much of the day he might be busy as a manufacturer, yet he could not give up the habit of experimental investigation. Curiosity drove him to research. At Newark, where he was his own master, experimentation became a daily and systematic, rather than intermittent, pursuit. From the summer of 1871 he began to keep a laboratory notebook, setting down almost day by day the exact record of his investigations, ideas, and even random reflections.

In his Newark years Edison gradually developed into one of the most accomplished technicians of the telegraph industry. The Edison Universal stock printer, improved by him over a period of several years, came into use in almost all financial offices and security exchanges in Europe as well as in America, speeding up the process of all speculation and investment.

His growing professional repute brought many an important entrepreneur to his shop. Not long after he had begun making stock printers, a young railroad and telegraph engineer named Edward H. Johnson turned up at the Ward Street shop bringing with him a model of a new type of automatic telegraph—invented by one George D. Little—which Edison was asked to examine and test. Little's device used a moving paper tape with perforations, corresponding to Morse dots and dashes, which controlled signals sent by a transmitting instrument and printed automatically by the receiver on another tape.

Edison tested the machine thoroughly over wires of the Pennsylvania Railroad and diagnosed its weaknesses. Instead of being faster than the ordinary Morse manual sender, it proved to be extremely "sluggish" because it was highly subject to electrostatic interference. Then Edison, after some study, made a number of proposals for correcting the defects of this apparatus. The mechanism, in his judgment, had splendid possibilities, and he appeared to Johnson both confident and very clearheaded in his plans for its "cure."

The group that had purchased Little's patent had already formed a stock corporation named the Automatic Telegraph Company to promote the invention. They had been on the verge of abandoning the whole project when Johnson delivered an ecstatic report on the young Newark inventor's plans for making their machine practical. Whereupon the company's directors hurried over to see Edison and entered into a contractual agreement with him. One of the directors of Automatic Telegraph was George Harrington, who, unknown to Edison, was reputed to be the financial agent of the sinister Jay Gould.

Harrington, on behalf of the Automatic Telegraph Company, advanced Edison forty thousand dollars. Edison thereupon, in partnership with Joseph T. Murray of Newark (as Edison & Murray), opened another shop, spent most of the money on special equipment and material, hired more men, and set to work. One stipulation was that Edward H. Johnson be assigned to assist him. Johnson, who had come only to consult Thomas A. Edison, would remain to work as his associate for more than twenty years.

A GREAT PART of the autumn of 1871 was devoted by Edison to the automatic, or high-speed, telegraph. In tests carried out during the winter of 1871–72 over lines between New York and Philadelphia, he was eventually able to transmit one thousand words a minute in Morse code signals.

On August 16, 1872, a patent application covering his own improvements and additions to the Little apparatus was filed and assigned to George Harrington.

It was Edison's most skillful performance so far and clearly foreshadowed the early development of a commercially practicable automatic telegraph of tremendous speed. Yet he was not satisfied. A big idea had come to him, and he must work it out at all costs. Since no human being could receive the messages coming at such speed over the lines, why not make the receiving instrument entirely automatic? Why send messages by an automatic transmitter in dots and dashes when they might be printed out at the other end of the line in Roman characters by combining the automatic telegraph with the mechanism of his own Universal stock printer?

He pushed on with his work, commenting on each experimental trial with notes such as:

A bully experiment by T. A. Edison, assisted by Charles Batchelor.... The sentence we took: "Now is the winter of our discontent"—with this we got 250 words per minute, but counting five letters to a word we got 228.

By the winter of 1873 the Automatic Telegraph people had reason to be jubilant over Edison's progress. He had performed more than he had promised. The completed models incorporated receiving instruments that printed letters on tape, and, before he finished, he gave the new system tests over long lines for 120 successive nights.

The messages were usually dispatched by Edison from a loft on lower Broadway, in New York, to Washington. On a number of occasions he delivered his automatically transmitted messages as far as Charleston, South Carolina, something of a feat in those days of poor wire.

Edison was given orders to start manufacturing the automatic apparatus, and an economic revolution of some sort impended for the telegraph industry. It was at this point that the mysterious Jay Gould, already known as "the destroying angel of Wall Street," stepped from behind the scenes and took over the ownership of the Automatic Telegraph Company, together with its new telegraphic patents that now promised such remarkable achievements.

By reimbursing Harrington, the principal stockholder of Automatic Telegraph, for his payments to Edison, and by ultimately acquiring that company, Jay Gould also acquired the services of Thomas A. Edison and rights to his automatic patents,

393

a powerful pawn in the campaign for the conquest of the nation's telegraph system. Of all this grand design the exalted young inventor probably knew less than anyone else.

BY 1871, when Edison had first appeared in Newark, the former tramp telegrapher certainly seemed to have come up in the world. But there were arrears in terms of private life of which he was increasingly aware. Prosperous though he was, he still lived in a furnished room in Newark; he had neither a home of his own nor a wife. It was said of him in those days that he was "timid in the presence of women"—but clearly not through lack of interest in them.

Science, alone, had been his chosen mistress for long years. But now he found himself exposed to the electromagnetic effects of daily contact with a beautiful young girl who worked in his shop. She was one of a number of women engaged in punching perforations into telegraph tape; but Edison did not look at the others. Her name was Mary Stilwell and she was then barely sixteen years of age; but she was tall and full of figure, and had a great pompadour of lovely golden hair. More and more often, his mind was distracted from his experiments by the person of Miss Stilwell.

His courtship was conducted in his own odd way and with his own "characteristic humor." Though he had scarcely ever spoken to her before, one day he gave her a sudden smile and inquired rather abruptly, "What do you think of me, little girl, do you like me?"

"Why, Mr. Edison, you frighten me. That is—I—"

"Don't be in a hurry about telling me. It doesn't matter much, unless you would like to marry me."

The young girl was both frightened and disposed to laugh at the same time. But Edison went on impetuously, "Oh I mean it. . . . Think it over, talk to your mother about it and let me know as soon as convenient; Tuesday, say. Next week, Tuesday, I mean."

Soon Edison and his new partner Joseph T. Murray were seen riding out in a carriage to call on Mary and her sister, Alice Stilwell, at the Sunday school where they taught—though the inventor cared nothing for church. When he duly asked her father for her hand, Edison was told that he would have to wait about a year because of her extreme youth.

They did not wait out the year, but within a few weeks, on Christmas Day of 1871, they were married at a small family ceremony in Newark. After the wedding lunch Edison brought his bride to the private house at Wright Street, Newark, which he had bought a few days before their marriage.

They were no sooner alone together than some defective stock tickers began preying on his mind. He related that "Just about an hour after the marriage ceremony had been performed," he could think only of those stock tickers! "I told my wife about them and said I would like to go down to the factory. She agreed at once. . . ."

The more famous legends about this incident suggest that he stayed on at his laboratory throughout the afternoon of his wedding and far into the night, while his young bride, frightened and tearful, waited alone in her strange new quarters. It was twelve when a friend rushed into the laboratory, exclaiming, "Tom, what are you doing at this late hour?"

"What time is it?" Edison asked vaguely.

"Midnight!"

"Midnight," he said in a dreamy way. "Is that so? I must go home then, I was married today." And with that he seized his hat and went off.

The next day the couple left for Niagara Falls. It seemed that Mary felt so young and inexperienced that she insisted that her elder sister Alice accompany her on her honeymoon trip.

Their first child, born a year later, was fair and blue-eyed, and was named Marion, after Edison's eldest sister. The next child, Thomas junior, arrived in 1876. In 1878 a second son was born who was given the name of William Leslie.

For a brief season, a measure of order and comfort were brought into the inventor's private life. On Sundays he usually managed to rest and often played with the children, becoming wildly gay. But as often as not his mind would be completely separated from his charming wife and his infant children.

He often returned home from work late for supper and, when

his work was very pressing, not until the early hours of the morning. Sometimes he would be away two or three days, sleeping on a bench or cot in his laboratory. Then he would appear at last, disheveled, pale, and too utterly worn to speak; and soiled as he was, he would throw himself upon a couch or bed in all his clothes.

Mary Edison was scarcely the woman who might have "improved" him. A gentle and affectionate being, she found herself wedded to a "great man" such as she had never imagined. He was older than she by almost ten years, strong-willed, and often transported by ideas she could never understand. She never required that he alter his way of life to conform with the needs of domesticity, but submitted entirely to his wishes.

For Thomas Alva there were no hobbies nor recreations. On the many nights when her husband was away Mary Edison had only the company of a few women friends and her sister Alice, who lived with the Edisons for several years prior to her own marriage. In this family the rule was that "father's work always came first."

In the early months of marriage the enraptured young inventor no doubt made some attempts to explain to his young wife something of what he was doing and what he aspired to do. But he must have found soon enough that he could not draw her attention to his problems. In his laboratory, in the early days, he often thought of her in moments of revery, and as he worked with his notebooks before him, sometimes scribbled affectionate nicknames for her.

IN 1873 AMERICA was on the threshold of an era of unrivaled material progress. The resourcefulness of her engineers and inventors was to be displayed only three years later at the great Centennial Exposition in Philadelphia. Here were giant steam engines, two crude examples of the electric arc light, George Westinghouse's air brake for railway trains, automatic printing and multiplex telegraphs by Edison, new gas stoves, fifty-ton locomotives, and new devices for cultivating the land, mining the earth, and making shoes.

The country, nevertheless, was in dire straits in 1873; neither its natural riches nor the industry of its population spared it the "hard times" which periodically recurred. At such periods capital disappeared, and not even the strongest of financiers seemed to have money to invest in the discoveries of inventors.

Edison at this time was on the verge of disaster. It was always difficult for him to manage the exact costing of new products, partly because of his peculiar ideas of bookkeeping. Nor did he easily brook criticism or interference by partners and associates, often becoming suspicious and angry.

One of a series of minor inventions with which he strove to keep himself afloat was a call-box system. Such devices gained a passing popularity because they seemed to offer protection against fire, burglary, and sudden illness. Another minor invention of 1874 was the Edison electric pen, operated by a small electric motor. As he described it in his patent application it "rapidly punctured a sheet of paper with numerous small holes, filling such holes with an ink, and pressing this upon the surface to be printed . . . against a steel plate." The advantage was that after letters or records had been thus written in perforations, many copies could be made. In the days before the typewriter came into commercial use, the electric pen achieved a considerable popularity.

Edison also relates that "toward the latter part of 1875 I invented a device for multiplying copies of letters called the Mimeograph." It was a simple machine for automatic stencil duplication, and he later sold it for a modest sum to A. B. Dick, of Chicago. Out of it grew one of America's largest office-equipment industries.

He was, above all, prolific. In the seven years after he came to New York he applied for and was awarded two hundred patents. But while small sums ventured by businessmen helped him in the initial development stages, there were usually long delays before profits were realized from these minor inventions.

THOUGH THE TIMES were bad, his heart was set on a truly big invention, that of a multiplex telegraph that would surpass all that had been done before in this field. The Morse circuit was still essentially a single-track affair operating at the speed of manual sending; but traffic swelled year by year, and it was difficult to keep pace with it. Therefore, Edison, throughout this period, thought only of realizing the full technical potential of the telegraph. What was galling to him, and would, in the end, drive him from the field, even though the telegraph was his first love, was the scientific and financial conservatism of those who had come to control the telegraph industry.

Early in 1873 Edison had written to William Orton, the president of Western Union, to suggest that the company back his experiments in duplex telegraphy. Orton thereupon invited him to come to his office to see what he could do to improve on J. B. Stearns's duplex devices. The company had bought patent rights to the Stearns apparatus in 1872; though workable, it had not turned out to be a profitable affair. Stearns's device could send two messages on one wire only *in opposite directions*. Orton agreed that if Edison's duplex invention-in-progress could send two messages *in the same direction* and thus double traffic, it would be a vast improvement over Stearns's device.

Edison then asked that he be allowed to use the facilities of the Western Union headquarters so that he could make experiments over their wires. This was agreed upon, with the understanding that inventions developed from these experiments be sold by Edison to Western Union.

All the winter and spring of 1873 the young inventor worked like a madman at a whole series of duplex devices in a large room in the basement of the Western Union building, often staying there all through the night when the wires were free.

After two months Edison announced promising results:

> I experimented 22 nights—tried 23 duplex systems, 9 failures, 4 partial success, 10 all right, 1 or 2 bad. . . .

At some time during the series of 1873 experiments, the idea came up that "if he succeeded in sending two messages in one direction, why would it not be as easy to duplex both transmitters as it would be to duplex one? And then there would be four?" Edison expressed the opinion that if one could be done the other could be done. Thus the real possibility of the quadruplex, which he had outlined for himself in earlier years, arose again and fairly haunted him.

In the spring of 1873 Edison interrupted his experiments on the "diplex," as he called it, to make his first trip to England, in an attempt to sell patent rights to the British for his other important invention, the automatic printing telegraph.

On his return he found the Panic of 1873 on, the sheriff after him, and no money in sight. When he tried to resume his series of experiments on the diplex telegraph at the Western Union headquarters, he could not find Orton—for he was away on a long business trip—and could not interest any of the other executives in his experiments. Western Union itself was having financial troubles; its stock was being pounded down in the market. For the time being the Western Union people seemed to have lost all interest in putting money into new inventions.

Thus a good many months passed during which the tantalizing problems of the diplex and quadruplex were allowed to rest. But they continued to obsess him. He wrote to Orton complaining that he had received no further cooperation from Western Union officials when he tried to renew these experiments in multiplex telegraphy; but he got no reply.

Finding himself in extremities Edison went back to work on other projects for the smaller, rival Automatic Telegraph Company headed by George Harrington and Josiah Reiff. Either he did not know or did not care that these men were really the agents of Jay Gould, the unconscionable war lord of American finance; nor did Edison then suspect that, since he was a free-lance inventor who alternately did work for both sides, his patents and his contracts would become central points of dispute in the "great telegraphic war" that now began between Gould and the Western Union interests and would continue for years.

But at some time in this period, it was later charged, Edison had *also* promised to sell rights to the multiplex telegraph invention to George Harrington. From these tangled business dealings with two rival interests in the telegraph industry arose the oft-repeated charge that Tom Edison had "harum-scarum notions about his contractual obligations."

When Orton finally reappeared, he gave orders that the

fullest cooperation be extended Edison; he also approved of the idea of Western Union's chief engineer, George B. Prescott, becoming Edison's partner—though Prescott was his subordinate and a high officer of Western Union, to whom the invention, if successful, would be sold. The conduct of both Prescott and President Orton, who advised him, reflected the low standard of business ethics during those robber-baron times. Edison's own recollection of the affair bore out this view:

> I wanted to interest the W.U. Telegraph Company [in the quadruplex] with a view to selling it, but was unsuccessful, until I made an arrangement with the Chief Electrician of the Company, so he could be known as joint inventor and receive a portion of the money. At that time I was very short of funds and needed it more than glory. This electrician appeared to want glory more than money, so it was an easy trade. . . .

After the deal with Prescott, experiment on the new type of duplex conceived by Edison went forward more rapidly, at Western Union's expense and with the help of its personnel.

Growing slowly in his own undisciplined way, Edison by now had reached a stage where his mind functioned in scientific work with great clarity as well as ingenuity. He had to use the most elaborate circuits—combining strong and weak currents with rapid changes in the direction of their flow—that were ever attempted in the era before electronic science was born. Yet this complicated scheme of the electrical currents was worked out in Edison's head. "He had really very little power of abstraction and had to be able, above all, to *visualize* things," one of his sons said of him in later years.

By early summer Edison was sending jubilant notes to Orton:

> I have struck a new vein. . . . Think 't will be a success.
> Two messages can be sent in the same direction.
> In opposite directions.
> Way stations can work on it. . . .

The design of the quadruplex was now complete. At one of his tests Edison rigged up two rooms constituting the near and far ends of the circuit, with a wire running out to Albany, a hundred and fifty miles distant, connecting them; it worked fairly well.

"Boys, she's a go!" he exclaimed to his assistants. But it was still a new thing and full of "baffling perversity" at times. "It must be used," he said, "to find out where the bugs are."

The turning point had come in the summer of 1874 when Edison got the two messages going in one direction on one wire and combined his own apparatus with the Stearns system, thus transmitting, all together, four messages on one wire (two in each opposite direction) at a rate of 142 telegrams per hour.

Edison, Prescott, and Orton then met at Orton's office, and Edison signed a preliminary agreement dated July 9, 1874, in which he designated Prescott as his "coinventor," the patent for the quadruplex to be filed jointly in their names. If the invention proved on further testing to be successful, Western Union was to buy the patent rights from Edison and Prescott on conditions it usually accorded to inventors, with any disputes over terms to be settled by an outside arbitrator.

Up to this time Edison had still received no payment from Western Union, but all through that summer he continued to work hard over the installation and testing of the new quadruplex apparatus on the company's long lines. At last, preparations were made for a full-dress exhibition before a board meeting of Western Union.

Edison relates:

> Under certain conditions of weather one side of the quadruplex would work very shaky, and I had not succeeded in ascertaining the cause of the trouble. . . . The day arrived, I had picked the best operators in N.Y. and they were familiar with the apparatus. I arranged that if a storm should occur and the bad side got shaky to do the best they could and draw freely on their imagination. They were sending old messages—about twelve o'clock everything was working fine, but there was a storm somewhere near Albany—Mr. Orton, the president, and Wm. Vanderbilt and other directors came in. I had my heart trying to climb up around my oesophagus. . . . But the operators were stars, they pulled me through. The N.Y. Times came out next day with a full account. . . .

On October 14, 1874, a published report of Western Union showed that the quadruplex device had been in operation over part of its lines, and that results thus far indicated it would double the company's existing facilities and yield economies amounting to many millions.

No wonder the great "barons" would continue for years to contend in court for its possession. It would bring dominance of the industry to whoever owned it.

DURING THE modern era of electronics the telegraph has been all but forgotten. Nonetheless, Edison's quadruplex was a strategic invention in its time and impresses us as the masterwork of his youth. It was surely the most complicated job Edison had done thus far, and therefore marks a decided jump in his own intellectual capacity. Up to now the twenty-seven-year-old inventor had been known to a small circle of clients who appreciated his budding talents. But when reports of his quadruplex were published in newspapers and technical journals in the autumn of 1874, his reputation began to spread among a mainly scientific public abroad as well as at home.

At this stage of his career Edison was prosperous; he suddenly found himself with a modest accumulation of capital, his debts paid off and some twenty thousand dollars to the good. He was also determined to bring about a sweeping change in his way of life. He must, at all costs, quit "business" and manufacturing and live in some quiet retreat where he could give himself entirely to the vocation he loved—inventive research.

IV. Menlo Park

IN THE EARLY spring of 1876 residents of the tiny hamlet of Menlo Park, New Jersey, saw with some surprise a new and rather oddly shaped building going up in an open pasture on a hill overlooking the main railway line between New York and Philadelphia. It was a plain wooden structure of two stories and rectangular in form. A tall white-haired man with a long nose directed the building operation; he was Sam Edison, the father of the inventor, who had been called from Michigan for this purpose. On weekends a slightly built, negligently dressed young man with a silk hat perched on his big head used to drive out to see how the work was going here.

By the end of May the structure was all but completed; it was a hundred feet in length by thirty in width, with white-painted clapboard sides, tall windows and a porch in front. Surrounding it was a stout picket fence. Before the paint was dry, great horse-drawn trucks thundered up from Newark, bringing equipment—boxes of chemicals, rolls of wire, loads of books, a Brown steam engine, and a gasoline converter that would supply gaslight. Finally the younger Edison came to install himself in the new building; and with him came his faithful retinue, Batchelor, Kruesi, John Ott, and a dozen other manly-looking, full-bearded workers.

In that homely barnlike structure, the inventor partitioned off a small office, a little library, and a drafting room on the lower floor; the floor above was a single room furnished with many tables covered with instruments, machines, and batteries, the walls being lined with shelves holding a great variety of materials and chemical jars of every color. On this floor there was a force of thirteen skilled mechanics working with fine steel and brass instruments, or electrical products of every kind. At their head, bent over a table, was Edison.

There, in effect, he hung out his shingle, announcing to the world that he, Thomas A. Edison, would undertake research and development work on *any and all inventions*.

It will be recalled that on first coming to New York he had formed the partnership of Pope, Edison & Company, as consultants in electrical engineering, perhaps the first concern of its kind. The establishment at Menlo Park was more ambitious; it was, in fact, the first industrial research laboratory in America, or in the world.

At that time there were only a few poorly equipped laboratories at some of the leading universities, and they were for teaching purposes or for purely scientific research. No one had ever heard of a research center directed solely toward *practical* inventions—an "invention factory" making inventions to order.

The traditional view was that invention was an act of God, a "divine accident," a stroke of genius. Here was a genius who held that there was no such thing as genius. And his bustling organization at Menlo Park was, in itself, one of the most remarkable of Edison's many inventions.

He told the physicist Dr. George Beard, in all seriousness, that he proposed to turn out at Menlo Park "a minor invention every ten days and a big thing every six months or so." Beard was dumbfounded and thought Edison was blowing. But the recent list of his patents ran to about forty a year. A number of them, covering the stock printer and quadruplex, had already brought him sizable revenues; there were others under way; and he knew in addition that leading capitalists of New York would seek him out, if only for the purpose of hiring him to test, improve, or perfect someone else's invention.

He was truly happy, he felt a blessed sense of freedom, when at last he found himself in the country in the month of June; and in this spirit he wrote to a patent lawyer of his acquaintance about his "brand-new laboratory . . . at Menlo Park, Western Div., Globe, Planet Earth, Middlesex Country, four miles from Rahway, the prettiest spot in New Jersey, on the Penna. Railway, on a High Hill. Will show you around, go strawberrying."

Edison purchased a plain farmhouse of six rooms, hard by the site of his laboratory, and installed Mary there with his two children. Two of the other six houses in the village were occupied by his principal assistants, Batchelor and Kruesi, who also had families. The one boardinghouse in the place, a Mrs. Jordan's, was soon filled with those laboratory mechanics who were bachelors. In effect, the whole small hamlet became a community devoted to experimental science. Edison Village, it was humorously called.

As at Newark, his men worked long hours, starting with the whistle at seven in the morning, sometimes sleeping on benches or on the floor during all-night vigils. On occasions when they worked late at night, a pleasant midnight collation was sent in by Mrs. Edison, and they would make merry, the place resounding with laughter.

Not only did Edison exert a powerful attraction upon his

co-workers, but the ambitious program of the next five years gripped their imagination more and more. Young workers, hearing of the remarkable deeds performed in this place under the leadership of the young inventor, eagerly came to apply for jobs.

The significance of the Menlo Park laboratory was that its master worked with a whole team, comprising not only machinists and technical men but also several persons with formal scientific training. He still adhered to his cut-and-try methods. But at Menlo Park, industrial invention depended not on the insights of the shopworker alone, but on a careful comprehensive search by a whole team under him. It is for this reason that his little organization served as a pilot model for the huge industrial research laboratories organized in later years, such as those of the Bell system and General Electric.

Edison's decision not to undertake inventions unless there was a definite market demand for them was of great historical importance, as a modern commentator, James G. Crowther, has written: "He was the first great scientific inventor who clearly conceived of invention as subordinate to commerce." In thus making his inventions conform to the necessities of human use and convenience, he also established a social and democratic criterion for applied science. "He began the advance toward a democratic theory in which invention would be cultivated in order to increase human happiness. . . ."

In choosing the "commercial" standard, Edison was by no means being "vulgar" or mercenary. He was determined to make his hazardous profession both businesslike and respectable. But no one was more satisfied than he, once there was a little money on hand, to make that little do for his needs and to live for the joy of inventive work.

EVER SINCE July of 1875, some months before his Menlo Park move, a wholly new field of investigation had absorbed Edison: that of the acoustic, or harmonic telegraph, which by use of tuning forks or reeds transmitted musical notes over a wire. By 1875 Elisha Gray had contrived a telegraph that carried nine to sixteen different musical notes, taken from tuning forks and transmitted to a receiving instrument. But if different musical notes could be sent over an electric wire, why not the sound of the human voice—why not a *speaking* telegraph? Gray, in fact, called his harmonic telegraph a "telephone."

In the meantime Alexander Graham Bell, a well-educated Scottish immigrant who was Edison's age, had had the same idea, and for several years struggled with the problem of making a metal disk, vibrating in response to sounds, convey and reproduce those sounds over an electrified wire.

By the summer of 1875 William Orton seems to have been alerted to the promise of the experiments being pursued by Gray, Bell, and others. Swallowing any hard feelings engendered by the bitter legal battle between Western Union and the Gould interests over the patents of that talented young "professional," Edison, he once again called him in. Already it was said of Edison, "He never fails in anything he seriously undertakes." Orton now invited him to investigate acoustic telegraphy for Western Union. Edison went to work, and shortly before moving to Menlo Park he devised an apparatus for analyzing waves produced by various sounds.

Edison was late in entering the race for the telephone; half a dozen expert men had begun the investigation of the speaking telegraph years before him. He also showed great courage in undertaking such work in view of the fact that he was very hard of hearing. Evidently his hearing loss was that of the eardrum and middle ear, for he seemed to be able to hear sound instruments by biting his teeth into them, thus allowing vibrations to be conducted through the bones of his head to the inner hearing nerve.

Alexander Graham Bell, meanwhile, had been making rapid progress. One afternoon in June 1875 his ear had caught a first feeble sound of words, the voice of his assistant speaking to him over the wire of a crude magnetotelephone. This clue was followed up closely until the morning of February 14, 1876, when Bell thought he had invented enough to apply for a patent covering his telephone. That same day, his nearest rival, Elisha Gray, walked into the Patent Office to outline exactly the same invention transmitting human speech. It is probably the most famous example of "parallel" invention made by two men working independently. The patent law, however, accorded the entire authorship and rights over one of the most valuable patents ever granted to Bell alone.

After the details of Bell's telephone were made public in March 1876, Edison went back and examined his own device for measuring sound waves. He now found that it was capable of transmitting sound, though crudely. If only he had had the ears to hear faint sounds of speech, he might have won the race for the telephone. He acknowledged himself fairly beaten.

In July 1876, at the Centennial Exposition in Philadelphia, Bell's demonstrations of his telephone made a tremendous public sensation. Now the Western Union magnates, who only a few months before had turned down Bell's offer to sell his patents at a reasonable price, began to feel uneasy. Again they decided to call in Edison. As he put it simply, they had found the 1876 telephone a crude affair, and "wanted me to make it commercial." It consisted only of two receivers used alternately for hearing and speaking; while one person talked the other listened. Bell thought it was pretty wonderful when the human voice was carried for a distance of two miles. The man "sending" had to shout each sentence three or four times in order to be heard above a good deal of "interference."

During the autumn of 1876 and the winter following, Edison puzzled over the problem of raising the telephone's volume while still controlling and balancing the current variations it induced. It was at the end of the first winter at Menlo Park that Edison had his big idea. The Bell magnetotelephone, for many reasons, could not be used effectively as both receiver and transmitter. What was needed was a separate transmitter in circuit with Bell's receiver, which when used alone for both purposes was too weak.

Edison then conceived of a second strategic innovation, that of introducing an induction coil so that electrical impulses of an enormously higher potential could be sent out on the main line by the secondary circuit of the coil. Instead of being limited to a few miles' range, the sound vibrations of Edison's transmitter could be heard over long distances.

Now he began a broad search for the right conducting substance for his transmitter. He divided this labor among his staff at Menlo Park and, beginning at the end of his stock of chemicals tried every one of them—some two thousand. If it took all summer, he would continue the search by such methods. And after that, throughout the autumn and the winter.

He was thoroughly familiar with the wonderful properties of carbon. His first rude transmitter used graphite electrodes and operated fairly well; but now he searched for a purer carbon. One day an assistant brought him a piece of broken glass incrustated with carbon black from a smoking lamp chimney. He scraped off the carbon, pressed it into a little cake and tried that. It was molded in the form of a button and introduced into the transmitter. Now the volume of sound was several times larger than in Bell's telephone and the articulation was sharp. Edison's carbon transmitter was, in fact, a *microphone*.

In a test that was a sort of full-dress rehearsal over a line 107 miles long, between New York and Philadelphia, in the presence of Western Union's directors, Edison's transmitter delivered speech "loudly." The effect was sensational. Everyone present felt that he had liberated the art of telephony—so hoarse and stuttering in its first two years—and had won a tremendous advantage over the limited Bell apparatus. One spoke into the separate Edison transmitter and at the same time also listened, through the receiver held at one's ear, to the speaker at the other end of the line. On that day in 1878 the telephone received its fundamental form, which was to remain virtually unaltered for almost half a century.

Edison now had begun to feel that "he ought to be taken care of . . . and threw out hints of this desire." Orton sent for him and asked him how much he wanted. Edison said he thought $25,000 might have been enough, but invited Orton to make him an offer. Orton thereupon said his company would pay the inventor $100,000, a tiny percentage of the wealth his invention was to bring in. Very well satisfied, Edison agreed on condition that the money be paid him in installments, during the life of the patent, of $6000 a year for seventeen years. Orton had no trouble agreeing to this, since the interest alone on

$100,000, at six percent, would have netted the inventor a similar sum. But to Edison it was just as well, since he believed that "inventors didn't do business by the regular process." He feared that if he received all the money at once, it might disappear quickly.

Meanwhile, the sale of his telephone transmitter patent in England brought further rewards, for there it was seen at once that Edison had a grip on half the telephone invention. He has related:

> One day I received a cable ... offering "30,000" for my interest. I cabled back I would accept. When the draft came I was astonished to find it was for 30,000 pounds sterling. I had thought it was dollars.

For "curing" (as Edison phrased it) Bell's magnetotelephone he gathered in altogether a quarter of a million dollars. The telegrapher who had come to New York threadbare ten years earlier was already the highest-paid professional among American inventors, one who, in a pinch, could be trusted to deliver almost any contrivance needed.

THE YEARS AT MENLO PARK, from 1876 to 1881, were by all odds the happiest and most fruitful of Edison's life. He was in his early thirties and at the very height of his creative power. The business of inventing was humming along; the combats of great Wall Street moneymen for possession of his patents testified to their importance to the industrial system.

There was a charm about life in this village of applied science that many who came here noticed. Here Edison enjoyed peace and freedom. He could meditate, permit his mind to wander, even "play" without interruption. "Edison is always absolutely himself," one visitor wrote. When he wished to inform himself on some special subject of moment to him, he would sometimes gather together a great mass of books, lay them out on the floor of his library and "pore over them for hours on end ... after which he would go back, refreshed, to the manual part of his task."

His life was simple and yet complete. His co-workers were

sworn friends and disciples who shared in his devotions. Moreover, his wife and children were close by. The eldest, Marion, as a girl of five or six, often played in the laboratory at her father's feet. On evenings when he returned home early for supper—rarely enough—he sometimes entertained his family with mechanical or musical toys of his own invention.

In his laboratory he was capable of pursuing a large variety of inventions under development at the same time. At one period, early in the eighties, there were said to have been forty-four of these under way, with different assistants in charge of each. Edison would study their progress daily, passing rapidly from one to another as he inspected them. In 1877, for example, we know that technical improvements were being worked out for various telegraph and submarine-cable devices; different types of telephones were being improvised; electric pens and mimeograph machines were being made; various sound-measuring instruments were being developed; many chemicals and drugs were under investigation; even a crude incandescent lamp was contrived, but was abandoned when it burned out in a few moments.

Edison appears to have sensed clearly the dependence of invention and discovery upon the total accumulation of knowledge. He was forever collecting curious and miscellaneous facts, and squirreling them away in his memory. In his work, to be sure, is all the evidence of methodical and close-gripping deduction.

But he also stressed the important role played by chance or accident in discovery. Pasteur, who had a deep understanding of the mental processes of discovery, said, "Chance favors the mind that is *prepared*." Edison, too, then must certainly have been prepared when, as he confessed, he met, "by the merest accident," with the opportunity for the most original invention he had ever conceived, one that would open up a wholly new and marvelous art to mankind.

THE STUDY of sound fascinated Edison—in that he was partially deaf. At this time, he has said, "my mind was filled with theories of sound vibrations and their transmission by diaphragms."

Some time before he had worked out the carbon transmitter he applied for a patent covering "An Improvement in the Automatic Telegraph," designed to permit the recording and repeating of telegraph messages at speeds of two hundred words a minute. This device consisted of a disk of paper laid on a revolving platen and rotating around a vertical axis, quite like the modern phonograph disk. An embossing point traveled over the disk embossing on it the dots and dashes of incoming telegraph messages.

Returning later to this telegraph repeater, he tried to improve its performance by changing over to an arrangement using continuous rolls of coated or paraffined paper tape. When this instrument raced along at high speed, the indentations of dots and dashes striking against the end of a spring sometimes gave off a noise, "a light musical, rhythmical sound, resembling human talk heard indistinctly."

The indistinct mutterings in the machine haunted him; the sounds it made were *almost human*, like those issuing from the first weak Bell telephones.

It *may* have been accident that caused the musical sound in the telegraph repeating instrument. But diaphragms were very much in his mind now. One day he took a tape of paraffined paper and placed it underneath a diaphragm having a small blunt pin attached to its center. As he related:

> I rigged up an instrument hastily and pulled a strip of paper through it, at the same time shouting "Halloo!" Then the paper was pulled through again so that its marks actuated the point of another diaphragm, my friend Batchelor and I listening breathlessly. We heard a distinct sound, which a strong imagination might have translated into the original "Halloo." That was enough to lead me to further experiment.

They had heard the first strangled cries of the infant talking machine struggling to be born.

This work was kept somewhat secret. There is evidence that he approached the Western Union people with his idea of reproducing and recording the human voice, but they saw no conceivable use for it!

411

It is under the date of August 12, 1877, that we first come upon an entry in Edison's notebooks using the word "phonograph"; and by early November there were indications of the pristine form of the talking machine:

> I propose having a cylinder ... 10 threads or embossing grooves to the inch ... cylinder 1 foot long.
> I have tried wax, chalk, etc.

A fortnight later the first accurate sketch in his own hand of the original talking machine is entered into the notebooks. He recalled incidents accompanying it with great vividness:

> Instead of using a disc I designed a little machine using a cylinder provided with grooves around the surface. Over this was to be placed tinfoil, which easily received and recorded the movements of the diaphragm. A sketch was made. . . . The workman who got the sketch was John Kruesi. I didn't have much faith that it would work. . . . When he was nearly finished, [he] asked what it was for. I told him. . . . He thought it absurd.

Others present bet the "Old Man" cigars that the contraption would not work. When the thing was completed, it was a solid job of brass and iron, with a three-and-a-half-inch cylinder on a foot-long shaft and a hand crank to turn it. Edison fixed a sheet of tinfoil around the cylinder, began turning the handle of the shaft, and shouted into one of the little diaphragms:

> *Mary had a little lamb,*
> *Its fleece was white as snow,*
> *And everywhere that Mary went*
> *The lamb was sure to go.*

Then he turned the shaft backward to the starting point, drew away the first diaphragm tube, adjusted the other in position to reproduce sound, and once more turned the shaft handle forward. Out of the machine came forth what everyone recognized as the high-pitched voice of Thomas A. Edison himself, "almost perfectly" reproduced, reciting the little Mother Goose rhyme. Kruesi turned pale and made some pious exclamation in German. All the onlookers were dumbfounded.

Edison declared afterward, "I was never so taken aback in all my life. Everybody was astonished. I was always afraid of things that worked the first time." After that, he tells us, they sat up all night fixing and adjusting it so as to get better and better results—talking into it and singing, testing different voices, then listening with unending amazement to the words coming back.

When, on December 15, 1877, he filed a patent for the phonograph, his most original invention, nothing remotely resembling such a machine was ever found to have been mentioned in all the voluminous records of the United States Patent Office, and the grant of patent was made in the unusually brief time of fifty-seven days.

When he had finished with his invention, Edison hardly knew what to do with it. These days his inventions were usually made on order; but no one had ordered this. Was it only a scientific toy, a curiosity? Yet the first raucous croaks of Edison's phonograph were heard round the world. People did not yet understand the 1876 telephone; now they were confronted with the phonograph, which seemed even more astounding.

FAME ENTERED the door of the Menlo Park laboratory at the end of 1877. The acclaim suddenly given the phonograph and its author was almost unprecedented. A "phonograph craze" flared up. Newspaper reporters, writers, and artists of popular magazines flocked out to Menlo Park in large numbers, and described the "nineteenth-century miracle" of the phonograph.

A leading journal in America saluted Edison in an editorial as being conceivably "the greatest inventor of the age," adding:

> We are inclined to regard him as one of the wonders of the world. While Huxley, Tyndall, Spencer and other theorists talk and speculate, he produces accomplished facts, and with his marvellous inventions is pushing the whole world ahead in its march to the highest civilization.

After the press had done its duty in telling the millions about the "speaking phonograph," the crowds who had read about "the New Jersey Columbus" came to Menlo Park to see him and his works. They came from cities and farms, by carriage or wagon and by train; indeed the railroad organized excursions. Menlo Park became the mecca of a continuous pilgrimage of scientists and curiosity hunters.

People crowded into the lower floor of the building and saw nothing but books, blueprints, and mechanical designs; then they tramped upstairs and gaped at the array of chemical jars, metals, batteries, and electrical machines. Overhead were tangled lines of telephone and telegraph wires that made strange cobwebs everywhere.

Edison himself demonstrated his invention and answered all questions promptly and clearly. Like a comedian, he entertained the crowds by showing them all sorts of tricks the talking machine could perform: he whistled popular airs, or he rang bells, coughed, and sneezed before the recording tube, then reproduced these assorted sounds.

Among the visitors were a good number who came to see with their own eyes if there were not some prestidigitator's trick about this new invention. One such was Bishop John Vincent, cofounder of the Chautauqua movement. After looking sharply all about the laboratory for a hidden ventriloquist, the bishop began to shout into the phonograph's recording tube with great rapidity a long string of jawbreaking Old Testament names. When the tinfoil record was played back to him, he announced emphatically that he was now satisfied there was no fraud by Edison, since not another man in the whole country could recite those biblical names with such speed as he had used.

Nothing would suffice, after all the newspaper stories of Edison's miracle, but that he must come to the nation's capital to exhibit his speaking phonograph before the notables of government and science. He accepted urgent invitations to Washington, and arriving there, first paid a call on Joseph Henry at the Smithsonian Institution. Here he demonstrated the phonograph in the scientist's parlor.

Later in the evening he made his appearance before a large gathering and allowed his machine to introduce itself. As Edison turned the crank its voice was plainly heard saying, "The speaking phonograph has the honor of presenting itself before the American Academy of Sciences."

The last stop during that triumphal tour of the capital was at the White House. As Edison relates:

> About 11 o'clock word was received from the President that he would be very pleased if I would come. . . . I was taken there and found Mr. Hayes and several others waiting. . . . The exhibition continued till about 12:30 a.m., when Mrs. Hayes and several other ladies who had been induced to get up and dress, appeared. I left at 3:30 a.m.

Little known hitherto, except in his profession, the youthful-looking inventor of the phonograph was now seen or talked about everywhere. At first sight the great public took him to its heart as it had never done with other men of science—at least since Ben Franklin's day. Edison was a plain, rough-hewn, democratic type—and yet, as all acknowledged, he certainly "knew his stuff." As he was written about in the press, exaggerated tales were spread of the extreme poverty of his boyhood and youth. Without schooling, without the help of friends or family, the former trainboy was said to have come to New York in his rags and conquered. He was the very type of the self-made man, whom so many Americans fervently believed in and sought to emulate.

Popular traditions about great inventors have long been woven around old legends of "magicians" endowed with super-human powers, from the ancient Titans in their caves to the witches and sorcerers of medieval times. The appellation of "Wizard" was now affixed to Edison; henceforth he was to be the Wizard of Menlo Park.

FOR A SEASON the young inventor seemed never to tire of experimenting with his phonograph. He was quite aware that the tinfoil was not a satisfactory material for recording; that some of the consonants came out "soft" or were wanting altogether; and that rotating the cylinder by hand at an even rate of speed was difficult. As one historian has concluded: "The phonograph, in truth, had been launched before its time. It was all very well to talk about dictating letters . . . or using it to read [books] to the blind, but not when a tin-foil cylinder would play for scarcely more than a minute." The new machine greatly needed development to realize its immense possibilities—which no one foresaw, least of all Edison, who was deaf and unmusical.

For a while, he investigated new substances for recording, such as wax, and a new form of record, shaped like a plate, or disk. But eventually Edison laid the phonograph aside, *abandoned* it for ten long years, leaving all the potential of this highly original device undeveloped. Here was one of the inventor's greatest blunders, one that in the end was to cost him dearly.

Within a year or two the phonograph was regarded only as a scientific curiosity. Edison himself in a newspaper interview described it as "a mere toy, which has no commercial value." Rival inventors, in his judgment, would not even bother to pirate his invention.

He had other ideas that engaged his full attention in the summer of 1878. One undertaking particularly gripped his imagination; it was described by one of his intimates as being that of dispelling "night with its darkness . . . from the arena of civilization."

IN THE LATE SPRING OF 1878 Edison felt very tired and ill. He had been working at the development of a dozen or more inventions at the same time. In seven years, since his brief honeymoon, he had had no real vacation. When an invitation came to him, through Professor George F. Barker, to join an expedition of scientists going to the Rockies to observe the total eclipse of the sun that summer, he gladly agreed to make the trip.

During their journey together, Professor Barker, who had become passionately interested in the possibilities of electric lighting, talked long and earnestly with Edison of recent developments in this field and urged him to investigate it for himself. "Just at that time I wanted to take up something new . . ." Edison recalled.

The problem of turning electric current into illumination had haunted men of science throughout the nineteenth century, ever since Sir Humphry Davy's famous demonstration before the Royal Society of London in 1808, when he ran a strong electric current (furnished by a battery of two thousand cells) through a small gap between two carbon rods, creating a brilliant blue-white light in that gap, in the form of an arc. But for many years after, progress in this field was slow for want of an abundant source of electrical current.

In America, somewhat later, at the Philadelphia exposition of 1876, Moses G. Farmer exhibited three glaring arc lights, burning in the open air, powered by his own rude dynamo. A year later Edison received a report on the new "electric candles" which Paul Jablochkov, a former Russian officer of engineers, had successfully introduced as streetlamps in Paris.

At the time (1877), Edison set to work experimenting with open arc lights having carbon strips as burners. He also investigated incandescent lights. The incandescent light was entirely different from the arc light in principle: it used a slender rod or pencil enclosed in a glass globe from which the oxygen had been exhausted, more or less. Electric current heated the pencil to incandescence, the absence of oxygen preventing the metallic or carbon rod from burning out or melting. As yet, only poor results had been obtained with incandescent lamps, after fifty years of desultory experimenting. Baffled by the perplexities of the task, Edison had dropped his electric light experiments to devote himself to the phonograph.

On his return from the West at the end of August 1878, he found a file of papers sent him by Grosvenor P. Lowrey, general counsel to Western Union, reporting on the Paris Exposition that summer and especially on the new electric candles of Jablochkov. By now a half mile of the Avenue de l'Opéra had been illuminated by those big arc lights; they were said to have provided the finest artificial light ever seen.

Now Lowrey joined Barker in urging Edison to undertake an investigation of the electric light. Early in September Edison agreed to go with Professor Barker to Ansonia, Connecticut, to visit the brass-manufacturing shops of William Wallace, partner of Moses Farmer and coinventor of the first American electric dynamo. After receiving the inventor and his party warmly, Wallace exhibited eight brilliant arc lights of five hundred candlepower each as well as the Wallace-Farmer dynamo of eight horsepower that supplied them.

As an eyewitness related:

> Edison was enraptured. . . . He fairly gloated. . . . He ran from the instruments to the lights and then again from the lights back to the electric instruments. He sprawled over a table and made all sorts of calculations. . . .

He then turned to Mr. Wallace and said challengingly, "I believe I can beat you making the electric light. I do not think you are working in the right direction." They shook hands in friendly fashion and, with a diamond-pointed stylus, Edison signed his name and the date on a wine goblet served by his host at dinner.

HE HAD MERELY PLAYED with the idea of making electric lights before this time. Now he was on fire. After examining the Wallace-Farmer arc lights, he relates, "I determined to take up the search again. On my return home I started my usual course of collecting data. . . ." Shortly afterward he said, "I saw *the thing had not gone so far but that I had a chance* . . . what had been done had never been made practically useful. The intense light [of the arc light] had not been subdivided so it could be brought into private houses."

A reporter for one of the leading New York dailies obtained a startling interview with the inventor. With soaring imagination, Edison communicated to the reporter his vision of a central station for electric lighting that he would create, and from which a network of electric wires would extend, delivering current for small household lights. The plans he announced were, in breadth and originality of conception, far in advance of anything earlier attempted in this field. Together with light, he would transmit energy for power and heat, to cook food, to run an elevator, a sewing machine, or anything else requiring a motor.

During the visit with Wallace the image of the central gashouse and its distributing system, of gas mains running to smaller branch pipes and leading into many dwelling places, had flashed into his mind. With the gas system a man could turn a single jet in one room on or off, or do so with a hundred jets. Edison was now aiming to duplicate the gas-distributing industry—with electricity!

"If you can replace gaslights, you can easily make a great fortune," a New York newspaper reporter remarked.

"I don't care so much about making my fortune," Edison replied tartly, "as I do for getting ahead of the other fellows."

There was the man, very much himself. To have more money meant little. But to stand as leader among the world's foremost inventors, to make again and again a great impact on society and industry—even to "change the world," if possible—meant everything.

THERE WERE two main avenues which experimenters seeking to develop the electric light had followed: that leading to the big arc light, and that of the small incandescent unit, the enclosed glow lamp. Though the arc light had recently been brought to the commercial stage, its limitations were many. Arc lights ran as high as three thousand candlepower, but they gave an almost blinding glare, emitted noxious gases, and could only be employed high overhead, in streets or in high-ceilinged factories or shops. Edison, seeing what the adapters of the arc light had not done, struck out for the incandescent light in a vacuum—the will-o'-the-wisp which so many inventors had pursued in vain during a half century.

In making his decision he was going against the stream, and "putting aside the technical advance that had brought the arc light to the commercial stage." For the problems of the incandescent light were entirely different from those of the arc light; it would need a different type of dynamo and a different kind of circuit, not to speak of many new safety devices. Meanwhile it remained for him also to find an incandescing substance that would endure a fierce heat, yet would not fuse or melt and burn out within a few minutes—the very thing that scientists had been seeking for fifty years.

He naturally turned to carbon in his first experiments, since he knew that it had a very high melting point. Strips of carbonized paper were tried as "burners"; they were made incandescent in the open air and quickly oxidized, merely to ascertain how much current was required. Then he used some glass jars, partially evacuated of air by means of a hand-worked pump, and managed to keep his carbon strips incandescent for "about eight minutes" before they went out. Accepting the prevailing view that carbon was easily destructible, he laid it aside for the time being.

He next tested various infusible metals, and out of a whole group chose platinum. On introducing a spiral of platinum wire into a globe partially exhausted of air, he was able to bring it to incandescence and achieve a brilliant light. However, at high heat the platinum burner quickly melted and the light went out.

After that he tried using an iridium-platinum composition for his incandescing substance. These early experimental lamps played exasperating tricks on the inventor, who studied them for long hours, brooding, distracted, letting his cigar go out, lighting it, letting it go out again.

To be sure, he was learning a good deal as he went on. The earliest notes on the electric light experiments show him already keenly aware of the importance of obtaining a higher vacuum, which he achieved by cementing the bottom of his leaky glass container. It was going to be a long, hard job, he realized, requiring added equipment, a larger staff, and a good deal of money.

GROSVENOR LOWREY had promised that if Edison undertook to invent a practical electric light he would approach the Western Union directors, who were his clients, for funds to finance Edison's research work. Lowrey, as an informed patent attorney and also a leading New York corporation lawyer, had fallen completely under the spell of the self-taught inventor and regarded him much as an ardent collector of paintings regards a great artist whose works he believes are destined to become immortal. On receiving assurances that Edison would actually undertake the work on the electric light, Lowrey began to form a syndicate of capitalists to back his inventive research. From the start of the lamp experiments, the lawyer went about buttonholing his well-heeled clients, assuring them that "Edison has discovered the means of giving us an electric light suitable for everyday use, at vastly reduced cost as compared with gas."

Edison, meanwhile, encouraged by Lowrey, called in the metropolitan newspaper reporters, and launched a full-scale press campaign designed to loosen Wall Street purse strings. To be sure, the inventor conceded, he needed time, perhaps several months, or a year, to "get the bugs out." Nevertheless he put on a show of his platinum-wire lamp. As a reporter described the scene, he turned on the Wallace-Farmer eight-horsepower dynamo and

> touched the point of a wire on a small piece of metal near the window casing . . . there was a flash of blinding white light. . . . "There is your steam power turned into an electric light," he said. Then the intense brightness disappeared, and the new light came on, cold and beautiful. . . . The strip of platinum that acted as a burner *did not burn*. It . . . glowed with the phosphorescent effulgence of the star Altair. A turn of the screw, and . . . the intense brightness was gone; the platinum shone with a mellow radiance through the small glass globe.

But if the artful Edison had not turned off that screw, the light would have gone out by itself within a few minutes.

Nonetheless, the repute of the Wizard of Menlo Park was so formidable that his published claims created a fair-sized financial panic on both the London and New York stock exchanges. Gaslight securities within a few days lost about twelve percent of their value, "owing to the publication of Professor Edison's discovery of the distribution of electric light," a cabled dispatch from London reported. It was now widely believed that, thanks to Edison's entrance into the field of electric lighting, the whole flourishing gaslight industry might soon enter into a decline.

On October 1 Lowrey wrote Edison that he had approached Hamilton W. Twombly, the son-in-law of W. H. Vanderbilt ("the richest man in America"), and told him that the inventor "was willing to sell half of this invention for $150,000." On the following day Lowrey was closeted for an hour and a half with Twombly and Vanderbilt, and that night he wrote Edison that he hoped to get for him a "clear $100,000" from the Western Union directors. He also solicited the interest of the partners of Drexel, Morgan & Company.

Evidently the sensational stories about Edison's plans helped the Western Union people make up their minds. They had narrowly missed buying the telephone patent of Bell and now could not get it at any price. They would not pass over the chance of Edison's light. On October 12, 1878, Lowrey was able to report he had a contract ready.

The contract, drawn up by Lowrey between Edison and the syndicate of capitalists who were to finance his researches, was one of the most noteworthy in the annals of American industry. In effect the Western Union people were buying rights, not in an existing invention, but in an unknown quantity, a promise. "Their money," Edison said, "was invested in confidence of my ability to bring it back again." The original investing group, who became directors of the new company, figured prominently in the Social Register and the New York financial district: Vanderbilt, Twombly, President Norvin Green of Western Union, Egisto Fabbri (partner of J. P. Morgan), Lowrey, and also Tracy Edson and James Banker, both important capitalists. Each of these men, under a preliminary agreement, invested a few thousand dollars cash by subscribing altogether to five hundred shares of the proposed company's stock, amounting to $50,000, which was paid over to Edison in installments.

The new company was to be known as the Edison Electric Light Company, and was originally to have 3000 shares ($300,000 capital stock), of which 2500 shares were to be given to Edison. For his part, he agreed to assign to the company all his inventions and improvements in the electric lighting field for a five-year period. If Edison's future inventions were successful, his stock would be worth a good deal; if he failed, it would be worthless. All that the backers risked was their original $50,000 cash—in return for which they had the chance of controlling all of

Edison's patents in this field and of developing a worldwide patent-holding and licensing company profiting from the inventor's patents in electric lighting. On this occasion they were showing real vision, though at other periods they were by no means consistently cordial to inventive research.

Behind the whole venture stood the figure of J. Pierpont Morgan, already the country's outstanding banker, who kept his name off the board of directors but had his partner Fabbri serving as director and treasurer of the new company. To have gained support for such a novel undertaking from America's leading financiers was decidedly a feather in the cap for Thomas A. Edison's little all-purpose "invention-factory" at Menlo Park. He was simply given a blanket order to create an electric lighting and distributing system, and to develop a pilot plant, or model, of that system.

AS SOON AS the new project was reported, other inventors, in Europe as well as in America, had become unusually active in this field. But one reason why Edison believed he would "get ahead of the other fellows" was that he had unbounded confidence in his laboratory, his superior scientific equipment, and his staff. All of this was rapidly expanded in 1878 when three sizable buildings were added to the original structure. One was a separate office and library; another, an engine house of brick construction, to contain two eighty-horsepower steam engines; a third was a glassblower's shed.

All that autumn, and through the winter of 1879 that followed, Edison studied the problems of high-resistance lamps and multiple circuits. He must contrive a light with a very high resistance to the current and using, therefore, but small quantities of it. He had known this from the beginning.

The investigation of electric lighting required a most arduous program of research: Edison and his staff made lengthy studies of the electrical resistances of various substances, and examined them for heat radiation. The effect of increasing or lowering resistance, and of changing voltage or amperage on such materials, and of using them in different forms, was also measured carefully.

At an early stage of this campaign, Edison, in a very revealing letter of November 1878, admitted that all sorts of unexpected difficulties were turning up.

> It has been just so in all my inventions. The first step is an intuition—and comes with a burst, *then* difficulties arise.—This thing gives out and then that—"Bugs" . . . show themselves and months of anxious watching, study and labor are requisite before commercial success—or failure—is reached . . . I have the right principle and am on the right track, but time, hard work and some good luck are necessary too. . . .

In January 1879 Edison designed and completed his first *high-resistance* lamp, having a very thin spiral of platinum wire as its incandescing substance set in a globe that was as effective a vacuum as he could get with an ordinary air pump. A second, improved model of this lamp dated from April 1879. The results so far were encouraging; those first lamps burned "an hour or two." He then tackled the dual problem of getting a higher vacuum and also improving the incandescing element, with which inventors had struggled for more than a generation.

The incandescing substance must resist a tremendous heat before it could give light; if the heat were too great it would melt. Carbon had the highest melting point: 3500 degrees C. But when he attempted to maintain a heat of no more than 1500 to 1700 C. in his first vacuum globes, the carbon incandescing substance tended to burn out around that level. He tried other materials: boron, chromium, molybdenum, and in fact "everything." He thought of tungsten, but found he could not use it with existing tools.

A thin wire of nickel seemed to offer promise, during a month of lengthy tests—but the enormous power of the light caused eye pains and almost ruined his eyesight. He was mortified at losing a whole day recovering.

Giving up the troublesome nickel, he came back to platinum, which, though having a lower melting point than carbon, seemed to show a longer life when incandescent. He resumed efforts to obtain a higher vacuum, which was a shrewd judgment for that time. In England, Sir William Crookes had lately made great progress toward very high vacuums by means of an improved type of pump, called the Sprengel pump. On learning of this, Edison got hold of one of the first of these new vacuum pumps to reach America. Now a vacuum was obtained that came within one or two millimeters of full exhaustion of air; in a globe having such a high vacuum the thin platinum wire gave forth a brilliant light of twenty-five candlepower and continued to do so for some time, whereas in the open air it melted at once when raised only to four candlepower.

By now he had reason to congratulate himself, having made considerable progress beyond the stage which had been reached by others attempting to perfect an incandescent lamp—though it was also true that he seemed to be meeting with fresh difficulties at every step. On April 12, 1879, he executed a new patent application for his first high-resistance platinum lamp having an improved vacuum.

But his money was now melting away more rapidly than he had expected. The task he had undertaken looked much longer than was anticipated. The spirits of his financial sponsors began to droop. Meanwhile the first arc lights, introduced in September 1878, were already blazing over lower Broadway in New York, and more were being installed elsewhere with impressive effect. The bankers now began to have serious doubts whether Edison had pursued the right course in trying for an unproved lighting system.

In very friendly spirit, Lowrey reported to Edison that at a recent meeting at Morgan's office, some of his financial backers had expressed serious misgivings. Lowrey urged that instead of trying to conceal any real troubles he faced, for fear that his sponsors might lose courage, the inventor should be as frank as possible. Finally, in mid-April of 1879, Edison agreed to hold a private demonstration of his high-resistance platinum lamp for the benefit of his financial partners.

As Francis Jehl, an assistant, relates:

> They came to Menlo Park on a late afternoon train from New York. It was already dark, when they were conducted into the machine shop where we had several platinum lamps installed in

series. . . . Mr. Morgan and Mr. Lowrey and the others stopped at the library for half an hour or so while our chief reported to them verbally on the results of his experiments so far.

After the conference, the group crossed the yard to the laboratory, where the "boss" showed them pieces of platinum coil he was using for his lamps, and pointed out the arrangements of lights on brackets along the walls. Then, the room having grown quite dark, Edison gave Kruesi the order to "turn on the juice slowly."

Today, I can see those lamps rising to a cherry-red, "like glow-bugs," one of the eye-witnesses wrote afterward, and hear Mr. Edison saying: "A little more juice" and the lamps began to glow. "A little more" . . . and then one emits a light like a star, after which there is an eruption and a puff, and the machine shop is in total darkness. We knew instantly which lamp had failed, and Batchelor replaced that with a good one. The operation was repeated two or three times, with about the same results, after which the party went into the library to talk things over until it was time to catch the train for New York.

It was a gloomy gathering that broke up on that cold, raw April evening. All of Lowrey's abounding faith would be needed to rally their spirits and persuade them to shell out more cash. Some rumors of the disappointing demonstration of his platinum lamps now leaked out; as a result, Edison Electric Light stock, which had risen to $600 a share, fell sharply, while gaslight securities began to recover. A leading New York daily reported that "well-informed electricians did not believe that Mr. Edison is even on the right line of experiments."

Edison had found out a good many things: how to make an improved vacuum; how to raise the resistance of his incandescing coil. But he realized that there were fatal defects in his first high-resistance light. Platinum, he saw, was really an obstacle in this hunt, and he had expended enormous effort in struggling with it.

In adversity he could be highly philosophical. "Even if you gave much time and labor to learning the hundreds of wrong

ways of doing a thing" he would say, it might lead, in the end, to the right way. But once he became convinced that he had mistaken his path, he could show great resolution and speed in retracing his steps.

"After that exhibition," Jehl said, "we had a general house-cleaning at the laboratory, and the . . . platinum lamps were stored away."

V. Toward the Light of the World

"THE ELECTRIC light has caused me the greatest amount of study and has required the most elaborate experiments," Edison said in recollection; "I was never myself discouraged, or inclined to be hopeless of success. I cannot say the same for all my associates." Edison at this point was directing his efforts on a much broader front of the area "under siege." For it must be remembered that it was not only a light he sought; he must try to create "a whole new industry with all its ramifications."

He now followed three main lines of investigation. First, the constant-amperage dynamo available then for arc lights must be adapted and redesigned to be suitable for his new system requiring a constant-voltage current. Second, he directed a group of assistants in the key assignment of perfecting the pumping methods used in exhausting air from his lamp globes to obtain a still higher vacuum. Third, another team, under his own watchful eye, carried out a long series of experiments in which about sixteen hundred materials were tested as incandescent elements in his sealed vacuum globes.

He was, meanwhile, afflicted by the very publicity he had once courted. The favorable public interest first aroused by news of his electric light venture had given way to bitter attacks, which charged that by his want of education and his "feverish methods of research accompanied by propaganda," he had placed himself before the world as a "charlatan"; his reputation as a scientist was "smirched."

Edison was as jubilant as a small boy when, in midsummer of 1879, the engineering of an improved constant-pressure dynamo was achieved. It bore the same relation to the electric light system as the cheap production of gas from coal did to gaslighting. He had thus laid a firm foundation for his multiple circuit of small high-resistance lights—to which the most exhaustive studies were being devoted at the same time.

But when the new dynamo was described and pictured in October, in a lead article in the *Scientific American*, there was a great scoffing and ridiculing of Tom Edison's "absurd claims." The hectoring of Edison by some of the leading American electrical experts, among them Dr. Henry Morton of Stevens Institute, now seems to us traceable to their own real ignorance of actual dynamo problems. Edison, on the other hand, was opening up new paths.

From the very outset of his work, Edison was guided by his concept of a *whole electric distribution system* of which all the parts must be fitted into place. In contrast with other inventors, who searched only for some magical incandescing substance, he worked out all the supporting structure of his system: its power supply, conductors, and circuit, and then came back to determine what kind of light would be demanded by it.

Reading Dr. Morton's positive predictions of failure for his whole enterprise, Edison grimly promised himself that, once he had it all running "sure-fire," he would erect at Menlo Park a little statue to his gloomy critic which would be eternally illuminated by an Edison lamp.

THE ALLEGED "MECHANIC" who was said to lack education was to be found reading scientific journals and institutional proceedings at all hours of the day or night. The new opportunities to test the incandescent qualities of metals and carbons, under the conditions of a vessel highly exhausted of oxygen, now allured Edison.

"There never has been a vacuum produced in this country that approached anywhere near the vacuum which is necessary for me," he wrote in his notebook. He had his boys pumping away for dear life, until by August 1879 he had all but one one-hundred-thousandth of an atmosphere expelled from his glass globe. A hundred-thousandth part was too much; the battle must go on. Then, in late summer, the Edison team succeeded in making a pump by which a vacuum of one-millionth part of an atmosphere was obtained.

With growing excitement he realized that two key positions had been won. He had his constant-voltage dynamo and a high vacuum. All that remained for him, then, was to discover an illuminant that would endure.

In early September, after about a year's search, Edison turned back to experimenting with carbon again as his illuminant, and this time for good. Carbon had the highest melting point and the highest resistance.

He was of course extremely familiar with the properties of carbon. In a shed in back of the laboratory there was a line of kerosene lamps always burning, and a laborer engaged in scraping the lampblack off the glass chimneys to make carbon cake. "Oh, Mr. Edison, the lamps are smoking," visitors to Menlo Park sometimes warned him.

"Yes, I must remind them to turn the wicks down," he would answer banteringly. But he did nothing of the sort. He had the cakes of carbon brought to him and kneaded them with his fingers into fine reeds.

After considerable calculation, Edison estimated that the carbon should not be over one sixty-fourth of an inch in diameter! He also estimated that the carbon filament should be about six inches long.

It was a bold undertaking: reducing the illuminant to the thinness of ordinary heavy sewing thread. Would so slender a reed of carbon support those high temperatures, where thick rods had melted? By grace of the improved vacuum, they hoped to succeed.

THROUGH THE SUMMER MONTHS Edison and his staff worked at the tantalizing job of making fine reeds of carbon lampblack mixed with tar behave properly in an incandescent lamp. His assistants kept kneading away at this puttylike substance for hours and hours.

Before long they were able to make threadlike filaments as thin as seven one-thousandths of an inch. They then tested them; the tests required infinite pains and were time-consuming. This was indeed promising; the threads lasted an hour or two before they burned out. But it was not yet good enough.

In the later stages of this long campaign, Edison drove his co-workers harder than ever; they held watches over current tests round the clock, one man taking a sleep of a few hours while another remained awake.

At this stage of his life Edison worked with minimum rest periods of three or four hours a day, his enormous recuperative powers helping to sustain him. He would doze off for a catnap on a bench, or even under a table, with a resistance box for his pillow, but his assistants had orders to waken him if anything occurred that required his attention.

Tension among the laboratory force increased during the late summer days of 1879, as the several components of Edison's incandescent lighting system were being perfected. But the "chief mucker" also knew how to divert their minds by serving some food and light wine after they had been working late at night, or by sitting down to swap stories with his men, or listen to music they made up for the squeaky tinfoil phonograph.

One of the assistants on one occasion regaled his companions by improvising a parody of Gilbert and Sullivan's *H.M.S. Pinafore* in Edison's honor:

> *For I am the Wizard of the Electric Light,*
> *And a wide-awake Wizard too. . . .*

THE IMPERSONAL RECORDS of the laboratory notebooks for October 1879 show Edison's mood of anticipation pervading the whole staff at this stage. He had been pushing on with hundreds of trials of extremely fine lamp filaments, so attenuated that no one could conceive of how they would stand up under terrific heat.

He had tried various methods for treating cotton threads before carbonizing them, but they would break. Finally he packed them with powdered carbon in an earthenware crucible which was then sealed with fire clay and heated at high temperatures. At last he had a firm, unbroken carbonized thread, or a filament. It was, however, very hard to handle, being then fastened by delicate clamps to the end of platinum lead-in wires. It was actually the ninth of a series of very fine incandescent filaments Edison had carefully constructed. Afterward, Edison related, it was necessary to take it to the glassblower's house in order to seal it within a globe.

> With utmost precaution Batchelor took up the precious carbon, and I marched after him, as if guarding a mighty treasure. To our consternation, just as we reached the glass-blower's bench the wretched carbon broke. We turned back to the main laboratory and set to work again. It was late in the afternoon before we produced another carbon, which was broken by a jeweler's screw driver falling against it. But we turned back again and before nightfall the carbon was completed and inserted in the lamp. The bulb was exhausted of air and sealed, the current turned on, and the sight we had so long desired to see met our eyes.

The trial of the No. 9 model of carbonized cotton filament was put on late during the night of October 21. There was no sleeping that night. The men looking on were thoroughly used to these things fizzling out. But the notebook entries for that night convey the results:

> No. 9 on from 1:30 a.m. till 3 p.m.—13 1/2 hours . . .

The tales that were woven about that triumph featured a "death watch" of "forty hours" maintained by Edison and five of his associates. The evidence of the records speaks only of an incandescent lamp that burned for more than half a day, that is, thirteen and a half hours; but there is frequent mention of a lamp having burned forty hours—very possible they wrote down no notes of this, in the excitement of the moment.

Contemporary accounts of this historic event, appearing soon afterward, described Edison turning on the current for the perfected lamp:

> Presto! a beautiful light greeted his eyes. He turns on more current, expecting the fragile filament to fuse; but no, the only change is a more brilliant light. He turns on more current and

still more, but the delicate thread remains entire. [Edison said, "We sat and watched with anxiety growing into elation."] Then with characteristic impetuosity and, wondering and marveling at the strength of the little filament, he turns on the full power of his machine. . . . For a minute or more the tender thread seems to struggle with the intense heat—that would melt diamond itself—then at last it succumbs and all is darkness. The powerful current had broken it in twain, but not before it had emitted a light of several gas jets.

As it went out the weary men waiting there jumped from their chairs and shouted with joy. Edison remained quiet, then said, "If it can burn that number of hours I know I can make it burn a hundred." He took up the broken filament and examined it under the microscope, noting how its structure had changed. He knew at last that the high-resistance element he wanted must be fibrous in structure, some form of *cellulose*. He would look for still better materials than cotton thread, which broke too readily.

The October 21, 1879, lamp gave but a feeble, reddish glow, but it was the best and most practical incandescent light contrived in more than fifty years of inventive effort, the future light of the world.

FOR ONCE he tried to be discreet and keep his discoveries a secret until he had improved upon his lamp filament. He wanted a more serviceable illuminant, and, since the cotton thread was a vegetable fiber, he reasoned that some other vegetable substance of fibrous character would provide the answer. His laboratory staff was then put to work testing a long list of similar materials, among them bagging, baywood, boxwood, cedar shavings, celluloid, fishline, flax, coconut shell, hickory, plumbago, punk, twine.

But in the end it was paper, in the form of tough cardboard, that proved most enduring and infusible when carbonized and reduced to a hairlike filament. Edison was exultant when this filament burned for 170 hours, and swore that he would perfect his lamp so that it would withstand 400 to 1000 hours of incandescence, before any news of it was to be published.

On November 1, 1879, he executed a patent application for a carbon filament lamp, which was quickly granted as U.S. Patent No. 223,898. It was not the "first" electric light, nor even the first incandescent electric lamp. It was the first practical and economical electric light for universal domestic use. It opened the way to the electrification of men's dwellings throughout the world, and introduced the large-scale production and sale of electric power itself.

It was early in November 1879 that the worried capitalists who had supported Edison's venture learned the secret of his success. Two of J. P. Morgan's partners paid a quiet visit to Menlo Park a short time later, and found that Edison's house was brilliantly illuminated by the new lamps.

During the first thirteen months Edison had expended $42,869.21 on experimental work, not counting legal, patent, and other expenses, most of which had been met by the Edison Electric Light Company. Now he raised the question of further money advances for experimental and development work, so that he might complete a pilot light-and-power station at Menlo Park.

Edison pointed out that he had spent out of pocket more money than he had been given and pleaded for continued support. But the directors were stony. They were uncertain, as yet, about the future of his invention. Was it "only a laboratory toy," as one of them charged? Would it not need a great deal more work before it became marketable?

The future electric light and power industry, now aching to be born, would be valued, for its American section alone, at roundly fifteen billion dollars at the time of the inventor's death. Yet there was prolonged haggling before another comparatively small sum was advanced to Edison, early in 1880, through loans by the original stockholders. And this was only obtained after Grosvenor Lowrey, still Edison's staunchest supporter, made the secret of the electric lamp public—prematurely, and over Edison's objections. The lawyer foresaw that the news would startle the world and convince doubters among his fellow capitalists.

But rumors had been spreading about the ill-kept secret for

several weeks. New Jersey neighbors told of brilliant lights blazing all night at Menlo Park; and railroad passengers between New York and Philadelphia also saw the bright lights, with astonishment, from their train windows. In Wall Street there was a flurry of speculation in Edison Electric stock, only a few shares of which were available as yet; the price rose, for a brief period, to a level of $3500 a share—on the mere hopes or prospects of Edison's success.

Then came the front-page story in the New York *Herald*, on Sunday, December 21, 1879:

EDISON'S LIGHT
THE GREAT INVENTOR'S TRIUMPH
IN ELECTRICAL ILLUMINATION

———

A SCRAP OF PAPER

———

IT MAKES A LIGHT WITHOUT GAS
OR FLAME, CHEAPER THAN OIL

———

SUCCESS IN A COTTON THREAD

The story of the inventor's fourteen-month struggle was now told to the world, and acclaim for Edison reverberated again on both sides of the Atlantic. As Lowrey had foreseen, the news "shook the scientific world to its foundations." Scarcely two years before, thanks to his phonograph, Edison had gained international celebrity. Now Menlo Park was again to be invaded by thousands of scientific pilgrims and plain curiosity seekers.

In the week following Christmas 1879, hundreds upon hundreds of visitors made their way to the world-famous New Jersey hamlet to see "the light of the future" and to pay homage to its good "Wizard." The closing nights of the year 1879 actually turned into a mass festival, which reached its climax on New Year's Eve, when a mob of three thousand sightseers flooded the place. The crowds never seemed to tire of turning those lights on and off, as they moved slowly through the rooms of the laboratory.

But they had also come to see Thomas A. Edison. The cry would go up, "There's Edison," and a rush would start toward him. As usual, he appeared in his working clothes, which were almost of a deliberate negligence, a white handkerchief at his throat in place of a cravat, and his vest half buttoned.

What they saw here was but a token of what was in store for them in the near future, the inventor promised. He was waiting for the completion of his new generator, he said, and intended to illuminate all the surroundings of Menlo Park, for a square mile, with eight hundred lights. After that he would light up the darkness of the neighboring towns, and even the cities of Newark and New York! His lamp would be sold for twenty-five cents, he predicted, and would cost but a few pennies a day to run. At the moment the lamps were very costly to produce, for it took two men six hours to pump a high vacuum for his globes, and only a few score lamps were on hand.

As a result of the wave of publicity the directors of the Edison company now willingly "coughed up" another $57,568 for the inventor's proposed development work in the next twelve months. He had won a great battle, yet the campaign was far from ended.

The future commercial value of the incandescent light was now established beyond question; but it remained for him to put a complete central-station lighting system in operation on a large scale. This would mean facing many more problems, inventing numerous electrical appliances then unknown, and in fact developing a whole new art. In such development work Edison would be driven to efforts even more original than the work on the lamp itself.

"Remember, nothing that's good works by itself, just to please you," he used to say; "you've got to *make* the damn thing work."

FROM THE FIRST, Edison had never ceased working over his larger plans for a complete *system* that would supply power and heat as well as light. For its components it would need new dynamos, safety fuses, power switches, insulating materials still in the experimental stages, meters to measure current, and a whole family of varied lighting fixtures, sockets, and service wiring for households. Without this system the miraculous incandescent lamp was a scientific toy until it could be commercially exploited and made useful as one of many thousands of such units functioning within a complete lighting circuit.

Although Edison had an overall plan for such a system in mind, the grand design of a central power station and spreading network of wire was to be achieved only after some three years of trial and error. It was only then that Edison would be ready to march on New York. It was only then that the completed "Edison system"—which eventually impressed informed persons as being so comprehensive, so "beautifully conceived" in all its detail—became what he had hoped for: a giant distributing mechanism as practical and economical as that of gas.

IN THE SECOND YEAR of the electric light campaign, things seemed to be moving all too slowly, though Edison was making a whole series of strategic inventions that were to bring his system to completion. During the one year, 1880, the indefatigable man applied for sixty patents, among them five covering auxiliary parts, six covering dynamos, thirty-two pertaining to improvements in incandescent lamps, and seven to advanced systems of current distribution. The last group of devices was scarcely exceeded in importance by the invention of his incandescent lamp. When one of them, the feeder-and-main system, was patented and demonstrated in England, Lord Kelvin, who was present at the demonstration, was asked why no one else had ever thought of it before, since it was so simple and yet eliminated the serious loss of pressure always expected in a parallel circuit. He is said to have replied, "The only answer I can think of is that no one else is Edison."

Some members of the Vanderbilt-Morgan syndicate, however, were rather alarmed at the way Edison used up about $150,000 that year—for machinery, steam engines, dynamos, copper wire, and sundry materials—merely to test a pilot plant at Menlo Park. But a new and enthusiastic supporter of Edison, who became first an investor and then a director of the Edison Electric Light Company, was the railroad magnate Henry

Villard. After having seen the first public exhibition of the incandescent lamp at Menlo Park, he encouraged the inventor by expressing high hopes for the future of the new industry. A few months later, in the spring of 1880, he appeared at Menlo Park and invited Edison to install an independent lighting plant in the new S.S. *Columbia*, then under construction for the Villard-controlled Oregon Railway & Navigation Company.

The contract for the S.S. *Columbia* required the installation of an independent lighting plant for a large steel ship of 3200 tons, and 334 feet in length. This was to be the inventor's first commercial lighting plant of the "isolated" type, improved versions of which would later be installed in hotels, stores, and private mansions. It also proved to be a most useful rehearsal for the larger central station work that was to follow. Edison and Batchelor supervised all the work, which was finished in time for the departure of the *Columbia* on its long voyage around Cape Horn to California. The ship made a most brilliant display by night as it sailed down Delaware Bay.

Henry Villard proved an enthusiastic supporter of another new project. In the spring of 1880 the residents of Menlo Park, inured though they were to strange sights and sounds, saw something wholly unexpected. A gang of laborers began laying ties and rails out in the open fields adjacent to the laboratory to make a narrow-gage railway track running out a third of a mile around a hill and then back to the starting point. Not long afterward, a little iron monster about six feet long and four feet wide was placed on the tracks. It was in fact the first full-sized electric locomotive ever made in America.

With the locomotive, Edison tried to give the impression that he was merely "playing on the job" while waiting for new machinery for his large light plant to be completed. But if it was sport, he entered into it with his usual verve. As an old railroader himself, Edison added a big searchlight to the head of the locomotive and a bell to warn off cows, while a small open-air passenger truck was coupled behind.

On the day of the trial run, Edison gave the order to switch current onto the railway track, and bravely mounted the locomotive. The light-fingered Batchelor was at the throttle, and some twenty persons in addition crowded aboard the loco-motive and truck.

"All aboard!" Edison cried in his high voice. "Fire her up!" The crowd hurrahed and waved handkerchiefs gaily, as Batchelor closed the switch. The little train started slowly, gathered speed, and bumped along on the rough track until it was brought to a halt at its terminal. But when the switch was reversed, in order to go back over the same course, Batchelor had to apply the lever with some force, so that the friction wheels burst and the locomotive was disabled. But within three weeks the loco-motive was again pulling well enough for Edison to demon-strate it before his financial backers, the directors of the Edison Electric Light Company.

Villard, a firm believer in electricity as a motive power for transportation, was most enthusiastic, and advanced the inventor forty thousand dollars, to cover extended experiments with an improved engine. But a whole combination of untoward circumstances brought Edison's pioneering work in railway electrification almost to naught. The patents for this group of inventions were eventually assigned to the Edison Electric Light Company, but the directors refused to invest any large sums in it. Also, Edison's electric railway patents turned out to be poorly drawn; interference suits were entered against him by a rival inventor, Stephen D. Field. The Edison company directors eventually decided that it was advisable to join forces with Field and thus settle the patent suits.

Edison took little part hereafter in the electric railway enter-prise, which was managed by Field, and had no part in the vast profits ensuing from it. For him the electric locomotive had been a distraction, a beloved "hobby"—during the intervals when he waited for the completion of the big machines and boilers needed for his lighting system.

STRENUOUS PREPARATIONS for a second "full-scale" demonstration of Edison's incandescent lighting system were again under way. The delays, unexpected breakdowns, and actual dangers met with in this undertaking would have been enough to dishearten any inventor. And one trouble was that Edison himself, eternally

dissatisfied, kept changing his plans; he saw greater economies to be won by more powerful engines and larger dynamos, and kept throwing out his old machines to order new ones.

"Our system is not a guess nor a hazard," Edison proclaimed. Unlike others, he had "no stock to peddle"; he would not move until his plan for domestic electric light distribution was complete and "figured down to the smallest item."

To help accomplish this he mapped out an area in Menlo Park of about half a square mile surrounding the laboratory and, along the lines of imaginary streets, set out white wooden lampposts. The half-dozen neighboring houses all were wired, as was the group of laboratory buildings and shops, for the installation of 425 lamps. Current was supplied from a central power station in an annex of the laboratory, consisting of eleven dynamos. Dissatisfied with this numerous array of small dynamos, Edison had the design of a large-capacity dynamo undertaken.

That Christmas of 1880 snow fell, and at last the central station at Menlo Park was ready, as hundreds of visitors arrived to see its promised illuminations. A contemporary relates:

> In every direction stretched out long lines of electric lights, whose lustre made wide white circles on the white-clad earth. One could not tire of gazing at those starry lines. Edison did not bother about his overcoat as he walked in the open air. In an instant all was dark ... in another instant the whole scene of fire and ice sprang into being again. "Eight miles of wire!" Edison exclaimed; and yet he observed, some people were not satisfied with his demonstration.

Meanwhile, the relations between the inventor and his bankers continued to be, at best, those of an uneasy coalition between opposing interests and temperaments. As he prepared to take up the next phase of development work, the lighting of great cities from central stations, Edison again felt himself held back by his financial sponsors. For months he had been pressing the directors of his company to furnish capital for new manufacturing enterprises that would supply incandescent lamps, light fixtures, sockets, switches, fuses, fuse blocks, meters, voltage regulators, and dynamos that were essential to his central-station lighting ventures. But the directors wanted none of the headaches or limited profits of manufacturing.

"Wall Street could not see its way clear to finance a new and untried business," he said later. "We were confronted by a stupendous obstacle. Nowhere in the world could we obtain any of the items or devices necessary for the exploitation of the system. Thus, I was forced to go into the manufacturing business myself."

In the summer of 1880 he set up a factory for making incandescent lamps—the first in the world—in an old barn across the tracks from the Menlo Park laboratory. It was started on a shoestring capital of ten thousand dollars, almost all raised by himself and his associates. At first about two hundred hand operations were needed in making these lamps, so that they cost $1.21 each; Edison, however, contracted to sell them to the Edison Electric Light Company for eighty cents. Within a year they were employing 133 men, turning out a thousand lamps a day, but "stacking up" half of them, since there were not enough users to buy them as yet.

Again Edison dipped deeply into his resources; selling some of his Edison company shares or borrowing against them, he organized more factories in which electrical accessories were to be made. Early in 1881 Edison's old mechanic, Sigmund Bergmann, went into equal partnership with him and opened a shop in New York which was to supply lamp sockets, switches, fuses, light fixtures, chemical meters, and other instruments, all devised by Edison. Bergmann, who proved to be an able manufacturer, had to expand his quarters within a year and employ three hundred men.

Next, Edison began making dynamos, a difficult and unfamiliar business, calling for huge factory space, much machinery and equipment, and a large labor force.

In the course of 1880 and 1881, Edison, by heavy borrowing, risked all the fortune he had in order to launch the manufacturing enterprises associated with an entirely new industry, that of electrical equipment. Though his Wall Street friends remained skeptical and declared themselves bewildered by his unorthodox business methods, he as an entrepreneur was doing the most constructive thing of all: carrying out the formation of new wealth, based on his own inventions.

Another important turn of events was the winning of a New York City franchise by the Edison parent company in April 1881, permitting it to lay underground mains in the streets of New York, and distribute and sell electric light. Economy tests revealing that Edison's light could be operated at a fraction of one cent per hour, or approximately the cost of gaslight, were heartening to the leaders of great banking, railway, and telegraph enterprises.

They loosened their purse strings and supplied the inventor with fresh funds, about eighty thousand dollars in all, with which he would be able to begin building the central station for New York City. For this purpose another subsidiary corporation, called the Edison Electric Illuminating Company of New York, was organized. This was the pygmy ancestor of the present-day Consolidated Edison Company.

During the winter of 1880 to 1881 the inventor kept rushing back and forth between New York and Menlo Park, attending to a multitude of affairs that were coming to a head. He saw that he would now have to establish himself in the great city in order to supervise the building of the first central station, upon which so much depended.

In February 1881 he returned to Menlo Park from a highly satisfactory conference with his "money men," as he called them, and to his associates seemed to be "boiling over with enthusiasm and energy."

"Come on," he cried to Charles Clarke, his chief engineer, "pack up and come with me to New York. We're going to begin business right away."

EDISON THOUGHT he was leaving the seclusion of Menlo Park only temporarily; but the remove to New York marked another turning point in his life and the beginning of a long period of furious activity. For his headquarters and showroom a large and ornate four-story mansion at 65 Fifth Avenue, just below Fourteenth Street, had been leased. It was near the center of the fashionable residential and shopping district of the city; its elegantly furnished and spacious rooms gave an impression of dignified luxury appropriate to the growing fame of the inventor and his company.

"We're up in the world now!" Edison exclaimed at this time to an old acquaintance. "I remember ten years ago I had to walk the streets of New York all night because I hadn't the price of a bed. And now think of it! I'm to occupy a whole house on Fifth Avenue."

Since Edison counted on a fairly long sojourn in the city he had brought his wife and the three children to live near him in a hotel adjacent to Gramercy Park. He had not much time for his family, however, for he was promoting the Edison system night and day. He had installed a small steam engine to run generators for a house lighting plant which made his Fifth Avenue place a brilliant show at night. After seeing the brave new lights at Edison's house, W. H. Vanderbilt and his wife ordered a similar electric plant for their palatial home on Fifth Avenue; thereupon J. P. Morgan ordered the same for his own residence on Madison Avenue.

Meanwhile, with an eye on future international business, Edison had some members of his Menlo Park staff in Europe preparing exhibitions of model lighting stations for expositions to be held later that year in Paris and London. It was thanks to Edward H. Johnson, who was supervising the work in London, that a young man named Samuel Insull arrived in the United States from his native England on March 1, 1881, to take up employment as Edison's private secretary. After having worked as a clerk at the Edison office in London for two years, the twenty-one-year-old Insull was sent to Edison, on the urgent recommendation of Johnson, as a youth with a real head for business. He would soon become Edison's financial factotum.

The new secretary's first impression was that Edison "was engaged in a gigantic undertaking." He was fighting the gas companies; he was struggling with the difficulties of getting the machinery he needed; he was taking over some large works and told Insull he counted on employing fifteen hundred men within a few months. All sorts of jobs were being done at the same time and with no little confusion. He had even established a school on the top floor of his Fifth Avenue headquarters to train men in the new art of electric lighting service.

IN THAT SUMMER one would often have found Edison in the back parlor at 65 Fifth Avenue, sitting on a high stool placed before a large wall map, about twelve feet high by fifteen feet wide, which he studied incessantly; it represented a chosen district of lower Manhattan. This he had selected as the area for his first city station. His first intention had been to cover a district of about a square mile, running south from Canal Street to Wall Street; but in the end he greatly reduced this area.

The power station he envisaged would be placed as nearly as possible in the center of this district, with its conductors in underground conduits running out in all directions to the outlets of consumers. After prowling all about the section, he determined upon a site at 255–257 Pearl Street, which he purchased early in August 1881.

Pearl Street had come down in the world since the days in the early nineteenth century when it was lined with fashionable taverns and thronged with fine carriages. Now it was squalid. Nor did the building at 255–257 add to its charms. Yet this homely edifice was to be the cradle of the modern electric light and power industry.

The arduous breaking of earth for underground mains began in the late fall when frost was almost upon them. Other early electrical services, from telegraph and burglar-alarm systems to arc lights, all used overhead wires strung on poles or simply running from roof to roof. It was a cheap method; and, in the opinion of many experts, it avoided leakage of electric current into the earth.

Edison insisted, however, that his plan would eliminate all danger of shock or fire from short circuits. "You don't lift water pipes and gas pipes on stilts," he protested. Though directors of his own company objected to the additional expense for insulation and tubing, Edison was determined that safe procedures be established at the outset.

There were fourteen miles of trenches to be dug and much

tubing to be laid in the district served. The illustrated newspapers of the time show Edison in a battered stovepipe hat directing this work and personally overseeing the installation of all couplings and safety-catch boxes.

Sometimes the day's work ended so late that Edison and some of his helpers slept in the cellar below the unfinished power station in Pearl Street. Two of the men who aided him, after sleeping in that cold and damp cellar that winter, became sick and died, while he himself, as he related, was never affected.

With the coming of winter, Edison and his labor gangs down in the trenches had been forced to halt excavation work. Time was passing, yet New York still waited for the opening of Edison's power station. The excavation work and laying of mains was resumed at a frantic pace in the spring of 1882, but the job was not completed until June.

Early the next month the central station at Pearl Street was furnished with four great boilers, six steam engines, and the first three of six improved jumbo dynamos, so named by Edison after P. T. Barnum's famous circus elephant. In addition, switchboards and control instruments were installed in the station, and, on an upper floor, a bank of one thousand electric lamps with which to test the system.

On July 6, 1882, Edison, having fired up the boilers several days before, threw the switch for a trial run of the first jumbo. Three days later, on a Sunday, when the business area was quiet, he connected a second jumbo dynamo to the first, admitting that his heart was in his mouth as the engines engaged.

One of those present has related:

> It was a terrifying experience. . . . The engines and dynamos made a horrible racket, and the place seemed to be filled with sparks and flames of all colors. It was as if the gates of the infernal regions had suddenly opened.

Edison later recalled that he grabbed the throttle of one engine while Johnson, the only other person present who kept his wits, caught hold of the other, and thus they shut off the engines. Not until new steam engines with specially designed mechanical governors were installed could the trouble be corrected.

THE PREMIERE AT PEARL STREET, so long awaited, so oft postponed, loomed up at last in the late summer of 1882. "I kept promising through the newspapers that the large central station in New York would be started at such and such a time," Edison confessed. "These promises were made more with a view to keeping up the courage of my stockholders, who naturally wanted to get rich faster than the nature of things permitted."

He recapitulated the events of that day and described his own inner tension:

> The Pearl Street station was the biggest and most responsible thing I had ever undertaken. It was a gigantic problem, with many ramifications. . . . All our apparatus, devices and parts were home-devised and home-made. Our men were completely new and without central-station experience. What might happen on turning a big current into the conductors under the streets of New York no one could say. . . . The gas companies were our bitter enemies in those days, keenly watching our every move and ready to pounce upon us at the slightest failure. Success meant world-wide adoption of our central-station plan. Failure meant loss of money and prestige and setting back of our enterprise. . . . I had been up most of the night rehearsing my men and going over every part of the system. . . .

For once, he avoided any ballyhoo in connection with the official opening at Pearl Street, for he was haunted by the fear that something might happen to spoil the party. Steam was admitted to one of the jumbo dynamo-steam units in operation; and at 3:00 p.m. on Monday, September 4, 1882, Edison gave the order to pull the switch. The current flowed forth through the underground conductors and the Edison lights went on in the first district against the full sunlight of a summer afternoon, therefore giving a rather feeble effect.

It was anticlimactic, after so many ardors and alarms. Despite the tall talk of a central station that was to light thousands of buildings through one circuit, the Edison Electric Illuminating Company opened for business with only eighty-five customers fully wired and a total load of only four hundred lamps.

Somehow the metropolitan newspapers had got wind of the affair, and their representatives were on hand to cover it with modest little stories destined for the inner pages. "Most of the principal stores from Fulton and Nassau Street," the *World* reported casually, "were lighted by electricity for the first time." And *The New York Times* observed: "It was not until about 7 o'clock, when it began to be dark, that the electric light really made itself known and showed how bright and steady it was." The *Times* itself already boasted of fifty-two Edison lamps in its editorial and counting rooms—"soft, mellow, grateful to the eye; it seemed almost like writing by daylight."

Edison's electric light and power business began in America's greatest city without fanfare and in the early years grew but slowly. "Look, the Edison lamps have been turned on," people said simply, at the start of the first city power station in America, and that was that. Only after many months and, indeed, years, had passed did men come to realize what Edison had wrought in that crude central station in dingy Pearl Street. It was, in fact, nothing less than the long-hoped-for industrial marriage of steam and electric force. Almost unaware, the world began to move out of the age of James Watt into the Electrical Age.

More than fifty years had passed since Michael Faraday had discovered the mechanical production of induced electricity and had been possessed by a vision of the future electric power. It needed Edison, however, as well as Faraday, Ampère, Arago, and other scientific explorers, to make the Electrical Age. For it was Edison who had finally *applied* the knowledge of electrical science that had been accumulating during those fifty years, creating new wealth immeasurable, new convenience and enjoyment, and a new tempo of life.

His campaign for his electric light and power system had consumed four years of Edison's life, roughly from age thirty-one to thirty-five. He was now gray-headed, but still youthful in appearance, his round smooth-shaven face unmarked and unlined, and strong as ever. He seems also to have been so highly stimulated by his recent activities that he fairly proliferated important inventions of all sorts in these years. On the opening day in Pearl Street he could say truthfully, with that pride in his workmanship that he never bothered to conceal, "I have accomplished all that I promised!"

VI. The Middle Years: Second Marriage

IN THOSE HURRIED YEARS of the earlier half of his career Edison had virtually no private life; the relaxed enjoyments of home, a personable wife, his young children, were things he tasted quickly and sparingly. It was in his "man's world," where all were masculine and bearded fellows who worked long and swore hearty oaths while they worked, that he was most himself and knew his greatest pleasures.

He clung to his old-fashioned notions of women's mental inferiority. "Women as a class are inclined to be obstinate. They do not seem to want to get out of the beaten path." Such opinions or prejudices were strengthened by his feeling about his first wife, Mary, a good and simple woman of limited education, who, as he fully realized, scarcely knew anything of what was going on in her husband's head.

Their married life might have been unhappy had Mary not been so gentle, so reconciled to her lot. In the small hamlet of Menlo Park, though it had become world-famous, her own life was one of dull loneliness. The Edisons lived in a substantial and comfortable home; there was a staff of two Negro servants and a coachman; a barn and stable with horses and carriages in the yard; a summer house on the big lawn. But Mary Edison, seeing all too little of her husband, and left much alone with her children, had only the wives of his married associates as her companions.

At the time of the electric light project Edison never came home at all for weeks on end, according to a close neighbor, who saw him finally one morning "coming along the plank path to his house walking as though he were asleep." Some carpenters were at work in the house and Mrs. Edison sent them away, saying, "He has gone into my spare room and rolled right over on the bed in all his dirt and grease, on my nice counterpane and pillow shams, but I don't care, as long as he gets rest and sleep."

By the 1880's new honors and dignities clothed her. Was she not the consort of one of America's first citizens, whose fame overleaped the oceans? Yet she remained modest and self-effacing. On the few occasions when she appeared at the laboratory the workmen regarded young Mrs. Edison, now grown quite stout, with unconcealed admiration. They were proud of her—for she had been one of their own rank in the Newark shop and yet remained as gracious and friendly as ever.

Though often quite distrait with his wife, Edison was far from indifferent; indeed he felt a strong attachment to her; she was, after his mother, the only woman in his life up to that time. She had shared the lean years with him. Now he was a rich man and he could bring Mary the most costly gifts. Thus, in her first year of residence in New York, she made an impressive appearance one day at a tea party—all bejeweled, dressed in a gown of the richest brocade.

When the pace of work permitted relaxation, Edison would devote his Sundays to his family, sometimes taking them to a nearby beach. In his lighter moments he could be merry enough, bantering his wife and teasing the children; on those Sunday excursions Mary Edison was always "proudly happy" as she rode off with her husband by her side. When at home on a Sunday, however, Edison's mind would go spinning along, absorbed in problems and experiments. At meals he would often say little to his family, eat quickly, and leave the table before the others.

The stories of his playing with his children date mostly from the earlier years of his first marriage. By way of toys he would bring a batch of old alarm clocks for them to "experiment" with. Sitting down on the floor, he would take the clocks apart and put them together again, bidding his boys to do likewise, hoping that they would become fascinated by the mechanical arts. Disappointingly, his small sons, Tom junior and William Leslie, showed no passion for rusty alarm clocks.

Usually Edison's love of mischief—which on occasion showed a vein of playful cruelty—came out in his games with his children. One day he brought home a little glass toy in the form of a swan and invited one of the children to put the tail of the swan in his mouth and blow. The child was not amused when, from the neck of the swan, water sprayed all over his face.

The children found their father not so much unkind as puzzling, and often "difficult." Marion, the eldest, being a girl, was not expected to become an inventor. She was tall, blond, pretty, and had her father's verve. Edison tended to be more affectionate with her than with his sons. When only ten she had her own pony and cart and used to drive about the village at a fast clip. Of the children only Marion was allowed to come into the laboratory, for she often brought her father his lunch at noon.

He would have liked his eldest son, who resembled him physically, to be keen of mind and aggressive and energetic like himself. The boy, however, turned out to be rather delicate and sickly. Sometimes he would put up a ten-foot pole and invite his own children and the neighbors' children to shinny up and win the coins he placed at the top. To the father's disappointment Tommy would always prove to be the weakest and the last at such games.

Edison's own father had been at best an indifferent sort of father, with little real understanding of his son. Of Thomas A. Edison his children recalled that he could be both warmly affectionate and playfully, unconsciously cruel, but that most of the time "he hardly ever saw us," or, "he never thought of us."

Unfortunately, his disappointment in his eldest son, and also in Willie, the younger one, revealed itself. Their upbringing, he may have felt, was not one of the best, possibly because of Mary's habitual overindulgence with her children, or her own lack of education. Mary was also somewhat self-indulgent. She could spend whole afternoons idly chatting with a woman friend and consuming an entire box of chocolates. It was bad for Mary Edison's figure—she became tremendously stout—and bad for her health.

Though not unforgiving, Edison could show a fierce temper. His family knew these moods too. There was, no doubt, a normal amount of anger and grief and forgiveness in his life with Mary. Then suddenly, tragically, she was gone from him.

In the winter of 1883–1884 Edison, suffering from neuralgia, made a vacation journey to northern Florida with his wife and daughter. The climate of St. Augustine proved beneficial. Soon his mind was racing back to the problems of the central station system; he would fire off letters or telegrams by the hour to Insull, such as: "Don't forget to have Tomlinson [his attorney] draw up contract with the engineers"; or "Let me know how the new pressure indicator works."

After the journey to Florida, the Edisons returned to New York; a few months later, Mary and the children went back to the Menlo Park house, which was still used as their summer home. Edison then was much occupied by work in the city and remained there most of the time. In July Mary contracted typhoid fever, which at first did not alarm her family; but soon she was under the constant care of a doctor and her sister Alice. When suddenly she began to sink, Edison was called, and he hurried back from New York to her bedside. On the morning of August 9, 1884, his daughter Marion recalls, she was wakened by her father, who had been up all the night before. "I found him shaking with grief, weeping and sobbing so he could hardly tell me that mother had died in the night."

From that day forward, he rarely came back to Menlo Park; it was as if he hated the place. He was an agnostic, and so could find no solace in praying for Mary's soul. As was his wont, he buried himself in work, and thus stoically put out of mind the tragedy of his beautiful young wife. She was not yet thirty when she died.

With the passing of Mary, Edison's way of life seemed to undergo a marked change. At thirty-seven he was no longer a hell-for-leather, free-lance inventor, but a man of substance, heading a big industrial enterprise that increased his wealth year by year. He was, in fact, a millionaire. By force of circumstances he assumed an outlook that was more worldly than before. When, not long afterward, he fell in love and married again it was with a woman wholly different from his simple and touching Mary.

FOUR YEARS after Edison had perfected his carbon filament lamp there were only twelve city stations, on the model of Pearl Street, in operation; in all America only 150,000 of his lamps were in use. Much more rapid progress had been made in selling isolated lighting plants for factories, stores, and hotels; by 1884 these numbered about two hundred. But all of it amounted to almost nothing compared with the huge gaslight industry which he had sworn to supplant. After the original Pearl Street station reached its full load limit, no more generators were added for several years; new business was simply turned away.

The trouble was obviously due to the extreme conservatism of Edison's financial backers. Henry Villard, who believed in the light, had overextended his railway holdings, was temporarily in financial difficulties, and unable to lend support; even Edison's old friend, Grosvenor Lowrey, had lately joined the conservative group.

How could Edison expand the business when others controlled its policy? And try as he would, he could not stir things up without the approval of the holding company which owned his lighting patents.

Nevertheless, in the autumn of 1885, in contrast with the preceding year of financial depression, business began to hum for the Edison electrical manufacturing companies. After moving to a larger factory space, the lamp company steadily reduced the number of manual operations and the labor time required. From an initial cost of $1.21 per lamp, when manufacture was started in 1880, the company had lowered the production cost to about thirty cents in 1885, when it turned out as many as 139,000 lamps. In the late eighties the company's output at last approached a million lamps annually, as Edison had prophesied in the beginning, and costs per unit were down to twenty-two cents.

By October 1, 1886, the combined Edison organization, with assets approaching ten million dollars, amounted to a big business for those days. More than five hundred of its isolated lighting plants were now in operation at various points throughout the country, using over 330,000 lamps. Central stations in large cities had risen from only twelve, in 1884, to a total of fifty-eight two years later. Similar facilities were being sold and installed in the great cities of Europe, South America, and Japan. Now revenues flowed from all over the world to the man who had created the practical incandescent lighting system.

His affairs were now so prosperous that at last he could look forward to relinquishing most of his purely business cares to other hands and going back to his laboratory table.

SIX MONTHS had passed since the death of Mary Edison; more and more the widower of thirty-eight felt the difficulty of his position. He was left with three motherless children whom he could not properly look after.

Marion, who attended a boarding school in New York, was nearest to him and much in his company during the wifeless interval. At thirteen she was almost full-grown, and went out with him a good deal to theaters, restaurants, or on Sunday carriage drives. "Why don't you come down to my shop to see me? You're not studying anyway," he would say, for he seemed lonely then. And she would leave her lessons and come to the machine works on the East Side, bringing him his favorite five-cent cigars.

The two boys, however, he saw much less of; Tom and Will, at this period, lived at Menlo Park with their Aunt Alice. Having formed strong prejudices against formal or academic education, Edison saw to it that his sons, as well as his daughter, had as little as possible of it. He would have liked the boys to acquire the training of a mechanic or an artisan, according to the principles expounded in Rousseau's *Émile*, which he had read with approval. The results in the long run were not such as to have gratified either Rousseau or Edison. The sons by the first marriage now had no mother and knew their father very little.

In his friendships Edison was given to sudden personal enthusiasms. At times different favorites, like new satellites, revolved around his sun. Where his associate, Edward Johnson, had formerly reigned, the stout Ezra T. Gilliland, a onetime telegrapher whom Edison had first known years before in Cincinnati, now sat as the master's first "apostle." The diligent young Insull, too, had become more and more a confidant.

Though Ezra Gilliland often came to New York to work with Edison, his home was then in Boston, for he had some profitable business of his own in telegraph and telephone patents. His accomplished and beautiful wife presided gracefully over their home, which Edison visited often in the winter of 1885. One of the new friends he often saw at the Gillilands' was the handsome young lawyer named John Tomlinson, who soon became Edison's trusted personal attorney.

Under the civilizing influence of the Gillilands and Tomlinson the formerly unsocial man of the laboratories was found going out to buy a sixty-five-dollar coat (very dear then) and dressing for the evening. He who was always formerly so pressed for time now sat for hours on end in a drawing room with elegant but idle ladies and gentlemen, enjoying light talk, listening to music, and even playing parlor games! With his new friends he would also go off to one of Boston's old music halls and sit in the "bald-head row," enjoying a display of "the usual number of servant girls in tights."

What had become of Thomas Edison, the man who labored like a Titan? How could he pass whole days in such frivolous diversions? Was he corrupted, bewitched? Certainly the charm of the Gilliland home and its circle held him at this period and distracted his mind. The thought that for all his fortune he lacked such a home with its cheerful talk and laughter, and such a homemaker as its mistress to care for his children and himself, was ever present in his mind. He was certainly one of America's most eligible widowers. At news of the death of his wife, scores of unknown ladies wrote him letters expressing their pity at his bereavement and freely offering him their hearts and their fortunes.

The Gillilands, evidently with the approval of Edison, now undertook to invite to their home a flock of marriageable females for the widower's inspection. By ones and twos they arrived in Boston from as far off as Ohio and Indiana and marched into the Gilliland parlor, while Edison examined them one after the other. The game grew more and more engrossing, though Edison remained coy.

"Come to Boston," he wired Sam Insull. "At Gill's house there is lots of pretty girls." Finally there appeared a striking brunette from Ohio, whom Mrs. Gilliland knew well, and whose visit was carefully planned. She was Mina Miller, the daughter of Lewis Miller, of Akron, Ohio, a wealthy manu-

facturer of farm tools. Mr. Miller was well known as an active and philanthropic churchman, for he was a cofounder—with Bishop John Vincent of the Methodist Church—of the Chautauqua movement.

As was often the case in American families of recent fortune, Lewis Miller's daughter Mina was sent to a finishing school in Boston, and then, for further improvement, on the "grand tour" of Europe, whence she had lately returned. She is described as having been in her youth "accomplished and serious, with a liking for charity and Sunday school work"—but also a veritable belle, with an imposing figure, "rich black hair and great dazzling eyes."

The first meeting of Edison and Miss Miller took place in the early winter of 1885; by prearrangement the girl was visiting with Mrs. Gilliland when the inventor arrived from New York. The Gillilands had told him all about her.

Edison was talking to several men in the parlor, when Gilliland said to him, "Mina Miller is here and she is going to play and sing for you." The beautiful eighteen-year-old Miss Miller swept into the drawing room like a great lady, greeted the famous inventor with dignity, and returned his gaze with the utmost composure.

On being asked to sing, she went at once to the piano and performed for the guests. She was far from being an accomplished musician, but what was impressive was the self-assurance with which Miss Miller did everything.

Edison, who was twice her age, on first exposure to Miss Miller felt, as he himself said, "staggered." Not long after meeting her he sent an urgent telegram to Insull, in New York, asking that two photographs of himself be sent to Miss Miller in Boston.

Later that winter, with his daughter Marion and the Gillilands, he went to Florida for a winter vacation. He would have returned North within a few days, but someone spoke to him of the tropical region of southwest Florida, of the Everglades and the Keys. Off he went, with his two friends and his daughter, for a journey of some four hundred miles on a rickety train.

After prowling about a sun-drenched scene of royal palms,

mangoes and giant tropical flowers for two days, he determined to take an option on a site of thirteen acres along the Caloosahatchee River near the village of Fort Myers and build a winter home there for himself.

Wherever he had been that season, he had spoken of the perfections of Mina Miller. So much so that, as he noticed, it made his daughter Marion fierce with jealousy.

In the Floridian jungle Edison had decided that he must marry Mina Miller, bring his bride there, and build not only a winter home but a new laboratory to be placed in that tropical setting. His diary shows him buzzing with romantic schemes for his castles in the Everglades.

On his return to New York in the spring of 1885, he found that the thought of Miss Miller permitted him no sleep. He wrote in his jocular manner, "Saw a lady who looked like Mina. Got thinking about Mina and came near being run over by a streetcar. If Mina interferes much more will have to take out an accident policy."

Determinedly he wooed the young lady "via the post office." Though he was uncommonly busy again that year with new lighting-plant installations and telegraphs for railroads and ships, he made prodigious efforts to see her. Her home was in Ohio; but in the summer the Millers regularly migrated to Jamestown, New York, to attend the Chautauqua gathering. Though Edison was "not much for religion," as he said, he determined to visit there in order to see her whom he now called "the Maid of Chautauqua."

Mr. Lewis Miller had been so long and closely associated with Bishop Vincent, the head of the Chautauqua movement, that their children had virtually grown up together. There was a rival suitor on hand, a younger man than Edison—the bishop's son, George Vincent, who was considered to be destined for Mina since boyhood.

But it was Edison who was at her side during a crowded steamer excursion on Lake Chautauqua. The throng surrounded them closely, they could not be alone; and he could not hear her save when he was very close to her. But the inventor was once more equal to the emergency. As he related:

My later courtship was carried on by telegraph. I taught the lady of my heart the Morse code, and when she could both send and receive we got along much better than we could have with spoken words, by tapping our remarks to one another on our hands.

Soon afterward, he managed to take her out alone with him in a small rowboat. Mina Miller feigned resistance to her ardent lover for a while, though with steadily weakening resolve. He then gained her parents' consent to have her join him in a long excursion by carriage through the White Mountains of New Hampshire, the Gillilands acting as her chaperones, while his daughter also accompanied them. It was during this drive through the mountains that Marion saw her father tap out his proposal on Miss Miller's hand, as he too testified:

I asked her in Morse code if she would marry me. The word "yes" is an easy one to send by telegraphic signals, and she sent it. If she had been obliged to speak she might have found it much harder.

Mina's consent was conditional upon her parents' approval. Therefore Edison, upon his return to New York on September 30, sent off a formal application for her hand to Mr. Miller. He had made his proposal after mature deliberation; and he declared in conclusion that he had learned to love Mina, and that his future happiness depended upon Mr. Miller's answer. The reply brought assurance of such happiness.

The news of Edison's forthcoming marriage to Mina Miller was soon out. In the autumn of 1885 the inventor was making extraordinary preparations for this new phase of his life. He was busy with plans for building a winter home in Fort Myers, Florida, and having lumber shipped for his projected laboratory. He was also engrossed in the purchase of a home magnificent enough for Mina, and for his own improved station in life. The simple house at Menlo Park was out of the question now. He had given her the option of living in a big town house in the city, or in the country, and she had expressed a preference for a country house.

On a day when the snow covered the ground he drove with

her to West Orange to see a large estate. It was called Glenmont, and had been built on a high ridge by a former millionaire merchant of New York at the staggering cost of $200,000. It was a veritable castle of brick and wood in a style loosely called American Romantic, with spacious rooms, numerous outbuildings, greenhouses, and broad, landscaped gardens. Glenmont apparently suited Miss Miller's ideas exactly.

All this, and the bride's jewels too, meant spending money like water, yet nothing daunted the inventor. Though not yet forty in 1886, he saw himself as one who was rising to the status of America's ruling industrial barons, one who stood at the head of a great industry he himself had created. Henceforth, all that he undertook must be planned on the grand scale. There was to be not only the great mansion in suburban New Jersey but also a vastly enlarged new laboratory to replace Menlo Park, furnished with the finest equipment in the world, and to be situated on the acres he had purchased in West Orange, within a half mile of his future home and his new wife.

ALL NORTHERN OHIO seemed to be agog over the event, as Edison arrived there to be wedded to an acknowledged belle of the region. From the entrance of the big Miller house in Akron Mr. Miller rolled out a red carpet extending several hundred feet to a knoll on the grounds that overlooked the city. By every train crowds of guests arrived, the spanking Miller carriages with their high-stepping horses bearing them away swiftly to the Miller home.

The big front parlor was ablaze with flowers and resounded with the music of an orchestra; a whole corps of waiters had been brought from Chicago to serve the wedding lunch. The ceremony was performed under an arch of roses. Later that afternoon the couple drove around Akron, cheered by crowds, and had their picture taken before boarding the train for Florida in the early evening.

In April they came back from Florida and Edison brought Mina to their new home in West Orange, that sprawling, red-painted chateau over which the second Mrs. Edison was to reign for many years. In character Glenmont was similar to those spacious residences of mixed architectural styles erected by the new rich of the 1870's and 1880's. It had a porte cochere and a broad vestibule, vast living rooms, rich chandeliers, wide staircases, heavy red-damask-covered furniture, and masses of bad statuary, oil paintings, and bric-a-brac collected by its former owner. To Mina Edison this place was the appropriate setting for genius.

Some pains had been taken with Mina's upbringing so that she might be fit to play her part in good society. She was a young woman of undeniable strength of character and will, who entered upon the adventure of marriage with full awareness that her mate was one of the most noted of living men. There was a good deal in her husband that she intended, nevertheless, to improve. Under her sway his rough exterior would be gradually smoothed, though it was a slow and difficult process. No power on earth could really turn this man into a tame parlor lion; to Mina's regret he continued to shun the kind of social life she would have enjoyed.

In his middle years the worker risen from the ranks of the poor was the lord of Glenmont and its handsome acres and possessed of a good and beautiful young wife of proper breeding. His ambitions nowadays bore a resemblance to those of the Carnegies and Rockefellers, the captains of industry who were his contemporaries.

To A. O. Tate, who became his private secretary after Insull's promotion to an executive post, he remarked, while gazing out of the windows of Glenmont, "Do you see that valley?"

"Yes, it's a beautiful valley," the other replied.

"Well, I'm going to make it more beautiful. I'm going to dot it with factories."

DURING THE BOOM TIMES of the late 1880's in America, the whole economy was growing at an unprecedented rate. Was there ever anything like the newly completed Brooklyn Bridge, or the young skyscrapers in Chicago, or Mr. Carnegie's steelworks in Pittsburgh? Like a good American Mr. Edison, too, felt the urge to do things on a truly continental scale.

At this period, in 1886, the Edison Machine Works was moved

from its location in New York City to vastly larger quarters at Schenectady, New York. The great presses and machine tools were transported to Schenectady, and within a year all the Edison generator, motor, tubing, and insulation work was being carried on there by some eight hundred hired hands. The Schenectady works grew with the rapidity of a Western boom-town, until they fairly overflowed with busy artisans and machines of every kind.

The next year there was the new laboratory to be built at a site in West Orange's quiet Main Street, a half mile from Edison's new home. The laboratory buildings, when completed, aggregated ten times the size of the humble establishment at Menlo Park. They constituted then the largest and most complete private research laboratory in the world.

The main brick building, 250 feet long and three stories high, contained large machine shops, an engine room, glassblowing and pumping rooms, chemical and photographic departments, rooms for electrical testing, stockrooms, and in its main wing a spacious office and library. The library contained ten thousand volumes, and with its glass cases of minerals and chemicals was a museum and sample room as well.

A staff of forty-five to sixty persons assisted the inventor at West Orange. They ranged from scientific specialists down to draftsmen, mechanical assistants, and unskilled laborers. Edison still kept a tight reign on everything being done in his laboratory, but inevitably the work had to be departmentalized. At Menlo Park he was able to see at a glance what every one of his dozen assistants was doing in the one long room. Now, every morning after going through his mail, he would have the men in charge of different experiments come into the library one by one and report on the work in progress. He was always able to shift his attention quickly from one line of investigation to another, asking questions, giving instructions, and making decisions rapidly. It was also his habit, at least once a day, to make a tour of the different departments and with his own eyes study the work being done.

His own passion for experimentation never flagged. From conferences with his assistants he often would escape to an upper room of the main building, a sparsely furnished place littered with instruments and materials. Here he would remain, engaged in lengthy studies of the favorite subject of the moment.

ONE OF HIS MAJOR PREOCCUPATIONS in the spring of 1887 was with renewed experimental work on his own phonograph. For nearly ten years the primitive tinfoil phonograph had remained only a scientific toy, now forgotten even by the entertainment parlors and country fairs that had once exhibited it. However, he had learned some months earlier that rival inventors working at the laboratory recently established by Alexander Bell were busily improving his phonograph and had been awarded patents for their innovations. He vowed he would not bother to sue his adversaries, but would *ruin* them—by making a better machine.

Thus, after having neglected his paternal duties toward his "baby," the phonograph, owing to the pressure of larger affairs, Edison went back to his laboratory table again. For most of two years, experiment with the phonograph was given priority in the laboratory over many other affairs claiming his attention. And he was happier thus, as the engineers phrase it, with "his belly at the drawing table again."

In the many clauses of his basic phonograph patent of 1878 Edison had enumerated various materials that could be used for records, waxed substances among them. As a substitute for the old tinfoil sheet, whose impressions were faint and easily effaced, he now devised a hollow cylinder of a prepared wax compound, with walls about a quarter of an inch thick. Wax permitted closer grooving. In place of the old recording needle Edison introduced a much harder cutting tool, a somewhat blunt sapphire stylus; he then devised an ingenious "floating weight" to replace the crude adjustment screws holding the needle in place.

In testing results on the improved phonograph Edison had the great problem of trying to hear distinctly despite his deafness, which was total in his left ear. He would place his right ear—whose hearing was limited—in contact with the instrument itself; or at times he would bite into the horn with his teeth, thus permitting the sound vibrations to be carried through the bones of his head to his hearing nerve. "It takes a deaf man to hear," he would say grimly.

The laboratory notebooks show him compiling a long list of "complaints" against his evolving phonograph:

> Crackling sounds in addition to continuous scraping due, either to blow-holes, or particles of wax not brushed off—poor recording—uneven tracking—dulling of the recorder point—breaking of glass diaphragm—knocking sound: chips in wax cylinder—humming sound, due to motor.

In painstaking fashion Edison worked to eliminate these defects one by one, inventing various new stratagems and devices by which the first simple talking machine became more responsive and lifelike. Though, in his judgment, the principal use of the phonograph would be as a business machine, for dictating letters, he tested his apparatus by making records of famous musical artists. The boy prodigy, Josef Hofmann, then twelve, came and played the piano. After him came Hans von Bülow, the most famous pianist of his era, to perform a Chopin mazurka and to listen through the tubes as it was played back.

Henry M. Stanley, the journalist of African fame, a sternly religious little man whom God had brought safely through the jungle, also visited the Edison Laboratory about this time and spoke a few grave words into the talking machine. Then he turned to the inventor and said, "Mr. Edison, if it were possible for you to hear the voice of any man known in history, whose voice would you prefer to hear?"

"Napoleon's," replied Edison without hesitation.

"No, no, I should like to hear the voice of our Saviour," said Stanley.

"Oh, well," laughed Edison, "you know, I like a hustler!"

ON MAY 31, 1888, at a time when the inventor was still overborne by the problem of the new phonograph, excitement of a different sort centered at Glenmont, for on that day the first of the three children Edison was to have by his second wife was born. It was a girl and was named Madeleine. Edison had interrupted his work to await the arrival of the child, remained for a time at his wife's bedside, then hurried back to his laboratory. A few days later he had gone into all-night sessions with his assistants, locked within the laboratory in what the newspapers called an "orgy of toil." The Edison team was making its last wild charge upon the sound-producing problems of the phonograph. On the morning of June 16, 1888, they emerged to announce success.

By now Mina Edison was more fully aware of what kind of great man she had married. Accustomed to a cheerful home and to a busy social life, she must now spend her days and nights much alone in the big mansion on the hill at Llewellyn Park. There were few diversions, no games, and almost never any social gatherings here. The children by Edison's first marriage did not enjoy staying at Glenmont. Marion, only a few years younger than her stepmother, attended boarding school or traveled in Europe with a governess. The two boys after a while spent much of their time in the home of their aunt, Alice Holzer, at Menlo Park, or at the farm of their uncle, Pitt Edison, in Michigan, when they were not away at school.

As Mina Edison said in later years, the conditions of her marriage constituted a great challenge. With her deep sense of duty she recognized that her husband's career always came first. Such efforts as she made to control him soon found their limits, for as he had once said, no woman could ever "manage" him. Evening after evening she would wait in vain for him to come home to dinner, then send him some warm food by the coachman. She was loyal, and he, despite his teasing habit, was most affectionate with her. But when they were grown old, she did not shrink from admitting publicly that he was "difficult."

Around the time of the coming of the new daughter and the new phonograph, Colonel George Gouraud, Edison's English impresario, arrived in West Orange for a business conference with the inventor. Shortly after he returned to London, he received from Edison, in place of the letter or cablegram he had expected, a dictated "phonogram" reporting with great satisfaction the safe arrival of both "babies."

At his offices in London, Gouraud gave demonstrations of the new apparatus that made a tremendous impression. These would begin with an introductory speech by Edison himself followed by records giving the silvery voice of Mr. William Gladstone, the Prime Minister; of Robert Browning reciting his verses; and of Sir Arthur Sullivan who was "terrified at the thought that so much hideous and bad music may be put on record forever."

Edison said, "I don't want the phonograph sold for amusement purposes. It is not a toy. I want it sold for business purposes only." Nevertheless it was the entertainment side of his invention that the world wanted most. A few years later it would be introduced into popular nickelodeons as a coin-in-the-slot machine, grinding out light music and comic dialogues for the multitudes. The brass bands, the music-hall tenors and sopranos resounding in thousands of the tinny 1888 models pointed the way to the future role of the phonograph as purveyor of music to the masses.

IN THE WINTER and spring of 1889 he had felt more tired than ever before. His young wife, attempting to minister to his health, tried for a long time to persuade him to rest. Then at last, to her great delight, he agreed to take a long holiday and go to Europe with her.

The vacation trip turned into a triumphal tour. They sailed on the French liner *La Bourgogne*, their first destination being Paris. Edison was to visit the great Universal Exposition in France, see the new Eiffel Tower and all the contrivances of the nineteenth-century inventors, including his own electrical, telegraph, telephone, and phonograph inventions.

On their arrival at the dock in Le Havre an official delegation representing the French Republic was on hand to meet them; reporters from newspapers of many European countries were there to interview them, and crowds cheered them on their way to the train. In Paris there were more and bigger crowds, and more government dignitaries to bid them welcome.

A crew of Edison men had arrived several months earlier to prepare a display of Edison products that covered a whole acre of the fairgrounds. Here a complete central lighting station had been erected, and was surmounted by a brilliant electric sign, made up of colored bulbs representing the flags of both France and the United States. But the longest lines of people, an estimated thirty thousand, were drawn to the new phonographs, which ranked second only to the Eiffel Tower as an attraction.

During the ten days in Paris the American inventor, with his big head, expressive features, and youthful bearing, became familiar to the people in the streets, who besieged the entrance of his hotel in the Place Vendôme to see him. At the opera house, as he entered a box—the guest of the President of the Republic—the orchestra played "The Star-Spangled Banner," while the audience cheered and called on him to speak. He seemed overcome with emotion, merely rose to his feet, bowed, and sat down.

Marion Edison, who had been studying at Geneva, joined her parents in Paris. She recalls that her father disliked the crowds and social life, but that her stepmother apparently could never have her fill of them. "Oh, they make me sick to my stomach!" Edison would exclaim on returning from those long dinners.

It was plain that the youthful Mrs. Edison and her high-spirited stepdaughter of seventeen agreed in "everything save their opinions." Marion was clearly "jealous" of the beautiful young woman who had taken not only her mother's place but, as she may have felt, her own place as well in her father's affections.

From Paris the Edison party went on to Berlin, and then late in September they arrived in London. The tycoons of the electrical industry were most eager to talk with Edison and entertain him in their big country houses, and in London he inspected the Edison central station at Holborn Viaduct.

On the return voyage, Edison was thoroughly relaxed. Immediately on his arrival in New York he hurriedly crossed the harbor in a launch to the Jersey shore, then rode by carriage to the laboratory at West Orange. He was burning to know the results of certain secret experiments that had been going on during his absence behind the locked door of Room 5. But Batchelor and another assistant, a young Englishman named

W. K. L. Dickson, had meanwhile put up a small new building in the laboratory compound for these new purposes. Proudly Dickson showed his chief into the studio and prepared to demonstrate what had been accomplished, in accordance with Edison's instructions, during his stay in Europe.

Edison sat down; the big room was darkened; Dickson went to a bulky apparatus at the back of the room that resembled a large optical lantern. Next to it, and attached to it, was a phonograph. Against the wall, facing Edison, there was a projection screen. Dickson turned a crank, and a vague flickering image of Dickson himself "stepped out on the screen, raised his hat and smiled, while uttering the words of greeting: 'Good morning, Mr. Edison, glad to see you back. I hope you are satisfied with the *Kineto-phonograph*.'"

The development of the first operable motion-picture camera —invented but not yet patented by Edison—was well under way. Connected with it, though rather rudely synchronized, was a model of his improved phonograph. Thus the first motion pictures were not silent, but were talking pictures.

VII. Dollars and Science

EDISON WOULD HAVE LOVED to pursue his fascinating experiments in the motion picture with undivided attention, but the work advanced far more slowly than his earlier inventions. "Dollars and science were so much mixed up" in his career, as he himself suggested. And at this point commercial ventures took precedence over inventive activities.

By 1888 Edison was actually one of America's ranking industrialists, employing between two thousand and three thousand workers. With so many on his payroll, he could not escape labor troubles.

In his relations with his workers he had the attitude of the old-fashioned entrepreneur. Since he himself was content to work eighteen hours a day, he reasoned that his hired hands should be willing to hustle for eleven hours. But the period of 1884 to 1887 was a time of marked labor unrest, when nearly one million workers entered the ranks of labor to fight for the union shop, the ten-hour day, and higher wages.

Edison paid average wages, plus incentive payments for extra effort, but he could never abide labor unions. As a small employer of a few dozen men, he had made his men like him and had known how to keep them interested in the work. Nowadays the factory system's division of labor characterized his electrical shops, where hundreds of workers were employed and no man made more than a fraction of any product.

Moreover, Edison and Insull, his financial lieutenant, were carrying fearful burdens. They had enormous orders and great difficulty in meeting payrolls and buying supplies, for rapid expansion left them short of capital. The company lawyer now remarked, "The danger is not that we won't have enough business, but won't be able to grow fast enough to handle it."

BY 1888 the largest of the Edison manufacturing companies, the machine works at Schenectady, was so busy that it was reported the workers were literally standing on one another's feet. Competition from "patent pirates" in the electrical manufacturing field was a growing threat. Patent infringement suits filed by Edison lawyers took years to drag through the courts, while every electrical company in America "jumped the Edison claims." The need for reorganization was urgent; the need for fresh capital was even more urgent.

Some effort had already been made to coordinate the selling and installation of lighting plants for the three companies that were making their main components—Edison Lamp, Edison Machine Works, and Bergmann's. But this manufacturing group was in constant friction with the parent company, Edison Electric Light, which held the Edison patents and licensed them to local light and power companies.

Henry Villard, now making his financial comeback, had perceived the difficulties the Edison industries encountered in their expansion. For two years he had been maturing a plan for a grand consolidation. His scheme was to buy in the "electrical shops" at a fair value. Knowing that he could not operate without the support of the Morgan group, which controlled the parent company, he sought to combine forces with them. In the spring of 1888 he then proposed the amalgamation of the several companies as the Edison General Electric Company.

While Edison was working to build up his manufacturing organization he had often been obsessed by the fear that he might be forced into bankruptcy. The necessity of meeting a weekly payroll for more than two thousand workers, week by week, harrowed his mind. At times "he was embarrassed in getting enough money to pay even for his household expenses." The proposals of Villard and his syndicate "to buy out the shops" were therefore received by Edison with a deep sense of relief from intolerable burdens.

After a good deal of haggling, Villard worked out a final agreement by which the Edison Electric Light Company was to be taken into the combination to be known as the Edison General Electric Company. The new company was described in the metropolitan press as one of the biggest consolidations ever carried out under the laws of New Jersey and as constituting an "electrical trust." After the whole deal was completed, Villard was elected president of Edison G.E.

Edison, owning a minority share of about ten percent of the stock, still was regarded as the company's inventive brain; he was also one of its directors. He had, nevertheless, little to say about its actual management. The improved incandescent lamp, for example, after 1888 was constructed with a cellulose filament, but showed uneven qualities because of imperfect producing methods. Edison would have liked to hunt down the "bugs." But now, it seems, it was necessary that he *ask permission* of his lamp factory's management before he could send an inspector into the plant who would report to him directly.

Edison now felt himself only a cog in a gigantic corporate machine. More significantly, perhaps, he was stubbornly opposed to one of the newest and most promising developments in the electrical field—the alternating-current generators and transformers that George Westinghouse and others among his competitors in America and Europe were then introducing. The a-c system, successfully applied, would make it possible to send high-voltage currents over long-distance transmission lines for many miles, and cheaply, and then, with the a-c transformer, step them down again to low voltages at the point of consumption. (With Edison's low-voltage direct-current system, transmission distance was limited to two miles.) Thus, it would eventually be feasible, with the a-c system, to place hydroelectric plants or steam generating plants at favorable locations for waterpower or coal supply. Younger engineers were dreaming already of harnessing the power of Niagara Falls and producing electrical energy in immense volume.

But Edison, back in 1880, had firmly opted for direct current at 110 volts as the safest form of electrical distribution—all the way from the powerhouse to the ultimate consumer. Now, claiming that the new high-voltage a-c system would destroy the reputation for safety he had tried to build up for his industry, he bitterly denounced all a-c advocates.

When President Villard of Edison G.E. sent Edison a German scientific article reporting advances in a-c systems in Switzerland and Germany, Edison replied, "The use of alternating current instead of direct current is unworthy of practical men."

It was perhaps Edison's greatest blunder (as he himself would admit twenty years afterward). He seemingly closed his mind and would go no further, resisting a-c systems much as the big gaslight companies earlier had rejected his incandescent electric light. "In 1879 Edison was a bold and courageous innovator," a modern commentator has said. "In 1889 he was a cautious and conservative defender of the status quo."

One of his chief competitors, the Thomson-Houston Company of Lynn, Massachusetts, had meanwhile obtained valuable transformer patents, developed "alternators," and, in competition with Westinghouse Company, begun to sell power on high-voltage lines. Moreover, whispers of an approaching coalition with one or the other of these big rivals began to spread. If they were true, he remarked to Villard,

> . . . then it is clear that my usefulness is gone. . . . Viewing it from this light you will see how impossible it is for me to spur my mind, under the shadow of possible future affiliations with competitors, to be entered into for financial reasons. . . .

The restless Edison now panted for new subjects to which he could apply his unique inventive talents, without the weight of a large organization bearing down upon him. It seemed to him that to "play" with his secret "kinetographic camera" or his improved phonograph, or that elephantine machine he had lately designed for the magnetic separation of iron ore would be an endless delight to his mind.

"Electric lights are too old for me," he remarked jocularly at this period. It was no mere jest.

One day, early in 1892, according to his private secretary, Edison was brooding in his library when a laboratory assistant came in and made some inquiry about electrical matters, to which he replied frankly that he did not know the answer. Brusquely he added that his scientific adviser, Dr. Arthur Kennelly, should be consulted. "He knows far more about [electricity] than I do. In fact, I've come to the conclusion that I never did know anything about it." His words were tinged with deep bitterness.

By the autumn of 1891 secret conferences about another big merger between Edison G.E. and Thomson-Houston Company finally approached their decisive phase. Edison G.E. was thus sold over the inventor's head. The new company, eventually to become one of the world's largest corporations, was to be called simply the General Electric Company, and the name of Edison was thus to be removed from its banner. He was known as the "father of electric lighting"; his name had been a great trade name. That it should now be removed from the title of the organization he had founded seemed not only unduly hard but ungrateful.

Up to the last hour, Edison hoped that the Edison Lamp Company would be treated differently from the other units and be kept under his control. But news of the transfer of all the Edison manufacturing units to the new company, without exception, suddenly reached him from a New York newspaper office in advance of its publication.

"I had never before seen him change color," his secretary, Tate, said afterward. "His complexion was naturally pale, but following my announcement it turned white as my collar."

MR. EDISON FROZEN OUT HE WAS NOT PRACTICAL ENOUGH FOR THE WAYS OF WALL STREET ran the headlines of a leading New York daily. He remained silent about what had happened; but he issued a brief public denial that he had been "mistreated" or "gulled." In reality, he had begun to retire from his company in 1889, when he reduced his ownership of its stock to about ten percent. After 1892 he unwisely sold the rest of it. He was elected a director of the General Electric Company; but he hardly ever attended any of its board meetings and soon resigned. Tate wrote:

> Something had died in Edison's heart. . . . He had a deep-seated, enduring pride in his name. And this name had been violated, torn from the title of the great industry created by his genius. . . .

One day, several weeks after the merger of the two companies into the General Electric "trust" had taken place, Edison, speaking with a companion, declared that he was done forever with electric lighting. "I am going to do something now," he said, "so different and so much bigger than anything I've ever done before that people will forget my name ever was connected with anything electrical."

IN THE FINAL DECADE of the nineteenth century two more sons were born to Edison: Charles, in 1890, a handsome infant who resembled his father; and Theodore, who came into the world in 1898. Edison's own father, Samuel Edison, died in 1896 at the ripe old age of ninety-two. Meanwhile, Tom junior, the eldest son, pursued an erratic career; he made an unfortunate marriage, and got into financial straits from which he had to be rescued with the aid of papa's checkbook. Finally, the large athletic Will, during the Spanish-American War, at twenty years of age, enlisted for service and came down with yellow fever. It all sounded like the lot of joy and sorrow befalling the average American family. But during all those years the baby that gave Edison the greatest concern was the "Ogden Baby" —his enterprise for separating ore magnetically, developed near the site of the old Ogden mines in Ogdensburg, New Jersey.

Edison gave at least five years of his life over the decade between 1890 and 1900 to a struggle to develop this invention from which he hoped to win a commanding position in the country's vital iron and steel trade. Iron ore was growing scarce; he thought his new ore-milling process would recapture economically the pure iron of exhausted mines in the Appalachian region. He sank about two million dollars in this venture, and his company went in debt to the tune of several hundred thousands more.

But while he labored to develop his magnetic ore separator, fabulous high-grade iron deposits, enough for most of America's needs over the next sixty years, were discovered in the Mesabi Range in Minnesota. Accordingly, in the late 1890's the price of iron dropped from $4.00 to $2.65 a ton.

On hearing this, Edison burst out laughing. "Well, we might as well blow the whistle and close up shop," he exclaimed.

It was an unmitigated disaster, the worst he had ever faced; he had lost not only years but the entire fortune accumulated by his inventive labors. Yesterday a millionaire several times over, today he was "busted."

One day in 1899 he returned to the mills to order the dismantling and disposal of the machinery. Where another might have been in a state of despair, he discussed his situation in the most jovial spirit. Though now fifty-three he remarked gaily enough that he could always find a job as a telegrapher at seventy-five dollars a month. Then, in more serious vein, he remarked that he had already arranged to put all that costly equipment, and the technical knowledge he had gained, to good use: the establishment of a modern portland cement works according to his own design.

He hoped in this way to settle the debts of about $300,000 the ore-milling concern was left with, adding: "No company I was ever connected with has ever failed to pay off its creditors." It was like him to waste not a moment in vain regrets, to forget the defeat, and with coldly rational courage apply himself at once to new undertakings.

About a year or two after they had dismantled the Ogdensburg ore-milling plant, Walter S. Mallory, his plant superintendent, happened to call his attention to newspaper articles of the current boom in Wall Street, during which General Electric stock had risen to $330 a share. Edison asked, "If I hadn't sold any of mine what would it be worth today?"

After some calculation Mallory replied, "About four and a quarter million dollars."

Edison was silent for a moment, plucking at his right eyebrow, then looked up, smiled broadly, and said, "Well, it's all gone, but we had a hell of a good time spending it!"

AT CERTAIN PERIODS, after having been much away from his laboratory, Edison would say, "I am tired of *industrial science*," and would promise to "rest himself" by taking up "pure science." Nature, he said, was often full of surprises, and it was fun to come upon them unexpectedly. In his laboratory notebooks there were observations of hundreds of curious, unexplained phenomena.

In November 1895 came the remarkable discovery by Professor W. K. Roentgen, the Netherlands physicist, of the so-called X rays emanating from a cathode tube. Their radiations could pass through the flesh and muscle tissue (though not the bones) of living animals and so make a shadow picture of the bones on a photographic plate. The value of such an instrument for surgery was grasped at once; soon many investigators were at work devising fluoroscopes, Edison one of the first among them.

Professor Michael Pupin, of Columbia University, appealed to him for help in discovering the most effective fluoroscopic chemicals. During a lull in activities at the ore mill, Edison went back to his laboratory and with his assistants tested crystals made out of about eight thousand different chemical combinations. Within a few weeks he sent the Columbia University scientist a fluoroscope with a tungstate-of-calcium screen—with which Pupin was enabled to make a clear shadowgraph of a man's hand that was filled with shotgun pellets. Guided by the Edison fluoroscope a surgeon promptly performed the first X-ray operation in America, with complete success.

Soon after, Edison was working up a variety of X-ray tubes

and donating a number of them to hospitals where surgeons had quickly taken up the new X-ray techniques.

Other scientific "distractions" were provided by intermittent development work on the phonograph, but surpassing all these activities in interest for Edison was his secret "toy," the motion-picture camera.

Our last glimpse of the motion-picture camera was in the locked room at Orange, when Edison had returned in October 1889 from his triumphs at the Paris exposition, to be shown by his assistants a "kineto-phonograph" that actually functioned. This balky and jerky kinetic camera was both intriguing and difficult; he could see no practical commerical future for it and yet could not bring himself to drop it.

FOR A CENTURY or more men had used a variety of mechanical tricks with pictures—usually a series of drawings or photographs of objects in successive stages of movement—to create the illusion of pictures in motion. Such pioneering efforts using the scientific phenomenon of persistence of vision set the stage, so to speak, for Edison.

He had set himself the further problem of recording movements in a continuous stream, and showing or projecting them. He began with a fairly visual idea of the kind of mechanism he would use. This is clearly shown by the document he wrote—October 8, 1888—to describe such an apparatus:

> I am experimenting upon an instrument which does for the eye what the phonograph does for the ear, which is the recording and reproduction of things in motion, and in such form as to be both cheap, practical and convenient. This apparatus I call a Kinetoscope, "moving view." ... The invention consists in photographing continuously a series of pictures occurring at intervals ... and photographing these series of pictures in a continuous spiral on a cylinder or plate in the same manner as sound is recorded on a phonograph.

He goes on to explain that when the picture was taken, the cylinder would be held at rest; then it would be rotated for a single step, halted again, and another exposure made. He remarks significantly enough, "A continuous strip could be used, but there are many mechanical difficulties in the way."

Edison himself overcame the many mechanical difficulties he had foreseen at the time. By the spring of 1889 he and his assistants had abandoned the photographically sensitized plaster cylinder and were experimenting with the recently created transparent celluloid film. These heavy sheets of celluloid coated with a photographic emulsion were cut into narrow strips, cemented together end to end, and fed across the focal plane of the camera.

Then came news that George Eastman of Rochester, New York, the inventor of the "Kodak," had improved celluloid film, making it tougher, yet light and flexible. Soon Eastman was producing strips of his new improved film for Edison's special use in rolls of fifty feet.

It was the summer of 1889, shortly before he was obliged to leave for Paris, that Edison designed a camera mechanism for advancing, or feeding, the roll of film forward at a given rate of speed, using perforations on one side of the film which were engaged by a sprocket wheel attached to a main shaft revolved by hand or motor. And it was with this machine, during Edison's absence, that his assistants managed to complete pictures lasting twelve seconds which W. K. L. Dickson showed to him on his return. After his motion-picture invention became known to the public, everyone exclaimed over the *simplicity* of his apparatus— the strip-film kinetograph which solved both basic problems of the motion-picture art: taking pictures of motion and exhibiting them.

Edison's first intention was to make sound pictures; he would synchronize the movement of the reel of film with a phonograph driven by the same motor powering the camera. There was to be singing or music accompanying a dance, or the sound of a voice as the film unrolled. "The establishment of harmonious relations between kinetoscope and phonograph," Dickson wrote later, "was a harrowing experience, and would have broken the spirit of inventors less inured to hardship and discouragement than Edison."

With the thought of making the apparatus "commercial," he

also devised a peep-show mechanism for exhibiting positive prints made from his kinetograph negatives, which he named the Kinetoscope. This consisted of a cabinet of substantial size with an eyepiece through which pictures on moving strips of film could be viewed.

In the year that followed, Edison had his assistants build a better and larger motion-picture camera. This ponderous machine, which was in use between 1890 and 1894, is the true father of all modern motion-picture cameras. The width of its film, 35 millimeters, is still standard today.

At this period of his life, in middle age, Edison worked much more slowly at his inventive tasks than in the past. Several different experimental projects were generally going forward at the same time. Four men, for example, worked on the motion-picture job in the early stages, while it was still more or less a secret. Edison was just then leaving the electrical manufacturing industry, was experiencing much difficulty with the phonograph business, and was already deeply involved in his nerve-wracking ore-separating work.

Thus he did not even file for a patent on his basic 1889 kinetograph and Kinetoscope until the end of July 1891, and those patent applications were, as it happened, incomplete and faulty. Two of his photographic assistants, not long afterward, left his employ to work for others who entered into competition with Edison in the new industry created by his invention. These competitors fought him in the courts to contest his patent claims.

He committed another and even more costly error by failing to take out foreign patent applications for his motion-picture camera in England and Europe. As a matter of routine his lawyer advised him to file for such foreign patents. But when told that it would cost $150, he is reported to have rejected the proposal, saying casually, "It isn't worth it."

These two legal errors opened the door wide to competition by many rival inventors, borrowers, infringers, and plain pirates. Once a model or even a drawing of Edison's motion-picture camera was available in Europe, anyone could imitate it and have it patented in his own name and offered in the

United States market as well as that of Europe. In short, his work on the motion-picture camera was more disputed and disparaged than almost anything he ever did.

AFTER HAVING NEGLECTED the motion-picture invention—in favor of low-grade iron ore and the phonograph—Edison's interest in the affair finally began to grow. By February 1, 1893, a strange building, dedicated to the new art, had appeared within the Edison Laboratory compound. It was something the like of which had never before been seen: a wooden structure of irregular oblong shape, with a sharply sloping roof hinged at one edge so that half of it could be raised to admit sunlight. The whole building, fifty feet in length, was mounted on a pivot, like a revolving bridge, and could be swung around slowly to follow the changing position of the sun and admit its full glare to the interior. The walls of this jerry-built affair were covered with black tar paper; a stage at one end of the single large room was also draped in black, so that the whole decor was funereal in the extreme. Such was the first building constructed especially as a *motion-picture studio*, officially called the Kinetographic Theater, but affectionately referred to by its staff as the Black Maria.

In this somber edifice a spate of pygmy motion pictures was ground out in 1893 and 1894. The performing artists strutted for a brief moment of glory—the shorts ran about a minute and a fraction—in the full glare of that sunlit stage, against a background so dark that the pictures were quite sharply defined. Among the early performers was "Gentleman Jim" Corbett, pugilistic idol of America, who provided a realistic exhibition of his art; the famous strong man Sandow; Japanese dancers; "Buffalo Bill," with accompanying Indians, recording a first Western; also acrobats, knife throwers, and diverse fowl recruited for cockfights.

In one of his frivolous moments Edison went off to Daly's Theatre in New York and persuaded its celebrated Gaiety Girls to come to his studio and dance before his kinetograph. After such efforts it was an easy step to film short comedy skits from the vaudeville stage, as well as picturesque renditions of an organ-grinder performing with his monkey, or of a patient in a dental parlor reacting to treatment with laughing gas.

The camera's eye was also pointed outside the windows of the Edison Laboratory to take realistic views of everyday life along Valley Road, West Orange. These might be called the first documentaries. Then one day the quiet of West Orange was shattered by the thunder of battle, as uniformed horsemen, simulating the British and the Boers in Africa, went charging over the empty lots outside the laboratory—to the vast amusement of the eternal American boy in Thomas A. Edison.

For several years, Edison's efforts to interest capitalists in promoting his new machine had been in vain. Edison's former Wall Street friends, such as Villard, would not go near his motion-picture invention; even Edison himself at the outset seemed a bit ashamed of its apparently delinquent character. Then, early in 1894, Thomas Lombard, who promoted the sale of coin-machine phonographs for Edison and had long seen commercial promise in the queer little peep-show box, turned up with a young capitalist named Norman C. Raff.

Raff, recently arrived in the East from gold-prospecting exploits in the Rockies, and his associate, Frank Gammon, whom he soon introduced, were speculators, backers of racetrack entries or theatrical shows. They saw the skits and prizefights, and in 1894, after organizing the Kinetoscope Company, entered into a contract with Edison to purchase a large number of his peep-show boxes for two hundred dollars each and exhibit them in Kinetoscope parlors.

The first of these parlors was opened on lower Broadway in New York, on April 14, 1894, and was billed as "The Wizard's Latest Invention." The first public showing created something like a riot. Crowds on Broadway waited all day and far into the night in long queues to see the pictures that moved for ninety seconds, through the eyeholes of five Kinetoscopes. Soon there were similar parlors opened in Chicago, Baltimore, Atlantic City, San Francisco, and other centers, which were also besieged by crowds. The exploitation of the motion picture was thus begun as a form of mass entertainment, following the commercial pattern of the earlier phonograph parlors.

Two years later, in 1896, following the development by Thomas Armat of Washington, D.C., of a successful projector (the vitascope) which was combined with the Edison motion-picture camera, preparations were made to open theaters with wall screens. The formal public presentation of the "enlarged Kinetoscope" took place on the night of April 23, at Koster & Bial's fashionable Music Hall on Herald Square, before a silk-hatted audience embracing many leading figures in the theatrical and business world. The presentation included ballet girls dancing with umbrellas, burlesque boxers, some vaudeville skits, and finally so realistic a scene of waves crashing upon a beach and stone pier that some of the viewers in the front row recoiled in fear. The audience was astonished and exhilarated by this newest "miracle of science," and sent up great cheers for Edison.

This event signalized the introduction of living pictures to the theaters of Broadway, and thereby to all the world. But the impact that this new entertainment medium was to have upon the minds and lives of hundreds of millions throughout the world was something unforeseen and unimagined—perhaps surpassing the effect of almost all other nineteenth-century inventions, by Edison or anyone else.

In the late nineties, after he had severed his connections with the General Electric Company, Edison had been on the verge of financial ruin, thanks to the failure of his ore-separating venture. In 1898, in response to a kindly letter from Henry Villard inquiring if he needed help, he had written cheerfully that he hoped to be able to clear off the debts he had incurred. "My three companies, the Phonograph Works, the National Phonograph Company, and the Edison Manufacturing Company (making motion-picture machines and films) are making a great amount of money, which gives me a large income." At that time he was still pouring his revenues into the ore-milling works.

But soon after he gave up that stubborn campaign, he was in the black again! Edison cared nothing for mere money, as against the joy of a new battle to wrest from nature more of her secrets—but he could always earn his way. By his wits, with the help of his ingenious Kinetoscope, and a few other tricks, he had saved himself again. With his recent winnings he could now afford to "plunge" into a new, a different, and a very hazardous experimental project.

VIII. A Stern Chase: the Storage Battery

THE AUTOMOBILE AGE had begun. In light coupés or phaetons, powered by steam and gasoline engines or electric motors, some three thousand Americans were already "burning up the roads." The first steam cars and gas buggies were noisy, hot, and bothersome; they stank and gave much trouble mechanically; yet every year they gained in following.

Edison tried the early gas buggies and steamers, and allowed that the horse was doomed; the future would belong to self-propelled carriages and trucks. He also ventured to predict that most of them would be driven by electric motors and storage batteries.

Why electric cars? A survey made in New York at the end of 1899 showed that of a hundred motorcabs in use in the downtown area, ninety were powered by storage batteries. Compared with cars using steam engines, which were heavy, or gas engines, then most unreliable, the electric runabout was clean, light, and quiet. Carriage builders were installing lead batteries and small motors in Studebaker or Columbia vehicles. But who knew as much as Edison about electrical machines? It was the right time, he judged, to enter this field and contrive a product more practical than any other.

A few years earlier, at a gathering of members of the Association of Edison Illuminating Companies, Edison met by chance a thin, long-legged young man with pale blue eyes, named Henry Ford. Ford was then employed as chief engineer at the Detroit Edison Company's powerhouse, and had been introduced to Edison by the head of that company, Alexander Dow. "There's a young fellow," said Dow, "who has made a *gas* car."

For long years Henry Ford had fairly worshipped Thomas A. Edison as the greatest of inventors, the example whom he desired to emulate. Now he was invited to sit next to this great man. He was shy, and usually dull in conversation. But when asked to describe his first automobile model, the young engineer became animated.

Edison, cupping his ear, listened and was impressed. He brought his fist down upon the table and said, "Young man, that's the thing! You have it—the self-contained unit carrying its own fuel with it. Keep at it!"

Ford went back to his machine shop in Detroit filled with inspiration; he would soon leave the Detroit Edison Company plant, find some financial backers, and in 1899 launch his first small automobile manufacturing concern. Though they did not meet again for several years, Ford believed that this first encounter was a turning point for him; his gratitude toward Edison endured and became something like idolatry.

In looking at the problem of the horseless carriage in 1900 Edison had concluded that the gasoline engine was "unscientific" and wasteful compared with the electric motor. But the batteries available as motive power also were inefficient, and the corrosion of metal by acid constantly limited durability. "I guess I'll have to make a battery," he said.

He defined the problem for himself: to attempt an entirely new voltaic combination that would make his "box of electricity" light, durable, undeteriorating, quickly chargeable, economical, and capable of storing a larger amount of energy than possible with the type of battery using lead electrodes. Such an instrument, he felt, would "open up a new epoch in electricity."

Having gathered personnel and equipment, he gave the signal for the hunt to begin. Beginning in 1901, hundreds of tests were made of various grades of copper and finely divided iron, and the results set down painstakingly in laboratory notebooks. The number of experiments mounted up into the hundreds, then to the thousands. A year, eighteen months went by, and they had not even a clue. After many more trials, they tried nickel hydrate and began to get better results. It was, however, a poor conductor. The tests continued.

At sixty, stout, round-faced, and deafer than ever, Edison

had nonetheless changed very little in spirit and method since he had invented the carbon filament lamp thirty years earlier. There was the same abandonment to studies. His temper, to be sure, was a little shorter nowadays, sometimes violent when a clumsy mechanic upset things; but he continued to show an unfailing patience in the face of repeated disappointments. In fact, it was a rule with him never to show grief or bitterness, even when some long-prepared experiment proved to be a failure. Things came to him nowadays, as in the past, mostly by hard work and taking the time to "try everything."

Sometimes he alluded to himself as a sort of Don Quixote, who was tilting at scientific windmills in order to liberate the good storage battery. His chief draftsman, John Ott, long in his service, he nicknamed Santcho-Pantcho.

Once, when a new employee respectfully asked to be informed about the laboratory rules and regulations, Edison spat on the floor (he was chewing tobacco) and expostulated, "Hell, there ain't no rules around here! We're tryin' to accomplish somep'n."

HE GAVE the utmost care to the design of an entirely new battery form. From rough sketches and models he evolved a novel structure of nickel-plated steel, the positive pockets being packed with nickel hydrate and the negative being of iron oxide.

At last, in 1903, he was ready to test his batteries in actual usage. He installed them in carriages with a small electric motor and chain drive, and ran these vehicles over the rough country roads near Orange. Records were kept on test sheets and closely scanned. In his laboratory Edison also set up an electrical apparatus that jolted his battery cells up and down, day and night, in simulation of heavy road usage. They were even thrown out the windows of the upper floors to test durability. He wanted his battery to be foolproof.

Finally, at Silver Lake, in the summer of 1904, a manufacturing plant was made ready, special machine tools were set out, and 450 workmen were engaged. Production slowly got under way, and in the first season several thousand cells of the first battery model, the "E," were turned out. The demand far exceeded what Edison could supply; merchants and transport concerns had the first Edison storage batteries installed in light delivery wagons and, at the outset, found their electric carriages and trucks highly convenient.

With his usual self-confidence Edison had started a rousing publicity campaign for his "revolutionary" storage battery even before he was ready to manufacture it. Thus, in interviews during 1903, and early in 1904, he announced that there would soon be "a miniature dynamo in every home . . . an automobile for every family." The new Edison battery had great power, weighed next to nothing, had neither acid nor lead, would not deteriorate when not in use, was almost endlessly rechargeable, and could withstand almost any mistreatment.

He concluded:

> . . . I hope that the time has nearly arrived when every man may not only be able to light his own house, but charge his own machinery, heat his rooms, cook his food, etc., by electricity, without depending on anyone else for these services.

In short, he had "revolutionized the world of power" the newspapers reported; he had brought forth the "age of stored electricity," destined to change sea travel, land transport, warfare, and agriculture. The outlook for the ill-smelling gas buggies seemed dark indeed!

Edison posed for news photographers standing beside a spanking little red sulky which had nickel-iron batteries and an electric motor. It was so easily run, he declared, that his twelve-year-old boy Charles could drive it. With that he leaped on board and sped away at twenty miles an hour.

However, bad reports soon began to come in from the first users; and then the reports grew steadily worse. After all the propaganda, it was a shock to learn that the battery containers leaked on being used in vehicles; that the cells were of uneven performance, and usually dropped about thirty percent in power. Defective batteries returned to the factory were broken up and examined. The electrical contacts in the positive element were found to be unreliable.

The truth about this fiasco was spreading. All the exuberant advance publicity had but made things worse. Moreover, Edison this time had raised $500,000 through friendly investors by giving a bond and mortgage on his other manufacturing properties; and these funds had all been exhausted by the work of research and the cost of setting up the factory.

He recognized that his battery still needed prolonged study before it could be marketed. But if he shut down his plant and set to overhauling the whole job in his laboratory, he faced a very heavy financial loss. Still worse, and most humiliating to him, would be the public admission of failure, after his sweeping claims of success.

After a brief discussion with his financial associates, he made his decision swiftly. He would shut down production at once and take back all the batteries that had proved defective, at his own cost. One of his associates questioned his wisdom in stopping production, pointing out that his batteries were still far in advance of the old-style lead ones. To such objections Edison replied flatly, "I stopped manufacturing because the battery was not satisfactory to myself. . . ."

It was an act of courage. And now, since the Edison Storage Battery Company had used up all its capital, he financed it out of his own pocket.

Fortunately the motion pictures were now booming, thanks to *The Great Train Robbery* distributed by Edison's studio in 1904. This film—now regarded as the classic prototype of the motion-picture *play*—generated a great new wave of popularity for motion pictures. A flood of Westerns and thrillers followed, and little motion-picture theaters and nickelodeons mushroomed all over the country.

Now, at Edison's command, virtually his whole laboratory force set to work to overcome the irregularities that had shown themselves in the first battery. The new series of experiments brought forth more variables, and were to engage the labors of Edison and his staff for five years more. But Edison vowed that he would find the right way to make a battery—"If it takes me seven years and $1,750,000"—alluding here to the cost of his recent education in iron-ore milling.

By the summer of 1905 Edison could report that he had again

made a "vast number of experiments, now reading 10,296," and that he "had found out a great many things."

Then in the winter of 1905, while working under great stress, he became very ill, and underwent what was then a fairly dangerous operation for mastoiditis. Henceforth he would be almost stone-deaf. Though the annual winter vacation at Fort Myers would have benefitted his health, and he longed to go, he returned instead to his laboratory to watch the testing of hundreds of new combinations for battery cells and examine the test sheets being compiled for them.

Though the road seemed to lead through all the turnings of an immense labyrinth, Edison insisted on preserving a mask of outward composure and good cheer. Nevertheless, the ten years' hunt for a good storage battery was a prevailingly somber period, Edison's associates recalled, despite his ideas about keeping up morale. Age was coming upon him; his long, thick hair grew very white, while his well-defined eyebrows remained very dark, accentuating his pallor.

In the year 1907 the newspapers reported that a Rolls-Royce car with a six-cylinder gasoline engine had passed a ten-thousand-mile endurance test. In Detroit, Henry Ford, working with a will as fierce as Edison's, perfected a cheap fifteen-horsepower four-cylinder engine for his Model N car, precursor of the celebrated Model T. The Model N went twenty miles on a gallon of fuel and cost only $600. "Hundreds of persons," it was reported, rushed to buy Ford's small car.

DURING THE YEARS of extreme tension created by the unrelenting campaign for the nickel storage battery the inventor's family found him more "difficult" than usual. An article in *Collier's Weekly*, based on a lengthy interview with Mrs. Edison, was titled "She Married the Most Difficult Husband in America." To the interviewer Mrs. Edison declared that she had dedicated her life to the service of her great man, "and thought it worth it a thousand times over." He had few friends and lived, she said, "a great deal by himself and in himself, shut out from the contacts open to most men." Neither hobbies nor amusements interested him. Mrs. Edison and the children "always put his work first," and his home and family life were organized to that end.

Mina Edison had great influence over her iron-willed husband. That he loved her greatly, and that he also esteemed her, was beyond doubt. Though time pressed, he would linger with her for some moments each day, in her garden or in the big conservatory at Glenmont. And every day when he left the house and when he returned, he would kiss her. If she were not nearby as he went to work, he would send a servant to call her.

To the young children of his second marriage, he was by turns teasingly affectionate or remote. "Sometimes it was as if he never saw us," his youngest son, Theodore, said long afterward. The distance from his children had an unfortunate effect on his two elder sons. But Mina Edison was determined that with *her* children, at least, it would be different, that there should be no such alienation from the father. She therefore encouraged her eldest son Charles to be with his father as much as possible and, during school vacation, to work in his laboratory, even at the humblest tasks, such as the "bottle monkey's."

IN THE years 1905 to 1908 the whole structure of the storage cell was redesigned. By prolonged experimenting Edison and his co-workers brought about one improvement after another, and helped to clarify the major problem. The stubborn riddle of drop-off in capacity from cycle to cycle of charging and discharging was finally solved sometime in 1908.

After they had tried hundreds of different additives, a small amount of lithium hydroxide was introduced. This had the effect of raising capacity and then holding it steady over a long period—"a real piece of magic" that could never have been calculated theoretically in Edison's time. His empirical work, carried out at a cost of a million dollars of his own money, was successful in the end.

"At last the battery is finished," Edison wrote in the summer of 1909, with evident relief. It seemed "an almost perfect instrument." A year later factory production was resumed on a large scale; in the first twelve months thereafter a million dollars' worth of the new A battery cells was sold, beginning a profitable career for the Edison Storage Battery Company that has continued to this day.

Several important carriage works hastened to produce electric runabouts and light trucks that were powered by an array of Edison cells. Department stores used such electric trucks for years. Light electric town cars were popular for a period because they were noiseless and fumeless; their radius was about sixty miles a day, and their Edison batteries could be fully recharged in seven hours.

However, when winter came it was common for many Edison-powered vehicles to become stuck in snowdrifts or on muddy roads. Meanwhile the far-ranging gas buggies of Ford and others, with their cheap, improved combustion engines, swept all before them.

On the other hand, the beautifully constructed Edison battery was found particularly useful where dependability and long life were important, as at power plants, and for railway signaling; or to provide current for miners' lamps, train lights, and other railway and marine appliances. Though the electric automobile had only a brief vogue, a remarkably wide field of usage was developed in industries such as mining and quarrying, on merchant vessels, and ships of war.

Was it worth the tremendous effort? Edison used to profess that his inventive work was guided only by the criterion of commercial success. But the profits were rather on the moderate side when measured against the "punishment" he had taken in that series of heartbreaking experiments lasting nearly ten years. The thought of calling a halt at some midway point and cutting his losses was never tolerated. Why did he go on and on? "I always invent to obtain money to go on inventing," he said simply.

HE "RESTED" at intervals, during the campaign for the storage battery, by turning his attention to a number of highly different inventive tasks. One such new departure was the sizable Edison Portland Cement Company. Edison foresaw a large expansion of reinforced concrete construction in America. In such spare moments as he had, he drew up engineering plans for an entirely new type of cement kiln. His plant, when completed in 1907, was designed to grind out a thousand barrels of cement every twenty-four hours, when the average cement kilns produced only two hundred barrels a day.

At about this same period the spreading phonograph "craze" kept his factories at West Orange working on a two-shift basis, and by 1914 the volume of Edison's phonograph business, stimulated by the countrywide ragtime mania, surpassed seven million dollars annually.

Motion pictures, made immensely popular by the star system, brought revenues that were even larger. A business dictating machine, the Ediphone, demanded another new manufacturing unit. To this he added the Telescribe, a machine combining the dictating phonograph and telephone, which recorded both sides of telephone conversations.

He kept control of his enterprises in his own hands, nowadays, and owed money to no man. He had reorganized his various industries and combined them in one corporation under the title of Thomas A. Edison, Incorporated. Thus in the closing years of his life he created a "family business" embracing about thirty different enterprises whose gross annual sales amounted to between $20,000,000 and $27,000,000.

Thanks to the phonograph and motion-picture industries, he now ranked as a member of the country's select group of multimillionaires. But while his industries earned, at times, as much as two million dollars of profit annually, he boasted that he "never paid any dividends." As fast as profits were realized from one invention, he would plow the earnings into research and development in new fields.

Probably no professional inventor was ever engaged in so many businesses, or in so much manufacturing, selling, and "meeting of payrolls." His son Charles, who was twenty-four in 1914, had studied at the Massachusetts Institute of Technology and was being trained to serve as an executive in various departments, so that he might eventually become head of the entire concern. Nonetheless, while he lived, Thomas A. Edison ran the whole business and the laboratory as well, according to his own lights.

THEY WERE DOING A LAND-OFFICE BUSINESS at the Edison works in West Orange, in 1914, when disaster struck without warning.

On the evening of December 9, 1914, Edison had gone home early for dinner, a clear sign of old age coming on. Just before 6:00 p.m. fire broke out in a small wooden structure in the factory quadrangle, where chemicals and inflammable motion-picture film had been stored. The factory fire squad quickly went into action, but water pressure in the village of West Orange was low.

Since most of the adjacent factory buildings were of reinforced concrete, then considered fireproof, it was hoped that the fire would not spread far. (Because of their "fireproof construction" he had had them insured at less than a third of their cost, which was more than a million dollars.) But the burning chemical products shot forth great geysers of green flame which soon enveloped neighboring buildings. Fire companies from eight nearby towns soon rushed to the scene, but falling water pressure balked all their efforts.

The several factories in the path of the wind were soon in full conflagration; one of them, Building 24, which was six stories high, contained large stores of chemicals which sent up spectacular flames from big tanks on its upper floor. Numerous firemen and volunteers were overcome; one Edison worker was killed.

Charles Edison, on hand to help direct emergency measures, was overwhelmed by the horror of the scene and his sense of despair. His father, called from the dinner table at Glenmont, came walking slowly into the yard, silent, impassive. The whole Edison "empire" was going up in green and yellow flames; yet he stood and watched it all with folded arms.

Fortunately the big library and main laboratory buildings were out of the path of the flames. But the administration building at one side of the yard, containing stores of valuable instruments, was partly on fire; and the firefighters and volunteers hastened to carry out such supplies as they could reach.

At last the Old Man spoke to his son Charles. "Where's Mother?" he asked. "Get her over here, and her friends too. They'll never see a fire like this again."

Charles began to lament the incalculable loss. But his father only said dryly: "Oh shucks, it's all right. We've just got rid of a lot of old rubbish."

However, he soon went into action, stayed up all night, and directed the removal of such valuable merchandise and machinery as could be saved. A crowd of ten thousand persons had gathered to watch the fire. Late in the night the fire was gradually extinguished. At dawn the place was still smoldering.

Many persons came to Edison, or telegraphed, expressing their sorrow at this catastrophe. To one such sympathizer Edison replied, "I am sixty-seven; but I'm not too old to make a fresh start." But to his son Charles he said: "I wonder what we will use for money?"

On the day after the fire he directed a crew of fifteen hundred men who cleared the ruins and removed the debris. He again worked with furious energy, as in his youth. Factory space was rented in nearby towns; machinery was set up, and men put to work. On the security of a large amount of receivables due him, he negotiated loans at banks. At news of his misfortune, Henry Ford hastened to New Jersey and generously lent Edison $750,000 in order to speed the work of reconstruction. Edison, over the years, repaid the debt in full.

Within three weeks the Edison factories had been restored to some semblance of order; and shortly after New Year's Day 1915 most of the personnel were at work in two shifts. The speed of recovery was almost as spectacular as the disaster.

IX. Canonization

A NEW PHASE OF GLORY as America's acknowledged folk hero had opened for Edison after the turn of the century as he approached his seventh decade, a glory that could at times be burdensome. The electric utilities—power companies such as the Chicago Edison Company now headed by his former financial manager, Samuel Insull—had become the new giant among industries, and had long since unofficially adopted Edison as patron saint. Edison symbolized electricity—thoughts and words soaring across great distances: energy freed from the engine and belt by smokeless motors; cities wreathed in light.

His legendary success story, like his expressive face, was familiar to all men. His very appearance, and his widely reported sayings—racy, humorous, and original in flavor—but strengthened the will of the multitude to idolize him. He was chosen repeatedly, in popular newspaper or magazine polls, as America's "greatest" or "most useful citizen." In short, he was almost universally regarded as one of the real makers of America, and so, well suited to serve as a folk hero.

Newspapermen could never resist him. At his annual birthday interviews, one of the reporters usually opened up by saying, "Happy birthday, Mr. Edison. How are you feeling today?" The question having been relayed to him, on one occasion, by his old secretary, W. H. Meadowcroft, Edison wheeled about suddenly, executed a high kick clearing his big laboratory table and all its paraphernalia, then brought his leg down to the floor and shouted, "Fine as silk!"

To what did he attribute his success? was one of the most oft-repeated questions. Was he not a genius? One of his justly memorable phrases in reply to such queries was, "Genius is ninety-nine percent perspiration and one percent inspiration."

His gospel was "Work—bringing out the secrets of nature and applying them for the happiness of man." He for his part would never retire "until the doctors brought in the oxygen cylinder." At seventy-five as at forty-five, he felt well because he worked "two shifts." Mrs. Edison, it seems, had cut down his hours to only sixteen a day.

In the late fall of 1910 a lively and prolonged controversy was provoked by Edison when he candidly professed himself to be a freethinker in religious matters. To the question put to him during an interview, "What does God mean to you?", he replied, "A personal God means absolutely nothing to me." Moreover, he declared himself an enemy of all superstition, deplored the fact that most people were "incurably religious," and pointed out that "billions of prayers" had brought no mitigation of natural catastrophes such as great wars.

Edison's mailbag at the Orange post office was soon swollen

with angry letters from pious folk. Ministers in their pulpits protested his materialistic bias. Believers beseeched him "not to take away their God." Business associates pleaded with him not to destroy the prestige of his great name and injure Edison industries. Some of his remarks, reflecting a spirit of levity toward the superstitious, were given circulation and further irritated the orthodox. To a minister's query as to the value of lightning rods as protection for his church spire, Edison replied, "By all means, as Providence is apt to be absentminded." In the face of attack, he held his ground staunchly, saying:

> The criticisms that have been hurled at me have not worried me. A man cannot control his beliefs. . . . I try to say exactly what I honestly believe to be the truth. . . . I have never seen the slightest scientific proof of the religious theories of heaven and hell, of future life for individuals, or of a personal God. . . . Proof! Proof! That is what I have always been after. I do not know the soul, I know the mind. If there is really any soul I have found no evidence of it in my investigations. . . . But I have found repeatedly evidence of mind. . . . I do not believe in the God of the theologians; but that there is a Supreme Intelligence, I do not doubt.

On the question of education, Edison's opinions aroused almost as fierce controversy as his idea on religion. What was abhorrent to him was all formal schooling and college training, such as he himself had managed so well to do without. "I can hire mathematicians at fifteen dollars a week," he had once said, "but they can't hire *me*."

School, for him, meant only teaching and learning by rote. He advocated that every child be encouraged to develop his faculties by *making things*, and by observing nature for himself, instead of having his mind crammed with memorized facts.

Edison also assailed the whole idea of teaching the liberal arts in higher institutions.

> What we need are men capable of doing work. I wouldn't give a penny for the ordinary college graduate, except those from institutes of technology. . . . They aren't filled up with

Latin, Philosophy and all that ninny stuff. America needs practical, skilled engineers, business-managers and industrial men.
In three or four centuries, when the country is settled and com-
mercialism is diminished there will be time for literary men.

What was not known at that period was that his attempts to
educate his own children had been a complete failure. (I speak
here of the elder children born of his first marriage; those of the
second marriage were quite differently brought up by Mina
Edison.)

On the strength of his own experience, he had discouraged
his eldest son, Tom junior, from going to college. Such schooling as he had did not reach beyond the high-school stage. As for
William Leslie, the second son, he showed no aptitude for
learning and was not interested in going beyond a preparatory
school. The spirit of the elder sons was undoubtedly affected
by the early loss of their mother in 1884. It was not easy to be
the son of such a father, so often obsessed by his work, and
seemingly so self-centered or remote.

Edison's second marriage, moreover, had introduced a painful
division in the family. Mina Edison was but a few years older
than her stepdaughter Marion and her stepson Tom and naturally found it difficult to impose her authority over them. Marion
had shown from the outset an adolescent hostility, or jealousy,
toward her young stepmother. Always an attractive and independent personality, Marion was never a problem to her parents,
and in her later years maintained very friendly relations with
the younger Edison children.

Tom junior had much sweetness of personality and showed
some little mechanical bent. Sad to say, he even tried to be an
inventor on his own. Later, like his brother Will, he drifted
away from the parental home. Though regularly supplied by
his father with enough funds to live on, Tom was often in
trouble, and for a period drank a good deal.

In 1904 Edison formally disowned Tom junior, because he
had allowed the Edison name to be exploited by dishonest
associates. But as Edison was, in reality, very fond of his eldest
son, a reconciliation was effected, and the prodigal youth was

brought back again, to be employed in various departments of the Edison industries.

William Leslie, a tall and athletic youth, created anxieties of a somewhat different nature for his parent. Will was sometimes described as headstrong and stormy; despite efforts on his father's and Mina Edison's part to encourage good relations, he maintained an attitude of hostility toward his stepmother.

The destiny of the later children, born of Mina Edison, proved to be far more fortunate than that of the elder ones. Their mother brought them up in her own Methodist faith, reared them with care and affection, and stoutly opposed her husband's counsels that their formal or religious education be limited. On the contrary, their daughter Madeleine was sent to Bryn Mawr College; Charles and Theodore attended good private schools, and completed their education at Massachusetts Institute of Technology.

In 1914 Charles had set to work in earnest learning the family business under his father, with whom he always got on well. Several years later he was made executive vice-president; on his father's retirement (in 1927) he was to succeed him as head of Thomas A. Edison, Incorporated—which had been the fond wish of Mrs. Edison all along.

Theodore Miller Edison, born in 1898, made an excellent record as an engineering student at the Massachusetts Institute of Technology, showing a passion for science. But to the elder Edison's dismay, his youngest child seemed determined to become a mathematical physicist—one of the breed that Edison had always belittled. This made for dissension in the family, for Theodore proved to be as strong-willed as his father, and in the face of paternal disapproval continued his studies of higher physics.

"Theodore is a good boy," the father said, "but I am a little afraid . . . he may go flying off into the clouds with that fellow Einstein. And if he does . . . I'm afraid he won't work with me."

"Is it not strange that a man who always did exactly what he pleased would not let his own children do anything that they wanted to do?" a member of the family is reported to have remarked at this time.

A FEW MONTHS AFTER THE OUTBREAK of war in Europe in August 1914, a newspaper reporter interviewed Edison and recorded his thoughts on the great conflict. Principally it made him "sick at heart" for mankind, as he said. "This war had to come. Those military gangs in Europe piled up armaments until something had to break." Reflecting American public sentiment, which was decidedly neutral in the first year of the war, he asserted that he would have no part in it. "Making things which kill men is against my fiber."

But in the late spring of 1915, at the time of the sinking of the S.S. *Lusitania* by a German U-boat, Edison changed his mind and allied himself with "preparedness" groups who were urging that we expand armaments and train military personnel for the eventuality of war.

The military services were already making plans for expansion. Secretary of the Navy Josephus Daniels attempted to organize an advisory board of scientists and inventors whose minds would be at the service of the military.

Since nothing could be more natural than that Edison himself should head such a board, Daniels wrote him inviting him to undertake "this very great service for the Navy and the country at large." President Woodrow Wilson approved of the proposal. Edison replied promptly with the equivalent of a cheerful "Aye, aye, sir." If his country needed his inventive skill to make her safe from attack, he would willingly respond.

On receiving his acceptance, Secretary Daniels hastened to West Orange and discussed the plan of the proposed board with Edison, who shrewdly advised that instead of just naming two or three famous inventors, such as himself and Wilbur Wright, as its members, Daniels should address himself to the country's leading scientific and engineering societies, and invite them to select outstanding persons in their different fields. This was done, and a rather impressive group was gathered together for the Navy Consulting Board. At the initial meeting at Washington, in October 1915, Edison was formally appointed its president. The board met only at rare intervals at first.

However, tension between the United States and Germany rose in the early months of 1916, and the scientists of the Navy

Consulting Board grew more active as the war came closer.

One of Edison's most significant proposals was that the Navy establish a scientific research laboratory for the development of new weapons. The nation's military services had never evinced any interest or spent any money on technical research, since the days of John Paul Jones. Improved weapons were adopted in a haphazard fashion, usually after experimental work by private ordnance manufacturers. Edison pushed his proposal to establish a naval research laboratory with characteristic tenacity and in the face of stout bureaucratic resistance, so that eventually such an institution was authorized by Congress. The Naval Research Laboratory was to be Edison's most vital contribution to the national defense; between the two world wars it would be the only American institution for organized scientific research in weapons, hence of enormous importance in preparing for the technological warfare of the 1940's.

Late in December 1916 Secretary Daniels called on Edison and told him in confidence that the Allies were fated to lose the war unless they could stop the German submarines. He now asked Edison to give all his time to inventing antisubmarine devices. Edison promptly turned over his business affairs to other hands and plunged into this work. He was thus occupied when the United States entered the war against Germany in April 1917.

Giving free rein to his fine mechanical imagination he contrived a whole series of defensive instruments against U-boats: a device for the quick turning of ships; one for locating guns and torpedoes; another for raising smoke clouds to cover merchant vessels; antitorpedo nets; hidden lights; turbine heads for projectiles; collision mats; and finally a sonic apparatus, employing a submerged phonograph diaphragm, to detect submarines.

When the war drew to its end the Navy, at Secretary Daniels's wish, tendered the Distinguished Service Medal to Edison, a rare honor for a civilian. He refused it, saying that he "did not wish to hurt anyone's feelings," and was aware that other civilian scientists who had helped in the war effort would believe they were entitled to equal honors.

He turned his attention again to his own business. After the wartime inflation, a depression was under way, and the Thomas A. Edison works, like other "war babies," needed to be trimmed down. He removed many hundreds of workers from his payrolls, but the old-timers, even the feeble ones, he insisted, must remain, especially in the laboratory.

X. Sunset, with Electric Illuminations

IN THE AUTUMN OF 1922 Edison visited the General Electric Company's huge plant at Schenectady after an absence of twenty-five years. The factories that had grown up out of the old Edison Machine Works now extended "for miles" and employed 18,000 workers who, at the order of President Gerard Swope, assembled to welcome and cheer Edison. Here hundreds of scientists and technicians were at work in fields of technology that Edison had only dimly imagined. Dr. Charles P. Steinmetz showed him around the laboratory and demonstrated his "lightning bolts," capable of discharging 120,000 volts at a bar of tungsten, causing it to "vanish" and turn into gas. W. R. Whitney, director of the laboratory, showed him a new process for converting tungsten into lamp filaments. The aged inventor sighed, and recalled what great troubles he had encountered in his own attempts to experiment with tungsten. Dr. Irving Langmuir also displayed new vacuum tubes for long-distance transmission; also a 100,000-candlepower lamp, and photoelectric mechanisms that reproduced sound on tape for motion pictures and phonographs. Edison declared that he had greatly enjoyed seeing "the old place, and the old boys," but admitted that it had changed, had grown up.

Some time after his visit to General Electric, Edison, old free lance that he was, declared that the "corporation laboratory" would not do. The inventor was now a "hired person," assigning to the corporation all his patents; such men worked in large groups and held many conferences. The "weight of organization" was too great, Edison observed shrewdly; and the results, he predicted, would not be as rich as in the case of individual inventors working in small organizations.

In his late seventies Edison gave most of his attention to the improved phonographs, business machines, and secondary and primary batteries. The fortunes of the Edison industries were at full tide during the postwar boom, toward 1923, then ebbing as radio came into general use and competing manufacturers placed on the market newly invented electronic phonographs, or even phonographs and radio receivers in combination. Edison could not abide the new recording instruments, and as for radio, he predicted people would want to listen to music of their own choice and the "radio craze" would soon pass.

The old mechanical phonograph business, however, was falling off rapidly; Edison's nationwide organization of thirteen thousand phonograph dealers threatened to disappear. His sons Charles (who by then was playing a leading role in the family business) and Theodore begged him to make both radio receivers and electronic phonographs. According to Theodore Edison, his father opposed the new ventures until it was too late to enter upon them.

His youngest son, Theodore, considered the most talented of his children, he regarded with mixed feelings of puzzlement and respect. There had been, at times, some lively disputes between them on the score of Theodore's addiction to mathematics and the method of theory and calculation. On one occasion, when no agreement seemed possible, the young man had packed his trunks and prepared to leave West Orange to look for a job somewhere else; but his father capitulated and agreed to have him work in his own way. An old shed was turned over to Theodore for use as a laboratory. After a while his work appeared impressive enough to warrant his transfer to a fully equipped laboratory, and eventually—two years after his father's retirement—to the post of technical director of the Edison Laboratory, as well as a member of the company's executive board.

In the autumn of 1926, when he was well along in his eightieth year, Edison at last announced that he had decided to retire. His son Charles would succeed him as the head of Thomas A. Edison, Incorporated and he would limit himself thereafter to laboratory experiments.

For several years the interest of the Old Man had been directed to an entirely new field of operations. It was to be a last "campaign" of experimentation to which he would surrender himself with all his unfailing enthusiasm. "I have had sixty years of mechanics and physics," he remarked as he now turned to another science, as much for his own pleasure and amusement as for any profit that might come of it. He was botanizing; but as always there was a practical object in view.

RUBBER HAD recently become one of the most important commodities for the modern industrial world, thanks to the automobile. It was produced in distant tropical regions and in wartime became scarce and extremely dear. Back in 1915, while visiting Luther Burbank's plantation in California with Ford and Harvey Firestone, Edison had remarked that if the United States entered the war, rubber would be the first product to be cut off. Ford had asked him to do something about creating a domestic supply, or a substitute, to which Edison replied, "I will—some day."

When rubber became costly again toward 1924–1925, owing to the British Far Eastern rubber-restriction scheme, Ford and Firestone renewed their pleas that Edison undertake a serious investigation of domestic sources of rubber, which they offered to finance. The Edison Botanic Research Company was organized in 1927, with the Ford and Firestone companies each advancing $93,500 to cover the costs of research, while Edison agreed to contribute his labor. Thus he was engaged once more in one of his famous hunts, "ransacking the world" for some plant, either existing or to be developed by crossbreeding, which contained sufficient rubber to be processed on a large scale. Once more the Old Man had a happy look in his eyes as he began his new studies at Fort Myers in the winter of 1927.

His mental powers, at eighty, showed no perceptible decline. He "got the whole subject of rubber into his head" so he could see every phase of his problem. The main source of supply was the *Hevea brasiliensis*, a tree native to Brazil, but successfully transplanted on a large scale to Malaya, Ceylon, and Africa. It was well known to scientists that numerous other plants, even those common to the North Temperate zone, contained latex in varying quantity. What Edison hoped to find was a crop native to the United States, and capable of being cultivated, harvested, and processed within a year or eighteen months, so as to provide a source of supply in the event of war or other emergency.

In less than a year Edison reported to Henry Ford that he had collected 3,227 wild plants and shrubs from points ranging between New Jersey and Key West, and that seven percent were found to have rubber in various quality and amounts. "Everything looks favorable to a solution. . . ." he concluded with his unvarying cheerfulness.

At the end of a second year's search, when some fourteen thousand plants had been examined and tested, of which about six hundred contained some rubber, Edison, after flirting with honeysuckle and milkweed, fixed on the domestic goldenrod as the most promising plant of all. Goldenrod yielded about five percent rubber. Edison selected the varieties that seemed most promising, and crossbred. It was time-consuming; but a giant goldenrod about fourteen feet tall yielding about twelve percent latex was ultimately developed. Ford was so greatly encouraged by Edison's reports that he purchased an extensive acreage in southern Georgia for the raising of goldenrod.

Edison worked on at his Florida botanical laboratory even in the heat of spring and early summer. Then, in the late summer of 1929, while at West Orange again, Edison fell ill; his whole digestive apparatus seemed affected and there was some indication of kidney malfunction and diabetes.

But he rose from his bed saying, "Give me five years and the United States will have a rubber crop." But who, now, could give Edison five years?

Oddly enough, not only Edison, but Henry Ford, the Du Pont Company, and Standard Oil of New Jersey, after 1925, received information about the new German chemical process for converting coal or petroleum derivatives into synthetic rubber. Government scientists thoroughly explored the possibilities of using vegetable materials such as Edison's variety of goldenrod, but reached the conclusion that processing such plants would be more difficult and costly than making synthetic, and would yield a product inferior to natural India rubber or the new synthetics.

Edison's goldenrod rubber project, therefore, was fore-doomed. If Henry Ford suspected this, the motor king would not have moved a hand to stop Edison's dying effort. Where Edison was concerned, Ford was all sentiment.

In 1929 Harvey Firestone, having received a shipment of the costly goldenrod latex from Fort Myers, obligingly turned out four rubber tires for the inventor's Model-A Ford touring car.

Edison did not recover quickly from his illness. He was suffering from uremia, yet worked in his botanical laboratory, assuring all and sundry that the solution of the rubber problem was at hand. "We are just beginning. . . ." he said.

THE NINTH DECADE of the inventor's life was a time for the erection of monuments in his honor, a time for the bestowal of medals, ribbons, decorations. He was a walking monument himself, in fact, an immortal. From the governments of Japan, Russia, Chile, and many nations lying between, honors were heaped on him, and on May 21, 1928, his own government, by a resolution in Congress, awarded him the Congressional Medal of Honor.

A signal event in Edison's old age was Henry Ford's decision to build an immense museum of the history of industry and invention, as a monument not only to himself but also to his friend Edison, in Ford's native town of Dearborn, Michigan.

Hence Ford began to gather up relics of the legendary Menlo Park laboratory, now in ruins. He not only scoured the New Jersey countryside for the very planks that had fallen off Edison's old sheds, but also gathered together a notable collection of original models of Edison's inventions, installing them in a section of Greenfield Village in Dearborn that was at first known as the "Edison Institute." These models were so well restored or, in some cases reproduced (with the advice of Francis Jehl, of the original Menlo Park team), that everything worked as before, the paper-carbon lamps as well as the 1882 dynamos. About three millions were thus lavished by Ford upon his collection of Edisonia alone, the total cost of Greenfield Village being more than ten million dollars.

Early in 1929, when the Ford Museum and Greenfield Village were nearing completion, Ford decided, with Edison's consent, to combine the dedication of his own institution with a celebration in honor of the fiftieth anniversary of Edison's incandescent lamp invention. He ordered his builders to rush the job on the great museum building, for it was to be the stage setting in October 1929 of the opening-day banquet.

When Edison finally stepped from the train at Dearborn, two days before the Golden Jubilee of Light was to open, he looked "like a benevolent old wreck," for he had been so gravely ill, in August 1929, with pneumonia that his life was feared for. Now as Edison beheld Greenfield Village and the transplanted Menlo Park, he smiled his broadest smile. The laboratory stood in its native red New Jersey clay (transported thither by train) and even had a heap of old metal junk lying outside. For had not Edison once said that what the good inventor needed was "imagination and a scrap heap"?

Here were all the old bulbs, telegraph instruments and stock tickers, the dynamos, the old generating plant of Pearl Street, and even an old mortar and pestle he had used and thrown away. There was not only the old laboratory, but also Mrs. Jordan's boardinghouse across the road from it; even the old railroad station at Smith's Creek, Michigan, where he had worked, and beside it a reproduction of a little Grand Trunk Railway train, including the baggage car with Tom Edison's little laboratory-on-wheels!

After Ford had shown him this truly monumental restoration Edison said, "Well, you've got this just about ninety-nine and one-half percent perfect."

"What is the matter with the other one-half percent?" Ford asked.

"Well, we never kept it as clean as this!" Edison drawled.

President and Mrs. Hoover, with attendant secret-service men, arrived on the morning of the twenty-first of October, at the head of a delegation including the nation's most eminent political and financial personages. At nightfall, after all the sights had been displayed to the distinguished guests, Edison appeared on the second floor of the "Menlo Park" laboratory to demonstrate how he made a carbonized thread and vacuum globe in 1879 and at a given moment turned it on.

The excitement had been wearing for the Old Man. But the festival was still to be topped off with a banquet for five hundred guests. President Hoover was to give the principal address. But at the door of the banquet hall Edison faltered and all but collapsed. Led to a settee in the corridor, he sat down and wept, overcome with emotion and fatigue.

"I won't go in," he said to Mrs. Edison. Only she could have overcome his resistance. They brought him some warm milk; he revived a little, entered the hall and took his place at the seat of honor. Messages from many nations were read, tributes were offered, while he heard nothing and ate nothing. President Hoover spoke.

"I have thought it fitting for the President of the United States to take part in paying honor to one of our great Americans. . . . Mr. Edison . . . has repelled the darkness . . . has brought to our country great distinction throughout the world. He has brought benefaction to all of us. . . . "

Edison spoke briefly, but with feeling, in reply. He was happy, he said, that tribute was being paid to scientific work.

"This experience makes me realize as never before that Americans are sentimental and this crowning event of Light's Golden Jubilee fills me with gratitude. As to Henry Ford, words are inadequate to express my feelings. I can only say to you, that in the fullest and richest meaning of the term—he is my friend. Good night."

Then he slumped into his chair and turned as white as death. Mrs. Edison and President Hoover's physician at once helped him to a room in the rear of the speaker's table, and laid him on a sofa. Drugs were administered, and he came to; then he was taken to the Ford residence and put to bed for several days. "I am tired of all the glory, I want to get back to work," he said.

During his recent illness he had permitted doctors to examine

him thoroughly. They had found that he suffered from a combination of uremic poisoning, Bright's disease, diabetes, and gastric ulcer. It was a mystery to the medical men how he had lasted so long.

His days in the laboratory were now definitely over, though none was supposed to mention that to him or anyone else. "Keep him going. Don't change anything, have the same people, don't let him stop," the family doctor advised.

HE ABSENTED HIMSELF for longer and longer intervals from his laboratory in the two years of life that remained. Often he stayed abed or sat in an easy chair at home, but still kept in close touch with his technical assistants, who daily brought him news of the progress of the goldenrod rubber experiment. Mrs. Edison watched patiently over his rest and diet, and maintained an almost daily routine of motor drives with him along the country roads of New Jersey.

In those last years of ill health and weakness Edison's interest in new "campaigns" never flagged. Having recently met Colonel Charles A. Lindbergh, he insisted on being taken to Newark Airport to learn something about the problems of airplane landing and takeoff. "The aviators tell me that they must find a means to see through a fog," he said. "I have an idea about it. I am waiting for a real fog—a water fog—and I will see if I can't penetrate it." Perhaps a rocket would do the trick?

At about this period he ventured the prophecy that "There will one day spring from the brain of Science a machine or force so fearful in its potentialities that even man, the fighter who will dare torture and death in order to inflict torture and death, will be appalled, and so will abandon war forever. . . ." He was greatly interested in the impact of Albert Einstein's formulations, but admitted that he couldn't understand any of them. "I am the zero of mathematics," he conceded ruefully. In one of his last interviews, he went on to say, "I am much interested in atomic energy, but so far as I can see we have not yet reached a point where this exhaustless force can be harnessed and utilized."

On August 1, 1931, he had a sudden sinking spell and lay at the point of death. He could absorb virtually no food at all—

but, to the astonishment of his physicians, he rallied and tried to rise from bed again. But as soon as he understood the real state of affairs, that he would never be well enough to go back to work, he seemed to lose the desire to live.

Now, for the first time, he ceased to fight; as he lay in bed reading or writing in one of his notebooks, the words or drawings wavered, the notebooks slipped from his hand.

In October, when the sharp-thrusting hills of the Orange Valley were truly daubed in orange, he sank again. Gloom hung over the mansion in Llewellyn Park. Edison slept, waked a little, and drowsed again. There were several eminent medical men attending him, and he persisted in discussing their method of treatment, inquiring of them what medicines they were trying, how his body was reacting—and why. After blood tests were taken he would insist that the chief physician bring him slides and microscope so that he too might examine them. When the chart was set up before him with its stabilized line, he could read it and follow his progress. After the first week of October, the line turned downward; he could see very clearly how the "campaign" was going.

One who ministered to him asked if "he had thought of a life hereafter."

"It does not matter," he replied in a low voice. "No one knows."

Now his mind became befogged at last, and from time to time he sank into a coma. At the brief intervals when he was conscious he was placed in a chair by one of the tall windows of his bedroom, overlooking a great sweep of lawn and handsome beeches. Could he still see? Mina Edison was the last person he appeared to recognize. She bent over the pale invalid and placed her mouth to his ear. "Are you suffering?" she asked. "No, just waiting," he replied. Once he looked toward the window and the last audible words he uttered were: "It is very beautiful over there."

Newspaper reporters maintained a deathwatch in the vicinity of Glenmont day and night. The room upstairs was kept dark at night, with a nurse sitting beside the patient; if the lights went on—then all the world must be told. In the last hours many of

Edison's laboratory associates waited in the hall downstairs, while Charles Edison would go up the great stairway, then down, to make his report. After his periodic visits to the sickroom, Charles used the same phrase spoken long ago by the watchers at the Menlo Park laboratory in October 1879: "The light still burns."

On October 17 his pulse dropped steeply; in the early morning hours of Sunday the 18th, at 3:24 a.m., the lights of his room went on, and the doctors and nurse came out to announce the end. The electromagnetic telegraph, the telephone, the radio, with all of which his life had been bound up, flashed the news to all the corners of the world.

Some thought was given in high places to the idea of commemorating his passing in some unusual way. The President of the United States, it was proposed, should order all electric current to be turned off for a minute or two, in streets, factories, public places, and homes throughout the nation. But no sooner was the thought uttered than it was realized that such action was unthinkable. Owing to the very nature of Edison's contribution to the technical organization of modern society, his now so vital system of electric power distribution—the blood circulation of the community—would have been arrested; there was risk of incalculable disaster in halting, even for an instant, the great webs of transmission lines, and the whole monster mechanism of power that had grown in a half century out of his discoveries. The idea of a momentary "blackout" was therefore abandoned. Instead the President suggested that lights be dimmed for a few minutes where possible, as in private residences, at 10:00 p.m. of the day of Thomas A. Edison's funeral. Many paid this last tribute, silently, and then the lights were turned on again.

HANS
CHRISTIAN
ANDERSEN

A CONDENSATION OF

HANS CHRISTIAN ANDERSEN

by
RUMER GODDEN

ILLUSTRATED BY
CHARLES RAYMOND

When Hans Christian Andersen went to Copenhagen at the age of fourteen he was a bewildered country boy with ill-fitting clothes, very little money and an absolute belief—which nobody else shared—that someday he would achieve universal fame. What he did not foresee was that acclaim would come as a result of his tales for children, which were written hastily and as diversions from his longer, more ambitious literary works.

Andersen was himself an "ugly duckling" whose life reads much like one of his own enchanting fairy tales—from the heartbreaks and misfortunes of his childhood to the rewards and honors that enriched his later years.

Here is Rumer Godden's affectionate portrait of one of the greatest storytellers of all time who, like "the staunch tin soldier," will be remembered always for his humor, his wisdom and his glowing heart. The designs at the beginning of each chapter are reproduced from his own paper cutouts.

Life itself is the most beautiful fairy tale.
—Hans Christian Andersen: "The Story of My Life"

PROLOGUE

ON THE SIXTH OF DECEMBER, 1867, in the great upper room of the city hall at Odense, the capital of Fyn, middle island of Denmark, a banquet was in process. The guest of honor was an old man, immediately noticeable because of his height, the size of his hands and feet, his curled hair, great forehead, and wise deep-set eyes. He was dressed with elegant care in black, and on his shirtfront were the Swedish Order of the North Star, the Order of the Red Eagle of Prussia; even the Order of Our Lady of Guadalupe from faraway Mexico. He had been made a state councillor, that honorable Danish title, and by his plate lay an affectionate telegram of congratulation from the King.

On his arrival from Copenhagen the day before, he had been met by the bishop and escorted by him to the palace. The town was decorated and all the schools were closed for a public holiday. Now the last toast had been drunk, the last speech had been made, and he was asked to step to the window. It was opened and he leaned out.

The city hall was in the town square with its big cobbled space lined on three sides with old houses; on the fourth side the cathedral of Saint Canute rose high above everything else.

517

That night the whole square was illuminated; candles were burning in every window, lanterns were at the doors; in the center of the square was a great bonfire and round it the guilds came marching with torches and banners; then came all the children of Odense singing "In Denmark I was born," the song the honored guest had written for his country. The young clear voices coming up on the night air sounded like all the children of the world.

They could have been. The children of almost any nation would have known him just the same; and not only children, grown-ups, from the simplest to the most gifted of every land. For this was Hans Christian Andersen, whose stories have become a part of our heritage. His fairy tales, in the hundred-odd years since he wrote them, have sold more copies than any other book in the world, except the Bible and Shakespeare and *Pilgrim's Progress;* there have been over seven hundred editions in more than eighty languages.

Andersen had many happy and triumphant days in his life, but none as happy as that of the illumination of Odense. This was the town where he had been born. He had gone shivering in his poor clothes and wooden shoes across the cobbles of the square, had looked longingly through the windows at the comfort and warmth inside its houses; he had been confirmed, almost as a pauper, in the glittering Saint Canute's; he was almost apprenticed to one of those guilds, the Tailors' Guild, bearing the torches below, and not far away from the window where he stood now honored and cheered was the rough mean room that had been his home in one of the small houses of the poorest streets.

There, almost sixty years ago, an old woman had told his fortune. His father had laughed at her but to his mother she had been an oracle and a comfort, because this big ungainly boy who had such strange ideas was a worry and a puzzle. When anyone tried to think what trade he should follow as he grew up, he always said, quite simply: "I shall be famous," which was, of course, ridiculous.

But the wisewoman had seemed to bear this out. "He will be a wild bird who shall fly high, great and noble in the world."

Then she had said: "One day the whole of Odense will be illuminated for him." His mother had repeated that everywhere and the good people had remembered it.

He stood at the window looking down. The cheers sounded in his ears, the flames from the bonfire and torches leaped in the square; important men pressed round him, his orders shone on his breast, he held the King's telegram in his hand; it seemed a long long way from that little room in the poor street.

CHAPTER I

HANS ANDERSEN'S FATHER and mother were so poor when they began housekeeping that they had to make most of their furniture themselves. The bed had originally been a wooden frame used to hold the coffin of a count; that awed them very much. But on April 2, 1805, on it lay a living crying child, a son, Hans Christian Andersen.

His father was only a boy himself, twenty-two when his son was born. He was a shoemaker, but so full of dreams that he could not do well in everyday life; his shoemaking seems to have been poor. Once he made a pair of shoes as a sample for the lady of one of the great manor houses; he was hoping for the post of cobbler there, which would bring a country cottage, a cow, hens, a garden. A piece of silk was sent to him, but he had to provide the leather himself. All the hopes of the little household were on those shoes; Hans Christian prayed for their success and when they were wrapped in a handkerchief and taken to the manor he waited expectantly for the good news. But his father came back pale and angry; the lady would not even try on the shoes and said he had wasted the silk. "Then I shall waste my leather too," he had said and had taken out his knife and cut the shoes to pieces.

Probably the elder Andersen felt he should not have been making shoes at all. Once Hans Christian saw tears in his eyes. It was when a boy from the grammar school came in to be measured for a pair of boots and boasted about all he was learning. Hans Christian saw his father turn away, his face quivering. "That is the way I should have gone!" he said.

These ambitions came from Hans Christian's grandmother, an old lady with fine ways that did not match the poverty in which she lived. She had a fluent tongue and told endless stories about her aristocratic descent. It was not until he was grown up that Hans Christian knew that they were only stories, but from the very beginning he realized there was a shadow over the family; his grandfather was a lunatic, harmless enough to go wandering about, which meant that everyone saw him.

Perhaps this was why they made no friends, Hans Christian and his father; his mother, Anne Marie, was always neighborly, but then she had not their pride. The young shoemaker was aloof; he gave all his love and time to his little son; sometimes it seemed as if there were not much difference in their ages. He read aloud endlessly to Hans Christian from the *Arabian Nights*, and made him toys and a puppet theater. This ability to amuse children, to make enchanting things for them, was in the family, and Hans Christian too, when he was older, made puppet theaters and cut paper into patterns as fine as lace, with trees, flowers, angels, ballerinas, little men, and swans.

Every Sunday in summer Hans Christian's father would take him to the woods and lie dreaming and brooding on the grass while the little boy played. Once a year, in May, the mother would go too; it was her single pleasure trip of the year. She would put on her only good dress, a cotton gown in which she went to Communion, and carry sandwiches and a pot of beer. In the evening, when it was time to go home, she would gather fresh beech boughs to plant behind the polished stove and Saint-John's-wort to put in the chinks of the beams; they were an omen; if they lived, her family would live too, through the year.

They had only one room and a tiny kitchen, but she made it comfortable and filled it with love. In his autobiography her son wrote: "Our one little room had nearly all the space filled up with the shoemaker's bench, the bed, and the folding crib on which I slept. The walls were covered with pictures and over the workbench was a cupboard containing books and songs; the little kitchen had a row of shining pewter plates, and the small space seemed big and rich to me. The door itself with landscape paintings on the panels was as much to me then as a whole art gallery."

Those paintings are in the story of "Wee Willie Winkie," who brings the children's dreams and squirts sweet milk in their eyes to make them sleepy.

Wee Willie Winkie touched the painting with his magic squirt, and the birds in it at once began to sing. The branches stirred in the trees, and the clouds scudded along; you could see their shadows drifting over the fields.

Willie Winkie took little Hjalmar and lifted him up to the picture-frame, and Hjalmar put his feet into the picture, right into the tall grass; there he stood with the sun shining down on him through the branches of the trees. He ran down to the water and got into a little boat that was lying there. It was painted red and white, and its sails shone like silver. . . .

Yes, it was a wonderful sail they went for. At one moment the woods were quite thick and dark, and then suddenly they were like a beautiful garden with flowers and sunshine, and there appeared great castles of glass and marble with princesses on the balconies who were all little girls that Hjalmar knew well and had played with. They reached out their hands, and each one was holding the nicest sugar-pig any sweetshop could sell.

The small Hans Christian liked to be put to bed, not in his own crib, but at the end of his parents' big four-poster bed. When the bed curtains were drawn they made a little house, but through them he could see the candlelight and firelight and hear his father reading, his mother's admiring or impatient

interruptions, and he lay half asleep, listening, letting the words sink into him while the simple room seemed the safest, happiest place on earth.

Anne Marie kept it scoured and tidy, and she taught her boy how to keep himself neat and clean in a simple economical way that was to serve him well. She dressed him carefully; his father's old suits were cut up for him, a handkerchief was tied round his neck in a bow, and his hair was washed and curled.

Anne Marie had the genuine peasant feeling for life; no matter how poor they were, on festival days she managed to serve the traditional food: rice porridge, a bit of roast goose, and apple cake at Christmas, ham and green kale at Easter.

Sometimes she used to look at Hans Christian and tell him how spoiled he was and how, as a child, she had been sent out to beg. Though she was ashamed and spent the whole day under a bridge crying, she had not dared to go home without having earned a single penny. That must have gone deeply into the little boy's heart; years afterwards he made that child live forever in "The Little Match-Seller."

Much of his childhood went into his fairy tales. From the kitchen, a ladder led up into the attic, and in the gutter between the tiled roofs of their house and the one next door was his mother's only garden, a box in which she grew herbs. In the story of "The Snow Queen" that garden still blooms.

In the great city—where there are so many houses and people that there isn't room for everyone to have a little garden of his own, so most of them have to be content with flowers in flower-pots—there lived two poor children who *did* have a garden a bit larger than a flowerpot. . . . Their parents were next-door neighbours, living in attics; at the point where their roofs were almost touching and the gutter ran along the eaves, each house had a window . . . you had only to step across the gutter to cross from one window to the other.

The parents of the two children each had a big wooden box outside and in this grew potherbs that they used and a little rose tree . . . they looked exactly like two banks of flowers. The sweet pea tendrils hung down, the rose trees put out long branches . . . it was almost a triumphal arch of greenery and flowers.

Hans Andersen grew up with flowers. "I am the most Danish of writers," he was to say, and one of the most characteristic things in Denmark is the national love of flowers. In every house or apartment the windows are filled with plants, lovingly tended; they are almost a part of the family. "You can't trust the opinion of pot plants," says the butterfly in one of Andersen's Tales. "They converse too much with humans." All through the countryside are nursery gardens and hothouses and markets where flowers are plentiful and cheap. Every Sunday, when Hans's grandmother came, she brought flowers with her, and he was allowed to arrange them in a vase to put on the cupboard shelf. It was remarkable how his big hands could do delicate things with great beauty.

His grandmother had charge of the garden of the lunatic asylum and sometimes Hans Christian was allowed to go there with her. But it was not only for the flowers that he went; with curiosity and terror he used to peep into the cells where the worst lunatics were kept. He was forbidden to go near them, but one day as he lay down looking through the crack under a door, he saw a lady lying on a straw bed; her hair hung down and she sang in a queer high voice that sent shivers down his back. All at once she sprang up and threw herself against the door; the little trap through which her food was put came open and she stretched out her arm; the tips of her fingers just touched Hans Christian, who lay screaming, paralyzed with fright.

Perhaps it was this fright that made him dread and fear his lunatic grandfather. The old man was well known in Odense and the country round it; the housewives gave him food, but the boys sometimes chased him and threw stones. Once Hans Christian heard them; he hid, shaking with terror and pity, and felt sick with shame.

Sometimes the boys teased Hans too; they jeered at his puppet theater and his stories, and more and more he came to love solitude. He would stretch his mother's apron across a broomstick and the one gooseberry bush in the yard and sit there making up stories. In spite of the boys he liked to tell these stories—after all it is no good having stories that nobody hears. So sometimes he went to a room near the asylum where poor women came to spin. They petted him and, better still, they listened. The old women said he was too clever to live, which pleased him enormously.

He did not look strong; he was over-tall and thin, long-legged like a young stork, his favorite bird, which he was to resemble all his life. His skin was delicate from staying so much indoors, and his eyes were so small that they seemed to peer at people under his shock of flaxen hair. He had no idea that anyone thought he looked odd, and he drank in the old women's flattery as well as the horrid stories they told him of witches and ghosts, and people who dropped down dead. Anne Marie too was full of macabre peasant superstitions, all of which she did her best to implant in her son.

The Great Comet of 1811 showed in the sky when Hans was six. His mother told him it would knock the earth to bits. Hans Christian shook as he looked at the mighty fireball with its large, shining tail, until his father came out and quietly told him what it was. Anne Marie did not believe it. To her, the things her husband was always saying were appalling. One day he closed the Bible and said: "Christ was only a man like us, but an extraordinary man." Anne Marie was terrified at his blasphemy, Hans Christian expected the roof to fall, but nothing happened and the words stayed with him. He remembered other things his father said too: "The worst devil is in ourselves," and "I am a freethinker." When he thought of them, they seemed to be pushing him on in a way he did not like, but no one can stay under his mother's apron always. The outside world, however big and frightening, has to be faced.

One memorable day Hans Christian was taken to the theater, and from that day the theater began to lure him. When there was no money to go inside, he would beg handbills and, sitting at home over them, imagine whole plays round the titles and lists of characters. From the stories under the gooseberry bush he had progressed to drama.

Then his father decided that his son should go to school; Anne Marie took Hans Christian to the dame school, stipulating that her boy was not to be touched with the rod. The dame taught Hans Christian his letters and to "read right" as it was called, and to spell aloud in as high a key as possible. He liked the lessons and there was a clock that he liked still more; little figures bobbed out when it struck the hours; he used to watch it and forget his spelling; the dame caned him and he took his book and went home.

He was sent next to a school for poor Jewish children. Even though the master was very kind to him he did not find happiness there. At the dame school he had been beaten for the first time but here something happened that hurt far worse. He was clever at drawing and one day he showed a picture of a castle to a little girl; he wanted to impress her as he had impressed the old spinning women, and he said it was a picture of his home and that, really, he was of high rank. When the child did not believe him, instead of stopping he tried to impress her more; he told her that God's angels talked to him. She drew away and said in a low voice to a boy near her: "He is mad like his grandfather." Hans Christian felt sick as he had when he had seen the boys throwing stones. It seemed as if outside his happy cozy homelife everything was hard and chill.

It was the time of the Napoleonic Wars. Napoleon was in everybody's mind and his picture hung even in the Andersens' little room. Hans Christian was always to remember how his father revered the Emperor. The shoemaker talked of signing up and Anne Marie cried. She knew that her delicate uncertain husband was not fit to be a soldier; but in a few days he had enlisted and Hans Christian heard him go away. He could not see the soldiers go because he was sick with measles in the big bed, but he heard the drums beating. Like other boys he had thought drums exciting, but now they were heartless and frightening; they were taking away his father, and his little world had fallen apart.

When, in time, the shoemaker came back, the last spirit had gone out of him. He talked no more of ambitions and hopes and he was so thin that the bones of his face showed. There came a day when Anne Marie sent Hans Christian, not for the doctor, but for the wisewoman. The wisewoman said incantations, tied a woolen thread round Hans Christian's wrist, and handed him a sprig of green that she said came from the tree that gave the wood for the Crucifixion. But on the third day after that the suffering emaciated man died. His corpse lay on the bed behind the calico curtains. Hans Christian and his mother shared the small bed and kept awake. A cricket chirped the whole night through.

"You needn't sing for him, he is dead," Anne Marie said to it. "The ice maiden has fetched him."

Hans Christian knew what she meant. The winter before, when the windowpanes had been frozen, his father had made peepholes with hot pennies. Looking through them they thought they had seen a young girl with outstretched arms. "She has come to fetch me," his father had said and laughed.

Now he was dead, a young man with an old tired face. His last wish for his son might have been an echo of his own wistful, wasted life. "No matter what the boy wants to be," he had told Anne Marie, "even if it is the silliest thing in the world, let him have his way. Let him have his way!"

While his father lived Hans Christian had had someone to whom he could look up. The elder Andersen could assess and criticize his son, but now Hans Christian was quite uncurbed.

His mother said openly that he was the most remarkable boy on earth. She often told of a time when they had gone gleaning on an estate where the overseer was well known for being rude and savage; as they picked up the fallen corn they saw this man coming with a whip in his hand. Anne Marie ran, but Hans Christian lost his wooden shoes and could not run in the stubble. The overseer had come up angrily and lifted his whip when the small boy looked up at him and said: "How dare you hit me when God can see it?" The overseer lowered his whip, patted Hans Christian's cheek and gave him money.

"My Hans Christian is a strange child," said his mother proudly. He certainly looked strange. He wore a long coat and a cap with a broken peak. He was so gawky and awkward that people laughed at him, and his habit of shutting his eyes when he thought made people think he was blind. He was wildly talkative, but there were few who understood that talk, and he was very lonely. His mother went out washing all day, standing up to her knees in the cold river water, and Hans Christian sat at home with his toy theater, made dolls' clothes, and read plays, a strange little solitary figure.

His mother sent him to school again, to the city school for poor boys, but he did not really learn. He could not resist telling stories and the boys often persecuted him. One day the whole class chased him through the streets jeering: "There runs the playwright." It filled him with horror. Was he really like his grandfather as the little girl had said? After that he clung to his few real friends, all grown-up.

Near the school was a house belonging to the widow and the sister of a pastor who had been a poet. Sent there one day on an errand, Hans Christian saw in the house more books than he had ever imagined could be in one home. His wonder and reverence attracted the attention of the two ladies and they invited him in. He was soon a welcome visitor. He came often to listen to their reading and borrow books, to talk and not be laughed at. He heard Shakespeare for the first time and began acting *Hamlet* on his doll stage. Unlike most children he loved people to die in a play, but it was not only the drama that stirred him; even in translation the poetry of Hamlet took hold of him. He was beginning to understand that it was something rare and great and splendid to be a poet. Fired, Hans Christian started writing plays of his own.

He was never shy about reading his work to anyone who had time to hear it. He also loved making lists, and he made a list, in his father's old army paybook, of all the plays he meant one day to write. He wrote poems too, but most of his time was spent in dreaming or reading.

This happy private life had to come to an end; Anne Marie said he must go to work and she apprenticed him to a weaver. His grandmother took him there the first day, and said bitterly that she had not expected to live to see the time when her grandson should mix with ragged boys and coarse men.

At first it was not as bad as she had made Hans Christian fear. The journeymen were not unkind to him; he was an original and amused them. When they found he had a gift for reciting and singing they would stop the looms and let him entertain them. He was happy until one day the journeymen said he must be a girl, his voice was so clear and high. Hans Christian fled home to his mother and refused ever to go there again. She tried him in a tobacco factory, but the jokes were the same and the tobacco dust hurt his chest and made him cough, so she took him away.

Anne Marie had been a widow for two years and she was a full-blooded lively woman. Now she married again and Hans Christian had to see everything his father had loved go to another man. The new husband was a shoemaker too and he worked at the bench Andersen had made, slept in his bed, called Anne Marie wife. Hans Christian had to share his mother's attention with this stranger. The stepfather's family thought the marriage beneath them and would not allow either Anne Marie or her son to come into their homes. It was very bitter that he, Hans Christian, the wonder child, was not thought fit to go into a workman's house! Proudly he said he did not care. He was going to be famous. But he said it almost in a panic.

The stepfather moved the household to a new home where the garden ran down to the river. Hans Christian used to stand there on one of the big stones his mother used for washing, and sing. One of the old washerwomen had told him that China lay under the Odense River, and he imagined how a Chinese prince might hear him and be so enchanted with his voice that he would come up through the river to take him down to wealth and fame on the other side of the world, letting him come back again, of course, to Odense, where he, Hans Christian, would build a great house like the prince's palace in China. It was a palace that came years after into the tale of "The Nightingale."

The Emperor's palace was the finest palace in the world, made entirely of delicate porcelain. . . . The garden was full of the rarest flowers, and the loveliest of these had little silver bells tied to them which tinkled so that no one should go by without noticing them. Yes, everything in the Emperor's garden was most carefully thought out, and it stretched so far that even the gardener had no idea where it ended. If you kept on walking you found yourself in a glorious wood with tall trees and deep lakes. The wood went right down to the sea, which was blue and deep; big ships could sail right in under the branches of the trees.

It was not only for the prince that Hans Christian sang, but for someone more practical. On the other side of the palings lay the garden of one of the town's rich men; Hans Christian knew that this burgher sometimes brought his visitors to listen quietly behind the palings to him, the poor boy. He had a very pleasing voice and soon people began to send for him to come to their houses and sing. Among them was a colonel of the dragoons, Colonel Höegh-Guldberg. The Guldbergs were perceptive learned people and the colonel noticed something in Hans Christian that struck him as more than just amusing and pre-cocious. He decided the boy should have an audience with the prince governor, afterwards King Christian VIII.

This is not as dazzling as it sounds, because in Denmark the royal family is on friendly and easy terms with the people. But for Hans Christian it was dazzling enough. Before the interview Colonel Guldberg told him, if the prince gave him an oppor-tunity, to ask to be sent to the grammar school. This dashed Hans Christian a little. He had come to despise school; Anne Marie boasted so much that her son could learn his lessons by taking one look in his schoolbooks that soon he never looked at them at all. He did not mean to waste this glittering oppor-tunity in talking about school and, standing before the prince in the long room at the palace, he said fearlessly that he should like the prince to help him to be an actor and immediately began to recite. The prince only said sensibly that though Hans Christian's reciting was good, there was no mark of genius and he would far better apprentice himself to a turner, as that was a respectable trade.

No one ever had more good advice than Hans Andersen. All his life people told him so many things for his own good that it is a wonder he managed to exist at all. It was not that he did not feel criticism; he did, inordinately, and he had a terrible way, that he could not prevent, of bursting into tears though they shamed him bitterly. But there was a certainty in him that was stronger than all the advice.

He managed not to cry at the palace but to bow to the prince and get himself out of the room, but he was deeply disap-pointed. What cut him to the heart, though, was that all his friends, Colonel Guldberg, the burghers at whose houses he had sung, even the pastor's widow, thought he should do as the prince said. Some of them told him plainly why; a boy who was so ludicrously lanky, they said, could never act and, even if he were better looking, there was his background of poverty and, they said more gently, of insanity. It was clearly impossible and when Hans Christian would not give in they thought him tiresome and, one by one, they dropped him.

Anne Marie sometimes thought he went out of his way to make trouble for himself. There were two confirmation classes every year in Odense, the dean's class and the chaplain's. A child was supposed to be allowed to choose either, but automatically the rich children, the children of quality, went to the dean, the poor to the chaplain. When the time came for Hans Christian to be confirmed he chose to go to the dean.

"But why the dean?" asked Anne Marie. "They will only look down on you." Hans Christian felt he belonged, by right, with the gentler, educated children, and he was also mortally afraid of the rough, poor boys. He went to the dean but he paid for it. The dean himself was coldly distant with him and found fault with everything he did and said; the other children sneered and made him feel he had pushed himself in where he did not belong; only one little girl looked kindly at him and once she gave him a rose. But it is a sign of the true poet that he would rather have one rose than a bouquet. To Hans Christian this was a very special gift, taking away the soreness and the unkind barbs.

The day of his confirmation arrived. Anne Marie and his grandmother came timidly to the great cathedral to hear their boy make his response. Hans Christian wore a made-over brown suit of his father's, a snowy white shirt, and, for the first time in his life, a pair of boots. His great fear was that everybody would not see them and he pulled them up outside his trousers. The boots creaked and that made him even more proud because he thought everyone in the congregation would hear and notice they were new. Then, with a pang, he realized that at this sacred moment he was thinking more about the boots than about God. He knew that was dreadful and he began to pray frantically, but found he was thinking of the boots again. Those boots are in the story of "The Red Shoes," in which little Karen, who wears them, is exactly as he was then.

> Everybody stared at her feet and, as she walked up the aisle to the chancel, she felt that even the old pictures over the tombs, those portraits of the clergy and their wives ... were fastening their eyes on the red shoes. It was these that filled her thoughts when the priest laid his hand on her head and spoke of holy baptism, of the covenant with God and of her duty now to become a fully fledged Christian ... and the organ played so solemnly and the children sang so beautifully ... but Karen thought of nothing but her red shoes.

The traditional savings bank of Danish children is a fat clay or china pig with a slit in its back. Hans Christian's held all the money he had saved in fourteen years, stray pennies he had been given, money from his singing or that he had earned by running errands. He had never touched it but, when his mother began to talk urgently of his becoming a tailor, he saw that something desperate must be done; he must break his pig open, take his money, and go to Copenhagen.

When the pig-money was counted it was found to be thirteen rigsdaler [the equivalent of about thirty shillings]. To Hans Christian it was wealth and he begged his mother to let him go.

"But what will you do there?" she asked in bewilderment.

He gave his perpetual answer. "I shall be famous."

"But how?" asked Anne Marie.

Hans Christian knew all about it. "First you suffer terrible things," he said, "but then you get to be famous."

He said "famous" so much as if it were the logical outcome that Anne Marie believed him. But there was a general outcry when it became known that she had said yes. The neighbors said it was a dreadful thing to allow so young a boy to go off to a big city where he knew no one. "Tell him to put it out of his head," said the neighbors. But he would not, and he reminded Anne Marie that his father had said: "If it's the silliest thing in the world, let him have his way."

Anne Marie was growing weary; her new husband was lazy

and instead of having someone to work for her she had to keep him as well as herself and Hans Christian. All day she stood washing in the river; the cold of the water was giving her rheumatism and she had begun to take nips of brandy. It was the only thing, she said, that kept out the cold but it cost money. Pathetically, it is probable that this was the first time she had wanted money for herself. She knew she could not afford to keep Hans Christian idle at home and also she did not really believe he would reach Copenhagen. "He won't get far," she said to the neighbors. "When he sees how rough the big sea is, he will come back."

Hans Christian made his plans. That summer some of the actors and singers of the great Royal Theater had come to Odense; they had filled his imagination, and he had heard of the ballet, where a solo dancer, Madame Schall, was the most popular. She had filled Hans Christian's imagination. Now he went to one of his friends, Iversen the printer, and asked him for a letter of introduction to Madame Schall. "But I don't know her!" said Iversen. To Hans Christian that did not matter in the least, and he went on pleading for the letter. The old man earnestly advised him not to go to Copenhagen at all but to learn a trade. "That would be a great sin!" said Hans Christian.

Impressed in spite of himself, Iversen wrote to Madame Schall. "But she won't help you," he said and told Hans Christian to go and see a Professor Rahbek, a director of the Royal Theater. Hans Christian hardly heard, he was so pleased with the precious letter.

His mother packed his clothes in a small bundle. She had made a bargain with the driver of a post carriage who agreed to take Hans Christian to Copenhagen with him for three rigsdaler if the boy would join the coach outside Odense and get down on the outskirts of the capital so that the driver could pocket the money himself.

One afternoon Anne Marie and Hans Christian went to the city gate. He wore his old shabby clothes; they thought his confirmation suit too smart for traveling. But he had on his boots and a hat so much too big for him that it fell down over his eyes. His little store of money was in his pocket; he carried his bundle in his hand, and he had a packet of bread to eat on the way. He was just fourteen years old.

His old grandmother had walked all the way to the gates to see him go. As the coach drew up, she sobbed without being able to say a word. Hans Christian could not speak either. He kissed her and Anne Marie over and over again, then swung himself up and the guard blew the horn. It was a glorious afternoon; the sun, as much as tears, blinded his eyes as he looked back and saw the figures of his mother and grandmother, clinging together and growing smaller and smaller in the distance. Hans Christian never saw his grandmother again; she died in 1822.

CHAPTER II

IT WAS FROM THE HILL of Frederiksberg, where the driver put him off, that Hans Christian first looked down on Copenhagen. In the fine September morning the city looked beautiful and promising with its pale green spires, its towers and buildings rising out of the early mists. Behind them the water of Öresund [the Sound], separating Denmark from Sweden, glinted in the sun.

For two days and nights he had traveled across Denmark's myriad scattered islands and narrow belts of blue sea, its meadows and wild marsh and heathlands. Its low-beamed farmhouses with their courtyards seemed like houses in a fairy tale, as did the manors that were reflected in lakes where swans floated.

When the coach had stopped at the small towns, and the other passengers had gone into inns, Hans Christian had had to stand outside, eating the dry bread Anne Marie had given him. He had not dared to spend any of his money. He did not know why he had not turned back a dozen times. But worst of all had been the ferry ride across the Great Belt, the strait which separates the island of Fyn from the island of Zealand, on which Copenhagen is situated. A small smack left at dusk and sailed all night. As Anne Marie had predicted, Hans Christian was terrified; he had stayed awake, thinking every moment they would go down to the bottom. When they reached Zealand, he felt so tired and forlorn that he knelt down on the dock behind a shed and asked God to help him.

There had been a woman in the coach, a wet nurse returning from Odense to Copenhagen, who had been kind to Hans Christian and had insisted on giving him her address. Now, on this sparkling morning, he could not believe he would need it, and carelessly stuck it in his pocket as, his bundle in his hand, he walked marveling through a great park, along an avenue of linden trees, and finally found himself at the West Gate of Copenhagen.

In those days the city, being walled, was guarded at the gates by soldiers and customs officers, who listed the travelers who came in. King Frederick VI liked to see these lists and it seemed quite fitting to Hans Christian that the King should know of his arrival. It was part of this glorious day, the day he first trod the streets of Copenhagen. They were cobbled like those of Odense but were far wider and some of the houses were six stories high, which seemed immensely tall after the one or two stories at home. The visitor to Copenhagen, now as then, is struck by the number of book shops and flower shops; there are few policemen in the streets, royalty can walk there without being stared at as if they were animals in the zoo. Tivoli, the big amusement park, is gay with the gaiety that springs from the people. This sense of fun is as fresh as the wind that blows over the islands. The people seem proud and happy to be Danes.

At first Hans Christian was so awed that he could only wander about and stare, and it was some time before he remembered that he had to find food and shelter. He found an inn just inside the gate, arranged to leave his bundle there and come back that night to a cheap garret room, and went out into the streets again.

They seemed unaccountably swarming and noisy even for a city. There were catcalls and screams, the smash of broken glass; then soldiers on horseback came charging through the crowd. He was in the middle of an anti-Jewish riot. Only one thing kept Hans Christian from running back to the inn: his burning desire to find the Royal Theater.

In Copenhagen, at that time, the theater was the center of Danish cultural life and fashion. It gave impetus to the arts of the whole country; the best of her writers, composers, painters, actors, singers, and dancers were drawn there. But to Hans Christian it was even more; he went there as a pilgrim to a shrine. When he found it, he walked round it, looking lovingly at the walls and praying fervently that this would be the place where God would let him be an actor.

The next day Hans Christian dressed carefully in his confirmation suit and the hat that came down over his eyes. He said a prayer, took the letter Iversen had written to Madame Schall, and set out to find the address. At last he found the right door, but before he pulled the bell-rope, he knelt down and prayed again that she would help him.

Madame Schall, having been in the theater till midnight, got up very late and Hans Christian, in his eagerness, had come very early; so that he had to wait for what seemed hours on the landing, in a horrible tension of apprehension and hope. When he was finally shown into the drawing room Madame Schall was resting on the sofa, and he felt awkward towering above her. The fashionable room had a Regency elegance; gilt chairs with spindle legs and satin seats, console tables and mirrors of the period. It must have looked disconcertingly fragile and glittering to the clumsy country boy. He stood in front of Madame Schall, trembling and blushing.

She was staring at him as if he were a monstrosity. Then he picked up his courage and began to tell her his hopes and schemes. He finished by telling her how his plan of coming to

Copenhagen to be an actor depended on her. Would she please help him?

She asked in a bewildered voice what parts he thought he could play. "Anything," said Hans Christian promptly. "I can show you. I shall play you a part from *Cinderella*. May I take off my boots?" he said seriously. "I am not light enough for the character with them on."

While she watched, helpless and a little frightened, he shook off his boots and, taking off his hat, which he used as a tambourine, began to dance and sing. He had seen the play when the Royal Theater Players gave it at Odense and he thought it would compliment Madame Schall if he danced the heroine's part, which he did with wild gestures and great leaps that shook the room.

There was no applause. Madame Schall stopped him and told him sternly to get dressed at once and go away. Tears rolled down his cheeks as he put on his boots and Madame Schall saw them and seemed sorry. She told him more gently that sometimes he could come and eat dinner at her house, a thing many Danish householders allowed poor students to do. Hans Christian wanted so much more than dinners that he turned away.

Outside he sat down on the stairs trying to think what to do. Old Mr. Iversen, he remembered, had advised him to see Professor Rahbek at the theater. Hope rose again as Hans Christian decided he had better do that.

Rahbek received Hans Christian in his office; but he told him shortly that it was the chief director who decided on the parts and admitted the students, and it was too late that day for an interview. Then he, too, told him to go. Hans Christian was dignified enough to hold back his tears in front of Rahbek, but alone in his garret at the inn he cried hopelessly.

In the morning his interview with the chief director was very short. The great man said coldly: "You are much too thin for the stage."

"If you will take me and give me a hundred-rigsdaler salary, I shall soon grow fat," Hans Christian said with new courage.

The chief director was not used to being answered back.

"You would be ridiculous on the stage," he said cuttingly, and added: "The theater accepts only educated young persons."

Hans Christian, his cheeks burning, asked desperately if he might join the Royal Ballet. The chief director must have thought him mad, and said even more coldly that the ballet accepted pupils only in May. Then the director rang the bell and Hans Christian was shown to the front door.

It was a frightened and miserable boy who found himself outside in the square. He took out his money; there were only a few coins left. It seemed no one wanted to help him. His confidence was gone. He stood alone in the September wind, a terrified forlorn child.

Among the coins was the address of the kind nurse in the coach. He asked his way to her house, and when she opened the door he told the whole story and asked her advice. "Take the first ship back to Odense," she said. "That is the only sensible thing to do." Everyone, it appeared, was sensible except Hans Christian. "I would rather die," he said.

He left her and wandered back to the theater square. Go back to Odense! He could hear the jeers and laughter: "There runs the playwright! He is mad like his grandfather." But what was he to do? What he did only someone with his spirit could have done. He put apart the money for his inn bill, gathered the remaining coins in his hand and went to the theater and bought a ticket.

The play was *Paul and Virginia*, and when the curtain went up, completely forgetting everything that had happened, he lived every moment of the story. When the lovers parted he burst into such violent crying that all the audience in the poor people's section turned to look at him. Some women tried to console him, saying it was only a play, and others began to share their food with him. Hans Christian, who always told everyone everything, told them that he was weeping because he was a Paul and the theater was his Virginia and he was separated from it forever. They thought it very touching and stuffed him with fruit and cake. Soon he began to feel surprisingly better.

But when he paid his bill at the inn the next morning he had only one rigsdaler left. He decided to swallow his pride and find work with a tradesman; perhaps to be an apprentice in Copenhagen was different from Odense. The nurse gave him a bed for the moment and she helped him to apprentice himself to a carpenter; but when the other apprentices and the journeymen began to make lewd jokes he decided he could not stay.

He felt he could not now go back to the nurse, and he aimlessly roamed the Copenhagen streets. Perhaps he walked down to look at the beautiful harbor with its ships and quays, then past the customshouses to the Langelinie, the waterfront promenade, where, aloof on a rock, the statue of his Little Mermaid now looks out to sea. He must have wandered back towards the theater, and down the Nyhavn, the canal where the sailors' shops and eating houses are. Perhaps he walked round by the fish market, where, in the early morning, fishwives in green serge skirts and white coif caps still sit selling fish and skinning eels. Perhaps he turned away to the fragrance and color of the flower market in the little Höjbro Square. There was the Stock Exchange with its twisted copper spire, and the sailors' church, Holmens Kirke. Behind them now is the Royal Library, where his manuscripts are kept as treasures.

Perhaps he dreamed a little as he walked, but his feet must have been sore, his bundle heavy. It would soon be evening, and he was homeless and hopeless.

It was then that he thought of his voice. Everybody had always praised his singing and he had heard that an Italian named Siboni was the director of the theater music school. Perhaps Siboni would help him? He gathered up his courage for a new try.

Hans Christian was in luck. Siboni was giving a dinner party; Professor Weyse the composer was there, Baggesen the poet, and other celebrated men. The housekeeper answered the door. She was about to tell Hans Christian to go away when, as with Madame Schall and the nurse, he poured out everything that had happened, how he had suffered, and his wish now to be a singer. The housekeeper forgot the dinner while she listened, and when at last she heard Siboni's impatient ringing, she told Hans Christian to stay where he was. Then she whisked into the dining room and repeated the whole story so well that Siboni had the boy brought in. His white face and shabby clothes made their own impression. Then Siboni told him to sing and Hans Christian lifted up his voice while they listened attentively, their wineglasses still. Then suddenly remembering where he was and why, Hans Christian burst into tears.

The men had dined well and they were perhaps easily touched but they were nearly all artists and there was a spark in this odd boy that they recognized. Siboni promised to take him as a pupil. The poet Baggesen was quite sincere when he said: "One day something will come of him"; but added gravely to the shabby, tear-stained, overgrown child: "Don't get vain when the public applauds you."

When the housekeeper let Hans Christian out that night, he was almost delirious with joy and hope. He begged her to tell him if Siboni meant what he had said; he told her he needed a salary, as he had only about seven pennies left. Kind and motherly, she advised him to see Professor Weyse in the morning.

When Hans Christian presented himself at the professor's lodgings he found that that understanding man, who had once been poor himself, had worked on the diners' emotions to take up a collection. He had over seventy rigsdaler for Hans Christian and Siboni's firm promise that the master would teach him singing and give him dinner every day at his house. "Get yourself a quiet decent lodging," said Weyse, "and every month I will give you ten rigsdaler."

On the composer's stairs Hans Christian kissed his own hand and lifted it up in gratitude to God. He was half mad with joy and relief but he was not surprised; in the end, the hero always was triumphant. When he reached the nurse's house, to which he felt now he could go back, he wrote his first letter to his mother.

Anne Marie showed Hans Christian's letter to everyone she knew in Odense. "You see!" she said. "He hasn't been there one week and his future is made!"

SIBONI WAS AN inspired teacher and he was generous; but the winter was cold and cruel. The boy had only one pair of boots and when they wore out he was walking literally in ice and slush. He caught a bad cold and his voice broke. Gently Siboni told him to face facts. He would never make a singer; he should go back to Odense and learn a trade.

Odense. A trade. Everyone said that to him. But to himself he was still a hero. He remembered that Colonel Guldberg, who had been kind to him in Odense, had a brother in Copenhagen, and that he was a professor and a poet. A poet! Hans Christian promptly wrote to Professor Frederik Guldberg and was told to come and see him.

Although Hans Christian for many years was poor in money, he was rich in friends; it was as if he touched people with some sort of magic. The busy overworked Professor Guldberg offered him lessons in Latin, German, and Danish, as it was clear from the letter that Hans Christian could not even write his own language. The boy accepted gratefully. He also went to see Dahlén, a dancer who had a school that had connections with the theater, and begged him for a place.

Dahlén began by being amused—Hans Christian showing his steps was like a ladder dancing—but he ended by being impressed; Dahlén saw that the boy's face had the peaked old look of beggar children; the broken boots with paper in the soles and the tight old coat told their story. Touched by Hans Christian's honesty and passion, Dahlén let him in.

There was no salary for student dancers and, while Hans Christian trained, he had to live. Guldberg got up a subscription for which the boy wrote the appeal himself. It read: "My need for a time compels me to lay my fate in the hands of noble friends of mankind since I feel most deeply attached to the art of acting and born only for the service of Thalia. . . . I hope I may stay in the ballet until I become an actor . . . I . . . ask for the gift of a little sum each month until I can support myself. I shall work hard to make the time as short as possible."

People responded. Professor Weyse contributed, which made Hans Christian happy as it showed that important men believed in him. But when Siboni's two maids came and offered part of their wages, Hans Christian felt not only happy but humbled; he was responsible to them all.

While he worked with Siboni, Hans Christian had been living

in an old crooked house in a disreputable part of the city. There were women at every window and visitors at odd hours. At first some of the women called out to him and made him blush but soon they grew used to him and let him alone. Hans Christian had been sleeping in a disused larder off a kitchen. It was not much bigger than a cupboard, and it had no window.

When the landlady heard of his new riches—and probably Hans Christian ingenuously told her about them himself—she was avid to keep him. Hans Christian stammered that he had hoped and dreamed of a better room. "It's true it is small," said the landlady, "but I shall give you board and let you sit in the kitchen, and here you are safe," and she began to tell him lurid things about the cheating Copenhagen landladies. Soon she had frightened him so much that he begged her to let him stay. She seized her opportunity and said that she could not take him for less than twenty rigsdaler a month. Hans Christian implored her to take him for sixteen, but she said that unless she had twenty rigsdaler in advance, out he could go to be fleeced and robbed, and she left the room.

Hans Christian could not keep back his sobs when he was left alone. But after a time the woman came back and said she would take sixteen rigsdaler. Perhaps she had been thinking it over and realized, wisely, there was not much money to be squeezed from the boy.

Hans Christian knelt down and kissed her hand and for a long time he thought of her as a benefactor. With all the low and dreadful people he met, with all the misery in which he lived, he kept a childlike faith, not only in life itself but in people. He was like his own little Match-Seller, left outside in the dark frozen street, who struck her match and, in the flame, saw another life, lit up, gracious, lovely, in the squalor of her own.

Ah, but a little match—that would be a comfort. If only she dared pull one out of the bunch, just one, strike it on the wall and warm her fingers! She pulled one out—ritch!—how it spurted and blazed! Such a clear warm flame, like a little candle, as she put her hand round it—yes, and what a curious light it was! The little girl fancied she was sitting in front of a big iron stove ... with such a warm friendly fire burning ... why, whatever

was that? She was just stretching out her toes, so as to warm them too, when—out went the flame, and the stove vanished. There she sat with a little stub of burnt-out match in her hand.

She struck another one. It burned up so brightly, and where the gleam fell on the wall this became transparent like gauze. She could see right into the room, where the table was laid with a glittering white cloth and with delicate china; and there, steaming deliciously, was the roast goose stuffed with prunes and apples. Then, what was even finer, the goose jumped off the dish and waddled along the floor with the carving knife and fork in its back. Right up to the poor little girl it came . . . but then the match went out. . . .

. . . In the cold early morning huddled between the two houses, sat the little girl . . . frozen to death on the last night of the old year.

It was his own glowing imagination that protected Hans Christian and brought him unharmed to his glory, as it brought the sad little Match-Seller to hers. "She was trying to get warm," the people said when they saw the used-up matches, but Andersen added: "Nobody knew what lovely things she had seen and in what glory she had gone. . . ."

He had need of all his matches in the months that followed. His landlady entertained men in the kitchen where she had told him he could sit. Often Hans Christian felt impelled to go to bed at six. He did not mind; he had a candle, a tray of supper, a book; and he had made another doll theater for which, with pennies the landlady gave him for running errands, he bought little dolls and dressed them in scraps of velvet and silk he begged from the milliners' shops.

He had no money for clothes and shoes; Professor Guldberg allowed him ten rigsdaler each month and Weyse helped with more, but still it was not enough. From one person to another Hans Christian was forced to go, holding out his hand. He was always matter-of-fact about his begging; he took what he needed and no more and, though he knew all the sordid small bitternesses of poverty, he never learned to be avaricious. "A poet should not gorge," he wrote in later life, but added: "And he should not starve!"

Hans Christian's appetite for reading was as strong as ever, and he took many books from the university library. Then he found the novels of Sir Walter Scott, and a new land, Scotland, seemed to become a part of him. In real life the world seemed slowly opening up to him too. Professor Guldberg persuaded an old actor to coach Hans Christian in drama. The pupil took his lessons very seriously, but his teacher said: "Feeling you certainly have, but you can never be an actor. What you will be, God knows."

Everyone unfortunately said the same thing. Copenhagen was then a little city and Hans Christian had already become known. Through one of her ladies-in-waiting, he met the crown princess. She suggested he appeal for a grant to the King, who attended personally to the petitions of even his humblest subjects. The petition was written, but the King asked the directors of the theater for a report; it was a bad one. Hans Christian Andersen, it said, had a most unfortunate appearance, and his singing, acting, and dancing were hopeless. The petition was dismissed.

But he got onto the stage in the ballet school. One night he was told that all the students were to be allowed to go on with the chorus, even he. This was the first time he really worried about his clothes. The confirmation coat was in holes; he could not straighten himself to his full height because his waistcoat was too short and left a gap between it and his trousers. Hans Christian could not let these difficulties prevent his going on-stage, but he kept well to the back, hoping to escape notice. Suddenly one of the singers, who was known as a wit, seized him by the hand and dragged him forward into the bright lights. "Allow me to present you to the Danish public," he cried. Hans Christian ran off the stage with tears running down his cheeks.

Then the good-hearted Dahlén gave him a tiny part in a ballet he had written; it was only as a troll in a group of trolls but at last he saw his name in print: TROLL—ANDERSEN! He carried the ballet program round with him and lay in bed and read his name by candlelight, his name in print!

Though his life was extremely uncomfortable, Hans Christian

had moments, in those days, of great happiness, even exhilaration. He was young, he was in Copenhagen, he was on his way! One day he walked through the park round the palace; it was two years since he had been into the open country, and the spring morning, the budding beech trees, and the streams filled him with exuberant joy. He began to sing and threw his arms round a tree and kissed it. "Are you mad?" a rough voice asked. It was one of the King's grooms, and Hans Christian was so startled that he ran away, but nothing could take away the ecstasy of that morning.

When Dahlén had regretfully to put him out of the ballet school, he went to see the master of the singing school and succeeded in getting a place in the choir. Soon he had more than one part though even he could see they were not brilliantly successful.

His talent for making exalted friends, however, always helped him. He had attracted the attention of Örsted, the gentle brilliant scientist who was to become one of his best friends. He had also come to know the Rahbeks, who led the Danish literary world. Mrs. Rahbek listened sympathetically to Hans Christian's verses and stories, which he had begun to write down and never tired of reading aloud. One day she gave him some flowers to take to a woman friend and said gracefully: "It will please her to get a bouquet from a poet's hand."

Hans Christian felt as if he were on fire. It was the first time anyone had called him a poet. Suddenly he saw what he must do: he must write his way to fame.

HE BEGAN NOW to write plays with feverish haste and proudly brought one to read to Mrs. Rahbek.

"But you have put in whole passages from two of the best-known Danish poets!" she protested.

"Yes, they are so beautiful," said Hans Christian complacently and went on reading.

Hans Christian was only sixteen. Writing intoxicated him and he began to skip his lessons and gave himself up to poetry and the theater. Who would not rather be praised by admiring ladies in drawing rooms and spend evenings in the theater than work in a little room at Latin grammar? As one of the Royal Theater chorus Hans Christian had a free seat in the pit and the temptation was irresistible; soon he was there every evening.

It was a strange, hectic, uncertain life he led in those days and he had to make desperate shifts to cover its discrepancies. Once, on a hot summer day, he went, in a blue coat someone had given him, to see some friends. It was much too big, especially across the chest; even when he buttoned it up to his chin there was still a great bag across the front. He filled it up with old theater programs, which made him look as if he had an enormous bosom; naïvely he thought no one would notice. He went jauntily into the drawing room but soon everyone was asking him what was the matter with his chest; why didn't he open his coat on such a hot day?

He had always seemed odd because of his quaint mannerisms, but he now had to make extraordinary contortions to hide a sleeve that had split, or to cover up one cracked shoe with the other foot, or to pull down cuffs that had ridden far up his bony wrists.

He had a superstition that what he did on New Year's Day he would do the whole year round; probably it was one of Anne Marie's omens. The theater of course was closed that night, but Hans Christian found his way down the corridors, up dusty steps, past stacked scenery, onto the stage. It was eerie as only an empty stage can be; he thought of ghosts, all the people who had been there, forgotten actors, singers silent now, who had once had hearts beating like his; he thought they were watching him from the wings. His skin pricked with terror, but he had come to act and he took an attitude. Not a single line could he remember, and he finally fell on his knees and said the Lord's Prayer aloud. He went out convinced that he would that year speak on the stage. Drama was what he ought to study. Never mind what people said.

Then Professor Guldberg began to resent the fact that Hans Christian was missing his lessons; he also suspected his pupil was not studying as he should. The professor had had more belief in Hans Christian than anyone else; he had gone out of his way to help him, and on his behalf had badgered other people. He was disappointed and angry at this ingratitude. Hans Christian begged to be forgiven, but the professor would not relent. "I have done with you," he said finally, and pushed Hans Christian out the door and shut it.

Every night Hans Christian had asked God: "Will it be better with me soon?" but he did not seem to be walking in God's way; now by his own fault he had lost his dearest patron.

In three months the funds subscribed for him were gone. His work in the chorus was meagerly paid and how he got through the winter of 1822 he never knew. At midday, he would go out and sit on a bench in the park, perhaps eating a piece of bread he had saved, getting up now and then to stamp his frozen feet, sitting again almost at once because he was so weak. But though he often went without food all day, he tried to hide his pitiable condition and he still persisted. He even wrote a play, *The Robbers of Vissenberg*, based on a folk tale and, trembling with hope, he submitted it under the pseudonym of William Christian Walter to the directors of the Royal Theater. William stood for Shakespeare, Christian for himself, and Walter for Sir Walter Scott. It was not vanity, he later explained. It was love; he loved Shakespeare and Scott and, naturally, he loved himself.

The play came back with a letter which read:

16 June, 1822.

To the author of the play:

Returning *The Robbers of Vissenberg,* as completely unsuitable for the stage, the directors wish the author to know that with the total absence of elementary culture and knowledge which this play shows on every page, it would be impossible for even the highest talents to produce it to a cultured public. They would be most content if this hint might induce the young man to seek the instruction without which the career he is so eager to adopt forever must and will be closed to him.

Holstein. Rahbek. Olsen. Collin.

At first Hans Christian was too wounded to take in the letter's meaning; then slowly it linked with other things in his mind: Colonel Guldberg in Odense telling him to ask to be sent to school, the chief director with his "the theater accepts only educated young persons," Professor Guldberg and his Danish lessons. Hans Christian saw closing down on him the thing he had shirked for so long: study.

But how? By what means? *With* what means? As if to put him deeper into despair, he was dismissed from the chorus.

Hans Andersen was often asked how he found the courage to go on. He might have said because he had no other choice. Now out of his hunger and despair he wrote another tragedy: *Alfsol* [The Elves' Sun].

It was hastily written. How hastily can be seen by a story that Captain Wulff, a naval officer who was an eminent translator of Shakespeare, often told of Hans Christian appearing like an apparition in his doorway and saying: "You have translated Shakespeare. I too have written a tragedy. Shall I read it?" Without waiting for an answer he opened a manuscript and started to read. Wulff was as much amused as angry; and at the end, asked the boy to come again. "I will, when I have written a new tragedy," said Hans Christian. Wulff remarked that that would take some time. "I think that in a fortnight I shall have another one ready," said Hans Christian.

Alfsol showed something more clearly than his earlier writings; something that could only be called quality. It was clumsy, but it was alive and, as he read it aloud to anyone who would listen, a few people were genuinely impressed. Already one of Hans Christian's friends had persuaded a newspaper to publish a short scene from *The Robbers of Vissenberg*, and when he saw himself in print as an author, it was even more heady than the theater program. He lay awake all night, staring at the printed piece, his heart beating. He decided to collect his works, under his chosen pen name.

Through another friend *Alfsol* was submitted to the directors of the theater. At the same time Hans Christian was told to go and see the most powerful of all the directors, State Councillor Jonas Collin. So Hans Christian furbished up his old clothes and went humbly to the house that was, more than any other, to become a home to him.

Jonas Collin, in his portrait, looks a calm, solid man with a high forehead, penetrating eyes, and a mouth that seems extraordinarily resolute and decisive, though not unkind. He did not seem amused as some others had been by Hans Christian's clothes; his comments were dry and he hardly spoke of *Alfsol*. Other people had appreciated it so much that Hans Christian had expected at least a little praise. He left feeling that there was no sympathy for him here; but a few days later he was called to see the directors of the theater.

What he expected Hans Christian would not have liked to have said; but in his inmost heart he thought it was possible, just possible, that *Alfsol* was to be produced. Why else had the directors sent for him? Perhaps he was to be attached to the theater as some few favored playwrights were. With dry lips and beating heart, he waited as Rahbek began to speak.

Alfsol was given back to him at once. The play, Rahbek said gently, was impossible for the stage. Quivering with disappointment, Hans Christian braced himself to hear what he knew was coming; he was about to be told, sternly, to go back to Odense and learn a trade. But what was this that Rahbek was saying?

The play showed a little real promise, Rahbek was telling Hans Christian, such promise that if he were prepared to study with his whole heart he might someday write something worthy of being acted on the Danish stage. The room was very still as those words were spoken; their grave import seemed to stir Hans Christian as nothing had before, and in that moment he had a glimpse of what it could mean to be a writer.

In a letter to the other directors Rahbek had written:

> 3 September, 1822.
> Andersen's *Alfsol* . . . is a collection of words and tirades without dramatic action, without plan, without characters, full of Icelandic and New German all mixed up, everyday phrases in everyday rhymes. . . .
> On the other hand, if it is taken into consideration that this play is a product of a person who is hardly able to write coherently . . . one cannot help wishing that a test be made of what this peculiar head might become by instruction. . . .

Rahbek went on briskly. The directors had decided to send Hans Christian to school.

School! After his inflated dream, his great vision, this reality was like a slap in the face. Hans Christian stared at Rahbek, dumb with astonishment. School! But he was a playwright and grown up; he was seventeen. School meant children, exercise books, classrooms. He felt offended; after all, he had lived on his own in this big city for almost three years, had been welcomed and asked to read his verses in Copenhagen drawing rooms. Then he saw, in a flash of insight, that all this was beside the point; what were important were those phrases that had burned themselves into his heart: "The theater accepts only educated young persons." "With the lack of elementary culture and education it would be impossible for even the highest talents to produce . . ." This was not unkindness, it was truth, and he looked with a new gratitude at the directors. These eminent men were donating money for him. And what were they asking of him? Very much. He would have to shed his little acquired privileges, his conceit, and go back to the beginning again. Half dazed, he managed to accept.

He was told to go and see Jonas Collin in a few days. A moment later he was outside in the square. Where, Hans Christian might very well wonder, was life taking him now?

CHAPTER III

IN THE DAYS THAT FOLLOWED, an extraordinary feeling of peace and relief came to Hans Christian. Slowly, he began to understand that he would for some years have enough to eat, that he would be given books, clothes that fitted him, shoes that kept water out, even that strange thing he had never had, pocket money. All this Collin made plain to him. The King had been pleased to grant him an allowance from public funds; Collin would send him more money, and he would get free instruction at the grammar school at the town of Slagelse. "Slagelse!" said Hans Christian and his face fell, but it seemed ungrateful to be disappointed.

Collin took Hans Christian home to dinner, where Mrs. Collin gave him a real welcome. The Collin children let few people into their circle, but this strange boy, whom their father had in a way adopted, they took in like a brother. And in Collin Hans Christian felt he had found another father. "Don't be afraid to write to me," said Collin. "Tell me anything you need and how you get on."

It was a heartened and hopeful Hans Christian who left Copenhagen by the stagecoach for school at Slagelse. The sleepy little backwater was smaller than Odense; even its main street was cobbled and its few red-roofed houses were set in rolling green fields and muddy lanes. It seemed very dull to the boy and he badly missed the beauty and excitement of Copenhagen. All the same, the room he found in Slagelse was clean and fresh and he could look out onto a garden and fields.

He had persuaded himself that it might be romantic to go to school and had written triumphantly to his mother and wished his father and grandmother were alive to hear this news which would have pleased them more than anything else. But soon he began to see what he had undertaken. There was nothing even remotely romantic about Slagelse Grammar School. It was humdrum and he was not used to sitting on a bench or working steadily or doing what he was told.

There was another thing that Hans Christian and perhaps the Royal Theater directors had not thought of. As he knew almost nothing, he would have to be placed in the second lowest class among the little boys. They hardly reached to his elbow and here he was, stumbling and stammering over easy words and sums that they could solve in a twinkling. He was too big for the benches and tables, and his awkwardness, his big head with its thatch of hair, the little eyes blinking behind the big nose, made him a perfect target for teasing. Yet they did not tease him as much as they might have done; there was something about him that made them desist—perhaps it was his palpable goodness and earnestness. Hans Christian never suffered as much from the boys as from the teachers.

After the first few weeks they found him, quite simply, exasperating. Overworked and badly paid, they resented this youth who was financed by a state grant; to them he had nothing to distinguish him but size and ignorance.

"I had a great desire to learn," he later wrote, "but for the moment I floundered about as if I had been thrown into the sea; one wave followed another; grammar, geography, mathematics." Hans Christian studied long after school hours were over; when he was stupid with sleep, he would wash his head with cold water or run about the little school garden to wake himself up. He worked desperately, fervently, and at the end of the first term his marks were not too bad.

Timidly he sent them to Professor Guldberg, to show he was really working now, and Guldberg wrote back a letter full of kindliness. "But as your friend," the professor added, "I tell you, don't write verses. Study."

That prohibition was echoed by the head of the school, Rector Simon Meisling, but not as gently. He was a thickset, dirty little man with red hair and a fat choleric face. He had the brain of a scholar and the tastes of a bull. Hans Christian had innocently gone to call on him and his big, rather blowsy wife; as usual, he had told them his hopes, his secret schemes, and read them poems and scenes from his plays. He very soon learned how silly he had been. Easy Mrs. Meisling had been impressed with him and soon became embarrassingly kind, but the rector, who had looked at him coldly as he read, began to make sarcastic gibes.

The whole school was afraid of Meisling, and now Hans Christian became his butt. "Shakespeare with the vampire eyes!" he would call him, and if, in spite of struggles, the fatal tears came, Meisling would send a boy to fetch a brick so that the great poet Andersen could wipe his eyes on it and make even a brick poetical. It sounds a stupid humor, but thundered in front of a room full of boys it was humiliating.

Hans Christian could not account for the rector's dislike, for never in his life had he felt jealousy. Meisling had cause to be jealous. Sponsored by the directors of the Royal Theater, Hans Christian was asked to such homes as that of Bernard Ingemann the poet, who was teaching at Sorö, not far away. Ingemann, though known throughout Denmark, was so charming and modest that he treated this over-big schoolboy as a serious fellow poet.

Meisling would himself have liked to know Ingemann. There were other people whom Mrs. Meisling would dearly have liked to know, but she had made herself so notorious in Slagelse by her brazen behavior that there were few houses to which she was asked. When she saw this charity boy welcomed, she complained to her husband, who told Hans Christian that if he went to those houses he would be expelled, but the rector did not dare stop him from going to Ingemann's. Worst of all, when at the end of the first year they all went to Copenhagen for the Christmas holidays, Meisling saw his pupil disappear into houses like Collin's, Rahbek's, Captain Wulff's—men whom the shabby burdened schoolmaster would never know.

Hans Christian had no idea of this; to him the rector was nearly as powerful as God. He quaked when Meisling came into class, and when it was Hans Christian's turn to recite, the little boys felt the whole bench shake; no matter how well he knew the lesson, and he always did know it, he could never say it in front of Meisling, who would then bellow at him and say he was a hopeless fool. Hans Christian grew so nervous that on a Christmas visit to Copenhagen he hardly dared to take his marks to Collin. They will think I am wasting the money, he had thought in misery. To his amazement, Collin was pleased. "You have shown industry and courage," he said and asked Hans Christian to dinner at his house, where once again the boy met the Collin children: Ingeborg, Gottlieb, Edvard, Louise, and Theodor.

Yes, there were gleams of happiness in spite of school. This visit to the capital was entirely happy, and in the spring the crown princess sent him the money for a visit to Odense. Coming back to those well-known streets, the one-storied timbered houses, the neighbors who struck him as unbelievably ragged and poor, he was able to measure how much he had accomplished in four years. He was well dressed, with money in his pocket, and his own mother meeting him in the street, did not know him at first; when the tall stranger spoke to her she wanted to curtsy.

Now people were saying that the shoemaker's son was not as mad as he seemed; they pointed him out, boasting they had known him as a child. Anne Marie said he was being honored as if he were the child of a count.

But the little triumph made the humiliations of school, when he went back, all the sharper. The chief use Meisling seemed to find for him now was as a nursemaid for his children. Hans Andersen, oddly enough, was never indiscriminately fond of children, and the little Meislings could not have been attractive. He must have wondered if this was what he was sent to Slagelse to do: separating noisy little quarrelers, amusing the older boys and girls, rocking the baby to sleep. Still, he would have done anything to appease the rector.

How much this man preyed on his mind is shown by reading his diary: "The rector said 'Good night' to me; oh, if only he knew how his friendliness encourages me. . . ."

But he could not even please the teachers; they had a pattern boy in their minds and anyone who did not fit it was wrong. They nagged and humiliated Hans Christian. Years afterwards in "The Ugly Duckling" he wrote a scene that might belong to those teachers; it is where the duckling is instructed by a hen and a cat.

They always used to say "We and the world" because they fancied that they made up half the world—what's more, much the superior half of it. The duckling thought there might be two opinions about that, but the hen wouldn't hear of it.

"Can you lay eggs?" she asked.

"No."

"Well, then, hold your tongue, will you!"

And the cat asked: "Can you arch your back or purr or give out sparks?"

"No."

"Well, then, your opinion's not wanted, when sensible people are talking."

And the duckling sat in the corner, quite out of spirits. Then suddenly he remembered the fresh air and the sunshine, and he got such a curious longing to swim in the water that—he couldn't help it—he had to tell the hen.

"What's the matter with you?" she asked. "You haven't anything to do—that's why you get these fancies. They'd soon go if only you'd lay eggs or else purr."

"But it's so lovely to swim in the water," said the duckling; "so lovely to duck your head in it and dive down to the bottom."

"Most enjoyable, I'm sure," said the hen. "You must have gone crazy. Ask the cat about it—I've never met anyone as clever as he is—ask him if he's fond of swimming or diving! I say nothing for myself. . . ."

"You don't understand me," said the duckling.

"Well, if we don't understand you, I should like to know who would. . . . You may take my word for it—if I say unpleasant things to you, it's all for your good; that's just how you can tell which are your real friends. Only see that you lay eggs and learn how to purr and give out sparks!"

"I think I'll go out into the wide world," said the duckling.

But Hans Christian could not go out into the wide world. He had to stay in the classroom at Slagelse. Examination time was coming and he was full of dread; he gave himself headaches and put himself into cold sweats, but he did well, was put up to the third class, and Meisling wrote a surprisingly good report to Collin. The crown princess sent money again and, in his second Christmas holidays, Hans Christian was able to pay another longed-for visit to Copenhagen, though Meisling said he could only be spared for a week.

When Hans Christian was happy he soared to dangerous heights, dangerous because in his naïveté he boasted of what he meant to do. He was up among the stars. He was away from the rector for a whole eight days, he was often at the Collins' house, the Rahbeks', the Wulffs'; he read and dreamed poetry and went to his beloved theater. Sooner than miss the performance the last Saturday, he let the mail coach go without him and walked all through the night and the next day to Slagelse to be in time to play with the rector's children as appointed on Monday morning.

Then as the New Year opened, the rector told him to come and live in his house. Hans Christian was now nearly twenty; Mrs. Meisling had found out how useful he was, and why, she asked her husband, should a landlady have that two hundred rigsdaler? She had another reason too.

Mrs. Meisling had always teased Hans Christian. Sometimes on Sundays the rector would play with his children and a few chosen pupils; it was boisterous, rough, and often questionable fun. He would insist on wheeling Hans Christian about in the perambulator and, as a forfeit, he would make Hans Christian kiss Mrs. Meisling under a blanket. Mrs. Meisling kissed thoroughly while Hans Christian flinched and blushed.

In the lax noisy Meisling house he seemed to live in an atmosphere of women, of swishing skirts, giggles, confidences. The maids knew what their mistress did and they behaved as they liked; they too thought it was fun to embarrass Hans Christian. They would come into his room, lean on his chair, interrupt him, and talk to him until Mrs. Meisling drove them away and took their place.

He had been given a room with a separate entrance to the courtyard, but now he found it had another door communicating with her bedroom and, with blushing cheeks and a beating heart, he would listen, dreading that she might be coming in.

Mrs. Meisling's behavior was probably the reason for her husband's savage temper and heavy drinking; after he was asleep, she would put on a peasant dress and go out into the streets or woods to see whom she could find. Everyone in Slagelse knew of it. Hans Christian tried to keep his respect for her but he could not. Every time she came near him he tingled. He was thankful when he could escape to Copenhagen for Christmas.

He had been asked to stay at the Wulffs'. "Do they know you are a charity boy?" sneered Meisling. Hans Christian answered gently that they did. "Wonderful!" said the rector.

It was almost too wonderful. Captain Wulff was in charge of the Naval Academy, in one of the palaces of the Amalienborg, and Hans Christian, shown to his room by a footman, looked down to where sentries stamped in the snow in front of the King's palace. Six years ago, he thought, I wandered in that square and no one knew me. Now I am staying in a house next the King!

Space and cleanliness, quiet and dignity fell blessedly on his raw nerves. Collin once again was pleased with his marks. Ingeborg joked with him; he was often with Edvard and he read a new poem to everyone. Then, in the midst of this excitement, he had a letter from the rector, who said he had heard Hans Christian was making himself ridiculous reading his poems and he would have a few things to say when he saw him again! Hans Christian went back sick with fright.

The rector was now posted to the town of Helsingör [Elsinore] and Hans Christian went with him. The students' examination at the university, equivalent to taking a degree, was to come in the next half year and the rector promised him coaching in Latin and Greek.

With the new place, the Meislings at first put on a new self-respect; the rector wore a frock coat, which he kept clean, and refrained from bullying the teachers and boys. The Helsingör ladies delighted Mrs. Meisling by calling on her but the neighborliness did not last; whispers quickly reached them and soon no invitations came. Mrs. Meisling relapsed into her old ways, and things were even more miserable in this beautiful little town than they had been in Slagelse.

The rector spoke to Hans Christian as if he were an idiot; when school was over, the house door was locked and Hans Christian had to stay in the schoolroom, or else play with the children or sit in his little room, where he went in fear of Mrs. Meisling. Though he had been poor all his life, he had never lived with dirt; now the house was filthy. The rector looked as if he slept in his clothes; the children stank.

To Hans Christian those days in Helsingör had an unconquerable sadness. Thoughts of his mother and himself as a child mingled in his mind. Anne Marie had had to be put in a home. She was crippled with rheumatism and drinking heavily; only brandy, she said piteously, would keep out the cold. She spent every penny she was given on the cheap raw spirits that were sold to the poor, and she had to be put under control. Everyone said she was a disgrace. Hans Christian wished he could die of his loneliness and misery.

After lessons the other boys could go home; he had to stay and look after the children. The squalor in the house grew even worse; he and another student boarder had to eat off the same plate. Living was dear in Helsingör, and now Meisling began complaining that the two hundred rigsdaler a year was not enough to keep an outsize lout of a boy who ate so much. Hans Christian hardly dared put a piece of meat on his plate and soon he looked as starved as in the old days in Copenhagen. Worse, Mrs. Meisling would not leave him alone; often she brought him coffee in the middle of the night, and once she frightened Hans Christian by coming into his bedroom in her nightgown, though she said it was only to fetch butter that she had hidden from the maids.

Hans Christian was driven at last to write to Collin and beg to be taken away. His letter was hysterical, but he could not bring himself to say a word about Mrs. Meisling. Collin, who knew the rector was bad-tempered, saw nothing more in it and answered in a normal sensible way that the rector really meant well and his harshness was only his manner.

The letter put Hans Christian into fresh despair. But now a young teacher of Hebrew began to visit Meisling for lessons; he saw the way Hans Christian was treated, the grudged and scanty helpings of food, and—the young teacher could hardly believe his eyes—the way Mrs. Meisling embarrassed him. In the Easter holidays this teacher called on Collin. Shocked and distressed, Collin arranged for Hans Christian to leave at once.

Hans Christian went to say good-by to Meisling. He held out his hand and said, with a falseness that probably came from fright: "Thank you for all the good you have done me."

The rector was more honest. He said what he hoped. "You will never become a student," he shouted. "Your verses will rot in a bookseller's attic and you will end your days in a madhouse."

It sounded like a curse. Hans Christian had to leave with it ringing in his ears.

CHAPTER IV

As THERE WERE ONLY a few months to go before the university examination, Collin decided it was not worth arranging for Hans Christian to go to another school; instead he found a private tutor, a young man called Müller, gifted and gentle. It was a new experience for Hans Christian and it was bliss to be in Copenhagen again.

He had rented a small garret, the garret in his *A Picture Book without Pictures*. It was in one of the narrowest streets, but "light is not wanting for me, for I live high up and I have a fine view over the roof." While the moonlight shone over the houses, he gazed until the chimney pots seemed to change to mountains and the gleam of the canal was a river winding far away. The whole world came to him there, through the moon, which said: "Paint what I tell you, and you will have a fine picture book.

"Last evening I was gliding through the clear atmosphere of India and reflecting myself in the Ganges . . ." said the moon. "Yesterday I looked down upon life in Paris." "I have followed the polar birds and the swimming whales to Greenland." "I will give you a picture of Pompeii." And the moon brought him other, deeper thoughts of birth and death and sorrow and love. All these were waiting for him; he was nearly ready; nearly, but not quite. There was still this stiff examination and Hans Christian had reluctantly to leave the moon and go back to the table where his Latin exercise lay.

To help keep expenses down he had dinner every day at one

of his friends' houses, but it was the Collin house that was his real home, and it was Edvard of whom he thought the most. Edvard was everything he, Hans Christian, was not; good-looking, controlled, modest. Hans Christian yearned to be like him. How Edvard felt it is difficult to know. He was always cool, composed, and withdrawn; but he was good-natured. He helped with the Latin compositions and the grammar that Hans Christian still found fearfully difficult. Next to Edvard it was Louise who touched him most. She had been a little girl when he first knew them; now she was fifteen and already womanly. While her sister and brothers were astringent and sometimes made Hans Christian feel stupid and awkward, she was always gentle and patient.

To his friends in the capital it must have seemed that it was the same Hans Christian who came back from school each time. He was over twenty-two, but he seemed to be as ebullient as ever, as brashly confident one moment, as despairing the next, as full of smiles and tears, as talkative; he still had a pocket stuffed with poems, and he still insisted on reading aloud. People thought it was conceit that made Hans Christian read aloud; it was not, it was necessity. A poet cannot tell the effect of his poem until he has heard it, seen its effect on an audience. It was the same later on with the Tales; as he read them, he was listening acutely to see where they lost pace; afterwards he would go home and correct them.

Slowly people began to see there was a change in Hans Christian. In his years away he had grown in judgment and knowledge, and his quiet suffering under much bullying had given him dignity, a queer legacy to have come from Meisling.

Mrs. Wulff was always trying to bring him to a sense of who he was. She had written to him at school, good sensible letters: "Dear Andersen, wake up and don't dream of becoming immortal for I'm sure you will only be laughed at." She talked to him in Copenhagen in the same way, of modesty, gratitude, good sense, and of knowing his place; Hans Christian tried to attend, but a moment after he would be swept away again.

Captain Wulff often made him feel that he thought him a waste of time, but the Wulffs' daughter, Henriette, became his fast friend. She was little and hunchbacked, but gay, intelligent, and exceedingly witty, a dear companion who drew out all the tenderness in him. She also shared his secrets. One day the captain came into the drawing room with a copy of a newspaper, *The Flying Post*. "There is something I want you to hear in this," he said to his wife. "Two poems that are really good. They are signed simply 'H.' Perhaps they are by Heiberg," and he read them aloud. It was Henriette who said: "They are by Hans Christian."

There was a moment of surprised silence; Hans Christian was expectantly glowing, but the captain put down the paper and left the room as if he were vexed; Mrs. Wulff was silent too and Hans Christian was so hurt that presently he went home.

Mrs. Wulff had often said that if he came to Copenhagen there would be too many visits, too few lessons, and soon Hans Christian began to understand their displeasure; they thought he had been writing poetry instead of working and he had to admit it was partly true. The examination date was close and suddenly Hans Christian knew he could not pass. Collin had looked grave at their last meeting and said if he failed it was the end; they could not ask the King for more support. Hans Christian had never felt his dependence more; other students, if they failed, disappointed only their parents and families, but bound up with his results was a whole circle of benefactors. Poems were forgotten and he worked frantically; on the day of the examination he fainted, but he forced himself to revive, and he passed.

Although another examination, a year later, would have to be passed before a student could enter a profession, Hans Christian Andersen had proved himself worthy of his friends. The sudden relief seemed to release a spring in him; to his friends it seemed that they had hardly had time to advise him what to do next when they found his thoughts had flown— "like a swarm of bees," he said—into his first book. It was the story of a walk. The tutor, Müller, lived in another part of the city, and in the long walks there and back Hans Christian had been writing in his head, as he had done long ago under his mother's apron, by the gooseberry bush.

A Walking Trip from Holmens Kanal to the East Point of Amager, a jumble of all the thoughts and associations that come into the mind as the body walks along, is perhaps one of the first attempts at stream-of-consciousness writing. It is a jumble of styles too. Sometimes it is in humorous verse, it has many of the stilted paragraphs that Hans Christian admired; occasionally it flows into a new style that is quick, almost colloquial, the beginnings of the style of Hans Andersen. The little book was fresh and gay and unquenchably young, and everybody was charmed.

He had to publish it himself because the publishers offered such poor terms. This he did by subscription and, after nearly the whole edition was subscribed, a publisher came with a good offer for a second. There was money for Collin to bank, but what made Hans Christian happier, the critics were kind.

That year everything seemed to smile on him; as if success brought success, a little vaudeville play, parodying those old tragedies he had once tried to imitate, was put on for a short run at the Royal Theater. It was on this stage that he had knelt down and prayed that New Year's Day. Now he was here again, not as an actor, but as the actor's mainspring, the playwright. Anxiety, responsibility, joy, and gratitude almost killed him.

Mrs. Collin was sitting alone that night when Hans Christian burst in on her and threw himself down into a chair, sobbing. She instantly guessed what had happened. "Hush! Hush!" she soothed him. "Well-known authors are often hissed."

"But they didn't hiss," cried Hans Christian. "They applauded. They cried: 'Long live Andersen!' They clapped!" It was chiefly a student claque, but that did not cloud his joy.

That whole spring and summer were radiant. He was invited to country houses, where he joined in picnics, garden parties, charades. "My hardships are over," he said. It seemed that all he had to do to be happy was to write and earn a little money, and it was writing that made him happiest of all.

Then he had a letter from Ingemann; the poet warned Hans Christian against frivolity. Ingemann knew that a social life is death to the artist, and he begged Andersen to give it up, and not to care so much for other people's opinions. Hans Christian was puzzled. What did Ingemann mean? What was wrong with sophistication? Nothing, if it did not take one's sense of values away. Hans Andersen ended by knowing this very well. In "The Swineherd" he was to write an ironic little indictment of society, in which a poor prince seeks to woo a wealthy princess by sending her his most precious possessions.

Growing on the grave of the Prince's father was a rose-tree—oh, such a lovely rose-tree. It only flowered every five years, and even then had but one solitary bloom. But this rose smelt so sweet that it made you forget all your cares and troubles. And the Prince also had a nightingale that could sing just as if it had all the loveliest tunes hidden away in its little throat. The Princess should have both the rose and the nightingale, he said; and so they were placed in big silver caskets and sent to her. The Emperor had them brought before him in the great hall . . . out came the lovely rose.

"Oh, isn't it pretty!" cried all the maids-of-honour.

"It's more than pretty," said the Emperor, "it's handsome."

But when the Princess touched it she nearly burst into tears. "Oh, Papa, what a shame!" she cried. "It's not artificial, it's real!"

"What a shame!" repeated all the court ladies. "It's real!"

"Come, let's see what's in the other casket before we get annoyed," suggested the Emperor. And then out came the nightingale. Its singing was so lovely that for the moment there wasn't a thing that could be said against it.

"*Superbe! Charmant!*" exclaimed the maids-of-honour, for they all talked French, the one worse than the other. "How the bird reminds me of Her late Majesty's musical box!". . . "All the same I can't believe that it's real," said the Princess.

"Yes, it is; it's a real live bird," said the one who had brought it.

"All right, then let it fly away," said the Princess and she wouldn't hear of the Prince being allowed to come to her.

Just before Hans Christian's first university examination he had met, at dinner, a young man who was so quiet and shy that it seemed certain he must have come from the country for the first time. "Are you going up for the examination at the university?" Hans Christian had asked in a slightly patronizing way.

"Yes," the young man had said with a smile. Hans Christian had talked to him encouragingly and had even boasted a little, but when the day arrived he had not been able to find the young man anywhere among the other students. He found him in the examiners' room; he was the professor who was to examine in mathematics.

The young professor's modesty made Hans Christian blush. They were much the same age, one a learned professor, the other a raw boastful student, and Hans Christian vowed to try to catch up, and never to brag or idle again. He went to work, and passed the examination. His friends were astonished that he said nothing about his marks, which were almost brilliant.

WITH HIS LAST EXAMINATION behind him he felt he was no longer Hans Christian the boy, but Andersen an avowed writer. There was no time for moonlight now; his grant from the King was finished. He had to live, and that for an artist is always the difficulty, how to balance dreams and living.

At Christmas he brought out the first collection of his poems; they hold what is perhaps the first indication of the Tales. Mrs. Ingemann, whose dark eyes saw farther than most people's, wrote to him about one poem: "The little elves of our childhood seem to me to be, on the whole, your good geniuses and when they live in the fancy and heart, then, I think, there is no fear of the stream of understanding losing itself among the glittering pebbles." Molbech, the most important critic of the day, praised the poems, but some of the other critics condemned them.

It is not wise for a writer to challenge his critics, but for a very young man, it is never easy to be wise. Andersen hit back violently; though the Collins said it was vanity and that he must not risk getting a name for that. Andersen would not listen. He had made new friends who praised him indiscriminately. Buoyed up by their encouragement, he decided to write a historical novel. In the summer of 1830 he went to stay with the widow of Iversen the old printer, but not a word of the novel did he write.

Mrs. Iversen had her granddaughters with her, a bevy of girls, all freshness, innocence, dewy beauty, and soft eyes. They played hide-and-seek in the old garden, and there seemed to be girls everywhere, peeping at him from behind bushes, dodging behind sundials that should surely have said: "I show none but sunny hours."

The garden had inscriptions on its stonework that told one what to think and feel in each place, but Andersen found he had no feelings at all. What was the matter with him? Was he incapable of love? Then in an old castle he saw a painting of a lady and, as he gazed at it, his heart ached unbearably. He could love her, if only she were alive! But she was paint and canvas. Everything now seemed meaningless and silly; he began to think he was an imitation of a man.

At last he left Mrs. Iversen and went to stay for a few days with a student friend, Christian Voigt.

The Voigts lived at Faaborg, a little town on the sea, in the beautiful south of Fyn. They were rich merchants and when Andersen saw the family house he was impressed. It seemed a thriving busy world with servants and journeymen, buyers and sellers going in and out, and no place for a poor poet; but Christian Voigt took him in, introduced him to his eldest sister, Riborg, and at once Andersen was reassured.

It was a summer morning, the room was quiet and sunny, full of books and flowers; its quiet was balm. Riborg poured coffee and Andersen found that she could talk appreciatively of his work. He supposed she was plain; her mouth was wide, her hair dark brown. Her eyes were brown too, but they lit up when she laughed.

She was with the two young men all day; they went sailing and picnicked on one of the wooded islands. Andersen, of course, read aloud to them, and Riborg made a wreath of oak leaves but was too shy to offer it to him herself; she asked her brother to give it to Andersen. The next day there was another picnic and, in the evening, a dance. Andersen, who could not dance, stood like a long shadow against the wall until Riborg came to him and they sat down together. They talked the evening away; it was not like other girls' talk; it was of poetry, music, philosophy, but with the womanliness that he revered, and he went to bed that night with his head in a tumult.

The next day Christian Voigt, beginning to guess what had happened to his friend, told him that Riborg was engaged to the son of the local apothecary; she would have been married by now but her parents did not approve. After a moment's silence, Andersen said he had better go back to Odense.

Before leaving he walked with Riborg in the garden, and told her he would call the heroine of his unwritten novel Riborg. He picked a bunch of flowers for her and went away. When he got back to Odense he was so dreamy and abstracted that the girls laughed at him and said: "In love at last!"

"Nonsense!" he said angrily.

It had to be nonsense. What had he to offer? He had no profession, no money to study for one; there was nothing he could do but write. And Riborg was engaged to someone else.

Back in Copenhagen he wrote a little of the novel, then stopped and began the libretto of an opera, then collected his new poems. He wrote to a friend in Odense: "People are puzzled by my latest poems, just fancy now; they think I am in love, everyone thinks so." It was not surprising. The poems were written for Riborg; among them was *Two Eyes of Brown* and such lines as:

> *You love me. I saw it in your eyes.*
> *Forget me now, it is your painful duty.*

When he heard that Riborg had come to Copenhagen, Andersen rushed to call on her; after that he went every day, always listening to every word she said and looking at her so intently that she blushed when she saw him. One evening when he left he kissed her hand; when he saw she was not angry he was sure she loved him. He managed to get home, though he could scarcely think for joy; now he knew that nothing mattered beside this fact of love. He was ready to give up his writing and learn a trade, or perhaps he could do both, write and work at a trade. He did not know how things could be arranged but he knew that he must tell Riborg that he loved her.

Though she was so near he could not bring himself to speak

to her. Instead he wrote a letter; in it he asked her, before God, to make sure she loved the other man. Her brother brought her answer. She wrote that she could not make the other man unhappy, they had waited and trusted so long. Andersen must try to understand.

What had made her change? In Faaborg, she had thought him wonderful, but in Copenhagen she had heard her poet laughed at, called "Lamppost," and "Stork," and perhaps she had grown unsure.

Hans Andersen was to fall in love more than once and each love, long afterwards, found a counterpart in one of his Tales. The one he was to write for Riborg, "The Top and the Ball," was harsh and a little bitter.

The ball thinks herself too good for the top. "You don't seem to realize," she says, "that my father and mother were morocco slippers and that I have cork inside me." The ball can bounce high, she is engaged to a swallow. . . . Long afterwards when the top is gilded he is accidentally thrown for a moment into a dustbin, where he finds a wrinkled old object that was once the ball. The maid comes and picks him out; the ball is left there. "The top came in for a lot of attention but nothing was said about the ball, and the top never spoke again of his old love. Love is, of course, bound to fade away when your sweetheart has spent five years in a gutter. You can't be expected to know her again if you meet her in a dustbin."

But years later, when she was happily married, he saw Riborg again. "Memories are very like amber beads," he wrote after this meeting; "if we rub them, they give back the old perfume."

When he died, a small wash-leather bag was found on his breast; in it was a letter from Riborg, perhaps the very letter in which she had refused his love; no one knows because young Jonas Collin, the grandson of old Collin, burned the letter unread. The bag is in the Odense Museum with copies of the love poems, Riborg's portrait, and a little bunch of flowers, dried now so that their colors are gone; they lie on a scrap of paper on which Riborg wrote: "From Andersen"; they are the flowers he picked for her in the garden in Faaborg.

Hans Christian had only known Riborg a little while but, now

he had lost her, he felt desolate. Perhaps it was Edvard Collin who, knowing more than anyone else what was going on, now told his father that Andersen needed a change. In the familiar quiet study Councillor Collin talked to Hans Christian and, after pondering, told him to use some of his savings and take a trip abroad.

HANS HAD ALWAYS dreamed of other countries. He loved the migrant birds, particularly the swallows and storks; they seemed to bring other lands close to him. Like the Viking's Wife in "The Marsh King's Daughter," he had been awakened by the rustling of wings. "Stork on stork, sitting on the roofs and out-buildings . . . flocks of them flying round in great circles. Then all together they took off."

"I feel a tingling in my wings," said the Mother Stork. Andersen knew that tingling now. He would go into a new world where no one knew him or could bring up his past and his faults.

On his first trip he went no farther than Germany, but like the stork he could stretch his wings. He saw mountains for the first time, heard strange tongues, and wandered in the great Gothic cathedrals. He was the perfect traveler; he had an open mind, a quick eye, a capacity for picking up conversations and little scenes. With the fervor he had brought to Shakespeare and Scott he began to read Goethe and Schiller, and he encountered some fairy tales written by the brothers Grimm.

When he returned to Copenhagen he wrote a travel book called *Shadow-Pictures of a Journey to the Harz and Saxon Switzerland.*

"It would take an Andersen to write a travel book after only six weeks abroad!" said the critics. And they refused to like it. Nothing he did now pleased them. But he was unquenchable. He thought his own works beautiful and believed in them with his whole heart.

It was true, at that time, that Andersen's writing was often bad and careless; he could not be made to see that grammar and spelling were important; he could not be bothered to look up the exact meaning of words. The plays with which he bombarded the Royal Theater came back and a new volume of poems went unnoticed. He was writing too fast in a desperate attempt to win back the position he had lost.

This was another of Andersen's bitter times. Word came that his mother had gone quite to pieces; no one had been able to keep drink from her and now she was so violent that she had to be shut up. Andersen went to Odense but the pitiful shambles of a woman hardly knew him. He told no one in Copenhagen about this fresh shame but he starved himself to send money to Anne Marie. He was writing now not only against poverty but against the specter of failure. He had done nothing to show anyone that he was a genius and he had to be a genius or else he was a daydreamer like his father, mad like his grandfather. Hour after hour he sat in his room holding his head in his hands, while the paper was blank in front of him or scribbled over with writing that was sterile, immature, mannered, straining to be Walter Scott... still, still not Andersen.

CHAPTER V

HANS ANDERSEN, it is said, could never tell the color of a woman's eyes. "He only sees the soul in things," complained a friend. But in 1832 he wrote a poem, *The Brown Eyes and the Blue*. The brown eyes were Riborg's, the blue were Louise Collin's. Andersen had found he could talk to her about his unhappiness, even about Riborg.

All the Collins had good faces: level almond-shaped blue eyes, the distinctive long straight Collin nose, and mouths that were

571

unexpectedly sensitive; to Louise, long silky brown hair and a very fair skin were added. *She is so white, my heart's dearest,* Andersen was soon writing in another poem. It is difficult to believe he really loved her; by her portrait in later life she looks so firmly respectable and bourgeoise, even a little ornate; but he had been hurt by Riborg, and Louise's gentleness soon made him think he should not be talking of an old love but of a new.

Though Andersen could never have brought himself to say the word "love" to a Collin, he could pour it out in writing and he began to send Louise letters and poems that showed his feeling in every line: "My whole life seems to me a poem and you are beginning to play quite a part in it. You are not cross about this, are you?" "Oh dear me, one need only let the heart speak to be a good poet!" He sent her *The Brown Eyes and the Blue*, and those poems that said quite plainly, "Heart's dearest."

Louise did not know what to do. She was a placid, good girl, and she looked forward to marrying a solid average man, not a tempestuous poet. She saw now where her sympathy had taken her and with quiet sense consulted Ingeborg, who was now married to Adolph Drewsen. Without hurting his feelings Ingeborg told him that all Louise's letters had to be shown to her, a common practice for a young girl in 1832. That stopped the letters and poems—Andersen shrank from writing emotionally in any letter that witty, merry Ingeborg was to see—but he still haunted the house trying to catch Louise alone. Only she never seemed to be alone. The blue eyes looked pityingly at him and she often seemed on the point of telling him something and drew back. Then she announced her engagement to a Mr. Lind, a solicitor, respectable and good like herself.

The engagement hurt Andersen. It was not only another unsuccessful love; he had been told nothing about it until it was public property and that made him feel shut out. He was not a man, he thought, but someone apart, and he was to say of Mr. Lind: "Little Denmark has given him more than all Europe can give this poet."

Invisible knives pressed into the Little Mermaid's feet when she walked, Andersen would write; she was always different from the humans round her though they loved her. "A mermaid hasn't any tears," wrote Hans Andersen, "and so she suffers all the more." Today on the shores of the Langelinie her statue sits, a small bronze figure on her rock, her face turned away from the busy happy people on land as she gazes perpetually out to sea. She looks ineffably lonely, and she might be called the statue of Andersen's heart.

He could think of only one way to hide his grief: to get away to the ends of the earth. He was advised to present one of his books to King Frederick and, if it were accepted, to ask the favor of a stipend for traveling. Andersen thought that monstrous. "What, give a book and at once ask a favor!"

Collin put things sensibly. "The King is a very busy man," he said. "He would rather you showed that indelicacy than bother him with a second interview."

"Well, where is your petition?" the old King asked bluntly when he had accepted the book.

"I have it here," said Andersen, but he was ashamed. "It seems to me dreadful that I should bring it with the book," he said. "They told me it was the only way, but it is not like me."

The King's gruffness disappeared; he laughed and took the petition and Andersen was granted a stipend for two years instead of the customary one, though he had no idea of what he wished to do.

His heart was still unbearably sore but he began to find renewed proof of the friendship the Collins felt for him. They knew Andersen had come to a point from which he must begin again. He was only twenty-eight but he had had two bitter love affairs and he had come full tilt against the critics. It was better, they told him, that he should be forgotten for a while and come back fresh. He himself felt he could hardly go on living. "I prayed . . . I might die away from Denmark," he wrote, and then with a flicker of his real self, "or else return strengthened in activity to win for me and my beloved ones joy and honor."

All the Collins came to see him off and, on the ship, as Copenhagen fell away, the captain brought him a letter. It was from Edvard and it said more than the distant contained Edvard had ever said:

Monday noon, 22 April, 1833.

Dear Friend,

. . . Believe me, I'm intensely sorry at your departure, I shall miss you dreadfully . . . I'll miss you in your seat at the table; still, I know, you will miss more, for you are alone; but . . . it is a consolation to know that one has friends back home who think of one, so you have this consolation, for we shall constantly remember you with love. Good-bye, my dear, dear friend! God let us meet again glad and happy in two years.

THE ROYAL LIBRARY in Copenhagen has a book it particularly prizes, Hans Andersen's Album, about which he wrote: "It accompanied me on all my travels and has since increased and become of great value to me." In Paris, Andersen, as well as keeping the Album, made small pen-and-ink sketches of the places he visited; Versailles, Napoleon's bedroom, the Opéra and the theater; each little drawing as vivid and alive as everything he touched.

He saw the quick fiery Paris of the restoration. Napoleon's military rule was over; the nobles with all their taste and elegance had come into power again, the arts flourished. Life was stimulating, extravagant, and gay; it must have been heady for Andersen, coming from the restraint and simplicity of Denmark, but soon not all its gaiety, good company, and theaters could hold him. He was a writer and there was something he wanted to write. He needed quiet and so he went to Le Locle, a little town high up in the Swiss mountains, where it snows even in August.

When the first views of the Alps opened in the mists, they seemed to Andersen like forms swimming high up in the air. What he had thought was a thick smoke came curling upwards to the coach; it was a cloud. Then, "through an opening in the mountains we saw far below a deep lovely green, a land such as you see in your dreams; it was Geneva, its lake as clear as the azure sky. . . . The mountains stood high over the horizon like waves of violet glass tipped with creamy foam." It might have been the country of the Ice Maiden.

He found the Swiss in the little watchmaking town friendly and hospitable. The children of the French family with whom he stayed grew so fond of him that they used to shout their dialect in his ears; they could not believe that such a sympathetic man could not understand them.

There was stillness and rest in the dark pine trees; there was beauty in the bright green grass and the juicy violet-colored crocus; there was peace in which to write a long poetic drama that he had begun in Paris.

Agnete and the Merman was taken from an old Danish folk song. Even as a child the old story of the double world of earth and sea had taken hold of Hans Christian; it was, of course, the first seed of "The Little Mermaid," but he was trying the theme now in a different form; he sent it home before leaving Le Locle for Italy. "*Agnete* is Danish in soul and mind," he wrote in the preface. "I send my dear child to my motherland, where she belongs. My friends, receive her kindly."

Agnete might be Andersen's best dramatic work; not an unworthy sister of "The Little Mermaid," but no one would take it. "Is *he* writing again?" the publishers said. "We were tired of him long ago." Edvard managed to get it printed in the end, but he suggested with asperity that Andersen's silly writing really should be given up. Andersen survived the attacks that were to be made on *Agnete* because he was already writing something else.

If Germany is the country of the heart, France of common sense, Italy is the land of imagination; in it Andersen breathed with an ease and happiness he had never known before. There was a quality in him that the North had chilled and stilled; now it was released and everything seemed larger, warmer, more free.

HE WENT TO Milan and Genoa, but it was in Florence that his eyes were opened. Looking at Michelangelo's sculpture, he wrote: "The marble has looked into my soul." Now he understood what he had refused to understand before, the necessity of form; he saw how blind he had been, and he wrote home: "I wish I were just seventeen years old and had the same sentiments and ideas as now; I would surely become something; now I only see that I don't know anything, and life is so short; how can I possibly learn so enormously much? . . ."

But he was catching up, growing more than he knew, and what Florence had begun, Rome completed. No one who has seen the vastness of Rome can be small again, and Andersen lived there for four months. When he left for Naples, he felt fresh and full of life, almost too full. Everywhere was this languorous, careless, tempting beauty. "From Cicero's villa," he wrote in his diary, "we saw the Garden of the Hesperides. I strolled in the warm air under the lemon and orange trees and threw the shining yellow fruit into the blue sea." At night he saw Vesuvius against the moonlit sky while scents from unknown gardens filled the night. And in this new, propitious atmosphere he began to write his first novel.

It was not only the beauty. In his years of study, of writing and poetizing, Andersen had lost touch with the ordinary people he had known as a child; now, as he traveled, he began to find them again; he seemed to see into the lives of husbands and wives, seamen, inn servants, beggars; and he thought often of his old home.

Then he had a letter from Collin telling him that Anne Marie had died. Andersen's first thought was: God, I thank Thee. Now her poverty is at an end. But soon he began to feel utterly alone; there was no one now whom he could call his own. Everybody round him had someone, a mother, father, children, a wife. He wrote in his diary: "Happy he who is married, who is engaged!"

That is what Andersen wanted, a wife. His body ached for fulfillment but he was fastidious. As many ugly men do, he could have found women over and over again, but not the delicacy and beauty that drew him. The kind of women he wanted, the Louise Collins, hardly thought of him as a man; they were fond of the child in him. It was the price he paid for his gift; one of the qualities of Andersen's writing, the one that makes it impossible for anyone to imitate him, is its purity of feeling, its innocence.

He came home from Italy, by way of Vienna and Munich, traveling slowly. He did not want to come home; he thought he knew what was waiting for him there—criticism, antagonism, that perpetual good advice. But it had to be faced; his last penny had been spent. "So tomorrow I travel towards the north. A strange sorrowful feeling possesses me. Northward, there where my dear ones live in snow and fog, lies the iron ring to be fastened to my foot."

There was one thing that brought him a feeling of hope—the novel he had started in Italy. He continued to work on it in Copenhagen, where he had taken rooms near the Nyhavn, on the sunless side because it was cheaper. "A cold shadow lies over my study," he wrote in a letter to Henriette Wulff, who was away in the Italy he missed, "but outside . . . I see a tall, leafy poplar; by moonlight it looks quite black; then I recall the dark cypresses and all the beautiful things I dreamt of the other day. Yes, I have dreamt so clearly that I was in Italy last year, so I must write my Italian story, exhale all that I dreamt and saw."

Soon he was able to finish his book and inscribe it "To the Conference Councillor Collin and his noble wife, in whom I found parents, whose children were my brothers and sisters, whose house was my home, I present the best that I possess." It was not only the best; at that moment it was all he possessed in the world.

Edvard took the novel to a publisher and bargained for his friend. Twenty pounds was all the publisher would give, and in installments only, but Andersen accepted. He had to; he had not paid his rent for a month, and he had no decent clothes or shoes.

Because he was so poor, so short of money, while he was waiting for *The Improvisatore*, as he called the novel, to go through the press, he wrote a little pamphlet, four fairy tales for children.

THOSE FIRST FAIRY TALES were "The Tinder-Box," "Little Claus and Big Claus," "Little Ida's Flowers," and "The Princess and the Pea," three adapted from folk tales, but all of them told in Andersen's own way. He sent them to Henriette Wulff to read—"The Princess and the Pea" was really a dig at her, who was so particular over small things. "Örsted says that if *The Improvisatore* will make me famous, these will make me immortal, but that of course I don't believe," he said.

All his hopes were on the novel. *The Improvisatore* is the story of a poor boy, an improviser of poems and tales, in fact Andersen himself, but called Antonio and living not in Denmark but in Italy. The transition into that sunny land seemed to have released a spring in him and he wrote this, his real autobiography, far more truthfully and deeply than he wrote the straightforward *Story of My Life*. It was vitally important to him; without it he would never have sloughed off the last of that poor fumbling ignorant boy, and emerged, free, as Hans Andersen. *The Improvisatore* had a form and pace which were new. It made a revolution in the history of the Danish novel, and it was the turning point of his life.

He waited with anxiety for it to come out, but there was nothing to fear. The critics could not help being favorable. There was a new feeling in the air—approval, something Andersen had not felt for a long time. And some of the approval was from men whose opinion he prized most. Even Captain Wulff, who had been so ungraciously silent long ago about the poem in *The Flying Post*, told everyone: "I couldn't put the book down!"

It ran into several editions, was translated into Swedish, German, and English. Before the year was out Andersen had finished another novel, *O.T.*, and begun yet another. "I want to be the first novelist of Denmark," he said. "Modest as ever!" groaned the Collins.

But life has a way of giving you what you want in such a curious fashion that you do not recognize it. "I shall be famous," Hans Andersen had said, yet when the fame began to come he hardly saw it. He was too busy with his novels.

O.T. was a poor dashed-off thing but he had made a name with *The Improvisatore* and the new book was not badly received. It did not sell well though, and as all the children he met seemed to know his first book of Tales, and it *was* selling, he wrote a second. Among the new stories was "Thumbelina." Like "The Princess and the Pea," it was written for tiny, witty Henriette Wulff, but, said Andersen, "Really I should drop these trifles and concentrate on my real work."

He still did not dream what that was, but slowly he became aware that people had begun to point him out in the street;

Above, pen-and-ink sketch of a bridge in Florence, made
by H.C.A. during his Italian travels of 1833-35; below, first
page of the original manuscript of "The Little Mermaid."

though it was often as the author of that charming Italian novel, it was far more often as the man who wrote the Tales. Children were stopped by their mothers and nurses and told: "Look, there is your Hans Andersen."

He was easy to recognize. He had always loved clothes from the day when his friends filled him with joy by giving him their secondhand ones; now he had a coat lined with velvet and a tall hat, and his hair was curled by a hairdresser. It was part of his naïveté, but it was also an attempt to get away as far as possible from the wooden shoes, the rags and patches, and the shame of desperate makeshifts, such as padding out that coat front with programs.

Elith Reumert, who wrote a loving study of Andersen in *Hans Andersen the Man*, gives a description of how, as a boy, he once saw Andersen in Copenhagen:

> I was a lad of fourteen when, one day . . . on my way to school, I . . . saw a tall and peculiar figure turning the corner . . . whom I at once, from the many pictures I had seen, recognized as Hans Christian Andersen, the poet. . . . When he passed me I stood at attention, and instinctively took off my cap most respectfully. To my surprise he returned my salute with such excessive politeness that I felt quite shy. He gave me a pleased and kindly smile, and when he slowly passed on, backwards, I was afraid he would stumble over his own legs. He kept swinging his hat towards me, nodding and smiling, until he disappeared.
>
> As I stood there I felt as if I was in a dream . . . to tell the truth I was not quite sure he had not been making fun of me.
>
> Now I know better. He who could be made happy by a friendly word and depressed by a hard one; he who with astonishing honesty had confessed to the world that his soul only felt happy when admired by everybody . . . he had, in the street, met one of those youngsters who in deep veneration and gratitude had paid him a child's homage, and in his childlike heart he felt at the moment this homage as a great joy. . . .

IT OFTEN SEEMS that children have a telegraphic system of their own, without any wires or delivery forms; a fashion spreads among them. And the Andersen Tales spread quickly, first over

Denmark, then into Germany, on to Sweden, England, and over the world. Soon they were found on the grown-ups' tables as well as in the nursery.

"I get hold of an idea and tell a story for the young ones," Andersen said, "remembering all the time that father and mother are listening and we must give them something to think about too." The result was beyond anything he had expected; when he brought out the third collection of Tales and the most sophisticated of critics declared "The Little Mermaid" and "The Emperor's New Clothes" to be the best things H. C. Andersen had ever written, the poet was completely bewildered. "The Little Mermaid" better than *Agnete?* Though it was true that nothing he wrote ever moved him as much as the fairy tale, it was written in a few days, while the long dramatic poem had taken months of work. He was not only mystified, he was a little annoyed.

People who have not read Andersen may ask, with him, what there was in these little tales that has placed them where they are. What is it that makes them so different from those of the brothers Grimm?

To begin with, each story has the essence of a poem: a distilling of thought and meaning into a distinct form, so disciplined and finely made, so knit in rhythm, that one word out of place, one word too much, jars the whole. It is this that gives the Tales their extraordinary swiftness, so that they are over almost before we have had time to take them in, and we have had the magical feeling of flying. The children, he remarked, always had their mouths a little open when he had finished; that is the feeling we have too.

But they were not written carelessly, were not the happy accidents that some people think them. Anyone who has studied the original manuscripts from the first short draft of a story, through all its stages of crossings out and rewritings in Andersen's small spiky handwriting, the cuttings and pastings together, until the last draft was ready for the printer, can see how each word was weighed, what discipline was there. Even the discipline was skillful; Andersen never let it kill the life in his style.

That life is his hallmark. A sentence from one of Hans Andersen's Tales is utterly different from a sentence by anyone else. "The children got in the coach and drove off," Grimm would have written, but Andersen wrote: "Up they got on the coach. Good-bye, Mum. Good-bye, Dad. Crack went the whip, whick whack and away they dashed. Gee up! Gee up!"

"It's not writing, it's talking," the irritated Molbech said, but, one after another, serious literary critics found in it a source of inspiration. "From that moment," said one, "a new prose was born in Danish literature; the language acquired grace and colour, and freshness of simplicity."

It is difficult for us abroad to realize this because that is what is lost most of all in English translations. No writer has been more mutilated by his translators. Andersen's writing has economy and strength; it is witty, ironical, and humorous, and, though it can be intensely poignant and poetical, it is always crisp. In most English translations he is made heavy and sentimental, the endings are sometimes changed. It is a wonder that any of his quality is left. However, the translation by R. P. Keigwin catches it, Danish scholars say, as never before.

Hans Christian was a philosopher; his stories are parables and have meanings that sound on and on after their last word is read. He was a poet; he knew the whole gamut of feeling from ecstasy to black melancholy and horror. He was a child; children have a godlike power of giving personality to things that have none—sticks and stones, banister knobs and footstools, cabbages. This power normally dies in them as they grow up, but Andersen never lost it. "It often seems to me," he wrote, "as if every . . . little flower is saying to me: 'Look at me, just for a moment, and then my story will go right into you.'" "Right into you," that is the clue. The daisy, the streetlamp, the beetle are suddenly breathing and alive.

Once upon a time there was a bundle of matches; they were tremendously proud of their high birth. Their family tree—that's to say, the tall fir tree that each little match-stick came from—had been a huge old tree in the wood. And now the matches lay on the shelf between a tinder-box and an old iron cook-pot, and they told the other two about the time they were young. "Ah yes," they said, "in those days, with the velvet moss at our feet, we really were on velvet. Every morning and evening we had diamond tea; that was the dew. And all day we had sunshine. . . . But then the woodcutters arrived; that was the great upheaval, and our family was all split up. Our founder and head was given a place as mainmast on board a splendid ship that could sail round the world if she liked; the other branches went to other places and, as for us, we've got the task of lighting up for the common herd; that's how we gentlefolk come to be in the kitchen."

"Well, things have gone differently with me," said the cook-pot which stood alongside the matches. "Right from the time I first came into the world, I've been scrubbed and boiled again and again. I've got an eye for the practical and, strictly speaking, I'm No. 1 in this house. My great delight, at a time like after dinner, is to sit clean and tidy on the shelf and have a nice little chat with my friends. But except for the water-bucket, who now and then goes down into the yard, we spend all our time indoors. Our one news-bringer is the market basket, but that goes in for a lot of wild talk about the government and the people. Why, the other day there was an elderly jug so flabbergasted by what the basket said that it fell down and broke in pieces. It's a real radical, that basket, mark my words!"

It is a whole live kitchen world. After reading it a kitchen never seems the same place again; one is almost afraid to take a shopping basket out for fear of what it might think; and notice in how few words the story is told. All the stories have this economy, this startlingly quick effect. None of the Tales, except "The Snow Queen," which is almost a novel, is long; Andersen is verbose and boring in his novels and autobiography, but these are his poems—for that is what he always was, a poet.

Not everyone approved. There were some bad reviews. "Although the reviewer has nothing against good fairy tales for grown-ups," said one, "he can only find this form of literature entirely unsuitable for children. Far from improving their minds," he said severely, "Andersen's Tales might be positively harmful. Would anyone claim that a child's sense of what is proper would be improved when it reads about a sleeping Princess riding on the back of a dog to a soldier who kisses her? As for 'The Princess and the Pea' it is not only indelicate but indefensible, as the child might get the false idea that great ladies must be terribly thin-skinned...."

We smile at such criticism, but there are others that threaten Andersen just as seriously; for instance, that children should be given books without shadows, books of lightness and laughter, nothing else. Perhaps the reason such books are so lifeless is that living things have shadows.

Andersen had his dark side; a legacy from his horror of his grandfather, from the tales with which Anne Marie and the spinning women had frightened him as a little boy and, more especially, from the customs of his time. One must remember he was writing in the first half of the nineteenth century and had spent his childhood among ignorant, crude, and superstitious people. Stories as vividly horrid as "The Girl Who Trod on a Loaf," as sad as "The Shadow," should perhaps be kept away from children altogether, but to expunge parts of them, to tell them in another way, is to destroy them. Andersen's "The Little Mermaid" is one of the saddest on earth, but it is also one of the very best loved.

In pictures and statues of Andersen, tiny children are shown listening to the stories. This is sentimentally false; the stories were not meant for tiny children. In Andersen's time, very little children were kept in the nursery when visitors came to the house; it was not until they were eight or nine years old that they were allowed to go down to the drawing room to meet Mr. Hans Andersen and perhaps hear his Tales. Even then they did not wholly understand them; they were not meant to. All Andersen wanted was that they should love them; presently, as they grew up, they would understand. To stop and explain—as conscientious mothers do—is to spoil the rhythm, the whole feeling. Let the children wonder; these are wonder tales.

Andersen understood children completely and knew what would please them. "It is easy," he once said of the Tales. "It is just as you would talk to a child. Anyone can tell them." Time has made it very plain that no one can tell them quite like Hans Andersen.

IT IS NOT A HAPPY THING to be a writer; imagination is a writer's greatest gift but it can be torture in everyday life. A poet never knows when or how his ecstasy or melancholy will seize him; the same people, the same place, the same things can fill him with joy one day, misery the next.

"No winter has passed so quietly and happily as this one," Andersen wrote to a friend. "*The Improvisatore* has procured me esteem from the most noble and best . . . I have no anxiety for my daily bread, thank God, and lately I have been able to enjoy life thoroughly. . . . I sit down wearing gay-coloured slippers and a dressing-gown, with my feet on the sofa, the stove purrs, the tea-urn hums on the table. . . . Then I think of the poor boy in Odense who wore wooden shoes, and my heart is soft and I bless the good God." And then it would be: "Oh, God! What a creature I am! . . . I often wish I had never been born or that I had not this erratic turn that makes me so unhappy."

Just as most people do not have transports of happiness that make them throw their arms round trees and kiss them, so they do not know this black melancholy. Andersen must often have looked on his equable, sensible friends, serene with that tough and cool serenity which seems to flourish in the North, and wished that he were they.

If he had had a wife it might have been easier, but how could he marry? The little affluence *The Improvisatore* had brought did not last; though the Tales brought in a steady sum, it was small as yet; at times Andersen did not know how to pay his rent or keep himself decently dressed, and before thinking of a wife he would need at least two thousand rigsdaler a year.

Edvard Collin had married a sparkling dark-eyed girl and perhaps this made Andersen look round again on the girls he knew. But what was the good?

One day as he sat brooding in his small room, somebody knocked at the door. It was the Count Conrad Rantzau-Breitenburg, a cabinet minister. He had read *The Improvisatore* and had been impressed. In any other country but Denmark a poor author would have been summoned to the minister; here the minister climbed the stairs to the author's rooms. It was Andersen's old fairy-tale luck; as they talked, the count looked round the room and saw how bare it was and presently, gently, he asked Hans Andersen if there was anything he could do for him.

Besides grants to the theater and schools and the stipends for traveling, Denmark sets aside a sum for pensions to be given to those writers, painters, and composers whose work is worthwhile, and who hold no state office. Andersen knew that most of the important poets had pensions, but they were older men and well established; even with the success of *The Improvisatore* Andersen could not say he was established—he did not count the Tales. But though he felt his claims were slender, he nerved himself to ask the minister for a little state support. His luck held; soon he heard he had been granted a pension of four hundred rigsdaler a year.

It was not much, but life in Copenhagen was simple and Andersen's way of living very cheap; it meant the end of forced writing, and the hope that he could marry. And it was more than money; it was recognition. "Now you *cannot* complain," said his friend Örsted. "Now you know you are appreciated. Your reputation is founded."

Even as uncertain a being as Hans Andersen began to feel it. The summer before, he had paid a visit to Sweden. When he made a second visit, to Lund, the university town, students came marching in hundreds to give him an ovation; they swept off their blue caps and stood bareheaded in front of him.

There was another recognition in these years, one that meant more to Andersen than anyone could know. He was on his way to dine, groomed in clean linen and a fashionable coat, when he met Meisling, his old rector, in the street. He had suffered more from this man than from anyone else in his life; now as he looked down on the fat, shabby little man with a red nose, whose breath was rank with drink, certain words must have rung on the air: "Your verse will rot in a bookseller's attic and you will end your days in a madhouse."

Meisling trembled and held out his hand. "I must tell you," he stammered, "that I know how wrong I have been." He could hardly get the words out; they were unmistakably sincere. Andersen took his old master's hand and all he felt was gladness that the strange inexplicable hatred was gone.

At last, Hans Christian Andersen was solidly founded— strange words for him. He gave up his rooms by the canal and moved into a good hotel opposite his loved Royal Theater; he bought dandified clothes, he went "elegantly to elegant dinners." Henriette Wulff teased him by saying he was nothing but a fine gentleman now, but often, even in these happy days, he was dark and haunted.

At this time Louise Collin's marriage was announced. Andersen had known that one day she must marry Mr. Lind, but it was hurtful. There was another happy couple for him to congratulate, to watch, to envy; another new little home to visit and go away from, back to his lonely rooms. "I have imagined so much and had so little," he was to say afterwards.

Over and over again this theme of being left out, of being different from anybody else, comes into his work; it is in "The Little Mermaid," "The Little Match-Seller," "The Ugly Duckling." There is a short, hardly known story called "Heartbreak" which in its little way sums up this theme: a tanner's widow had a pug dog who died; the grandchildren made him a grave,

. . . so beautiful that it must have been quite pleasant to lie in it; it was bordered with broken flowerpots, strewn with sand, and at its head a broken beer bottle was stuck upside down; it was so beautiful that all the boys and girls were invited to look at it, the only price of admission being one trouser button, a thing every boy would have and which he could give. . . .

So all the children from their street, and from the back lane as well, came along and paid their buttons. . . . and it was well worth the expense.

But outside the tanyard, right against the gate, was a little ragged girl, standing so gracefully there, with the prettiest curls and delightfully clear blue eyes. She didn't say a word, and she didn't cry, but every time the gate opened she looked in as far as she could. She hadn't a button—she knew that—and so she was left standing sadly outside, standing there till the others had all had their look at the grave and had gone away. Then at last she sat down, held her small brown hands before her face, and burst into tears; she alone had not seen the dog's grave. That was heartbreak, as bitter for her as it may sometimes be for one who is grown up.

Now Andersen's own lonely heart drove him to travel again. For the rest of his life he was to take these journeys, constantly, year after year. A look in Hans Andersen's Album shows that he belongs not only to Denmark but to the whole world. There are contributions from all nationalities, all ages. The Album has bars of music from Liszt, Schumann, Weber; letters from Dickens, Mendelssohn, Jenny Lind. There are portraits of Balzac, Victor Hugo, Dumas, George Sand; there are notes and pictures from Heine and Schiller, and a part of the manuscript of *William Tell*.

Andersen's fourth journey was longer and more adventurous than any he had taken; this time he traveled on the railways and confessed to a feeling he called "railway fever"—"I must say that the first sensation was as if a child's hand drew a little carriage. The speed increases imperceptibly. . . . You look out of the windows and discover you are careering away as with horses at full gallop; . . . you seem to fly . . . and soon we are suddenly under a roof where the train stops. It is Leipzig; we have come seventy miles in three hours!"

With a grant of money sent him by the King, Andersen took a ship from Italy to Greece and then on to Turkey. He brought home with him the new book of travels, *A Poet's Bazaar*, but more important were two smaller books that were published before he went away: *A Picture Book without Pictures* and a fourth collection of Tales, "The Wild Swans," "The Daisy," and "The Staunch Tin Soldier."

A little of Hans Andersen is in all his Tales; in some of them as obviously as his unhappiness in "Heartbreak," his sufferings in "The Ugly Duckling," his ambition in "The Fir Tree," but in "The Staunch Tin Soldier" a quality shines out that might be called the soul of Andersen; a little fantastic, and so gay and crisp that one almost forgets the steadfastness that is the point of the whole story. It was staunchness that molded the one-legged tin soldier, at last, into a glowing tin heart, and stead-fastness that was beginning to make the scattered, complex Andersen into a whole poet.

IN THE SUMMERS of his middle years, Andersen would leave Copenhagen and stay at the great manor houses of the country. These were like whole villages, spreading in farms and work-shops over two or three acres, the manor house itself rising in gables and turrets. Where once upon a time Anne Marie would have thought herself privileged to help with the washing, where Andersen the father had not been good enough to be the cob-bler, their son was now welcomed as an honored guest.

"In the homes of what are called the greatest families of the country I met some kind, warmhearted people, who appre-ciated . . . me and admitted me to their circles, let me participate . . . in their rich summer life; independent, I could there quite surrender to nature . . . and to the life in a manor house; . . . there I wrote most of my Tales. In this world of quiet lakes in the woods, and the green grass fields . . . nature around me and within me preached my mission to me."

Book by book, more Tales came out, "The Ugly Duckling," "The Top and the Ball," "The Fir Tree," "The Snow Queen," "The Snow Man," "The Ice Maiden," "The Rose Elf." All together there are one hundred and sixty-eight Tales, of which one hundred and fifty-six were printed in Andersen's own time.

Each year brought him more fame; soon he was staying in palaces. He went to Weimar where Goethe had lived, and there

met the handsome blue-eyed young man Carl Alexander, grand duke of Weimar; from the first moment they were friends. The duke and his young duchess taught Andersen some things about royalty that he had not dreamed of and that perhaps helped him to make his own princes and queens so human; he must have smiled when he remembered the stilted made-up language he had once invented for them. The grand duchess picnicked with her children in the woods, and they, the little Prince Carl August and his brothers and sisters, gathered round Andersen clamoring for stories as if they were little Drewsens or Collins, or his own landlady's daughter at home.

He was naïvely happy in these royal friendships. "After all," he makes the nightingale say of the Emperor, "there is something holy about a crown"; but to his friends, especially the sensible Collin family, it seemed snobbish and extravagant. It never occurred to them that what would have been extravagant for them, or for Hans Christian the foundling, was not extravagant for Hans Andersen the poet. Never, to the end of their lives, did the Collins know Andersen's full stature. For all their faithfulness, they were smug; it made them limited, and Andersen, though he was their devoted friend as long as he lived, had outgrown them.

Once he might have gone to people's houses to amuse them, one might almost say with his antics; now he went as an equal. His studies, his travels, his constant meetings with gifted, cultured men and women, had mellowed him; he was no longer crude and raw.

Even his looks had altered. His ugliness had weathered into a dignity and nobility that was striking. He was sought after, not only because of his Tales, but for himself. He seemed integrated, whole.

But in him there was still the dissatisfied restless longing. Those languorous days in the old manors and palaces, the picnics and music, the bare shoulders and laces, the diamonds sparkling in scented hair, had wakened him again; as in the old garden at the Iversens' and in those warm Neapolitan nights, he quivered with feeling; after all he was not forty and had the strength of the untried. "What do I live for?" he sometimes asked. "Am I not a man?" It seems fitting that at this moment, in a small party given by the master of the Royal Ballet, Andersen should meet a shy, serious young woman, whose face seemed plain until she spoke; then, startlingly, she was almost beautiful.

"Watch a woman who can be beautiful and ugly," says the proverb, "she is rare." Very often that evening Hans Andersen found himself watching this one. She sang, and he was so strangely moved that he could not stay in the room. A few nights later he heard her at the Royal Theater; when she sang the staid Copenhagen audience rose to its feet and gave her such an ovation that Andersen, standing among them, was giddy and deaf. That night his toast was drunk with hers in champagne and he knew he was in love—not in love again—this was something utterly new and fresh.

The girls he had loved till now had been good ordinary Danish daughters, brought up to be housewives. This new girl was like no one he had known; she was unique, a revelation; though she was only twenty-three, her knowledge and wisdom were extraordinary; they seemed to come from the same natural fountain as her singing. Denmark called her the Swedish Nightingale; her name was Jenny Lind.

She was tall, slender, and graceful. In Andersen's Album there is a picture of her wearing a low-cut dress and deep lace collar; her auburn hair falls in a galaxy of ringlets and her head is poised with singular grace on a very long neck. People have said that her gray eyes changed remarkably as she sang.

Her career was extraordinary in that it had no reverses. As a child she used to sit in the window of her grandmother's apartment in Stockholm and sing to the cat. People passing in the street stopped to hear and wonder, among them the maid of one of the dancers at the Royal Opera House. "You talk of your opera singers," the maid told her mistress. "You ought to hear that little girl with the cat."

The dancer heard her and at once sent her to the director of singing. From that day the Royal Opera House at Stockholm took charge of Jenny Lind; it educated and trained her and finally sent her abroad, where Copenhagen, Berlin, Paris, Milan, London, New York, one after another, went mad over her.

She and Andersen were good companions. Once, on one of their walks in Copenhagen, feeling hungry, they went into a baker's shop and ate hot buns and milk. The baker recognized them and refused to be paid, saying he was honored enough by a visit from two such celebrities, but Jenny paid him. Standing by the counter in the little shop, she sang one of her famous folk songs for him, and then she and Andersen went on for their walk.

From the beginning Andersen knew he had very little hope. As she boarded the ship that was to take her away for the first time, he put a letter in her hand, "a letter that she must understand." She understood it so well that she thought it better not to answer it. A year or two afterwards he tried again; when they were staying in the country he carefully separated her from the others on a walk, meaning to propose, but before he could speak she said briskly: "Come along, Andersen, don't let's get left behind," and ran on.

In December of 1845 he went to Berlin, where she was singing, hoping to spend Christmas with her, but though she knew he was there she did not send for him. He sat alone in his hotel room and wrote miserably in his diary: "She takes so little notice of me, who came to Berlin chiefly for her sake. It is Christmas Eve. How happy the home is where the husband has a hearth! The Christmas tree is lighted; his wife stands with the youngest in her arms. . . ." When at last she did send for him and they spent New Year's Eve together, he knew it was no use. For the first time they were quite alone; she lighted the Christmas tree for Andersen and with her lovely voice sang peace and happiness into his soul, but she made it quite clear that she could give him nothing else.

He has told a little of what she meant to him in "The Nightingale." He wrote many fairy tales for Jenny Lind, "The Angel," "Under the Willow Tree," but none like this, as telling, or as poignant. It tells of the nightingale who sang in the wood and how the Emperor learned to prize his free little brown bird, with the throbbing living song in its throat, more than the glittering jeweled one with its clever musical box. "I can't make my home in the palace," said the nightingale, "but let me come when I want to; then I'll sing of an evening on this branch by the window, and my singing can make you both gay and thoughtful. I shall sing of those that are happy, and of those that suffer; I shall sing of the good and the evil that are here lurking about you."

Andersen saw Jenny Lind many times again, but she married Otto Goldschmidt, the pianist. And by that time Andersen had quietly accepted that he was to be alone.

CHAPTER VII

IT WAS IN THE SUMMER OF 1847 that Andersen traveled in a new direction, to England. "London is the city of cities," he wrote. "Here is Paris but with a mightier power; here is the life of Naples but not its bustle." Not bustle but bedlam: he was terrified of traffic. "Omnibus after omnibus passes . . . teams, carts, hansoms and elegant carriages. . . ." He found the city tiring, but the people unfailingly courteous and kind.

He had brought no letters of introduction, but the Danish ambassador, Count Reventlow, on whom he called the first morning, told him he did not need any. "Everybody knows you," said the count.

That seemed true; from the first night Andersen was heaped with invitations. The season was in full swing and he was invited every day for dinner, or for the evening, and after that to balls; he was even obliged to go out to breakfast, a common thing in England then, and there were crowds everywhere.

The English way of life certainly seemed costly and complicated to simple Hans Andersen. He liked the ordinary people; but the enormous contrast between rich and poor horrified him. He had never seen so many famished men and women. "They glide by like shadows," he wrote home, "and place themselves in front of a person and gaze at him with hungry sad expressions on their pale pinched faces." At the same time he had never seen such elaborate dresses and houses. "Almost everywhere the principal figures are the same," he wrote, "only varying in gold, satin, lace, and flowers."

The longing for fragrance and freshness overpowered him and he escaped to see Jenny Lind. "The topic of the day in London was Jenny and only Jenny," he wrote. In an attempt to achieve privacy she had hired a little house, with a low hedge shutting out the street. But he found out where it was and went. People were standing outside trying to get a glimpse of Jenny Lind, and that day they had a chance; she recognized Andersen from the windows, and ran out and shook both his hands, forgetting the crowd. "We hastened into the house, which was pretty and rich," wrote Andersen. "Elegantly bound books lay on the table. She showed me my own *True Story of My Life*." They talked of home and when she saw how exhausted and tired Andersen was, she said: "Now you know what it is like to be at a perpetual feast," and she was silent and sighed.

Not many years later, at the height of her fame, in full career, still young, Jenny Lind suddenly retired. No one could understand why but Andersen, who loved her. In "The Nightingale" he had written of how the marvelous little bird, after her triumph, was sentenced to "remain at court and have her own cage, with leave to go out for two walks in the daytime and one at night. She was given twelve attendants who each held on tightly to silk ribbon fastened round her leg. There was absolutely no fun in a walk like that."

Jenny had always had a profound effect on Andersen. After being with her he was able to single out what was valuable and true in the lavishness and glitter, and remember what it was that he had come to England to do. For years he had wanted to meet Dickens. Another dream was to go to Scotland, which for Andersen was only one thing, "Walter Scott's country."

To King Christian VIII he wrote, "My stay in England and Scotland floats before me like a fantasy of joy and sunshine."

It ended with a visit to Dickens's retreat at Broadstairs. For Hans Andersen, the English author was too haloed with admiration and sentiment to have any faults; but that Dickens criticized his Danish friend was shown only too plainly. Andersen was not an easy guest. To begin with he was that hostess's dread, the guest who can never be left alone. Fortunately the children did not mind being pressed into service; "and we have plenty of those," said Dickens. Then he was so ridiculously sensitive. Mrs. Dickens found him one day, sobbing full-length in the grass, a newspaper clutched in one hand. "Is one of your friends dead?" she asked, but it was "a perfectly nasty review" of one of his novels. There was also the difficulty of the language; he could not learn to speak English. The Dickens girls said he was a "boney bore," and in the end it was only kind Mrs. Dickens who cared for him. When he had gone, Dickens stuck a card up on the dressing-table mirror: "Hans Andersen slept in this room for five weeks; it seemed to the family ages."

Andersen was quite unaware of this; the time seemed to him idyllic. "The whole landscape is like a garden," he wrote home, "there is a fragrance of clover, the elder tree is in blossom, and the wild roses have an odor of apples so fresh and strong." He basked in the family life; both his host and hostess personified to him "the spirit of true amiability," and he confidently kept Dickens on his long and growing list of famous friends.

But Andersen was not as confident of his friends at home and he had some reason to think his own country was not fair to him. The Danish press had unaccountably refused to publish any of the articles or pictures that appeared about him abroad, and when he had come back from England he heard someone say, pointing him out in the street: "Look, our orangutan, who is so famous abroad, is back!"

In 1845 his friend Hauch, led by jealousy and spite, had pilloried him in a novel, *The Castle on the Rhine*. In the book there was a poet so fantastically vain that he rushed up and introduced himself to people, read aloud relentlessly, made parents bring their children forward so that he could tell them stories. The poet traveled abroad to get appreciation; in the end he went mad, and when the jeering riffraff put him in a cart and dragged him off to the madhouse, he still proudly believed they were honoring him as the greatest poet in the world.

It was a cruel portrait; much of it was true. "People in Copenhagen keep asking me: 'What have you done to Hauch?'" Andersen wrote to Ingemann. "And I have answered that Hauch never had me in mind, that he has a noble and magnanimous disposition and bears friendship and kindness to me." But Andersen had not then read the book; all Copenhagen waited to see what would happen when he did. They expected an outcry, but Andersen sent another letter to Ingemann so full of dignity that Ingemann felt obliged to go to Hauch with it.

> Copenhagen, 16 September, 1845.
>
> . . . I've seen this figure [of the poet]; they are right to say "It is Andersen!" Here all my weaknesses are collected! I think and hope that I have lived through this period; but everything that this poet says and does, I might have said and done; I felt shockingly impressed by this crude portrait, which showed me in my misery. Still, I believe that . . . Hauch . . . appreciates the good that is in me; I have the greatest confidence in him and affection for him still and will keep it. What has shocked me, what scorches my thought . . . is the end of the miserable poet. My own grandfather was insane, my father's mind was affected shortly before his death. There is nothing to do, nothing to say; it is a breaker I have to let wash over me; the most bitter part of it is that I, being a little more sensible than my caricature, must try hereafter to be a little less open; but that is said to be good and prudent. Remember me cordially to Hauch.
>
> > Affectionately yours,
> > H. C. Andersen.

The effect of his own large-mindedness stayed with Andersen down the years; criticism pained him as much as ever but he was able to meet it with dignity. And if, on a second English visit, Dickens sometimes appeared to avoid his guest, Andersen shut his eyes to it. He knew he was tiresome and knew, equally well, that in spite of it, he was loved.

There was one love that was new to him; he, who had adored

so many young girls, was now adored and, more surprisingly still, by a Collin, Jonna Drewsen, Ingeborg's daughter. She had been a thin leggy little girl with large dark eyes that always seemed fixed on Andersen's face when he went to the Drewsens'. At first he thought of it as a child's love, but she grew up with the same swiftness that had surprised him in her Aunt Louise. It was a strange last gift for him but he loved Jonna enough to encourage her to marry someone else: Henrik Stampe, the son of the Baroness of Nysö.

The young baron saw Jonna first in the box that Collin, as a director, had at the theater. It was Andersen who introduced them, who carried their letters and persuaded the disapproving baroness to give her consent, and he put all three of them into "The Shepherdess and the Chimney-Sweep."

Jonna is the little china shepherdess. ". . . She wore golden shoes and looped up her gown fetchingly with a red rose. Her hat was gold, even her crook was gold. She was simply charming." Her young man was a chimney-sweep made of the finest porcelain. ". . . If the china-makers had wanted to, they could just as easily have turned him out as a prince, for he had a jaunty way of holding his ladder. . . . The chimney-sweep and the shepherdess stood close together on a table and they became engaged because they suited each other exactly. . . ."

Jonna was, for Andersen, a little piece of intelligence and idealism in years when the world seemed full of stupidity and ugliness. For the second time in two decades Denmark was at war with Prussia, causing Andersen to suffer the peculiar torments of someone who has dear friends on both sides. It was known that Hans Andersen was an admirer of Germany. He was called unpatriotic, which hurt him, but how could he, who had made himself international, have the blind patriotism of those who knew only Denmark? Hate the Germans? He thought they were wickedly, disastrously wrong, but he could not hate men and women in whose houses he had been an honored guest, children to whom he had told his Tales. "You don't find me fervent enough in my Danishness, dear Jonna," he wrote, for even Jonna had joined in. "Perhaps it arises from the fact that I am just to everybody. Is that a crime?"

Though he refused to enter the bitter partisanship, his heart was torn for his little country. Almost every day troops of young men marched off and he wrote the song "I cannot stay, I have no rest" for them; it became a popular war song. His deepest feelings were poured into the "Hymn for Denmark," the last stanza of which reads:

> O land where I was born, to me so homely,
> where clings the root whence all my being flows,
> whose accents are my mother's, soft and comely—
> no music ever stirred my heart like those.
> > You smiling Danish strand,
> > that swans have built their nests in,
> green islands that my heart finds perfect rest in,
> 'tis you I love—Denmark, my native land!

In a letter from the front, one of his friends told him how, in a town where all the houses were riddled with cannonballs and grapeshot, on one roof was a stork's nest, holding a new stork family. It seemed to Andersen a symbol. The storks made him hope that peace would come back again to Denmark.

AS TIME PASSED, the people of Denmark seemed to identify Andersen more and more with his Tales. The novels and travel books, though they had several editions, faded slowly into the background. Andersen still agonized over this, but he began to accept the verdict and let his lifework be the Tales.

The defeat of 1864, when Denmark had to yield Schleswig-Holstein to the Prussians, was bitter for any Dane, but the Tales were already in German nurseries as well as Danish ones; wars had nothing to do with them, for they were universal. The children of England and America had them, and so did the children of France.

Even in Andersen's lifetime first editions were rare; they had been handled by so many children that most had fallen to pieces. In Paris Andersen was asked double the original price for a tattered edition of *A Picture Book without Pictures*, and the bookseller was overwhelmed when told who his customer was.

At the end of "The Ugly Duckling" comes that description of how the clumsy, ugly, grayish bird is recognized as a swan.

He felt positively glad at having been through so much hardship and want; it helped him to appreciate all the happiness and beauty that were there to welcome him ... and the great swans swam round and round and stroked him with their beaks.

Some little children came into the garden and threw bread and grain into the water and the smallest one cried out: "There's a new swan!".... and they clapped their hands with delight ... and everyone said: "The new one is the prettiest" and the old swans bowed before him.

This made him feel quite shy and he tucked his head away under his wing ... he was too, too happy but not a bit proud, for a good heart is never proud ... and the lilacs bowed their branches to him right down into the water and the sunshine felt so warm and kindly. Then he ruffled his feathers on his neck and rejoiced from his heart. "I never dreamed of such happiness when I was the ugly duckling."

Andersen had ease and comfort now. His pension was raised as a tribute and later he was given the title of Professor. His life now seems like a kaleidoscope in which the pictures come and go so quickly that it is hardly possible to separate the years. He had craved fame, and he was given it, brimming over. Ovations met him everywhere he went.

But there were dark days of mourning too. Andersen and young Jonas Collin, the son of Edvard, were in Lucerne together when word came that old Councillor Collin was dying; they reached Copenhagen in time for the funeral. To be included, at such a moment, as one of the family touched and gratified Hans Andersen deeply and he never forgot it; it was as a son that he looked down on the calm kind face of his benefactor in the coffin and as a son he mourned.

There were other losses; Ingemann died and Andersen went to Sorö to be with his widow. Örsted died. Worst of all, in 1858 his old friend Henriette Wulff had been on her way to America in the steamship *Austria* when it caught fire in mid-Atlantic and sank. Andersen wrote about it in his diary. He had read Henriette's last letter to her sister in which "she had said she felt some repugnance for the journey—which was odd in one who loved the sea so passionately and had crossed to America before—that she had almost turned back but shamed herself out of her weakness and went on." There were descriptions of the fearful scenes by the few who were saved, but little feeble Henriette was not among them; she had been seen going to her stateroom and it was thought she had been suffocated by the smoke.

The news tortured Andersen; he mourned for his little gay friend and ever afterwards, for fear of fire, he carried a rope with him when he traveled. Henriette's death too made him even more afraid of the sea.

For a long time letters of praise and thanks had been coming across the Atlantic, and many invitations to come to America. Dickens had gone to America, and Jenny Lind; Henriette Wulff had always urged Andersen to come. "There is the vast ocean between us," he had written in answer to one of her letters, "fourteen days of broad angry sea where I should for days be seasick in return for my money out of pocket." He was frightened too of America itself: "I should not know how to make even a fairy behave herself with propriety there," he said.

He never went. Henriette's death had shaken him and he felt that, with his travels and eminent circles, he had neglected his old friends; now their ranks were thinned, they seemed dearer than ever and he clung to them. He took Collin grandchildren with him on his travels, Viggo Drewsen, who was Ingeborg's son and Jonna's brother, or young Jonas, the son of Edvard; nothing in his life gave him more pleasure than to benefit these young men, to give back some little part of all he had been given.

The Queen Dowager asked him to stay with her in her palace; another new king, Christian IX—Andersen lived through four reigns—made him a state councillor, the very title old Collin, Jonas's grandfather, had had.

Then, on the sixth of December, 1867, Hans Andersen was invited to Odense to be given the freedom of the city, to stay at the bishop's house for the ceremony, to be guest of honor at a banquet, a public holiday with children singing and illuminations. "He will be a wild bird who shall fly high. . . . One day the whole of Odense will be illuminated for him," the wisewoman had said. It had come true at last.

CHAPTER VIII

AT SIXTY-TWO ANDERSEN was a tired and nervous old man; his hard life, the poverty and underfeeding he had endured as a boy, the tension at which he lived, had worn him out.

His nerves were a torment; there was the fear of the sea; another visit to England was out of the question. There was the fear of fire; his terror of having left candles alight made him go again and again to look into any room he had left. There were fears of death; perhaps because there was an outbreak of cholera in the city or, equally, because a mosquito had bitten him. There were fears of missing trains; on his travels he nearly drove young Jonas frantic by insisting on getting to the station hours before the train started.

He still traveled with his rope and battered valises; something of his wildness had never died in him. He made new friends; he called on Elizabeth Barrett Browning in Italy and he saw Jenny Lind again. "I heard her singing and it was the same soul, the same fountain of music, the song of a jubilating warbling bird; the nightingale cannot whistle like that, the thrush cannot quiver." But Andersen was not beguiled. "She has left the stage, that is a wrong," he wrote, "it is to give up her mission, the gift God chose for her."

Hans Andersen's sense of God was always unquestioning, simple, and direct. In one of the strangest and most beautiful of his stories, "The Marsh King's Daughter," Andersen makes the storks tell the heroine, little Helga, who has grown careless and proud, the legend of the ostrich.

All the ostriches had once been very beautiful, with big strong wings. Then one evening the largest birds in the wood said to the ostrich: "Brother, mightn't we, God willing, fly tomorrow to the river and drink?" And the ostrich answered: "I'm willing!" So at dawn they flew off; at first, high in the air towards the sun, God's eye; all the time higher and higher, with the ostrich flying on far ahead of all the others. Proudly it flew towards the light, trusting in its own strength and not in Him who gave it; the ostrich wouldn't say "God willing." Then the avenging angel drew aside the veil from the blazing sun, so that the bird's wings were burnt up in a flash, and it sank miserably to earth. Ever since then no ostriches have been able to rise into the air. They stampede in a panic, rush wildly about, but can never leave the ground. It is a warning to all of us, whatever we think or do, to say "God willing."

Hans Andersen, like the wise storks, never forgot God.

When he was at home in Copenhagen, he still liked, as in his penurious days, to eat his dinner at different houses every day. "Monday calls me to friends of many years' standing, State Councillor Edvard Collin and his family; Tuesday takes me to the Drewsens, where Ingeborg is always a steadfast sister to me; on Wednesday to Örsted's home; he himself is gone, but his wife and youngest daughter, Mathilde, are still there." Andersen also had met two new families, who were cultured, liberal, and kind: the Henriques and the Melchiors. Both families took him into their intimate circle.

The Collins would have looked down their noses at what the Melchiors and Henriques not only allowed but encouraged; Andersen had all the attention, and had to be served first at table or he became annoyed. The indulgence was not good for him; when he had been with the astringent Collins he had written his finest work; with the Henriques and Melchiors, the Tales grew weak; they were charming but had not the crispness of the older ones. But he still made his paper cutouts and scrapbooks for the Henriques and Melchior children, arranged flowers, and endlessly read his stories aloud.

In the King's Garden at Copenhagen, that garden which surrounds the romantic castle of Rosenborg, there is a statue of

A collage page from a scrapbook made by H.C.A. for little
Agnete Lind, daughter of Louise Collin Lind. It includes
the title page from "Fairy Tales Told for Children," Part II;
a cutout design made by H.C.A.; a drawing of a theater
audience clipped from a newspaper; and a picture of a
snake captioned "Here lies the snake of knowledge of
good and evil."

Hans Andersen reading aloud to some children. It is so eloquent that the figure of Andersen seems to speak. On the side of the base is a scene from the tale of "The Ugly Duckling"; it is of the moment when the duckling, grown to his full size, looks into the water and sees himself a swan.

The Melchiors had raised a subscription for this statue to be put up and Andersen was asked to choose the design himself, but most of the sketches submitted by sculptors irritated him by their pretty sentimentality. "I could not bear to have children climbing on my back or sitting on my lap while I read," he said. They had to stand or sit properly, everything had to be in order.

This ceremony, the importance of paying attention, enhances storytelling for children. Andersen understood that very well, and everywhere he went children flocked to see him, brought him wreaths and kisses, wrote to him. Once, when he was talking jokingly to a composer friend about the funeral march that would one day have to be written for him, he said: "Most of the people who walk after me will be children; make the beat keep time with little steps."

In those last years there were more ceremonies, more honors. On the fiftieth anniversary of Andersen's arrival in Copenhagen there was a public banquet, and on his seventieth birthday a wonderful private dinner at the Melchiors'.

"My birthday was a day rich in sunshine and blessing," Andersen wrote to the editor of the New York *Tribune*, who had sent a gift of books from the children of America. "From every part of my beloved motherland and far away beyond its boundaries came beautiful presents, letters, and telegrams. For what an infinite amount of goodness I have to be thankful." But in his letter to the grand duke of Weimar he said that though it was a great and splendid day, he was very ill and could hardly receive the deputations and visitors. "God willing," he said, "I shall soon leave town. Only country quiet and summer warmth can help me now."

The Melchiors took him to their summer villa, Rolighed, which means "quietude"; it looked over the blue waters of the Sound and had a garden that stretched down to the sea; at first

Andersen was able to walk about and sit out in the sun, then he had to stay in bed.

His last work was for a child. Though very weak, he dictated a poem, *Springe in Kjöge*, to Mrs. Melchior for her little daughter Charlotte; after that he was silent, only smiling at anyone who helped him or came near him. Once, when Mrs. Melchior brought him a white rose, he kissed her hand.

On the fourth of August, 1875, Melchior sent a telegram to Edvard: "At eleven o'clock this morning, our beloved mutual friend passed peacefully away."

In Denmark, for a funeral, flowers are strewn up the aisle of the church; it is as if it were a wedding, a new beginning.

Hans Andersen is buried in Copenhagen, but people do not often go to see his grave; they go to the King's Garden to see his reading statue, to the Langelinie to see the Little Mermaid. There are often fresh flowers in her arms. In Odense the house where he was born has been made into a museum, and so many visitors ask the way to it that the red-and-white signposts of the city have an extra arm that reads: *Andersens Hus*.

In "The Last Dream of the Oak Tree," the oak and the mayfly talk of death, when life will be over.

> "Over, what is over?" asks the little fly. "Will all the beauty in the world die when you die?" she asks the tree.
>
> "It will last longer, infinitely longer than I am able to imagine," says the great oak tree.

ILLUSTRATION CREDITS